Studien und Texte zu

Studies and Texts in Antiquity and Christianity

Herausgeber/Editor:
CHRISTOPH MARKSCHIES (Berlin)
MARTIN WALLRAFF (Basel)
CHRISTIAN WILDBERG (Princeton)

Beirat/Advisory Board
PETER BROWN (Princeton) · SUSANNA ELM (Berkeley)
JOHANNES HAHN (Münster) · EMANUELA PRINZIVALLI (Rom)
JÖRG RÜPKE (Erfurt)

88

Galen's
De indolentia

Essays on a Newly Discovered Letter

Edited by

Clare K. Rothschild and
Trevor W. Thompson

Mohr Siebeck

CLARE K. ROTHSCHILD, born 1964; 1986 B.A. University of California, Berkeley; 1992 M.T.S. Harvard University; 2003 Ph.D. University of Chicago; currently Associate Professor of Theology at Lewis University, Romeoville, IL.

TREVOR W. THOMPSON, born 1975; 1998 B.A. Oklahoma Christian University; 2002 M.A., M.Div. Harding University Graduate School of Theology; 2007 M.A. University of Chicago; 2009 Ph.D. (candidate) University of Chicago; currently Instructor of New Testament at Abilene Christian University.

ISBN 978-3-16-153215-3
ISSN 1436-3003 (Studien und Texte zu Antike und Christentum)

Die Deutsche Nationalbibliothek lists this publication in the Deutsche Nationalbibliographie; detailed bibliographic data are available on the Internet at *http://dnb.dnb.de*.

© 2014 by Mohr Siebeck, Tübingen, Germany. www.mohr.de

This book may not be reproduced, in whole or in part, in any form (beyond that permitted by copyright law) without the publisher's written permission. This applies particularly to reproductions, translations, microfilms and storage and processing in electronic systems.

The book was typeset by Martin Fischer in Tübingen using Times New Roman typeface, printed by Laupp & Göbel in Nehren on non-aging paper and bound by Buchbinderei Nädele in Nehren.

Printed in Germany.

The Editors dedicate this volume to the memory of

Paraskevi Kotzia (1951–2013) †

Ὅσον ζῇς φαίνου
μηδὲν ὅλως σὺ λυποῦ
πρὸς ὀλίγον ἐστὶ τὸ ζῆν
τὸ τέλος ὁ χρόνος ἀπαιτεῖ.*

Paraskevi Kotzia was an Associate Professor of Classics at Aristotle University, Thessaloniki, where she also led the Center for Aristotelian Studies. She studied Classics at Aristotle University completing postgraduate studies in Classics, Philosophy, and Paleography at the Free University of Berlin. Her main research interests included Aristotle, the Aristotelian exegetical tradition, Plato and the Neoplatonists, ancient medicine, and ancient theories of language. She left behind extensive and multi-faceted contributions, most notably, *Ο σκοπός των Κατηγοριών του Αριστοτέλη (The Aim of Aristotle's Categories)*, *Περί του μήλου ή Περί της Αριστοτέλους τελευτής (Liber de pomo)*.

Her last major work was a critical edition of Galen's *De indolentia*.

---

* Seikilos, funeral epitaph; first-second century CE; Copenhagen inv. 14897

Acknowledgments

New discoveries are certainly not an ancient historian's bread and butter. They are in fact so rare that most historians exhaust entire careers without experiencing the thrill. It has been so long since Trevor first called me with news of the discovery of Galen's *De indolentia* that the precise date has vanished from memory. The excitement I felt on that day, however, never seems to wane as weekly I learn of a new dispute over the critical text, become embroiled in a debate over interpretation, or have the opportunity to share the discovery with someone who has not yet heard. It was four years ago that Trevor and I decided to translate the text together. This volume represents an unexpected journey prompted by this initial commitment.

The manuscript was collaboratively edited and prepared by Clare K. Rothschild (Lewis University) and Trevor W. Thompson (Abilene Christian University) between June 2012 and October 2013. We received excellent direction and feedback on aspects of this work from the authors and others. Other individual colleagues to whom we are grateful are Johan Thom (Stellenbosch) and L. Curt Niccum (Abilene Christian University). We also wish to thank Dean Ken Cukrowski (ACU College of Biblical Studies) for generously permitting Trevor to take on a time-consuming publication project. Finally, we wish to express utmost gratitude to Dr. Henning Ziebritzki at Mohr Siebeck for his interest in and special attention to the details of this manuscript and to Prof. Drs. Christoph Markschies and Christian Wildberg for its recommendation to the STAC series.

Chicago/Abilene, October 20, 2013   Clare K. Rothschild
                                          Trevor W. Thompson

Table of Contents

Acknowledgments VII
Abbreviations and References XI

Galen of Pergamon 1

CLARE K. ROTHSCHILD / TREVOR W. THOMPSON
Introduction (with illustration of Vlatadon 14) 3

I. English Translation

CLARE K. ROTHSCHILD / TREVOR W. THOMPSON
Galen: "On the Avoidance of Distress" 21

II. Interpretive Essays

Manuscript Evidence

VÉRONIQUE BOUDON-MILLOT
Vlatadon 14 and *Ambrosianus* Q 3 Sup: Two Twin Manuscripts 41

DANIEL DAVIES
Some Quotations from Galen's *De indolentia* 57

Realia

MATTHEW C. NICHOLLS
A Library at Antium? 65

ALAIN TOUWAIDE
Collecting Books, Acquiring Medicines: Knowledge Acquisition
in Galen's Therapeutics 79

Philosophy

PARASKEVI KOTZIA (†)
Galen, *De indolentia*: Commonplaces, Traditions, and Contexts 91

ELIZABETH ASMIS
Galen's *De indolentia* and the Creation of a Personal Philosophy 127

JANET DOWNIE
Galen's Intellectual Self-Portrait in *De indolentia* 143

Irony

RALPH M. ROSEN
Philology and the Rhetoric of Catastrophe in Galen's *De indolentia* ... 159

CLARE K. ROTHSCHILD
The Apocolocyntosis of Commodus or The Anti-imperial *Tendenz*
of Galen's *De indolentia* 175

Christian Trajectories

JOHN T. FITZGERALD
Galen's *De indolentia* in the context of Greco-Roman Medicine,
Moral Philosophy, and Physiognomy 203

L. MICHAEL WHITE
The Pathology and Cure of Grief (λύπη): Galen's *De indolentia*
in Context 221

RICHARD A. WRIGHT
Possessions, Distress, and the Problem of Emotions:
De indolentia and the Gospel of Luke in Juxtaposition 251

III. Ancillary Material

TREVOR W. THOMPSON
Collation of the Critical Editions of Galen's *De indolentia* 277

Index of Ancient Authors and Texts 315
Modern Author Index 332

Abbreviations and References

Ancient sources generally follow the abbreviations in *The SBL Handbook of Style: For Ancient Near Eastern, Biblical and Early Christian Studies*, Peabody, Mass.: Hendrickson, 1999. For works in the *Corpus Galenicum,* the titles and abbreviations follow Appendix 1 and Appendix 2 in R. J. Hankinson, ed., *The Cambridge Companion to Galen*, Cambridge University Press, 2008. Minor changes have been made to the titles of Galen's works to reflect the *The SBL Handbook of Style*. Each reference to the *Corpus Galenicum* includes, if available, its location in the standard edition of Karl Gottlob Kühn, ed., *Claudii Galeni Opera Omnia*, Leipzig: C. Cnobloch, 1821–33. Arabic numerals for Kühn references offer fastest access through the *Thesaurus Linguae Graecae*. In certain instances, individual contributors cite other critical editions, such as Johannes Marquardt, Iwan Müller, and Georg Helmreich, eds., *Galeni Pergameni Scripta Minora* (*SM*). Leipzig: Teubner, 1884–93; *Corpus Medicorum Graecorum* (*CMG*), Leipzig and Berlin: Teubner, 1914–present; the new Budé Galen series published by Les Belles Lettres. In such cases, we have supplemented the critical edition used by the author with the Kühn reference.

Galen of Pergamon

129 CE	Birth in Pergamum to a wealthy family of architects
143/144	Galen begins to study philosophy
145/146	Dream of Galen's father; Galen begins to study medicine
148	Death of Galen's father
149–157	Galen's travel and study of medicine in Smyrna, Corinth, and Alexandria
157	Galen returns to Pergamum
157–162	Physician to gladiators at Pergamum
161	Galen leaves Pergamum
162–166	First Roman Period
166–168	Return to Pergamum
168–169	Summoned to Aquileia; cares for victims of the great plague
169	Second Roman Period begins
169–176	Court physician to the Imperial family
192	Great Fire in Rome
ca. 216/217	Death

Clare K. Rothschild / Trevor W. Thompson

Introduction

I. Discovery

Introduction
The long-lost treatise *De indolentia* (Περὶ ἀλυπησίας/ἀλυπίας) or *On the Avoidance of Distress* is a letter from Galen to an unspecified addressee in which he describes how he responded to the fire that destroyed much of his library and medicines in 192 CE.[1] The manuscript, catalogued in the Vlatadon monastery as codex 14, is of unspeakable value to scholars of antiquity. As one of the foremost specialists on ancient medicine, Vivian Nutton observes:

> The discovery in 2005 by a French research student of Vlatadon 14 in a monastic library in Thessalonica must rank with one of the most spectacular finds ever of ancient literature.[2]

Vlatadon Monastery
Today, the property of the Vlatadon/Vlataion monastery in Thessaloniki encompasses twenty-two acres of rocky and steep terrain with panoramic views of the surrounding area. It is heralded as the spot on which Paul established the Thessalonian church *ca.* 51 CE. The present monastery was founded *ca.* 1351 by Dorotheos and Markos Vlat(t)is. These brothers were priest-monks and members of the intellectual circle gathered around Gregory Palamas (1296–1359), a monk from Mount Athos who became the Archbishop of Thessaloniki. The church retains a number of the features of the original building. Its interior includes the well-known fresco, "Three Children in the Fiery Furnace." Relics kept in the monastery include a few purportedly belonging to Athanasius (296–373 CE) and Gregory Nazianzus (329–391 CE). On the premises of the monastery, there is a bookstore, hostel, and museum. The monastery also houses the Patriarchal Institute for Patristic Studies.[3]

---

[1] For Galen, see Véronique Boudon-Millot, *Galien de Pergame: Un Médecin Grec à Rome* (Paris: Les Belles Lettres, 2012) and Vivian Nutton, *Ancient Medicine* (2d. ed.; London: Routledge, 2013).

[2] Vivian Nutton, "Embodiments of Will," *Perspectives in Biology and Medicine* 53, no. 2 (2010): 271–88.

[3] Bibliography on Vlatadon monastery: Panteleimon Rodopoulos and Konstantinos Voloudakes, *Holy Royal Patriarchal and Stauropegic Monastery of Vlatadon* (Thessaloniki: Monastery

Vlatadon 14; f. 10v. with the permission of the Abbot of Vlatadon Monastery
(Copyright Vlatadon Monastery)

Catalogue of Eustratiades

In 1918, Sophronius Eustratiades created a catalogue of the holdings of the Vlatadon Monastery. In January 2005, Antoine Pietrobelli, a graduate student at the Sorbonne in Paris, visited the Patriarchal Institute to examine microfilm of manuscripts held at Mount Athos. He hoped to find additional evidence with which to prepare a critical text of *In Hippocratis de acutorum morborum victu* – his dissertation project under the direction of Véronique Boudon-Millot (doctorate received in 2008). While waiting for the microfilm, he examined Eustratiades's catalogue.[4] In it, he observed that codex 14 (see Table 1 on page 6) contained

---

Vlatadon, 1999); Georgiou Stogioglou, *The Patriarchal Monastery of Vlatades in Thessaloniki* (Thessaloniki: Patriarchal Institute for Patristic Studies, 1971).

[4] Concerning Vlatadon 14, see Sophronius Eustratiades, Κατάλογος τῶν ἐν τῇ μονῇ Βλατέων (Τσαοὺς-Μοναστήρι) ἀποκειμένων κωδίκων (Thessaloniki 1918), 57, who unfortunately forgot to mention Περὶ ἀλυπίας among the works by Galen contained in Vlatadon 14. This catalogue

Galenic treatises either nowhere else extant (*De propriis placitis*) or extant in only one other place (*De libris propriis*).

A few months later in March 2005, Véronique Boudon-Millot and Jacques Jouanna traveled to Thessaloniki to see the catalogue, microfilm, and codex.[5] In her inspection of codex 14 on the microfilm, Boudon-Millot noticed important discrepancies between the titles listed in the catalogue and the works appearing in the codex. In the catalogue, Eustratiades listed only twenty-three of twenty-eight Galenic texts.[6] The catalogue is represented in Table 2 on page 7. The five overlooked treatises are underlined.

---

was also published under the title 'Κατάλογος τῶν ἐν τῇ μονῇ Βλατέων (Τσαοὺς-Μοναστήρι) ἀποκειμένων κωδίκων' in *Γρηγόριος ὁ Παλαμᾶς* 2 (1918) 97–107, 224–37, 274–83, 326–30, 386–404, 437–43, 473–75, 503–07, 708–17; 3 (1919) 29–45, 74–91, 137–50. Both catalogues are mentioned in Marcel Richard, *Répertoire des bibliothèques et des catalogues de manuscrits grecs* (3rd ed. rev. and corr. by J.-M. Olivier; Turnhout: Brepols, 1995), 782. However, Vlatadon does not appear in the catalogue of Hermann Diels (*Die Handschriften der antiken Ärzte. I. Teil: Hippokrates und Galenos* [Berlin: Die Königliche Akademie der Wissenschaften, 1905].

[5] Cf. Véronique Boudon-Millot and Jacques Jouanna (with Antoine Pietrobelli), *Galien: Ne pas se chagriner* (Budé; Paris: Les Belles Lettres, 2010), vii–ix. See Antoine Pietrobelli, "Variation Autour du *Thessalonicensis Vlatadon* 14: un manuscript copié au *xénon* du Kral, peu avant la Chute de Constantinople," *Revue des etudes byzantines* 68 (2010): 95–126 [esp. 114]. The codex dates to the 15th century and is probably from Constantinople. It is written in a miniscule script; Pietrobelli later attributed folios 10v–18v to the hand of Andreiômenos. The manuscript has 281 folios and measures 305 × 220 mm (12.0079 x 8.6614 inches).

[6] The number is twenty-one if the three books of *De crisibus* [On Crises] are combined. The codex also includes two pseudo-Galenic texts. The first four pages of the codex are an unusual combination of strange medical comments, blank pages, a Greek botanical lexicon, another blank page, extracts of Hippocrates' *De morbis mulierum*, another blank page, at which point appears *De sectis* (folio: 1r). Eustratiades counted 276 folios, but there are actually 281. Pietrobelli's text separates one text into two, making six. The total number of complete Galenic texts is twenty-seven.

ΣΩΦΡΟΝΙΟΥ ΕΥΣΤΡΑΤΙΑΔΟΥ
ΠΡ. ΛΕΟΝΤΟΠΟΛΕΩΣ

Thessalonike, Monē Blateōn

ΚΑΤΑΛΟΓΟΣ

ΤΩΝ ΕΝ ΤΗι ΜΟΝΗι ΒΛΑΤΕΩΝ

(ΤΣΑΟΥΣ-ΜΟΝΑΣΤΗΡΙ)

ΑΠΟΚΕΙΜΕΝΩΝ ΚΩΔΙΚΩΝ

« Τὸ ἀναστηρίζειν ταῖς ἀναμνήσεσι τὰ ὑπορρέοντα τῷ μήκει τοῦ χρόνου καὶ ὅση δύναμις ἀντιμάχεσθαι τῇ φθορᾷ, παρ' οἷς οὐ δεκάζει τὰς ψήφους ὁ φθόνος, πολλῆς ἀξιοῦται τῆς εὐφημίας.»

(Κῶδ. Ω 133 φ. 1α τῆς Μεγίστης Λαύρας).

ΕΝ ΘΕΣΣΑΛΟΝΙΚΗι
Τύποις **Σ. Παντελῆ** καὶ **Ν. Ξενοφωντίδου**
1918

Table 2

— 37 —

14

Γαληνοῦ περί αίρέσεων

Χαρτ. 30Χ32. αἰῶν. ιε' φύλ. 276

1) φ. 1α Περί αιρέσεων. 2) φ. 13α περί τέχνης. 3) φ. 50α περί τῶν ἐν ὀφθαλμοῖς συνισταμένων παθῶν. 4) φ. 56α Γαληνοῦ ἐπιλήπτῳ παιδὶ ὑποθήκη. 5) φ. 59α περί τῶν ἑαυτῷ δοκούντων. 6) φ. 62α περί τῆς οὐσίας τῶν φυσικῶν δυνάμεων. 7) φ. 62β περὶ τῶν ἰδίων βιβλίων 8) φ. 67α περί τοῦ διὰ τῆς μικρᾶς σφαίρας γυμνασίου. 9) φ. 68β ὅτι αἱ ποιότητες ἀσώματοι. 10) φ. 70β πρὸς τοὺς περὶ τύπου γράψαντας. 11) φ. 75β περὶ μελαίνης χολῆς. 12) φ. 80β περὶ τῆς τῶν καθαιρόντων φαρμάκων δυνάμεως. 13) φ. 83α περί πλήθους. 14) φ. 92β περὶ τοῦ προγινώσκειν. 15) φ. 99α περί προγνώσεως. 16) φ. 101α πῶς χρὴ ἐξελέγχειν τοὺς προσποιουμένους νοσεῖν. 17) φ. 101β τίνας δεῖ καθαίρειν καὶ ποίοις καθαρτηρίοις καὶ πότε. 18) φ. 104α περὶ κρίσεων βιβλίον α'. (ἐντεῦθεν ἡ γραφὴ ἄλλης χειρός). 19) φ. 118β περὶ κρίσεων βιβλίον β'. 20) φ. 133α περὶ κρίσεων βιβλίον γ'. (τρίτης χειρὸς γραφή). 21) φ. 149α εἰς τὸ περὶ διαίτης ὀξέων Ἱπποκράτους, οἱ δὲ περὶ πτισάνης, οἱ δὲ πρὸς τὰς χνιδείας γνώμας ἐξήγησις Γαληνοῦ Κλαυδίου Περγαμηνοῦ. (γραφὴ ἄλλης χειρός). 22) φ. 191β Γαληνοῦ εἰς τὸ περὶ διαίτης ὀξέων νοσημάτων. 23) φ. 239β Γαληνοῦ ὑπόμνημα εἰς τὸ πρῶτον βιβλίον προρρητικὸν Ἱπποκράτους (τὸ τέλος ἐξέπεσεν).

15

Γρηγορίου τοῦ Θεολόγου λόγοι μετὰ σχολίων

Μεμβρ. 29Χ22 δίστηλ. αἰῶν. ιγ' φύλ. 321

1) φ. 3α λόγος εἰς τὸ ἅγιον Πάσχα. 2) φ. 27β εἰς τὴν νέαν Κυριακήν. 3) φ. 34β εἰς τὴν ἁγίαν Πεντηκοστήν. 4) φ. 47β εἰς τοὺς Μακχαβαίους. 5) φ. 58β εἰς Κυπριανὸν μάρτυρα. 6) φ. 70β εἰς τὸν ἀρχιεπίσκοπον Ἀλεξανδρείας Ἀθανάσιον. 7) φ. 94α εἰς τοὺς λόγους καὶ εἰς τὸ ἐξισωτὴν (Ἰουλιανόν). 8) φ. 104α εἰς τὰ γενέθλια τοῦ Κυρίου 9) φ. 115α ἐπιτάφιος εἰς τὸν μέγαν Βασίλειον. 10) φ. 175α εἰς τὰ ἅγια Φῶτα. 11) φ. 188α εἰς τὸ βάπτισμα. 12) φ. 221α εἰς Γρηγόριον Νύσσης τὸν ἀδελφὸν Βασιλείου. 13) φ. 225β εἰς τὴν παρουσίαν τῶν ἑκατὸν πεντήκοντα ἐπισκόπων συντακτήριος καὶ ἐξιτήριος. 14) φ. 242β περὶ φιλοπτωχίας. 15) φ. 267α εἰς τὸν πατέρα σιωπῶντα διὰ τὴν πληγὴν τῆς χα-

Vlatadon Codex No. 14[7]
2 *De sectis* (Περὶ αἱρέσεων; f. 1r–4v*)*
3 *Ars Medica* (Τέχνη ἰατρική; f. 5r–10r)
4 *De indolentia* (Περὶ ἀλυπίας; f. 10v–14v)
5 *De causa affectionum* (Περὶ αἰτίας παθῶν; pseudo-Galen; f. 15r–18v)
6 *Introductio sive medicus* (Εἰσαγωγὴ ἢ ἰατρός; pseudo-Galen; f. 19r–44v, l. 13 and f. 50r, l. 5–53)
7 *De morborum temporibus* (Περὶ ἐν ταῖς νόσοις καιρῶν; The manuscript entitles the first part: Περὶ τῶν ἐν τοῖς παραοξυσμοῖς καιρῶν. The second part, although belonging to the same work, is entitled Περὶ τῶν τοῦ ὅλου νοσήματος καιρῶν. f. 44v, l. 14–50r, l. 4 and f. 53v, l. 2 *ab imo*–56r, l. 17*)*
8 *Puero epileptico consilium* (Ἐπιλήπτῳ παιδὶ ὑποθήκη; f. 56r, l. 18–58v, l. 3)
9 *De propriis placitis* (Περὶ τῶν ἑαυτῷ δοκούντων; f. 59r–62v, l. 18);
10 *De libris propriis* (Περὶ τῶν ἰδίων βιβλίων; f. 62v, l. 18–65v, l. 8 *ab imo*)
11 *De ordine librorum suorum* (Περὶ τῆς τῶν ἰδίων βιβλίων τάξεως; f. 65v, l. 8 *ab imo*–67r, l. 8)
12 *De parvae pilae exercitio* (Περὶ τοῦ διὰ τῆς μικρᾶς σφαίρας γυμνασίου; f. 67r, l. 9–68r)
13 *Quod qualitates incorporeae sint* (Ὅτι αἱ ποιότητες ἀσώματοι; f. 68v–70v, l. 26)
14 *Adversus eos qui de typis scripserunt* (Πρὸς τοὺς περὶ τύπου [τύπων] γράψαντας; f. 70v, l. 27–75v, l. 3)
15 *De atra bile* (Περὶ μελαίνης χολῆς; f. 75v, l. 4–80v, l. 17)
16 *De purgantium medicamentorum facultate* (Περὶ τῶν καθαιρόντων φαρμάκων; f. 80v, l. 18–83r, l. 18)
17 *De plenitudine* (Περὶ πλήθους; f. 83r, l. 19–92v, l. 3)
18 *De praecognitione* (Περὶ τοῦ προγινώσκειν; f. 92v, l. 3–99r, l. 2)
19 *De praenotione* (Περὶ προγνώσεως; f. 99r, l. 3–100r)
20 *De dignotione ex insomniis* (Περὶ τῆς ἐξ ἐνυπνίων διαγνώσεως; f. 100v–101r, l. 8)
21 *Quomodo morbum simulantes sint deprehendendi* (Πῶς χρὴ ἐξελέγχειν τοὺς προσποιουμένοις νοσεῖν; f. 100v–101r, l. 8)
22 *Quos, quibus catharticis medicamentis et quando purgare oporteat* (Τίνας δεῖ καθαιρεῖν καὶ ποίοις καθαρτηρίοις καὶ πότε; f. 101v, l. 6 *ab imo*–103v, l. 4)
23 *De crisibus* (Περὶ κρίσεων; f. 104r–147r; book 1 105r, l. 17–118v, l. 2 *ab imo*: book 2 f. 118v, l. 1 *ab imo*–133r, l. 11; book 3 133r, l. 11–147r)
24 *In Hippocratis de victu acutorum commentarii* (Εἰς τὸ περὶ διαίτης ὀξέων Ἱπποκράτους ὑπόμνημα; f. 149r–239v, l. 11; correct order: book 1 f. 149r–169r; book 2 f. 169r–172 213r–220v; 181r–191v; book 3 191v–212v; 173r–174r, l. 23; book 4 174r, l. 24–180v, 221r–228v, 261r–268v, 242r–249v; 235r–239v, l. 11)
25 *In Hippocratis prorrheticum I commentarii III* (Εἰς τὸ πρῶτον βιβλίον προρρητικὸν Ἱπποκράτους ὑπόμνημα; f. 239v, l. 11–103v l. 4; correct order: f. 239v–241v, 273r–276v, 269r–272v, 258r–v, 258/1r v, 259r–260v, 229r–234v, 250r–257v)

The missing treatise occupying folios 10v to 14v has the title Περὶ ἀλυγισίας.[8] Boudon-Millot provisionally identified it as Περὶ ἀλυπίας/*De indolentia* – Galen's lost letter-treatise on moral philosophy. This identification was later confirmed by comparison with a paraphrase-summary of *Ind.* preserved in Arabic and Hebrew. In 2007, in a volume honoring Jouanna, Boudon-Millot published an initial version of the Greek text with a preliminary French translation (hereafter: B-M). In 2010, Boudon-Millot and Jouanna collaborated on a critical edition published by Budé (hereafter: BMJ). This volume is part of a new Budé series (now four new text-translations) on the Galenic corpus.

---
[7] Adapted from Pietrobelli, "Variation Autour du Thessalonicensis Vlatadon 14," 97–100.
[8] Modern Greek: ἀλυγισία, "stiff."

Modern Language Translations
Immediately following Boudon-Millot's first 2007 publication, translations into modern languages began to appear. Christopher P. Jones translated part of the text into English in an article in the *Journal of Roman Archaeology* (2009).[9] Pier Luigi Tucci also translated sections of the text in two articles in *JRA* (2008, 2009).[10] Vivian Nutton translated the entire piece into English based on his own reconstruction of the Greek text. A selection of Nutton's translations can be found in BMJ's commentary, Christopher Gill's *Naturalistic Psychology in Galen and Stoicism*,[11] and elsewhere. Cambridge University Press will publish the translation and commentary as the first volume in a series of Galen translations sponsored by the Wellcome Trust Programme under the leadership of Philip van der Eijk. Van der Eijk and his team aim to provide a coordinated series of English translations in a uniform format, accompanied by introductions, explanatory notes, bibliographies, glossaries, and indices.[12] Nutton's translation will appear in a volume entitled, *Galen: Psychological Works* edited by Peter N. Singer. With *Ind.*, this volume will include *Psychological Affections, Psychological Errors, Character Traits*, and *The Faculties of the Soul Depend on the Mixtures of the Body/The Soul's Dependence on the Body*. Nutton's translation pending, in 2011, we (Rothschild and Thompson) attempted to provide a diplomatic translation as a tool for getting the text out to a wider audience and encouraging further work. Our English translation based on the Greek text of BMJ appeared in *Early Christianity*, a relatively new journal published by Mohr Siebeck (Tübingen) and dedicated to the field of early Christian studies.[13] We have since modified the translation incorporating newer recent readings and emendations.

Finally, at about the same time, Paraskevi Kotzia and Panagiotis Sotiroudis of Aristotle University in Thessaloniki constructed their own Greek critical edition of *Ind.* on the basis of the codex[14] with a translation into modern Greek. A de-

---

[9] "Books and Libraries in a Newly-Discovered Treatise of Galen," *Journal of Roman Archaeology* 22 (2009): 390–8.

[10] "Galen's Storeroom, Rome's Libraries, and the Fire of A. D. 192," *Journal of Roman Archaeology* 21 (2008): 133–49 and "Antium, the Palatium, and the Domus Tiberiana Again," *Journal of Roman Archaeology* 22 (2009): 398–401.

[11] Christopher Gill, *Naturalistic Psychology in Galen & Stoicism* (Oxford: Oxford University Press, 2010).

[12] Until 2011, the Loeb Classical Library had published only Galen's *On the Natural Faculties* (1916). Under the leadership of Jeffrey Henderson, however, three volumes comprising Galen's *Method of Medicine* appeared in that year translated by Ian Johnston and G. H. R. Horsley (*Galen:* Method of Medicine [3 vols.; LCL; Cambridge, Mass.: Harvard University Press, 2011]). Ian Johnston is currently working on two new Loeb volumes that will include Galen's *De sanitate tuenda, Ars Medica*, and *Ad Glauconem de methodo medendi* (planned publication in 2015).

[13] Clare K. Rothschild and Trevor W. Thompson, "Galen: 'On the Avoidance of Grief,'" *EC* 2, no. 1 (2011): 110–29.

[14] Paraskevi Kotzia and Panagiotis Sotiroudis, "Γαληνοῦ περὶ ἀλυπίας," *Hellenica* 60 (2010): 63–148.

tailed collation of both critical editions, plus an even more recent Italian diglot by Ivan Garofalo and Alessandro Lami are included at the end of this volume (see "Collation").[15]

Recent Surge of Interest in Galen
With the discovery of *Ind.*, the world has witnessed a surge of interest in Galen. In addition to the various publication series noted above, the new annual journal *Galenos* is dedicated to Galenic studies[16] and several conferences have convened on the topic of Galen's life and work including: (1) "International Colloquium on Galen and the Vlatadon Codex at Vlatadon Monastery" in Thessaloniki on May 14, 2010; (2) "Seminario sul nuovo Galeno del codice Thessalonicensis 14 (XV sec.)" in Florence on November 22, 2010; (3) "New Approaches to Galen," hosted by the American Philological Association (session organizer, Rebecca Fleming) in San Antonio, TX from January 6–9, 2011; and, (4) "Books and Quotes: Scientific Works and Scholarly Editions in the 2nd Century AD," at the Berlin-Brandenburgische Akademie der Wissenschaften from September 28–29, 2012.

II. Text and Context

English Title
In keeping with scholarly conventions in the field of Classics, this volume primarily refers to the newly discovered work by its Latin title, *De indolentia*. That said, a significant number of different English titles are in use among which are: *On the Avoidance of Grief, On Freedom From Grief, Avoiding Grief,* and *On Being Free of Sorrow/Pain*. The main source of the variety is that no single word in English adequately captures the wide range of meanings and possible nuances of the λυπ- word group in Greek. The alpha privative only multiplies possibilities. The English title, *On the Avoidance of Grief,* was established by the first English translations of Galen's *On My Own Books* (*Lib.Prop.* 19.45) in which Galen lists *Ind.* among his written works.[17]

---

[15] Ivan Garofalo and Alessandro Lami, *Galeno: L'anima e il dolore*. De indolentia, De propriis placitis (BUR Rizzoli. Classici greci e latini; Milan: Biblioteca Universale Rizzoli, 2012). We note also that Mario Vegetti published an Italian translation based on the Greek text of BMJ; see Vegetii, *Galeno: Nuovi scritti autobiografici* (Rome: Carocci, 2013). Numerous other emendations to the critical editions have been proffered, either individually or in groups, in books, articles, and papers (see "Bibliography").

[16] *Galenos: Rivista di filologia dei testi medici antichi* (beginning in 2007).

[17] On the complicated nomenclature of the Galenic corpus in general, see "Appendix I: A Guide to the Editions and Abbreviations of the Galenic Corpus" and "Appendix II: English Titles and Modern Translations," in *The Cambridge Companion to Galen* (ed. R. J. Hankinson; Cambridge: Cambridge University Press, 2008), 391–403, and "Notes on Conventions," in

Authenticity
The evidence points strongly, if not certainly, toward the authenticity of the Vlatadon 14 text of *Ind.* Four points are salient. First, as noted, in *Lib.Prop.* (K 19.45), Galen refers to a work entitled, περὶ ἀλυπίας as one of his writings.[18] Second, comparison of the Greek text of Vlatadon 14 with the contents of Arabic and Hebrew epitomes of this work dated to the thirteenth-century confirms that the text in Vlatadon 14 is Galen's long-lost work. Third, miscellaneous biographical content of the treatise including details about the fire, Galen's age when he first arrives in Rome (i.e., "thirty-three," *Ind.* 34), and Galen's comments about his father and grandfather (*Ind.* 59) – accords with what we know about Galen's life from other works. Finally, the style and thought of *Ind.* are consistent with Galen's oeuvre. Treatment of the topic of λύπη in *De propriorum animi cuiuslibet affectuum dignotione et curatione* (*Aff.Dig.*), for example, demonstrates close agreement with treatment of λύπη in *Ind.*[19] To our knowledge, authenticity of the newly discovered text has not yet been seriously disputed.

Date of Composition
Scholarly consensus quickly established 192–193 CE as the most probable date of composition of *Ind.* This date is based upon at least the following two factors. First, the treatise focuses on Galen's response (or lack thereof) to a fire in the city of Rome during the year 192 CE – a disaster attested by multiple sources (e.g., Cassius Dio 72.24; Herodian 1.14.2–6). Moreover, near the beginning of the treatise, Galen refers to the fire as "very recent" (*Ind.* 2). The fire, thus, functions as a solid *terminus post quem* for the treatise and the treatise seems to have been written not long after this catastrophic event. Second, however, *Ind.* 54–55 describes "recent" actions of Commodus in an unflattering light. Since Commodus continually threatened members of the royal court, the logic is that Galen would not have been openly critical of the emperor until after his death on December 31, 192 CE. Cumulatively, a date in the first half of 193 CE seems most likely for the composition of *Ind.*

Galenic Psychological Oeuvre
According to Galen, *Ind.* is part of a larger body of literature he classifies as moral philosophy (ἠθικά φιλοσοφία; K 19.45–46), including the following seventeen works:

Galen and the World of Knowledge (eds. C. Gill, T. Whitmarsh, and J. Wilkins; Cambridge: Cambridge University Press, 2009), ix–xv.
[18] περὶ ἀλυπίας ἕν – "*On the Avoidance of Grief* in one book."
[19] Cf. esp. *Aff.Dig* (K 5.37, 43)

(1) *On the Diagnosis and Cure of the Passions and Errors of the Soul* (listed as a single work in two volumes)
(2) *Moral Character*
(3) *Against Favorinus' Attack on Socrates*
(4) *On the Avoidance of Grief*
(5) *Purpose of Philosophy*
(6) *The Relationship to his Hearers of One Making Public Demonstrations*
(7) *People who Read in Secret*
(8) *To Make the Punishment Fit the Crime*
(9) *Encouragement*
(10) *The Discourse with Bacchides and Cyrus in the Cilla of Menarchus*
(11) *Attendance at Dialogues*
(12) *To Orators in the Forum*
(13) *Pleasure and Pain*
(14) *What Follows from each Chosen Aim in Life*
(15) *Things said in Public to the Adherents of Sects*
(16) *Things said in Public Against Flatterers*
(17) *Things said in Public in the Presence of Pertinax*

With regard to specific philosophical positions held, Galen is consistently appreciated as a paradigmatic example of eclecticism. That said, his approach may be more accurately described as personal philosophy (see essay by Asmis in this volume).[20] At times, his thinking picks up on Stoic (ἀπάθεια) or Epicurean (ἀταραξία) ideas. At other times, his comments indicate strong affinities with Aristotle. In the larger oeuvre, his discussions of the ψυχή favor the Platonic tri-partite model as opposed to the more unified Stoic approach. He also famously argues against the Stoics that the rational part of the ψυχή resides in the head. Although these issues do not arise *per se* in *Ind.*, (e.g., *Ind.* 76), Galen does discuss the ψυχή following the first citation of Euripides in *Ind.* 52, after which point ψυχή plays a prominent role.[21] Other important terms from Stoicism include: φαντασία, γυμνάζειν (54), προσδοκεῖν (55), and παρασκευάζειν (2; 55); and the Epicurean expression, ἀοχλησία is the topic of discussion in *Ind.* 68:

> Some suppose that freedom from disturbance is the good'. I myself believe that neither I, nor any another human being, nor any living creature exhibits. I observe that every living thing is compelled to perform its own functions both with respect to body and soul. I also treated this point with copious explanatory notes in some other works, especially in my *Against Epicurus*.

---

[20] According to *Aff.Dig.*, Galen received a broad philosophical training in Pergamum. He learned from a Stoic (a student of Philopator), a Platonist (a student of Gaius), and a pupil of Aspasius the Peripatetic, and an Epicurean from Athens (K 5.415–42).
[21] E.g., 56–57; 60; 62; 68; 75; 76; 77; 81.

Epistolography

The generic classification of *Ind.* is somewhat uncertain. To be sure, the text begins as a response to a letter: "I received your letter in which you urged me to reveal to you what training, arguments, or doctrines prepared me never to be distressed" (*Ind.* 1). Yet the work, in its present form, does not contain the most common epistolary elements such as prescript (i.e., sender, address, or greeting), or proemium (prayer-wish for health or well-being, thanksgiving, remembrance, or expression of joy). Also, in the only occurrence of the common epistolary exhortation παρακαλεῖν in this text, Galen is the object not the (more typical) epistolary subject (*Ind.* 1).[22] In *Ind.*, Galen does not request anything from the reader and indicates no pending travel plans. The work contains no closing with epilogue (e.g., concluding advice or plans for a visit) or postscript (i.e., greetings, wishes, signature, or date), although it does conclude with a reference to "sending" (*Ind.* 84). Current evidence does not permit definitive conclusions about the original form of *Ind.* The text could originally have included the typical introductory and concluding epistolary features, removed by an editor or copyist later on.

Throughout *Ind.*, Galen addresses the intended reader in the second-person singular. Although the addressee is never identified, Galen offers a few clues to his identity. He had apparently been in Rome with Galen (*Ind.* 1), remained in communication with people in Rome (*Ind.* 1), and was educated with Galen (*Ind.* 51, 57). Likewise, Galen addresses his reader in the second-person singular in *Aff.Dig*, a work viewed as a tractate not a letter. In that work, Galen openly acknowledges an easy collapse between the public and private divide among publications. This may suggest that he ultimately expected *Ind.* to have a wide publication:

> As for the question of how to discover them all, I could give an account of how I found them out in my own case, but will at present refrain, *since this pamphlet may at some point fall into the hands of others* – they too should first exercise themselves to find out their own errors. (*Aff.Dig.* [K 5.5], emphasis added)[23]

Like Seneca, Galen's letters were probably intentionally both public and private – written originally with a single individual in mind to address a question posed by that person, but eventually intended for a much wider audience. We choose, therefore, to identify the text as a "letter-treatise" – a tentative conclusion recognizing the problems of classification and leaving the door open for further research and reflection.

---

[22] At *Ind.* 56, Galen does, however, "recommend" (παρακελεύεσθαι) – common to letters.

[23] ET: Peter N. Singer, *Galen: Selected Works* (Oxford World's Classics; Oxford: Oxford University Press, 1997), 102.

Consolation Literature
Although *Ind.* contains *topoi* common to consolation literature, this classification is problematic for at least a few reasons. First, Galen repeatedly affirms in this work, either by restating an observation of his reader or by his own statement, that he has never been distressed (*Ind.* 4–5, 29). He needs no consolation. Furthermore, the work offers no consolation or method of consolation for its intended reader – should he need it. On the contrary, Galen seems to intentionally create distress in the opening half of the work in his enumeration of items lost in the fire (see the essay of Rosen in this volume). This narration of loss builds in a kind of rhetorical crescendo. First, Galen notes the loss of an important dictionary. Next, he describes even greater losses, including limited editions and commentaries. Then, he poses the rhetorical question of what could be worse than what he has listed thus far (*Ind.* 31) – at which point he describes how he lost various irreplaceable items (*Ind.* 38). The *coup de grâce* is delivered when Galen finally describes the loss of two invaluable recipe collections. Even this, however, Galen says he bore very easily. He concludes, however, that one should not deduce from what he has said that he is impervious to distress. In an important caveat, he lists things that would distress him (*Ind.* 72a). In such cases, he explains that he would only be able to manage if he had food, water, shelter, and a book or a friend. In the case of severe physical pain, he says he could hope only to survive (78a–b, 79a).

Books, Literature, and Libraries
De indolentia provides important evidence for second-century literary culture (see the essay by Nicholls in this volume). The text covers a range of topics in this area of study, including Galen's aptitude for distinguishing genuine from false texts (*Ind.* 16), his nuanced lexical debates with other physicians (*Ind.* 23b–26), and his prolific scholarly activity (*Ind.* 14). Above all, however, this treatise offers information about ancient library culture. Nicholls refers to the text as "an invaluable new source for the book and library historian."[24] Among other things, the reader learns of (1) rare editions and collections in the city of Rome held at the Palatine libraries; (2) rental by Roman intellectuals of nearby warehouses to store books and other valuable materials; (3) presence of catalogues in ancient libraries as aids to book patrons; and (4) Galen's access to and use of texts held in the libraries on the Palatine. In addition, Galen describes the activities of friends in Pergamum who, like his friends in Rome and other cities, placed copies of his works in the local public libraries (*Ind.* 21; see the essay of Touwaide in this volume).

---

[24] Matthew C. Nicholls, "Galen and Libraries in the *Peri Alupias*," *Journal of Roman Studies* (2011): 123–42 [esp. 124].

Study of the Emotions, Passions, and Affections
Thanks to the work of scholars such as William V. Harris, Robert A. Kaster, and David Konstan, the last decade has witnessed increased attention to implications of the emotions, passions, and affections in ancient texts.[25] Taking the lead from contemporary science, scholars in a variety of fields are addressing the range of feelings implied by concepts of emotion in and throughout history. *De indolentia* contributes generously to this discussion in so far as it exemplifies an array of emotions grouped under the single expression, λυπή.

Early Christian Literature
On account, perhaps, of the facts that he flourished at the end of the second century and issued polemical statements against Christians, Galen's writings are often neglected in comparative studies of Early Christian literature, even though the two corpora treat many of the same topics. The following three comparative points offer a sample of questions for further research.

- Second-century use of parchment codices to preserve valuable texts (*Ind.* 34) may be comparable to early Christian preference for the codex.
- Like *Ind.*, more than one early Christian text preserves elements of an ancient epistle in the absence of standard epistolary elements (e.g., Hebrews, Epistle of Barnabas, 1 John). Since Galen has both private and public distribution in mind for his writings, these Christian texts might have similar publication aims.
- The 'hermeneutics of self-interpretation' is an important new trajectory in investigations of early Christian literature. Like Paul in 1 Corinthians (5:9–13), Galen recommends that his reader consult prior works on related topics to fully comprehend and/or correctly interpret his meaning in the present letter-treatise (*Ind.* 84). Galen's recourse to this hermeneutical strategy is, thus, another similarity he shares with early Christian literature (*Ind.* 67).

Bibliography

De indolentia: Texts and Translations

Véronique Boudon-Millot. "Un traité perdu de Galien miraculeusement retrouvé, *Le Sur l'inutilité de se chagriner*: texte grec et traduction française." Pages 72–123 in *La science médicale antique: Nouveaux regards. Études réunies en l'honneur de*

---

[25] William V. Harris, *Restraining Rage: The Ideology of Anger Control in Classical Antiquity* (Cambridge, Mass.; Harvard University Press, 2001) and William V. Harris, ed., *Mental Disorders in the Classical World* (Columbia Studies in the Classical Tradition 38; Leiden; Brill, 2013); Robert A. Kaster, *Emotion, Restraint, and Community in Ancient Rome* (Classical Culture and Society; Oxford University Press, 2005); David Konstan, *Pity Transformed* (London: Duckworth, 2001) and David Konstan, *The Emotions of the Ancient Greeks: Studies in Aristotle and Classical Literature* (Robson Classical Lectures; University of Toronto, 2006). Cf. Philippus R. Bosman, *Mania: Madness in the Greco-Roman World* (Pretoria: Classical Association of South Africa, 2009).

Jacques Jouanna. Edited by Véronique Boudon-Millot, Alessia Guardasole, and Caroline Magdelaine. Paris: Beauchesne, 2007.
Véronique Boudon-Millot and Jacques Jouanna (with Antoine Pietrobelli). *Galien:* Ne pas se chagriner. Collection des universités de France, publiée sous le patronage de l'Association Guillaume Budé. Paris: Les Belles Lettres, 2010.
Ivan Garofalo and Alessandro Lami. *Galeno: L'anima e il dolore.* De indolentia, De propriis placitis. BUR Rizzoli. Classici greci e latini. Milan: Biblioteca Universale Rizzoli, 2012.
Paraskevi Kotzia and Panagiotis Sotiroudis. "Γαληνού περὶ ἀλυπίας." *Hellenica* 60 (2010): 63–148.
Vivian Nutton. "Avoiding Distress." Pages 43–106 in *Galen: Psychological Works.* Edited by Peter N. Singer. Cambridge: Cambridge University Press, 2014.
Clare K. Rothschild and Trevor W. Thompson. "Galen: 'On the Avoidance of Grief.'" *EC* 2, no. 1 (2011). 110–29.
Mario Vegetii. *Galeno: Nuovi scritti autobiografici.* Rome: Carocci, 2013.

De indolentia: Other Works

Anargyros Anastassiou. "Galen, de indolentia, § 71, S. 21, 17–19 Boudon-Millot, Jouanna = § 27, S. 79, 321–322 Kotzia, Sotiroudis = § 71, S. 44 Garofalo, Lami." *Galenos: Rivista di filologia dei testi medici antichi* 6 (2012): 49–51.
Ioanna-Maria Athanasopoulou, Antonis A. Kousoulis, and Effie Poulakou-Rebelakou. "How to Cope with Disaster Loss and Mourning: Galen's Paper which was Lost for Centuries." *Vesalius* 17, no. 2 (2011): 99–101.
Francesco Becchi. "La psicopatologia di Galeno: il περὶ ἀλυπίας." Pages 23–31 in *Studi sul* De Indolentia *di Galeno.* Edited by Daniela Manetti. Vol. 4 of *Biblioteca di "Galenos": Contributi alla ricerca sui testi medici antichi.* Pisa: Fabrizio Serra, 2012.
– "Dalla τέχνη ἀλυπίας di Antifonte al Περὶ ἀλυπίας di Plutarco e di Galeno: evolucione storica di un ideale di vita." *Studi italiani di filologia classica* 10 (2012): 88–99.
Anna Maria Ieraci Bio, Klaus-Dietrich Fischer, Ivan Garofalo, Alessandro Lami, Lorenzo Perilli, and Amneris Roselli. "Congetture e emendamenti inediti sui testi medici." *Galenos: Rivista di filologia dei testi medici antichi* 2 (2008): 135–42 [esp. 137–8; proposed emendations of *De indolentia* by Garofalo and Roselli].
Véronique Boudon-Millot (in collaboration with Antoine Pietrobelli). "De l'arabe au grec: un nouveau témoin du texte de Galien (le manuscript *Vlatadon* 14)." *Comptes-rendus des séances de l'Académie des Inscriptions et Belles-Lettres* 149, no. 2 (2005): 497–534.
Véronique Boudon-Millot. "The Library and the Workshop of a Greek Scholar in the Roman Empire: New Testimony from the Recently Discovered Galen's treatise *Peri alupias.*" Pages 7–18 in *Asklepios. Studies on Ancient Medicine: Between Craft and Cult.* Edited by Louise Cilliers. Baltimore, MD: The Johns Hopkins University, 2008.
– "Galien de Pergame et la pratique épistolaire: à quelles conditions une médecine par correspondance est elle possible?" Pages 113–32 in *Les écritures de la douleur dans l'épistolaire.* Edited by Patrick Laurence and François Guillaumont. Leuven: Peeters, 2010.
– "La Vita Galieni de Jean de Procida: un nouveau jalon dans l'histoire du texte du Ne pas se chagriner de Galien." *Galenos: Rivista di filologia dei testi medici antichi* 6 (2012): 165–72.

- "What Is a Mental Illness, and How Can it Be Treated? Galen's Reply as a Doctor and Philosopher." Pages 129–46 in *Mental Disorders in the Classical World*. Edited by William Harris. Leiden: Brill, 2013.

Gianluca Del Mastro. "Μέγα βιβλίον. Galeno e la lunghezza dei libri (περὶ ἀλυπίας 28). Pages 33–61 in *Studi sul* De Indolentia *di Galeno*. Edited by Daniela Manetti. Vol. 4 of *Biblioteca di "Galenos": Contributi alla ricerca sui testi medici antichi*. Pisa: Fabrizio Serra, 2012.

Tiziano Dorandi. "'Editori' antichi di Platone." *Antiquorum Philosophia* 4 (2010): 161–74.

Klaus-Dietrich Fischer, Ivan Garofalo, Alessandro Lami, and Vito Lorusso. "Congetture e emendamenti inediti." *Galenos: Rivista di filologia dei testi medici antichi* 6 (2012): 181–90 [esp. 183; proposed emendation of *De indolentia* by Lorusso].

Ivan Garofalo. "Emendamenti al *de indolentia*." Pages 63–67 in *Studi sul* De Indolentia *di Galeno*. Edited by Daniela Manetti. Vol. 4 of *Biblioteca di "Galenos": Contributi alla ricerca sui testi medici antichi*. Pisa: Fabrizio Serra, 2012.

Christopher Gill, Tim Whitmarsh, and John Wilkins. "Introduction." Pages 1–18 in *Galen and the World of Knowledge*. Edited by Christopher Gill, Tim Whitmarsh, and John Wilkins. Cambridge: Cambridge University Press, 2009.

Christopher Gill. *Naturalistic Psychology in Galen & Stoicism*. Oxford: Oxford University Press, 2010 [esp. 243–329].

- "Philosophical Therapy as Preventive Psychological Medicine." Pages 339–62 in *Mental Disorders in the Classical World*. Edited by William V. Harris. Leiden: Brill, 2013.

Jean-Baptiste Gourinat. "'Le Platon de Panétius' À propos d'un témoignage inédit de Galien." *Philosophie antique* 8 (2008): 139–51.

Abraham S. Halkin. "Classical and Arabic Material in Ibn 'Aḵnīn's 'Hygiene of the Soul.'" *Proceedings of the American Academy for Jewish Research* 14 (1944): 25–147 [esp. 60–65, 110–15].

George W. Houston. "Galen, his books, and the Horrea Piperataria at Rome." *Memoirs of the American Academy in Rome* 48 (2008): 45–51.

William A. Johnson. "Libraries and Reading Culture in the High Empire." Pages 347–63 in *Ancient Libraries*. Edited by Jason König, Katerina Oikonomopoulou, and Greg Woolf. Cambridge: Cambridge University Press, 2013.

Christopher P. Jones. "Books and Libraries in a Newly-Discovered Treatise of Galen." *Journal of Roman Archaeology* 22 (2009): 390–8.

- "Galen's Travels." *Chiron* 42 (2012): 399–419.

Jacques Jouanna. "Présentation du nouvea Galien, *Ne pas se chagriner*, dans la *Collection des Universités de France*." *Bulletin de l'Association Guillaume Budé* no. 2 (2011): 22–40.

Paraskevi Kotzia. "Galen περὶ ἀλυπίας: title, genre and two *cruces*." Pages 69–91 in *Studi sul* De Indolentia *di Galeno*. Edited by Daniela Manetti. Vol. 4 of *Biblioteca di "Galenos": Contributi alla ricerca sui testi medici antichi*. Pisa: Fabrizio Serra, 2012.

Alessandro Lami. "Il nuovo Galeno e il fr. 964 di Euripide." *Galenos: Rivista di filologia dei testi medici antichi* 3 (2009): 11–19.

Carlos Levy. "Médicine et philosophie: à propos de l'édition du *De Indolentia* de Galien dans la C. U. F." *Bulletin de l'Association Guillaume Budé* no. 1 (2011): 198–210.

Carlo M. Lucarini. "Congetture al nuovo Galeno." *Philologus* 154, no. 2 (2010): 331–7.

Daniela Manetti, ed. *Studi sul* De Indolentia *di Galeno*. Vol. 4 of *Biblioteca di "Galenos": Contributi alla ricerca sui testi medici antichi*. Pisa: Fabrizio Serra, 2012.

- "Galeno περὶ ἀλυπίας e il difficile equilibrismo dei filologi." Pages 9–11 in *Studi sul* De Indolentia *di Galeno*. Edited by Daniela Manetti. Vol. 4 of *Biblioteca di "Galenos": Contributi alla ricerca sui testi medici antichi*. Pisa: Fabrizio Serra, 2012.
Susan P. Mattern. *The Prince of Medicine: Galen in the Roman Empire*. Oxford: Oxford University Press, 2013 [esp. 220–4; 261–7].
Matthew Nicholls. "Parchment Codices in a New Text of Galen." *Greece and Rome* 57, no. 2 (2010): 259–67.
- "Galen and Libraries in the *Peri Alupias*." *Journal of Roman Studies* 101 (2011): 123–42.
Vivian Nutton. "Galenic Madness." Pages 119–28 in *Mental Disorders in the Classical World*. Edited by William Harris. Leiden: Brill, 2013.
Luigi Piacente. "Sul prestito librario nell'antica Roma." *Segno e Testo* 9 (2011): 35–51.
Antoine Pietrobelli. "Variation Autour du *Thessalonicensis Vlatadon* 14: un manuscript copié au *xénon* du Kral, peu avant la Chute de Constantinople." *Revue des etudes byzantines* 68 (2010): 95–126.
Ioannis Polemis. "ΔΙΟΡΘΩΤΙΚΑ ΣΤΟ ΠΕΡΙ ΑΛΥΠΙΑΣ ΤΟΥ ΓΑΛΗΝΟΥ." *Επιστημονική Επετηρίς της φιλοσοφικής σχολής του Πανεπιστημίου Αθηνών* 43 (2011/12): 371–8.
Enzo Puglia. "La Rovina dei Libri di Anzio nel *De Indolentia* di Galeno." *Segno e Testo* 9 (2011): 1–10.
Tommaso Raiola. "'Asini per uccelli': una nota a *de Indolentia* 61." *Galenos: Rivista di filologia dei testi medici antichi* 5 (2011): 21–26.
Marwan Rashed. "*Aristote à Rome au IIe siècle: Galien, De indolentia*, §§ 15–18." *Elenchos* 32, no. 1 (2011): 55–77.
Amneris Roselli. "Libri e biblioteche a Roma al tempo di Galeno: la testimonianza del '*De indolentia*.'" *Galenos: Rivista di filologia dei testi medici antichi* 4 (2010): 127–48.
- "Galeno dopo l'incendio del 192: bilancio di una vita." Pages 93–101 in *Studi sul* De Indolentia *di Galeno*. Edited by Daniela Manetti. Vol. 4 of *Biblioteca di "Galenos": Contributi alla ricerca sui testi medici antichi*. Pisa: Fabrizio Serra, 2012.
Clare K. Rothschild and Trevor W. Thompson. "Galen's *On the Avoidance of Grief*: The Question of a Library at Antium." *Classical Philology* 107, no. 2 (2012): 131–45.
Antonio Stramaglia. "Libri perduti per sempre: Galeno, *De indolentia* 13; 16; 17–19." *Rivista di Filologia e di Istruzione Classica* 139, no. 1 (2011): 118–47.
Pier Luigi Tucci. "Galen's Storeroom, Rome's Libraries, and the Fire of A. D. 192." *Journal of Roman Archaeology* 21 (2008): 133–49.
- "Antium, the Palatium, and the Domus Tiberiana Again." *Journal of Roman Archaeology* 22 (2009): 398–401.
- "Flavian libraries in the City of Rome." Pages 277–311 in *Ancient Libraries*. Edited by Jason König, Katerina Oikonomopoulou, and Greg Woolf. Cambridge: Cambridge University Press, 2013.
- "Galen and the Library at Antium: The State of the Question." *Classical Philology* 108, no. 3 (2013): 240–51.
Alexei V. Zadorojnyi. "Libraries and *paideia* in the Second Sophistic: Plutarch and Galen." Pages 377–400 in *Ancient Libraries*. Edited by Jason König, Katerina Oikonomopoulou, and Greg Woolf. Cambridge: Cambridge University Press, 2013.

I. English Translation

Clare K. Rothschild / Trevor W. Thompson

Galen: "On the Avoidance of Distress"[1]

Our first publication ("Galen: 'On the Avoidance of Grief,'" *EC* 2, no. 1 [2011]: 110–29), offers a close diplomatic rendering in English of the Greek text in Véronique Boudon-Millot and Jacques Jouanna (with Antoine Pietrobelli), *Galien:* Ne pas se chagriner (Budé; Paris: Les Belles Lettres, 2010; hereafter: BMJ with references in the following format: section.page.line). The following English translation represents an idiomatic version of the earlier work, revised in light of the subsequent Greek text of Paraskevi Kotzia and Panagiotis Sotiroudis, "Γαληνού περὶ ἀλυπίας," *Hellenica* 60 (2010): 63–150 (hereafter: KS; references in the format: line number), to our knowledge the only critical edition based upon the codex as opposed to digital images. The present ET also interacts with the Italian diglot of Ivan Garofalo and Alessandro Lami (*L'anima e il dolore.* De indolentia, De propriis placitis [BUR Rizzoli. Classici greci e latini; Milan: RCS libri, 2012]) as well as various other proposed emendations published after the appearance of our first translation. In difficult passages, we have supplied the Greek text in footnotes as an aid to the reader. When our reading departs from BMJ, we supply both the Greek text and its source with grounds for decisions in the notes. Readings of Kotzia-Sotiroudis or Garofalo-Lami occasionally distort BMJ's section breaks. A compilation of critical texts at the end of the present volume (pages 277–314) should assist the reader interested in tracking all choices.

1 I received your letter in which you urged me to reveal to you what training, arguments, or doctrines prepared me never to be distressed. You said that, when you were here, you witnessed how I lost the slaves I kept on hand in Rome during a severe bout of long-lasting plague.[2] You also heard that such a thing had already happened to me before. I encountered severe losses to my belongings three or four times.

2 You said that you saw I was not even a little disturbed. However, the very recent event that happened to me – when all of my possessions deposited in the storehouses on the Sacred Way were destroyed in the great fire – surpassed everything prior.

3 You said you knew how important these objects were but learned from a messenger that I am still not in the slightest bit troubled, remaining cheerful and carrying out my customary activities as before.

---

[1] We would like to thank both Paraskevi Kotzia and Ian Johnston for carefully reading and commenting on prior iterations of this translation. All flaws are our own.

[2] Plague ca. 166 CE.

4 Of items deposited in the storehouses destroyed in the fire, what surprised you was not that I appeared to endure without distress silver, gold, silver-plates, and many contracts, but a considerable number of my writings, a wide assortment of medicines both simple and compound, and various instruments.

5 Of the instruments lost, some were standard medical equipment. Although as I just said they were lost, I expect to be able to replace them. Others, however, were one of kind (pieces of) medical equipment[3] that I invented. After forming their molds from beeswax, I gave them to blacksmiths to forge. It is no longer possible to recover these items without significant time and substantial effort.

6 Likewise, it is no longer possible to recover the books – both the ancient works corrected by my hand and those that I composed – and the so-called remedies, of which you said you knew I had many. It is especially impossible to recover the so-called 'theriac' of eighty pounds in weight, the cinnamon, of a quantity surpassing all the retail-dealers (in Rome) put together, and, likewise, all the other rare (therapeutic substances) I had in abundance.

7 You also learned that when Philides[4] the grammarian's books were destroyed in the fire, he wasted away and died as a result of discouragement and distress. What is more, for quite some time, people went around in black garments – thin and pale like mourners.

8 Being confident that the storehouses along the Sacred Way would certainly not succumb to fire, people used to deposit their most valuable possessions in them. They trusted them because they were not made of wood apart from the doors, were not in the vicinity of a private house, and were guarded by a military garrison since the district archives of four procurators of Caesar were stored there.

9 For this very reason, those of us who leased the units paid more rent, confidently storing very valuable possessions there.

10 Yet, in addition to this shared misfortune, something else – a private misfortune – befell me. When I went to Campania, I placed[5] everything at home in the storehouse – instruments, medicines, books, and not a few silver vessels – for safekeeping while I was abroad. For that reason, the entire inventory – plus the (above-mentioned) valuables – were destroyed. You said that you learned these things happened in this way, but wanted to hear about it from me for greater certainty.

11 It seemed remarkable to you that I was not troubled, even though all my valuables were destroyed by fire.[6] Obviously, you are correct in what you have

---

[3] Vlatadon: χρήματα προσευρημένα τῶν ἀρμένων.

[4] This grammarian's name is most likely corrupt. See discussion in BMJ (p. 41–42). BMJ 7.4.6 and KS 29: Φιλίδης; Garofalo and Lami: Φιλι<στ>ίδης (p. 10).

[5] KS 43: κατεθέμην.

[6] Τὸ γὰρ μηδὲ τῶν τοιούτων ἁπάντων ἁπτομένων ἀνιαθῆναί με θαυ(μα)σι(ώ)τερον ἐδόκει σοι. We read τῶν τοιούτων ἁπάντων ἁπτομένων as a genitive absolute. Alternatively, τῶν

written. In Campania, when I learned that everything[7] had been destroyed, I bore the matter very easily being not even a little disturbed. However, when I went back up to Rome,[8]

12a I was in need of everything. Without my possessions, it was impossible to prepare remedies in a timely manner. I felt annoyed then,[9] just as I still feel now, finding myself in need of one thing or another – a book, instrument, or medicine – every day.

12b Even still the most tragic thing escaped you. Compounding the calamity of my books was the fact that all of the libraries on the Palatine also burned on that day, precluding hope of their replacement.

13 Therefore, it is impossible to replace the rare books to which there was limited access or the publicly available books sought out for their clarity – the Callinian, Atticianan, Pedoucinian, and certainly the Aristarchean collections, including two Homeric works, Panaetius' Plato, and many other such works. Those collections preserved the very words that the collectors themselves either wrote or copied in each volume. In fact, autograph copies[10] by many ancient grammarians, rhetoricians, physicians, and philosophers were among them.[11]

14 In addition to these (losses) – catastrophic on a grand scale – on the same day I lost all the books full of obscurities and errors in the texts that, after correction, had been copied on to a clean manuscript because I intended to publish

---

τοιούτων ἁπάντων ἁπτομένων θαυμασιώτερον may serve as the genitive complement for the comparative, θαυμασιώτερον: "It seemed to you more remarkable that I was not troubled, than that all my possessions burned."

[7] KS 49: ἅπαντα.

[8] KS 50–1: Ἐπεὶ δ᾽εἰς Ῥώμην ἐπανῆλθον.

[9] KS 52: <ἐν> βραχεῖ <δὲ> χρόνῳ τῆς δ[υσχερείας]. Cf. *De placitis Hippocratis et Platonis* (*PHP*) 5.7.48. Or perhaps: δυσχωρία "disadvantageous ground?"

[10] Vlatadon: αὐτόγραφα. The claim to be in contact with autographs may represent Galenic exaggeration. See Matthew C. Nicholls, "Galen and Libraries in the *Peri Alupias*," *Journal of Roman Studies* 101 (2011): 123–42 [130–1 n. 40]. Kotzia opts for αὐτόγραφα. In private correspondence, she notes that, because exaggeration is a central feature in Galen's report about his losses, and because she views the claim to possess autographs as a trend among Galen's contemporaries. Kotzia offers the following examples for comparison: (1) Pliny the Elder writes, "I have seen documents in the hand of Tiberius and Gaius Gracchus written nearly two hundred years ago; while as for autographs of Cicero, of the divine Augustus, and of Virgil, we see them repeatedly (*Tiberi Gaique Gracchorum manus apud Pomponium Secundum ... uidi annos fere post ducentos*)" (Pliny *Nat.* 13.83); and (2) Aulus Gellius *Noct. att.* 2.3–5: *ostendisse mihi librum Aeneidos secundum mirande vetustatis emptum in sigillariis uiginti aureis, quem ipsius Vergili fuisse credebatur.*

[11] We understand an elision of βιβλία with σπάνια καὶ ἀλλαχόθι μηδαμόθεν κείμενα (likely anticipating τὰ βιβία at the end of the sentence; 13.6.4). More importantly, there is an elision of σπάνια καὶ ἀλλαχόθι μηδαμόθεν κείμενα between the οὔτε and τῶν μέσων (13.5.20). Understanding the elision balances the οὔτε ... οὔτε clauses, makes sense of the ἐστιν (deleted in BMJ), and supplies an understood object of δυνατόν ἐστιν εὑρεῖν in the second οὔτε clause. Result: οὔτε <σπάνια καὶ ἀλλαχόθι μηδαμόθεν κείμενα> τῶν μέσων (cf. the insertion of <τινὰ> in KS 59). Our reading also preserves Vlatadon's ἐν τοῖς (cf. BMJ ἐντός and KS ἔν τισι).

them. The writings were carefully corrected, so that nothing was added, or left out,[12] not even a *paragraphos*, single or double, or a *coronis* – a siglum appropriately placed between books. What should[13] we say about the period or comma,[14] as you know, of such importance in obscure books that the one who pays attention to them does not need a commentator.[15]

15 These included the works of Theophrastus, Aristotle, Eudemus, Clytus,[16] Phaenias, the majority of what Chrysippus wrote – and all the ancient physicians.[17]

16 Further, these things will especially distress you. Namely, that I found among the book rolls inventoried on the outside according to their titles in the so-called *Pinakes* – in both the libraries on the Palatine and those in Antium – some works clearly not belonging to the author after whom the book roll is inventoried. They are dissimilar from that author in both style and thought – for example, the works of Theophrastus, in particular (his) works on scientific matters.[18]

17 Everyone has his [Theophrastus's] books on plants expounded in two extended treatises. But, there was a work by Theophrastus in complete agreement with Aristotle[19] that I found (i.e., in the libraries on the Palatine) and copied, which is now lost. In the same way, as those books by Theophrastus, I also found works of some of the other men of old *not* inventoried in the catalogues,[20] some that, although inventoried in the catalogues, no longer appear in the libraries.[21]

---

[12] Vlatadon: χρήματα. We accept Vlatadon here, taking χρήματα to mean something like τι.

[13] Ioannis Polemis, "ΔΙΟΡΘΩΤΙΚΑ ΣΤΟ ΠΕΡΙ ΑΛΥΠΙΑΣ ΤΟΥ ΓΑΛΗΝΟΥ," *Επιστημονική Επετηρίς της φιλοσοφικής σχολής του Πανεπιστημίου Αθηνών* 43 (2011/12): 371–8: τί δεῖ λέγειν (p. 372).

[14] KS 72: ἅς.

[15] Punctuation in BMJ and KS is different. We take only the first phrase as a question.

[16] Polemis: Κλύτου (p. 372).

[17] Nicholls, "Galen and Libraries in the *Peri Alupias*," 11 n. 58.

[18] This section is variously reconstructed. We follow BMJ with the exception of reading "in Antium." BMJ 16.6.21–7.5 Λυπήσει δέ σε καὶ ταῦτα μάλιστα ὡς τῶν ἐν τοῖς καλουμένοις πίναξι [τῶν] γεγραμμένων βιβλίων ἔξωθεν εὑρόν τινα κατά τε τὰς ἐν τῷ Παλατίῳ βιβλιοθήκας καί τ<ιν>α[ς] ἐναντίω<ς> ἃ φανερῶς <οὐκ> ἦν οὗπερ ἐγέγραπτο, <οὔτε> κατὰ τὴν λέξιν οὔτε κατὰ <τὴν> διάνοιαν ὁμοιούμενα αὐτῷ. Καὶ τὰ Θεοφράστου καὶ μάλιστα τὰ κατὰ τὰς ἐπιστημονικὰς πραγματείας 17 – ἔστιν ἄλλα τὰ περὶ φυτῶν βιβλία κατὰ δύο πραγματείας ἐκτεταμένας ἡρμηνευμένα – πάντες ἔχουσι. For the reading of "in Antium" [ἐν Ἀντίῳ] here and in the following two sections see Clare K. Rothschild and Trevor W. Thompson, "Galen and the Library at Antium," *CP* 107, no. 2 (2012): 131–45. Contrast, Pier Luigi Tucci, "Galen and the Library at Antium: The State of the Question," *CP* 108, no. 3 (2013): 240–51.

[19] According to Sotiroudis, Vlatadon reads Ἀριστοτέλους. KS supplies τῇ. The tractate referred to here would have been a rare find; it is now evidently lost.

[20] Cf. Plutarch *Sull.* 26.2: ἀναγράψαι τοὺς νῦν φερομένους πίνακας.

[21] It seems that Galen refers in this section to three groups of book rolls in the libraries on the Palatine and Antium: (1) book rolls inventoried in the *Pinakes* but containing other un-inventoried works; (2) book rolls not inventoried in the *Pinakes*; and (3) book rolls inventoried in the Pinakes but missing in the library. The inventoried but missing works may have been subsumed within other book rolls of different inventory label. The point is that no catalogue

I found, then, many of these works in the libraries on the Palatine, which I prepared in Antium.²²

18 In fact, those on the Palatine were destroyed the same day as mine. The fire not only burned the storehouses on the Sacred Way, but also before them, the libraries by the Temple of Peace, and after them, both those on the Palatine and the so-called House of Tiberius in which there was also a library full of many other books. At the time I first went up to Rome, some in Antium were on the verge of ruin on account of the negligence of those continually robbing them by false pledges.²³

19 Copying these books required no small amount of effort. As it is, the papyri are completely useless and cannot even be unrolled because they have become glued together by decomposition since the region is both marshy and low-lying, and stifling in the summer.

20 Loss of the Attic glossary, especially the most frequently occurring terms, was likewise a source of distress.²⁴ There are two parts, as you know, one from Old Comedy and another from prose writers. However, just by chance, copies of the latter had been brought to Campania. If, in fact, those at Rome had burned two months later, the copies of all my works would have arrived in Campania.

21 All my works intended for circulation were already transcribed in duplicate, not counting those (only) intended to remain in Rome. Friends at Pergamum requested I forward all my works in order to place them in public libraries²⁵ as other friends had done in other cities. I also intended to keep copies of everything in Campania.

22 For this reason, there were duplicate copies of all my works, excluding those meant to be housed [only] in Rome (i.e., not for circulation), as I said.

23a The fire, then, broke out at the end of winter. I planned, at the beginning of summer, to transport books to Campania, both those copies to be kept there and those to be sent to Asia when the Etesian winds blow.

23b–24a Fortune, then, ambushed me, depriving me of many of my other books, not least the Glossary of nouns that I excerpted from the whole of Old Comedy. **24a** As you know,²⁶ Didymus (Chalcenterus)²⁷ previously explained

---

will allow, as in 80 CE, the librarians in Rome to ever recover (through, for example, copies made at another reputable library and transported to Rome) what was lost in this fire because so much remained uncatalogued.

²² Galen restocked Antium's library by copying books from the Palatine library.

²³ Antonio Stramaglia. "Libri perduti per sempre: Galeno, De indolentia 13; 16; 17–19." *Rivista di Filologia e di Istruzione Classica* 139, no. 1 (2011): 118–47 [140–2].

²⁴ KS 101–2: Ἴσως δὲ ἐλύπει <σε ἂν> καὶ ἡ τῶν Ἀττικῶν ὀνομάτων καὶ ὅσα πολιτικὰ πραγματεία. We understand ἡ <ἀπώλεια> τῶν Ἀττικῶν ὀνομάτων ("loss of the Attic glossary").

²⁵ Polemis: ὅπως ἐν βιβλιοθήκαις δημοσίαις θῶσι (p. 373).

²⁶ Vlatadon: ἦν δ' ὡς οἶσθα.

²⁷ Grammarian from Alexandria (second half of the first century BCE to the beginning of the first century CE).

both the frequently occurring and all the rare terms from Old Comedy in fifty books. From these books, I had composed an epitome in six thousand lines.

24b–25 It seemed to me that such a composition was useful to both orators and grammarians, in short, whoever wished to apply Attic words more generally to practical matters.[28] This recent example supports my claim: one of the renowned physicians in Rome said that the word "groat"[29] did not occur in the Hippocratic period and, for this reason, claimed that Hippocrates preferred to use the word "tisane"[30] from among all terms for grain in *On Regimen in Acute Diseases*. This physician assumed that if, in fact, the word "groat" was known to the Greeks, Hippocrates would not have chosen a different word (i.e., "tisane").

26–27 However, the word "groat" is recorded in *On Regimen in Health* – which some attribute to Hippocrates, but others to Philistion, and still others to Ariston, both ancient physicians. What is more, the word "groat" is also recorded in the authors of Old Comedy. Ἀβυδομην and Ἀβύστακινεῖν[31] – all such words unclear to listeners were defined in my work – including words that Didymus formerly explained well, such as emmer, grasspeas (chickling vetch), bitter vetch, groat, and other seeds of Demeter, vegetables, late summer fruits, wine from the remains of pressed grapes, 'seconds,' trees, fruits, plants, living things, instruments, equipment, tools, other practical expressions, and all proper nouns.

28 All the other books that comprise this epitome excerpting old Comedy were not transported to Campania prior to the fire. By chance, those by prose writers had already been transported. They are in forty-eight large book rolls. It will perhaps be necessary to split into two those with a length exceeding four thousand hexametric verses.[32]

29 (Loss of) none of these books troubled me – although there were many useful limited editions. Neither was I troubled by the destruction of my commentaries.[33] The commentaries were of two types. Some were useful to others, whereas others were useful for me alone, having the same preparatory sketch for aid in memorization.[34]

---

[28] Vlatadon: ἢ οἵτινες ὅλως ἀττικίζειν βούλοιντο τινα καὶ τῶν εἰς τὰ πράγματα χρήσιμα διαφερόντων (with ἀταικίζειν corrected). We understand οἵτινες ἀττικίζειν βούλοιντο after καί. Alternatively, it is possible to translate: "or whoever wishes to use Attic words at all, including words relevant for practical use." BMJ 24b.9.201 records ἢ οἵτινες ὅλως ἀττικίζειν βούλοιντο <ἢ> τινα: "or whoever wishes to use Attic words at all or words from among those relevant for practical use."

[29] χόνδρος i.e., hulled grain broken into fragments.

[30] πτισάνη i.e., crushed barley.

[31] The text is evidently corrupt here. Polemis suggests Ἀβυδοκόμης ("informer's-haircut") and ἀβυρτάκη ("leek sauce"). Galen evidently selected two obscure terms from the beginning of the alphabetical list for rhetorical effect.

[32] Cf. Vlatadon: ἐξάριθμον ("supernumerary," "exceeding the norm").

[33] ὡς οὐδὲ ἡ τῶν ἡμ<ετέρ>ων ὑπομνημάτων ἀπώλεια

[34] BMJ 29.11.4–5: καίτοι τὴν αὐτὴν ἔχοντα παρασκευὴν εἰς ἀνάμνησιν.

30 In addition, there were many summaries or synopses of a great number of medical and philosophical books. Yet not even these losses distressed me.

31 What then, would you say, could be painful enough to cause me distress, more than all the things I have said? Well, I will tell you: I was entrusted with the most remarkable medical recipes that no one in the entire Roman world had. Fortune contributed some; I made up the rest.[35]

32 As a matter of fact, Fortune granted me recipes twice. The first occurrence took place as follows. A rich man in our circle was so eager to acquire knowledge about effective medications that he paid more than one hundred gold pieces for certain recipes. Not only did he purchase[36] recipes prized by physicians in Asia today, but also [physicians] of the past.[37]

33 All of these medical recipes were carefully recorded in two parchment codices. One of his heirs – a very good friend of mine – gave them to me without my asking.

34 This, then, was my first windfall of medical recipes. Listen to the second occurrence. It was as follows. When I arrived in Rome for the first time, I was thirty-three years old. I discovered that a fellow citizen and classmate of mine named Teuthras was staying in the city. He had inherited the parchments of the physician Eumenes.[38] Eumenes was a Pergamene who loved pharmacology and was more knowledgeable about it than all other physicians.

35 These very parchments[39] were gathered together in one place from all over the world thanks to Eumenes' travels, after which he came to Rome where he remained until his death. When Teuthras was dying in the first bout of plague, he left me these parchments. This was shortly after my arrival, as I said, the first time I had come to Rome.

36 Thanks to these provisions, I was easily able to exchange two or three of my recipes for an effective recipe belonging to someone else.

37 Not only, then, were all of these parchments destroyed in the fire – I, in fact, still considered this trivial – but I lost my own highly accurate treatise, *On the Composition of Drugs according to Kind*, in which, I explain how[40] to prepare

---

[35] Alessandro Lami *apud* Vivian Nutton (also KS 154): συμπροθυμηθέντος ("in part my joint zeal").

[36] Vlatadon (KS 159): κατὰ τὴν οὐσίαν. We understand, with Kotzia, that the phrase κατὰ τὴν οὐσίαν is synonymous with ἀξιόλογος.

[37] If one understands an elided ὅσα in the second half of the sentence as well (so: ἀλλὰ καὶ ὅσα τῶν παλαιῶν), this sentence may refer to two groups of medical recipes: "He went about this task by purchasing not only all the effective recipes prized by physicians (today), but also (those) by those (physicians) of the past." This interpretation is also recommended by the πάντων of 33 as well as Galen's reference in that passage to two parchment codices.

[38] Eumenes does not appear elsewhere in Galen. Perhaps Eudemus of Pergamum is the person intended.

[39] KS 169: αἱ διφθέραι.

[40] Nutton (*apud* BMJ) reads ἐμήνυον.

the most trustworthy medicines step by step. Only a few recipes, lent to friends beforehand, are preserved.

38 Perhaps then you will say that your interest is piqued.[41] Because each one of these losses, in and of itself, would have been insurmountably distressing to others, you yearn to know how I, despite having lost such a great variety of my possessions, was not troubled as others were, but endured everything that happened.[42]

39 I will give you a double reply to this request. First, I begin with this recollection. Surely, you remember, having frequently heard me offer such anecdotes. Extravagant Aristippus[43] was not satisfied with a thrifty way of life. On the contrary, he was only satisfied with expensive things: buying delicacies every day, each time bestowing quantities of silver upon the more attractive prostitutes,[44] yet, equally often, begging for something from the crowd – what a fellow![45]

40 Once he was returning from Piraeus (to Athens) – it was always his custom to walk, not just on short roads like this, but also on long ones. Since he observed that the slave was unable to keep up on account of his load – a leather bag full of gold – he ordered him to empty out a considerable amount so that what remained would be manageable for him.

41 With the same resolve, he also did as follows. Although he owned four fields in his home country,[46] he lost[47] one of them during some kind of crisis, leaving only three.

42 When a fellow citizen met him, he was about to express consolation for the loss. Laughing at him, Aristippus said, "Why exactly would *you* console me[48] when I own three good fields and you own hardly one? Should I not be consoling you?" This anecdote[49] demonstrates very well what you often heard me say, namely that a person should not dwell on what is lost,[50] but consider how those who inherit three fields from their father cannot bear to see others with thirty.

---

[41] Polemis: ἐπιτετάσθαι [374].
[42] Garofalo: ἀλλὰ πᾶν ἤνεγκα τὸ συμβάν. Cf. BMJ 38.13.7–8: ἀλλὰ πάνυ <ῥαδίως> ἤνεγκα τὸ συμβάν and KS 184: ἀλλὰ πάνυ ἤνεγκα τὸ συμβάν.
[43] Student of Socrates (c. 430–355 BCE).
[44] Garofalo and Lami: ταῖς θερμοτέραις τῶν κατ' αὐτὸν ἑταιρῶν (pg. 28).
[45] KS 189: ὀψωνῶν ἑκάστης ἡμέρας. BMJ 39.13.13 emends to ὄψων [ἄν]. We retain πολυτελείαις (Vlatadon) as opposed to emending to πολυτελῶς (KS) by supplying an elided ἀρκούμενος taking the dative. This preserves a balanced οὐκ ... ἀλλὰ καὶ construction.
[46] I.e., Cyrene.
[47] KS 198: ἀπώλεσεν.
[48] KS 200: συλλυπεῖ σύ.
[49] We understand ὁ λόγος as the elided subject of ἐνδεικνύμενος; cf. 39.13.11.
[50] Plutarch *Tranq. an.* 469B includes this saying with an additional piece (LCL ET: "It is the act of a madman to be distressed at what is lost and not rejoice at what is saved"); this saying seems also to be preserved in Arabic; BMJ's apparatus includes: "but what has remained" (ἀλλὰ πρός τι τῶν σῳθομένων).

43 Even if they own thirty fields, they will see others with fifty. And, in turn, when they acquire that amount, they will see others with seventy. And, if they then obtain that number, they will see others with more than one hundred. Advancing little by little, they eventually desire everything and will, in this respect, always be poor – their desire unfulfilled.[51]

44 However, if someone focuses on fields sufficient to meet his own expenses, instead of focusing continually on the number of fields belonging to someone else, he will bear the loss of the excess without distress.[52]

45 If someone with only a single field loses it, he will be utterly destitute. As a result, he will be justifiably troubled. However, if he has four fields and loses one, he will be brought down to equal terms with those who only ever had three. Therefore, it isn't a significant accomplishment not to be distressed, if someone has three fields left. However, it *is* a significant accomplishment, when someone with not even a single field endures poverty without distress, as Crates did. And, it is even more significant, if he has no house and is without distress, as in the case of Diogenes.

46 It is not, then, a great achievement for me not to be troubled at all by the loss of property[53] when what is left is always more than enough.

47 Rather, it is fitting to pity the person who pays out ten thousand drachmae regularly from an income of one hundred thousand,[54] but is distressed at the loss of thirty thousand, since it is natural, losing ninety thousand annually, not to be troubled, given that ten thousand would be sufficient to feed him.

48 The insatiability of such spendthrifts amazes me, I who have done nothing amazing. Nevertheless, it is fitting for me to be amazed at all of those who, having lost everything, are not troubled in any way. As they say, Zeno of Citium lost everything in a shipwreck. Yet, when it was reported to him, he declared: "You do well, O Fortune, driving us to the mantle and the portico!"

49 Hence, I have accomplished nothing significant by shunning the manifold loss of my possessions, just as I shun life in the imperial court. Not only did I not aspire to such a life back then, but in point of fact I held my ground against it – not once, not twice, but many times. Fortune drew me into it by force.

---

[51] Content expressed in 42b–44 contains parallel ideas to Plutarch *Cupid. divit.* 524A–D.

[52] The reading of Vlatadon (ἀκίλως) is corrupt. We follow Garofalo and Lami: τὴν τῶν περιττῶν ἀπώλειαν ἀλύπως οἴσει (p. 32). Cf. BMJ 44.15.2: τὴν τῶν περιττωμάτῶν ἀπώλειαν ἀκηδῶς οἴσει.

[53] BMJ punctuates as a question; KS punctuates as a statement. Translated as a question: "So why is it a great achievement for me not to be troubled at all by the loss of money?"

[54] Cf. Garofalo and Lami: τὸν ἀναλίσκοντα μὲν <ἐν> ἐνιαυτῷ μυρίας δραχμὰς ἐκ προσόδου μυριάδων δέκα ("who in a year wastes ten thousand drachmae from an income of one hundred"; p. 32).

50a It was not even a great achievement not to be driven utterly mad by the many aged royals in the imperial court.[55]

50b But I lost all of my medicines, my books – including effective medical recipes and published editions about these recipes – along with many other treatises, each one of which alone demonstrated the industry of a lifetime.[56] Still, not to become distressed (at such a loss is not a significant achievement); rather, it represents a privileged upbringing. And above all, it exemplifies high-mindedness.

51 What initially led me to such high-mindedness you yourself know based on the fact that you were raised and educated with me from the beginning (in Pergamum), and second, as you mentioned,[57] based on the experience of events in Rome.[58]

52 You are well aware that political spectacles also educate through experience, recalling the art of medicine. No maxim is more effective than the one Euripides placed in the mouth of Theseus. Hearing the verses, you will recognize them:[59]

> Having learned from a certain wise man,[60]
> I thrust misfortunes into my mind,[61]
> Adding to myself exile,
> Untimely deaths,[62] and other forms of adversity,
> In order that,[63] if I ever suffered[64] any of the things I was imagining,
> Coming upon me anew,[65] it might not bite[66] my psyche.[67]

---

[55] Polemis: μέγα μὴ μανῆναί τὴν <αὐτὴν> μανίαν πολλοῖς τῶν ἐν αὐλῇ βασιλικῶν καταγηρασάντων (p. 375).

[56] Cf. Garofalo and Lami: <ἂν> ἐπεδείκνυτο ("would have demonstrated"; p. 34).

[57] Vlatadon: ἔφης.

[58] Cf. Lucian *Imag.* 17: τὴν δὲ ἐκ τῆς Μιλήτου ἐκείνην Ἀσπασίαν, ἧ καὶ ὁ Ὀλύμπιος θαυμασιώτατος αὐτὸς συνῆν, οὐ φαῦλον συνέσεως παράδειγμα προθέμενοι, ὁπόσον ἐμπειρίας πραγμάτων καὶ ὀξύτητος εἰς τὰ πολιτικὰ καὶ ἀγχινοίας καὶ δριμύτητος ἐκείνῃ προσῆν, τοῦτο πᾶν ἐπὶ τὴν ἡμετέραν εἰκόνα μεταγάγωμεν ἀκριβεῖ τῇ στάθμῃ.

[59] Fragment from an unidentified play. Also quoted in *PHP* 5.418; Plutarch [*Cons. Apoll.*] 112D; Cicero *Tusc.* 3.29. See also Euripides fr. 963: μηδ' εὐτύχημα μηδὲν ὧδ' ἔστω μέγα, | ὅ σ' ἐξεπαρεῖ μεῖζον ἢ χρεὼν φρονεῖν, | μηδ' ἥν τι συμβῇ δυσχερές, δουλοῦ πάλιν· | ἀλλ' αὐτὸς αἰεὶ μίμνε τὴν σαυτοῦ φύσιν | σῴζων βεβαίως ὥστε χρυσὸς ἐν πυρί. Cf. Plutarch [*Cons. Apoll.*] 102F.

[60] Vlatadon: σοφοῦ τινος. It is τινος σοφοῦ in BMJ 77.23.7 and KS 346.

[61] Vlatadon: εἰς φροντίδα συμφορὰς ἐβαλλόμην. With BMJ and KS, we omit Vlatadon's ἐκ. KS 246–53 adopts readings from Kannicht and *PHP*. See KS critical apparatus.

[62] Vlatadon: τε.

[63] Vlatadon: ἵν'. ἵνα in BMJ 77.23.11 and KS 350.

[64] BMJ 52.17.8 (KS 252): πάσχοιμι.

[65] For this phrase, Vlatadon reads μάτην at BMJ 77.23.12; KS 351.

[66] BMJ 52.17.9: δάκῃ. Cf. KS 253: δάκοι (Vlatadon δάκνη).

[67] Three assumptions operative in KS's restoration for this citation which we cannot confidently accept: (1) that the text from Euripides is accurately restored in Kannicht; (2) that Galen had Kannicht's restored version or knew it by memory; and (3) that Galen would have wanted to cite the same form of the quotation in both of his texts.

53 The wise man continually reminds himself of what it is possible to suffer. However, even the person who is not a sage – provided he is not living like an animal[68] – is himself somehow roused to an understanding of reality by day-to-day occurrences.

54–55 You are persuaded, I think, that in all of recorded history[69] there have never been atrocities as severe as those encountered[70] recently during the brief reign of Commodus.[71] Witnessing each of them day after day, I trained my imaginative faculties for the loss of everything I own, expecting to be judged[72] – just as others who have done nothing wrong – and sent to a deserted island. When someone anticipates banishment to a deserted island, together with the loss of all of his possessions, he prepares himself to endure it. If somehow[73] (he would have anticipated) losing only part of his possessions[74] – deprived of none others[75] – he would have been distressed.[76]

56 That is why, having tested others, I consider[77] the saying of Euripides to be the most effective and, therefore, recommend that you train your *psyche*'s imaginative faculties as often as possible.

57 This training is only an option for those predisposed to courage by nature and beneficiaries of the finest education. The latter good fortune granted me. Moreover, since you were educated with me, you know the kind of person[78] my father was.[79]

58 Every time I remember him,[80] I sense my soul (*psyche*) strengthening. There was no one who revered justice and temperance (as he did); and thanks to this reverence, he accrued these qualities naturally, that is, apart from the teachings of philosophy.

---

[68] Cf. *Protrepticus* (*Protr.*) 14.28–29.

[69] παρ' ὅλον τὸν χρόνον, ὡς τὰς ἱστορίας ἔγραψαν οἱ τοῦ' ἔργο<ν> ἔχοντες

[70] Vlatadon (KS 259): ἔπραξας.

[71] KS 259: Κομμόδου. Cf. Vlatadon: κωμῴδου.

[72] Polemis: Μετὰ τοῦτο καὶ αὐτὸς δικασθῆναι προσδόκα (p. 376).

[73] Vlatadon (KS 265): εἴ που. We understand the elision of προσεδόκησε (cf. προσδοκήσας at 55.18.7) in the protasis of a past unreal condition. We accept BMJ's emendation to κατά τι ἀπολέσας (55.18.11) from Vlatadon's καταπολέσας. Alternatively, BMJ 55.18.11–13 emends to ἢ που κατά τι ἀπολέσας γοῦν μηδενὸς τῶν ἄλλων κτημάτων ἀφαιρεθείς, <οὐκ ἄν> ἔμελλε λυπηθήσεσθαι: "Whenever someone, expecting to be exiled to such as island together with the loss of all his possessions, prepares himself to endure it. He would surely, despite having lost a portion – although deprived of none of this other possessions – not be distressed."

[74] The sense here is the individual has only trained for the loss of some possessions.

[75] Vlatadon: μηδενὸς τῶν ἄλλων κτημάτων ἀφαιρεθείς. As above, the context is one of banishment.

[76] BMJ 55.18.13: ἔμελλε λυπθήσεσθαι.

[77] We understand an elided verb of thought (e.g., ἡγέομαι).

[78] Vlatadon (BMJ 57.18.20): ὁποῖον.

[79] Taking ἦν μοι πατὴρ with οἶσθα ὁποῖον. Cf. BMJ, p. 149, where the editors offer an elided construction of the identical type.

[80] Vlatadon: ὧν.

59 For he was not acquainted with philosophers in his youth. He was trained in both virtue and architecture from childhood by his father, my grandfather, to whom these things were (likewise) hereditary.[81] My father used to say that his father lived in the same virtuous manner. And, he, in turn [i.e., Galen's grandfather], (used to) said that *his* father, the grandfather of my father, had lived likewise. The former, [i.e., Galen's grandfather], was an architect and the latter, [i.e., Galen's great-grandfather], a surveyor.

60 You should understand, then, that by nature I too live this same virtuous life, resembling my father's side. Being educated in the same way as them I have a similar condition of the soul.

61 Furthermore, I am aware that my father looked down upon human affairs as trivial, as I, especially now in my old age, have also had to do.

62 My father regarded those who lead lives of pleasure to be nothing more than the birds[82] we see in the city of Rome led around by their owners to mount females for a price. Yet my father likewise did not praise[83] those who dismissed such pleasures, satisfied to feel neither pain nor distress with regard to their souls. He was never persuaded to claim that there was something greater and better, that is, the good, with a unique nature, not merely defined as the absence of pain or distress.

63 But, even if someone – departing from these views – holds the position that the good is, for example, knowledge of divine and human affairs, I observe that human beings partake of the least possible amount of this good. If it is the least amount, then it is clear that we do not have accurate knowledge about everything.

64 Specifically, the person unable to fully discern what is human and what is divine does not know, either at the level of the universal or the particular, what to accept and what to flee. Because of this, I am of the opinion that politics, that is, preoccupation with human affairs is futile. At the same time, I observe that few profit from the zeal of good and noble men.

65 Consistently raised with this kind of reasoning, I consider everything (human) to be ultimately trivial. Otherwise, I would assume leisure, instruments, medicines, books, reputation, and wealth were vital.[84] But, for the one who takes

---

[81] Polemis: ἀσκηθεὶς, ἐν αἷς καὶ αὐτὸ ἐκείνῳ ἦν πατρῷον (p. 376).

[82] Vlatadon: οἰωνῶν. Cf. Aristotle *Hist. an.* 5.2 (539b25–540a3) and 6.2 (560b16–5561a3). Tommaso Raiola, "'Asini per uccelli': una noterella al testo di de Indolentia," *Galenos: Rivista di filologia dei testi medici antichi* 5 (2011): 21–26, emends to ὄνων ("asses"). The text may be corrupt in the manner suggested by Raiola. However, we have chosen to follow the reading of Vlatadon (cf. BMJ 62.19.17).

[83] Vlatadon (KS 290): ἔπεισεν.

[84] KS 303–4: Καὶ σχολὴν καὶ ἄρμενα καὶ φάρμακα καὶ βιβλία καὶ δόξαν καὶ πλοῦτον <καὶ οὐκ> ἄξια σπουδῆς ὑπολάβοιμι <ἄν>. On our reading, the insertion of καὶ οὐκ and ἄν is unnecessary. We understand an elided protasis supplied from the prior sentence. BMJ (65.20.15–17) punctuates the sentence as a question.

everything (human) to be trivial, what thought should there be for the presence or the absence of these things?

66 The consequence for the one who assumes that things of true value have been taken from him is to be perpetually distressed and anxious. Whereas the consequence for the one who continually dismisses these (things) as trivialities, is never to be distressed.[85]

67 Each of the things I mentioned above, I conclusively demonstrated, not generally but with precise definitions, to be trivialities. I have writings on each of these topics. Going through them you will find[86] that I composed them, by the gods, neither with effort nor as writing something particularly profound, but as a pleasant diversion.

68 Some suppose that freedom from disturbance is the good, something I myself believe that neither I, nor any another human being, nor any living creature exhibits. I observe that every living thing is compelled to perform its own functions both with respect to body and soul. I also treated this point with copious explanatory notes in some other works, especially in my *Against Epicurus*.

69 So I think I have answered your question about the avoidance of distress in full. Nevertheless,[87] I believe it is necessary to add one distinction.

70 Perhaps you think that because some philosophers profess that a philosopher[88] will never suffer distress – not even in the current circumstances – I too make this claim (to be a philosopher), and even more, since you say you have never seen me distressed.

71 For my part, I cannot say if such a wise man exists, unaffected in every way. But, I do have accurate knowledge of the kind of person I am.[89] I can overlook the loss of money – up to the point of being banished to a deserted island, deprived of everything – and I can overlook bodily pain, up to the point of professing that I disregard the bull of Phalaris.

72a–b[90] A homeland destroyed, a friend punished by a tyrant, and anything else like this will distress me and I pray to the gods that none of these things ever happens to me. You have never seen me distressed because up to now none of these things has happened to me.

73 I marvel at Musonius who, as they say, was accustomed at every opportunity to proclaim: "O Zeus, send me a crisis." I, on the contrary, pray continually: "O Zeus, do *not* send a crisis that is able to trouble me!"

---

[85] BMJ 66.20.22 inserts μηδέποτε λυπεῖσθαι.
[86] Vlatadon: ἃ διελθὼν εὑρήσεις ἀλλὰ μὰ.
[87] Vlatadon: αὐτάρ.
[88] Polemis: τὸν φιλόσοφον (p. 377).
[89] BMJ 71.2118–19: τοῦ δ' αὐτὸς εἶναι τοιοῦτος ἀκριβῆ γνῶσιν ἔχω. Contrast KS 321–2: τοιοῦτος ἀκριβῆ γνῶσιν ἔχω τοῦ δ' αὐτὸς <μὴ> εἶναι.
[90] We follow the punctuation of KS 327: τοιαῦτα, καὶ θεοῖς εὔχομαι; cf. BMJ 72a–72b.22.4: τοιαῦτα. 72b Καὶ θεοῖς εὔχομαι.

74 Thus, I pray continually about my physical condition that my body will be healthy. I would never pray to demonstrate perseverance by having my head smashed to the ground. Even though I resolved to train my imagination for every affliction, so as to endure them with moderation, I would not pray to encounter anything able to distress me.

75 By closely monitoring its state, I accurately sense the condition of my body and mind. Therefore, I do not wish for an external cause great enough to destroy my health or a crisis powerful enough to overcome my state of mind.

76 I do not neglect the health of my body and mind, endeavoring, insofar as I can, to instill in both sufficient strength to withstand whatever distresses them. For although I neither expect my body to have the strength of Hercules, nor my mind – which wise men tell me exists – to have such strength, I think it is best never to intentionally forgo any training.

77 For I praise very highly the message of Theseus who speaks on Euripides' behalf[91] in the following verses:

> Having learned from a certain wise man,[92]
> I thrust thoughts of misfortunes into (my) mind,[93]
> Adding to myself exile,
> Untimely deaths, and[94] other forms of adversity,
> In order that,[95] if I ever suffered[96] any of the things I imagine,
> Coming about, it may bite[97] my mind in vain.[98]

78a–b This alone I find effective for painful situations. To be sure, I am not above all of them. What is more, I never make claims I cannot demonstrate. I

---

[91] For the odd expression ὑπὲρ Εὐριπίδου, see Aristophanes *Thesm.* 542: παρρησίας κἄξον λέγειν ὅσαι πάρεσμεν ἀσταί, εἶτ' εἶπον ἀγίγνωσκον ὑπὲρ Εὐριπίδου δίκαια, διὰ τοῦτο τιλλομένην με δεῖ δοῦναι δίκην ὑφ' ὑμῶν; also, 649: τὸ πέος διέλκεις πυκνότερον Κορινθίων. ὦ μιαρὸς οὗτος· ταῦτ' ἄρ' ὑπὲρ Εὐριπίδου ἡμῖν ἐλοιδορεῖτο.

[92] Vlatadon: τινος σοφοῦ.

[93] Vlatadon: εἰς φροντίδα συμφορὰς ἐβαλλόμην. With BMJ and KS we strike ἐκ. KS 246–53 adopts readings from Kannicht and *PHP*. See KS critical apparatus.

[94] Vlatadon: τε.

[95] Vlatadon: ἵνα.

[96] KS 350: πάσχοιμι.

[97] Vlatadon: δάκῃ.

[98] Vlatadon: μάτην. Although Vlatadon does not suggest it, Sotiroudis strikes the second citation of Euripides, presuming that that the second quote has entered the text from the margin in an antecedent of the manuscript. In private correspondence, Kotzia generously offers the following defense of their decision: (1) He does not think that Galen would ever repeat a relatively lengthy quote in so short a text; (2) the second quote is not naturally integrated in its context; (3) τὸ Θησέως is sufficient as a reference to a passage quoted previously; and (4) the Greek in the phrase introducing the quote is almost impossible, esp. ὑπὲρ Εὐριπίδου(ς) (KS 345 and BMJ 77.23.6) and ταύτην (KS 352; BMJ 78a.23.13) has no obvious referent. Kotzia does not find Jouanna's explanation that "le mot sous-entendu" is ἄσκησις (p. 178) tenable. Kotzia poses ὁδόν as the referent of ταύτην. Space limitations imposed by the editors of *Hellenica* prevented them from offering such explanations in their publication.

repeatedly tell my companions that I can only dismiss the loss of all money if enough remains to prevent hunger, cold – *insert thirst here after πεινῆν μήτε ῥιγοῦν;*[99] and I can only dismiss sufferings if I am able[100] to converse with a friend and understand the words when someone reads a book to me.

79a If strong pains overcome me, I will be happy if I can demonstrate perseverance in them.[101]

79b Writing elsewhere on the avoidance of distress, I offered advice on matters which thanks to nature and education are superfluous to mention to you, someone I know has exercised simplicity in food and clothing since you were young. You have also maintained a controlled approach to sexual pleasures. Slaves to such things[102] are relentlessly driven to want more.

80 If they do not have an excess,[103] they first lament and moan day and night. Then, obtaining[104] these things, they are forced to lie awake considering how to fulfill their desires (again). When they don't obtain these things, they wail;[105] when they do get them, they are not satisfied. Therefore, falling victim to their insatiable desires, they incline themselves toward a very wretched life.[106]

81 In contrast, some grasp at honor, riches, reputation, and political power in a moderate way. If, however, such a one is found grasping at these things without moderation, he is compelled to live most wretchedly. He does not know the first thing about the virtue of the mind. In fact, he increases[107] the vices in it because he is unable to obtain the objects of his desire. All the while, he remains distressed.

82 For it is true that the most powerful desires have an insatiable goal that no one who lives according to nature should trust them or those reliant on them.[108]

---

[99] The Greek poses a difficulty: BMJ 78.24.5 ὅτι χρημάτων μὲν ἀπωλείας ἁπάσης καταφρονῶ μέχρις ἂν ὑπολείπηται τοσαύτη κτῆσις αὐτῶν ὡς μήτε πεινῆν μήτε ῥιγοῦν <μήτε διψῆν> [τὸ γὰρ διψῆν ὑπάρχει καὶ αὐτὸ τούτοις ἕπεσθαι]. It seems that the third component of the well-known triad: hunger, thirst and cold is missing. Thirst (ἡ δίψα) may have been omitted for any number reasons. Perhaps it was left out of an original draft or was deleted by *homoioteleuton*. KS suggests striking ἕπεσθαι. In any case, it seems possible that this unusual phrase, τὸ γὰρ διψῆν ὑπάρχει καὶ αὐτὸ τούτοις ἕπεσθαι, arises as a copyist's or other individual corrector's marginal note (or speaker's direction to a scribe taking dictation): "thirst belongs, add it here after these."

[100] BMJ 78b.24.7: [τοῦ]τὸ δύνασθαι.

[101] BM: οἱ γὰρ ἰσχυροὶ πόνοι τούτων ἡμᾶς περιέχουσι. We understand the antecedents of τούτων as σῶμα (76.23.2) and ψυχή (76.23.3). Alternatively, one could understand τούτων as referring to hunger and cold: "Strong pains of these types (i.e., hunger and cold)."

[102] BMJ 79b.24.14–15 and KS 364–65: οἷς οἱ δουλεύοντες.

[103] KS 365 (following BM): Εἰ {τε} δέ.

[104] Polemis: εὐπορήσουσιν (p. 377–8).

[105] Polemis: ὀδύρονται (p. 377–8).

[106] We read προσγίνονται in BMJ 80 rather than 81. KS 369–71: περιπίπτουσι <καὶ> ταῖς ἀπλήστοις ἐπιθυμίαις προσγίνονται. 30 Τινές οὖν οὐχ ὡς οἱ πολλοὶ λυποῦνται. BMJ 80–81.25.5–7: περιπίπτουσι ταῖς ἀπλήστοις ἐπιθυμίαις. 81 Προσγίνονται τινὲς οὖν [οὐχ ὡς οἱ πολλοὶ λυποῦνται]

[107] Vlatadon (KS 374): αὐξήσει.

[108] BMJ 82.25.15: ὥσπερ οὐδὲ τῷ ποτε πιστεύοντι; Garofalo and Lami emend to ὥσπερ οὐδ' ἐγώ ποτ' ἐπίστευόν τι (p. 50).

83 But, experience is the ultimate authority on (such) unimaginable things. I dared to beg from someone who possessed thousands of drachmas – seven thousand or more. But, (apparently) he neither shares what he has with others, nor partakes of it himself.[109] The man replied: "Just as we carefully protect the parts of our body, so also everyone must carefully protect their money."

84 Shocked at the man's statement, I departed. Subsequently, as is my custom, I dictated a book *On Money-Loving Rich People* and I am sending it to you.

---

[109] Cf. KS 380–81: ἀπολαύοντος.

II. Interpretive Essays

Manuscript Evidence

VÉRONIQUE BOUDON-MILLOT

Vlatadon 14 and *Ambrosianus* Q 3 Sup: Two Twin Manuscripts

Introduction

The purpose of this essay is to provide a more precise indication of the origin and history of *Vlatadon* 14 manuscript, and to try to identify the various sources used by different copyists. Among these, the most important source, which had also been used by a manuscript preserved in Milan, *Ambrosianus* Q 3 Sup, may now be fairly precisely reconstituted owing to new evidence provided by *Vlatadon*. It furthermore provides details on the intellectual environment in which *Vlatadon* evolved.

History of a discovery

Before focusing on the origin and history of *Vlatadon* 14 (henceforth *Vlatadon*), it may be useful to add some words about the circumstances of its discovery in Thessaloniki eight years ago. The story of how the lost text by Galen, Περὶ ἀλυπησίας (*De indolentia;* On Avoidance of Grief) was found, begins in January 2005 when I sent one of my PhD students, Antoine Pietrobelli (now a lecturer at the University of Reims), in preparation for his thesis – an edition of the commentary of Galen *In Hippocratis de acutorum morborum victu* – to the library of the monastery of the Vlatades at Thessaloniki to consult the microfilms of the manuscripts of Mount Athos which are kept there, and which concern his text.[1] While waiting for the microfilms to be brought to him, he had the idea of consulting the catalogue of the manuscripts of Vlatadon published by Eustratiades in 1918, which had a very limited circulation.[2] This catalogue only contains a single medical manuscript (*Vlatadon* 14 of Galen); the remainder are exclusively patristic manuscripts. The catalogue of Eustratiades has thus remained unknown

---

[1] On the circumstances of this discovery, see Antoine Pietrobelli, "Variation autour du *Thessalonicensis Vlatadon* 14: un manuscrit copié au xénon du Kral, peu avant la chute de Constantinople," *Revue des Etudes Byzantines* 68 (2010): 95–126.

[2] Sophronius Eustratiades, Κατάλογος τῶν ἐν τῇ μονῇ Βλατέων (Τσαοὺς-Μοναστήρι) ἀποκειμένων κωδίκων (Thessalonique, 1918). See also "Κατάλογος τῶν ἐν τῇ μονῇ Βλατέων (Τσαοὺς-Μοναστήρι) ἀποκειμένων κωδίκων," in Γρήγοριος ὁ Παλαμᾶς 2 (1918): 97.

to medical specialists. In this catalogue, *Vlatadon* is very rapidly described: none of the treatises of Galen present in the manuscript are described, and, in particular, *De indolentia* has been omitted. After locating *Vlatadon* in the catalogue, Antoine Pietrobelli sent me an email the same evening asking whether this manuscript was known, or whether he had made a discovery. But, as he had to return soon to France, he did not have time to see it. In fact, Pietrobelli's stay at Thessaloniki was complete, he was obliged to leave the next day, and didn't have the time to examine the manuscript in detail.

On this news, Jacques Jouanna and I went to Thessaloniki in March 2005 to see the manuscript. Unfortunately we were only allowed to see the microfilm, and, so far, despite much effort, several requests, and two other visits to the site, the last in May 2010, we have not been permitted to examine the manuscript directly. On this first visit, I began to read the microfilm, and noted that the catalogue of Eustratiades is very incomplete, and *Vlatadon* contains many more treatises than are indicated by Eustratiades in his catalogue. And above all, I discovered the entirely new treatise *De indolentia* the title of which was already well known to me thanks to Galen's treatise *De libris propriis* where the physician of Pergamum mentions it. At the time, I was preparing an edition in the *Collection des Universités de France* (*CUF*).[3]

By reading the microfilm, I discovered that *Vlatadon* likewise preserves for us the complete text of the two bibliographic treatises by Galen, *De ordine librorum suorum* and *De libris propriis*, which were only available in a unique manuscript (*Ambrosianus* Q 3 sup.; henceforth *Ambrosianus*) that is very seriously lacunose for those treatises. *Vlatadon* also contains the complete Greek text of Galen's *De propriis placitis* that Vivian Nutton edited in the *Corpus Medicorum Graecorum* series from the Arab-Latin translation.[4] *Vlatadon* is thus a new and very important witness for four texts of Galen that were either thought lost, or known only in a very lacunose form.

The discovery of *Vlatadon* had the effect of a bombshell in the select world of philosophers and Galenists. Even though several articles have already appeared

---

[3] Véronique Boudon-Millot, *Galien: Introduction générale. Sur l'ordre de ses propres livres. Sur ses propres livres. Que l'excellent médecin est aussi philosophe* (Budé; Paris: Les Belles Lettres, 2007). The Greek title in *Vlatadon* 14 is corrupt. We read Περὶ ἀλογισίας at the beginning and Περὶ ἀλογισίας at the end of the Greek text, instead of Περὶ ἀλυπίας in *De Libris Propriis*. On the question of the correct title (Περὶ ἀλυπησίας), see Véronique Boudon-Millot and Jacques Jouanna (with Antoine Pietrobelli), *Galien: Ne pas se chagriner* (Budé; Paris: Les Belles Lettres, 2010), 27–29.

[4] Vivian Nutton, *Galen: On My Own Opinions* (*CMG* 5.3.2; Berlin: Akademie Verlag, 1999). Now add Véronique Boudon-Millot and Antoine Pietrobelli, "Galien ressuscité: Edition *princeps* du texte grec du *De propriis placitis*," *Revue des Etudes Grecques* 118 (2005): 168–213, with Greek text and French translation. See also Ivan Garofalo and Alessandro Lami, *Galeno: L'anima e il dolore. De indolentia, De propriis placitis* (BUR Rizzoli. Classici greci e latini; Milan: Biblioteca Universale Rizzoli, 2012), with Greek text and Italian translation.

and others are in preparation, *Vlatadon* has by no means revealed all its secrets.[5] The source or, more likely, the sources used by *Vlatadon* remain shrouded in mystery. In other words, what might have been the source(s) relied on by the various copyists of *Vlatadon,* and where had they been able to find treatises by Galen as rare as the *De indolentia* (until then quite unknown in Greek), *De propriis placitis* (of which only some fragments in Greek had been known) or *De ordine librorum suorum* and *De libris propriis,* so far only transmitted by a unique and incomplete manuscript in Milan?

Two Twin Manuscripts

A comparison of *Vlatadon* and the Milan manuscript, *Ambrosianus*, might provide some additional clues.[6] Following the discovery of *Vlatadon*, I have, in fact, again examined *Ambrosianus*, which I had already used for my edition in the CUF series of the *De ordine librorum suorum* and *De libris propriis.* This renewed examination in December of 2009 in the Ambrosiana Library in Milan, allowed me to present in greater detail the close ties between *Vlatadon* and *Ambrosianus. Ambrosianus* is generally thought to date from the 14th century.[7] It had been acquired in Thrace in 1466 by a certain Dimitrios Angelos and it therefore predates *Vlatadon*, which, as suggested by Pietrobelli, dates from between 1448 and 1453.[8]

From the table given in Appendix, it can immediately be seen that *Ambrosianus* and *Vlatadon* have in common a series of eleven Galenic treatises, num-

---

[5] A recent bibliography is given in Daniela Manetti, "Galeno περὶ ἀλυπίας e il difficile equilibrismo dei filologi," in *Studi sul* De indolentia *di Galeno* (ed. D. Manetti; Biblioteca di "Galenos" Contributi alla ricerca sui testi medici antichi 4; Pisa/Roma: Fabrizio Serra, 2012), 9–22 [esp. 21–22].

[6] On this topic, see also Boudon-Millot, *Galien: Introduction générale.* Sur l'ordre de ses propres livres. Sur ses propres livres. Que l'excellent médecin est aussi philosophe, 44–47.

[7] Notably by Emidio Martini and Domenico Bassi, *Catalogus Codicum Graecorum Bibliothecae Ambrosianae* (2 vols.; Milan: U. Hoepli, 1906), 2:738–40; Dieter Harlfinger in *Galen,* De Plenitudine: *Kritische Edition, Übersetzung und Erläuterungen* (ed. Ch. Otte; Serta Graeca 9; Wiesbaden: Ludwig Reichert Verlag, 2000) 7, who suggests a date between 1320 and 1380, and Beate Gundert, *Galen:* Über die Verschiedenheit der Symptome (*CMG* 5.5.1; Berlin: Akademie Verlag, 2009), 6; but Nutton, *Galen:* On My Own Opinions, 17, suggests a later date around 1400 and, in Vivian Nutton, *Galen:* On Prognosis (*CMG* 5.8.1; Berlin: Akademie Verlag, 1979), 16, even later around 1450.

[8] Pietrobelli, "Variation autour du *Thessalonicensis Vlatadon* 14," 126. See also Brigitte Mondrain, "Jean Argyropoulos professeur à Constantinople et ses auditeurs médecins, d'Andronic Eparque à Démétrios Angelos," in *Polypleuros nous: Miscellanea für Peter Schreiner zu seinem 60. Geburtstag* (ed. C. Scholz and G. Makris; Byzantinisches Archiv 19; München/Leipzig: K. G. Saur, 2000), 223–50, and Brigitte Mondrain, "Demetrios Angelos et la médecine: contribution nouvelle au dossier," in *Storia della tradizione e edizione dei medicigreci, Atti del VI Colloquio Internazionale Paris 12–14 Aprile 2008* (ed. V. Boudon-Millot, A. Garzya, J. Jouanna, and A. Roselli; Naples: M. D'Auria, 2010), 293–322.

bered from 21 (κα´) to 33 (λγ´) in *Ambrosianus*, which, in *Vlatadon* begins with the *De propriis placitis* and ends with the *De praenotione ad Epigenem.* I shall begin by looking at this series before reverting to the two other sets that flank it at the beginning and the end of *Vlatadon*.

But first, I would like to point out that, as I have already shown elsewhere concerning *De ordine librorum suorum* and *De libris propriis, Ambrosianus* is not the model of *Vlatadon* for the treatises they have in common, but that *Ambrosianus* and *Vlatadon*, in fact, derive from a common source.[9] Moreover, the two manuscripts most felicitously complement each other and thus inform us of the condition of their common source and make it possible to reconstitute its original state. In fact, the complete series originally consisted of at least twenty-three Galenic treatises, and perhaps a few more. A careful examination of *Ambrosianus* allowed me to discover an ancient numeration of the treatises. I have indicated these numbers in the middle column of the table below, placing those that are no longer decipherable in the Milan manuscript, and which I had to reconstitute, within square brackets.

The series in *Ambrosianus* begins with *De symptomatum differentiis*, numbered 3 (in the middle column). Thus, the first two treatises are missing. It is legitimate to suppose that they concern *De morborum differentiis* and *De causis morborum*, two treatises that customarily constitute a whole set with the following two, *De symptomatum differentiis* and *De symptomatum causis,* to form a complete set of four treatises on the causes and symptoms of diseases that are often found together in our medieval manuscripts. For similar examples, please see the recent edition of *De symptomatum differentiis* by Beate Gundert in the *Corpus Medicorum Graecorum* (*CMG*), and the reference to ten manuscripts in which we find together the same four treatises, respectively *Marcianus gr.* 275 from the 15th century, *Laurentianus gr.* 74, 16 from the 12th/13th centuries, *Parisinus gr.* 2157 from the 15th century, *Scorialensis* 85 from the 15th century, *Scaligerianus gr.* 18 from the 16th century, *Phillippicus gr.* 1991 from the 16th century, *Ambrosianus gr.* 420 from the 15th century, *Parisinus gr.* 2169 from the 16th century, *Marcianus App. Cl.* V, 4 from the 15th century and the *Mutinensis gr.* 237 from the 16th century. I shall revert later to a lexicon and diagrams also found there. It will be noted that the numbering of *De symptomatum causis* is 6 (ς´) since each of the three books has been counted. The numbering of the six books of *De locis affectis* has followed the same logic; but, starting with folio 82, the copyist began to number the chapters as well, arriving at a total of 7 (ζ´) to 17 (ιζ´). As for the three books of *In Hippocratis de praedictionibus I*, they were correctly numbered from 18 (ιη´) to 20 (κ´).

---

[9] See Boudon-Millot, *Galien: Introduction générale. Sur l'ordre de ses propres livres. Sur ses propres livres. Que l'excellent médecin est aussi philosophe*, 44–47.

The Series of the Treatises Common to
Ambrosianus and *Vlatadon 14*

The series of the treatises common to *Ambrosianus* and *Vlatadon* begins with the following treatise and *De propriis placitis*. If my hypothesis of a common source is correct, how can it be explained that the copyist of *Vlatadon* chose to copy the series starting with the number 21 (κα′) in the middle column? The copyist of *Vlatadon,* who had already copied five medical treatises in the first part of the manuscript (treatises nos. 6 to 10 in the right-hand column), would certainly not have thought it necessary to add another four treatises on nosology and symptomology. The sheer size of *De locis affectis* (six books) which contrasts with the brevity of the other transmitted treatises, has probably also discouraged the copyist of *Vlatadon*. As to *In Hippocratis de praedictionibus I,* it has been transferred to the end of *Vlatadon* (no. 29), possibly to constitute a set with *In Hippocratics de acutorum morborum victu.*

The series common to our two manuscripts, therefore, begins in *Vlatadon* with *De propriis placitis* (no. 21 in *Ambrosianus*) with, however, the significant difference that only *Vlatadon* has preserved the complete original Greek text for us. In fact, the loss of several folios in that part of *Ambrosianus* resulted in the loss of the entire beginning of the treatise. Therefore, *Vlatadon* constitutes an important testimony for *De propriis placitis,* as well as for the following two treatises (*De libris propriis* and *De ordine librorum*), both of which also reveal an important *lacuna* in the *Ambrosianus,* again as a result of a material accident. The rest of the series, namely treatises nos. 26–33, proceed in parallel in the two manuscripts, except for the notable exception of the *De sophismatibus penes dictionem* (no. 28), which the scribe of *Vlatadon* had omitted for some unknown reason and without resulting from a material accident, since the two treatises, no. 27 (*Quod qualitates incorporae sint*) and no. 29 (*Adversus eos qui de typis scripserunt*), of the series are copied in *Vlatadon* without interrupting the continuous flow to the *verso* of folio 70. It should also be noted that the beginning of *De purgantium medicamentorum facultate* (no. 31) precedes the beginning of the *Adversus eos qui de typis scripserunt* (no. 30) in *Ambrosianus,* but that this inversion may in fact be explained by a new accidental disruption in the sequence of the folios in *Ambrosianus*. Finally, it will be noted that, if the series in *Ambrosianus* is interrupted with *De praenotione*, the end of which is missing, this is again solely owing to a material accident and the loss of the entire final section of the manuscript.

Vlatadon 14: Unique Testimony for the End of the Series

Thus, *Vlatadon* represents our unique testimony as regards the continuation of this series, which in the common source of the two manuscripts consisted of at least five additional treatises, from *De praenotione* to *De causis procatarcticis*, *Vlatadon* having preserved only the first two lines of that latter treatise. This brusque interruption at the end of folio 103v in *Vlatadon* is a possible indication that this may be the result of an accident, a hypothesis that might only be confirmed through a direct analysis of the manuscript by examining the pattern of the quires. The loss of the *De causis procatarcticis* is all the more regrettable as the treatise had only become available through a 14th century Latin translation by Nicolo da Reggio.[10] It seems more unlikely that the original series extended well beyond this, without also concluding on the loss of a significant number of folios in that part of *Vlatadon*. The most likely explanation is again that the original series and the common source relied on for *Ambrosianus* and *Vlatadon* must have consisted of some 30 treatises.

As for treatises preserved in the final part of *Vlatadon*, they are of a different kind in both magnitude and subject theme, as confirmed also by a different style of writing at that point. For, it is also here that a second copyist intervenes to take over from Constantin Lascaris, responsible for the preceding series. However, the second copyist is none other than Dimitrios Angelos, who has already been referred to earlier as the purchaser of *Ambrosianus* in 1466. Of the three treatises copied at the end of *Vlatadon* (nos. 27 to 29), one of them, *In Hippocratis de praedictionibus I*, goes back to the same source as that used by *Ambrosianus* (no. 4). In fact, we have seen that this commentary was originally placed in sixth position within the original series and in fourth position within *Ambrosianus*. For his part, the copyist of *Vlatadon* preferred to group it here at the end of the manuscript with two other treatises. But, as I have been able to verify by collating the text of that commentary both in *Ambrosianus* and *Vlatadon*, it is beyond doubt that our two manuscripts again derive from the same common source. In contrast, concerning *In Hippocratics de acutorum morborum victu*, Pietrobelli has demonstrated in his thesis that *Vlatadon* had close links to the Athonite manuscript *Iviron* 184 (late 13th to early 14th centuries).[11] The enquiry must be pursued concerning *De crisibus*.

---

[10] R. J. Hankinson, *Galen:* On Antecedent Causes (Cambridge Classical Texts and Commentaries 35; Cambridge: Cambridge University Press, 1998).

[11] Antoine Pietrobelli, "Histoire du texte, édition critique et traduction annotée du livre I du commentaire de Galien au *Régime des maladies* aiguës d'Hippocrate" (Ph.D. diss., Université Paris-Sorbonne, 2008), cxxxiii–xclviii.

The Treasures Preserved in the First Part of the Vlatadon Manuscript

I shall now come to the first part of *Vlatadon* manuscript that I have purposely left aside until now and which also harbours a number of treasures. Three sets must be distinguished: a first set composed of *De sectis* and *Ars Medica,* copied by the principal copyist of the whole manuscript, Constantin Lascaris; a second set similarly composed of two treatises (*De indolentia* and *De causa affectionum*), copied by a scribe whom Pietrobelli identified as a scribe named Andreiomenos, and a third set composed of five treatises again essentially copied by Constantin Lascaris. The portion copied by this new scribe, Andreiomenos, thus appears to be an additional insertion into the set copied by Constantin Lascaris. The presence of a blank folio at the end of the portion copied by Andreiomenos reinforces the hypothesis of a subsequent addition into this set originally copied by Lascaris. Here again, only a direct examination of the manuscript and of the pattern of the quires would allow us to validate definitively this hypothesis.

The project pursued at the beginning of *Vlatadon* appears, in any event, very coherent since, with *De sectis* and *Ars Medica,* the copyist had started to recopy the first two titles of the Alexandrine Canon (the selected works by Galen collected in Alexandria at the turn of the 6th century to serve as the basis for the teachings of medicine in that city) before adding the *Introductio,* a Pseudo-Galenic treatise, the title of which again clearly indicates the advantage of propaedeutics for medical students.[12] As I have already demonstrated in a recently published article, the copyist of *Vlatadon* 14 had used a manuscript similar to *Palatinus gr.* 199 as a model for *Ars Medica.*[13] After verification, I was able to observe that the same is true for *De sectis.*

As for the following treatises (treatises 6 to 10 in *Vlatadon*), they appear in that same order in *Parisinus gr.* 2271, where, as Caroline Petit points out, the same separate arrangement of the chapters of the *Introductio* (1–15 on the one hand, and 16–20 on the other) had been adopted as in *Vlatadon.* I should add that this Parisian manuscript, which was part of the collection of Antoine Eparque, a nobleman born on Corfu in 1492, had been written entirely by Dimitrios Angelos, whom we have already mentioned earlier because he intervened at the end of *Vlatadon.*[14]

Last, but not least, I shall now examine two small treatises copied by Andreiomenos, two true gems, one of which is especially precious as it is absolutely

---

[12] Caroline Petit, *Galien:* Le médecin, Introduction (Budé; Paris: Les Belles Lettres, 2009).

[13] Véronique Boudon-Millot, "Un nouveau témoin pour l'histoire du texte de l'*Ars medica* de Galien: le *Vlatadon* 14," in *L'Ars medica (Tegni) de Galien: Lectures antiques et médiévales* (ed. N. Palmieri; Mémoires [Centre Jean Palerne] 32; Saint-Etienne: Publications de l'Université de Saint-Etienne, 2008), 11–29.

[14] When the Turks attacked Corfu in 1537, Eparque, ruined, had to flee to Venice where he began to sell his valuable collection of manuscripts, many of which were bought around 1540 by Guillaume Pelicier for the Royal Library in Fontainebleau.

unique. They are *De indolentia,* on the one hand, and *De causa affectionum,* on the other. The extent of the curiosity and enthusiasm generated among Galenists by the discovery of *De indolentia,* a treatise, moreover, until then unknown, does not need to be emphasized. However, it is much more difficult to determine where Andreiomenos had been able to uncover such a treasure. At most, one might attempt to learn a little more about *De causa affectionum,* the second in this couplet. Though not of the same exceptional order as the discovery of *De indolentia,* the Pseudo-Galenic treatise *De causa affectionum* had so far only been known through a single manuscript, *Marcianus App. Cl.* V, 12 (coll. 1317), which the section of interest to us dated from the 11th century (or somewhat later).[15] Jouanna has relied on this treatise in his edition of the Hippocratic treatise *On breaths,* since the *De causa affectionum* presents four parallel passages to the Hippocratic treatise.[16] His evaluation of the text of the *De causa affectionum* in the review of the *Marcianus* is as follows: "It proceeds from a source at a very high level of the *stemma,* as it sometimes agrees with A against M, and sometimes with M against A, and thus also presents particular lessons against A or M."[17] The publishers of Hippocrates would have recognized in "A" and "M" the two famous Hippocratic manuscripts, namely the *Marcianus gr.* 269 (10th century) and *Parisinus gr.* 2253 (11th century). What can be said concerning the recension preserved in *Vlatadon?* It appears that, following the collation, the text of *De causa affectionum* preserved in *Vlatadon* belongs to the same tradition as that of *Marcianus App. Cl.* V, 12, with which it shares the errors and omissions, but also the same good lessons going back to the same common ancient source. However, one will also note that in *Vlatadon* the text of the *De causa affectionum* breaks off brusquely before the end at the bottom of folio 18bv. There follows a blank unnumbered folio. Here again, it would be desirable to be able to examine the manuscript to determine the exact nature of this interruption, which appears very likely to have been caused by the loss of several folios (but how many?) in the wake of another material accident. If, with respect to *De causa affectionum,* the incomplete text transmitted by *Vlatadon* necessarily appears as inferior to the complete text transmitted by the *Marcianus,* the folios missing in *Vlatadon* at the end of *De causa affectionum* permits the conclusion that the set, now limited to two treatises copied by Andreiomenos at folios 10v–18bv, had originally comprised a larger collection. But here also, as long as it is not possible to directly examine the manuscript, it is impossible to be more precise. It is nevertheless

---

[15] See Elpidio Mioni, *Codices in classes a prima usque ad quintam inclusi* (vol. 1, part 1 of *Codices graeci manuscripti Bibliothecae divi Marci Venetiarum;* Indici e cataloghi; Rome: Istituto Poligrafico dello Stato, 1972), 271–3. However, Anargyros Anastassiou and Dieter Irmer, *Testimonien zum Corpus Hippocraticum, Teil II, Band 1* (Göttingen: Vandenhoeck & Ruprecht, 2001), xx, mention the 14th century (with a question mark).

[16] Jacques Jouanna, *Hippocrate:* Des Vents, (Budé; Paris: Les Belles Lettres, 1988), 78–83.

[17] Jouanna, *Hippocrate:* Des Vents, 79.

plausible that at that point in *Vlatadon*, not only was the end of *De causa affectionum* lost, but also one or even several other treatises. Such a loss, if it were to be confirmed, would seem even more regrettable as, for the first two volumes in the series (*De indolentia* and *De causa affectionum*), Andreiomenos seems to have relied on one or more particularly rare and ancient source(s).[18]

Ambrosianus and *Vlatadon* share one last characteristic: the presence of a lexicon and diagrams, even though, as has to be pointed out at the outset, they are not identical in the two manuscripts. In fact, *Ambrosianus* has transmitted an outline of a Greek-Arabic lexicon[19] (folio 11r) under the Greek title Ἀραβικῶς αὗται αἱ λέξεις λέγονται, while *Vlatadon* (folio 2r) has preserved parts of a Greek-Turkish lexicon. Similarly, *Ambrosianus* (folios 10r and 11v) has preserved a collection of diagrams intended to illustrate the properties of the soul (αἱ δυνάμεις τῆς ψυχῆς). This illustration is presented in the same dieretic form as that adopted in *Vlatadon* (folio 147v) in the diagram drawn by Constantin Lascaris to illustrate the latitude of health (ὑγείας πλάτος), a diagram that it is in relation to the lessons given by John Argyropoulos to Xenon of the Kral at Constantinople.[20]

In fact, the name of Argyropoulos (ca. 1393/1394–1487), a philosopher and professor teaching in Constantinople between 1448 and 1453, is the true link between the individuals who intervened in *Vlatadon*: foremost Constantin Lascaris, the principal copyist of *Vlatadon* and a pupil of Argyropoulos, just as Dimitrios Angelos who intervened both in our two manuscripts, the *Ambrosianus* and *Vlatadon*, but also Andreiomenos whom Pietrobelli suggests we consider as a contemporary of Constantin Lascaris.

The paradox of *Vlatadon* is that this work of a copyist, which one might characterize as "schoolish," has preserved for us truly unique documents. *Vlatadon* is, in effect, our only testimony (complete or partial) concerning Galen's four treatises: *De indolentia* and *De propriis placitis,* moreover unknown in Greek; and *De ordine librorum suorum* and *De libris propriis* already known by *Ambrosianus* but the complete text of which has been preserved only by *Vlatadon*, without forgetting *De causis procatarcticis,* of which *Vlatadon* is also alone in having transmitted certain Greek phrases.

The copyists of *Vlatadon*, therefore, had access to sources that were both exceptionally rare and diversified. We have attempted to show that, (1) Treatise

---

[18] Conversely, this is not so concerning the recipes copied by the same Andreiomenos at the very beginning of *Vlatadon* (f. 3r) that are actually extracts from the *De morbis mulierum* 1.75 (Émile Littré, *Hippocrates*: *Opera Omnia* [10 vols.; Paris: J. B. Baillière, 1839–61] 8:17–168 [164]) that follow the review of *Parisinus gr.* 2254 (D with Littré), a recentior descending from M.

[19] Offering the Arabic translations (transliterations) for ὑγρότης, ψυχρότης (μπαριτ for *bârid*), ξηρότης, θερμότης, αἷμα (τὲμ for *dam*), ξανθὴ χολή, μέλαινα (σαβδὰ; for s*ouda'*) and φλέγμα.

[20] On this diagram, see Mondrain, "Jean Argyropoulos professeur" (see n. 8), 223–50.

nos. 2 and 3 (*De sectis* et *Ars Medica*) go back to a manuscript comparable to the current *Palatinus gr.* 199; (2) Treatise no. 5 (*De causa affectionum*) but perhaps also no. 6 (*De indolentia*) go back to an ancient and unknown source, also relied on by *Marcianus App. Cl.* V, 12; (3) Treatise nos. 6 to 10 go back to a source comparable to *Parisinus gr.* 2271; (4) Treatise nos. 11 to 26 (as well as no. 29) go back to a source also relied on by *Ambrosianus* and which originally contained a series of at least 23 treatises, of which 16 have been preserved in *Ambrosianus* and 17 in *Vlatadon,* and 12 of which are common to both manuscripts (also counting the *In Hippocratis de praedictionibus I,* transferred to the end of *Vlatadon*); (5) Treatise nos. 27 and 28 at the end of the manuscript go back to one or possibly two different sources (of which one is comparable to the *Iviron* 184).

From Where Could the Copyists Draw All or Part of Such Wealth?

Among the sources used, the *Palatinus gr.* 199, for a long time thought to have originated in the south of Italy, is most likely of Byzantine origin. Brigitte Mondrain suggests we situate the copy in Frankish Morea, without excluding Xenon of the Kral at Constantinople.[21] Similarly, the *Parisinus gr.* 2271, copied by Dimitrios Angelos, contains beside the famous diagram on the latitude of health, a short text by John Argyropoulos (folio 157v) on the causes of pulses.[22] *Ambrosianus* Q 3 Sup, acquired in 1466 by the same Dimitrios Angelos who had extensively completed and restored the manuscript, also directs us to the same John Argyropoulos whose pupil he was. Finally, as we have seen, the most important scribes to intervene in *Vlatadon* all also belonged to the circle around John Argyropoulos, whose pupils they were in that same Xenon of the Kral.

Given this setting, it is most likely that the copyists of *Vlatadon* had drawn their documentation essentially from the rich collections of the library of the Kral, which was a centre of study, teachings and also of health and well-being, prior to the dispersion of these precious books, of which a portion at least has now been saved from oblivion owing to the exceptional testimony of *Vlatadon*.

In conclusion, my own analyses on the origin and sources of *Vlatadon* concur with those undertaken by Pietrobelli on the copyists to perceive in *Vlatadon* a collective work, realized by non-professional scribes from among the followers of John Argyropoulos between 1448 and 1453.

---

[21] Brigitte Mondrain, "Nicolas Myrepse et une collection de manuscrits médicaux," in *I testi medici greci: Tradizione e ecdotica* (ed. A. Garzya; Collectanea 17; Napoli: M. D'Auria, 1999), 402–18 [esp. 412].

[22] Mondrain, "Jean Argyropoulos professeur," 226–7.

Appendix

The "*" designate the treatises transmitted only through *Ambrosianus* or *Vlatadon*, respectively.

Ambrosianus gr. Q 3 Sup		*Vlatadon* 14
		f. 2r (paginated 3/1) Greek-Turkish lexicon[1]
		1 f. 3r (paginated 4/1) Ἐκ τῶν Ἱπποκράτους κυητήρια[2]
	cf. *Pal.* 199	**2** ff. 1r–4v (paginated 5α–12α) *De sectis*[3]
		3 ff. 5r–10r (paginated 13α–23α) *Ars Medica*[4]
		4 ff. 10v[5]–14βv *De indolentia**[6]
	cf. *Marc.* V,12	**5** f. 15βr–18βv *De causa affectionum*[7]
		A blank unpaginated folio
	cf. *Par.* 2271[8]	**6** ff. 19βr–44v *Introductio seu medicus* (Petit 77.6)[9]
		7 ff. 44v–50r *De morborum temporibus*[10]
		8 ff. 50r–53v *De oculorum affectionibus* (= end of the *Introductio*; Petit 77.7–105.8).
		9 ff. 53v–56r *De totius morbi temporibus*[11]
	n° in Q3Sup	**10** ff. 56r–58v *Puero epileptico consilium*[12]
[*De morborum differentiis*][13]	[α] = 1	
[*De causis morborum*][14]	[β] = 2	
1 ff. 1r–10r *De symptomatum differentiis*[15]	γ = 3	
f. 11r Ἀραβικῶς αὗται αἱ λέξεις λέγονται		
f. 10r and 11v αἱ δυνάμεις τῆς ψυχῆς		
2 ff. 12r–44v *De symptomatum causis* (3 books)[16]	ς[17] = 6	
3 ff. 45r–128v *De locis affectis* (6 books)	ζ-ιζ = 7–17	

Ambrosianus gr. Q 3 Sup		Vlatadon 14
4 ff. 129r–184v *In Hippocratis de praedictionibus* (3 books)[18]	ιη-κ = 18–20	
5 f. 185r̄v *De propriis placitis* (c. 13 only)	[κα] = 21	**11** ff. 59r–62r *De propriis placitis* (1–13)*
6 ff. 185v–187r *De substantia facultatum naturalium* (= *Prop. Plac.* c. 14–15)[19]	κβ = 22	**12** ff. 62r–62v *De substantia facultatum naturalium* (= *Prop. Plac.* c. 14–15)
7 ff. 187r–197r *De libris propriis*[20]	κγ-κδ = 23–24[21]	**13** ff. 62v–65v *De libris propriis**
8 ff. 197r–200r *De ordine librorum suorum*[22]	κε = 25	**14** ff. 65v–67r *De ordine librorum suorum**
9 ff. 200r–202v *De parvae pilae exercitio*[23]	κς = 26	**15** ff. 67r–68r *De parvae pilae exercitio*
10 ff. 202v–207v *Quod qualitates incorporeae sint*[24]	κζ = 27	**16** ff. 68v–70v *Quod qualitates incorporae sint*
11 ff. 207v–210v *De sophismatis** f. 211 blank (note of Demetrios Angelos)	κη = 28	
12 ff. 212r–231r *Adversus eos qui de typis scripserunt*[25]	[κθ] = 29[26]	**17** ff. 70v–75v *Adversus eos qui de typis scripserunt*
13 ff. 231r–237v *De atra bile*[27]	[λ] = 30[28]	**18** ff. 75v–80v *De atra bile*
14 ff. 225r–238r *De purgantium medicamentorum facultate*[29]	[λα] = 31	**19** ff. 80v–83r *De purgantium medicamentorum facultate*
15 ff. 238r–265r *De plenitudine*[30]	[λβ] = 32	**20** ff. 83r–92v *De plenitudine*
16 ff. 265r–272v *De praenotione ad Epigenem*[31] The end is missing	λγ = 33[32]	**21** ff. 92v–99r *De praenotione ad Epigenem*
	[λδ] = 34	**22** ff. 99r–100r *De praenotione* (= *De constitutione artis medicae* c. 17–20)[33]
	[λε] = 35	**23** ff. 100v–101r *De dignotione ex somniis*[34]
	[λς] = 36	**24** ff. 101r–101v *Quomodo simulantes morbum deprehendendi*[35]
	[λζ] = 37	**25** ff. 101v–103v *Quos, Quibus catharticis medicamentis et quando purgare oporteat*[36]
	[λη] = 38	**26** f. 103v *De causis procatarcticis** (only two lines)[37]
		27 ff. 104r–147r *De crisibus* I–II–III[38] f. 147v diagram ὑγείας πλάτος
	cf. *Iviron* 184[39]	**28** ff. 149r–239v *In Hippocratis de acutorum morborum victu*[40]
		29 ff. 239v–276v *In Hippocratis de praedictionibus* (the end is missing)[41]

¹ I thank Marwan Rashed for the message of 8/12/2009 confirming that this is indeed Turkish, that *kizel iakout* is written in one place for *kizil yâqût* (red ruby), and sometimes there is even a transliteration from modern Greek. This lexicon shows a language mix of half Persian-Arabic, half Greek.

² An extract from Hippocrates *De morbis mulierum* I.75 (Littré, *Hippocrates*, 8:164.17–168.15).

³ K 1.64–105. After verifying this in the thesis dissertation by Daniel Béguin, " *Introduction, édition, traduction et commentaire du* De sectis *de Galien*," (Ph.D. diss., Université Paris-Sorbonne, 1989), 1:99 and 120, it seems that *Vlatadon* is comparable to *Vaticanus Palatinus gr.* 199, notwithstanding the absence of its numerous errors and omissions. In particular, the text of *De sectis* is interrupted a few words before the end in *Vlatadon* at the same spot as in *Palatinus*.

⁴ K 1.305–412 (Véronique Boudon-Millot, *Galien:* Exhortation à l'étude de la médecine; Art medical [Budé; Paris: Belles-Lettres, 2000]). The text of the *Ars* medica reveals an interpolation (from a text by Aetius) also found in the *Vaticanus Palatinus gr.* 199. See Boudon-Millot, "Un nouveau témoin pour l'histoire du texte de l'*Ars medica* de Galien: le *Vlatadon* 14," 17–19.

⁵ Starting with f. 11r, we observe the addition of the sign b after the foliation number.

⁶ Boudon-Millot and Jouanna (with Pietrobelli), *Galien:* Ne pas se chagriner, 27–29.

⁷ Pseudo-Galen, *De causa affectionum* edited by Georg Helmreich (Ansbach: Programm des Königliche Humanistischen Gymnasiums, 1910/1911), 3–19. This treatise is found in only one other manuscript: *Marcianus* V, 12 (ff. 136v–147r) regarding which, see Mioni, *Codices manuscripti bibliothecae*, 271–3, who identifies five copyists. Our treatise, in *Marcianus*, is written by the second copyist (11th century) for ff. 136–45, and by the fourth (14th century) for the last two folios. See also Mariarosa Formentin, *I codici greci di medicina nelle tre Venezie* (Padova: Liviana, 1978), 68–69, who presents the treatise as the work of an anonymous Byzantine epitomizer (but ignores the Helmreich publication). Finally, see the edition of Hippocrates' *On Breaths* by Jouanna (78–83), who emphasizes the age and the importance of this testimony. The text preserved under that title in *Vlatadon* is incomplete and breaks off at the end of f. 18bv (most likely after the loss of one or several folios) with the words μετὰ κρίσιν ὑποστροφῶδεα, οἱ μὲν πλανῆται πυρετοῖ καὶ διὰ πλῆ(θος) (Helmreich 17.4). This seems to indicate that the section copied by Andreiomenos was originally longer. This loss is even more cause for regret for the philologist as Andreiomenos relied on a most precious source which contained extremely rare treatises.

⁸ Three manuscripts, *Parisinus gr.* 2271, *Marcianus App. Cl.* V, 9 and *Vaticanus gr.* 285 maintain close ties with the students of Argyropoulos and contain the same diagram to demonstrate the latitude of health. However, *Parisinus gr.* 2271 appears to be the best candidate because it displays the division of the chapters of the *Introductio* into two parts (absent in the *Marc. App. Cl.* V, 9) and it stood as a model to *Vaticanus gr.* 285, and it stood also as a model to *Vlatadon* for the *Introductio,* according to the stemma given by Petit in her edition. Henri Omont, *Inventaire sommaire des manuscrits grecs de la bibliothèque nationale de Paris* (Paris: E. Bouillon, 1883–98), 2:227, does not mention that it includes the *De totius morbi temporibus*, but does only mention *De morborum temporibus* (but this is an error of Omont).

⁹ K 14.674–797 (Petit, *Galien:* Le médecin, Introduction). The Pseudo Galen *Introductio* breaks off at chapter 15 (K 14.766).

¹⁰ K 7.406–39.

¹¹ K 7.440–62.

¹² K 11.357–78.

¹³ K 6.836–80. Square brackets [ ] signify that the treatises are missing from *Ambrosianus*, but that they have been there originally, before the loss of the first folios. In fact, in many manuscripts the three treatises *De morborum differentiis*, *De causis morborum* and *De symptomatum differentiis* constitute a set, as for instance in the *Ambrosianus* G 97 Sup (420) from the 16th century.

¹⁴ K 7.1–41.

[15] K 7.42–84 (Gundert, *Galen:* Über die Verschiedenheit der Symptome [*CMG* 5.5.1]).
[16] K 7.85–146 (book 1); 147–204 (book 2); 205–272 (book 3).
[17] This treatise is numbered stigma (λόγος ς) namely 6 on f. 25v, 26v, 28v, 39v up to 44v since it is composed of three books, each of which is counted separately.
[18] K 16.489–840 (Hermann Diels, *Galeni in Hippocratis Prorrheticum I commentaria III* [*CMG* 5.9.2; Leipzig/Berlin: Teubner, 1915]).
[19] Nutton, *Galen:* On My Own Opinions; Boudon-Millot and Pietrobelli, "Galien ressuscité;" Garofalo and Lami, *Galeno: L'anima e il dolore.*
[20] K 19.8–48 (Boudon-Millot, *Galien: Introduction générale.* Sur l'ordre de ses propres livres. Sur ses propres livres. Que l'excellent médecin est aussi philosophe).
[21] The chapter in the *De libris propriis* entitled Περὶ τῶν ἱπποκρατείων ὑπομνημάτων (red ink) has been numbered in the margin κδ (24) as it had perhaps been considered as an independent set (even though other subtitles, also noted in red, did not lead to such a confusion).
[22] K 19.49–61 (Boudon-Millot, *Galien: Introduction générale.* Sur l'ordre de ses propres livres. Sur ses propres livres. Que l'excellent médecin est aussi philosophe).
[23] K 5.899–910.
[24] K 19.463–84.
[25] K 7.475–512.
[26] Numbering hidden by the reinforcement strips glued onto that area.
[27] K 5.104–48 (Wilko De Boer, *Galeni De propriorum animi cuiuslibet affectuum dignotione et curatione. De animi cuiuslibet peccatorum dignotione et curatione. De atra bile.* [*CMG* 5.4.1.1; Leipzig/Berlin: Teubner, 1937]).
[28] The sequence of the two treatises has been inversed in *Ambrosianus*, probably following rebinding, but just before the title of *De Atra Bile* (f. 231r) it is possible to read the end of *Adversus eos qui de typis scripserunt* and just before the title of *De plenitudine* (f. 238r) one can read the end of *De purgantium medicamentorum facultate.*
[29] K 11.323–42 (Jürgen Ehlert, "Galeni De Purgantium Medicamentorum Facultate: Überlieferung und Edition" [Ph.D. diss., Georg August-Universität, Göttingen, 1959]).
[30] K 7.513–83 (Christoph Otte, *De plenitudine* [Serta Graeca 9; Wiesbaden: Reichert, 2001]).
[31] *De praenotione ad Epigenem* (K 14.599–673). The text is incomplete in *Ambrosianus* and is interrupted in K 14.627.13 (Nutton, *Galen:* On Prognosis).
[32] The numbering reappears here (f. 265r) following a lengthy interruption due to the bad condition of conservation of the manuscript.
[33] K 1.224–304 (Stefania Fortuna, *Galeni De constitutione artis medicae ad Patrophilum* [*CMG* 5.1.3; Berlin: Teubner, 1997]).
[34] K 6.832–5. (Giulia Guidorizzi, "L'opuscolo di Galeno *De dignatione ex insomniis,*" Bollettino del Comitato per la preparazione dell'ëdizione nazionale dei Classici grecie latini n.s. 21 [1973]: 81–105).
[35] K 19.1–7.
[36] K 11.343–56.
[37] Kurt Bardong, *Galeni De Causis Procatarcticis Libellus a Nicolao Regino in Sermonem Latinum Translatus* (*CMG* Suppl. 2, Leipzig/Berlin: Teuber, 1937); Hankinson, *Galen:* On Antecedent Causes, 1998.
[38] K 9.550–766 (Bengt Alexanderson, *Galeni de Crisibus* [Studia Graeca et Latina Gothoburgensia 23; Göteborg/Stockholm: Elanders/Almquist Wiksell, 1967]). The fact that this commentary is not part of the preceding sequence is recognizable by a different pagination and presentation, notably the presence of decorative banners above the title (f. 104r).
[39] Concerning medical texts, this manuscript only includes *In Hippocratis de acutorum morborum victu.* Therefore, it cannot be similarly taken into account as regards the two other treatises copied at the end of *Vlatadon.*
[40] K 15.418–919 (Georg Helmreich, *De Bonis Malisque Sucis* [*CMG* 5.9.2; Leipzig/Berlin: Teubner, 1915]). Note, in particular, the presence of these same decorative banners as in the preceding treatise (f. 149r).

⁴¹ An important lacuna is common to all manuscripts, except one, which therefore cannot be taken to point to a parental link between *Ambrosianus* and *Vlatadon*. The treatise is very incomplete due to the loss of several folios. It is difficult to say whether the source of this treatise in *Vlatadon* is identical with that for *Ambrosianus,* where it ranks sixth within the sequence (now No. 4). The affirmative seems likely as it benefits from the same presentation for the title and script as the other treatises in that sequence (f. 239v) in *Vlatadon*. The absence of banners, a distinctive element in the two preceding treatises, also seems to support this.

DANIEL DAVIES

Some Quotations from Galen's *De indolentia*

Galen's philosophical works exerted considerable influence on medieval Arabic philosophy. Many of his works are noted by the great translator Ḥunayn ibn Isḥāq, from whose pen derived a number of Arabic and Syriac translations of Galen.[1]

The portions related here are taken from two Jewish philosophers, one of whom, Joseph ben Judah ibn Aqnīn (c. 1150–1220), quoted directly from the Arabic translation and the other, Šem Tov ben Joseph ibn Falaquera (c. 1225–95), translated into Hebrew.[2]

The Arabic quotations are taken from ibn Aqnīn's *Hygiene of the Suffering Souls and Remedy of the Sound Hearts* (*Ṭibb al-Nufūs al-Alīma wa-Muʿālaja al-Nufūs al-Salīma*).[3] Little is known of Ibn Aqnīn's life. He was born in Barcelona but emigrated to North Africa. His influence on later Jewish thinkers seems to have been small, although a number of his works were translated into Hebrew. The *Hygiene of the Souls* stands in a tradition of Arabic ethical treatises, in which the doctrines espoused by both Muslim and Jewish writers were similar, if some of the proof texts differed.[4]

179. Galen said: worry is the annihilation of the heart and distress is sickness of the heart. <Then he explained this and said> distress is about what has been and worry is about what will be.

180. He also said: grief is about what has passed and worry is about what will come. Beware of distress, for distress is the departure of life. Do you not see that someone whose face is distressed is ruined by distress?

---

[1] For a history of the translation movement, see Dimitri Gutas, *Greek Thought, Arabic Culture: The Graeco-Arabic Translation Movement in Baghdad and Early ʿAbbāsid Society (2nd–4th/8th–10th centuries)* (New York: Routledge, 1998).

[2] Ḥunayn wrote a letter in which he lists the works of Galen that he has translated along with those that he has not. He translated *Ind.* into Syriac himself, and he explains that Hubayš translated it into Arabic. See Gotthelf Bergsträsser, *Ḥunain ibn Isḥāq über die syrischen und arabischen Galen-Übersetzungen* (Abhandlungen für die Kunde des Morgenlandes 17.2; Leipzig: Deutsche Morgenländische Gesellschaft, 1925), 15–19.

[3] Abraham Halkin published the aphorisms that ibn Aqnīn quoted from earlier sources, along with a translation, and study. "Classical and Arabic Material in Ibn ʿAknīn's 'Hygiene of the Soul,'" *Proceedings of the American Academy of Jewish Research* 14 (1944): 25–147. The passages quoted here are on pages 110–4, and the paragraph numbers included there are retained.

[4] See Halkin, 28. Franz Rosenthal points to ibn Aqnīn's use of al-Ghazālī in *Knowledge Triumphant: The Concept of Knowledge in Medieval Islam* (Leiden: Brill, 2007), 294.

181. Galen said in *Avoidance of Distress* that disasters befell him, including the loss of his possessions and the incineration of his books in a building that fell in the fire, with contracts,[5] instruments, remedies and many pastes that he had crafted, and he was not distressed over this. He urged relinquishing distress and applying rest to the soul [to help] against distress. This is the opinion of the early sages. (cf. BMJ § 4.3.3–9/ KS § 2.66.13–17)[6]

182. It is told that Aristippus had four villages. Something happened by reason of which one of them was lost and three remained. One of the people of his town met him and showed distress because of the loss that had befallen him. He laughed at him, said to him, "Why are you of a mind to be distressed for me when I have three villages? You do not have the like of one of them and I will not be distressed for you." (cf. BMJ § 41.13.22–14.7/KS § 18.74.196–201)

183. Galen said, he [Aristippus] did well in this. I say that a person ought not to focus on the amount lost but focus on the amount that remains, and to reflect and consider to himself that those who inherit three villages from their fathers do not bear nor tolerate seeing people who have thirty villages. And if they get to the point that they have thirty they look to other people who have seventy villages, and if they get to the point that they also have a similar amount, they turn their eyes to other people who have more than one hundred villages until the matter grows in them, a desire hatches, and they long for themselves to have more than everyone. Because of this their whole time is poor unless their desires are not opposed. But if a person does not focus on the amount of possessions of another, and sets his sights on whether or not his possessions suffice for his expenses, the loss of his surplus possessions will be easy. It is as if a person has one village, which he loses, and he remains dispossessed and penniless; if he grieves his grief is reasonable. (cf. BMJ § 42–43.14.8–15/KS § 18.74.202–4)

184. Galen also said in his treatise on *Avoidance of Distress*, my father used to disdain all human matters and derided them, and this is something that happened to me in my old age. (cf. BMJ § 61.19.14–16/KS § 25.77.284–6)

185. He also said: distress and constant thought will necessarily attach to someone who considers that he is dispossessed of significant bodily things. As for someone who considers that he is only dispossessed of base, worldly things, he continues without being distressed. (cf. BMJ § 61.20.19–22/KS § 26.78.305–7)

186. He said that focusing on good food and drink, excellent garments, and sex compels those who give in to them to need to gather many possessions. Since they are not satisfied they first take to lamenting and moaning day and night and, afterwards, when they reflect on how [to fulfill] their desires with what they still possess.They are sleepless all night. If they do not attain them they weep and cry, and if they do attain them they are equally unsatisfied. Those whose desires are not opposed are stronger than the first. That is because many people care immoderately about honor, praise, riches, power, and authority. Someone who loves any of these excessively is compelled to the utmost of

---

[5] Lit: "memoranda."

[6] BMJ = Véronique Boudon-Millot and Jacques Jouanna (with Antoine Pietrobelli), *Galien: Ne pas se chagriner* (Budé; Paris: Les Belles Lettres, 2010); KS = Paraskevi Kotzia and Panagiotis Sotiroudis, "Γαληνοῦ περὶ ἀλυπίας," *Hellenica* 60 (2010): 63–148.

searching in his way of life, until he does not know that the soul has virtues and forgets what in it is evil. With this he is constantly deeply grieving. He does not reach what he intended, and that is because the goal is not achieved in the desire for recalcitrant, excessive desires. (cf. BMJ § 79b–82.24.14–25.14/KS § 29–30.81.364–77)

Šem Tov ben Joseph ibn Falaquera

The Hebrew quotations are taken from Falaquera's *Balm of Sorrow* (*Ṣeri ha-Yagon*). Falaquera possessed a knowledge of the Arabic and Greek philosophers that was perhaps unrivalled by other Jewish authors of his time. He considered himself a follower of Aristotle, whom he read with Averroes' commentaries, but his works also include translations of many other Arabic sources.[7]

During this period, Jewish centers in the Latin Christian world were growing.[8] Whereas previous great Jewish philosophers had been comfortable in their vernacular Arabic and had been integrated sufficiently into their Islamic cultural surroundings to read Arabic science and philosophy, most Jews of Western Europe neither knew Arabic nor were they part of the Latin scientific tradition. Furthermore, aside from being unable to access Arabic philosophical works, the great philosophical works of their own rabbinic Jewish tradition were also closed off as they were written in Judeo-Arabic. A desire to read Maimonides' *Guide for the Perplexed*, moved leaders of the Lunel Jewish community to commission a Hebrew version from Samuel ibn Tibbon (c. 1165–1232), whose father, Judah, had already translated a number of works from Arabic to Hebrew. But understanding the *Guide* requires background knowledge in the Arabic tradition, and so Ibn Tibbon set about his project of creating a philosophical tradition in Hebrew, through translations and original works.[9]

Falaquera was a part of this translation tradition. He wrote introductory works designed to educate Jewish readers in the sciences.[10] In order to help them study science to a more advanced level, he wrote an encyclopedia, in which he both translates and weaves sources together, sometimes paraphrasing rather than rendering the original passages literally. Mauro Zonta identified the passages presented here as possibly deriving from Galen's *Avoidance of Distress*.[11] He

---

[7] Steven Harvey, "Shem Tov ibn Falaquera's *De'ot ha-Filosofim*: Its Sources and Use of Sources," in *The Medieval Hebrew Encyclopedias of Science and Philosophy* (ed. S. Harvey; Dordrecht: Kluwer Academic Publishers, 2000), 211–37.

[8] Robert Chazan, *The Jews of Medieval Western Christendom 1000–1500* (Cambridge: Cambridge University Press, 2006).

[9] See James T. Robinson, "Maimonides, Samuel Ibn Tibbon, and the Construction of a Jewish Tradition of Philosophy," in *Maimonides after 800 Years: Essays on Maimonides and His Influence* (ed. J. M. Harris; Cambridge, Mass.: Harvard University Press, 2007), 291–306.

[10] Steven Harvey, *Falaquera's* Epistle of the Debate*: An Introduction to Jewish Philosophy* (Cambridge, Mass.: Harvard University Press, 1987).

[11] Mauro Zonta, *Un Interprete Ebreo della Filosofia di Galeno: Gli scritti filosofici di Galeno nell'opera di Shem Tob ibn Falaquera* (Turin: Silvio Zamorani Editore, 1995), 115–23.

states that many are equivalent to passages in al-Kindī's *On the Device for Dispelling Sorrows* (*Fī al-Ḥīla li Dafʿ al-Aḥzān*).[12] However, he notes that there are also other passages attributed to a certain "sage," and that this is an appellation that Falaquera often uses for Galen, although he also refers to Galen by name on other occasions. Two of the passages are quoted without attribution to "the sage," but Falaquera sometimes relates narrative passages without specifying their sources.[13]

14. VI:13–17[14]
The sage says: whoever wants to live will prepare a stout heart for troubles.
And he said: a person needs to disdain his life, and to believe that the way of the world is sometimes good and sometimes bad, and opposite to what the person wants. Therefore, the careful and intelligent individual needs not to be happy when his venture succeeds and not to worry at a time that it does not succeed, since he knows that it is all extinguished and that the time is short.

15. VIII:24–28
The sage[15] said: whoever knows that "passing away" rules his being, will bear troubles lightly.
And he said: necessity requires that everything that has a beginning has an ending. And the wise man constantly reminds himself what can happen to him. But the fool who is like an animal, even though he does not walk on all fours like the animals, will not realise the human matters in things that happen to them every day.

16. VIII:28–30
Worry and rumination never leaves the man who thinks that he has lost great and dear things, but someone who thinks that he has lost a deficient and lesser thing does not worry. (cf. BMJ 20.19–22/KS 305–7)

17. VIII:30–IX:3
They mentioned that one of the philosophers had four villages. He happened to lose one of the villages and was left with three. He met someone from his village who showed him that he was worried about what he [the philosopher] had lost. The philosopher laughed at him and said to him, "Why do you worry about me when I have another three villages? You do not have even one of them and I am not worried about you." (cf. BMJ 13.22–14.7/KS 196–201)

---

[12] There is an English translation of al-Kindī's letter. Ghada Jayyusi-Lehn, "The Epistle of Yaʿqūb ibn Isḥāq al-Kindī on the Device for Dispelling Sorrows," *British Journal of Middle Eastern Studies* 29 (2002): 121–35. The Arabic was edited by Hellmut Ritter and Richard Walzer, "Studi su al-Kindī II: Uno scritto morale inedito di al-Kindī," *Atti Della Reale Accademia Nazionale dei Lincei, Anno* 334, *Memorie Della Classe Di Scienze Morali, Storiche E Filologiche* ser. 6, vol. 8 (1938): 5–63.

[13] Zonta, *Interprete Ebreo*, 114.

[14] These quotations are included in Zonta, *Interprete Ebreo*, 115–23. They are given with the passage numbers in Zonta's book, followed by references to the edition of Roberta Klugman-Barkan, "Shem Tob ben Joseph Ibn Falaquera's 'Sori Yagon' or 'Balm for Assuaging Grief:' Its Literary Sources and Traditions" (Ph.D. diss., Columbia University, 1971).

[15] Moses ibn Ezra quotes the first sentence in Aristotle's name in *The Book of Discussion and Conversation* (*Kitāb al-Muḥaḍara wal-Muḏakara*). See Zonta, *Interprete Ebreo*, 115.

18. IX:3–5
If someone with little knowledge happens to have three villages, he says to himself, "Why do I not have thirty?"

19. IX:22–28
The sage said: someone who knows that coming to be and passing away come one after another to all things, will not worry when troubles come over him, because it is impossible [to escape] them. He will take them lightly, since it is not in his power to push them back.
And he said: time generates and destroys, and the passing away of one is a cause of coming to be for another.
And he said: some bad luck is difficult to bear. When someone bears it at a time that it happens to him, it indicates the greatness of his soul. Some of it is easy to bear. When it happens to a person and he does not bear it, it indicates the lowliness of his soul.

20. XI:8–11
One of the philosophers, when the king issued a command to kill him and before killing him to make him suffer by cutting out his tongue, did as follows. When the philosopher understood that the king wanted to make him suffer by cutting out his tongue, he preempted him, cut it out, and sent it to the king, and showed everyone that he was not afraid of suffering.

21. XI:13–24
And they mentioned that one of the kings of Persia captured another king. He issued a command to light a very large fire and throw him there. Meanwhile, as his slaves were busy lighting the fire, rain fell and doused the fire, and they neglected to guard him because of the abundant rain. He escaped, fled to his land, and returned to his kingdom as before, complacent in peace and tranquility. He followed his heart's whim and did not recall the troubles that befell him.
One of his sages said to him, "My lord king, do not rest on your laurels and do not trust to good fortune, for they both change suddenly." He did not heed his words and followed his desires. So it was that on one night in his dream he saw himself washing in water and drying off in the sun. When it was morning his spirit was piqued, and he sought to know the story of the dream and its solution. He told it to his daughter, who said to him, "they will hang you from a tree, and you will be exposed to the eye of the sun." It was but a few days before the Persian king imprisoned him, and commanded that he be hung from a tree.

22. XII:2–4
And the sage says: like the days, neither happiness nor sorrow endure, and worry about what has been is degeneration of the intellect. And he said: Fear of trouble before it comes is fatigue from nature.

23. XIX:27–28
And the sage said: with worry there is no reason.

Realia

MATTHEW C. NICHOLLS

A Library at Antium?

The rediscovery of Περὶ ἀλυπίας (or *De indolentia*) has provided a wealth of new information about the contents and, to an extent, the operation of libraries in Rome in the late Antonine era. The treatise contains valuable information on book formats and lengths, the ways in which Galen stored and consulted books in his own collection and in nearby libraries, the means by which he procured, read, compared, and corrected books, and the uses to which he put them. The first half of the *Ind.* in particular dwells on this topic at length, wearing its philosophical mantle of consolation rather lightly; despite the work's conceit of unruffled acceptance of disaster, Galen goes to some pains to detail what he has lost and the works on which his own burned books were based. It seems likely, then, that one of the purposes of the *Ind.* was to document the range and scale of Galen's intellectual enquiries now that the fruits of his labours had been irrevocably lost, and perhaps to establish a defence both of his own reputation and those of his sources against spurious works that might have sprung up to fill the void, in the same way that *De libris propriis* attempts to safeguard his oeuvre against plagiarism and misattribution.

Galen was also determined to circulate accounts of his own working practices as a scholar, and the details he gives us are crucial to our understanding of how reading, writing, and intellectual enquiry were conducted in second-century imperial Rome. The range of enquiries listed in *Ind.* is impressive in its breadth (as it was intended to be): Galen names in particular books he had read by a number of Peripatetic scientific and writers (*Ind.* 15–17), and also "grammarians, orators, doctors and philosophers" (*Ind.* 13); his own lost writings included lexicographical works on the Attic vocabulary of old comedy and prose, the latter of which alone occupied some 48 volumes (*Ind.* 28). A part of his intent, therefore, is to establish the large range of books he had consulted and that were now lost. He is also keen for his readers to understand that these books had been in general of the highest quality (*Ind.* 13), and that when they had fallen short of his high standards, or been misattributed, his own diligent work had corrected them (*Ind.* 14).

The city of Rome is the setting of this work in *Ind.* Galen assumes that his notional addressee and his wider readership will understand his topographical references to, for example, the "warehouses on the Sacred Way" (e.g., *Ind.* 2, 8), the "libraries of the Palatine" (e.g., *Ind.* 12), the Temple of Peace and the "so-called Domus Tiberiana" (18). The account of *Ind.* provides a picture of busy scholarly activity in buildings (public and private) in the area around the Forum at Rome, a picture corroborated through references elsewhere, by Galen and others, to the libraries of the Temple of Peace and Palatine Hill, and to the booksellers whose stalls occupied the streets leading to these public complexes.[1] The image that Galen wishes to create is of a well-connected reader and writer, reading the peerless collections of the imperial libraries and sending his own works to grateful recipients across the empire.

Although *Ind.* is set in Rome, other places in Galen's widespread world of intellectual and medical activity are mentioned: friends "back home" in Pergamum and in other places were placing authenticated copies of Galen's work into the public libraries that were built in many second-century cities in the Greek east, and Galen himself was planning to send some of his books to a summer residence in Campania (*Ind.* 21) – an interesting combination of a traditional Roman elite self-presentation of *otium* with the busy civic striving of the Greek second sophistic.

It is possible that Galen mentions another place in *Ind.* as part of his self-portrait of well-connected reading and writing. The Vlatadon ms of *Ind.* is corrupt, and the process of producing critical editions, not always from autopsy, continues. One particular set of apparent errors has generated a lively debate. *De indolentia* 16, 17, and 18, all apparently corrupt, contain forms of the word ἐναντίος: τας ἐναντίω 16, τὰ' ἐναντία 17, τὰ δὲ ἐναντίω 18. The Budé edition amends this troubling phrase to the common Galenic adverb ἐναντίως, and I have been inclined to follow that reading elsewhere, translating as something like "on the other hand."[2] Others, though, have followed a reading first proposed by Christopher P. Jones, who suggested that each of these occurrences be read as ἐν Ἀντίῳ ("in Antium"), which he assumes to be a reference to the imperial palace known to have existed there. This reading has the benefit of requiring little or no emendation of the text in each case, and has gained much support.[3]

---

[1] On this geographical clustering, see Matthew C. Nicholls, "Galen and Libraries in the *Peri Alupias*," *JRS* 101 (2011): 123–42 [129–30].

[2] As have others: Véronique Boudon-Millot, "Un traité perdu de Galien miraculeusement retrouvé, *Le Sur l'inutilité de se chagriner*: texte grec et traduction française," in *La science médicale antique. Nouveaux regards. Études réunies en l'honneur de J. Jouanna* (ed. V. Boudon-Millot, A. Guardasole, and C. Magdelaine; Paris: Beauchesne, 2008), 72–123; Véronique Boudon-Millot and Jacques Jouanna (with Antoine Pietrobelli), *Galien:* Ne pas se chagriner (Budé; Paris: Les Belles Lettres, 2010); Pier Luigi Tucci, "Galen's Storeroom, Rome's Libraries, and the Fire of A. D. 192," *Journal of Roman Archaeology* 21 (2008): 133–49; Pier Luigi Tucci, "Antium, the Palatium, and the Domus Tiberiana Again," *Journal of Roman Archaeology* 22 (2009): 398–401; Pier Luigi Tucci, "Galen and the Library at Antium: The State of the Question," *CP* 108, no. 3 (2013): 240–51.

[3] Christopher P. Jones, "Books and Libraries in a Newly-Discovered Treatise of Galen," *Journal of Roman Archaeology* 22 (2009): 390–7; Antonio Stramaglia, "Libri perduti per sempre: Galeno, 'De indolentia' 13; 16; 17–19," *Rivista di Filologia e di Istruzione Classica* 139 (2011): 118–47; Clare K. Rothschild and Trevor W. Thompson, "Galen's *On the Avoidance of*

I remain unconvinced by this conjecture, though I agree that it makes good philological sense of a series of difficult passages of Greek and could well be correct. I have said elsewhere that it introduces "rather a leap" into a treatise that is about literary endeavour and fire at Rome, though others disagree:[4] introducing a separate library in a different place into the work seems to me to undermine the tragedy of the irreplaceable losses in the fire at Rome, which is the driving theme of the work as a whole as is made plain by Galen at *Ind.* 12. However, it is true that Galen also gives an account of the near-destruction of the books at "Antium" so, as scholars including Rashed point out, the overall argument of the work could be seen as preserved, or indeed amplified, by this double destruction:

> Pour que l'effet soit complet, Galien doit convaincre son interlocuteur que l'incendie a causé des dommages irréparables. Il lui faut donc expliquer pourquoi les fonds manuscrits d'Antium ne permettront pas de remédier au désastre de Rome. C'est parce que les livres de la bourgade côtière se trouvent dans un état déplorable.[5]

I therefore find myself in (very cordial) disagreement with some other scholars of this text, including the editors of the present volume, whose generous correspondence on the subject has been stimulating and helpful. However, the Antium reading is gaining ground and, if it is to be accepted, we need to consider what its implications are for our understanding of books, libraries, and scholarship in the late second century CE. The editors of this volume were kind enough to suggest that my thoughts on these matters would be of interest to them, and I propose, therefore, to examine the passages in which Galen appears to refer to an "Antium" library with this in mind, leaving aside for the present purpose the vexed (and already copiously discussed) question of whether or not the Antium reading is itself correct.

The text and translation that follows for the three relevant passages is therefore based largely on that proposed by Rothschild and Thompson in their recent *Classical Philology* article,[6] with one significant change in the first passage:

Grief: The Question of a Library at Antium," *Classical Philology* 107, no. 2 (2011): 131–45; Enzo Puglia, "La rovina dei libri di Anzio nel De Indolentia di Galeno," *Segno e Testo* 9 (2011): 53–62; Anna Maria Ieraci Bio, Klaus-Dietrich Fischer, Ivan Garofalo, Alessandro Lami, and Amneris Roselli, "Congetture inedite sui testi medici," *Galenos: Rivista di filologia dei testi medici antichi* 2 (2008): 135–42 [esp. 137–8]; Daniela Manetti, "Galeno περὶ ἀλυπίας e il difficile equilibrismo dei filologi," in *Studi sul* De indolentia *di Galeno* (ed. D. Manetti; Biblioteca di "Galenos": Contributi alla ricerca sui testi medici antichi 4; Pisa/Roma: Fabrizio Serra, 2012), 9–22; Christopher P. Jones, "Galen's Travels," *Chiron* 42 (2012): 399–419.

[4] E.g., Rothschild and Thompson, "The Question of a Library at Antium," 135.

[5] Marwan Rashed, "Aristote à Rome au IIe siècle: Galien, *De indolentia*, §§ 15–18," *Elenchos* 32 (2011): 55–77 [71].

[6] Rothschild and Thompson, "The Question of a Library at Antium."

De indolentia 16 Vlatadon text: τας ἐναντίω

Λυπήσει δέ σε καὶ ταῦτα μάλιστα ὡς τῶν ἐν τοῖς καλουμένοις πίναξι [τῶν] γεγραμμένων βιβλίων ἐκσωθέν<τα>[7] εὗρόν τινα κατά τε τὰς ἐν τῷ Παλατίῳ βιβλιοθήκας, καὶ **τὰς ἐν Ἀντίῳ** ἃ φανερῶς <οὐκ> ἦν οὗπερ ἐγέγραπτο, <οὔτε> κατὰ τὴν λέξιν, οὔτε κατὰ <τὴν> διάνοιαν ὁμοιούμενα αὐτῷ.

And what will particularly grieve you is that of the books recorded in the so-called catalogues I found some preserved in the libraries on the Palatine and some in Antium which clearly do not belong to the author to whom they are ascribed, similar to him [i.e., the author] in respect of neither style nor thought.

De indolentia 17 Vlatadon text: τὰ δ' ἐναντία

Τούτων οὖν ἐγὼ πολλὰ μὲν ἐν ταῖς κατὰ τὸ Παλάτιον βιβλιοθήκαις εὗρον, **τὰ δ'ἐν Ἀντίῳ** κατεσκεύασα.

I found, then, many of these [books] in the libraries on the Palatine, and others I prepared in Antium.

De Indolentia 18 Vlatadon text: τὰ δ' ἐναντίῳ

Διεφθάρη δὲ νῦν τὰ μὲν ἐν τῷ Παλατίῳ κατὰ τὴν αὐτὴν ἡμέραν τοῖς ἡμετέροις, τῆς πυρκαϊᾶς οὐ μόνον ταῖς κατὰ τὴν ἱερὰν ὁδὸν ἀποθήκαις λυμηναμένης ἀλλὰ καὶ πρὸ αὐτῶν μὲν ταῖς κατὰ τὸ τῆς Εἰρήνης τέμενος, μετὰ ταῦτα δὲ ταῖς κατὰ τὸ Παλάτιον τε καὶ τὴν Τιβεριανὴν καλουμένην οἰκίαν ἐν ᾗ καὶ αὐτῇ βιβλιοθήκη τις ἦν, πολλῶν μὲν καὶ ἄλλων βιβλίων μεστή, τὰ δὲ ἐν Ἀντίῳ διὰ τὴν ἀμέλειαν τῶν ἑκάστοτε ληστευομένων ἐκ διαδοχῆς αὐτὰ (…) καθ' ὃν χρόνον ἐγὼ ἀνέβην εἰς Ῥώμην πρῶτον ἐγγὺς ἦν τοῦ διεφθάρθαι.

But now the books on the Palatine perished on the same day as my own, when the fire ravaged not only the repositories by the Sacred Way, but first those at the Temple of Peace, and later those on the Palatine and the so-called House of Tiberius, where there

---

[7] ἔξωθεν is yet another point of difficulty. Stramaglia, "Libri perduti per sempre," 131, proposes ἐκσωθέν⟨τα⟩ and I follow that here as it seems to make best sense of what follows in this context: the passage from *Ind.* 17 seems to recapitulate a statement that Galen found these books at the Palatine and (for the sake of argument here) at Antium. BM (Boudon-Millot, "Un traité perdu de Galien miraculeusement retrouvé, *Le Sur l'inutilité de se chagriner*"), BMJ (Boudon-Millot and Jouanna, *Galien:* Ne pas se chagriner), Rothschild and Thompson, and Jones retain ἔξωθεν and read it as an adverb ("I found certain books from the Catalogue outside [the library]"). In the Rothschild-Thompson reading, Galen is taken to mean that he has found books outside the libraries which he has compared to catalogues at Rome and at Antium, but I have said elsewhere that I believe this Catalogue to be a single definite entity (see below and Nicholls, "Galen and Libraries in the *Peri Alupias*," 135–7); the logic of this difficult section of *Ind.* seems to be that the loss of books preserved at Rome and at Antium (at least initially) is what has caused irreparable loss to Galen. Still other readings are possible: Nutton takes ἔξωθεν to be a preposition ("I found certain books outside (i.e., not in) the Catalogue"); I have followed this latter reading elsewhere but it is hard to sustain if Galen's "on the other hand" is removed in favour of inserting Antium. See Boudon-Millot and Jouanna, *Galien:* Ne pas se chagriner, 65–66.

was also a library which was filled with many other books, whereas those in Antium through the negligence of those continuously robbing them ... was nearly destroyed at the time at which I first came to Rome.

What library was this?

If we accept the Antium reading for the sake of this discussion, we have to contend with the fact that Galen does not specify what manner of collection, library, or place he has in mind. Antium is mentioned nowhere else in the extant *corpus Galenicum*, so we have nothing with which to compare these references. Galen appears to refer to "libraries" in the plural at Antium at *Ind.* 16, where his τὰς ἐν Ἀντίῳ balances out the plural τὰς ἐν τῷ Παλατίῳ βιβλιοθήκας. This need not mean that he is referring to more than one institution or collection. As Stramaglia observes, and I have noted elsewhere,[8] references to libraries can use the singular or plural almost interchangeably to refer to single institutions or the collections within them.

So what was this library or book collection at Antium? Commentators on this passage have followed Jones in assuming that, if we read Antium here, Galen must be referring to the library attested in the imperial villa there. In fact, he does not say this; he merely refers to the name of the town of Antium as if his reader is expected to know which library or book collection this refers to. The imperial villa library is probably the best guess, but it should be pointed out that it is not explicitly named, and that when other Greek authors write ἐν Ἀντίῳ they generally mean the town itself.[9] While successive emperors enjoyed a villa retreat at Antium which was enormously enlarged in the first century CE and upgraded again by Commodus during Galen's lifetime (alterations not commented on by him), the town and its surrounding area had many other rich inhabitants, attracted in part by the prestige (and infrastructure) of the nearby imperial villa: during Nero's enlargement of the villa he sent a colony of the richest praetorian veterans to settle there, and "surely their social status ... was reflected in well appointed villas."[10] It is thus possible – indeed, likely – that other villas in the area had private libraries (Cicero had certainly kept a book collection there in a previous age).[11] We know, moreover, that several Italian provincial towns had public

---

[8] Stramaglia, "Libri perduti per sempre," 133–4; Matthew C. Nicholls, "*Bibliotheca Latina Graecaque*: on the Possible Division of Roman Public Libraries by Language," in *Neronia VIII Bibliothèques, livres et culture écrite dans l'empire romain de César à Hadrien* (ed. Y. Perrin; Latomus 137; Bruxelles: Éditions Latomus, 2010), 11–21 [13 n. 6].

[9] Plutarch *Cor.* 26.1.1; *Brut.* 21.1.2; Dionysius of Halicarnassus *Ant. rom.* 10.21.5.2; Cassius Dio 17.57.60.4; 58.25.2.2 (this last perhaps the villa: Tiberius is celebrating a marriage there).

[10] Annalisa Marzano, *Roman Villas in Central Italy: A Social and Economic History* (Leiden: Brill, 2007), 173. Nero's veterans: Suetonius *Nero* 9, cf. Tacitus *Ann.* 14.27.

[11] Cicero *Att.* 4.41; 4.5.4; 4.8.2; 5.3.3.

libraries of their own,[12] and it is not impossible that Antium had one too, just has Galen speaks later in *Ind.*, without particular emphasis, of the βιβλιοθήκη δημοσίᾳ that might be found in ἄλλαις πόλεσιν.[13]

Nonetheless, the imperial villa library remains the best guess: it is attested elsewhere, and the bare mention of the name "Antium" suggests (*a priori*) a particularly well-known place, as if one were to speak of "Monticello," or "Windsor," in the context of books and libraries. That said, we do not know an enormous amount about the imperial library at Antium. If we could attach Galen's testimony to this library, it would provide valuable new insights into its holdings and operation.

The *Fasti Antiates ministrorum domus Augustae* show us that in the first half of the first century CE, the imperial villa library at Antium was provided with at least a modest staff of specialists including two freedmen and two slaves titled *a bybliothece* between 37 and 48 CE.[14] In 32 CE there was a *librarius* – a copyist or scribe, suggesting an active library with either an expanding book collection, or maintenance of existing stock, or the copying out of texts as a service to others.[15] In 38 CE there were two *glutinatores*, men probably concerned with the binding or repair of papyrus books. This suggests a carefully organised and well-maintained library with a certain quantum of books, enough to justify a staff of named specialists to see to their maintenance, though it need not have been an exceptionally large establishment; Cicero, in his own Antium villa library, used three *librarioli glutinatores* loaned by Atticus.[16]

In the generation after these staff members had worked at the Antium villa, Nero radically remodelled it. Evidence for the continuation of the villa library after this date comes from Philostratus in his *Vita Apollonii* (20.8):

> This book [a volume of Pythagorean lore obtained from the oracle of Trophonius at Lebadea] is preserved in Antium, a place on the Italian coast, which is much visited for this reason. I concede that I heard this from the inhabitants of Lebadea; but I give here

---

[12] E.g., Tibur, Aulus Gellius *Noct. att.* 19.5; library at Comum: Pliny the Younger *Ep.* 1.8 and *CIL* 5.5262; at Suessa Aurunca: *CIL* 10.4670.

[13] *Ind.* 21.

[14] *CIL* 10.6638 = *Inscriptiones Italiae* 13.2.26: *l(ibertu)s a by(bliothece)*, freedman, 37 CE, which appears in Degrassi's text at I.III line 12 [Attilio Degrassi, *Inscriptiones Italiae. Volumen XIII, Fasti et Elogia. Fasciculus I, Fasti consulares et triumphales* (Rome: La Libreria dello stato, 1947)]; *Claud(ius) Atimetus a byb(liothece)*, freedman, 43 CE, II.III.22; *Chresimus a byb(liothece)*, slave, 44 CE, II.III.29; *Bathyllus ver(na) Capr(ensis) a bybl(iothece)*, slave, 48 CE, III.3; *librari(us)* I.II.2; *Eros glutinat(or) Aphrodisius glutinat(or)* II.II.4–5. See also George W. Houston, "The Slave and Freedman Personnel of Public Libraries in Ancient Rome," *TAPA* 132, no. 1/2 (2002): 139–76 [148–50], who notes that *glutinatores* are not unambiguously to be ascribed to book repair; and George W. Houston, "Tiberius and the Libraries: Public Book Collections and Library Buildings in the Early Roman Empire," *Libraries & the Cultural Record* 43, no. 3 (2008): 247–69 [249].

[15] Cf. Cicero *Fam.* 16.22; *Att.* 12.14.3, 13.44.3; Nepos *Att.* 13.3.

[16] Cicero *Att.* 4.4a; 4.5.4; 4.8.2; 5.3.3; Nepos *Att.*13.3–4.

my opinion on this book, that it was subsequently conveyed to the Emperor Hadrian at the same time as some of the letters of Apollonius, though by no means all of them; and it remained in the palace at Antium, which was the one out of his Italian palaces which most pleased him.

Apollonius' statement is not particularly reliable. He admits that he has not seen the book in question and appears uncertain about where exactly it is: he uses the same vague formula as Galen (ἐν Ἀνθίῳ) before asserting that in his opinion it was put by Hadrian into his palace library there. If this is right – or if, as seems easier to accept, it seemed plausible to Philostratus and his readers – then this account both conforms with Galen's picture of a library of useful books open to readers such as himself, and undermines his account of its demise, since Philostratus seems to presume that the book is still there and still accessible to the many people who visit Antium on its account.[17] Galen's account of destruction and loss over the decades in which he knew the library does not accord with Philostratus' account, written about thirty years later, of a book that had survived there for around a century.

Of the architectural form of this library we know nothing. Several imperial villas contained spaces which have been identified as libraries by analogy with the better-known architecture of public library buildings, which consisted for the most part of large, monumental halls with book cupboards let into wall niches,[18] but this rationale is not particularly convincing (what we know of villa libraries, from the remains at Herculaneum or Pliny's description of his Laurentine villa, does not absolutely conform to this pattern).[19] At Antium the space conventionally identified as the villa library, and attributed to a Domitianic phase of building, is in fact almost certainly a nymphaeum,[20] and although other parts of the vast palace complex may suggest themselves as libraries, no certain identification can be made.

Galen's testimony, if we accept that he is referring to an imperial villa library at Antium, therefore fills in a chronological gap in our knowledge of the villa library's life, telling us that it was still in operation but severely compromised in the latter half of the second century CE by various problems. It shows us that the books there were nevertheless of use to Galen in his researches and included unique items whose loss was irreparable. The "Antium" books were therefore comparable to the public library collections at Rome that are the principal con-

---

[17] Philostratus' verbs are in the present tense: ἀνάκειται, σπουδάζεται.

[18] See e.g., Lorne Bruce, "Palace and Villa Libraries from Augustus to Hadrian," *Journal of Library History* 21, no. 3 (1986): 510–52.

[19] Pliny the Younger *Ep.* 2.17.

[20] For the identification of this room as a library, see Valnea Santa Maria Scrinari; Maria Luisa Morricone Matini, *Mosaici Antichi in Italia. Regione Prima: Antium* (Roma: Istituto poligrafico dello Stato, 1975), 13. Contra: Alessandro Jaia, "Anzio: La villa imperial," in *Residenze imperiali nel Lazio: atti della Giornata di studio, Monte Porzio Catone, 3 aprile 2004* (ed. M. Valenti; Tusculana 2; Frascati: Libreria Cavour Editrice, 2008), 73–80 [73].

cern of the *Ind.*, and this near parity between private and public imperial libraries casts interesting light on both of them, particularly since their books holdings seem in this case to have been similar.

What books were these?

The sections of the *Ind.* that bear on the "Antium" question concern the comparison of sets of books to those recorded in "the so-called catalogues" (τοῖς καλουμένοις πίναξι, *Ind.* 16). At *Ind.* 16 Galen discusses misattribution of books in these Catalogues, saying that he has read books on the Palatine and at "Antium" that were not written by "the author whose name they bore" since the "style and thought" of the works makes the attribution (in Galen's view) untenable. He develops this theme further in *Ind.* 17, adding that there he had identified works not recorded in the Catalogues and found some that were mentioned there but which were somehow considered to be missing (μὴ φαινόμενα δ' αὐτά).

In between these two passages he gives details of what these missing or misattributed books contained. They seem to have been part of a collection of Peripatetic scientific writings, particularly by Theophrastus and Aristotle; some were well-known but others survived uniquely in these lost libraries and are therefore now gone for ever. Galen seems to expect his correspondent to know which Catalogue he is referring to (in the same way that the mere mention of "Antium" is apparently enough to signal which library was meant), so it was presumably a bibliographical document with a life outside the libraries which Galen visited, an authoritative list of canonical works rather than an operational shelf-list for particular libraries. I have written elsewhere that a good candidate for such a Catalogue is the list of Aristotle's books drawn up in Republican Rome, which was still current in second century CE Rome.[21] If this is correct, and Galen was right in searching for a correspondence between the books recorded in this document and those on the shelves of the Palatine and Antium libraries, it would imply that at least some of Aristotle's books were housed there, having endured a somewhat turbulent history before and after being brought to Rome by Sulla.[22]

This would be an interesting addition to our understanding of how imperial-era Roman libraries acquired their books. The rump of the Aristotelian-Sullan collection may have been acquired by Cicero,[23] and would then have probably

---

[21] Plutarch *Sull.* 26. See Nicholls, "Galen and Libraries in the *Peri Alupias*," 136.

[22] Strabo *Geogr.* 13.1.54 and prior note.

[23] Cicero may have purchased them from a financially embarrassed Faustus Sulla, though this is not certain: *Att.* 9.11.4 and Plutarch *Cic.* 27.3l; Shackleton Bailey's note on *Att.* 4.10.1 (David R. Shackleton Bailey, *Cicero's Letters to Atticus, Volume II* [Cambridge: Cambridge University Press, 1965], letter 84); Raymond J. Starr, "The Used Book Trade in the Roman world," *Phoenix* 44, no. 2 (1990): 148–57 [155 and nn. 27–29]; Anthony J. Marshall, "Library Resources and Creative Writing at Rome," *Phoenix* 30 (1976): 252–64 [259–60]; Carnes Lord,

passed into Octavian's hands through confiscation. It would then seem to have been divided at some subsequent point between the Palatine library in Rome and the villa library at Antium. Elsewhere in *Ind.* (13) Galen suggests that notable book collections – the Ἀττικιανὰ, Καλλίνια, and Πεδουκίνια – were preserved intact in the Palatine library, suggesting an acquisition and curatorial policy that favoured keeping named collections together. Here we see something different, the splitting of the remains of a famous collection, or at least of books which might naturally have been grouped together by author and subject material, and which could be compared to a known Catalogue, across two different sites, one a public library and one (probably) an imperial villa library in Antium.[24] This fits with the interpretation of the imperial library 'system', at least in its early days, suggested by Houston in his discussion of the staffing arrangements[25] – a progression from a private household library, or series of such libraries, to the first public institutions, staffed by personnel drawn from the *familia* and holding books drawn from the same sources as those that filled the imperial palace libraries.

Galen says that he spent much time and trouble making copies of these books (ἐγγραφομένοις, *Ind.* 19; see n. 30 below) early on in his Roman career; at *Ind.* 17 he uses the verb κατεσκεύασα in relation to this activity.[26] It therefore seems that he could visit the books at Antium and make copies of the books there, or have them made, just as he did in Rome. The process seems to have been similar in both Rome and Antium: Galen was able to browse among the books (since the Catalogue was not a shelf-list nor even, in his view, a reliable guide to the contents of the volumes held in each place: he had to see them for himself). He was able to identify large numbers of texts relevant to a particular subject area, in this case Peripatetic science, which suggests that there may have been some sort of grouping of texts by genre or subject area (or by collection, if at least some of these books were thought of as belonging to the group covered by the "so-called Catalogue"). Given his need to rent a storage space in Rome close to the libraries, and his moralising attitude to the depletion of the Antium library by neglect and possible theft (for which see below), it is unlikely that he was permitted to remove the books from the libraries, and this means that the "no little effort" (*Ind.* 19) he spent in correcting and copying these precious works

---

"On the Early History of the Aristotelian Corpus," *AJP* 107 (1986): 137–61. An alternative route to imperial ownership is through the downfall of the Pompeian faction in the civil war.

[24] If this chapter were not committed to exploring the implications of the "Antium" reading of *Ind.*, this could be used as an argument against accepting it.

[25] Houston, "Tiberius and the Libraries."

[26] "Obtained," or "made": Rothschild and Thompson, "The Question of a Library at Antium," 138 n. 34; Jones, "Books and Libraries in a Newly-Discovered Treatise of Galen," 396; Rashed, "Aristote à Rome au IIe siècle," 69. Boudon-Millot and Jouanna, *Galien:* Ne pas se chagriner, 7 – who reject Antium – translate *je me les suis procurés*, and suggests in their commentary that this relates to purchases in commercial bookshops (71).

was spent in the library itself: we must envisage a place furnished with space and equipment for writing by Galen (who says at *Ind.* 6 that his literary works were at least corrected "by my own hand") and probably also, given the scale of his enterprises, by assistants or slaves; perhaps he was able to command the services of the successors to the *librarius* mentioned in the *Fasti Antiates*.

This adds substantially to our understanding of how palace libraries might have functioned and what they were for. They seem to have been open to readers other than the emperor. Galen, of course, was high in the favour of the Antonine court and as such hardly a member of the "public," but his account is compatible with Philostratus' claim that a lot of people travelled to Antium to read the books there, and that these books included a prized rarity that drew many readers in. It seems that serious literary reading in some areas of intellectual enquiry in the Roman world involved travel to libraries to view rare books that were, or were at least supposed to be, confined there. In an earlier age the great private collectors had opened their villas for this purpose to favoured coteries of writers (as might be argued from the book collection preserved at the villa of the Papyri in Herculaneum), sometimes in quite large numbers, anticipating the public libraries of the imperial era.[27] Emperors might well have deployed the collections in their private estates in a similar way on occasion, and it seems from the *Ind.* that the public libraries in Rome and those at Antium all functioned similarly, as places where trusted manuscripts and rare books could be read and copied. This worked better in some libraries than others; Galen is full of praise for the holdings of the Palatine libraries as late as the fire of 192, but plainly regards the managements of the Antium library in the preceding decades as disastrous, as we will see. The lineaments of the operation of each library, though, seem to have been broadly the same; Galen, in dropping in casual references to "Antium," sees no need to explain that his working habits there were different or to tell his correspondent how the emperor's private library operated: he seems to assume that this will all be well-known. Again, the implied similarity with his working methods in the public libraries of Rome is interesting.

Decline: "now they are completely useless."

Galen's account of the Antium library charts a sorry decline in the condition of its books. It was already "near to destruction," ἐγγὺς ἦν τοῦ διεφθάρθαι, when he first came to Rome in 162 CE (*Ind.* 18). The reason for this initial poor condition seems to have been human failures, through either neglect or theft on the part of readers or of successive generations of library staff. The manuscript passage concerning these human reasons for the poor state of the "Antium" books is

---

[27] Plutarch *Luc.* 42.

itself – with a certain irony – corrupt. Boudon-Millot and Jouanna, who worked from reproductions of the manuscript rather than autopsy, preserve the following reading:

τ<ιν>ὰ δὲ ἐναντίως διὰ τὴν ἀμέλειαν τῶν ἑκάστοτε λῃστευομένων ἐκ διαδοχῆς αὐτὰ (…)

We have already seen the amendment to ἐν Ἀντίῳ. Further effort has been expended on the troublesome λῃστευομένων and its relationship to αὐτά, with a consensus developing that the reference here is to neglect on the part of the library's staff ("those entrusted successively" with responsibility for the books).[28] This makes better sense of the notion of 'neglect', ἀμέλειαν, though other readings are possible: Stramaglia retains λῃστευομένων and suggests on the basis of a further restitution that the books have disappeared from Antium through readers' failure to honour their pledges to return them, while Rashed, with a different restitution of the same corrupt passage, offers the picturesque possibility that the books have been eaten by mice.[29]

Either reading works grammatically and helps to resolve a difficult passage, but the notion of theft seems to go against what logic can be salvaged from the remains of Galen's Greek, which seems to run as follows: there had been at Antium in the early 160s a useful collection of books, though nearly ruined by negligence. Despite the poor condition of the library in 162 CE, or perhaps because of it, Galen spent much effort working on the books there. He had done his best to transcribe or correct these books,[30] in much the same way that he took on the task of copying out and correcting books from the Palatine libraries and elsewhere. The books, therefore, were in the library when Galen first arrived, and they or the copies made by Galen remain in the library, albeit in a terrible condition, "νυνί." It is hard to reconcile this with the idea that a large number of

---

[28] ἑκάστοτε πιστευομένων: Garofalo, "Congetture inedite sui testi medici," 137. ἑκάστοτε' ἐμπιστευομένων: Amneris Roselli, "Libri e biblioteche a Roma al tempo di Galeno: La testimonianza del *De indolentia*," *Galenos: Rivista di filologia dei testi medici antichi* 4 (2010): 127–48 [146]. See also Puglia, "La rovina dei libri di Anzio nel De Indolentia di Galeno," 55–56; Rashed, "Aristote à Rome au IIe siècle," 69; Stramaglia, "Libri perduti per sempre," 136–7. The two solutions – theft and neglect of librarians' duties – are of course not incompatible, as Marcus Aurelius' famous apparent endorsement of illicit borrowing through bribery implies (Fronto *Ep.* 2.5).

[29] Stramaglia, "Libri perduti per sempre," 141–3, adds μεσι[τείαι]ς in the lacuna on the basis of the extra letters μ[.]σι[……] discerned from inspection of the actual manuscript by Paraskevi Kotzia and Panagiotis Sotiroudis, "Γαληνού περὶ ἀλυπίας," *Hellenica* 60 (2010): 63–148 [70]. The word μεσιτεία, "ampiamente diffuso nella lingua burocratica dei papiri documentari," means a pledge, and would mean that the books have disappeared as borrowers have failed to honour their pledges to return them. Rashed, "Aristote à Rome au IIe siècle," 72, uses the same letters to reconstruct μ<υ>σὶ <βεβρωμένα>.

[30] The verb is ἐγγραφομένοις, which could refer either to copying out or to annotation and correction ("mark in or on" – LSJ, sv ἐγγράφω): perhaps the latter, if the books stayed on the shelves in Antium.

books had been stolen; the point that Galen seems to be making is not that the books have disappeared, but that the librarians at Antium have failed to ensure proper conditions of ventilation for the longevity of their physical fabric.[31]

In order to warrant inclusion in *Ind.*, and to amplify rather than undermine the treatise's primary account of the terrible double loss in Rome of private book collection and public library source material, these original books and Galen's copies or emendations must, by the time of writing, have become equally inaccessible. This seems to have been brought about by another problem in the library, the damp caused by the marshy and low-lying nature of the place, which was causing the papyrus books rolls to stick together:

νυνὶ δὲ τελέως ἐστὶν ἄχρηστα μηδὲ ἀνελιχθῆναι δυνάμενα διὰ τὸ κεκολλῆσθαι τὰς χάρτας ὑπὸ τῆς σηπεδόνος· ἔστι γὰρ ἑλῶδές τε καὶ κοῖλον τὸ χωρίον ἐς τὰ μάλιστα, καὶ διὰ θέρους πνιγηρόν.

De indolentia 19

This was certainly a threat known to Roman library-builders and librarians.[32] The passage of *Ind.* that discusses the fate of these books contains a troublesome lacuna,[33] but overall it seems likely that this description of damp in *Ind.* 19 applies to the books of the library mentioned before this gap, whether that library

---

[31] Puglia, "La rovina dei libri di Anzio nel De Indolentia di Galeno," 58–59, offers a similar logic.

[32] Puglia, "La rovina dei libri di Anzio nel De Indolentia di Galeno," 61, writes with grim relish of the mushy, fungal condition of damp papyrus books whose keepers have neglected to air them. Libraries at Ephesus and Rome appear to incorporate air gaps behind the bookroom walls to prevent or limit the penetration of groundwater; cf Vitruvius 6.4.1. There has been much discussion about whether this description of a damp location is compatible with Antium. Rothschild and Thompson, "The Question of a Library at Antium," 143, write that "both standard usage and contextual cues suggest that the best interpretation of τὸ χωρίον in *Ind.* 19 is 'region' [rather than 'building']" and adduce various sources to suggest that Galen's description of this "region" as marshy and low-lying is consistent with what we know of Antium. Tucci ("Galen's Storeroom, Rome's Libraries, and the Fire of A. D. 192;" "Antium, the Palatium, and the Domus Tiberiana Again;" "Galen and the Library at Antium: The State of the Question," *Classical Philology* 108, no. 3 [2013]: 240–51) disagrees strongly, arguing that Antium itself is not described in these sources as marshy but was in fact well known as a suitable resort for luxury villas; he prefers to see Galen's description here as pertaining to the site of the Domus Tiberiana library in the Roman Forum. The clifftop imperial villa at Antium certainly seems, as Tucci says, an airy and pleasant location, but it remains at least possible that a library room was inadvisably located in a damp part of the huge and sprawling palace complex. This argument is not entered into further here since it has been thoroughly considered by these authors and essentially bears on the question of whether the Antium reading is correct; we have already decided to accept this reading for the purposes of this essay. The fact remains that the villa was extensively rebuilt in the Antonine period (Jaia, "Anzio"), and the problematical library therefore could have been, but apparently was not, moved as part of this redevelopment: a puzzling omission if Galen had brought the library's deficiencies to the attention of the emperor.

[33] See n. 29.

is the one in the Domus Tiberiana at Rome (as Tucci argues)[34] or that at Antium (as is presumed in this essay).

If one accepts this overall reading of these deeply corrupted and difficult passages, the picture that emerges is as follows: there was, at "Antium," a library that contained substantial holdings complementary to those in the public libraries in central Rome, that Galen used as part of his extensive reading and correction of precious manuscripts, particularly in Peripatetic science (all the books he mentions, as is almost universally true of his entire oeuvre, are in Greek), despite problems there caused firstly by human faults and latterly by problems of damp. He seems to have used libraries in both places in much the same way, not deeming any differences of access or usage worthy of comment – an interesting reflection on the way that they were understood to operate not just by the privileged Galen, but by his reader(s). Galen spent a lot of time and effort correcting or copying the books at Antium, uncovering there errors of attribution and missing items just as he did at Rome. Had he made private copies for his own use he could have removed them from Antium, preserving their contents (unless they had, by chance, perished in the storage room in Rome).[35] He does not tell us that he did this, however, so it seems most likely that he corrected existing manuscripts, or made fresh copies that then seem to have stayed on the shelves there[36] – an interesting testimony to his role in maintaining this important imperial library collection, or at least arresting its decline; he must have been granted the right to interfere with the library collection in this way, presumably by the emperor and presumably in response to his own observations on its perilous condition. If Galen felt any responsibility for having left these precious books to decline over the decades in a fetid and paludinous atmosphere he does not, typically enough, reproach himself.

These passages are, frustratingly, deeply corrupt: we cannot get much further, and the readings proposed here are only one of several possible interpretations. We can at least say that the library at "Antium" seems to have suffered a fairly catastrophic decline – indeed, to make the mention of Antium fit into *Ind.* at all it must be the case that Galen cannot recover from there works which his correspondent might otherwise have assumed he could rescue after the fire at Rome. The Antium library is therefore known to Galen's audience, but its sad present condition has to be explained. By contrast, the public libraries in Rome remained in good order up until their destruction by fire and this, I would suggest, is the

---

[34] Tucci, "Antium, the Palatium, and the Domus Tiberiana Again."

[35] Boudon-Millot and Jouanna, *Galien:* Ne pas se chagriner, 74, suggest that the damp books were copies procured by Galen and stored in his lock-up depot on the Sacred Way is not tenable, given that the contents of this storage warehouse were destroyed by fire, not damp, and that Galen goes out of his way in *Ind.* 8–9 to praise the apparent security of the building and its suitability for storing books and other goods.

[36] See n. 30 above.

most interesting single insight that results from the acceptance of the Antium reading in *Ind.* Despite Hadrian's apparent favour for the Antium property and its library, the Antonine dynasty seems to have neglected properly to maintain the books there for many years, notwithstanding their immense investment in the villa of which it was a small part. On the other hand, the public libraries of Rome itself were much more carefully maintained right up until the fire of 192 CE, containing rare and precious books prized for the accuracy of their contents (*Ind.* 12–13). In their treatment of book collections, then, the emperors of the mid and late second century seem to have followed the lead of the library-founding emperors of earlier dynasties, seeing political or cultural value in maintaining prestigious collections of books in public libraries at Rome even when their own private collections were allowed to decline.

ALAIN TOUWAIDE

Collecting Books, Acquiring Medicines: Knowledge Acquisition in Galen's Therapeutics

Galen's recently rediscovered treatise *De indolentia* (*On Not Feeling Grief*) is an extraordinary document on the libraries in Rome, their catalogues and books, the circulation of written works, and also on Galen's use, production of, and care for, books and texts. *De indolentia* has been thoroughly scrutinized from this viewpoint. It has already revealed a certain number of the mysteries it still contains because of its poor conditions of preservation in the past and its careless writing, and may help clarify some *vexatae quaestiones* in the history of ancient books, collections and scientific tradition, in spite of its dramatically corrupted text and the still unsuccessful efforts to restore obscure passages. Some aspects of this multifaceted letter have not yet been investigated, however, such as Galen's methods for knowledge acquisition. In this essay I would like to venture in this area, with a particular focus on Galen's ways of collecting formulae for medicines and drugs for the preparation of such medicines.[1] I will argue that there is a striking similarity between Galen's search for, and care of, books and texts on the one hand and his quest for formulae for medicines and new medicines on the other hand. A first hint in that sense is provided by the words *books* and *medicines* which are associated in five occurrences throughout the letter, with φάρμακα coming first in three of such passages.[2]

On this question of the search for formulae for remedies, *Ind.* is a truly unique piece, one that compensates for a dramatic lacuna in the substantial body of literature devoted to drugs and medicines compiled during the period prior to Galen, which includes such works as the *Compositiones* by Scribonius Largus,

---

[1] I use the term "formula for medicine" for γραφή in Greek instead of "prescription" or "recipe." See 31.11.9–10; 35.12.12; 50b.16.12 in Véronique Boudon-Millot and Jacques Jouanna (with Antoine Pietrobelli), *Galien:* Ne pas se chagriner (Budé; Paris: Les Belles Lettres, 2010); references refer to the section, page, and line number.

[2] See the following occurrences: 7.4.23–24 (φάρμακα καὶ βιβλία); 12.5.14 (βιβλίου ... φαρμάκου); 50b.16.19 (φάρμακα ... βιβλία); 65.20.16 (φάρμακα καὶ βιβλία). Note also 4.3.6–7 and 7, although it offers a lexical variant for the books (... τῶν ὑπ' ἐμοῦ συ<γγε>γρα<μ>μένων ... φάρμακα). I should add that, in all passages except in 50b, the two terms βιβλία and φάρμακα are accompanied by a reference to surgical instruments (ἄρμενα), with the three elements books/formulae for medicines/instruments forming a significant recurrent triad. I will not comment on surgical instruments in this essay, however tempting it may be to establish a parallelism.

Naturalis historia by Pliny and *De materia medica* by Dioscorides. Even Galen's immense oeuvre is scant in details on this point, however abundant it is on *materia medica* and medicines with such treatises as *De simplicium medicamentorum temperamentis ac facultatibus*, *De compositione medicamentorum secundum locos*, *De compositione medicamentorum per genera*, *De remediis parabilibus*, and *De antidotis*.[3]

Although some studies have been devoted to ancient pharmacology,[4] be it in Galen's work or in other physicians', none of them has properly tackled the question of how Galen acquired his knowledge of remedial therapy.[5] Nevertheless some publications developed the theme of pharmacological experimentation in Galen's treatises. This is the case in an article by Mirko D. Grmek and Danielle Gourevitch[6] and in the short book by Mirko D. Grmek on biological experimentation in antiquity[7] about experimentalism and experimental science. Grmek's book probably overemphasizes this aspect by focusing on rare passages and isolating them, in the case of Galen, from the vast oeuvre in which they are included. Complementarily, an article by Armelle Debru brings to light the fact that Galen may have taken some of his information from daily practice and popular wisdom.[8]

More specifically, Cajus Fabricius' historical inquiry has stressed the vastness of the collection of data brought together by Galen in his treatises on therapeutics and *materia medica*, and the multiplicity of the sources consulted to assemble

---

[3] To this list I could add *De theriaca ad Pisonem* and the treatises on toxicology (*De venenis* and *De animalibus virus eiaculantibus*) that I have brought to light and presented in Alain Touwaide, "Galien et la toxicologie," *ANRW* 37.2:1887–1986.

[4] I do not use the term *pharmacology* here in the technical meaning it has acquired in the 19th century with Rudolf Buchheim (1820–79) and even more Oswald Schmiedeberg (1828–1921), but in its non-technical etymological meaning of "science of *farmaka*."

[5] See for example the several articles by Jerry Stannard (1926–88), collected in the volume *Pristina Medicamenta: Ancient and Medieval Medical Botany* (Variorum Collected Studies Series 646; Aldhershot and Brookfield: Ashgate, 1999); those by John M. Riddle reproduced in the volume *Quid Pro Quo: Studies in the History of Drugs* (Variorum Collected Studies Series 367; Aldhershot and Brookfield: Ashgate, 1992) and, more recently, those published by John Scarborough, grouped in the volume *Pharmacy and Drug Lore in Antiquity: Greece, Rome, Byzantium* (Variorum Collected Studies Series 904; Aldhershot and Brookfield: Ashgate, 2010). See also the proceedings of the 1995 Galen Colloquium: Armelle Debru, ed., *Galen on Pharmacology: Philosophy, History and Medicine: Proceedings of the Vth International Galen Colloquium, Lille, 16–18 March 1995* (Studies in Ancient Medicine 16; Leiden: Brill, 1997).

[6] Mirko D.Grmek and Danielle Gourevitch, "Les expériences pharmacologiques dans l'antiquité," *Archives internationales d'histoire des sciences* 35 (1985): 3–27.

[7] Mirko D. Grmek, *Il calderone di Medea: La sperimentazione sul vivente nell'Antichità* (Lezioni italiane, Fondazione Sigma-Tau 14; Rome and Bari: Laterza, 1996). French translation: *Le chaudron de Médée: L'expérimentation sur le vivant dans l'Antiquité* (Collection Les empêcheurs de penser en rond; Le Plessis Robinson: Synthélabo, 1997).

[8] Armelle Debru, "The Gardener and the Lady: Therapeutics and Society in the Age of Galen," in *The Pharmacy: Windows on History* (ed. R. Pötsch; Basel: Editiones Roche, 1996), 23–33.

such an impressive mass of information.⁹ At the same time, however, he made clear that Galen used earlier bodies of data, warning against the temptation to attribute to Galen himself the collection of all the material he included in his works. An investigation conducted on *De materia medica* of Dioscorides reached a similar conclusion.¹⁰ Such scholarly research invited caution on the part of modern readers and interpreters of ancient pharmacological literature not necessarily to credit ancient authors with the merit of having collected themselves the multiple fragments of earlier works assembled in theirs.

De indolentia makes a substantial contribution to this question of knowledge acquisition in the field of *materia medica*, formulae for medicines and therapeutics, and provides significant keys for the reading of the body of ancient literature on these topics and its subsequent tradition through history, particularly if the information retrieved from Galen's letter is compared to the explanation provided by Dioscorides in the preface of *De materia medica* on the way he collected information.

Galen is known to have traveled to collect in person some of the drugs that were used in his time. The episode of his expedition(s) to Lemnos to inquire about, and collect, the famous Lemnian earth is well known and does not need to be reported again here.¹¹ Not so known, but equally – if not more – significant is the passage in *De theriaca ad Pisonem* in which Galen reports how he tests the quality of a medicine – actually, a theriac – by giving it to some roosters but not to others and then exposing them all to vipers' bites.¹² Beyond these and some other passages substantially similar on the method of knowledge acquisition, nothing else has been transmitted by Galen in his immense oeuvre on the way he worked on pharmacology. Similarly, not much can be gleaned from the *Naturalis historia* of Pliny, even though we know that the work relies on extensive reading of a whole range of specialized literature and that relevant extracts were collected in a way that we might want to identify as "cut and paste." The case of *De materia medica* of Dioscorides is, however, slightly different. Whereas the work itself does not provide much information on how its author acquired the information contained in it, its preface is explicit on this point. Strangely enough,

---

⁹ Cajus Fabricius, *Galen Exzerpte aus älteren Pharmakologen* (Ars Medica 2 Abteilung Griechisch-lateinische Medizin 2; Berlin and New York: Walter de Gruyter, 1972).

¹⁰ Marie-Hélène Marganne, "Nouvelles perspectives dans l'étude des sources de Dioscoride," in *Médecins et médecine dans l'antiquité, avec, en complément, les Actes des Journées d'étude sur la médecine antique d'époque romaine* (ed. G. Sabbah; Mémoires 3; Saint-Etienne: Publications de l'Université de Saint-Etienne, 1982), 81–84.

¹¹ On these frequently cited expedition(s), see most recently Véronique Boudon-Millot, *Galien de Pergame: Un médecin grec à Rome* (Paris: Les Belles Lettres, 2012), 106–8, for the chronology and 115–19 for the report and analysis of the expedition. More generally, see Boudon-Millot, *Galien de Pergame*, 103–19, for Galen's scientific travels, aimed to collect and study some natural products used for therapeutic purposes.

¹² *Ther.Pis.* 2 (K 14.215.5–12).

however, it has not received the attention it deserves in modern scholarship despite a detailed study by John Scarborough and Vivian Nutton.[13] We shall return to Dioscorides' preface later in this essay.

If we examine book and text collecting in *Ind.*, we observe a scholar accustomed to living in a city with large libraries. Such a method was only possible in a metropolis. Whatever the extent of their collections, not all libraries at that time had as many books and texts as Rome. Galen indirectly witnesses to the limitations in the collections of other libraries – even public ones – when he reminds the recipient of *Ind.* that he arranged for books to be produced for some of his friends.[14] As a reader using such libraries, Galen was accustomed to consulting their catalogues[15] to detect items he had not seen in any other institutions,[16] to request and to read them, even cursorily, and to check the precision of the catalogue attributions.[17] In so doing, he was able to identify works that escaped the attention of cataloguers[18] or that were incorrectly identified.[19] He could also identify works that were supposedly lost and were not recorded in the catalogues.[20] This is the behavior of an assiduous reader who spends hours, if not days, in libraries, scrutinizing their catalogues, requesting numerous items, and sometimes barely opening them if their content corresponded to their title or, instead, sometimes interminably delving into them, introducing bookmarks, occasionally also – and almost involuntarily – annotating the books and, in any case, taking notes.

Such behavior is probably no surprise from somebody like Galen who lived in Pergamum, well known for its library, and studied in Alexandria, home to the most famous library of antiquity and the birthplace of library science. The names of Eratosthenes and Callimachus were probably still famous during Galen's years at the local school of medicine and, with them, the methods for book cataloguing, alphabetizing titles of works and other literary material or – to mention just a few – the screening of texts searching for rare, difficult or obsolete words. Of these aspects of book culture we find abundant traces in *Ind.*, especially his references to scrutinizing the catalogues to find texts no longer in circulation or the compilation of lists of words, technical terms and other rarities, not only in scientific, but also in literary texts.[21]

---

[13] See John Scarborough and Vivian Nutton, "The Preface of Dioscorides' *De Materia Medica*: Introduction, Translation and Commentary," *Transactions and Studies of the College of Physicians of Philadelphia* 5, no. 4 (1982): 187–227.
[14] 21.8.23–9.4.
[15] 16.7.1; 17.7.12–13.
[16] 13.5.19.
[17] 17.7.12–13.
[18] 17.7.12–13.
[19] 16.7.3–4.
[20] 17.7.13–14.
[21] 23b–28.9.11–10.24.

The portrait of Galen as a *rat de bibliothèque* – albeit not one of those who may have eaten pages of the Vlatadon manuscript and some of its precious information[22] – that emerges from these allusions scattered through *Ind.* is complemented by other affirmations in the text about Galen as a visitor and most probably also a client of publishers and bookshops.[23] The episode in which he evidently overheard two visitors of a bookshop wondering if a book they were flipping through was by Galen or not is well known.[24] Thanks to *Ind.* we learn that Galen knew the best editions of ancient works; we even discover what we should properly call a publishing company that was previously unknown.[25] He was, thus, well acquainted with the milieu of book production and a good client of the best publishers and bookshops.

Galen's book consumption was not only passive, as his frequentation (probably assiduous) of bookshops seems to indicate, but active, suggesting real bibliomania. Nevertheless, Galen was an engaged reader as well as a copyist,[26] corrector,[27] and even editor[28] of the texts he was interested in, including ancient authors.[29] Without entering into the subtleties of this aspect of his activity, I shall stress his method in revising texts neither excessively nor insufficiently, aiming at precision.[30] Also, he classified his own works in two groups, those for diffusion and those for personal use,[31] besides the others that he obtained and had possibly revised, but may have kept for his personal use, and his notebooks.

Such an attitude toward books, book-consumption, interest in information from books, information-collecting, and knowledge acquisition was not only that of a scholar, but also a city dweller, who had access to vast libraries with substantial holdings, duly organized with efficient and accurate catalogues and cataloguing instruments, and also had access to important publishing companies and bookshops. He probably also frequented smaller treasure troves of old and less-valuable books where experts were able to locate obscure jewels. Texts of this nature belonged in larger cities, a fact of which Galen was very much aware

---

[22] On this point, see the developments by Marwan Rashed, "Aristote à Rome au IIe siècle: Galien, *De indolentia*, §§ 15–18," *Elenchos* 32 (2011): 55–77 [esp. 70].

[23] See 13.5.21–22 about the products of different "publishers" and 17.7.15–16 for acquisitions (purchase?) of books.

[24] See Galen *Lib.Prop.* Intro. (K 19.8–9.17 = BM 134.11–14; Véronique Boudon-Millot, *Galien: Introduction générale. Sur l'ordre de ses propres livres. Sur ses propres livres. Que l'excellent médecin est aussi philosophe* [Budé; Paris: Les Belles Lettres, 2007]).

[25] See the reference to the *Pedoukinia* editions 13.5.22 with the related note of commentary.

[26] 6.3.15–16; 19.8.6–7.

[27] 6.3.15; 14.6.8–9.

[28] 14.6.9 and also 55b.16.13.

[29] 6.3.16.

[30] 14.6.11–13.

[31] 29.11.1–4.

since he took the time to send books to his friends living in smaller towns where such resources were not available.³²

Interestingly enough, the portrait of Galen as book consumer and, at the same time, book producer as copyist and corrector is closely reciprocated in the image that Galen gives of himself about remedies in *Ind*. The parallelism is close and begins immediately with the very first statement about the extent of his losses in Rome. In his report of the fire, he brings together books and remedies, both owned by Galen in significant quantities: "the mass of writings" (πλῆθος ... τῶν ... συ<γγε>γρα<μ>μένων) and "all the medicines of all sorts" (φάρμακα ... παντοῖα πάμπο<λ>λα).³³ This initial affirmation is followed by details concerning the nature of the books and the medicines, with a further implicit, but nonetheless clear, parallelism.³⁴ Indeed, the books Galen lost comprised three different types of works: (1) those of ancient authors copied by Galen himself (διὰ τῆς ἐμῆς χειρὸς ἀνδρῶν παλαιῶν τὰ συγγράμματα); (2) Galen's own works (τά ... ὑπ᾽ ἐμοῦ συντεθέντα); and, (3) those works that Galen corrected (τὰ ἐπηνωρθωμένα). Similarly, the medicines are (1) antidotes, particularly theriac (τὰς καλουμένας ἀντιδότους ... μάλιστα δὲ τὴν θηριακὴν), which can be compared to the works of ancient authors as it was a historical preparation; (2) ingredients for compound medicines (which recall the works written by Galen himself since these ingredients had been acquired to prepare medicines); and, on the basis of the parallelism between books and medicines, we may deduce that (3) Galen modified the formulae for medicines he had received just as he corrected the texts he was reading.³⁵

The first comparison is further stressed by two occurrences of the couple φάρμακα/βιβλία³⁶ the second of which comes immediately before the description of the ways Galen obtained the books he lost in Rome fire.³⁷ If some of these books were discovered by surprise (since they were not listed in the library catalogues or were considered lost whereas they were not),³⁸ others had been acquired³⁹ and revised and corrected,⁴⁰ and others were copies made to be sent to friends.⁴¹ The description of the works that Galen himself had devoted to lexicology constitutes a deft transition to the description of the formulae for medicines that were lost in the fire thanks to the mention and short discussion of

---

[32] 21.8.21–9.4.
[33] 14.6.6–8.
[34] 6.3.15–17.
[35] 6.3.17–4.5.
[36] 10.4.23–24 and 12a.5.14.
[37] 12b–22.5.15–9.7.
[38] 17.7.12–13.
[39] 17.7.15–16.
[40] 14.6.8–13.
[41] 21.8.21–9.7.

terms for vegetables.⁴² This segment of the text concludes with a reaffirmation that the books Galen lost were of two types: some had been revised and were aimed at diffusion, whereas others were for his own use.⁴³ Having explained this, Galen shifts from books to formulae for medicines.

Just as he had acquired works difficult to find and collections of rare words before the fire, he had more remarkable formulae for medicines than any others (θαυμασιωτέρας),⁴⁴ obtained by chance (τύχη)⁴⁵ – even a double chance (διττὴ τύχη)⁴⁶ – thanks to his reputation (κἀμοῦ συμπροτιμηθέντος).⁴⁷ One of Galen's fellow-citizens (ἀνήρ τις πλούσιος τῶν παρ' ἡμῖν)⁴⁸ gained knowledge of interesting formulae for medicines⁴⁹ (and spent huge amounts of money to buy some),⁵⁰ not only those in use at his time but also past ones,⁵¹ in a way that recalls a library collection, all the more so because these formulae had been recorded in a book that Galen received.⁵² As for the second chance, it consisted in receiving a collection of formulae assembled during travels worldwide (ἐξ ὅλης τῆς οἰκουμένης)⁵³ by the physician Eumene from Pergamum.⁵⁴ Besides these donations – whose fortuitousness recalls the discoveries in the library catalogues, Galen also had formulae that he prepared himself just as he authored original works.⁵⁵ To complete his therapeutic arsenal, he also exchanged formulae,⁵⁶ taking from the collections he had received in a way that might be compared to exchanging books.

The implicit comparison of formulae for medicines with books that runs through the lines is confirmed at the end of the descriptive section of *Ind.*,⁵⁷ where the sequence φάρμακα/βιβλία appears twice with a significant play on a repetition that generates the assimilation (πάντα μέν ... φάρμακα, πάντα δὲ <τά> βιβλία) and, further on, a rupture of the parallelism that introduces two different elements (value: ἀξιόλογα φάρμακα; and personal work: ἐκδόσεις) that generates an implicit transfer of the information about *value* from φάρμακα to βιβλία and conversely of personal work from βιβλία to φάρμακα. This brings to

---

⁴² 23b–28.9.12–10.24.
⁴³ 29.11.1–4.
⁴⁴ 31.11.10.
⁴⁵ 31.11.12.
⁴⁶ 32.11.13.
⁴⁷ 31.11.13.
⁴⁸ 32.11.15.
⁴⁹ 32.11.16–17.
⁵⁰ 32.11.16–17.
⁵¹ 32.11.19–20.
⁵² 33.11.21–12.3.
⁵³ 35.12.12.
⁵⁴ 34–35.12.4–17.
⁵⁵ 37.12.20–13.1.
⁵⁶ 36.12.18–20.
⁵⁷ 50b.16.10–13.

the readers' mind the fact that Galen had prepared new collections of valuable formulae for medicines on the basis of books he received by chance, akin to his "discovery" of books in the library collections in Rome.

Although the comparison is implicit, there is nevertheless a clear process of knowledge acquisition running through the lines of *Ind.* It is presented as the sum of his recipes collected from all over the world by individuals, one having acquired these formulae by paying for them with significant sums of money, the other having personally traveled to collect the formulae himself. Galen's method of knowledge acquisition contrasts with these two models, and also with his own in earlier years, when he traveled to Lemnos, for example. However, when writing *Ind.*, he may be a senior physician no longer able to take the risks incurred by extended journeys, particularly trips by sea. Also, it is typical of a scientist with a well established reputation to receive unsolicited donations, including those of precious information as Galen specifies he received, and to synthesize previous knowledge on the basis of material collected in this way.[58] Notions of value (δοκιμώτατα),[59] quantity (παμπό<λ>λας and τοσοῦτον ὅσον οὐδὲ παρὰ πᾶσιν),[60] and reputation (θαυμασιωτέρας,[61] θαυμασίων,[62] and also ἀξιολόγων[63]) associated with the formulae for medicines Galen mentions throughout this work confirm his status as a physician.

Galen's pharmacology is urban in nature, that is, of a context no longer in direct contact with natural resources; rather, of a context in which ingredients are either brought from the outside – collected, prepared, dried, and stocked for further use or (when they were not of foreign origin) procured on the market as available. We find further traces of the urban nature of his pharmacology in his development of compound medicines not only broad-spectrum remedies, but long-lasting, storable ones. Also, the lists of ingredient substitutions attributed to, but not necessarily by Galen, although they may have been written by a contemporary, attest nonetheless to this transformation in the science of pharmacology in his day insofar as they too acknowledge the transfer of medicine preparation from places where the ingredients were collected to places where the ingredients were merely stored.[64] This transfer from one milieu to another implies a transformation in methods for information collection. In pre-urban pharmacology, the source of the information and the source of the *materia med-*

---

[58] 37.12.20–13.2.
[59] 37.13.1.
[60] 6.4.1, 3–4.
[61] 31.11.10.
[62] 36.12.18–19.
[63] 50b.16.12.
[64] On this transformation, see Alain Touwaide, "*Quid pro Quo*: Revisiting the Practice of Substitution in Ancient Pharmacy," in *Herbs and Healing from the Ancient Mediterranean through the Medieval West: Essays in Honor of John M. Riddle* (ed. A. van Arsdall and T. Graham; Medicine in the Medieval Mediterranean 4; Farnham: Ashgate, 2012), 19–61.

ica were almost always identical. The medicinal substances – mainly plants – were grown by healers or by their patients in the surrounding of homes. Whoever mixed the remedies knew by personal and direct contact the herbs that were chosen, their properties, proper dosages, and possible mixtures. Subsequently, in the cities of the Roman Empire, this kind of personal contact was no longer possible, although some wealthy landlords created extraordinary gardens of the type leading Pliny to remark that certain of his contemporaries had imported nature to the cities.[65]

In these conditions, we see thus that Galen's method of knowledge acquisition is mainly book-based, emphasizing information gleaned from earlier collections some of which relied on a personal observation, travels, and sometimes direct contact with the original purveyors of the medical formulae. The method of collecting drug recipes that Galen claims for himself in *Ind.*, is backed by his encyclopedic pharmacological works, which also witness to his patient collection and proper identification, and arrangement of textual materials – almost to the point of creating a catalogue, including alphabetizing texts according to a library scheme rather than their possible intrinsic parameters, as in the case of *materia medica*. Although efficiency in locating information increased – as is the case with catalogues – the sum total of information itself was reduced as it was limited to the content of an entry in the catalogue or resulting system. As a consequence, the library-inspired, book-based system of Galen's urban pharmacology depleted overall stores of information available for the healing of patients.

This claim will be clearer if we compare Galen's with Dioscorides' method, itself not dissimilar from that of Teuthras' method, at least as Galen describes it.[66] In the preface of *De materia medica*, Dioscorides describes the way he collected the massive quantity of data that gives substance to his work.[67] Characteristically, he denounces alphabetizing information because it disconnects drugs with their most salient properties.[68] Regarding his method of information collecting, Dioscorides is precise: it consisted of extensive travel[69] permitting personal experience of most of the *materia medica* (with the significant term ἐμπειρία and

---

[65] On this question, see Alain Touwaide, "Art and Sciences: Private Gardens and Botany in the Roman Empire," in *Botanical Progress: Horticultural Innovation and Cultural Change* (ed. M. Conan and J. K. Kress; Dumbarton Oaks Colloquium Series in the History of Landscape Architecture 28; Washington, DC: Dumbarton Oaks, 2007), 37–49.

[66] 34–36.12.4–17.

[67] For this preface, see the edition by Max Wellmann, *Pedanii Dioscuridis Anazarbei:* De materia medica libri quinque (3 vols.; Berlin: Weidmann, 1906–14), 1:1–5. A modern English translation is now available: Lily S. Beck, *Pedanius Dioscorides:* De Materia Medica (Altertumswissenschaftliche Texte und Studien 38; Hildesheim, Zürich, and New York: Olms-Weidmann, 2005). For the preface, see pages 1–5.

[68] § 3 (1.2.13–14). I have translated ἐνέργεια by "property" for the sake of convenience here.

[69] § 4 (1.2.17–18). I will not discuss here the question of the supposed link of Dioscorides with Roman troops as this is outside the topic of this essay.

the no less significant expression δι' αὐτοψίας).⁷⁰ The rest of the information Dioscorides needed he probably gleaned from anonymous ἱστορία (perhaps referring to written documentation), which he would have consulted and compiled, trying to identify a common body of data for each item. He would have submitted such information to critical analysis in collaboration with the natives of the place where the *materia medica* grew (τὰ δὲ ἐξ ἱστορίας τῆς πᾶσι συμφώνου καὶ ἀνακρίσεως τῶν παρ' ἑκάστοις ἐπιχωρίων ἀκριβώσαντες).⁷¹ Dioscorides' method for obtaining information concerning effective *materia medica* is that of a person in the field not a library – even if he may have consulted some written documentation (ἱστορία). There is a sharp contrast, thus, between Dioscorides' and Galen's methods, probably best characterized by the difference between urban and rural milieux as the sources and context for knowledge acquisition.

Be that as it may, there is probably also another component that determined the ways these two pharmacologists acquired knowledge of *materia medica*: they had different purposes. Whereas Dioscorides aimed to collect all possible information about *materia medica* – and he assembled the largest collection ever made in antiquity if we can judge from preserved texts – Galen had a much bigger project. He aimed to assemble massive quantities of data and medicines, to circulate information about remedies (as he repeatedly affirms in *Ind.*), to compile his own lists of *valuable* and *admirable* medicines – that is, efficacious ones, probably confirming his ability as therapist – *and* to analyze and organize the resulting information according to his own theoretical system. This system was based on the properties of the *materia medica* (not necessarily neat in each drug, but sometimes mixed as the title *De temperamentis ac facultatibus simplicium medicamentorum* indicates), including their basic qualities, textures, and other physical qualities of their components. In creating and maintaining this system, Galen operated an important transformation in pharmacology, transferring it from its purely observational status (probably not much different from the discipline called *pharmacognosy* that lasted up until the 19th century) to an analytical one (perhaps corresponding more to contemporary *pharmacology* in the technical meaning of the word) – what I refer to in an earlier essay as a move from *pharmaco-centrism* to *medico-centrism*.⁷² In this sense, Galen was not necessarily as interested in descriptive pharmacology as Dioscorides. He was content to apply book-based knowledge as *Ind.* suggests.

---

[70] § 5 (1.3.7 and 8) respectively.

[71] § 5 (1.3.7–9).

[72] Alain Touwaide, "La thérapeutique médicamenteuse de Dioscoride à Galien: du pharmaco-centrisme au médico-centrisme," in *Galen on Pharmacology. Philosophy, History and Medicine. Proceedings of the Vth International Galen Colloquium, Lille, 16–18 March 1995* (ed. A. Debru; Studies in Ancient Medicine 16; Leiden, New York, Köln: Brill, 1997), 255–82.

Philosophy

Paraskevi Kotzia (†)

Galen, *De indolentia*:
Commonplaces, Traditions, and Contexts

Galen's Περὶ ἀλυπίας (or *De indolentia*), a letter to a Pergamene friend that the author classes among his ethical treatises,[1] is a text of a markedly personal, autobiographical character. The theme of ἀλυπία, providing this relatively short work with its title, is briefly raised at the very beginning during Galen's rehearsal of the request that his correspondent had addressed to him (BMJ 1.1–15/KS 1–10),[2] but is only taken up for discussion in the second part (BMJ 13.3–26.3/KS 181–384), the intervening section being given over to an extended description of the losses Galen suffered during the great fire of 192 C. E. in Rome.[3] Everything said in the second part of the treatise amounts in effect to a kind of theoretical accreditation of the "absence of grief" Galen had been able to display in the face of his losses. The reader has the impression of being already acquainted or indeed familiar with almost all of it.

First of all, the reader recognizes views known from other works of the Galenic corpus. Reasonably enough, there are similarities, on occasion even *verbatim* ones, to be found here with his treatment of the subject of λύπη in the *De animi cuiuslibet affectuum dignotione et curatione* (*Aff.Dig.*), a work which Galen in his *De libris propriis* (*Lib.Prop.*) categorizes in the same class of writings as *Ind*. The kind of ἄσκησις that Galen recommends as a preventive method effective against λύπη, namely prior familiarization with possible future disasters at the level of the imagination (BMJ 52.1–56.16/KS 245–69), receives detailed dis-

---

[1] *Lib.Prop.* 12 (K 19.45 = BM 169.13; Véronique Boudon-Millot, *Galien: Introduction générale. Sur l'ordre de ses propres livres. Sur ses propres livres. Que l'excellent médecin est aussi philosophe* [Budé; Paris: Les Belles Lettres, 2007]): περὶ τῶν τῆς ἠθικῆς φιλοσοφίας ἐζητημένων.

[2] References to the text of *Ind.* are to both of the critical editions in existence: the first number refers to the edition of Véronique Boudon-Millot and Jacques Jouanna (with Antoine Pietrobelli), *Galien: Ne pas se chagriner* (Budé; Paris: Les Belles Lettres, 2010); the second, to the edition of Paraskevi Kotzia and Panagiotis Sotiroudis, "Γαληνοῦ περὶ ἀλυπίας," *Hellenica* 60 (2010): 63–148. In the case of the former (hereafter BMJ), the section number is provided followed by the line number on the page. In the case of the latter (hereafter KS), the line number is provided.

[3] On the mixture of literary genres in the Περὶ ἀλυπίας see Paraskevi Kotzia, "Galen *περὶ ἀλυπίας*: Title, Genre and Two *Cruces*," in *Studi sul* De indolentia *di Galeno* (ed. D. Manetti; Biblioteca di "Galenos": Contributi alla ricerca sui testi medici antichi 4; Pisa/Rome: Fabrizio Serra Editore 2012), 69–91 [esp. 69–70].

cussion in *De placitis Hippocratis et Platonis* (*PHP*), a work composed some thirty years earlier than *Ind.*, in the period 162–6, in the context of a Posidonian critique of Chrysippus' theory in Περὶ παθῶν.

Second, most of the themes touched upon are also present as τόποι in other works of ethical philosophy having as their object the therapy of emotions, and in particular that of λύπη. Given that the πραγματεία ἡ θεραπευτικὴ τῶν παθῶν, as we read in *PHP* deals with the prevention of πάθη, that is, with how to guard against the arousal of painful emotions, as well as with their cure once they have arisen,[4] it is natural that commonplace themes, expressions, and argumentative strategies we come across in a text which aims at the prevention of λύπη, as is the case with *Ind.*, should also turn up in texts which aim at the alleviation of this same emotion, that is, in consolatory works.

Such standard themes – as well as clichés, commonplace anecdotes, and *exempla* – are present in all treatises of ethical philosophy not addressed to philosophers, but aiming at moral education. Margaret R. Graver's assessment with respect to consolatory literature also applies *mutatis mutandis* to Galen's treatment of "absence of grief:"

> The consolatory letters and treatises of antiquity are not, on the whole, philosophically ambitious. They may appeal to 'What Philosophy Says,' but their content usually tends towards the philosophical commonplace, platitudes of general application such as will find ready acceptance with the bereaved and perhaps provide some comfort.[5]

In texts belonging to the genre of the therapy of emotions, scholars usually trace the presence of commonplace ideas to the Stoic-Cynic tradition. This is not unreasonable given, on the one hand, the decisive contribution Stoics made to the study of the πάθη, and, on the other hand, the κοινωνία that existed between the Stoic αἵρεσις and its Cynic counterpart (Diog. Laert. 6.104). Yet, the fact remains that the same commonplaces are also employed by non-Stoic authors, such as Plutarch and Favorinus.

Of course, the common elements shared between *Ind.* and other works are not all equally revealing of Galen's indebtedness to an established tradition. For instance, Galen's invocation of the typical *exempla* of πενία – the Cynics Diogenes and Crates (BMJ 45.7–10/KS 216–18) – carries a different weight than the quotation from Euripides (BMJ 52.4–9/KS 248–53) deployed in connection with the ἄσκησις he recommends in *Ind.*, of which mention was made earlier. The fact that the same verses also turn up not just in Galen's own *PHP*, but, likewise, in

---

[4] *PHP* 4.7.22–23 (K 5.420–1 = *CMG* 5.4.1.2 284–7). Phillip De Lacy, *Galen: On the Doctrines of Hippocrates and Plato* (3 vols.; *CMG* 5.4.1.2; Berlin: Akademie, 1980–4): καὶ τὴν γένεσιν αὐτῶν κωλύσειε καὶ γενομένας παῦσαι δυνηθείη ... κωλύσομέν τε τῶν παθῶν ἕκαστον γίνεσθαι καὶ γενόμενον ἰασόμεθα.

[5] Margaret R. Graver, "The Weeping Wise: Stoic and Epicurean Consolations in Seneca's 99th Epistle," in *Tears in the Graeco-Roman World* (ed. T. Fögen; Berlin: De Gruyter 2009), 235–52 [235].

the Stoic-oriented third book of Cicero's *Tusculanae disputationes* as well as in the *Consolatio ad Apollonium* ascribed to Plutarch, and in advancement of the same theme, namely the pre-rehearsal of possible future disasters, suggests the employment of a common source, while at the same time shedding light on the transformations to which such thematic elements were subject in their migration from text to text.[6]

Given that, of the several attested works which bore the title Περὶ ἀλυπίας, Galen's is the only one extant,[7] a close study of the commonplaces and, more generally, the subject matter it shares with other works belonging to the same genre offers a promising approach toward a more concrete appreciation of the theme of "absence of grief." Another helpful line of approach would be to focus on the intertextuality between *Ind.* and Plutarch's *De tranquillitate animi*, as well as Seneca's *De tranquillitate animi*, since the "absence of grief" represents a basic factor and, in a certain way, a precondition of εὐθυμία.[8] The same holds also for the similarities our text displays with Plutarch's *De cupiditate divitiarum*, since the theme of "love of wealth" is crucial to Galen's argument. Moreover, it is Galen himself who prompts the comparison, since as a complement to *Ind.* he also forwards to his correspondent another work of his entitled, Περὶ τῶν φιλοχρημάτων πλουσίων (BMJ 84/KS 382-4).

---

[6] *Tusc.* 3.13: et primo, si placet, Stoicorum more agamus, qui breviter astringere solent argumenta; 3.22: Haec sic dicuntur a Stoicis ... sententiis tamen utendum eorum potissimum, qui maxime forti et, ut ita dicam, virili utuntur ratione atque sententia. ET: Margaret R. Graver, *Cicero on the Emotions: Tusculan Disputations 3 and 4* (Chicago: The University of Chicago Press, 2009), 12, "That is how the Stoics make their points ... Yet I will continue to rely primarily upon Stoic views, since among philosophers their reasoning is the strongest and, if I may say so, the most virile."

[7] Treatises Περὶ ἀλυπίας are attributed to Eratosthenes of Cyrene (3rd cent. BCE), to Diogenes of Babylon (2nd cent. BCE) – teacher of Panaetius – to Plutarch (Lamprias' Cat. no. 172), and to someone referred to as "Aristophanes the Peripatetic;" see Kotzia, "Galen Περὶ ἀλυπίας: Title, Genre and Two *Cruces*," 71, 74.

[8] The notions of ἀλυπία and εὐθυμία are frequently associated in our sources; cf. characteristically Musonius fr. 17: Τί ἄριστον γήρως ἐφόδιον; ET: Cora Lutz, "Musonius Rufus: 'The Roman Socrates,'" *Yale Classical Studies* 10 (1947): 32–147 [110]: "What is the best viaticum for old age?" ... ζῆν ἀλύπως ... οὕτω γὰρ ἂν καὶ εὐθυμότατος εἴη ... ἀλύπως βιοῦν ... πλοῦτος γὰρ ἡδονὰς μὲν οἷός τε παρέχειν ἀνθρώποις ἐστὶ ... οὔτε δὲ εὐθυμίαν οὔτε ἀλυπίαν οὐδαμῶς τῷ κεκτημένῳ παράσχοι ἄν. μάρτυρες δὲ πολλοὶ τῶν πλουσίων λυπούμενοι καὶ ἀθυμοῦντες; cf. Plutarch *Tranq. an.* 465A–B. Of course, εὐθυμία is something clearly more active than ἀλυπία, joy being its primary connotation. The adjective which best fits the condition of εὐθυμία is φαιδρός. See Galen *San.Tu.* 6.186.14: κατὰ τὴν ψυχὴν εὔθυμος τε καὶ φαιδρός· *Aff.Dig* 10 (K 5.54 = *CMG* 5.4.1.1 36.3; Wilko De Boer, *Galeni De propriorum animi cuiuslibet affectuum dignotione et curatione. De animi cuiuslibet peccatorum dignotione et curatione. De atra bile.* [*CMG* 5.4.1.1; Leipzig/Berlin: Teubner, 1937]). Cf. the text in n. 13. See also Hesychius ι 528: ἱλαρῶς· εὐθύμως φαιδρῶς; also Philo *Virt.* 5.68 (Leopold Cohn, *Philo von Alexandria: Die Werke in deutscher Übersetzung* [Berlin: Walter de Gruyter, 1962]): ἐκ τῆς κατὰ ψυχὴν εὐθυμίας φαιδρὸς καὶ γεγηθώς.

My precise aim in this paper is to discuss the commonplace thematic elements which come to light in *Ind.* in the context of the extant literature on the therapy of emotions, making parallel use (in an attempt to interpret *Galenum ex Galeno*) of the comparable views expounded by Galen in the longer and definitely more ambitious *Aff.Dig.*, as well as *PHP.*

Galen and His "Absence of Grief"

As mentioned earlier, *Ind.* is a conspicuously personal text, in the sense that the theoretical discussion of the subject of ἀλυπία was instigated by and is based upon the absence of grief that the author maintained in the face of the devastating losses he incurred in the conflagration. Its focus of concern is in reality the factors responsible for securing this "absence of grief."

In the opening lines of his letter, Galen enumerates repeated losses he endured ἀλύπως in the past (BMJ 1.5–12/KS 2–7). He has, he says, effectively demonstrated in practice (as his correspondent – the contents of whose letter he rehearses here – is aware) that ἀλυπία constitutes for him a settled form of emotional response to material loss. Galen has, he says, good reason to be proud of this, insofar as he regards "absence of grief" as an internal condition desirable to all people without exception – something that they would prefer even to "the riches of Cinyras and Midas."[9] Galen claims "all people regard λύπη as an evil, just as they do bodily pain."[10] Besides, the precepts his father bequeathed to him as a legacy stipulated that "absence of grief" should be the first goal which Galen ought to pursue in life: for whereas the pursuit of the virtues may be simply apparent, the pursuit of ἀλυπία is instead the only genuine goal that is universal for all people.[11] Not surprisingly, then, "absence of grief" is a topic that Galen returns to again and again. The arguments he invokes in *Ind.* are all ones that his correspondent had heard him put forward on many occasions. In effect, Galen's letter serves as a reminder.[12]

---

[9] *Aff.Dig* 9–10 (K 5.52 = *CMG* 5.4.1.1 35.2–4): τίς γὰρ οὐκ ἂν ἐθελήσειεν ἄλυπος εἶναι παρ' ὅλον αὑτοῦ τὸν βίον; ἢ τίς οὐκ ἂν τοῦτο προέλοιτο τοῦ πλουτεῖν Κινύρου τε καὶ Μίδου μᾶλλον. Note the reference to the two kings whose wealth was proverbial; cf. Tyrtaeus, fr. 12.6: πλουτοίη δὲ Μίδεω καὶ Κινύρεω μάλιον. Martin L. West, ed., *Callinus, Mimnermus, Semonides, Solon, Tyrtaeus, Minora Adespota* [vol. 2 of *Iambi et elegi graeci ante Alexandrum Cantati*; 2nd ed.; Oxford: Oxford University Press, 1992], 157.

[10] *Aff.Dig.* 7 (K 5.37 = *CMG* 5.4.1.1 25.14): ἡ λύπη δ' ἅπασι φαίνεται κακόν, ὥσπερ ὁ πόνος ἐν τῷ σώματι. Cf. Cicero *Tusc.* 4.82: in ea (*sc.* aegritudine) est enim fons miseriarum et caput.

[11] *Aff.Dig.* 8 (K 5.43 = *CMG* 5.4.1.1 29.6–12).

[12] BMJ 39.10–11/KS 86–87: πολλάκις ἀκηκοέναι διερχομένου τοιούτους λόγους, ὧνπερ νῦν ἄρξομαι τῆς ἀναμνήσεως; cf. BMJ 42.7–8/KS 201–2: ὃ πολλάκις ἤκουσας παρ' ἐμοῦ λεγόμενον; cf. *Aff.Dig.* 9–10 (K 5.52 = *CMG* 5.4.1.1 35.5–6): Ἐγὼ μὲν οὖν καὶ ταῦτα καὶ ἄλλα πολλὰ διῆλθον ἐκείνῳ τε καὶ ἄλλοις ὕστερον πολλοῖς.

The ἀλυπία Galen customarily displayed was noticed and admired by people in the various places he lived and worked. Some even turned to Galen for instruction in this regard, as we see in *Aff.Dig.* with the young man tortured by distress (ἀνιώμενος) over trivial matters or the older man who importuned Galen for a "crash course" in ἀλυπία.[13] The addressee of *Ind.* is also, in effect, asking Galen for instruction, as suggested both by the similarity of his question to that posed by the young man of the *Aff.Dig.* as well as by the form that Galen's answer takes.[14] For from the treatment he reserves to his subject, it becomes clear that on the one hand, Galen is proposing himself to his correspondent as an exemplar. Yet, on the other hand, his argumentation is explicitly deployed for the purpose of personal exhortation and instruction.[15] In this approach we recognize one of the techniques which were regularly employed in texts of moral education and conformed to particular specifications, as is characteristically shown by a passage from Favorinus' consolatory treatise, *De exilio*:

> The one who, aiming at virtue, maintains a placid spirit in such situations is both capable of managing them himself and pre-eminently suited to advise another, exhorting him not only through argument, but through personal example: he fashions arguments that are teachers of actions, as he proffers actions that are consonant with his arguments.[16]

Vis-à-vis his correspondent in *Ind.*, Galen appears to take on something of the function of the supervisor (ἐπόπτης) and tutor (παιδαγωγός) that he recommends in the *Aff.Dig.*[17] He reminds, he encourages, he exhorts, and all along the man-

---

[13] *Aff.Dig.* 7 (K 5.37 = *CMG* 5.4.1.1 25.15–20): καί τις τῶν συνηθεστάτων ἐμοὶ νεανίσκων ἐπὶ σμικροῖς ἀνιώμενος ... εἰς ἀνάμνησιν ἀφικέσθαι μου μηδ' ἐπὶ <τοῖς> μεγίστοις οὕτως ἀνιωμένου, ὡς ἐπὶ τοῖς μικροῖς αὐτός ... ἠξίου μαθεῖν, ὅπως μοι τοῦτο περιεγένετο; *Aff.Dig.* 10 (K 5.54 = *CMG* 5.4.1.1 36.2–5): καὶ γὰρ οὖν καὶ οὗτος, ἐπειδὴ <διὰ> πολλοῦ χρόνου καθ' ἑκάστην ἡμέραν ἑώρα <με> φαιδρόν, αἰσθόμενος ἑαυτοῦ κακοδαι<μονοῦντος>, ἐδεῖτο διδάσκειν, ὅπως ἂν αὐτὸς μὴ ἀνιῷτο.

[14] BMJ 1.3–5/KS 1–2: Ἔλαβόν σου τὴν ἐπιστολήν, ἐν ᾗ παρεκάλεις με δηλῶσαί σοι τίς ἄσκησις ἢ λόγοι τίνες ἢ δόγματα παρεσκεύασάν με μηδέποτε λυπεῖσθαι; cf. *Aff.Dig.* 7 (K 5.37 = *CMG* 5.4.1.1 25.15–20): ἠξίου <δ' οὖν> μαθεῖν, ὅπως μοι τοῦτο περιεγένετο, πότερον ἐξ ἀσκήσεως ἢ τινων δογμάτων ἢ φύντι τοιούτῳ.

[15] See BMJ 56.15–16/KS 268–9: ἀσκεῖν παρακελεύομαι τὰς φαντασίας σου τῆς ψυχῆς μόνον οὐ καθ' ἑκάστην καιροῦ ῥοπήν; cf. BMJ 79b.11–14/KS 362–4: Τὰ δ' ἄλλα <ἃ> γράφων εἰς ἀλυπίαν συνεβούλευσα, περιττὰ σοὶ λέγειν, ὃν ἐξ ἀρχῆς οἶδα καὶ φύσει καὶ παιδείᾳ τοῖς εὐτελέσιν ἐδέσμασι καὶ ἱματίοις ἀεὶ χρώμενον, ἀφροδισίοις τε ἐγκρατέστατον.

[16] Translation mine. ὅστις δ' ἀρετῆς ἐφιέμενος ἐν τοῖς τοι|ούτο[ις] εὐθυμεῖται, αὐτὸς μὲν ἱκανὸς προσ[δέ]ξασ|[θ]α[ι], εὐφυέστατος δὲ καὶ ἄλλῳ ξυμβουλεῦσαι οὐ λό|γῳ μόνον, ἀλλὰ καὶ τῷ οἰκείῳ παραδείγματι | προτρέπων, τοὺς μὲν λόγους τῶν ἔργων διδασ|κάλους ποιούμενος, τὰ δὲ ἔργα ἀκόλουθα τοῖς λόγοις παρεχόμενος (96.2). Adelmo Barigazzi, *Opere [di] Favorino di Arelate* (Florence: F. Le Monnier, 1966), 376.23–377.3.

[17] *Aff.Dig.* 10 (K 5.53 = *CMG* 5.4.1.1 35.11–14): ὅστις ἑκάστοτε τὰ μὲν ἀναμιμνήσκων αὐτόν, τὰ δ' ἐπιπλήττων, τὰ δὲ προτρέπων τε καὶ παρορμῶν ἔχεσθαι τῶν κρειττόνων, ἑαυτόν τε παράδειγμα παρέχων ἐν ἅπασιν, ὧν λέγει τε καὶ προτρέπει, δυνήσεται κατασκευάσαι λόγοις ἐλευθέραν τε καὶ καλὴν τὴν ψυχήν.

ner in which he personally endured loss serves to confirm in practice what he is advocating in theory. The coordinates within which the subject of *Ind.* will be treated are already laid down in the question addressed to him by his correspondent, which is identical to the one posed by the young man of *Aff.Dig.*:[18] the instruction to be provided by Galen is to comprise λόγοι, δόγματα, and a proposal on the type of ἄσκησις to be followed.

Λόγοι and Δόγματα

Galen's correspondent invokes λόγοι and δόγματα in his question. These terms are commonly associated in our sources. Λόγοι or rational arguments either support a correct δόγμα and demonstrate its correctness, or, conversely, refute a mistaken δόγμα.[19] The latter term, which Cicero renders into Latin as *decretum*, may assume in philosophical texts any one of the wide range of meanings possessed by the phrase δοκεῖ τινι ("what seems good or right to someone"), as determined each time by the context. Thus, depending on the occasion, δόγμα may have the meaning of: "belief," "philosophical belief," "philosophical tenet," "doctrine," "principle," "philosophical principle," "judgment," "practical or evaluative judgement,"[20] "basic doctrine,"[21] or "dynamic principle of reason and judgement."[22]

---

[18] See the texts cited in n. 14.

[19] See e.g., Plutarch *Tranq. an.* 476C: ... οὐ μοχλοῖς οὐδὲ κλεισὶν οὐδὲ τείχεσιν ἐθάρρυνεν ἑαυτόν, ἀλλὰ δόγμασι καὶ λόγοις ὧν πᾶσι μέτεστι τοῖς βουλομένοις; Plutarch *Pyth. orac.* 402E: ὅτι πρότερον μὲν ἐν ποιήμασιν ἐξέφερον οἱ φιλόσοφοι τὰ δόγματα καὶ τοὺς λόγους; Alexander of Aphrodisias *De fato* 212.1–8: παραπλήσιοι δὲ τούτοις καὶ ὅσους ἄλλους εἰς σύστασιν τοῦδε τοῦ δόγματος λόγους παρατίθενται ἐπὶ πλέον; Ammonius *In Anal. pr.* 4.6, 8.19–20 (*Commentaria in Aristotelem Graeca*; hereafter *CAG*): τά τε δόγματα αὐτῶν καὶ τοὺς λόγους οἷς κεχρημένοι τὰ ἑαυτῶν, ὡς οἴονται, δόγματα κρατύνουσιν; Epictetus *Diatr.* 4.1.170: Ταῦτα μελέτα, ταῦτα τὰ δόγματα, τούτους τοὺς λόγους, εἰς ταῦτα ἀφόρα τὰ παραδείγματα, εἰ θέλεις ἐλεύθερος εἶναι. Cf. also *Pecc.Dig.* 3 (K 5.72 = *CMG* 5.4.1.1 49.17–18): αἱ ὁμοιότητες τῶν ψευδῶν λόγων πρὸς τοὺς ἀληθεῖς αἰτίαι τῶν ψευδῶν δογμάτων εἰσί.

[20] See the exceptionally informative analysis of this notion by Jonathan Barnes, "Pyrrhonism, Belief and Causation: Observations on the Scepticism of Sextus Empiricus," *ANRW* 2.36.4:2608–95 [esp. 2627–31]. Cf. Ian G. Kidd, "Moral Actions and Rules in Stoic Ethics," in *The Stoics* (ed. J. Rist; Berkeley: University of California, 1978), 247–58 [253]: "*Decreta* are also like principles or general truths in being strongly allied to truth values: they infer truth by demonstration and proofs; they are required to demonstrate what is good and evil by rigorous proof; they involve judgment of good and evil, and are connected with understanding and teaching."

[21] Geert Roskam, *On the Path to Virtue: The Stoic Doctrine of Moral Progress and Its Reception in (Middle) Platonism* (Leuven: Leuven University Press, 2005), 36.

[22] Phillip Mitsis, "Natural Law and Natural Right in Post-Aristotelian Philosophy: The Stoics and Their Critics," *ANRW* 2.36.7:4812–50 [4848]: "For the Stoics, *decreta* somehow embody active dynamic principles of reason and judgement."

In contrast to the term λόγοι,[23] δόγμα does not appear anywhere in Galen's analysis in *Ind.* What one does find, however, is the content of that which in the *Aff.Dig.* is characterized as a δόγμα: the mistaken belief in the value of material goods, leading to the passion (πάθος) of insatiability (ἀπληστία). Galen's use of δόγμα there appears close to the use in Cicero[24] and Epictetus, who writes:

> It is not things themselves that disturb men, but their judgements (δόγματα) about things. For example, death is nothing terrible, otherwise Socrates would have thought so; what is terrible is the judgement (δόγμα) that death is terrible. So whenever we are impeded or disturbed or distressed, let us blame no one but ourselves, that is, our own judgements (δόγματα).[25]

To achieve the desired condition of "absence of grief," it is necessary to abandon the mistaken δόγματα which are responsible for the πάθος of λύπη and to adopt the right ones. The pertinent rational arguments (λόγοι) play a decisive role in this by refuting the former and making a convincing case for the value of the latter. In order for the correct δόγματα to become conducive to the prevention of grief, it is necessary that they should form the basis of a regular ἄσκησις. Important roles are, of course, also played by the φύσις of the individual concerned, as well as by his παιδεία. Although the factor of φύσις does not enter into the question raised by Galen's correspondent, *Ind.* does contain – as does the *Aff. Dig.*[26] – a rather extensive reference to Galen's own φύσις, which is traceable to the φύσις of his ancestors, to his upbringing and education, and especially to the positive example furnished by his father (BMJ 57.17–62.2/KS 269–92).

Galen begins his long-postponed reply (BMJ 38/KS 181–4) to his correspondent's question by introducing a positive *exemplum*, the Cyrenaic Aristippus.[27] Galen offers a pair of very well-known anecdotes concerning him. Prominent personalities of the past functioning as *exempla* are a typical feature of the genre

---

[23] BMJ 39.11/KS 187. Cf. the text in n. 12.

[24] *Tusc.* 3.24: Est igitur causa omnis in opinione nec vero aegritudinis solum, sed etiam reliquarum omnium perturbationum; 3.25: aegritudo est opinio magni mali presentis.

[25] *Ench.* 5.1 (ET: Anthony A. Long and David N. Sedley, *The Hellenistic Philosophers, Vol. 1: Translations of the Principal Sources with Philosophical Commentary* [Cambridge: Cambridge University Press, 1987], 418): Ταράσσει τοὺς ἀνθρώπους οὐ τὰ πράγματα, ἀλλὰ τὰ περὶ τῶν πραγμάτων δόγματα· οἷον ὁ θάνατος οὐδὲν δεινόν (ἐπεὶ καὶ Σωκράτει ἂν ἐφαίνετο), ἀλλὰ τὸ δόγμα τὸ περὶ τοῦ θανάτου, διότι δεινόν, ἐκεῖνο τὸ δεινόν ἐστιν. ὅταν οὖν ἐμποδιζώμεθα ἢ ταρασσώμεθα ἢ λυπώμεθα, μηδέποτε ἄλλον αἰτιώμεθα, ἀλλ᾽ ἑαυτούς, τοῦτ᾽ ἔστι τὰ ἑαυτῶν δόγματα; cf. *Ench.* 16.1: Ὅταν κλαίοντα ἴδῃς τινὰ ἐν πένθει ἢ ἀποδημοῦντος τέκνου ἢ ἀπολωλεκότα τὰ ἑαυτοῦ, πρόσεχε μή σε ἡ φαντασία συναρπάσῃ ὡς ἐν κακοῖς ὄντος αὐτοῦ τοῖς ἐκτός, ἀλλ᾽ εὐθὺς ἔστω πρόχειρον ὅτι ʽτοῦτον θλίβει οὐ τὸ συμβεβηκός (ἄλλον γὰρ οὐ θλίβει), ἀλλὰ τὸ δόγμα τὸ περὶ τούτου.ʼ

[26] *Aff.Dig.* 7 (K 5.37 = *CMG* 5.4.1.1 25.21–4): ἀπεκρινάμην οὖν [τ᾽] αὐτῷ τἀληθῆ. καὶ γὰρ καὶ τὴν φύσιν ἐν ἅπασιν ἔφην [εἰ] δύνασθαι μέγα ἐν τῇ τῶν παιδίων ἡλικίᾳ <καὶ τὴν> τοῖς συζῶσιν ὁμοίωσιν, εἶθ᾽ ὕστερον τά τε δόγματα καὶ τὴν ἄσκησιν.

[27] On the problematic transmission in Vlatadon 14 of the passage introducing the reference to Aristippus, see Kotzia, "Galen Περὶ ἀλυπίας: Title, Genre and Two *Cruces*," 79–87.

to which *Ind.* belongs. The purpose that they serve Plutarch accurately describes in *De Tranq. an.*[28] As he says, it is of great importance for the attainment of εὐθυμία that one should give due consideration to the fact that the people we celebrate did not suffer at all in similar calamities:

> For just as in a fever everything we eat seems bitter and unpleasant to the taste, and yet when we see others taking the same food and finding no displeasure in it, we no longer continue to blame the food and the drink, but accuse ourselves and our malady; so we shall cease blaming and being disgruntled with circumstances if we see others accepting the same events ἀλύπως and cheerfully.[29]

The first Aristippus anecdote, the one in which the philosopher commands his servant who is struggling under his load – a leather bag filled with gold coins – to empty out as much of the bag's contents as will allow him to carry the rest with ease, (BMJ 40/KS 191–5) is obviously intended to demonstrate Aristippus' independence from money. The same anecdote serves a comparable purpose in Horace, who cites it in his *Satirae* in order to contrast Aristippus' independence from wealth with the φιλοπλουτία of Staberius. The latter regarded poverty as the greatest ill:

> What does such a man have in common with the Greek Aristippus, who in the midst of Libya ordered his slaves to throw away his gold because, loaded down by the weight of it, they were traveling too slowly. Who is the crazier between these two?[30]

Diogenes Laertius, who recounts the same anecdote in his *Life of Aristippus*, there names his source:[31] it is the *Diatribes* of Bion, a "sophist of many colours" (Diog. Laert. 4.47: σοφιστὴς ποικίλος). While a student of Crates, Bion had initially opted for the teachings of the Academy. He decided in due course to

---

[28] Cf. Cicero *Tusc.* 3.56–58, where the method *per exempla* is proposed as an alternative to the method by argument (3.56: aut a disputandi subtilitate orationem ad exempla traducimus. Hic Socrates commemoratur, hic Diogenes). The *exempla* demonstrate that painful circumstances can be endured, since others have endured them and continue to do so (3.57: tolerabilia esse quae et tulerint et ferant ceteri). Two names cited as *exempla* of assuring oneself against grief are those of Theseus and Anaxagoras. Cf. Seneca *Tranq.* 16.2: vide quomodo quisque illorum tulerit et, si fortes fuerunt, ipsorum mos animo desidera.

[29] ET: Helmbold (modified), LCL: 467E: Διὸ καὶ τοῦτο πρὸς εὐθυμίαν μέγα, τὸ τοὺς ἐνδόξους ἀποθεωρεῖν, εἰ μηδὲν ὑπὸ τῶν αὐτῶν πεπόνθασιν. 468F–469A: ὡς γὰρ ἐν τῷ πυρέττειν πικρὰ πάντα καὶ ἀηδῆ φαίνεται γευομένοις, ἀλλ' ὅταν ἴδωμεν ἑτέρους τὰ αὐτὰ προσφερομένους καὶ μὴ δυσχεραίνοντας, οὐκέτι τὸ σιτίον οὐδὲ τὸ ποτὸν ἀλλ' αὑτοὺς αἰτιώμεθα καὶ τὴν νόσον, οὕτως καὶ τοῖς πράγμασι παυσόμεθα μεμφόμενοι καὶ δυσχεραίνοντες, ἂν ἑτέρους τὰ αὐτὰ προσδεχομένους ἀλύπως καὶ ἱλαρῶς ὁρῶμεν.

[30] ET: Sidney Alexander, *The Complete Odes and Satires of Horace* (Princeton, NJ: Princeton University, 1999), 265–6. *Sat.* 2.3.99–102 (*Socratis et Socraticorum reliquiae* IV A 80; hereafter *SSR*): quid simile isti | Graecus Aristippus? qui servos projicere aurum | in media iussit Libya; quia tardius irent | propter onus segnes. uter est insanior horum?

[31] Diog. Laert. 2.77 = *SSR* IV A 79 = Bion fr. 40 (Jan F. Kindstrand, *Bion of Borysthenes: A Collection of the Fragments with Introduction and Commentary* [Studia Graeca Upsaliensia 11; Stockholm: Olmquist, 1978]).

adopt the Cynic way of life, but subsequently became a student of the Cyrenaic Theodorus and eventually attended Theophrastus' lectures as well (Diog. Laert. 4.51–52). It was from Bion that Horace too, in all probability, drew the anecdote. Aristippus figures prominently in the work of Horace, who knew Bion's works.[32] Now whether the presence of Aristippus in the work of Bion is due to the influence of the Cyrenaic Theodorus[33] or to traditions portraying Aristippus with Cynic features[34] cannot be determined with certainty. Bion may well have adopted the Cyrenaic interpretation of the maxim ἀρκεῖσθαι τοῖς παροῦσιν ("be satisfied with what is at hand"), but it should nevertheless be pointed out that in Teles, to whose digest we owe our knowledge of Bion's *Diatribes*, a stance comparable to the one that the anecdote in Horace and the two in *Ind.* ascribe to Aristippus, is attributed to Crates:

> And therefore Crates replied to the man who asked, "What will be in it for me after I become a philosopher?" "You will be able," he said, "to open your wallet (φασκώλιον) easily and with your hand scoop out and dispense lavishly instead of, as you now do, squirming and hesitating and trembling like those with paralyzed hands. Rather, if the wallet is full, that is how you will view it; and if you see that it is empty, you will not be distressed (οὐκ ὀδυνήσῃ). And once you have elected to use the money, you will easily be able to do so; and if you have none, you will not yearn for it, but you will live satisfied with what you have (ἀρκούμενος τοῖς παροῦσι), not desiring what you do not have nor displeased with whatever comes your way."[35]

---

[32] *Ep.* 2.2.60: *Bioneis sermonibus*. Cf. John L. Moles, "Philosophy and Ethics," in *The Cambridge Companion to Horace* (ed. S. Harrison; Cambridge: Cambridge University Press, 2007), 165–80.

[33] Thus, John L. Moles, "The Cynics and Politics," in *Justice and Generosity: Studies in Hellenistic Social and Political Philosophy, Proceedings of the Sixth Symposium Hellenisticum* (ed. A. Laks and M. Schofield; Cambridge: Cambridge University Press, 1995), 129–60 [150], "The main influence must have been another of his mentors, the Cyrenaic Theodorus. He (*sc.* Bion) also adopted the Cyrenaic interpretation of the tag 'use the things that are present,' whereby these can include riches as well as poverty, rather than the hard Cynic view of 'the things that are present' as the bare necessities."

[34] See Ronald F. Hock, "Simon the Shoemaker as an Ideal Cynic," *Greek, Roman and Byzantine Studies* 17 (1976): 41–53 [48 n. 44]. Reprinted in Margarethe Billerbeck, *Die Kyniker in der modernen Forschung: Aufsätze mit Einführung und Bibliographie* (Bochumer Studien zur Philosophie 15; Amsterdam: B. R. Grüner, 1991). For differing evaluations of the Aristippus-Diogenes relationship, see John L. Moles, "Cynic Cosmopolitanism," in *The Cynics: The Cynic Movement in Antiquity and Its Legacy* (ed. R. Bracht Branham and M.-O. Goulet-Cazé; Berkeley: University of California, 1996), 105–120 [109 n. 19, contains the pertinent bibliography].

[35] ET: Edward N. O'Neil, *Teles: The Cynic Teacher* (Missoula, Mont.: Scholars Press, 1977). Teles Περὶ συγκρίσεως πενίας καὶ πλούτου (*A Comparison of Poverty and Wealth*) 38.4–39.1. Otto Hense, *Teletis reliquiae* (2nd ed.; Tübingen: Mohr, 1909): διὸ καὶ ὁ Κράτης πρὸς τὸν ἐπιζητοῦντα 'τί οὖν μοι ἔσται φιλοσοφήσαντι;' 'δυνήσῃ' φησί 'τὸ φασκώλιον ῥᾳδίως λῦσαι καὶ τῇ χειρὶ ἐξελὼν εὐλύτως δοῦναι, καὶ οὐχ ὥσπερ νῦν στρέφων καὶ μέλλων καὶ τρέμων, ὥσπερ οἱ παραλελυμένοι τὰς χεῖρας· ἀλλὰ καὶ πλῆρες ὂν αὐτὸ οὕτως ὄψει καὶ κενούμενον ἰδὼν οὐκ ὀδυνήσῃ, καὶ χρᾶσθαι προελόμενος ῥᾳδίως δυνήσῃ καὶ μὴ ἔχων οὐκ ἐπιποθήσεις, ἀλλὰ βιώσῃ ἀρκούμενος τοῖς παροῦσι, τῶν ἀπόντων οὐκ ἐπιθυμῶν, τοῖς συμβεβηκόσιν οὐ δυσαρεστῶν.'

What Teles reports concerning Crates exhibits obvious parallels with what can be inferred from the two anecdotes in *Ind.* regarding the stance of Aristippus: for Aristippus is profligate when in possession of cash (BMJ 39.12–15/KS 188–91), but he does not, for all that, attach importance to money, just as he does not attach importance to loss. The view that "you should not desire what you do not have, nor be displeased with whatever comes your way" is one of the main lines of Galen's argumentation. Moreover, the probability of a Cynic derivation for the first anecdote of Aristippus in *Ind.* – for reasons other than the presence in Teles of the relatively scarce word φασκώλιον, which may just be coincidental – perhaps accounts for the fact that Aristippus displays a typical Cynic characteristic: he covers the distance from Piraeus to Athens on foot, as did Antisthenes, the founder of Cynicism.[36]

The second anecdote, which relates how Aristippus faced the loss of one of the four fields in his possession, is also recounted – indeed, with striking similarities of expression – in Plutarch's *Tranq. an.*[37] In the Plutarchean version, Aristippus' reaction to his loss is contrasted to the usual response of the πολλοί, who focus on what is distressful and bereave their loss without taking joy in the goods still remaining to them:

> Most persons, in fact, do pass by the excellent and palatable conditions of their lot and hasten to those that are unpleasant and disagreeable. Aristippus, however, was not one of these, but was wise enough, like one who weighs things in a balance, by weighing the bad against the better, to rise above the conditions in which he found himself and thus to lighten his spirits. At any rate, when he had lost a fine estate …

The point of the anecdote is the same in both authors and carries the full approval of Galen, who declares that it constitutes one of his habitual arguments[38] and makes it the starting point of his analysis in *Ind.* As he himself asserts in the

---

[36] See BMJ 40.16–8/KS 191–2: ἀνιὼν ποτε ἐκ Πειραιῶς–εἰώθει <γὰρ> ἀεὶ βαδίζειν οὐ μόνον τὰς οὕτω βραχείας ὁδοὺς ἀλλὰ καὶ τὰς μακράς; cf. Diog. Laert. 6.2 (= *SSR* V A 12): οἰκῶν τ' ἐν Πειραιεῖ (*sc.* Ἀντισθένης) καθ' ἑκάστην ἡμέραν τοὺς τετταράκοντα σταδίους ἀνιὼν ἤκουε Σωκράτους, παρ' οὗ καὶ τὸ καρτερικὸν λαβὼν καὶ τὸ ἀπαθὲς ζηλώσας κατῆρξε πρῶτος τοῦ κυνισμοῦ.

[37] *Tranq. an.* 469C–D (*SSR* IV A 74). ET: Helmbold, LCL. καὶ γὰρ οἱ πολλοὶ τὰ χρηστὰ καὶ πότιμα τῶν ἰδίων ὑπερβαίνοντες ἐπὶ τὰ δυσχερῆ καὶ μοχθηρὰ τρέχουσιν. ὁ δ' Ἀρίστιππος οὐ τοιοῦτος, ἀλλ' ἀγαθὸς ὥσπερ ἐπὶ ζυγοῦ πρὸς τὰ βελτίονα τῶν ὑποκειμένων ἐξαναφέρειν καὶ ἀνακουφίζειν αὐτόν· χωρίον γοῦν ἀπολέσας καλὸν χωρίον γοῦν ἀπολέσας καλὸν ἠρώτησεν ἕνα τῶν πάνυ προσποιουμένων συνάχθεσθαι καὶ συναγανακτεῖν 'οὐχὶ σοὶ μὲν χωρίδιον ἓν ἔστιν, ἐμοὶ δὲ τρεῖς ἀγροὶ καταλείπονται;' συνομολογήσαντος δ' ἐκείνου, 'τί οὖν' εἶπεν 'οὐ σοὶ μᾶλλον ἡμεῖς συναχθόμεθα;' cf. BMJ 42.5–7/KS 200–1.

[38] BMJ 42.7–9/KS 201–3: πάνυ καλῶς ἐνδεικνύμενος (*sc.* Ἀρίστιππος) ὃ πολλάκις ἤκουσας παρ' ἐμοῦ λεγόμενον, ὡς οὐ χρὴ πρός τι τῶν ἀπολλυμένων ἐμβλέπειν; cf. Plutarch's comment on the same anecdote, *Tranq. an.* 469D: μανικὸν γάρ ἐστι τοῖς ἀπολλυμένοις ἀνιᾶσθαι μὴ χαίρειν δὲ τοῖς σῳζομένοις.

PHP, criticizing Chrysippus and siding with Posidonius,³⁹ the decisive factor in the "therapy of emotions" – be it preventive or remedial – is the discovery of the causes (αἰτίαι) giving rise to them. If this is successful, then Galen thinks it reasonable to assume that their therapy becomes feasible. Given that once the causes of things are identified and rendered inactive, the things themselves either fail to arise or cease to exist.⁴⁰

In an argument inspired by the anecdote of Aristippus' fields, Galen hints at the cause of λύπη, suggesting that it must be insatiability (ἀπληστία), before referring to it explicitly (BMJ 48.19/KS 225: ἡ τῶν τοιούτων ἀνθρώπων ἀπληστία). As we shall see, the more discursive discussion of the same theme in the *Aff.Dig.* clarifies that the mistaken δόγμα giving rise to grief is the "belief regarding insatiability," that ought to be replaced by the correct "belief regarding self-sufficiency (αὐτάρκεια)."

Treatment of the notion of insatiability in *Aff.Dig.* seems to be related to a tradition that also includes Aristippus as may be adduced from a passage in Plutarch's *Cupid. divit.*, attributing to Aristippus a variation on the medical analogy of dropsy (ὕδρωψ). Although a commonplace,⁴¹ this analogy must derive from Cynic sources as the evidence suggests. The insatiable person is likened to a sufferer of dropsy, the *tertium comparationis* being the inability of both ever to be "filled,"⁴² that is, to obtain a feeling of satiety. The earliest thinker to whom the analogy is attributed is Diogenes the Cynic,⁴³ although it is also attested for

---

³⁹ Fr. 150b (Ludwig Edelstein and Ian G. Kidd, *Posidonius I: The Fragments* [Cambridge Classical Texts and Commentaries 13 ; Cambridge: Cambridge University Press, 2004]) = *PHP* 5.6.14 (*CMG* 5.4.1.2 328–9 = K 5.471); fr. 161 Edelstein and Kidd = *PHP* 5.6.17 (*CMG* 5.4.1.2 330–1 = K 5.472); fr. 168 Edelstein and Kidd = *PHP* 5.6.19 (*CMG* 5.4.1.2 330–1 = K 5.472–3). Note the use of the first person οἶμαι (see the following note) and see Ian G. Kidd, *Posidonius II: The Commentary* (Cambridge: Cambridge University Press, 1988), 603.

⁴⁰ *PHP* 4.7.21–22 (*CMG* 5.4.1.2 284–5 = K 5.420–1): καίτοι τό γε συνέχον ὅλην τὴν πραγματείαν τήν τε τῶν λογικῶν ζητημάτων καὶ τὴν θεραπευτικὴν τῶν παθῶν οὐδὲν ἄλλο ἐστὶν ἢ τὸ τὰς αἰτίας ἐξευρεῖν, ὑφ' ὧν γίνεταί τε καὶ παύεται τὰ πάθη. οὕτω γὰρ ἄν τις, οἶμαι, καὶ τὴν γένεσιν αὐτῶν κωλύσειε καὶ γενομένας παῦσαι δυνηθείη. συναναιρεῖσθαι γὰρ εὔλογον οἶμαι ταῖς αἰτίαις τάς τε γενέσεις καὶ τὰς ὑπάρξεις τῶν πραγμάτων. Cf. Cicero *Tusc.* 3.23 (on *aegritudo*/λύπη in particular): Doloris huius igitur origo nobis explicanda est, id est causa efficiens aegritudinem in animo ... causa aegritudinis reperta medendi facultatem reperimus, and cf. also *Tusc.* 3.61, 4.82.

⁴¹ Besides the authors discussed here, see also Horace *Carm.* 2.2.13–16; Seneca *Helv.* 11.3; Polybius 13.2.2.

⁴² In any discussion of ἀπληστία there are always words present that refer to its etymological root, thereby making the analogy more transparent. Cf. Plutarch *Cupid. divit.* 524B: πληρούμενος μηδέποτε, ἀπλήρωτος; Galen *Aff.Dig.* 9 (K 5.49 = *CMG* 5.4.1.1 33.6–7): ἀπληστίαν μὲν ἀπὸ τοῦ τὰς ἐπιθυμίας ἀπληρώτους ἔχειν; *Ind.* BMJ 43.17–18/KS 209: μὴ πληρουμένης αὐτῶν τῆς ἐπιθυμίας; cf. BMJ 80.4–5/KS 369–70: οὐκ ἐμπίπλανται, ἀπλήστοις ἐπιθυμίαις.

⁴³ Stobaeus *Ecl.* 3.10.45: Διογένης ὡμοίου τοὺς φιλαργύρους τοῖς ὑδρωπικοῖς. ἐκείνους μὲν γὰρ πλήρεις ὄντας ὑγροῦ ἐπιθυμεῖν ποτοῦ τούς τε φιλαργύρους πλήρεις ὄντας ἀργυρίου ἐπιθυμεῖν πλείονος, ἀμφοτέρους δὲ πρὸς κακοῦ. ἐπιτείνεσθαι γὰρ μᾶλλον τὰ πάθη, ὅσῳ τὰ ἐπιθυμούμενα πορίζεται.

Bion. If someone wants to release either himself or someone else from poverty, the solution is not to go after money:

> For it is, says Bion, as if someone who wants to relieve the thirst of a man suffering from dropsy would not treat the dropsy but would supply him with springs and rivers. For the sufferer would sooner burst with drinking than be cured of thirst. And this man could never be satisfied, since he is insatiable, thirsting for fame, and superstitious.[44]

In the passage from *Cupid. divit.* alluded to earlier, Plutarch reproduces an argument "standardly deployed by Aristippus" (524B: εἰώθει λέγειν) in which he introduces into the medical analogy, alongside the people who drink incessantly without being able to assuage their thirst, those who have an analogous problem with food;[45] their common need for therapy is likened to the situation of those suffering from a comparable psychical affection, namely the ἄπληστοι:

> Those who part with nothing, though they have great possessions, but always want greater, would strike one who remembered what Aristippus said as even more absurd. "If a man eats and drinks a great deal," he used to say, "but is never filled, he sees a physician, inquires what ails him, what is wrong with his system, and how to rid himself of the disorder; but if the owner of five couches goes looking for ten, and the owner of ten tables buys up as many again, and though he has lands and money in plenty is not satisfied but bent on more, losing sleep and never sated by any amount, does he imagine that he does not need someone who will prescribe for him and point out the cause of his distress?"[46]

Facets of Aristippus' reworking of the theme of insatiability, as recorded in the testimony of Plutarch, are also on display in Galen's treatment of the same theme both in *Ind.* and in *Aff.Dig.* To begin with *Ind.* and the argument based on the anecdote of the ἀγροί, the symptomatology of insatiability described is very similar to that which Plutarch ascribes to Aristippus (εἰ δέ τις ἔχων πέντε κλίνας δέκα ζητεῖ, καὶ κεκτημένος δέκα τραπέζας ἑτέρας συνωνεῖται τοσαύτας, καὶ χωρίων πολλῶν παρόντων καὶ ἀργυρίου οὐ γίνεται μεστός). Yet what is even

---

[44] Teles, Περὶ συγκρίσεως πενίας καὶ πλούτου (*A Comparison of Poverty and Wealth*) = Bion fr. 34 (Kindstrand; ET: O'Neil, *Teles*, 41): ὅμοιον γάρ, φησὶν ὁ Βίων, ὡς εἴ τις τὸν ὑδρωπικὸν βουλόμενος παῦσαι τοῦ δίψους, τὸν μὲν ὕδρωπα μὴ θεραπεύοι, κρήνας δὲ καὶ ποταμοὺς αὐτῷ παρασκευάζοι. ἐκεῖνός τε γὰρ ἂν πρότερον πίνων διαρραγείη ἢ παύσαιτο τοῦ δίψους, οὗτός τε οὐκ ἄν ποθ᾽ ἱκανωθείη, ὅταν ᾖ ἄπληστος καὶ δοξοκόπος καὶ δεισιδαίμων.

[45] Cf. also Xenophon *Symp.* 4.37 (= *SSR* V A 82.14–16): τούτους μὲν οὖν ἔγωγε (*sc.* Antisthenes) καὶ πάνυ οἰκτίρω τῆς ἄγαν χαλεπῆς νόσου. ὅμοια γάρ μοι δοκοῦσι πάσχειν ὥσπερ εἴ τις πολλὰ ἔχοι καὶ πολλὰ ἐσθίων μηδέποτε ἐμπίμπλαιτο.

[46] 524A–B (ET: De Lacy and Einarson, LCL): τοὺς δὲ μηδὲν ἀποβάλλοντας ἔχοντας δὲ πολλὰ πλειόνων δ᾽ ἀεὶ δεομένους ἔτι μᾶλλον θαυμάσειεν ἄν τις τοῦ Ἀριστίππου μεμνημένος. ἐκεῖνος γὰρ εἰώθει λέγειν, ὅτι 'πολλὰ μέν τις ἐσθίων πολλὰ δὲ πίνων πληρούμενος δὲ μηδέποτε πρὸς τοὺς ἰατροὺς βαδίζει καὶ πυνθάνεται τί τὸ πάθος καὶ τίς ἡ διάθεσις καὶ πῶς ἂν ἀπαλλαγείη· εἰ δέ τις ἔχων πέντε κλίνας δέκα ζητεῖ, καὶ κεκτημένος δέκα τραπέζας ἑτέρας συνωνεῖται τοσαύτας, καὶ χωρίων πολλῶν παρόντων καὶ ἀργυρίου οὐ γίνεται μεστὸς ἀλλ᾽ ἐπ᾽ ἄλλα συντέταται καὶ ἀγρυπνεῖ καὶ ἀπλήρωτός ἐστι πάντων, οὗτος οὐκ οἴεται δεῖσθαι τοῦ θεραπεύσοντος καὶ δείξοντος ἀφ᾽ ἧς αἰτίας τοῦτο πέπονθε;'

more interesting is that the further step we find in Plutarch's testimony concerning Aristippus, namely the notion that the πάθος of insatiability is something which – by analogy with the recourse to physicians⁴⁷ sought by those who "eat and drink a great deal but are never filled" – requires therapy, is also the starting point of the discussion of ἀπληστία in *Aff.Dig.* Galen, in fact, begins his enquiry "with the insatiable appetite for food," and proceeds as an expert to give a detailed medical account of the purpose fulfilled by food and the harmful effects of excessive eating: "Our enquiry will begin with the insatiable appetite for food. For excessive consumption of food is described in this way."⁴⁸

Discussion of ἀπληστία in *Aff.Dig.* helps us to obtain a better understanding of the mistaken δόγμα which in *Ind.* is merely illustrated. What it amounts to is the erroneous belief that excessive wealth is a good thing. The counterproposal articulated in *Aff.Dig.* is the adoption of the correct δόγμα regarding self-sufficiency (αὐτάρκεια),⁴⁹ which is inextricably linked with ἀπληστία. Provided one has been previously persuaded that the self-sufficiency doctrine is indeed the correct one (ἀναπεπεισμένοι πρότερον ὀρθῶς εἰρῆσθαι), one must put it into action through exercise. In other words, one's individual actions should reflect the doctrine concerned:

> First of all, one should keep constantly at hand the doctrine (δόγμα) regarding self-sufficiency, which obviously is intimately connected with that regarding insatiability: for to hate insatiability is to love self-sufficiency. Now if being free from grief (ἄλυπον) lies solely in this and this is something up to us (ἐφ' ἡμῖν), then it is entirely up to us (ἐφ' ἡμῖν) to become free from grief (ἀλύποις), provided that we keep constantly at hand the doctrines regarding insatiability and self-sufficiency, and that we commit ourselves to the daily exercise of the particular actions which follow from these doctrines.⁵⁰

---

⁴⁷ The same thematic element of recourse to physicians is also introduced in the dropsy analogy by Horace in *Ep.* 2.2.146–9: Si tibi nulla sitim finiret copia lymphae, | narrares medicis; quod quanto plura parasti | tanto plura cupis, nulline faterier audes? / "If no amount of water could quench your thirst, you would tell your story to the doctor: seeing that the more you get, the more you want, do you not dare to make confession to any man?" (ET: Fairclough, LCL). As Brink correctly points out: Horace's employment of the commonplace shows characteristic similarities both with the testimony of Bion and Aristippus (according to Plutarch). Cf. Charles O. Brink, *Horace on Poetry: Epistles Book II: The Letters to Augustus and Florus* (Cambridge: Cambridge University Press, 1982), 362–3.

⁴⁸ ET: Peter N. Singer, *Galen: Selected Works* (Oxford: Oxford University Press, 1997), 121. *Aff.Dig.* 8–9 (K 5.45 = *CMG* 5.4.1.1 30.22–23): Θεασώμεθα γάρ, ἔφην, ἐπὶ σχολῆς, ὁποῖόν τι πάθος ἐστὶν ἡ ἀπληστία. τὴν δ' ἀρχὴν τῆς σκέψεως ἡ περὶ τὰς τροφὰς ἀπληστία παρέξει.

⁴⁹ Cf. Plutarch *Cupid. divit.* 524C–D: ἀλλ' ἀπληστία τὸ πάθος αὐτοῦ καὶ φιλοπλουτία διὰ κρίσιν φαύλην καὶ ἀλόγιστον ἐνοῦσα. The κρίσις in this passage is not identical with the emotion, it is simply involved in it as its cause (διὰ κρίσιν); by contrast, for Chrysippus emotions *are* κρίσεις; see *SVF* 3.456 (Diog. Laert. 7.111): δοκεῖ δ' αὐτοῖς τὰ πάθη κρίσεις εἶναι, καθά φησι Χρύσιππος ἐν τῷ Περὶ παθῶν· ἥ τε γὰρ φιλαργυρία ὑπόληψίς ἐστι τοῦ τὸ ἀργύριον καλὸν εἶναι; cf. Cicero *Tusc.* 4.26: *est autem avaritia opinatio vehemens de pecunia ... haec autem opinatio est judicatio se scire, quod nesciat.*

⁵⁰ ET: Singer, *Galen: Selected Works*, 124–5 (modified). *Aff.Dig.* 9–10 (K 5.52 = *CMG* 5.4.1.1 34.20–26): πρῶτον μὲν <οὖν> ἀεὶ πρόχειρον ἔχειν δεῖ τὸ περὶ τῆς αὐταρκείας δόγμα

How Galen understands αὐτάρκεια as it applies to his own case is something that he himself clarifies in his διορισμός (see below). Ἀλυπία for him means retaining complete indifference towards material loss, on the limiting condition that he continue to have available the resources necessary to his self-preservation: "he should not be hungry, or cold, or thirsty" (ὡς μήτε πεινῆν μήτε ῥιγοῦν μήτε διψῆν). This formula, which encapsulates the basic necessities of life, appears to have acquired proverbial status, as suggested in the first place by its presence in a whole series of sources,[51] but possibly also by the fact that in *Aff.Dig.* 8 (K 5.44 = *CMG* 5.4.1.1 30.12–13) Galen expounds the same overall view using the identical formula. The view is one he conformed to in his own life, having inherited it as a precept from his father, "who did not consort with philosophers" (οὐκ ὡμίλησε φιλοσόφοις). As for the notion of αὐτάρκεια that Galen delineates in his διορισμός, it is clearly of a Cynic type, being assimilated to the satisfaction of the bare necessities,[52] and exhibiting marked similarities with the description of Antisthenes' self-sufficiency provided by Xenophon in his *Symposium*:

> Yet I have enough so that I can eat until I reach a point where I no longer feel hungry and drink until I do not feel thirsty and have enough clothing so that when out of doors I do not feel the cold any more than my superlatively wealthy friend Callias here.[53]

συνημμένον δῆλον ὅτι τῷ περὶ τῆς ἀπληστίας. ὁ γὰρ μισήσας τὴν ἀπληστίαν ἐφίλησε τὴν αὐτάρκειαν. εἴπερ οὖν ἐν τούτῳ μόνῳ κεῖται τὸ ἄλυπον εἶναι, τοῦτο δ᾽ ἐφ᾽ ἡμῖν, ἤδη πᾶν ἐφ᾽ ἡμῖν ἀλύποις γενέσθαι, πρόχειρον μὲν ἔχουσι τὸ περὶ τῆς ἀπληστίας τε <καὶ> αὐταρκείας δόγμα, τὴν δ᾽ ἐπὶ τῶν κατὰ μέρος ἔργων ἄσκησιν ἑκάστης ἡμέρας ποιουμένοις ἐπὶ τοῖσδε τοῖς δόγμασιν. The influence of Epictetus on this passage of Galen is evident even at the level of terminology (πρόχειρον; ἐφ᾽ ἡμῖν; δόγμα περί + gen.); cf. e.g., *Diatr.* 4.5.29–30: οὐκ ἄλλο ἢ τοῦτο, τὸ δόγμα τὸ περὶ τυραννίδος, τὸ δόγμα τὸ περὶ φυγῆς, ὅτι τὸ μὲν ἔσχατον τῶν κακῶν, τὸ δὲ μέγιστον τῶν ἀγαθῶν, and above n. 25. See also John Sellars, *The Art of Living: The Stoics on the Nature and Function of Philosophy* (Aldershot: Ashgate, 2003), 119 n. 52.

[51] See e.g., Xenophon *Mem.* 2.1.17; *Symp.* 4.37; Epicurus fr. 33 in Graziano Arrighetti, *Epicuro: Opere* (2nd ed.; Turin: Giulio Einaudi, 1973); cf. fr. 200 in Hermann Usener, *Epicurea* (Leipzig: B. G. Teubner, 1887). On the evidence of this phrase in Greek literature see Véronique Boudon-Millot, "De Pythagore à Maxime Planude en passant par Galien: la fortune exceptionnelle de l'adage médico-philosophique ὡς μήτε πεινῆν μήτε ῥιγοῦν μήτε διψῆν," in *Officina Hippocratica: Beiträge zu Ehren von Anargyros Anastassiou und Dieter Irmer* (ed. L. Perilli, C. Brockmann, K. D. Fischer, and A. Roselli; Berlin: De Gruyter 2011), 3–28.

[52] See the classic paper by Audrey N. M. Rich, "The Cynic Conception of αὐτάρκεια," *Mnemosyne* 9 (1956): 23–29. The view in question is compared with 1 Tim 6:8: ἔχοντες δὲ διατροφὰς καὶ σκεπάσματα, τούτοις ἀρκεσθησόμεθα (23 n. 2). Cf. Edward N. O'Neil, "De Cupiditate Divitiarum (Moralia 523C–528B)," in *Plutarch's Ethical Writings and Early Christian Literature* (ed. H. D. Betz; Leiden: Brill, 1978), 321.

[53] Xenophon *Symp.* 4.37 = *SSR* VA 82.17–20 (ET: Todd, LCL): ὅμως δὲ περίεστί μοι καὶ ἐσθίοντι ἄχρι τοῦ μὴ πεινῆν ἀφικέσθαι καὶ πίνοντι μέχρι τοῦ μὴ διψῆν καὶ ἀμφιέννυσθαι ὥστε ἔξω μὲν μηδὲν μᾶλλον Καλλίου τούτου τοῦ πλουσιωτάτου ῥιγοῦν. For more similarities between Galen's argumentation and that of Antisthenes in the *Symposium*, see also notes 45, 54, and 55.

Cynic-Stoic Succession

One of the basic characteristics of ἀπληστία, as Galen points out in *Ind.*, is the progressive expansion of desire towards all things, which has the result that the insatiable always remain poor. Once again we are in the presence of a commonplace: "the poor man is the one who always craves for more."[54] The implied contrast between a poverty which is in the mind of the ἄπληστοι and a poverty of actual impecuniousness[55] informs the distinction Galen proceeds to draw between "superfluities" (περιττώματα) and "what is sufficient" (ἐξαρκοῦντα):[56] a distinction which he deploys in order to discriminate in value between the negligible ἀλυπία of the wealthy Aristippus in response to the loss of a single field, (BMJ 45.6–10/KS 215–8: ὥστε τούτῳ μὲν *μέγα οὐδὲν* μὴ λυπεῖσθαι τρεῖς ἀγροὺς ὑπολοίπους ἔχοντι), the highly estimable ἀλυπία of the unpropertied Cynic Crates (*μέγα δὲ τὸ τὸν μηδὲ ἕνα κεκτημένον ἀγρὸν ἀλύπως φέρειν πενίαν, ὡς ὁ Κράτης ἔφερε*), and finally the supremely estimable ἀλυπία of Diogenes, whose poverty was absolute. Galen's own "absence of distress" in response to loss of money is analogous to that of Aristippus. He too concentrates on the amounts left over after his loss, on the λειπόμενα, which greatly exceed his needs: *οὐκ οὖν ἐμοί τι πρᾶγμα μέγα μηδόλως ἀνιαθέντι διὰ χρημάτων ἀπώλειαν· ἦν γὰρ ἀεὶ τὰ λειπόμενα πολὺ πλέω τῶν ἱκανῶν*.[57] Hence, his "absence of grief" is ultimately not worthy of admiration, given that grief over the loss of superfluities is not "in accordance with nature" (κατὰ φύσιν),[58] as well as an indication of ἀπληστία.

---

[54] BMJ 43.16–18/KS 208–10: Ὥστε κατὰ βραχὺ προϊόντες ἁπάντων ἐπιθυμήσουσιν· καὶ κατὰ τοῦτο ἀεὶ πένητες ἔσονται, μὴ πληρουμένης αὐτῶν τῆς ἐπιθυμίας; cf. *Aff.Dig.* 9 (K 5.50 = *CMG* 5.4.1.1 33.29–30): ὥστ' οὐ πάντων πλουσιώτερος ἀλλ' ἀεὶ πένης ἔσῃ διὰ τὰς ἀορίστους ἐπιθυμίας. On the commonplace cf. Xenophon *Symp.* 4.35 (= *SSR* V A 82.4–7, Antisthenes): ὁρῶ γὰρ πολλοὺς μὲν ἰδιώτας, οἳ πάνυ πολλὰ ἔχοντες χρήματα οὕτω πένεσθαι ἡγοῦνται ὥστε πάντα μὲν πόνον, πάντα δὲ κίνδυνον ὑποδύονται, ἐφ' ᾧ πλείω κτήσονται; Horace *Carm.* 3.16.28: magnas inter opes inops; Seneca *Ep.* 2.6: non qui parum habet, sed qui plus cupit, pauper est; *Helv.* 11.4: qui naturalem modum excedet, eum in summis quoque opibus paupertas sequetur; see also Margarethe Billerbeck, *Der Kyniker Demetrius: Ein Beitrag zur Geschichte der frühkaiserzeitlichen Popularphilosophie* (Leiden: Brill, 1979), 25.

[55] Plutarch draws an explicit distinction between πενία ψυχική and πενία χρηματική: *Cupid. divit.* 524D–E; cf. Xenophon *Symp.* 4.34 (Antisthenes): οὐκ ἐν τῷ οἴκῳ τὸν πλοῦτον καὶ τὴν πενίαν ἔχειν, ἀλλ' ἐν ταῖς ψυχαῖς.

[56] Cf. Plutarch *Cupid. divit.* 524D: οὐ παύσονται δεόμενοι τῶν περιττῶν, τουτέστιν ἐπιθυμοῦντες ὧν οὐ δέονται.

[57] BMJ 46.10–13/KS 219–20; cf. *Aff.Dig.* 8 (K 5.43–44 = *CMG* 5.4.1.1 29.17–30.8): οὔτ' οὖν ἀπώλειά τινος ἱκανὴ λυπῆσαί με, πλὴν εἰ παντελῶς ἀπολέσαιμι τὰ κτήματα (τοῦτο γὰρ οὐδέπω πεπείραμαι), ... κατὰ τοῦτ' οὖν, ἔφην, οὐδὲ λυπούμενον εἶδές μέ ποτε, <εἴ γε> μήτε χρημάτων ἀπώλεια συνέπεσέ μοι μέχρι δεῦρο τηλικαύτη τὸ μέγεθος, ὡς μηκέτ' ἔχειν ἐκ τῶν ὑπολοίπων ἐπιμελεῖσθαι τοῦ σώματος ὑγιεινῶς ... τάχα δὲ καὶ σοὶ δόξω <διὰ τὸ> μηδὲν ἄχρι δεῦρο μέγα πεπονθέναι διὰ τέλους ἄλυπος ... οὔτε γὰρ ἀφῃρέθην ἁπάντων τῶν χρημάτων.

[58] BMJ 47/KS 220–4: Ἀλλὰ μᾶλλον ἄξιόν ἐστιν ἐλεῆσαι τὸν ἀναλίσκοντα μὲν ἐνίοτε μυρίας δραχμὰς ἐκ προσόδων μυριάδων δέκα, λυπούμενον δὲ ἐπὶ τρισμυρίων ἀπώλειαν. Κατὰ φύσιν γὰρ ἦν μηδὲ εἴ τις τὰς ὑπολοίπους ἐννέα μυριάδας ἀπολλύοι ἑκάστοτε, μηδὲ οὕτως ἀνιᾶσθαι

The Cynics Crates of Thebes and Diogenes of Sinope, who are introduced by Galen as *exempla* of ἄλυπος πενία, were related to each other as student and teacher. They are frequently mentioned together in our sources, principally in connection with their voluntary poverty.[59] According to the biographical tradition, it was Diogenes who persuaded the wealthy Crates to renounce his fortune (Diog. Laert. 6.87 = SSR 2 V H 4–17). Crates' conversion to πενία is very interestingly depicted in some fragments of philosophical poetry that he himself composed:

> Crates strips Crates of wealth: Crates sets Crates the Theban free, so that stronger things do not overmaster the master. Bless you, Fortune, teacher of noble things, for the ease with which I restrict myself to a cloak.[60]

In Crates' case, it was his voluntary renunciation of property that opened the way to philosophy. In contrast, it was the loss of his entire fortune in a shipwreck that opened the way to the same vocation for Crates' student Zeno, the future founder of the Stoa.[61] Zeno is the Stoic who in *Ind.* is adjoined to the Cynic duo in a well-known anecdote (see *SVF* 1.277), present in both Plutarch (*Tranq. an.*) and Seneca (*Tranq.*) and integrated into a discussion on the proper stance to take vis-à-vis unwished for events (ἀβούλητα), yielding, in the end, a positive outcome.[62] Together, Diogenes, Crates, and Zeno constitute a Cynic-Stoic succession,[63] usually present in contexts involving the positive outcome of ἀβούλητα:

τῶν γε μυρίων ἱκανῶς αὐτὸν τρεφουσῶν; cf. *Aff.Dig.* 9 (K 5.48 = *CMG* 5.4.1.1 32.12–15). As O'Neil, "De Cupiditate Divitiarum," 326, points out, "κατὰ φύσιν (i.e., things according to nature) – a common expression, esp. in Cynic-Stoic writings – constituted the very basis of αὐτάρκεια; "anything that is παρὰ φύσιν violates αὐτάρκεια."

[59] See e.g., Teles Περὶ αὐταρκείας (*On Self-Sufficiency*) fr. 2 (Hense 14): Καὶ τί ἔχει δυσχερὲς ἢ ἐπίπονον ἡ πενία; ἢ οὐ Κράτης καὶ Διογένης πένητες ἦσαν; καὶ πῶς ῥᾳδίως διεξήγαγον; cf. Plutarch *Tranq. an.* 466E (= *SSR* V H 46.5–7) on the cheerfulness with which Crates bore his poverty: Κράτης δὲ πήραν ἔχων καὶ τριβώνιον παίζων καὶ γελῶν ὥσπερ ἐν ἑορτῇ τῷ βίῳ διετέλεσε.

[60] Fr. 16. Ernst Diehl, *Anthologia Lyrica graeca* 1 (Leipzig: Teubner, 1954) = Hugh Lloyd-Jones and Peter J. Parsons, *Supplementum Hellenisticum* (Texte und Kommentare 11; Berlin: Walter de Gruyter, 1983), 365.

[61] Compare Zeno's remark occasioned by the loss of his ship (BMJ 48.34–35/KS 229–30): εὖ γε ποιεῖς, ὦ τύχη, συνελαύνουσα ἡμᾶς εἰς τὸν τρίβωνα καὶ τὴν στοάν with Crates' verse comment on his voluntary "emancipation" from his fortune: εὖ γ', ὦ Τύχη μοι τῶν καλῶν | διδάσκαλε, | ὡς εἰς τρίβωνα ῥᾳδίως συστέλλομαι.

[62] Seneca *Tranq.* 14.3: ... damna non sentiat, etiam adversa benigne interpretetur. Nuntiato naufragio Zenon noster ...; Plutarch *Tranq. an.* 467C–D: προσηκόντως δέχεσθαι τὰ γινόμενα παρὰ τῆς τύχης ... ἔξεστι γὰρ μεθιστάναι τὴν τύχην ἐκ τῶν ἀβουλήτων. ἐφυγαδεύθη Διογένης· 'οὐδ' οὕτως κακῶς'· ἤρξατο γὰρ φιλοσοφεῖν μετὰ τὴν φυγήν. Ζήνωνι τῷ Κιτιεῖ μία ναῦς περιῆν φορτηγός. The example of Diogenes, whom exile led to philosophy, is one we also find in Musonius, Ὅτι οὐ κακὸν ἡ φυγή ("That Exile is not an Evil"). Musonius fr. 9: ἤδη δέ τισι καὶ παντάπασι τὸ φεύγειν συνήνεγκεν, ὥσπερ Διογένει, ὃς ἐκ μὲν ἰδιώτου φιλόσοφος ἐγένετο φυγών (Lutz, "Musonius Rufus," 75).

[63] See Eusebius *Praep. ev.* 15.13.8: ... Διογένης ὁ Κύων, ὃς καὶ αὐτὸς θηριωδέστατα φρονεῖν δόξας πολλοὺς ἐπηγάγετο. τοῦτον Κράτης διεδέξατο· Κράτητος δὲ ἐγένετο Ζήνων ὁ Κιτιεύς, ὁ

Some, too, have made banishment and loss of property a means of leisure and philosophic study, as did Diogenes and Crates. And Zeno, on learning that the ship which bore his venture had been wrecked, exclaimed, "A real kindness, O Fortune, that you, too, join in driving us to the philosopher's cloak!"[64]

Ἄσκησις

On one hand, Galen contrasts Zeno's reaction to his wholesale loss of fortune (once again in value) with his own inconsequential, as he deems it, disregard of the miscellaneous loss of possessions he suffered in the fire: Ὥστε οὐδ' ἐμοὶ μέγα τι πέπρακται καταφρονήσαντι παντοδαπῆς ἀπωλείας κτημάτων (BMJ 49.3–4/KS 231–2). On the other hand, Galen views as of some consequence, and indicative of both his nobility and magnanimity (μεγαλοψυχία), his "absence of grief" in the face of the loss of those items which ultimately constituted his identity as a physician and author: his drugs, books, medicinal recipes, instruments, and manuscripts.

Μεγαλοψυχία was classified by the Stoics as one of the minor virtues, a subdivision of courage (ἀνδρεία). Chrysippus defines it as "knowledge which makes one be above those things which happen to good and base persons alike."[65] It was precisely the virtue of μεγαλοψυχία that enabled Galen to rise above grief in confronting his loss (see below). Galen attributes this virtue to two factors: first, his φύσις and his παιδεία,[66] and second, the experience (ἐμπειρία) of all the horrors that occurred during the tyrannical reign of Commodus. This second source of παιδεία (see BMJ 52.21/KS 245: παιδεύει), ἐμπειρία, served as an ἄσκησις, an "exercise of the imagination," in the sense of a preparation for what he himself did not in the slightest hold in disregard: a possible wholesale loss

---

τῆς τῶν Στωϊκῶν φιλοσόφων αἱρέσεως καταστὰς ἀρχηγός; cf. Diog. Laert. 6.15: Οὗτος (sc. Antisthenes) ἡγήσατο καὶ τῆς Διογένους ἀπαθείας καὶ τῆς Κράτητος ἐγκρατείας καὶ τῆς Ζήνωνος καρτερίας. On the Cynic-Stoic connection, see Aldo Brancacci, "I koine areskonta dei Cinici e la koinonia tra cinismo e stoicismo nel libro VI (103–105) delle Vite di Diogene Laerzio," ANRW 2.36.5.4049–75 [esp. 4066–71].

[64] Plutarch Inim. util. 87A (ET: F. C. Babbit, LCL): ἔνιοι δὲ καὶ πατρίδος στέρησιν καὶ χρημάτων ἀποβολὴν ἐφόδιον σχολῆς ἐποιήσαντο καὶ φιλοσοφίας, ὡς Διογένης καὶ Κράτης· Ζήνων δέ, τῆς ναυκληρίας αὐτῷ συντριβείσης, πυθόμενος εἶπεν, 'εὖ γ', ὦ τύχη, ποιεῖς, εἰς τὸν τρίβωνα συνελαύνουσα ἡμᾶς.' Cf. Simplicius In Epict. Ench. 1.23 (= SSR V B 514): Ὀλίγαι γάρ εἰσι φύσεις, καὶ σωμάτων καὶ ψυχῶν, αἱ ἀθρόως μεταβαίνειν δυνάμεναι ἀπὸ τῶν χειρόνων ἐπὶ τὰ εἰλικρινῆ ἀγαθά· ὅπερ Διογένει, καὶ Κράτητι, καὶ Ζήνωνι …· 45.25–34: τί δὲ ἡ ἄκρα πενία ἠνάγκασε τῶν μὴ καλῷ καὶ ἀγαθῷ ἀνδρὶ πρεπόντων ποιῆσαι; οὐχὶ δὲ καὶ Διογένης, καὶ Κράτης, καὶ Ζήνων, τότε γνησίως ἐφιλοσόφησαν, … ὅτε τὴν ἄκραν ἀκτημοσύνην ἀντὶ τῆς εὐπορίας ἠλλάξαντο;

[65] SVF 3.269: μεγαλοψυχία ἐστὶν ἐπιστήμη ὑπεράνω ποιοῦσα τῶν πεφυκότων ἐν σπουδαίοις τε γίνεσθαι καὶ φαύλοις; see also SVF 3.265 (Diog. Laert. 7.92); 3.270, 274–5.

[66] To which he will later revert with a detailed reference, (BMJ 57.17–62.2/KS 269–92); cf. Aff.Dig. 7–8 (K 5.37–41 = CMG 5.4.1.1 25.24–28.8).

of his fortune.⁶⁷ The ἄσκησις that in *Ind.* is presented as the consequence of a particular lived experience constituted, as is well known, a specific meditative technique forming part of the preventive therapy of painful emotions. It is what came to be known as the "pre-rehearsal of future ills" or, in the formulation of Cicero, the *praemeditatio futurorum malorum* (*Tusc.* 3.29). Advance preparation against detrimental emotions rendering consolation superfluous is a standard postulate in works on practical ethics. According to Epictetus:

> If you have these thoughts always at hand and go over them again and again in your own mind, and keep them in readiness, you will never need a person to console you, or strengthen you. For disgrace ... [consists] in not having reason sufficient to secure you against fear and against grief.⁶⁸

This "training of the imagination" – that in his own case, as he claims, was necessitated by the political situation – is precisely the ἄσκησις Galen prescribes to his correspondent (BMJ 56.15–16/KS 268–9: ἀσκεῖν παρακελεύομαι τὰς φαντασίας σου τῆς ψυχῆς μόνον οὐ καθ' ἑκάστην καιροῦ ῥοπήν) in response to the latter's request (BMJ 1.4/KS 1: τίς ἄσκησις). From the variety of sources referring to the pre-rehearsal of future ills as a mental exercise effective at forestalling the intense emotional reactions that are provoked by unexpected painful circumstances, the following two passages from Seneca are characteristic:

> For it is the unexpected that puts the heaviest load upon us. Strangeness adds to the weight of calamities, and every mortal feels the greater pain as a result of that which also brings surprise. Therefore, nothing ought to be unexpected by us. Our minds should be sent forward in advance to meet all problems, and we should consider, not what is wont to happen, but what can happen.⁶⁹

> As it is, fleeing to that which is able to lighten all sorrows, I have surrendered myself to wise men and, not yet being strong enough to give aid to myself, I have taken ref-

---

⁶⁷ BMJ 54.5–6/KS 260–1: ἐγύμνασά μου τὰς φαντασίας πρὸς ἀπώλειαν πάντων ὧν ἔχω; BMJ 55.10–11/KS 264: πάντων ἀπωλείᾳ τούτων ὧν εἶχε.

⁶⁸ Epictetus *Diatr.* 3.24.115–6: Ταῦτα ἔχων ἀεὶ ἐν χερσὶ καὶ τρίβων αὐτὸς παρὰ σαυτῷ καὶ πρόχειρα ποιῶν οὐδέποτε δεήσῃ τοῦ παραμυθουμένου, τοῦ ἐπιρρωννύντος. καὶ γὰρ αἰσχρὸν οὐ τὸ φαγεῖν μὴ ἔχειν, ἀλλὰ τὸ λόγον μὴ ἔχειν ἀρκοῦντα πρὸς ἀφοβίαν, πρὸς ἀλυπίαν (ET: W. A. Oldfather, LCL). Cf. Plutarch *Tranq. an.* 465B–C: οὕτω καὶ τῶν λόγων ὅσοι πρὸς τὰ πάθη βοηθοῦσι, δεῖ πρὸ τῶν παθῶν ἐπιμελεῖσθαι τοὺς νοῦν ἔχοντας, ἵν' ἐκ πολλοῦ παρεσκευασμένοι μᾶλλον ὠφελῶσι· Favorinus *De exil.* fr. 96.1 in Barigazzi, *Opere [di] Favorino di Arelate*: Ἀνὴρ δὲ ἐν μεγαλοψυχίᾳ ἀληθινῇ καὶ φιλοσοφίᾳ τεθραμμένος πρὸ τῶν ξυμφορῶν τὴν εὐθυμίαν ἐν τῇ γνώμῃ ἀπόθετον ἔχει. τὸ δὲ ἐπὶ τοῖς δεινοῖς τῆς ἐξ ἑτέρου παρηγορίας χρῄζειν τὸν καιρὸν τῆς εὐθυμίας ὑπερβαίνει; Cassius Dio 38.18.4: ... μὴ οὐ προπαρεσκευάσθαι πρὸς πάντα τὰ ἀνθρώπινα, ἵν' εἴ τι καὶ παράλογόν σοι προσπέσοι, μήτι γε καὶ ἄφρακτόν σε εὕροι. [...] οὐ γάρ που καὶ ἀπαξιώσεις παραμυθίου τινὸς παρ' ἑτέρου τυχεῖν. εἰ μὲν γὰρ αὐτάρκης ἑαυτῷ ἦσθα, οὐδὲν ἂν ἡμῖν τῶν λόγων τούτων ἔδει.

⁶⁹ *Ep.* 91.3–4 (ET: R. M. Gummere, LCL): Inexpectata plus adgravant: novitas adicit calamitatibus pondus, nec quisquam mortalium non magis quod etiam miratus est, doluit. Ideo nihil nobis inprovisum esse debet. In omnia praemittendus animus cogitandumque non quidquid solet, sed quidquid potest fieri. Cf. *Ep.* 76.34: Praecogitati mali mollis ictus venit.

uge in the camp of others – of those, clearly, who can easily defend themselves and their followers. They have ordered me to stand ever watching, like a soldier placed on guard, and to anticipate all the attempts and all the assaults of Fortune long before she strikes. Her attack falls heavy only when it is sudden; he easily withstands her who always expects her. For the arrival too of the enemy lays low only those whom it catches off guard; but those who have made ready for the coming war before it arrives, fully formed and ready armed, easily sustain the first impact, which is always the most violent.[70]

Recourse to wise men (*sapientibus viris*) alluded to in the second Senecan passage is in all probability an indirect reference to the Euripidean verses Galen cites in *Ind.*,[71] and that obviously had acquired commonplace status within the pre-rehearsal of future ills. As already mentioned, the same verses resurface, in analogous contexts, in three different texts exhibiting marked similarities that clearly indicate a common source: Cicero's *Tusc.*, the Plutarchean [*Cons. Apoll.*], and Galen's own *PHP*.

The earliest of the three texts is the third book of Cicero's *Tusc.*, the central theme of which is *aegritudo* (λύπη).[72] Cicero attributes the practical principle of *praemeditatio* to the Cyrenaic philosophers,[73] while later he clarifies that this

---

[70] *Helv.* 5.2–3 (ET: John W. Basore, LCL): ... Nunc, quod satis est ad omnis miserias leniendas, sapientibus me viris dedi et nondum in auxilium mei validus in aliena castra confugi, eorum scilicet, qui facile se ac suos tuentur. Illi me iusserunt stare adsidue velut in praesidio positum et omnis conatus fortunae, omnis impetus prospicere multo ante quam incurrant. Illis grauis est, quibus repentina est: facile eam sustinet, qui semper expectat. Nam et hostium aduentus eos prosternit, quos inopinantis occupauit ; at qui futuro se bello ante bellum parauerunt, compositi ef aptati primum, qui tumultuosissimus est, ictum facile excipiunt. On the notion of *praemeditatio* in Seneca, see Charles E. Manning, "Seneca's 98th Letter and the *Praemeditatio Futuri Mali*," *Mnemosyne* 29 (1976): 301–4; Mireille Armisen-Marchetti, "Imagination and Meditation in Seneca: The Example of *Praemeditatio*," in *Seneca: Oxford Readings in Classical Studies* (ed. J. G. Fitch; Oxford: Oxford University Press, 2008), 102–13.

[71] BMJ 52.4–9/KS 248–53 = fr. 964. See Richard Kannicht, *Tragicorum Graecorum Fragmenta. Volume 5. Euripides* (Göttingen: Vandenhoeck & Ruprecht, 2004), for a compendious survey of scholarly opinion on the identity of the Euripidean tragedy from which the verses derived; cf. also Christopher Collard, *Euripides, Vol. VIII: Oedipus-Chrysippus & Other Fragments* (LCL 506; Cambridge: Harvard University Press, 2008).

[72] *Tusc.* 3.29: apud Euripidem a Theseo dicta laudantur; licet enim, ut saepe facimus, in Latinum illa convertere: Nam qui haec audita a docto meminissem viro, Futuras mecum commentabar miserias.

[73] *Tusc.* 3.28: Cyrenaici non omni malo aegritudinem efiici censent, sed insperato et necopinato malo; 3.31: Quare accipio equidem a Cyrenaicis haec arma contra casus et eventus, quibus eorum advenientes impetus diuturna praemeditatione frangantur, simulque iudico malum illud opinionis esse, non naturae; 3.52 (cited in the following note). If, under the term *Cyrenaici*, Cicero is attributing *praemeditatio* to Aristippus, then the presence of the two Aristippus anecdotes in *Ind.* acquires new meaning. However, the further specification of Cicero's Cyrenaics is a subject of scholarly dispute. On the basis of testimonies that depict Aristippus advising against concern with either the past or the future (see Athenaeus *Deipn.* 12.544; Aelian *Var. hist.* 14.6 = *SSR* IVA 174), a number of scholars express doubt that the particular method should be attributed to him; on the relevant discussion, see Robert J. Newman, "*Cotidie meditare*: Theory and Practice of the *meditatio* in Imperial Stoicism," *ANRW* 2.36.3:1473–1517 [1477 n. 8]. For

was also the view of Chrysippus.⁷⁴ This explicit ascription of an advocacy of *praemeditatio* to Chrysippus receives, perhaps, some implicit corroboration in the fact that Galen in the *PHP* cites the familiar Euripidean verses in the context of his exposition of the Posidonian critique of Chrysippus:

> He (*sc*. Posidonius) asks why it is not the belief that evil is present, but only the fresh belief, that causes distress; and he asks why all that is unprepared for and strange, falling on a person in a sudden burst, confounds him and causes him to abandon his earlier judgments, but if prepared for, made familiar and prolonged either it does not upset him at all, so as to cause an affective movement, or it does so to a very limited extent. That is the reason why he says to 'dwell on' things 'in advance' and to behave toward things not yet present as though they were present. The word προενδημεῖν means in Posidonius to imagine, as it were, in advance (προαναπλάττειν) and to prefigure in one's mind (προτυποῦν) what is going to happen, and to bring about a gradual habituation to it, as to something that has happened before.⁷⁵

Cicero in *Tusc*. and Galen in *PHP*, both introducing the Euripidean verses into the discussion of the *praemeditatio*, associate them with a much-cited *dictum* of Anaxagoras,⁷⁶ who, upon being informed of his son's death, declared, "I knew I

---

an interesting interpretation that "reconciles" these testimonies with the possibility that *praemeditatio* may indeed have been advocated by Aristippus, see Margaret R. Graver, "Managing Mental Pain: Epicurus vs. Aristippus on the Pre-rehearsal of Future Ills," *Proceedings of the Boston Area Colloquium in Ancient Philosophy* 17 (2002): 155–77 [esp. 165–70].

⁷⁴ *Tusc*. 3.52 (= *SVF* 3.417): Cyrenaicorum restat sententia; qui tum aegritudinem censent existere, si necopinato quid euenerit. est id quidem magnum, ut supra dixi; etiam Chrysippo ita uideri scio, quod prouisum ante non sit, id ferire uehementius.

⁷⁵ *PHP* 4.7.7–8 (K 5.417–8 = *CMG* 5.4.1.2 282.5–14). ET: De Lacy: καί φησι διὰ τί πᾶν τὸ ἀμελέτητον καὶ ξένον ἀθρόως προσπῖπτον ἐκπλήττει τε καὶ τῶν παλαιῶν ἐξίστησι κρίσεων, ἀσκηθὲν δὲ καὶ συνεθισθὲν καὶ χρονίσαν ἢ οὐδὲ ὅλως ἐξίστησιν, ὡς κατὰ πάθος κινεῖν, ἢ ἐπὶ μικρὸν κομιδῇ· διὸ καὶ προενδημεῖν <δεῖν> φησι τοῖς πράγμασι μήπω τε παροῦσιν οἷον παροῦσι χρῆσθαι. βούλεται δὲ τὸ προενδημεῖν ῥῆμα τῷ Ποσειδωνίῳ τὸ οἷον προαναπλάττειν τε καὶ προτυποῦν τὸ πρᾶγμα παρὰ ἑαυτῷ τὸ μέλλον γενήσεσθαι καὶ ὡς πρὸς ἤδη γενόμενον ἐθισμόν τινα ποιεῖσθαι κατὰ βραχύ. In the foregoing text, the subjects of several verbs are insufficiently perspicuous. On this, see e.g., De Lacy, *Galen:* On the Doctrines of Hippocrates and Plato 3.649: "Understand Chrysippus as the subject of φησι ... Posidonius is interpreting Chrysippus' term" (sc. προενδημεῖν); Kidd, *Posidonius: Commentary*, 2.601: "I have little doubt that προενδημεῖν was a metaphor coined by Posidonius, which has to be explained" (cf. Hendrik Lorenz, "Posidonius on the Nature and Treatment of the Emotions," *OSAP* 40 (2011): 189–211 [206]: "But that Chrysippus is meant to be the subject of φησι ... seems rather implausible. The subject of φησι ... is obviously Posidonius ..."); Teun Tieleman, *Chrysippus' On Affections: Reconstruction and Interpretation* (Philosophia antiqua 94; Leiden: Brill, 2003), 118 n. 111: "Posidonius may have been the first to use the term 'dwelling in advance;'" cf. "that is why he [Chrysippus?/Posidonius?] says that one should dwell in advance ..." (312). In my view, De Lacy's interpretation – according to which the infinitive προενδημεῖν must already have occurred in Chrysippus while its proposed equivalents (προαναπλάττειν and προτυποῦν) are attributable to Posidonius – is the one that corresponds to the letter of the text.

⁷⁶ In our sources, the *dictum* is also attributed to other sages; see e.g., Diog. Laert. 2.13, 55; 9.20.

had begotten a mortal" (Anaxagoras 59 A 33: ᾔδειν θνητὸν γεννήσας).⁷⁷ Behind the words spoken by Theseus, Cicero informs us, lies Euripides himself, who had been an *auditor* of Anaxagoras. Hence Anaxagoras was the σοφός from whom the Euripidean Theseus, and Euripides himself, learned the technique of pre-rehearsal. Galen's testimony is along the same lines:

> And that is why he (Posidonius?⁷⁸) cited here the story about Anaxagoras, that when someone brought him the news that his son was dead, he said with great composure "I knew I had begotten a mortal"; and he mentioned also how Euripides took this idea and portrayed Theseus as saying: *"Taught by a certain sage ..."*⁷⁹

Taken in isolation from the Euripidean verses, Anaxagoras' *dictum* serves ultimately as a catchphrase for a human being's imperative need to identify the ills that Fortune may bring. A passage from Plutarch's *Tranq. an.* illustrates this use, combining, as it does, the injunction to "employ what is at hand" (χρῆσθαι τοῖς παροῦσι) and the possibility of loss – both themes also manifest in *Ind.* – with the exhortation to imitate (μιμεῖσθαι) Anaxagoras' position:

> His confidence and the absence of fear that their loss would be unbearable cause him to make most pleasant use of present advantages. For it is possible not only to admire the disposition of Anaxoragas, which made him say at the death of his son, "I knew that my son was mortal," but also to imitate it and to apply it to every dispensation of Fortune: "I know that my wealth is temporary and insecure."⁸⁰

Sometimes the presence alone of the word ᾔδειν/*sciebam*⁸¹ suffices to indicate the importance that the anticipation of possible disasters has for experiencing them without grief:

---

⁷⁷ Hermann Diels and Walther Kranz, *Die Fragmente der Vorsokratiker griechisch und deutsch* (Berlin: Weidmannsche Buchhandlung, 1903). Cf. *Tusc.* 3.30: Quod autem Theseus a docto se audisse dicit, id de se ipse loquitur Euripides: fuerat enim auditor Anaxagoras, quem ferunt nuntiata morte filii dixisse "sciebam me genuisse mortalem."
⁷⁸ If my understanding of the meaning of the phrase βούλεται τῷ Ποσειδωνίῳ (see above) is correct, then, in accordance with the syntax, the subject of παρείληφεν would appear to be Posidonius (not Chrysippus, as De Lacy, *Galen: On the Doctrines of Hippocrates and Plato* 3.649, suggests). See further discussion below.
⁷⁹ *PHP* 4.7.9 (K 5.418 = *CMG* 5.4.1.2 282.14–17). ET: De Lacy: διὸ καὶ τὸ τοῦ Ἀναξαγόρου παρείληφεν ἐνταῦθα, ὡς ἄρα τινὸς ἀναγγείλαντος αὐτῷ τεθνάναι τὸν υἱὸν εὖ μάλα καθεστηκότως εἶπεν 'ᾔδειν θνητὸν γεννήσας' καὶ ὡς τοῦτο λαβὼν Εὐριπίδης τὸ νόημα τὸν Θησέα πεποίηκε λέγοντα "ἐγὼ δὲ <τοῦτο> παρὰ σοφοῦ τινος μαθών." Anaxagoras' *dictum* is also cited in the Plutarchean [Cons. Apoll.] (118D); in fact so are the Euripidean verses (112 C–D), although no connection is drawn between the two.
⁸⁰ Plutarch *Tranq. an.* 474D (ET : Helmbold, LCL): τοῦτον ἥδιστα ποιεῖ χρῆσθαι τοῖς παροῦσι τὸ θαρραλέον καὶ μὴ δεδιὸς αὐτῶν τὴν ἀποβολὴν ὡς ἀφόρητον. ἔξεστι γὰρ τὴν Ἀναξαγόρου διάθεσιν, ἀφ' ἧς ἐπὶ τῇ τελευτῇ τοῦ παιδὸς ἀνεφώνησεν 'ᾔδειν θνητὸν γεννήσας,' μὴ θαυμάζοντας μόνον ἀλλὰ καὶ μιμουμένους ἐπιλέγειν ἑκάστῳ τῶν τυχηρῶν 'οἶδα τὸν πλοῦτον ἐφήμερον ἔχων καὶ οὐ βέβαιον.' Cf. Seneca *Tranq.* 11.6.
⁸¹ Seneca *Ep.* 76.35: Ideo sapiens adsuescit futuris malis ... sapiens scit sibi omnia restare. Quidquid factum est, dicit: "sciebam."

Immediately the thought that it was not unexpected will be the first thing to lighten the burden. For in every case it is a great help to be able to say, "I knew that the son whom I had begotten was mortal." For that is what you will say, and again, "I knew that I was mortal," "I knew that I was likely to leave home," "I knew that I might be sent off to prison."⁸²

The opposite stance to the one recommended by the *dictum*, namely an after-the-fact realization that one had not even imagined the ill that has since befallen, is once again indicated by means of a stereotype, this time negative expressions evocative of ἤδειν (e.g., οὐκ ἂν ᾤμην, ταῦτ' οὐ προσεδόκων, *non putavi hoc futurum*). However, the plea of ignorance is inadmissible: undesired events (ἀβούλητα) must not under any circumstances be unexpected (ἀπροσδόκητα) as well.⁸³ In counterpoint to any such disingenuous approach to the human condition, the pseudo-Plutarchean [*Cons. Apoll.*] cites the Euripidean verses:

> "But I cannot," he says, "for I never expected or looked for this experience." But you ought to have looked for it, and to have previously pronounced judgement on human affairs for their uncertainty and fatuity, and then you would not now have been taken off your guard as by enemies suddenly come upon you.⁸⁴ Admirably does Theseus in Euripides appear to have prepared himself for such crises, for he says: *But I have learned this from a certain sage*." (112C–D)⁸⁵

Although, as Galen's *PHP* suggests, the Anaxagorean *dictum* certainly appeared in Posidonius' treatise Περὶ παθῶν, we also have a vague report from Plutarch that Panaetius transformed it into a moral precept. From Diogenes Laertius we

---

⁸² Epictetus *Diatr.* 3.24.105 (ET: Oldfather, LCL): εἶτα ἄν τι γένηται τῶν λεγομένων ἀβουλήτων, εὐθὺς ἐκεῖνο πρῶτον ἐπικουφίσει σε, ὅτι οὐκ ἀπροσδόκητον. μέγα γὰρ ἐπὶ πάντων τὸ 'ᾔδειν θνητὸν γεγεν<ν>ηκώς'. οὕτως γὰρ ἐρεῖς καὶ ὅτι 'ᾔδειν θνητὸς ὤν,' 'ᾔδειν ἀποδημητικὸς ὤν,' 'ᾔδειν ἔκβλητος ὤν,' 'ᾔδειν εἰς φυλακὴν ἀπότακτος ὤν.' Note the protreptic tenor of the passage, comparable to that of Plutarch *Tranq. an.* 474D: ἔξεστι ... μιμουμένους ἐπιλέγειν ἑκάστῳ τῶν τυχηρῶν. An interesting connection between the Anaxagorean *dictum* and the theory that the cause of λύπη is a mistaken δόγμα (see above) is made by Simplicius *In Epict. Ench.* 54.22: Ἀναξαγόρας δέ, ἀκούσας, ὅτι τέθνηκεν αὐτοῦ ὁ υἱός, γαληνῶς ἅμα καὶ μεγαλοφρόνως, Ἤιδειν, φησί, θνητὸν γεννήσας. Τί οὖν θλίβει τοῦτον; Τὸ δόγμα τὸ περὶ τοῦ συμβεβηκότος, ὅτι κακόν· τοῦτό ἐστι τὸ θλῖβον αὐτόν. Τὸ δὲ δόγμα, ἡμέτερόν ἐστιν. Ὥστε θλίβει μὲν ὄντως τὸ κακόν· τοῦτο δὲ οὐκ ἐν τοῖς ἐκτός, ἐν τοῖς ἐφ' ἡμῖν ἐστι.

⁸³ See Plutarch *Tranq. an.* 474E: αἱ γὰρ τοιαῦται παρασκευαὶ καὶ διαθέσεις, ἐάν τι συμβῇ τῶν ἀβουλήτων μὲν οὐκ ἀπροσδοκήτων δέ μὴ δεχόμεναι τὸ 'οὐκ ἂν ᾤμην' καὶ τὸ 'ἀλλ' ἤλπιζον' καὶ τὸ 'ταῦτ' οὐ προσεδόκων; cf. 474E–F (on Carneades): πᾶν καὶ ὅλον ἐστὶν εἰς λύπην καὶ ἀθυμίαν τὸ ἀπροσδόκητον; Seneca *Tranq.* 11.9: Sero animus ad periculorum patientiam post pericula instruitur. "Non putavi hoc futurum," et "Umquam tu hoc eventurum credidisses?"; Seneca *Ira* 2.31.4: ... ego turpissimam (sc. excusationem) homini puto.

⁸⁴ Cf. the passage from the *Helv.* 5.2–3 (cited above in n. 70): velut in praesidio positum ... nam et hostium aduentus eos prosternit, quos inopinantis occupauit ... compositi et aptati primum.

⁸⁵ ET: F. C. Babbitt, LCL: "Ἀλλ' οὐ γὰρ ἤλπιζον," φησί, "ταῦτα πείσεσθαι, οὐδὲ προσεδόκων" ... καλῶς γὰρ ὁ παρὰ τῷ Εὐριπίδῃ Θησεύς. Note the contrast between παρεσκευάσθαι and ἀνασκήτως διακειμενοι (112E).

learn as well that Panaetius referred to the episode of Anaxagoras' life that inspired it in his treatise, Περὶ εὐθυμίας.⁸⁶

Cicero makes concise reference to "pre-rehearsal" in a very interesting passage of the *De officiis*, in which he counterpoints the theme of "οὐκ ᾔδειν" with that of the virtue of magnanimity (μεγαλοψυχία), which the Περὶ ἀλυπίας also associates with "pre-rehearsal:"

> It is the mark of a truly brave and constant spirit (*fortis vero animi et constantis est*) that one remain unperturbed in difficult times, and when agitated not be thrown, as the saying goes, off one's feet, but rather hold fast to reason, with one's spirit and counsel ready to hand. That is the mark of a great spirit (*ingenii magni*); but this is the mark also of great intellectual talent: to anticipate the future by reflection (*praecipere cogitatione futura*), deciding somewhat beforehand how things could go in either direction, and what should be done in either event, never acting so that one will need to say, "I had not thought of that" (*non putaram*). Such is the work of a spirit not only great and lofty (*magni animi et excelsi*) but also relying on good sense and good counsel. (1.80–81)⁸⁷

Whereas in the above passage of *Off.* the reference to "pre-rehearsal" clearly pertains to the wise man,⁸⁸ Galen's comment immediately following the Euripidean verses in *Ind.* introduces an important new dimension. It distinguishes among three categories of people: (1) the σοφοί, (2) the ignorant, and (3) an intermediate category of people who, while they are not σοφοί, yet do not "live as animals."⁸⁹ Of these, who are the ones who are capable of learning from experience, from what happens to them in real life? Not the σοφοί: they already have established convictions about the good and the bad, and are in no danger on account of πάθη (see below). They simply make sure to remind themselves constantly of the possibility of future disaster.⁹⁰ The "pre-rehearsal of future ills" as a technique is something that they can "teach," as did the σοφός who

---

⁸⁶ Plutarch *Cohib. ira* 463D: δεῖ δ', ὥς που καὶ Παναίτιος ἔφη, χρῆσθαι τῷ Ἀναξαγόρου (= Panaetius fr. 115; Modestus van Straaten, *Panaetii Rhodii Fragmenta* [Leiden: E. J. Brill, 1962] = 85 Francesca Alesse, *Testimonianze* [Naples: Bibliopolis, 1997]); Diog. Laert. 9.20 (= Panaetius fr. 45 van Straaten = 86 Alesse): φησὶ δὲ Δημήτριος ὁ Φαληρεὺς ἐν τῷ περὶ γήρως καὶ Παναίτιος ὁ Στωικὸς ἐν τῷ περὶ εὐθυμίας ταῖς ἰδίαις χερσὶ θάψαι τοὺς υἱεῖς αὐτόν (*sc. Xenophanes*), καθάπερ καὶ Ἀναξαγόραν.

⁸⁷ ET: Miriam T. Griffin and E. Margaret Atkins, *Cicero:* On Duties (Cambridge: Cambridge University Press, 1991), 168.

⁸⁸ Cf. Seneca *Ep.* 76.34–5: Hoc ut scias, ea quae putaverunt aspera, fortius, quum adsuevere, patiuntur. Ideo sapiens adsuescit futuris malis et quae alii diu patiendo levia faciunt, hic levia facit diu cogitando. Audimus aliquando voces imperitorum, dicentium: "Sciebam hoc mihi restare?"; sapiens scit sibi omnia restare. Quidquid factum est, dicit: "sciebam."

⁸⁹ BMJ 53.10–14/KS 254–7: Ὁ μὲν οὖν σοφὸς ἀνὴρ ἑαυτὸν ἀναμιμνήσκει διὰ παντὸς ὧν ἐνδέχεται παθεῖν, ὁ δὲ μὴ σοφὸς μέν, οὐ μὴν ὥσπερ βόσκημα ζῶν, ἐκ τῶν ὁσημέραι γινομένων ἐπεγείρεταί πως καὶ αὐτὸς εἰς τὴν τῶν ἀνθρωπίνων πραγμάτων γνῶσιν.

⁹⁰ Cf. *PHP* 4.7.6 (K 5.417 = *CMG* 5.4.1.2 282.1–5). Cf. Emmanuele Vimercati, *Posidonio. Testimonianze e frammenti: testo latino a fronte. Introduzione, tradizione, commento e apparati* (Milan: Bompiani, 2004), 636.

inspired Theseus in the verses of Euripides.[91] Of coure, the ignorant are also not capable of learning from experience. Rather, it is only people of the third category, intermediate between the first two categories, who are educated through experience. In this third category, Galen seems to include not only the addressee of his letter-treatise *Ind.*, but also himself. For he too belongs to those whom the events of daily life (BMJ 53.12/KS 255–6: ἐκ τῶν ὁσημέραι γινομένων) lead to an understanding of the human condition. His ἐμπειρία of πολιτικὰ πράγματα,[92] which he acquired as a witness to the atrocities of Commodus – the second, important cause of his μεγαλοψυχία – served as a training of his φαντασίαι regarding the possibility of exile with a wholesale loss of his fortune. Such an incessant ἄσκησις τῶν φαντασιῶν is what he also recommends to the addressee of his letter.[93]

The three categories of men that Galen refers to do, indeed, recall the three kinds of βίοι that Aristotle discusses in the *Ethica nichomachea* (1.3 1095b 14–1096a 7), as Amneris Roselli suggests.[94] Nevertheless, Galen's intermediate category, of interest here, offers no points of comparison with Aristotle's equivalent category of men who choose the βίος πολιτικός, notwithstanding the presence of a clear verbal reminder of Aristotle.[95] On the contrary, Galen's

---

[91] BMJ 52.4/KS 248: παρὰ σοφοῦ τινος μαθών; cf. Seneca *Helv.* 5.2: *sapientibus me viris dedi* (the text is cited above in n. 70).

[92] The ability to exploit the experiences of life for good is what seems to characterize the Stoic σοφός in contrast to the φαῦλοι, according to the classic twofold distinction of the old Stoa; see *SVF* 1.216; 3.567 (= Stobaeus *Ecl.* 2.99.9–12; Curt Wachsmuth and Otto Hense, *Ioannis Stobaei Anthologium* [Berlin: Weidmannos, 1884–1912]): Ἀρέσκει γὰρ τῷ Ζήνωνι καὶ τοῖς ἀπ' αὐτοῦ Στωικοῖς φιλοσόφοις δύο γένη τῶν ἀνθρώπων εἶναι, τὸ μὲν τῶν σπουδαίων, τὸ δὲ τῶν φαύλων ... Καὶ τὸν μὲν σπουδαῖον ταῖς περὶ τὸν βίον ἐμπειρίαις χρώμενον ἐν τοῖς πραττομένοις ὑπ' αὐτοῦ πάντ' εὖ ποιεῖν ... τὸν δὲ φαῦλον κατὰ τοὐναντίον κακῶς; 2.102.20–22: Πάντα εὖ ποιεῖ ὁ νοῦν ἔχων ... ταῖς περὶ τὸν βίον ἐμπειρίαις χρώμενος συνεχῶς. Nevertheless, as regards the second of Galen's categories, the emphasis is not on the practical exploitation of life experiences, but on their educative role.

[93] BMJ 54.5–6/KS 260–1: ὥστε καθ' ἑκάστην ἡμέραν κἀγὼ θεώμενος ἕκαστον αὐτῶν ἐγύμνασά μου τὰς φαντασίας πρὸς ἀπώλειαν πάντων ὧν ἔχω; BMJ 55.8–9/KS 263: εἰς νῆσον πεμφθῆναι ἔρημον; BMJ 56.15–16/KS 268–9: ἀσκεῖν παρακελεύομαι τὰς φαντασίας σου τῆς ψυχῆς μόνον οὐ καθ' ἑκάστην καιροῦ ῥοπήν.

[94] Cf. characteristically BMJ 53.12/KS 255: ὥσπερ βόσκημα ζῶν and Aristotle *Eth. nic.* 1.3 1095b 20: βοσκημάτων βίον προαιρούμενοι; see Amneris Roselli, "Galeno dopo l'incendio del 192: Bilancio di una vita," in *Studi sul De indolentia di Galeno* (ed. D. Manetti; Biblioteca di "Galenos": Contributi alla ricerca sui testi medici antichi 4; Pisa/Rome: Fabrizio Serra Editore 2012), 93–101 [esp. 99–100].

[95] Verbal reminders are characteristic of Galen's style of writing. *Ind.* contains a comparable verbal reminder from Plato's *Phaedrus* in connection with Galen's attitude towards his literary production; BMJ 67.40–5/KS 311: ἐν παιδιᾶς μέρει συνέθηκα; cf. *Phaedr.* 276d–e, 277e 6.

category recalls the προκόπτοντες of the Stoa,[96] who on their road to virtue find themselves between the wise and the ignorant.[97]

Διορισμός

To round out his treatment of "absence of grief,"[98] Galen proceeds to specify further his own personal stance on the subject by adding a διορισμός. The διορισμός, a comprehensive and coherent distinction and qualification, constitutes for Galen a basic methodological tool which lessens the danger that his words will be misunderstood, whether in the field of pharmacology or, as with *Ind.*, in the field of ethics.[99]

Galen's first clarification concerns the characteristic virtue of the Stoic σοφός, ἀπάθεια or the complete expunging of πάθη,[100] which, as is self-evident, entails an absolute ἀλυπία.[101] Galen casts doubt on the actual existence of any instantiation of this ideal,[102] seeing that he can find no confirmation of one. At any rate,

---

[96] The distinction between wise men and those making moral progress is present in Galen; see *PHP* 4.7.6 (K 5.417 = *CMG* 5.4.1.2 282.1–5 = Posidonius, fr. 165 Edelstein and Kidd = *SVF* 3.481): τῶν τε σοφῶν καὶ τῶν προκοπτόντων. On the Stoic notion of moral progress see Brad Inwood and Pierluigi Donini, "Stoic Ethics," in *The Cambridge History of Hellenistic Philosophy* (ed. K. Algra, J. Barnes, J. Mansfeld, and M. Schofield; Cambridge: Cambridge University Press, 1999), 675–738 [724–35]; Roskam, *On the Path to Virtue*, 15–138; John T. Fitzgerald, "Introduction," in *Passions and Moral Progress in Greco-Roman Thought* (ed. J. T. Fitzgerald; London: Routledge, 2008), 15–16.

[97] Note a distinction analogous to that of Galen between ἀπαίδευτοι ("totally vicious" or "ignorant"), προκόπτοντες ("progressing") and πεπαιδευμένοι ("perfectly virtuous" or "educated") in Proclus *In Plat. Alcib.* 3.158; Victor Cousin, *Proclii Philosophi Platonici opera: e. codd. miss. biblioth. reg. Parisiensis* (Paris: J. M. Eberhart, 1820–7) = *SVF* 3.543. Proclus attributes it to the Stoics (ὀρθῶς οἱ ἀπὸ τῆς Στοᾶς λέγειν εἰώθασιν); the English equivalents of the three terms come from David Konstan; see Ilaria Ramelli, *Hierocles the Stoic: Elements of Ethics, Fragments, and Excerpts* (trans. D. Konstan; Atlanta: Society of Biblical Literature 2009), liii.

[98] See BMJ 69.10–11/KS 316: Τελέως μὲν οὖν <οἶμαι> ἀποκρίνασθαί σοι πρὸς τὴν ἐρώτησιν ἣν ἐποιήσω περὶ τῆς ἀλυπίας.

[99] On the concept of διορισμός as a general principle of accuracy in Galen's work, see Heinrich von Staden, "Inefficacy, Error, and Failure: Galen on δόκιμα φάρμακα ἄπρακτα," in *Galen on Pharmacology: Philosophy, History and Medicine. Proceedings of the Vth International Galen Colloquium, Lille, 16–18 March 1995* (ed. A. Debru; Leiden: Brill 1997), 59–84 [esp. 73–74]; cf. Philip J. van der Eijk, *Medicine and Philosophy in Classical Antiquity* (Cambridge: Cambridge University Press, 2005), 279–99 ("Galen's Use of the Concept of 'Qualified Experience' in His Dietetic and Pharmacological Works").

[100] See *SVF* 3.443–55; 3.448 (= Diog. Laert. 7.117): Φασὶ δὲ καὶ ἀπαθῆ εἶναι τὸν σοφόν, διὰ τὸ ἀνέμπτωτον εἶναι; cf. also *SVF* 1.422, 434; 3.144, 201.

[101] On the ἀλυπία of the wise man according to the Stoics, see the syllogisms cited by Cicero *Tusc.* 3.14: non cadet ergo in sapientem aegritudo; 15: At aegritudo perturbatio est animi; semper igitur ea sapiens vacabit; 18: et sunt illa sapientis: aberit igitur a sapiente aegritudo.

[102] Cf. also *Aff.Dig.* 2 (K 5.11 = *CMG* 5.4.1.1 9.12–13): … ὅπου γὰρ οἱ δι' ὅλου τοῦ βίου τὴν ἀπάθειαν ἀσκήσαντες οὐ πιστεύονται τελέως αὐτὴν ἐσχηκέναι, *Aff.Dig.* 3 (K 5.14 = *CMG* 5.4.1.1 11.12): μηδένα φάσκων ἔξω παθῶν ἢ ἁμαρτημάτων εἶναι, *Aff.Dig.* 3–4 (K 5.15 = *CMG*

he knows well that he himself does not by any means live up to it. The ἀλυπία that he has always displayed up until now does not imply that he has done away with the emotion of λύπη: his "absence of grief" *was* contingent upon specific preconditions.[103] Such indifference to pecuniary loss does not, however, imply that Galen will also remain ἄλυπος in the face of a wholesale loss of his fortune, especially if this is combined with exile to some deserted island. Similarly, his indifference to bodily pain does not imply that he embraces the Epicurean and Stoic slogan of the σοφός claming to be able to remain happy even inside the bull of Phalaris.[104] Ἀνιαραὶ περιστάσεις (BMJ 78a.13–14/KS352) – situations which would actually cause him distress – comprise also the devastation of his homeland and the punishment suffered by one of his friends at the hands of a tyrant.[105]

These are all traditional motor-causes of distress that constituted independent themes of discussion and offered themselves as the subjects of separate treatises (and different literary subgenres), as Cicero bears witness:

> For there are certain remarks which it is customary to make about poverty, and others about living without office or esteem, and then there are particular disputations for each of the various topics of exile, destruction of one's homeland, servitude, physical impairment, blindness, and every other occurence that is generally regarded as unfortunate. The Greeks divide these up into individual disputations and treatises. (*Tusc.* 3.81)[106]

5.4.1.1 11.22–23): κἂν τὴν τοῦ σοφοῦ (*sc.* ψυχήν) μὴ δυνάμεθα σχεῖν; cf. Seneca *Tranq.* 7.4: ... Ubi enim istum invenies, quem tot saeculis quaerimus? Pro optimo sit minime malus.

[103] BMJ 72b.5–7/KS 327–8: καὶ διότι μέχρι τοῦ δεῦρό μοι μηδὲν τοιοῦτον συνέβη, διὰ τοῦτο ἄλυπόν με τεθέασαι. See also the discussion above.

[104] See fr. 601 Usener (esp. *Tusc.* 2.17: sed Epicuro, homini aspero et duro, non est hoc satis, in Phalaridis tauro si erit, dicet: Quam suave est, quam hoc non curo!; Seneca *Ep.* 66.18: Epicurus quoque ait sapientem, si in Phalaridis tauro peruratur, exclamaturum: "dulce est, ad me nihil pertinet ... dulce esse torreri); but cf. also *SVF* 3.586 (= Gregory of Nazianzus *Ep.* 32): Ἐπαινῶ δὲ τῶν ἀπὸ τῆς Στοᾶς τὸ νεανικόν τε καὶ μεγαλόνουν, οἳ μηδὲν κωλύειν φασὶ πρὸς εὐδαιμονίαν τὰ ἔξωθεν, ἀλλ' εἶναι τὸν σπουδαῖον μακάριον, κἂν ὁ Φαλάριδος ταῦρος ἔχῃ καιόμενον.

[105] Note an analogous enumeration pertaining to the ἀλυπία of the σοφός in Seneca *Dial.* 10.4 (*De Constantia Sapientis*): Alia sunt quae sapientem feriunt, etiam si non pervertunt, ut dolor corporis et debilitas aut amicorum liberorumque amissio et patriae bello flagrantis calamitas. Haec non nego sentire sapientem; nec enim lapidis illi duritiam ferriue adserimus; cf. also Dio Chrysostom *Aegr.* (Περὶ λύπης) 3.1–4, as well as Galen's own enumeration of situations arousing λύπη, *Hipp.Prog.* 18b.19: λυποῦνται δὲ οἱ μὲν ἀποθανόντων τέκνων ἢ οἰκείων ἢ συγγενῶν ἢ φίλων, οἱ δὲ προσδοκῶντες ἑαυτοὺς ἢ μόνους παθεῖν ἢ καὶ τὴν πατρίδα πᾶσαν ἀνάστατον ἔσεσθαι· λυποῦνται δὲ καὶ οἱ φιλοχρήματοι χρημάτων στερούμενοι καὶ οἱ φιλότιμοι τιμῆς καὶ τῶν ἄλλων ὡς ἕκαστος.

[106] ET: Graver, *Cicero on the Emotions*, 36. Sunt enim certa quae de paupertate, certa quae de vita inhonorata et ingloria dici soleant: separatim certae scholae sunt de exsilio, de interitu patriae, de servitute, de debilitate, de caecitate, de omni casu, in quo nomen poni solet calamitas. Haec Graeci in singulas scholas et in singulos libros dispertiunt. Of the literature of exile which Cicero mentions, several samples survive, e.g., those by Teles Περὶ φυγῆς (= fr. 3 Hense), Seneca *Helv.*, Musonius, Ὅτι οὐ κακὸν ἡ φυγή 9.41–51 (Otto Hense, *C. Musonii Rufi reliquiae* [Leipzig: Teubner, 1905] = Lutz, "Musonius Rufus," 68–77), Plutarch (*Exil.*/Περὶ φυγῆς) and Favorinus (*De exil.*); on this see the especially informative paper by Heinz-Günther Nesselrath,

Some of the personally distress-inducing circumstances that Galen enumerates in order to distinguish his ἀλυπία from the complete ἀπάθεια of the Stoic wise man consist in well-known typical cases of Stoic ἀδιάφορα (indifferents). Health (ὑγίεια) and wealth (πλοῦτος), as well as their opposites, disease (νόσος) and poverty (πενία), are all said by the Stoics to belong to this category. The first pair they further class as προηγμένα (preferred indifferents), the second as ἀποπροηγμένα (dispreferred indifferents).[107] As states of affair (or objects), contributing to neither virtue nor vice, the ἀδιάφορα are assessed as neither goods nor evils. They are οὐδέτερα (neutral). Hence, they exert no influence on the wise man, but are directly connected instead with his ἀπάθεια.

Especially deserving of interest is Galen's laconic reference to the possibility that his country might be destroyed (BMJ 72a.2–3/KS 325–6). Comparison with a well-known passage from Cicero's *Acad.* – where the Roman author criticizes Antiochus of Ascalon for having adopted the Stoic dogma of ἀπάθεια – confirms, on the one hand, that Galen does indeed differentiate his own stance in specific ways from the ἀλυπία exemplified by the Stoic σοφός. On the other hand it reveals that, in this case as well, Galen is in all probability following a standard argument:

> What about the views they (*sc.* Antiochus and Zeno) agree on? Can we approve them as established truths? *The wise person's mind is never moved by appetitive desire or transported with pleasure.* Come on! But suppose I allow that this is persuasive; what about the next one? *He is never afraid or feels grief.* Won't the wise person fear his country's destruction or grieve if it is destroyed? That's a harsh view, though one Zeno can't avoid, since he allows nothing except what is honourable to count as a good. (*Acad.* 2.135)[108]

Although it is evident that in his διορισμός Galen is discriminating his own stance from well-known Stoic views, he chooses to leave these in anonymity, with the single exception of a reference to the Stoic Musonius (BMJ 73.7–9/ KS 329–30). It is to Musonius that Galen attributes the saying, ὦ Ζεῦ, πέμπε περίστασιν, known to us from Epictetus: φέρε νῦν, ὦ Ζεῦ, ἣν θέλεις περίστασιν (*Diatr.* 1.6.37). Galen, however, inverts Musonius' wish: for himself, he wishes precisely that no adversity (περίστασις) should befall him that might cause him

---

"Later Greek Voices on the Predicament of Exile: From Teles to Plutarch and Favorinus," in *Writing Exile: The Discourse of Displacement in Greco-Roman Antiquity and Beyond* (ed. J. F. Gaertner; Leiden: Brill 2007), 87–108. Again from Cicero (*Tusc.* 3.54) we have a notification about a text belonging to the theme of *interitus patriae*, namely the words of consolation Cleitomachus sent to his countrymen upon the fall of Carthage.

[107] See Zeno *SVF* 1.190–2; Chrysippus *SVF* 3.117–23, 127–39.

[108] ET: Charles Brittain, *Cicero: On Academic Scepticism* (Indianapolis: Hackett 2006), 79. Quid? illa, in quibus consentiunt, num pro veris probare possumus? Sapientis animum numquam nec cupiditate moveri nec laetitia efferri. Age, haec probabilia sane sint: num etiam illa, numquam timere, numquam dolere? Sapiensne non timeat, si patria deleatur? non doleat, si deleta sit? Durum, sed Zenoni necessarium, cui praeter honestum nihil est in bonis.

distress and[109] – with a slight trace of humor – also disclaims any wish to display the Cynic-Stoic virtue of endurance (καρτερία).[110] He does, of course, adopt the ἄσκησις for the εὐεξία[111] of his body and soul, as Musonius used to recommend,[112] but adapted to his own individual characteristics of body as well as of soul, and in full awareness of his personal limits. He pursues his training without hoping to attain "the strength of Heracles:"[113]

> For even if I do not hope to acquire either in body or in soul the strength of Heracles, a strength which the wise claim that I do possess, I believe that it is better not to omit **any** exercise voluntarily.

This passage – that has caused significant difficulty due to its transmitted form in the manuscript[114] – provides, in my opinion, evidence that Galen is here differentiating himself from a particular Stoic source, namely Epictetus.[115]

Heracles, as an exemplar of strength both of body and of soul, is present in the same *Diatribe* in which the saying Galen attributes to Musonius appears. In the text of Epictetus, there is also a prior reference to Heracles. Epictetus' argument

---

[109] BMJ 73.9–11/KS 330–1: ὦ Ζεῦ, μηδεμίαν μοι πέμψῃς περίστασιν ἀνιᾶσαί με δυναμένην.

[110] BMJ 74.12–13/KS 332–3: εὔχομαι ... οὐ καταγείσης τῆς κεφαλῆς ἐπιδείξασθαι καρτερίαν; cf. *SVF* 3.264–5, 269–70.

[111] προηγμένον ἀδιάφορον, see *SVF* 3.127 (= Diog. Laert. 7.106).

[112] See Musonius Περὶ ἀσκήσεως 6:24.9–14 Hense = 54.2–7 Lutz, "Musonius Rufus," 75: ἐπεὶ τὸν ἄνθρωπον οὔτε ψυχὴν μόνον εἶναι συμβέβηκεν οὔτε σῶμα μόνον, ἀλλά τι σύνθετον ἐκ τοῖν δυοῖν τούτοιν, ἀνάγκη τὸν ἀσκοῦντα ἀμφοῖν ἐπιμελεῖσθαι (cf. BMJ 76.21–22/KS 339–40: Οὐ μὴν ἀμελῶ γε τῆς εὐεξίας αὐτῶν). Cf. also Diog. Laert. 6.70: Διττὴν δ' ἔλεγε (*sc*. Διογένης ὁ Σινωπεύς) εἶναι τὴν ἄσκησιν, τὴν μὲν ψυχικὴν τὴν δὲ σωματικήν; for Musonius' ἄσκησις as Cynic see Marie-Odile Goulet-Cazé, *L'ascèse cynique: un commentaire de Diogène Laërce*] VI 70–71 (Paris: Vrin, 1986), 185–8, and Marie-Odile Goulet-Caze, "Le Cynisme à l'Époque Impériale," *ANRW* 2.36.4.2720–833 [2810].

[113] BMJ 76.2–5/KS 342–4: Καὶ γὰρ εἰ μήτε τὸ σῶμα τὴν Ἡρακλέους ῥώμην ἕξειν ἐλπίζω μήτε τὴν ψυχήν, ἣν ἐμοί φασι ὑπάρχειν οἱ σοφοί, βέλτιον εἶναι νομίζω μηδεμίαν ἄσκησιν ἑκόντα παραλιπεῖν. Cf. also *Aff.Dig.* 4 (K 5.15 = *CMG* 5.4.1.1 11.20–21): Δεῖται δ' ἀσκήσεως ἕκαστος ἡμῶν ... καίτοι τὴν Ἡράκλειον εὐεξίαν οὐ δυνάμενος σχεῖν ... εἰ καὶ μὴ τὸ τοῦ Ἡρακλέους (sc. σῶμα).

[114] Cf. Boudon-Millot and Jouanna, *Galien:* Ne pas se chagriner, 176. Jouanna rightly construes the accusatives τὸ σῶμα and τὴν ψυχήν as accusatives of specification, but at the same time, he also proposes emendation of οἱ σοφοί to τοῖς σοφοῖς, which leaves unresolved – as he himself admits – the problem posed by the presence of the word ἐμοί. The dative τοῖς σοφοῖς is also adopted by Ivan Garofalo, "Emendamenti al *De indolentia*," in *Studi sul De indolentia di Galeno* (ed. D. Manetti; Biblioteca di "Galenos": Contributi alla ricerca sui testi medici antichi 4; Pisa/Rome: Fabrizio Serra Editore 2012), 63–68 [esp. 64–65]), who adds the clever (from a palaeographic point of view) emendation of ἐμοί to ἔνιοι, giving the following form to the passage: ἣν ἔνιοί φασιν ὑπάρχειν τοῖς σοφοῖς. The emended text does indeed provide a comprehensive meaning, but not the meaning of the passage of the Περὶ ἀλυπίας.

[115] Galen knew Epictetus' writings, indeed he once wrote a treatise entitled *In Defence of Epictetus against Favorinus*, which has not survived; see *Lib.Prop.* 11 (K 19.44 = BM 168.11–12): ὑπὲρ Ἐπικτήτου πρὸς Φαβωρῖνον ἕν; cf. also *Opt.Doct.* 1.41 K (= *SM* 82–83; Johannes Marquardt, *Claudii Galeni Pergameni Scripta minora* [Leipzig: Teubner, 1891]).

is that the περιστάσεις Heracles faced (i.e., his labours) were the exercises he needed to perform in order to acquire the virtues:

> But since they did exist and were found in the world, they were serviceable as a means of revealing and exercising our Heracles. Come then, do you also, now that you are aware of these things, contemplate the faculties which you have, and, after contemplating say: "Bring now, O Zeus, what difficulty you want; for I have an equipment given to me by you and resources wherewith to distinguish myself by making use of the things that come to pass." (*Diatr.* 1.6.32–34)[116]

In his use of the first person (ἐμοί) (BMJ 76/KS 340), Galen is responding to the second person of address intrinsic to the diatribic style of Epictetus' text (Ἄγε οὖν καὶ σύ), with which its author is not, of course, addressing the σοφοί, but rather the not-wise, for whom his "diatribe" is intended. The διορισμός ends with an exposition by Galen of his overall view on facing up to ἀνιαραὶ περιστάσεις. He does not claim to possess the μεγαλοψυχία of the σοφός.[117] But he is in a position to assure that what does characterize him is an agreement between his λόγοι and his ἔργα: the theoretical views that he argues for are always ones that he can demonstrate in practice.[118]

Conclusion

At this time, we may sum up the characteristic features of the treatment Galen accords to the theme of the "absence of grief" in *Ind.* by enumerating our observations. As our comparative presentation of the sources has revealed, Galen's treatment consists, in large measure, of commonplaces standard to materials on the theme of ἀλυπία, and traceable, in the main, to the Cynic-Stoic tradition. Compatible with this is, moreover, the διορισμός where Galen delineates pre-

---

[116] ET: Oldfather [modified], LCL: γενόμενα δὲ καὶ εὑρεθέντα εὔχρηστα ἦν πρὸς τὸ δεῖξαι καὶ γυμνάσαι τὸν Ἡρακλέα. Ἄγε οὖν καὶ σὺ τούτων αἰσθόμενος ἀπόβλεψον εἰς τὰς δυνάμεις ἃς ἔχεις καὶ ἀπιδὼν εἰπὲ 'φέρε νῦν, ὦ Ζεῦ, ἣν θέλεις περίστασιν· ἔχω γὰρ παρασκευὴν ἐκ σοῦ μοι δεδομένην καὶ ἀφορμὰς πρὸς τὸ κοσμῆσαι διὰ τῶν ἀποβαινόντων ἐμαυτόν.'

[117] As may be inferred from the use of the word ὑπεράνω; see discussion above (esp. n. 64).

[118] The cliché of the agreement between λόγοι and ἔργα, which Galen is here invoking, appears more particularly to have constituted a motif in texts of practical philosophy; see e.g., Seneca *Ep.* 108.35–36: Sic ista ediscamus, ut quae fuerint verba, sint opera. Nullos autem peius mereri de omnibus mortalibus iudico quam qui philosophiam velut aliquod artificium venale didicerunt, qui aliter vivunt quam vivendum esse praecipiunt, and the passage from Favorinus *De exil.* cited above, n. 16; cf. the incompatibility between λόγοι and ἔργα for which Philiscus criticizes the "grieving" exiled [exiled?] Cicero, in conjunction with his observation (see n. 68) that had Cicero "prepared himself for life's adversities," he would not have had need for the consolation which Philiscus is about to offer him (Cassius Dio 38.18). On this topic, see Jo-Marie Claassen, "Dio's Cicero and the Consolatory Tradition," *PLLS* 9 (1996): 29–45; Jo-Marie Claassen, *Displaced Persons: The Literature of Exile from Cicero to Boethius* (London: Duckworth 1999), 86–88.

cisely how he diverges from the traditions he follows. A direct Epicurean influence cannot, in my opinion, be traced in *Ind.* On the contrary, Galen criticizes the Epicurean ἀγαθόν of ἀοχλησία,[119] while also alluding to his own anti-Epicurean writings on this particular subject (BMJ 68.8–10/KS 314–5).[120] Furthermore, the Stoic ἄσκησις of preparing for future evils, that Galen emphatically recommends, met with strong opposition from Epicurus, according to the testimony we possess.[121] The Aristotelian-Academic doctrine of "moderation of emotions" may be what Galen is hinting at with the goal that his incessant ἄσκησις aims to achieve; as his wording in the διορισμός suggests, ἀσκεῖν <δ'> ἀξιώσας τὰς φαντασίας εἰς ἅπαν δεινόν, ὡς μετρίως ἐνεγκεῖν αὐτό. Moderation in emotion (μετριοπάθεια) – in sharp contrast to absence of emotion (ἀπάθεια) – is also the response Crantor advocates to grief, as may be inferred both from Cicero[122] and from the parallel passage in the Plutarchean [*Cons. Apoll.*].[123] The Aristotelian notion of the mean may be what underlies the assessment that those who pursue honours, riches, glory, and power μετρίως are not in danger of suffering the customary distress of the πολλοί.[124]

Epilogue

Nevertheless, some of the views Galen formulates in *Ind.* permit the hypothesis that any divergence from the Stoic tradition ultimately nourishes the ethical treatises belonging to this genre and may occur by way of a Stoic current exhibiting differences with both Ancient and New Stoicism. I have in mind the so-called Middle Stoa (according to the periodization of Schmekel[125]) and the Stoicism of Panaetius and Posidonius. As already mentioned, Galen criticizes Chrysippus, aligning himself with Posidonius, whose work, Περὶ παθῶν he discusses in detail

---

[119] BMJ 68.5–8/KS 311–314; cf. also BMJ 62/KS 289–92. See Epicurus *Ep. Men.* 127, cf. 131.

[120] The manuscript reading κἀν τῷ κατ' Ἐπικούρῳ is problematic. My emendation to κἀν τοῖς κατ' Ἐπικούρου (KS 315) is based on the section Τὰ πρὸς τὴν Ἐπικούρου φιλοσοφίαν ἀνήκοντα in *Lib.Prop.* 15–16 (K 19.48 = BM 172.12–173.4) and on the pertinent titles mentioned therein: Περὶ τοῦ κατ' Ἐπίκουρον εὐδαίμονος καὶ μακαρίου βίου δύο, Ὅτι τὰ ποιητικὰ τῆς ἡδονῆς ἐλλιπῶς Ἐπικούρῳ λέλεκται ἕν.

[121] See *Tusc.* 3.28; 32: nec fieri praemeditata (sc. mala) leuiora, stultamque etiam esse meditationem futuri mali (= fr. 444 Usener).

[122] See *Tusc.* 3.12; 3.71 (= Crantor fr. 3b Mette); cf. *Acad.* 2.135 and below.

[123] 102C–D (= Crantor fr. 3a Mette): Οὐ γὰρ ἔγωγε συμφέρομαι τοῖς τὴν ἄγριον ὑμνοῦσι καὶ σκληρὰν ἀπάθειαν, ἔξω καὶ τοῦ δυνατοῦ καὶ τοῦ συμφέροντος οὖσαν ... Τὸ δὲ πέρα τοῦ μέτρου παρεκφέρεσθαι καὶ συναύξειν τὰ πένθη, παρὰ φύσιν εἶναί φημι, καὶ ὑπὸ τῆς ἐν ἡμῖν φαύλης γίνεσθαι δόξης ... τὴν δὲ μετριοπάθειαν οὐκ ἀποδοκιμαστέον.

[124] BMJ 81.7–9/KS 371–3; see Aristotle *Eth. nic.* 2.6 1106b 16–24; 3.14 1119a 16–18; 4.7 1124a 5–7; cf., however, Democritus fr. B 191, see n. 153.

[125] August Schmekel, *Die Philosophie der mittleren Stoa in ihrem geschichtlichen Zusammenhange dargestellt* (Berlin: Weidmannsche Buchhandlung, 1892).

in the *PHP*, today the most important source of fragments of this work. By contrast, Posidonius' teacher Panaetius is never mentioned by name in the Galenic corpus. The only exception, as of now, is Πλάτων τοῦ Παναιτίου referred to in *Ind.* (BMJ 13/KS 61), one of the rare books belonging to Galen, which perished in the fire.[126] Posidonius is commended in the *PHP* for adopting Platonic views in the course of what, according to Galen,[127] is his criticism of Chrysippus.[128] Yet Panaetius too was ἰσχυρῶς φιλοπλάτων καὶ φιλοαριστοτέλης and had, moreover, written two works touching upon the theme expressed in *Ind.*[129] The first was a consolatory letter to Q. Tubero on the subject of the endurance of grief (*De dolore patiendo*) in which, according to the testimony of Cicero, he recommended as of vital importance to the management of grief the work *De luctu* (= Περὶ πένθους) by the Academic Crantor: "a book which one ought to learn by heart."[130] The other work by Panaetius was Περὶ εὐθυμίας. As noted earlier, the themes of ἀλυπία and εὐθυμία cut across each other, a fact that explains the presence of the same topics and commonplaces in works dealing with either theme. This, at any rate, is what may be inferred from the similarities we have pointed to thus far between Galen's *Ind.*, Plutarch's *Tranq. An*, and Seneca's *Tranq*. For anyone seeking to reconstruct Panaetius' thought, Cicero's *Off.* is a further important source. According to his own statement, Cicero relied on Panaetius' Περὶ τοῦ καθήκοντος for the first two books of this work.[131] It is impossible to determine

---

[126] On this topic, see Jean-Baptiste Gourinat, "'Le Platon de Panétius.' A propos d'un témoignage inédit de Galien," *Philosophie Antique* 8 (2008): 139–51; Tiziano Dorandi, "'Editori' antichi di Platone," *Antiquorum Philosophia* 4 (2010): 161–74.

[127] As regards the degree of faithfulness characterizing Galen's reproduction of Posidonius' views, the opinion which appears to prevail among scholars is that Galen presents a biased picture and that, in reality, Posidonius does not reject orthodox Stoic doctrines, but reinterprets and enriches them; see, e.g., Tieleman, *Chrysippus' On Affections*, 198–287; Roskam, *On the Path to Virtue*, 51–60.

[128] See, e.g., *PHP* 4.7.23 (K 5.421 = *CMG* 5.4.1.2 284.31–286.4 = T 97 Edelstein and Kidd): ταῦτα καὶ τοῦ Πλάτωνος θαυμαστῶς γράψαντος, ὡς καὶ ὁ Ποσειδώνιος ἐπισημαίνεται θαυμάζων τὸν ἄνδρα καὶ θεῖον ἀποκαλῶν ὡς καὶ πρεσβεύων αὐτοῦ τά τε περὶ τῶν παθῶν δόγματα.

[129] See Philodemus *Index Stoicorum* (PHerc1018), col. 61.2–4 Dorandi (= fr. 1 van Straaten = T 1 Alesse / fr. 57 van Straaten). Cf. Cicero *Fin.* 4.79 (van Straaten fr. 55 = Alesse 79). See also *Tusc.* 1.79 (van Straaten fr. 56 and 83 = Alesse 120).

[130] See Cicero *Acad.* 2.135 (the sequal to the passage is cited above): Legimus omnes Crantoris veteris Academici De luctu. Est enim non magnus, verum aureolus et, ut Tuberoni Panaetius praecipit, ad verbum ediscendus libellus; *Fin.* 4.23 (van Straaten fr. 113 = Alesse 83).

[131] Relied on, not translated literally (see *Off.* 2.60: quem multum in his libris secutus sum, non interpretatus), while making certain corrections (see *Off.* 3.7: Panaetius igitur, qui sine controversia de officiis accuratissime disputavit quemque nos correctione quadam adhibita potissimum secuti sumus). On the relationship of *Off.* with Panaetius, see Andrew R. Dyck, *A Commentary on Cicero*, De Officiis (Ann Arbor: University of Michigan, 1996), 17–21; Teun L. Tieleman, "Panaetius' Place in the History of Stoicism with Special Reference to his Moral Psychology," in *Pyrrhonists, Patricians, Platonizers: Hellenistic Philosophy in the Period 155–86 BC* (ed. A. M. Ioppolo and D. N. Sedley; 10th Symposium Hellenisticum; Naples: Bibliopolis, 2007), 107–42.

precisely the Panaitian-Posidonian influence on Galen's *Ind.*, given that Galen does not reveal his sources. The fact, for example, that we can state with certainty that the Euripidean verses constituting an important element of Galen's argument concerning "pre-rehearsal" were cited and discussed in Posidonius' Περὶ παθῶν is *not* something we know from *Ind.*: this information stems from the explicit testimony of the *PHP*.[132]

In order to avoid the danger of overinterpreting the possible similarities that appear to exist between views formulated in *Ind.* and those attributed to Panaetius, I shall limit myself in what follows to views our sources *explicitly* assign to Panaetius. In *Ind.*, Galen exhorts a man exhibiting the characteristics of a προκόπτων, that is, a person who is on the road to virtue,[133] while simultaneously taking pains to distance this person from the exemplar of the σοφός. Today it is almost universally admitted by scholars, (so as to constitute a, so to speak, "traditional view"),[134] that Panaetius' originality consists primarily in his shift away from the σοφός of the Old Stoa towards the ordinary man making moral progress in his effort to achieve virtue.[135]

The *locus classicus* for this assessment is Seneca's *Ep.* 116:[136]

> I think Panaetius gave a charming answer to the youth who asked whether the wise man would fall in love: "As to the wise man," he said, "we shall see. What concerns you and me, who are still a great distance from the wise man, is to ensure that we do not fall into a state of affairs which is disturbed, powerless, subservient to another and worthless to oneself."

---

[132] Nor from the [*Cons. Apoll.*], nor even from Cicero, who in *Tusc.* is evidently employing the same source as Galen, and who regards Posidonius as his teacher (see *Fat.* 5; *Nat. d.* 1.6).

[133] See n. 15.

[134] See Max Pohlenz, *Antikes Fuhrertum. Cicero De officiis und das Lebensideal des Panaitios* (Leipzig and Berlin: Teubner, 1934), 72; Philip De Lacy, "The Four Stoic Personae," *Illinois Classical Studies* 2 (1977): 163–73 [166 n. 7]; Griffin and Atkins, *Cicero: On Duties*, 168; Dyck, *A Commentary on Cicero, De Officiis*, 17; Fitzgerald, "Introduction," 24 n. 102; Emmanuele Vimercati, *Il mediostoicismo di Panezio* (Milan: Vita e pensiero, 2004), 162; Roskam, *On the Path to Virtue*, 37–38, 42.

[135] Notwithstanding that the term προκόπτων does not appear in any of Panaetius' fragments. Conversely, both the term and the notion appear in the fragments of Posidonius; see fr. 174–9 Edelstein and Kidd. See also Kidd, *Posidonius II: The Commentary*, 2.643–58.

[136] Seneca *Ep.* 116.5 = fr. 114 van Straaten = 82 Alesse (ET: Long–Sedley, *The Hellenistic Philosophers*, 423). Cf. also the passage from Cicero *Off.* 1.46, which is regarded as exhibiting Panaetian influence: Quoniam autem vivitur non cum perfectis hominibus planeque sapientibus, sed cum iis, in quibus praeclare agitur, si sunt simulacra virtutis: etiam boc inlelligendum puto, neminem omnino esse negligendum, in quo aliqua signification. "Since life is passed not in the company of men who are perfect and truly wise, but those who do very well if they show likenesses of virtue, I think it must be understood that no one should be entirely neglected in whom any mark of virtue is evident" (ET: Long–Sedley, *The Hellenistic Philosophers*, 424). One who radically disagrees on the prevailing assessment of the evidence from Seneca is David N. Sedley, "The School, from Zeno to Arius Didymus," in *The Cambridge Companion to the Stoics* (ed. B. Inwood; Cambridge: Cambridge University Press, 2003), 7–32 [24 n. 35].

According to Aulus Gellius, Panaetius gave up on Stoic ἀπάθεια:

> "For ἀναλγησία and ἀπάθεια not only in my judgement," said he, "but also in that of some of the wise men of that same school (such as Panaetius, a serious and learned man) are disapproved and rejected."[137]

More particularly as regards the emotion of grief, Panaetius, in his consolatory letter to Q. Tubero, appears not to have treated the subject in the manner expected (at least by Cicero, to whom we owe the testimony). He did not attempt to show that *dolor* is *not* something bad. Instead, he specified its nature and suggested a method for dealing with it.[138]

Another point of differentiation between Panaetius and Posidonius, on the one hand, and orthodox Stoicism, on the other, appears to have been – at least according to Diog. Laert. 7.128 – their reevaluation of the doctrine regarding the self-sufficiency (αὐτάρκεια) of virtue for human happiness (εὐδαιμονία),[139] accomplished through a reexamination of the ἀδιάφορα (see the discussion above):[140]

> However, Panaetius and Posidonius do not admit that virtue has this sufficiency of itself, but say that there is also need of good health, material goods, and physical strength.

It cannot be excluded that Panaetius was the one who conjoined the *dictum* of Anaxagoras to the Euripidean verses which "testified" to the value of "pre-rehearsal" in Chrysippus' Περὶ παθῶν and were discussed in his own Περὶ παθῶν by Posidonius. In any case, the fact remains that Panaetius was the first, as far as we know, to employ (in his work Περὶ εὐθυμίας) the Anaxagorean saying, (ren-

---

[137] Aulus Gellius *Noct. Att.* 12.5 = fr. 111 van Straaten = 84 Alesse (ET: J. C. Rolfe, LCL): "ἀναλγησία enim atque ἀπάθεια non meo tantum," inquit "sed quorundam etiam ex eadem porticu prudentiorum hominum, sicuti iudicio Panaetii, gravis atque docti viri, inprobata abiectaque est."

[138] Cicero *Fin.* 4.23 (= fr. 113 van Straaten = 83 Alesse): Homo in primis ingenuus et gravis, dignus illa familiaritate Scipionis et Laelii, Panaetius, cum ad Q. Tuberonem de dolore patiendo scriberet, quod esse caput debebat, si probari posset, nusquam posuit non esse malum dolorem, sed quid esset et quale, quantumque in eo inesset alieni, deinde quae ratio esset perferendi.

[139] See Zeno (*SVF* 1.187), Chrysippus (*SVF* 3.49), Hecato (fr. 3 Heinz Gomoll, *Der stoische Philosoph Hekaton, seine Begriffswelt und Nachwirkung unter Beigabe seiner Fragmente* [Bonn: F. Cohen, 1933]).

[140] Diog. Laert. 7.127–8 (= fr. 110 van Straaten = 74 Alesse); Posidonius fr. 173 Edelstein and Kidd: ὁ μέντοι Παναίτιος καὶ Ποσειδώνιος οὐκ αὐτάρκη λέγουσι τὴν ἀρετήν, ἀλλὰ χρείαν εἶναί φασι καὶ ὑγιείας καὶ χορηγίας καὶ ἰσχύος; cf. also Diog. Laert. 7.103 (= Posidonius fr. 171 Edelstein and Kidd). This testimony was accepted in respect of Posidonius by a series of major scholars (see Kidd, *Posidonius II: The Commentary*, 2.639–41). Kidd (2.639–641), however, doubts its validity; cf. also John M. Cooper, "Posidonius on Emotions," in *The Emotions in Hellenistic Philosophy* (eds. J. Sihvola and T. Engberg-Pedersen; Dordrecht: Kluwer Academic Publishers, 1998), 71–112 [100] (= John M. Cooper, *Reason and Emotion: Essays on Ancient Moral Psychology and Ethical Theory* [Princeton: Princeton University Press, 1999], 500). Although with some reservation, Richard Sorabji, *Emotion and Peace of Mind: From Stoic Agitation to Christian Temptation* (Oxford: Oxford University Press, 2000), 107, accepts the testimony.

dered in effect autonomous from the verses of Euripides), subsequently applied widely in texts advocating preparation for distress – inducing circumstances (see above). The fact that *Ind.* does not mention the *dictum* of Anaxagoras, but only the verses of Euripides, should not give rise to perplexity: in this work Galen simply limits himself to the "absence of grief" in relation to the loss of material goods.

Apart from the similarities that *Ind.* exhibits with positions that our sources assign to Panaetius, parallels are also discerned with views ascribed to him in modern scholarship, stemming mainly from Cicero's *Off.* The notion of "magnanimity" is a case in point.[141] Galen's formulation, μὴ λυπηθῆναι γενναῖον ἤδη τοῦτο καὶ μεγαλοψυχίας ἐχόμενον ἐπίδειγμα πρῶτον (BMJ 50b.15–17/KS 240–1; see above), recalls – even in its phrasing – a passage from Aristotle's *Eth. nic.* on the dignified way to confront calamities.[142] Comparable formulations reappear in the section of Cicero's *Off.*, dealing with magnanimity (1.61–92), a section thought to have been inspired by Panaetius. In one passage, included among the fragments of Panaetius,[143] magnanimity (*fortis animus et magnus*) has, as its first characteristic, the disregarding of externals (*rerum externarum despicientia*),[144] a motif constantly reprised in *Ind.*[145] to reflect Galen's detached relationship to material things. The way in which Galen refers to the notion of μεγαλοψυχία is identical to Cicero's in the specific passage of the *Off.*, while differing from Aristotle's, for whom the proper attitude towards wealth and other "external" goods is not one of disregard but moderation.[146] As for the second characteristic of magnanimity

---

[141] On the importance of the notion of μεγαλοψυχία for Panaetius, who elevated it to one of the primary virtues, substituting it for ἀνδρεία in the traditional quartet of virtues, see Andrew R. Dyck, "On Panaetius' Conception of μεγαλοψυχία," *Museum Helceticum* 38 (1981): 153–61; Elizabeth Asmis, "Seneca's On the Happy Life and Stoic Individualism," in *The Poetics of Therapy: Hellenistic Ethics in its Rhetorical and Literary Context* (ed. M. Nussbaum; Apeiron 23; Edmonton: Academic Printing & Publishing, 1990), 219–55 [226–32]; Tieleman, "Panaetius' Place in the History of Stoicism with Special Reference to his Moral Psychology," 234.

[142] *Eth. nic.* 1.11 1100b 3: ἐπειδὰν φέρῃ τις εὐκόλως πολλὰς καὶ μεγάλας ἀτυχίας, μὴ δι' ἀναλγησίαν ἀλλὰ γεννάδας ὢν καὶ μεγαλόψυχος. See Kotzia in Kotzia and Sotiroudis, 127; Roselli, "Galeno dopo l'incendio del 192," 98.

[143] Cicero *Off.* 1.66 (= fr. 106 van Straaten = 71 Alesse).

[144] Cf. *Tusc.* 3.19: quis fortis sit, eundem esse magni animi ... eum res humanas despicere atque infra se positas arbitrari.

[145] καταφρονεῖν; see BMJ 49.3/KS 231, BMJ 61.14/KS 284, (BMJ 62.20/KS 289), BMJ 66.21/KS 307, BMJ 71.20/KS 323, BMJ 71.1/KS 324, and BMJ 78b.3/KS 355–6. Commenting on *Off.* 1.66, Dyck, "On Panaetius' Conception of μεγαλοψυχία," 196, notes, "The despising of external goods is, of course, a specifically Stoic attitude," and adds, "For the ability of the μεγαλόψυχος to surmount evil, cf. Democritus 68B 46DK: μεγαλοψυχίη τὸ φέρειν πραέως πλημμέλειαν" (cf. n. 152 below). On μεγαλοψυχία in the Περὶ ἀλυπίας, cf. Christopher Gill, *Naturalistic Psychology in Galen and Stoicism* (Oxford: Oxford University Press, 2010), 264, "Which (sc. μεγαλοψυχία) he (sc. Galen) characterizes in Stoic terms, as courageous indifference to misfortune, rather than Aristotelian terms."

[146] See *Eth. nic.* 4.7 1124a 13–15: περὶ πλοῦτον καὶ δυναστείαν καὶ πᾶσαν εὐτυχίαν καὶ ἀτυχίαν μετρίως ἕξει and Dyck, "On Panaetius' Conception of μεγαλοψυχία," 197.

in the Ciceronian passage, this can be identified as φιλοπονία (*res geras, magnas illas quidem, et maxime utiles, sed et vehementer arduas, plenasque laborum*), also a Stoic virtue, another subdivision of ἀνδρεία (*SVF* 3.269);[147] Galen also associates it with his own μεγαλοψυχία (BMJ 50b.14–15/KS 239–40: τὴν καθ' ὅλον τὸν βίον ἱκανὴν φιλοπονίαν ἐδείκνυτο).

The same section of *Off.*[148] contains what seems like a virtual summary of the line taken by Galen in *Ind*. In this passage disdain for money, when money is not to be had (*pecuniam contemnere, si non habeas*),[149] is recommended. Moreover, the avoidance of φιλοχρηματία (*pecuniae fugienda cupiditas*) and φιλοπλουτία (*amare divitias*) are condemned, while the use of money for beneficent purposes (*ad beneficentiam liberalitatemque conferre*),[150] provided money is to be had, is urged. In a series of papers, Christopher Gill attempts a reconstruction of Panaetius' Περὶ εὐθυμίας by combining the points of similarity that Cicero's *Off.* shares with Seneca's *Tranq.* and Plutarch's *Tranq. an.*, judging all three works, and not just the first, to be based on Panaetius.[151] The upshot of his investigation is that Panaetius' Περὶ εὐθυμίας must have combined Stoic and Democritean/Epicurean views, without diverging from orthodox Stoicism.[152]

Although, as mentioned earlier, *Ind.* has a distinctly anti-Epicurean tenor, and although the common elements that can be identified with the ethical fragments of Democritus[153] appear to consist of commonplaces,[154] it is worth bringing up

---

[147] See Asmis, "Seneca's On the Happy Life and Stoic Individualism," 231 n. 43.

[148] Quam ob rem et haec videnda et pecuniae fugienda cupiditas; nihil enim est tam angusti animi tamque parvi quam amare divitias, nihil honestius magnificentiusque quam pecuniam contemnere, si non habeas, si habeas, ad beneficentiam liberalitatemque conferre.

[149] Cf. BMJ 78b.2–3/KS 355: Χρημάτων μὲν γὰρ ἀπωλείας καταφρονῶ.

[150] Cf. BMJ 83.18–19/KS 380: οὔτε κοινωνοῦντος ὧν εἶχεν ἑτέροις; also *Aff.Dig.* 9 (K 5.48 = *CMG* 5.4.1.1 32.19–21):

[151] See in particular Christopher Gill, "Panaetius on the Virtue of Being Yourself," in *Images and Ideologies: Self-definition in the Hellenistic World* (ed. A. Bulloch, E. S. Gruen, A. A. Long, and A. Stewart; Berkeley: University of California Press, 1993), 330–53; Christopher Gill, "Peace of Mind and Being Yourself: Panaetius to Plutarch," *ANRW* 2.36.7.4599–640.

[152] Given that Panaetius' counterproposal to the ἀπάθεια of Ancient Stoicism, εὐθυμία, appears to have been inspired by Democritus' Περὶ εὐθυμίης. Scepticism as to the probability of recovery of substantial material belonging to Democritus' Περὶ εὐθυμίης from Seneca's *Tranq.* and Plutarch's *Tranq. an.* is expressed by James Warren, *Epicurus and Democritean Ethics: An Archaeology of Ataraxia* (Cambridge: Cambridge University Press, 2002), 32 n. 14); cf. Walter Leszl, "Democritus' Works: From Their Titles to Their Contents," in *Democritus: Science, the Arts, and the Care of the Soul* (ed. A. Brancacci and P.-M. Morel; Philosophia antiqua 102; Leiden: Brill, 2007), 11–76 [71–76].

[153] In spite of the general misgivings as to the authenticity of the ethical fragments and the caution this imposes, see e.g., fr. 68 B 286: Εὐτυχὴς ὁ ἐπὶ μετρίοισι χρήμασιν εὐθυμεόμενος, δυστυχὴς δὲ ὁ ἐπὶ πολλοῖσι δυσθυμεόμενος; B 191: Ἀνθρώποισι γὰρ εὐθυμίη γίνεται μετριότητι τέρψιος καὶ βίου συμμετρίῃ· τὰ δ' ἐλλείποντα καὶ ὑπερβάλλοντα μεταπίπτειν τε φιλέει καὶ μεγάλας κινήσιας ἐμποιέειν τῇ ψυχῇ ... ἐπὶ τοῖσι δυνατοῖς ὧν δεῖ ἔχειν τὴν γνώμην καὶ τοῖσι παρεοῦσιν ἀρκέεσθαι; see also nn. 123, 145.

[154] On the phrase τοῖσι παρεοῦσιν ἀρκέεσθαι in particular, see above; cf. Zeph Stewart, ("Democritus and the Cynics," *Harvard Studies in Classical Philology* 63 [1958]: 179; Leszl,

one basic observation from Gill's reconstruction, by way of conclusion. According to Gill, Panaetius must have given special emphasis in Περὶ εὐθυμίας to the theme of "being yourself." Among the evidence to which he appeals in order to support this particular conclusion, a passage from Cicero's *Off.* – the message of which is that we ought to follow our personal nature – fits perfectly with the explanation Galen provides in *Ind.* regarding the limits of his "absence of grief":

> Each person should hold firmly to his own qualities, provided they are individual without being immoral, so that the propriety that we are looking for may be maintained. We must act in a way that does not conflict with our common human nature,[155] but which (with this proviso) allows us to follow our own individual nature. So we should use our own nature as the yardstick for our choice of projects, even if other projects are weightier and better.[156]

In his διορισμός, the limits Galen sets on his ἀλυπία have to do with his knowledge of his own individual characteristics of both body and soul: his knowledge of the peculiar quality of his ἕξις.[157]

"Democritus' Works," 91), concerning the possible role of the Cynics in the preservation of Democritus' ethical fragments.

[155] *universam naturam*; on the fact that this expression refers not to "cosmic nature" but to "our common human nature," see Gill, "Panaetius on the Virtue of Being Yourself," 342; Gill, "Peace of Mind and Being Yourself: Panaetius to Plutarch," 4605 n. 22; Roskam, *On the Path to Virtue*, 35 n. 14.

[156] ET: Gill, "Panaetius on the Virtue of Being Yourself." Cicero *Off.* 1.110 = fr. 97 van Straaten = 62: Alesse Admodum autem tenenda sunt sua cuique non vitiosa, sed tamen propria, quo facilius decorum illud, quod quaerimus, retineatur. Sic enim est faciendum, ut contra universam naturam nihil contendamus, ea tamen conservata propriam naturam sequamur, ut, etiamsi sint alia graviora atque meliora, tamen nos studia nostra nostrae naturae regula metiamur; neque enim attinet naturae repugnare, nec quicquam sequi, quod adsequi non queas.

[157] BMJ 75.16–18/KS 335–7: Αἰσθάνομαι γὰρ ἀκριβῶς ἐγὼ παρακολουθῶν τῇ ποιότητι τῆς ἐμῆς ἕξεως ἣν ἔχω κατὰ τὸ σῶμα καὶ τὴν ψυχήν; cf. BMJ 75.20–21/KS 339: οὔτε περίστασιν ἰσχυροτέραν τῆς κατὰ τὴν ἐμὴν ψυχὴν ἕξεως.

Elizabeth Asmis

Galen's *De indolentia* and the Creation of a Personal Philosophy

Galen wrote a well-known little treatise entitled *Quod optimus medicus sit quoque philosophus* (*The Best Doctor is also a Philosopher*); and he clearly thought of himself as being both a top-notch physician and a philosopher. He had the emperor's word for it: Marcus Aurelius used to say, as Galen reports, "he was first among physicians, and the only one who was a philosopher."[1] The idea of combining medicine and philosophy goes back to the time of Hippocrates; but it kept changing along with changes in the two disciplines. *De indolentia* helps us to obtain insights into this evolution.

A few of us might grant Galen the status of a philosopher; but most would resist. An intellectual, yes. But a philosopher? If we count him as a philosopher, what is his affiliation? Some scholars classify him as a middle Platonist.[2] Mostly, he has been regarded as an "eclectic." This is something of a catchall label for hard-to-pin-down philosophers from around 100 B. C. E. to the end of the second century C. E.[3] In the case of Galen, the label has been justified partly on the

---

[1] *Praen.* 11.8 (K 14.660 = *CMG* 5.8.1 128.27–28): διετέλει [τε] περὶ ἐμοῦ λέγων ἀεί, καθάπερ οἶσθα καὶ σύ, τῶν μὲν ἰατρῶν πρῶτον εἶναι, τῶν δὲ φιλοσόφων μόνον. I take the second part of the judgment to mean that he was the only physician among philosophers. Vivian Nutton translates: "... the only philosopher among philosophers" (*Ancient Medicine* [2d. ed.; London: Routledge, 2004], 233).

[2] So Phillip De Lacy, "Galen's Platonism," *AJP* 93 (1972): 27–39; and Pierluigi Donini, "Motivi filosofici in Galeno," *La Parola del Passato* 35 (1980): 333–70, who is opposed by Riccardo Chiaradonna, "Galen and Middle Platonism," in *Galen and the World of Knowledge* (ed. C. Gill, T. Whitmarsh, and J. Wilkins; Cambridge: Cambridge University Press, 2009), 243–60. Heinrich von Staden offers a meticulous dissection of the variety of influences, including the physicalist theories of early Hellenistic thinkers, that went into Galen's views on the relationship of body to soul in "Body, Soul, and Nerves: Epicurus, Herophilus, Erasistratus, the Stoics, and Galen," in *Psyche and Soma: Physicians and Metaphysicians on the Mind-Body Problem from Antiquity to Enlightenment* (ed. J. P. Wright and P. Potter; Oxford: Oxford University Press, 2000), 79–116 [esp. 105–16].

[3] There is just one philosopher, Potamo of Alexandria, who was labeled as an "eclectic" in antiquity; Diogenes Laertius (1.21) writes that he introduced a "certain eclectic sect." In her detailed study, *Potamo of Alexandria and the Emergence of Eclecticism in Late Hellenistic Philosophy* (Cambridge: Cambridge University Press, 2011), Myrto Hatzimichali concludes that "Potamo's eclecticism was an attempt to draw together and incorporate into his doctrines (ἀρέσαντα) what seemed to him worthwhile and "most accurate" from the different philosophical traditions (178)." This conclusion, which fits the very sparse information we have about

ground that he speaks of himself as "selecting" the best doctrines.[4] Despite the widespread use of the term, however, there has been considerable dissatisfaction with it, both in general and specifically for Galen. In the words of Paul Moraux, Galen's so-called eclecticism is "nothing other than the result of the application" of certain scientific criteria.[5] Michael Frede suggests that it may be unfair to see Galen as an "eclectic:" for "Galen himself at least saw his eclecticism as a result of critical judgment, attachment to the truth, and moral strength."[6] Others have added the term "syncretic," to make clear the selection isn't just a random collection, but has a historically based cohesion.[7]

I would like to try out a new label: "personal philosophy." I hasten to add an immediate disclaimer: I do not intend the label in the weak sense in which just anyone can be said to have a "personal philosophy." What I call "personal philosophy" is not popular philosophy, or merely an outlook on life. Using

---

Potamo, may serve as a starting-point for assessing the wealth of information we have about so-called "eclectic" philosophy in general.

[4] Michael Frede, for example, writes that Galen is "an eclectic in his own words," citing *Lib. Prop.* 1 (K 19.14 = *SM* 2.95.6–14 = BM 138.16–139.10) and *Aff.Dig.* 8 (K 5.41–42 = *CMG* 5.4.1.1 28.10–29.12); and "Introduction," in *Galen: Three Treatises On the Nature of Science* [ed. R. Walzer and M. Frede; Indianapolis: Hackett, 1985], xvi). The term "select" occurs only in the first of these places. See note 34 below. Nutton calls Galen "avowedly eclectic" (*Ancient Medicine*, 228–9).

[5] Paul Moraux, "Galien comme philosophe: la philosophie de la nature," in *Galen: Problems and Prospects* (ed. V. Nutton; London: Wellcome Institute for the History of Medicine, 1981), 87–116 [105].

[6] Frede, "Introduction," xvi–xvii. In a detailed discussion of Galen's eclecticism, Frede argues that it is set off from the general eclecticism of the time by two features: (1) strong anti-dogmatism; and (2) skepticism on certain basic philosophical beliefs, such as the nature of the soul ("On Galen's Epistemology," in *Galen: Problems and Prospects* [ed. V. Nutton; London: Wellcome Institute for the History of Medicine, 1981]: 65–86 [71]). Frede proposes that eclecticism in general has its origin in (1) the disintegration of the Athenian schools of philosophy at the end of the second and beginning of first century B. C. E.; (2) Academic skepticism; (3) neo-classicism, and (4) selectivity (esp. 67–70). Eduard Zeller previously saw ancient eclecticism as the "Rückseite" (549) of Hellenistic skepticism, displacing skepticism from the first century BCE, while combining previously separate strands of thought; he viewed it as a decadent movement (that is, an "Ermattung des Denkens," 564), which placed an unphilosophical reliance on self-consciousness as the criterion of judgment (*Die Philosophie der Griechen in ihrer geschichtlichen Entwicklung* [4th ed.; Leipzig: Fues, 1909], 3.1:547–64). John Dillon calls Galen's doctrine "truly eclectic" (*The Middle Platonists* [Ithaca: Cornell University Press, 1977], 339); but he eschews the label "eclectic" on the ground that it suggests selection on the basis of personal preference rather than on the basis of a coherent theory of the historical development of philosophy (xiv). See Donini on the history of the term "eclectic" since the Renaissance ("The History of the Concept of Eclecticism," in *The Question of "Eclecticism:" Studies in Later Greek Philosophy* [ed. A. A. Long and J. M. Dillon; vol. 3 of *Hellenistic Culture and Society*; Berkeley: University of California Press, 1988], 15–33); and Hatzimichali, *Potamo of Alexandria and the Emergence of Eclecticism in Late Hellenistic Philosophy*, 9–24, on the use of the term both in antiquity and in modern scholarship.

[7] Thus R. J. Hankinson considers Galen "not so much an eclectic, in the mildly pejorative sense of the word, as a creative syncretist" ("Galen's Philosophical Eclecticism," *ANRW* 36.5:3505–22 [3519]).

"philosophy" in a strong sense, I view "personal philosophy" as the opposite of "school philosophy:" it addresses the same concerns, but is rooted in each person's examination of an unbounded range of positions, which he reshapes as a guide for himself. Instead of accepting the judgment of others, a person asserts the freedom to guide his own life on the basis of his own judgment. Because he accepts some of the results obtained in the past, the procedure may be called eclectic. However, he does not merely make a selection: in the process of judging, he also corrects what was previously proposed and adds conclusions of his own. Overall, he creates a new construct. The label "eclectic" obscures not only the element of personal judgment but also the element of originality in what is newly put together. It also overlooks the impulse to fit one's position to one's life. Pro-choice and anti-authority, an individual uses his personal powers of judgment to fashion a personal way of life.

I associate five features with "personal philosophy," as applied to the three centuries between ca. 100 B. C. E. and 200 C. E. First, it is *critical*. By this I mean that a person relies on his or her own powers of judgment to assess a position. She won't accept philosophical tenets on faith, but aims to submit every aspect to her own judgment. Second, it is *oriented toward the past*. The past is viewed as a source of wisdom, along with gaps and errors. The wisdom of the past needs to be uncovered and augmented by one's own judgment. Third, it is *far-ranging*. Going beyond the boundaries of any particular school or area of inquiry, a person surveys a wide range of positions that have been taken in the past, whether by philosophers or by other thinkers. Fourth, it is *constructive*. Influenced by both dogmatic and skeptical thinkers, a person puts together a clearly demarcated system of truths that are partly taken from others and partly added by herself, while recognizing a limit to the discovery of truths. Fifth and last, it is *integrated with one's life*. By this I mean that it permeates all aspects of one's life. Philosophical activity is not separate from other endeavors; it may be combined with any occupation – farming, politics, running a household, teaching, medicine, whatever. To summarize: confronted by a huge wealth of ideas that have been handed down from the past, a person puts together a system of truths as a guide for one's own life. She lives her philosophy in all that she does, thus serving as an exemplar of her philosophy.

These five features, I suggest, apply to so-called ancient "eclectism" in general. As a personal philosophy, it admits of considerable variation from one person to the next. Frede has stressed that Galen's so-called eclecticism is very different from that of anyone else, and this is surely right.[8] Galen is especially insistent that he is not an adherent of any particular school; and he stands out in his demand for logical method, his ambition as a medical researcher, and his self-assertiveness. But he is no more exceptional than Antiochus, for example, who

---

[8] "On Galen's Epistemology," 71 n. 4.

is generally placed at the start of the "eclectic" period, or Philo of Alexandria, who has also been labeled an "eclectic." We know of Antiochus, who rebelled against the skepticism of the Academy, only through the writings of others; and we have only scanty reports about most so-called "eclectics." When we rely on the reports of others, we must be wary of the doxographic tendency to classify a thinker as belonging to one school or another, despite differences; classification tends to elide the perspective of the individual. By contrast, much of what is called "eclectic" philosophy looks highly idiosyncratic. If we substitute the term "personal" for "eclectic," we can better see the reason for this phenomenon.

One might well object that all philosophy is more or less "personal." I do not dispute this point. It has also been said that every founder is "more or less eclectic."[9] The difference is a matter of degree. A comparison with religion, which is inextricably linked with ancient philosophy, may be helpful. In his pioneering book, André-Jean Festugière distinguished between civic and personal religion: the former is manifested in group rituals; the latter, which coexists with the former, approaches divinity as an object of personal devotion. Philosophical schools represent a variety of systems, each of which unites its followers by common tenets.[10] But each system is also accompanied by a personal stance, which tends to draw inspiration from some teachings while ignoring others. The Stoic Cleanthes, whom Festugière cites as an example of personal religion, is a case in point.[11] From the second century B. C. E. on, philosophers looked increasingly beyond the boundaries of a particular school, asserting their freedom to draw inspiration from various schools. Personal philosophy, one might say, split off from school philosophy, building up its own set of dogmas. This is not to deny that some philosophers (including Antiochus at the beginning of this movement and Galen toward the end) saw themselves as recapturing an original unity. But to "follow" a precursor took on a new meaning: it was to see another as a model rather than as an authority.[12] Emulation won out over authority; and this resulted in a bridging of doctrinal differences as well as the attempt to add something of one's own.

---

[9] Donini quotes Diderot as saying that "there is no leader of a sect who has not been more or less eclectic" ("The History of the Concept of Eclecticism," 19).

[10] André-Jean Festugière, *Personal Religion among the Greeks* (Berkeley: University of California Press, 1954).

[11] Festugière, *Personal Religion among the Greeks*, 110–2.

[12] David N. Sedley has argued that throughout the Hellenistic and Roman periods, philosophical movements shared a "virtually religious commitment to the authority of a founder figure," with few exceptions ("Philosophical Allegiance in the Greco-Roman World," in *Philosophia Togata I: Essays on Philosophy and Roman Society* [ed. J. Barnes and M. Griffin; Oxford: Oxford University Press, 1989], 97–119 [97]). Although I agree that there was something of a religious commitment, I draw a distinction between authority and emulation; the latter allows for greater flexibility and a shifting of boundaries. Cf. Sedley's own remarks on first century BCE Academics invoking Socrates and Plato as "providing authority for the practice of never relying on authority" (102).

My plan in this paper is, first, to examine what is philosophical about *Ind.* and, second, to see how this fits Galen's notion of philosophy in general. Let us, then, start looking at Galen's *Ind.* There is an immediate surprise. The title suggests a discussion of ἀλυπία in general – like an essay by Seneca or Plutarch.[13] Instead, we find it is all about Galen himself, from beginning to end. The text consists of a reply to a boyhood friend, who wrote a letter to Galen saying how astonished he was that Galen did not feel any distress at the huge losses he suffered in the great fire at Rome in 192. This fire destroyed the depository in which Galen had stored many of his most valued belongings. Galen summarizes the content of the letter. As he reports, the friend noted that Galen's loss was so much greater than any that he had suffered before. In Galen's words, the friend asked: "What practice (ἄσκησις) or what arguments (λόγοι) or doctrines (δόγματα) prepared [you] never to be distressed" (1)?[14] The friend also drew a contrast with the grammarian Philides, who died of grief at the loss of his books in the same fire (7). Others went around the city dressed in black, like mourners.

After confirming that he did not indeed suffer any distress, Galen gives a full accounting of his losses: they were even greater, indeed much greater, than his friend thought (12–37). Galen's inventory is not only very detailed, but also rhetorically structured to heap up ever more severe losses. It culminates in the worst loss of all (of which the friend had no inkling), a unique collection of the greatest medical recipes from all over the world, supplemented by a work of his own (31–37). We are now almost halfway through the entire text. Having set the record straight, Galen now rephrases his friend's question (38): given that he suffered such a great variety of losses, any one of which would have filled another with the greatest distress, how is it that he was not troubled but bore it all?

His answer, he says, will be "twofold" (διττή, 39). First, he will tell the sort of discourses (λόγους) that his friend has often heard from him before. This section begins with two anecdotes about Aristippus (39–42), the hedonist founder of the Cyrenaic school of philosophy, then continues with the argument that it is easy to suffer a loss if it leaves one with more than one can use. It follows that it was no big deal for him never to be upset by the loss of any of his property (46). Galen offers this kind of reasoning elsewhere in his writings; and we can well imagine that it was a frequent topic of conversation with his friends. Galen never says explicitly what the second part is about, nor does he set it off explicitly from the first part. He makes clear, however, what he has in mind. For he gradually builds up a distinction between two kinds of losses: those that leave one with sufficient means and are easy to bear; and those that are a serious deprivation and require

---

[13] Véronique Boudon-Millot and Jacques Jouanna (with Antoine Pietrobelli), *Galien:* Ne pas se chagriner (Budé; Paris: Les Belles Lettres, 2010), x–xi, cite Plutarch's *De tranquillitate animi*, which is a reply to a letter asking Plutarch to write something on that topic. Plutarch offers a general disquisition on the topic.

[14] I use the numbering of Boudon-Millot and Jouanna, *Galien:* Ne pas se chagriner.

special fortitude.[15] The former can readily be brushed off; the latter demands great moral strength. One might object that the distinction is hard to pin down: one person's superfluous assets are another's necessities, and vice versa. However, it is of basic importance to get it right; and Galen puts himself forward as one who got it right. With the right moral attitude, losses that devastate others can be borne with ease.

Galen gradually prepares the second part of his answer by turning from Aristippus to philosophers of sterner stuff, in particular, the Cynics Crates and Diogenes, who were unfazed by exceptional poverty (45). The crowning example is the Stoic Zeno, who praised fortune for reducing him to having just a tunic and the stoa (48). Zeno, it is implied, lacked nothing so long as he could still teach and practice Stoic philosophy. Immediately after mentioning Zeno, Galen turns the spotlight on himself. He does so with considerable rhetorical flourish (49–50). Two negative clauses are followed by a third, positive clause, introduced by adversative "but." Galen writes: it was not a big achievement for him to think nothing of his financial losses; nor was it a big thing not to be driven mad by the numerous slanderers at court; but not to feel distress at what he has just now lost – and here he summarizes again what he lost – "this is altogether noble and a proof of the first rank linked to μεγαλοψυχία."[16]

The final assertion (as quoted) is the climax of the entire treatise. We can now see why Galen does not mark off the second part of his twofold answer. The beginning of the second part merges with the end of the first in a rhetorical build-up that masks the division. When it does arrive, the new topic bursts upon the reader with special force: it consists, in a word, in Galen's incredible nobility of mind, his μεγαλοψυχία. Amid all the many outpourings of self-praise in his writings, Galen assigns μεγαλοψυχία to himself only in this text, as far as a *Thesaurus Linguae Graecae* (TLG) search shows. Defined by the Stoics as the disposition of being superior to circumstances,[17] it had been elevated by Cicero into one of the four main virtues, taking the place of courage.[18]

So far, Galen has done little philosophical work in his exposition. He has sprinkled his text with philosophical anecdotes and drawn a distinction that was dear to philosophers. But mostly he has built himself up as a paragon of virtue. The discussion becomes more philosophical after this. After proclaiming his μεγαλοψυχία, Galen goes on to explain how he, personally, acquired it. He identifies two stages (51): his upbringing, and his experience at Rome. The first focuses on the education provided by his father (57–62). The second turns on the practice (ἄσκησις) of imagining future misfortune (52–56); this was a practice

---

[15] Boudon-Millot and Jouanna, by contrast, note that there seems to be no second part (*Galien:* Ne pas se chagriner, 114).
[16] 50: γενναῖον ἤδη τοῦτο καὶ μεγαλοψυχίας ἐχόμενον ἐπίδειγμα πρῶτον.
[17] *SVF* 3.264.
[18] *Off.* 1.61–92.

developed by the Cyrenaics and endorsed also by the Stoics. Galen highlights it as a means of coping with disaster.

In telling about his upbringing, Galen provides an example of ethical analysis. His father, he says, derided those who lived for pleasure (62); this is a put-down of Aristippus, among others. His father also supposed "that there is something better than freedom from bodily and mental pain," the goal proposed by the Epicureans. What, then, is this? His father "divined," Galen says, that this is "the good, having a nature of its own" (62). Faced with a conundrum, Galen tries out one possible answer: knowledge (ἐπιστήμη) of divine and human affairs. This idea of the good, which is identical with the Stoic definition of wisdom,[19] is too lofty for Galen. Siding with Plato, Galen denies that humans can know universals; hence they cannot make choices with knowledge (ἐπιστημονικῶς). Next, he considers the alternative of going into politics. He rejects this option, both because of its difficulty and because he doesn't see the masses benefitting from the efforts of good men (64). It is tempting to see here an homage to the emperor Marcus Aurelius. In consequence, Galen goes on, he thought everything "small" – his work as a physician, fame, money – all his successes. Echoing Plato, he says he wrote his books by way of "play" (67).[20]

What is left? Galen now returns to a candidate that his father rejected, freedom from trouble. He knows, he says, that no one – not he, nor any human, nor indeed any living creature – could bear such a life. For he sees that all want to be active in both body and soul (68). Galen does not elaborate further; he simply refers us to numerous discussions in other books, including a book (not extant) against Epicurus. He clearly gives a nod, however, to the Aristotelian conception of the human good as action in accordance with virtue.[21] He bases this judgment on an empirical criterion: his experience of himself, together with his observation of others.

All this is rather casual. Covering a large amount of territory very quickly, it is a recapitulation of what Galen had said many times before. At the end, Galen considers that he has given a complete answer to his friend (69). Let us pause a moment, therefore, to take stock. In the second part of his "two-fold" answer, Galen offers a much-needed clarification of his theme, ἀλυπία. On the Epicurean view, freedom from mental pain is part – indeed the dominant part – of the good. Galen objects: as a passive condition, it falls short of the good; for this requires action. This, however, is not all that is missing from Epicurean ἀλυπία. What is missing is the good in itself, conceived as virtue. As he demonstrates by his own example, Galen links ἀλυπία with the virtue of μεγαλοψυχία; and in this he

---

[19] *SVF* 2.35–36. Galen cites the definition at *MM* 1.1 (K 10.2).
[20] See *Phaedr.* 276d.
[21] Cf. Galen's list of possible goals at *Pecc.Dig.* 1 (K 5.61 = *SM* 47–48 = *CMG* 5.4.1.1 42.20–43.11); they include pleasure, lack of trouble (ἀοχλησία), virtue, and activity in accordance with virtue.

comes close to a Stoic position. Drawing on the Stoic definition of μεγαλοψυχία, he refers repeatedly to his contempt for possessions and other material conditions.[22] Does he then go over to Stoicism altogether? On the Stoic view, λύπη, distress, is one of the four irrational feelings (πάθη) and needs to be eradicated altogether. Is Galen willing to go this far?

Further clarification is needed; and that is why, even though Galen claims to have given a complete answer, he adds a sequel, consisting in a further distinction. His friend, indeed, prompted the sequel, by asking, to begin with, what prepared Galen "never to be distressed" (1). Galen sees a complication: his friend might suppose that he, Galen, will *never* feel distress – not just now, but never at any time (70), as some philosophers propose. So Galen sets his friend straight: he is not saying that he will never, ever, feel distress. How far, then, is he willing to go? He draws the line very clearly. Staking out a position against Stoic orthodoxy, he says: he has no way of telling, on the one hand, whether there is a person so wise as to be wholly without emotions (ἀπαθής); he has precise cognition (ἀκριβῆ γνῶσιν ἔχω), on the other hand, that he is not of this kind. Thus, he will suffer distress at extreme misfortune, such as being exiled to a deserted island, or suffering extreme torture, or having a friend punished by a tyrant. Setting up a contrast with the Stoic Musonius, who was reportedly in the habit of praying "O Zeus, send me a reversal (περίστασιν)," Galen says that he always prays: "O Zeus, send me no reversal that is able to pain me" (73). One might see here a bit of mockery, worthy of Lucian, a contemporary of Galen. At any rate, Galen seems to be putting the Stoic method of rewriting a well-known text to his own use, that of subverting a Stoic position.

This, then, is Galen's full answer. How philosophical is it? Overall, Galen has produced an autobiographical narrative that stakes out a moral position along a continuum of losses. He demarcates three kinds of losses: those that are easy to bear; those that require special fortitude; and those that are so extreme that he, personally, would not be able to bear them. Galen's ἀλυπία reaches extraordinarily far along the kinds of losses, but not all the way to the end. In his initial question (1), his friend listed three methods of self-preparation: practice (ἄσκησις), arguments (λόγοι), and doctrines (δόγματα). Galen has dealt with all of them, though in a sporadic manner.

Taken by itself, the text seems rather thin as a philosophical discourse. To judge its contribution, we need to put it in a wider context. Let us first consider Galen's other ethical writings. *De indolentia* is one of two extant works out of a list of twenty-six ethical works compiled by Galen in *De libris propriis* (K 19.45–46 = *SM* 2.121–22 = BM 169–70).[23] The other is comprised of two

---

[22] 49, 61, 66, 71, and 78.

[23] One of the works listed here, περὶ ἠθῶν, is extant only in a rather extensive Arabic epitome (translated by John N. Mattock, "A Translation of the Arabic Epitome of Galen's Book Περὶ

books: *De propriorum animi cuiuslibet affectuum dignotione et curatione* (*Aff. Dig.*; *On the Diagnosis and Cure of the Passions of the Soul*) and *De animi cuiuslibet peccatorum dignotione et curatione* (*Pecc.Dig.*; *On the Diagnosis and Cure of the Errors of the Soul*). *De indolentia* dovetails nicely with the first of these books. Written before the great fire of 192, *De propriorum animi cuiuslibet affectuum dignotione et curatione* offers a much more methodical view of ἀλυπία by placing it in the context of the passions in general.

After dealing at length with anger and desire, which belong respectively to the spirited and desiring faculties of the soul, Galen rounds out the discussion with a detailed analysis of distress, λύπη (*Aff.Dig.* 7–10 [K 5.37–57]). Again, Galen holds himself up as a model of cheerfulness: this is such as to prompt others to ask him how he maintains his composure (*Aff.Dig.* 7, 10 [K 5.37, 54]).[24] As in Περὶ ἀλυπίας, he credits his father with taking an interest in philosophy himself, making sure that his son received a well-rounded philosophical education (*Aff. Dig.* 7–8 [K 5.40–43]). His father took a special interest in ἀλυπία. All philosophers, his father said, want to appear virtuous even if they aren't, but the one thing they really want is ἀλυπία; consequently, Galen should practice it first of all (*Aff.Dig.* 8 [K 5.43]). Importantly, Galen's father considers this only a first step; he recognizes, as Galen points out in Περὶ ἀλυπίας, that there is a higher goal. Galen took his father's message to heart. He argues that λύπη has only one cause, ἀπληστία, "insatiability" (*Aff.Dig.* 9 [K 5.45]). Just as in his treatise on ἀλυπία, he draws a distinction, embellished with mathematical calculations, between what one needs and what is superfluous (*Aff.Dig.* 9–10 [K 5.45–52]). He also puts himself forward as an example: he has never yet lost so much money or social standing as to suffer distress (*Aff.Dig.* 8 [K 5.43–44]). Galen does not here use the word μεγαλοψυχία, nor does he attempt to draw a boundary between losses that can be borne, even if only with the greatest fortitude, and those that cannot.

De indolentia supplements this analysis by bringing in a new personal experience: the especially severe test of Galen's ἀλυπία in the fire of 192. Because of this test, Galen is now in a position to say more on the limits of ἀλυπία. Going far beyond what anyone could reasonably expect, Galen showed himself wholly

---

Ἠθῶν," in *Islamic Philosophy and the Classical Tradition* [ed. S. M. Stern, A. Hourani, and V. Brown; Columbia: University of South Carolina Press, 1972], 235–60; see also Richard Walzer, "New Light on Galen's Moral Philosophy [From a Recently Discovered Arabic Source]," *CQ* 43 [1949]: 82–96); here Galen treats the thymoetic and appetitive faculties of the soul in detail, but says very little (mostly in section 234) on distress (λύπη). Galen mentions at *Aff.Dig.* 6 (K 5.27) that he demonstrated in this treatise how to use the thymoetic faculty to control the desiring faculty of the soul.

[24] At *Aff.Dig.* 7 (K 5.37), Galen implicitly likens himself to Socrates (Plato *Prot.* 310a–d), by having a young friend come to him early in the morning (after spending a sleepless night) to consult him about his cheerfulness.

unperturbed by his losses, thus giving proof of the virtue of μεγαλοψυχία. There is, however, a limit. Galen knows, on the basis of his own experience, that he could not be a Stoic wise man: he has stretched ἀλυπία as far as it could possibly be expected in real life.

Let us now take the two texts together and check them against the list of five features that I associated with "personal philosophy." There is: (1) criticism, consisting in Galen's endeavor to judge ἀλυπία through logical analysis of what lies within his own experience; (2) a look at past philosophical positions; (3) a wide range of inquiry, covering a large variety of thinkers; (4) the construction of a position of his own, consisting in a demarcation of losses and corresponding ethical attitudes; and (5) the integration of this position in the whole of Galen's life. Following on the more formal exposition in *De propriorum animi cuiuslibet affectuum dignotione et curatione*, *Ind.* is a kind of apology for Galen's entire career as a physician. What matters to him is how he conducts his life, not what he gains or loses in the form of externals – books, wealth, and fame. He owes this contrast between inner disposition and external circumstances to a long philosophical tradition, with a special debt to the Stoics. But he worked it out himself with special reference to his own life, with a view to exemplifying it in his own person.

This is still a very restricted view of Galen's ethics. Despite the loss of most of Galen's explicitly ethical works, we know a great deal about his ethics from his voluminous other writings, which are crammed with ethical reflections. Concerning ἀλυπία in particular, he touches on it in his commentary on the Hippocratic *Epidemics*, with an example from the great fire at Rome. Just like the friend in *Ind.*, he cites another person, a certain Kallistos, who died from chagrin at the loss of his books in the great fire at Rome (*CMG* 5.10.2.2 486.19–24). He cites others, too, who died through physical illness arising from psychological distress (*CMG* 5.10.2.2 486–7). In *Praen.* 6 (K 14.631–3), he offers further examples, including the case of a love-sick woman whose illness he diagnosed as caused by her love for a certain dancer. In general, Galen keeps putting himself forward as an exemplar of virtue while castigating his enemies for insatiable greed and a boundless appetite for fame.

Our assessment, however, is still incomplete. We also need to consider how *Ind.*, and Galen's ethics in general, fits his philosophy as a whole. The number of ethical works listed by Galen is far exceeded by the number of works listed under the heading of "demonstration" in *De libris propriis* (K 19.39–45 = *SM* 2.115–21 = BM 164–9). There are about three times as many. In addition, Galen lists books on Plato, Aristotle, the Stoics, and Epicurus, and he ends with a list of grammatical and rhetorical works (*Lib.Prop.* 13–17 (K 19.45–48 = *SM* 2.122–24 = BM 170–3). The last group qualifies, on the Stoic view at least, as part of logic. There is no category of books dealing with the physical branch of philosophy as such. From this list, it looks as though Galen gave much more attention to logic, in particular demonstration, than the other two generally recognized branches of philosophy, physics and ethics.[25]

This impression, however, needs correction. As just mentioned, ethics permeates all of Galen's writings. Further, logic has instrumental value as a method of discovering truths, whether physical or ethical. As a means of discovery, it does not preclude a strong interest in physics and ethics. As for physics, there is indeed little (if anything) that can be grouped under this branch of philosophy if we exclude Galen's enormous output of medical writings from it.[26] There is, however, no reason to exclude the bulk of these writings. Medical research is an integral part of philosophical physics; for it deals with the human body, which is a part of physics. As such, moreover, it deals with the primary constituents of the physical world as well as the ultimate subject matter of physics, the governance of the world.[27] Accordingly, Galen held that Hippocrates laid the foundation of physics, on which Plato, Aristotle, and the Stoics built subsequently (*MM* 1.2 [K 10.14–17]). Plato, he claims, agreed with Hippocrates on the most important doctrines;[28] Aristotle was an "exegete" of Hippocratic physics, beginning with the four elementary qualities; and the Stoics, too, will award the "crown" in physics to Hippocrates. In sum, Hippocratic physics (φυσιολογία) "wins the victory" according to Plato, Aristotle, and the Stoics. Galen sees himself as continuing this tradition of physical inquiry. Following Hippocrates as "our guide for all that is good,"[29] he sees his work as extending over the whole of physics, from the four basic qualities to its culmination, divine governance.

In Galen's view, medical research provides sure evidence for key physical doctrines. Along with other areas of research, such as astronomy and geography, it is a pillar of knowledge about the physical world. This leaves a large area where one cannot know the truth: we cannot know, for example, what is the nature of the soul (even though we can know that it has three main faculties, and where they are located), or the nature of god (even though we can know that there is a provident creator), or how many worlds there are, or whether the world is eternal.[30]

---

[25] Jonathan Barnes notes that logic did not play a significant role in medical studies before Galen ("Galen on Logic and Therapy," in *Galen's Method of Healing* [ed. F. Kudlien and R. J. Durling; Leiden: Brill, 1991], 50–102 [53]).

[26] Cf. Moraux, "Galien comme philosophe: la philosophie de la nature," 87.

[27] At *UP* 17.1 (K 4.360–1), Galen notes that the study of the parts of the body is useful not only to the physician but much more to the philosopher, who seeks knowledge of the whole of physics.

[28] So also at *UP* 1.8 (K 3.7–9).

[29] *Praen.* 1 (K 14.602 = *CMG* 5.8.1 70.15–17).

[30] For example, Galen distinguishes between what he knows and what he doesn't in *De propriis placitis* 2.1–4.1, 7.1–5, 11.1–5, and 14.4–15.5 (*CMG* 5.3.2 56–65, 76–81, 90–95, and 114–21). According to Nutton, Galen makes a triple distinction in *De propriis placitis*: there are things he knows for certain, things that are plausible, and things on which he cannot yet make up his mind (*Galen, On My Own Opinions: Edition, Translation, and Commentary* [*CMG* 5.3.2; Berlin: Akademie Verlag, 1999], 47–48). See also *Pecc.Dig.* 3 (K 5.67 = *SM* 1.52

Galen delimits a proper area for physics on the basis of what human research can accomplish.

If we include, then, Galen's medical research under the heading of physics, it follows that much of what he wrote is on logic and much more is on physics. Much, too, is on ethics. Galen's writings deal extensively with every branch of philosophy. His logic permeates the physics and ethics, which consist in the application of logical principles. His ethics, in turn, permeates all the rest. It is generally held that Galen's philosophical innovations lie primarily in the field of logic; but if we take into consideration his medical discoveries, there is no doubt that he made a huge contribution to physics as well. In the field of ethics, his theoretical contributions are admittedly slight. But what matters here is the practice, not the theory. What theory there is springs out of the practice. Galen puts himself forward as an exemplar of ethical principles in virtually all his writings. Ethics looms large as something he teaches by personal example. This is how we see him in *Ind.,* and more or less insistently in all his writings. Just as he emphasizes the need for a personal mentor to serve as an example of what he says,[31] so he presents himself throughout his writings as a kind of mentor, exemplifying the lessons he teaches.

This view of Galen's philosophical contributions is supported by what Galen himself says in his book *Quod optimus medicus sit quoque philosophus.* Citing Hippocrates as a model, he assigns all three branches of philosophy to the physician (3 [K 1.60 = BM 290.9–291.5] with my divisions):

> What else is needed, then, for a doctor to be a philosopher, so long as he practices the craft in a manner worthy of Hippocrates? For if it is appropriate (a) to be trained in logical theory in order to discover the nature of the body, differences among diseases, and indications of remedies, and (b) to scorn money and to practice temperance in order to persist with love of hard work in the practice of these things, he has all the parts of philosophy: logic, physics, and ethics.

As Galen sees it, philosophy supplies the physician with the logical and moral tools to discover the truth about the body, diseases, and remedies. It follows that the physician has all three parts of philosophy: logic, physics, and ethics. No branch of philosophy is missing. By including physics, Galen himself makes clear that medical research belongs to the realm of physics. In general, philosophy provides the manner in which, or "how," the medical art should be pursued. In Galen's words, physicians require philosophy in order to pursue the art "well" (καλῶς); otherwise they are simply suppliers of drugs, out to make money (*Opt.Med.* 3 [K 1.61 = BM 291.5–21]). Elsewhere, Galen speaks of practicing

---

= *CMG* 5.4.1.1 46.12–47.1) and *De placitis Hippocratis et Platonis* K 5.783 (*CMG* 5.4.1.2 576.29–578.7) and K 5.815 (*CMG* 5.4.1.2 600.12–19).

[31] The mentor "presents himself as an example (παράδειγμα) in everything he says and urges" (*Aff.Dig.* 10 [K 5.53]).

medicine "in a philosophical manner" (φιλοσόφως).[32] In agreement with Stoic theory, philosophy has, so to speak, an adverbial role, determining how a person conducts his life.

Galen's type of philosophy, as I mentioned at the beginning, has generally been called "eclectic." In support of this label, it has been said that Galen called himself an eclectic.[33] This claim, however, is not entirely accurate. It is based primarily on a passage from *De libris propriis*, in which Galen says that he calls "slaves" all who declare themselves "Hippocratics," "Praxagoreans," or by the name of any other physician; by contrast, he "selects" (ἐκλέγοιμι) what is "fine" (καλά) in each.[34] Galen here draws a contrast between unthinking submission and the freedom of thinking out things for oneself; "selection" implies personal judgment. Accordingly, Galen emphasizes the need to "judge" and "test." Another passage makes clear his full meaning: a person trained in his books, Galen writes, will be able to "judge" (κρίνειν) the works of other medical writers and "bring to light (φωρᾶσαι) what has been said well by them and whether they made any mistakes."[35] Galen keeps repeating that one needs to "test" (βασανίζειν) all doctrines by recourse to experience.[36]

Galen insists just as much on testing philosophical dogma as the assertions of doctors. Thus he tells that his father took him to study with representatives of the main dogmatic schools – a Stoic, Platonist, Peripatetic, and Epicurean – and admonished him "not to commit yourself rashly to one sect, but learn over a large period of time and judge them." Consequently, Galen says, he made every effort to submit philosophical doctrines to strict examination.[37] Inspired, it seems, by Plato's *Protagoras*, he took pleasure in staging contests between some twenty philosophers of different persuasions ("slaves" to philosophical sects) and an equal number of persons trained in logic, and seeing the latter defeat and humiliate the former.[38] It's not that the philosophers didn't recognize some basic truths, but that they clung obstinately to dogmas that could not be justified.

Galen himself provides us with a much more accurate way of labeling his relationship to the past. In his own words, repeated numerous times, he aims to

---

[32] *Praen.* 1.9 (K 14.602 = *CMG* 5.8.1 70.26). At *Ord.Lib.Prop.* 4 (K 19.59 = *SM* 2.88 = BM 99.10–100.20), Galen lists the personal requirements for combining medicine and philosophy as: having a sharp mind and good memory, being hard-working, and being fortunate; cf. *CAM* 6.9–11 (K 1.244–5 = *CMG* 5.1.3 71–72) and *Nat.Fac.* 3.10 (K 2.179).

[33] See note 3 above.

[34] *Lib.Prop.* 1 (K 19.13 = *SM* 2.95 = BM 138.6–139.9). Similarly, Galen speaks of "selecting" what is "true and clear" from medical writers, and leaving aside what is not (*Loc.Aff.* 2.8 = K 8.90). See also *Opt.Med.Cogn.* 9.1 (*CMG* Suppl. Or. IV).

[35] *Ord.Lib.Prop.* 3 (K 19.58 = *SM* 2.87). See also *UP* 5.5 (K 3.365–6).

[36] See, for example, *Cris.* 1.16 (K 9.620); and *MM* 5.15 (K 10.375).

[37] *Aff.Dig.* 8 (K 5.42–43 = *SM* 1.32–33); cf. *Pecc.Dig.* 4 (K 5.78–79 = *SM* 1.60–61 = *CMG* 5.4.1.1 53.12–54.15). On the need for testing and judging both medical and philosophical doctrines, see also *Nat.Fac.* 1.14 (K 2.52–53) and 3.10 (K 2.179), and *Us.Puls.* 1 (K 5.149).

[38] *Pecc.Dig.* 5 (K 5.92–93 = *SM* 1.72–73 = *CMG* 5.4.1.1 61.21–62.29).

"complete" (τελειῶσαι) what was begun in the past; and this requires both the elimination of errors and the addition of new discoveries. "Selection" is only a means to this goal. "It is not possible," Galen says, "for the same person to begin something and complete it." Therefore, "one should praise those who interpret well what has been said and who add anything that has been left out" and blame those who refuse to learn anything from the past out of an ill-conceived desire for innovation (*Nat.Fac.* 2.9 [K 2.141]). Galen defends the past as a beginning, not as the last word; and he inveighs against trendiness that is blind to the past. Erasistratus and the Methodists are the chief culprits.[39] In his view, Hippocrates set out the right path. He acknowledges that Aristotle and Theophrastus, and their schools, nearly completed the task. Still, no one has yet completed it; most in fact contaminated what Hippocrates said (*MM* 2.6 [K 10.117–8]). In general, it is up to the successors to complete Hippocrates' method by making additions over many years (*Hipp.Aph.* 17b.352). Galen prompts the reader to see him as completing the method himself. As though engaged in a contest with the Muses, he sets himself the goal of "discovering and completing" the method "that has long been sought but not yet written out accurately." The way to do so is not to succumb to the laziness that now prevails (*MM* 1.9 [K 10.77]).

It has been said that Galen, while showing much independence of mind, looked backward rather than forward.[40] I would prefer to see him as looking to the past as a basis for looking forward. Like a relay runner, he looks toward the goal, while knowing that his place in line has been secured by the efforts of others. Galen's relationship to the past is one of rivalry, not of supplanting. Immense admiration for Hippocrates, together with some of his successors, goes along with the desire to improve upon their findings. He proclaims his own achievements in *De propriis placitis,* in which he demarcates his opinions from those of his precursors. What emerges is a system of thought that Galen has formed anew out of materials taken from the past and augmented by himself.

Let us now go back, for a last time, to the five features with which I began. How do they apply to Galen's philosophy as a whole? The first feature, (1) "critical," depends on the full development of one's cognitive abilities, including a rigorous knowledge of logical method and intensive personal observation. The second, (2) "oriented toward the past," consists in the effort to complete what was achieved in the past, through an examination of what is true or false, what needs to be added, and what cannot be known. The third, (3) "far-ranging," con-

---

[39] At *MM* 1.1 (K 10.5), Galen reiterates that "the ancients introduced a method of healing, and those who followed attempted to complete it," while attacking the Methodist Thessalus for throwing over past learning in order to follow crude and new-fangled methods.

[40] Frede describes Galen as having a "backward looking, rather than a forward-looking independence, which tends to choose from among the old rather than create the new" ("Introduction," xvii). Cf. Barnes who suggests that Galen saw himself as a "champion of ancient orthodoxy" ("Galen on logic and therapy," 52).

sists in taking as wide a view as possible, encompassing a variety of intellectual disciplines. The fourth, (4) "constructive," consists in putting together selected features and making additions of one's own. Constrained by the inherent limits of one's cognitive abilities (however great), the construct has a limit; beyond it, there is nothing sound. The fifth, (5) "integrated," consists in the pursuit of truth in all that one does. Galen puts himself on display as an exemplar of someone who cares only about the truth. What makes his philosophy "personal" rather than "eclectic" or "syncretic" is that he derives inspiration from his predecessors – Hippocrates in the first place, followed by a succession of others – to stake out a position of his own, using his particular abilities to finish what they had begun.

I suggest, although I cannot pursue this topic here, that "personal" philosophy occupies a broad intermediate range between allegiance to skeptical philosophy at one end and allegiance to a dogmatic school on the other. There are no sharp boundaries. Those who call themselves Stoics or Platonists, or even Epicureans, discard some tenets of their schools and adopt those of others, even though they may insist on their loyalty to the founder of their school. Seneca absorbed some Epicurean doctrines into his Stoicism; and Epictetus was hospitable to Cynicism. Skeptics, on the other hand, veer toward acceptance of doctrines to live by.[41] "Personal philosophy" has its own hero, Socrates, who becomes the favorite all-round model of a philosopher. In general, admiration for a predecessor takes the form of emulation rather than adherence. Within the range of "personal" philosophy, Galen's philosophy stands out in its devotion to medical research and its self-assertiveness. Galen doesn't merely judge for himself; he flaunts his personal powers of judgment. Antiochus' personal stance is something of a mystery. But what we know of him does not rule out that, similarly to Galen's relationship to Hippocrates, he saw himself as helping to complete a philosophy that was begun by Plato.[42] To take a final example, Galen's friend and supporter

---

[41] I am thinking particularly of Cicero, who excuses his doctrinal tendencies partly as consistent with skepticism (*Off.* 2.7–8) and partly as lapses (*Acad.* 2.66).

[42] There has been much discussion of Cicero's description of him as "bringing back the old Academy" (*vetus Academia revocata est*) at *Acad.* 2.70. There is a consensus that he established a school which he regarded as a continuation of the Old Academy, but there is debate on whether he was ever head of the Academy. See David N. Sedley, "The End of the Academy," *Phronesis* 26 (1981): 67–75 [70]; Jonathan Barnes, "Antiochus of Ascalon," in *Philosophia Togata* (ed. J. Barnes and M. Griffin; Oxford, 1989), 51–96 [57–58], and Robert Polito, "Antiochus and the Academy," in *The Philosophy of Antiochus* (ed. D. Sedley; Cambridge: Cambridge University Press, 2012), 31–54 [39]. Antiochus is generally viewed as a syncretist who did not make any innovations (so Barnes, "Antiochus of Ascalon," 90). I suggest that Antiochus set up his own, privately run school (that is, a school in an ordinary sense, as Epictetus later set up a school) in which he presented Plato as the initiator of a philosophical movement that still required some "correction" (as attempted by the Stoics, *Acad.* 1.35 and 43); some of the efforts of the Stoics were regarded by him as misguided, others (particularly in the field of epistemology) as improvements or completions.

Marcus Aurelius is much indebted to the Stoics; but he does not fit tidily into a Stoic niche.[43] He selects some elements from Stoicism, and questions or discards others; and he takes something from Plato, Heraclitus, skeptical thinkers, and many others. Throughout, he tries to build up a philosophy that is tied to his own circumstances. He integrates his philosophical concerns with his day-to-day activities as emperor. Marcus has both a personal religion, as Festugière pointed out, and a highly personal philosophy.[44]

In conclusion, it has been argued by Pierre Hadot that ancient philosophy is primarily a way of life rather than a body of discourse.[45] This judgment seems to me to fit best the period from around 100 B. C. E. to 200 C. E., including Galen. Galen's voluminous writings are an especially detailed expression of a way of life. At the same time, they are a critical response to a rich cultural tradition. I have called this "personal philosophy," as distinguished from adherence to a particular philosophical school. By focusing on Galen's engagement with the past, we can see how he contributed to the growth of philosophy as well as the medical art. His philosophy is not simply a reconfiguration of past insights, nor is it a fundamentally new creation, but an attempt to emulate the great figures of the past in the devotion to truth.

---

[43] As J. M. Rist points out, Marcus Aurelius never identifies himself as a Stoic ("Are you a Stoic? The Case of Marcus Aurelius," in *Jewish and Christian Self-Definition* [ed. B. F. Meyer and E. P. Sanders; vol. 3 of *Self-Definition in the Graeco-Roman World*; London: SCM Press, 1982], 23–45 [23]).

[44] Festugière, *Personal Religion among the Greeks*, 112–7.

[45] See esp.: "on est philosophe non pas en fonction de l'originalité ou de l'abandonce du discours philosophique ... mais en function de la manière dont on vit" (*Qu'est-ce que la philosophie antique?* [Paris: Gallimard, 1995], 266). See also Lloyd P. Gerson, review of Pierre Hadot, *What is Ancient Philosophy? Bryn Mawr Classical Reviews* 9.21.2002.

JANET DOWNIE

Galen's Intellectual Self-Portrait in *De indolentia*

In his most extensive ethical treatise on the passions and errors of the soul, when Galen considers what sort of calamity might test his self-control and temperate judgment, he imagines material loss: "there is no loss," he says "that has the power to cause me grief (λυπῆσαι) – except perhaps if I should lose all my possessions – for this I have not yet experienced."[1] As it turned out, he would face a version of this moral test some years later, in 192 CE – not, to be sure, total devastation of his physical livelihood and security, but the destruction of an important collection of books, writings and professional materials in a fire that consumed the contents of his storehouses on the Sacred Way at Rome. In the wake of this disaster, Galen wrote – at the request of a friend – the moral epistle known as *De indolentia* (*On Not Being Grieved*) in which he revisits in a personal context the question he had raised in more abstract terms in the earlier treatise: what habits of mind enabled him to face this particular loss with emotional and mental discipline?[2]

Two features make *Ind.* distinctive as a response to this question: first, the text's autobiographical mode. For, while Galen's earlier treatment of the ethical problem of grief includes subjective reflection, *Ind.* is all about Galen: here, philosophy is mediated through personal experience.[3] The second distinctive

---

[1] *Aff.Dig.* 8 (K 5.43): οὔτ' οὖν ἀπώλειά τινος ἱκανὴ λυπῆσαί με, πλὴν εἰ παντελῶς ἀπολέσαιμι τὰ κτήματα (τοῦτο γὰρ οὐδέπω πεπείραμαι). The text is often treated as two works: *De propriorum animi cuiuslibet affectuum dignotione et curatione* (*Aff.Dig.*; *The Passions of the Soul*) and *De animi cuiuslibet peccatorum dignotione et curatione* (*Pecc.Dig.*; *On the Diagnosis and Cure of the Errors of the Soul*).

[2] Véronique Boudon-Millot and Jacques Jouanna date *Ind.* to early 193, after the death of Commodus, and maintain that *Ind.* was written after the *Passions and Errors of the Soul*, on the grounds that if the fire at Rome had already occurred, Galen would have mentioned this when he details previous losses in the *Passions and Errors of the Soul*. See Boudon-Millot, and Jouanna (with Antoine Pietrobelli), *Galien:* Ne pas se chagriner (Budé; Paris: Les Belles Lettres, 2010), lviii–lxi, for an account of the difficulties of establishing this relative chronology, and Christopher Gill, *Naturalistic Psychology in Galen and Stoicism* (Oxford: Oxford University Press, 2010), for the reverse order.

[3] As Véronique Boudon-Millot, "Galen's Bios and Methodos: From Ways of Life to Path of Knowledge," in *Galen and the World of Knowledge* (ed. C. Gill, T. Whitmarsh, and J. Wilkins; Cambridge: Cambridge University Press, 2009), 175–89, points out, autobiographical material is generally not ornamental in Galen's writing; rather, it has "a real epistemological role" (188). The point is crucial in this text. See also Véronique Boudon-Millot, "Un traité perdu de Galien miraculeusement retrouvé, *Le Sur l'inutilité de se chagriner*: texte grec et traduction française,"

feature is the attention Galen pays to the nature of his loss. As he makes clear in this treatise, the fire of 192 destroyed possessions that were not just material but also intellectual: his scholarly manuscripts and equipment. For this reason, Galen's professional life is at the center of the text, and this complicates his philosophical response. Prompted by disaster to weigh the trappings of professional productivity against the intellectual process itself, in *Ind.* Galen sounds the depths of his compulsion for scientific research.[4]

In the first half of the epistle Galen accounts for what he has lost, describing in some detail not just the contents of the storerooms, but also the work they represented. As a consequence, when he professes an ethics of detachment in the treatise's second half, this stoic pose seems not entirely convincing. It is out of tune with the Galen glimpsed in the first half of the text, and familiar from his other writings – a figure who is professionally ambitious, seriously prolific, and a careful curator of his own literary legacy, as evidenced by his bio-bibliographical treatises, *De libris propriis* and *De ordine librorum propriorum*. On the one hand, of course, by pointing out its non-material aspects, Galen heightens the value of his loss and enhances his claim to remarkable self-control. On the other hand, however, when the philosophical argument of the text's second half culminates in a description of his writings as mere "entertainment" (παιδία), this seems like a paradoxical assertion. At this crucial juncture, I suggest, Galen offers this revised evaluation of his work not simply as a moral argument, but as a way of connecting this moral stance to his scientific understanding of what animates human beings, and living creatures more generally: relentless, dynamic activity (ἐνέργεια). In a sense, the loss Galen suffered as a result of the fire at Rome requires him to think dynamically about his "intellectual property" as well. In *Ind.*, he elaborates a philosophical framework for reasoning about loss that is consistent, ultimately, with the empirical results and the guiding principles of his scientific research.

A Professional Inventory

In his bio-bibliographical treatise *Lib.Prop.*, Galen lists *Ind.* among his writings on moral philosophy.[5] From the subject matter – the problem of grief – we might have expected either an analytical work, or something along the lines of

---

in *La science médicale antique. Nouveaux regards. Études réunies en l'honneur de J. Jouanna* (ed. V. Boudon-Millot, A. Guardasole, and C. Magdelaine; Paris: Beauchesne, 2008).

[4] For Galen's self-presentation as a practicing physician, see Susan P. Mattern, *Galen and the Rhetoric of Healing* (Baltimore: Johns Hopkins University Press, 2008). Both his therapeutic and his scientific engagements are important facets of Galen's personality as it emerges across his oeuvre in anecdotes and moments of autobiographical reflection.

[5] *Lib.Prop.* 12 [K 19.45.17]. For the reference, see Boudon-Millot and Jouanna, *Galien:* Ne pas se chagriner, 27.

pseudo-Plutarch's *Consolatio ad uxorem* on the death of his son.[6] In fact, Galen writes not to console or exhort, but to offer – at his friend's request – an account of his own immunity to grief.[7] After losing so much of his library, so many of his own writings, research tools, data, and *materia medica*, his correspondent has asked (1), "what training (ἄσκησις), or which arguments (λόγοι), or what teachings (δόγματα) prepared [Galen] never to be distressed (λυπεῖσθαι)?"[8] Galen insists throughout the text that he dealt easily with the situation he faced, and he offers an account in two parts, outlining first what property he lost, and then why this did not affect him. Linking the text's two halves is the underlying problem: what, precisely, was the nature and value of his loss?

At the beginning of the epistle, Galen gives a sense of the volume and range of the possessions that have been destroyed, going through a detailed inventory of the contents of his storeroom. The effect at first is to remind the reader that grief would have been a natural response – for the list is long. More than that, however, the important point is what these belongings represented. As he notes, his friend was not amazed at Galen's ability to come to terms with the loss of gold and silver and other purely material goods, but rather at his equanimity faced with the destruction of his writing, medicines, and instruments – in other words, the products and the tools of his scholarly research (4–5). He laments the loss of a number of "rare" books, as well as manuscripts he had copied and emended with the intention of preparing his own edition (14). He had worked these over to such a point of accuracy, he says, that not the slightest mark of punctuation, "not even a *paragraphos* – single or double – nor a *coronis*" was out of place (14). He enumerates other products of long labor – commentaries, summaries of medical and philosophical books, a treatise of his own on the composition of medicines – as well as editorial projects that were cut short by the fire. Likewise, when he mentions pharmacological recipes, ingredients, and models for the manufacture of medical instruments, he reminds his audience that his was a professional life in vigorous motion, and that the fire represents a serious setback for research and learning.

---

[6] Though, the fact that Galen refers to another text by the title *Consolation* suggests that he thought of this as a different kind of project.

[7] In the ancient literary, rhetorical, and philosophical tradition, most consolations were offered in an attempt to assuage the grief of others, but note Cicero's consolation (not extant) written to comfort himself on the death of his daughter Tullia.

[8] Galen reports being asked nearly the same question by another interlocutor in his *Aff.Dig.* 7 (K 5.37.10–12). See Boudon-Millot and Jouanna, *Galien:* Ne pas se chagriner, xlv–xlvii and 29–30. Translations from *Ind.* are my own, but I have consulted Clare K. Rothschild and Trevor W. Thompson, "Galen: 'On the Avoidance of Grief,'" *EC* 2, no. 1 (2011): 110–29, as well as Boudon-Millot and Jouanna. References to *Ind.* follow the division in the critical edition of Boudon-Millot and Jouanna. An alternative system is available in the edition of Paraskevi Kotzia and Panagiotis Sotiroudis, "Γαληνοῦ περὶ ἀλυπίας," *Hellenica* 60 (2010): 63–148.

His friend's enquiry gives Galen the opportunity, first, to enhance his professional profile by bringing all these materials before the eyes of the reader and, second, to enhance his moral profile by emphasizing what a feat it was to maintain philosophical composure: the greater the loss, the greater the philosophical challenge. In this sense, it is not exactly the magnitude of his loss, but its distinctly intellectual quality that matters. To corroborate this point, Galen compares himself to a fellow professional who handled the same situation with much less equanimity than he did himself: a scholar named Philides, he reports, who had also entrusted valuable possessions to the storehouses on the Sacred Way, was so afflicted that he "wasted away from discouragement and grief, and actually died" (7).[9] Philides' reaction – excessive and humorous – offers a foil for Galen's own, and an illustration of the danger of failing to assess one's scholarly work with appropriate detachment. But it also functions as a pathetic reminder of the scholar's natural response to intellectual loss. Galen underscores this point by projecting the grief he abjures upon his epistolary interlocutor, suggesting, for example, that his friend will be particularly "grieved" (λυπεῖν) at bibliographical irregularities turned up by Galen's research (16, 20). Scholarly pursuits matter, Galen insists, and it is for this reason that the destruction caused by the fire occasions the philosophical problem of grief.

Παιδία and Σπουδή

Halfway through the treatise, Galen has given a lengthy inventory of what was destroyed, highlighting its intellectual character, but he still has offered no clue as to how he managed to avoid the fate of Philides. As he points out, the extensive inventory has probably only enhanced his correspondent's curiosity. At the midpoint of the text, he restates his original question, but with a twist. Galen transfers to his friend the very problem of insatiable desire (ἐπιθυμία) that he will go on to examine in the text's second half: "Perhaps then you will say that your desire (ἐπιθυμία) is enjoined even more to want to know how, despite having lost such a great variety (ποικιλία) of my possessions – each of which alone, in and of itself, would have been most distressing (λυπηρότατος) for other human beings – I was not troubled like some others. Rather I very easily endured what

---

[9] Boudon-Millot and Jouanna, *Galien: Ne pas se chagriner*, 41–42, accept the manuscript reading of the name, though Philides is not known outside this text. They note that Galen stresses the importance of γνώμη for health in other texts too. At *In Hippocratis librum sextum Epidemiarum Comentarii* (extant in an Arabic version), he mentions a grammarian named Kallistos who died when his works were lost in the fire at Rome. In *De compositione medicamentorum per genera* he tells the fate of two doctors after they lost their books of medical recipes: one died, while the other gave up practicing medicine.

happened" (38).¹⁰ Just as he implicated his correspondent in the grief of scholarly loss (16, 20), so too he implicates him in the destructive force of insatiable desire that is the cause of un-philosophical grief.

Galen purports to offer a "double reply" (39: διττήν ἀπόκρισιν) in response to his friend's enquiry.¹¹ As Boudon-Millot and Jouanna point out, these two points are not clearly marked in the text that follows. He does, however, distinguish between the philosophical resources required to face material loss, and those required to face loss in the intellectual realm, and I propose that this is what he means by a "double reply."¹² He begins by pointing out the dangers of ἀπληστία – a state of insatiable desire in which the disordered soul has no self-generated sense of what is sufficient for its material needs. But from there he makes a leap to introduce the more elusive and complex virtue of μεγαλοψυχία – "greatness of soul" – in an attempt, it seems, to address the problem that unlike material goods, which are interchangeable and have no specific, inherent value, intellectual possessions of the sort destroyed by the fire are in some sense irreplaceable. To train oneself to avoid ἀπληστία in the context of material life is a basic philosophical task; to nurture the μεγαλοψυχία – the greatness of soul – that makes it possible to extend this attitude of philosophical detachment to concerns beyond the material is a rather higher claim. In the first part of his "double reply" Galen deals with the proper attitude towards material necessities, and the second part he attempts to outline a philosophical position with respect to intellectual endeavors.

First, to illustrate success in avoiding ἀπληστία, Galen tells two stories about Aristippus, the famous student of Socrates who lived a life of luxury, but in a spirit of philosophical detachment. According to legend, Aristippus thought nothing of unloading gold at the roadside when he noticed his slave struggling under the burden of a heavy load as they walked back from the Piraeus (40). He gave up landed property with equal grace: losing one of his four fields still leaves him with three, as he points out to one of his fellow Cyrenians who offers sympathy (συλλυπεῖσθαι) for his loss; since it is only reasonable to feel distress (ἀνιᾶσθαι) if one is left truly without means, Aristippus maintains, grief in this situation would be out of place (41–42). In both of these stories, Aristippus reduces wealth to its functional, instrumental value, and makes the point that human needs are real and limited. To adopt a needs-based approach to mate-

---

¹⁰ ἴσως ἂν οὖν φήσεις ἐπιτάττεσθαί σου τὴν ἐπιθυμίαν καὶ βούλεσθαι μᾶλλον γνῶναι πῶς ἀπολέσας τοσαύτην ποικιλίαν κτημάτων ὧν ἕκαστον αὐτὸ καθ' ἑαυτὸ μόνον λυπηρότατον ἂν ἐγένετο τοῖς ἄλλοις ἀνθρώποις, οὐκ ἠνιάθην ὡς ἕτεροί τινες, ἀλλὰ πάνυ <ῥᾳδίως> ἤνεγκα τὸ συμβάν.

¹¹ The two stages seem to be cued, here, by his reference to his interlocutor's "desire" (ἐπιθυμία) and to the "variety" (ποικιλία) of his possessions.

¹² Boudon-Millot and Jouanna, *Galien:* Ne pas se chagriner, 114, point out the lack of clarity and treat the second half of the treatise as one continuous argument. See the introduction to their volume for an outline of the epistle's structure (xvi–xxii and xxxix–xlv).

rial goods is freeing, and unless people understand what is sufficient, Galen interprets, they will always feel poor, "their desire (ἐπιθυμία) being unfulfilled" (43).[13] The connection to Galen's own situation is obvious: "why is it a great achievement for me not to be troubled (ἀνιᾶσθαι) at all by the loss of money? For what was left was always much more than enough" (46). He extends the point in the following paragraphs to a wider range of material and social goods – belongings of all sorts (παντοδαπή), and status at court, for example. Such benefits might come and go without affecting the fundamentals of Galen's existence. If anything, their impermanence helps him to attend – as Aristippus also did, famously – to pursuits beyond the material.

Galen uses Aristippus here as a model for avoiding the excessive ἐπιθυμία that he describes as ἀπληστία. However, the stories he chooses limit his example to the loss of material goods that are not unique. These anecdotes are insufficient when it comes to illustrating how Galen avoided grief for his intellectual possessions. For, it was its variety of unique qualities (ποικιλία) that was the prime characteristic of his Sacred Way inventory when he recapped his friend's philosophical enquiry at the center of the treatise (38). He could have invoked other stories of Aristippus, as he does in *Protrepticus*, where Aristippus keeps company with Homer, Hippocrates, and Plato, modeling divinely-sponsored self-sufficiency in intellectual terms. There, Galen describes Aristippus' reaction when he was shipwrecked and came ashore on the coast of Syracuse. Rejoicing to see a geometrical diagram on the sand, he took this a sign that he had landed in a place in which people engaged intellectual pursuits and sent this moral admonition back to his family in Cyrene: "Tell them to acquire such possessions as would float with them in the case of a shipwreck." Galen does not cite this story in *Ind.*, but it shares a related point: namely, that it is only by understanding the virtues of intellect and spirit as able to "float" free of their material trappings that Galen can remain unaffected by his loss of property in the fire at Rome, and thus stand above a figure like the scholar Philides, who seems to have confused intellectual values with material ones.

Because Galen does not cite the shipwreck story in *Ind.*, the Aristippus anecdotes and the notion of ἀπληστία in general, have a limited range. They offer a caution against succumbing to insatiable desire and a way of understanding a healthier dynamic based on the satisfaction of real needs – but it is not clear that the intellectual affairs that are his most pressing concern fit easily into a morality based on need. Galen's concern with intellectual matters in this treatise requires him to face the question of positive goods: what is the aim of human life for which intellectual pursuits are valuable? For this reason, in the second part of his "double" account, he introduces a positive virtue – μεγαλοψυχία, or greatness of

---

[13] The danger Galen names here is the "desire" (ἐπιθυμία) he has playfully imputed to his interlocutor at the transition to the second half of the treatise (38; see n. 9, above).

soul. This is not the positive complement of ἀπληστία, but rather a moral virtue in its own right, realized through a combination of innate personal qualities and long training.[14] What is unusual about μεγαλοψυχία, as Galen presents it here, is that it requires disciplining not a negative impulse (like desire), but rather a positive virtue: industry, or "love of work" (50–51: φιλοπονία). This goes to the heart of the challenge Galen faced in light of the fire at Rome. For, the writings and scholarly paraphernalia he lost demonstrated "the considerable industry (φιλοπονία) of my entire life." Galen has spent the whole first half of the treatise building up the picture of his life of intellectual industry. Why is it that to be able not to grieve over this is, as he says, "characteristic of one who is well bred and a preeminent example demonstrating greatness of soul (μεγαλοψυχία)"? The fire seems to have thrown into question the lasting value of intellectual industry and Galen needs to find a way to justify it in philosophical terms.

After the build-up of the first half of the treatise, it seems that Galen's ideal of philosophical detachment now requires him to undermine the value of his intellectual endeavors. Therefore, as he comes to the second part of his "double" explanation, he reaches the crux of the treatise as a whole. Galen explains that not only did he identify the ordinary triggers of distress and anxiety as "trivial" in his ethical treatises, separating essential concerns from those that are negligible, but he also is compelled to recognize the treatises themselves as trivial efforts. These works, and his other scholarly pursuits, were not worthy of serious effort (σπουδή) (67–68):

Ὅτι δὲ ἕκαστον ὧν εἶπον σμικρῶν εἶναι οὐχ ἁπλῶς ἀπεφηνάμην ἀλλὰ μετὰ πολλῆς ‹ἀκριβείας› εἴσει τὰ γεγραμμένα μοι περὶ τούτων ἑκάστου διελθὼν ἃ εὑρήσει(ς· ἀλλὰ) μὰ τοὺς θεοὺς οὐδὲ αὐτὰ μετὰ σπουδῆς, οὐδὲ ὡς μέγα τι πράττων, ἀλλ' ἐν παιδιᾶς μο(ίρᾳ) συνέθηκα.

Τὴν γὰρ ἀοχλ‹ησ›ίαν τινὲς ἀγαθὸν νομίζουσιν εἶναι ὃ οὔτε ἐμαυτὸν οὔτε ἄλλον ἄνθρωπον οὔτε ζῷόν τι φέρον οἶδα· πάντα γὰρ ἐνεργεῖν ὁρῶ βουλόμενα καὶ κατὰ σῶμα καὶ κατὰ ψυχήν· ἀλλὰ τοῦτ' αὐτὸ διὰ πολλῶν ὑπομνήσεων ἐπεστησάμην ἐν ἄλλοις τέ τισι κἂν τῷ κατ' Ἐπίκουρον.

And you will know, when you go through the writings that you find on each of these topics, that I revealed – not simply but very precisely – that each of the things I spoke about was slight. But, by the gods, I neither composed them with effort, nor as if producing something great; rather I composed them by way of entertainment.

For some suppose that freedom from trouble is good – but I know that neither I myself nor another human being nor any living thing supports this. Actually, I observe that everything wants to be active both in body and *psyche*. But this very thing I established by way of many remarks in other works, especially in the work *Against Epicurus*.

---

[14] Boudon-Millot and Jouanna, *Galien: Ne pas se chagriner*, 135, remark that this is a rare use of the word μεγαλοψυχία in a positive sense in Galen's corpus.

At the heart of this passage, and indeed of the whole treatise, Galen makes the paradoxical assertion that the writings that constitute a major part of his life's work were composed "by way of entertainment." This sounds flippant, or perhaps merely clever, since Galen has spent the first half of *Ind.* cataloguing his scholarly efforts in great detail. But he gives his statement weight by linking it with, on the one hand, his father's teaching and example in his early moral formation and, on the other hand, his own scientific discoveries.

As he has explained in the paragraph that precedes this, Galen learned as a child to train (ἀσκεῖν) his imaginative faculties, as a way of furnishing his soul in advance with the resources he would need to deal with suffering and loss (56). This training in withdrawal prepared Galen to avoid the experience of pain, but even more important was the influence of his father, who maintained (against the Epicureans) that there was a greater good in human life that could not be defined merely in terms of the absence of pleasure and pain.[15] Galen does not explain here what his father thought this good consisted in, but he offers his own answer in the second paragraph of the passage quoted above: ἐνέργεια, or dynamic activity. He offers his observation of the dynamic condition of humans and animals as an explanation (γάρ) for the paradoxical statement that he undertakes his intellectual and scientific work in a spirit of play. He calls his work a kind of entertainment not precisely because it is trivial, but rather because it manifests the truth that living beings are defined by activity. If the pursuit of activity is a primary characteristic of life, it does not matter whether he describes his work as earnestly intended or playfully intended – it is simply characteristic of Galen as a human being and as, by extension, a part of the wider network of the natural world. By pointing to his own scientific observation that "everything wants to be active both in body and ψυχή," Galen establishes a relationship between his ethical and professional endeavors.

These two concepts – of the defining role of activity, and the position of human beings, body and soul, in a wider natural landscape – are indeed fundamental to the scientific view of the world that Galen articulates across his writings. In the treatise, *De temperamentis,* when he discusses the body's composition in terms of the kinds of humoral balance that are conducive to human health, he points out that the healthy state depends upon a body's ἐνέργεια. As he explains, there are different degrees of health, which may be assessed along a continuum, but it is crucial to consider this in the context of an assessment of an organism's activities:

> ... a sufficient indication of the healthy state of imbalance is that there is not yet any definite damage to any of the animal's activities (ἐνέργεια). The gap between perfect performance of the activities and definite damage to the activities thus defines the

---

[15] For commentary on Galen's account of his father's philosophical inclinations in this passage, see Boudon-Millot and Jouanna, *Galien:* Ne pas se chagriner, 149–56.

extent of the latitude in our conception of health, and the degree of imbalance to be admitted.[16]

The notion of activity, or ἐνέργεια, is fundamental to Galen's concept of the functioning body – and it is also fundamental to his concept of the healthy and functioning soul, because he conceives of the intellectual faculties as part of the "integral human being" in its connection with the wider world of living things.[17] All human faculties, including the intellectual ones, are oriented towards, and manifest in, actions. So, in his treatise *De consuetudine*, Galen argues that the reason ἄσκησις (or training) works is that faculties have a natural capacity to be increased and strengthened with exercise, and – conversely – to be damaged with inactivity. This is as true for the intellect as for the body: he describes the correspondence in *Cons.* by way of an analogy between research and the exercise of running (Dietz 115.11–22):[18]

> The following also may occur. People who are unused to learning, learn little, and that slowly, while those more accustomed do much more and do it more easily. The same thing also happens in connection with research. Those who are altogether unfamiliar with this become blinded and bewildered as soon as their minds begin to work: they readily withdraw from the inquiry, in a state of mental fatigue and exhaustion, much like people who attempt to race without having been trained. He, on the other hand, who is accustomed to research, seeks and penetrates everywhere mentally, passing constantly from one topic to another; nor does he ever give up his investigation; he pursues it not merely for a matter of days, but throughout his whole life. Also by transferring his mind to other ideas which are yet not foreign to the question at issue, he persists till he reaches the solution.[19]

Galen speaks from experience – from his scientific observation of the physical body and, presumably, from personal experience of his own life's scholarly work. Because he regards dynamism – activity, or ἐνέργεια – as basic to both the life of the body and the life of the mind, he invokes the principle of ἐνέργεια to explain his instinct towards research, writing, and scholarship. When he describes his literary output as being "by way of entertainment," this sounds paradoxical. Ultimately, however, it is a way of placing his professional pursuits – including his writings – in a position consistent with the principles explored and articulated within them.

---

[16] *Temp.* 3.4 (K 1.609). Translation in Peter N. Singer, *Galen: Selected Works* (Oxford: Oxford University Press, 1997).

[17] See Jacques Jouanna, "Does Galen have a Medical Programme for Intellectuals and the Faculties of the Intellect?" in *Galen and the World of Knowledge* (ed. C. Gill, T. Whitmarsh, and J. Wilkins; Cambridge: Cambridge University Press, 2009), 190–205 [191].

[18] Fridericus R. Dietz, *Galeni de dissectione musculorum et de consuetudine libri* (Leipzig: L. Voss, 1832).

[19] Arthur J. Brock, *Greek Medicine: Being Extracts Illustrative of Medical Writers from Hippocrates to Galen* (London: Dent, 1929), 185.

Intellectual "Property" and the Dynamic Intellect

When Galen says, at the crux of this treatise, that he has composed his texts "not with effort," but "by way of entertainment," he invokes an opposition that was common in Greek, between παιδία and σπουδή – jest and seriousness.[20] For this he has a good model, and one that he invokes elsewhere: Socrates. Galen writes at the beginning of *De usu partium* that "it is characteristic of the Socratic muse constantly to mingle seriousness and jest."[21] In this opening book of one of his fundamental works on anatomy and physiology (a text, moreover, that he was working on around the time of the fire),[22] Galen recalls Socrates, in Xenophon's *Symposium*, arguing over beauty with the most handsome men of his time.[23] One might assume, Galen says, that this was a light and playful conversation, undertaken in jest. However, because Socrates understands physical beauty as a function of bodily construction oriented perfectly toward action (ἐνέργεια), what seems merely superficial is also serious. Galen appropriates this Socratic anecdote for his analysis of the human organism in *UP*, where he sets out to account for every part of the human body in terms of its ability to perform the action or the function (ἐνέργεια) for which it is destined and ordered by nature. He begins with an extensive praise of the hand which, in its every detail, illustrates the correlation of structure and action – formed as it is for those activities that make the human being characteristically human: hunting, playing musical instruments, writing laws, and theory. The correlation of structure and action, asserts Galen, is the measure and criterion of proper form, and as a consequence: "true beauty is nothing but excellence of construction."[24]

When he articulates the relationship between the beauty and the utility of human life in *UP*, Galen characterizes this as a Socratic move because it links the apparently trivial with the most fundamental processes of human life. As we have seen, he makes a similar gesture in *Ind.*, when he makes ἐνέργεια crucial to the ethics of intellectual pursuits. When Galen refers to his written works, in *Ind.*, as παιδία, his tone does not seem to be one of outright dismissal.[25] Rather, he suggests a dynamic relationship between παιδία and σπουδή, evoking the Socratic paradox in Socratic style. It is fitting, then, that in a brief *envoi* at the very end of the epistle, Galen describes a quasi-socratic encounter that distills issues that are central to the ethical problem he has dealt with in the text: "I dared," he

---

[20] Boudon-Millot and Jouanna, *Galien:* Ne pas se chagriner, 161.

[21] K 3.25.14–15: αὕτη γὰρ ἡ Σωκράτους μοῦσα, μιγνύειν ἀεὶ τὴν σπουδὴν ἐν μέρει παιδιᾶς. The translation is modified from Margaret T. May, ed. and trans., *Galen:* On the Usefulness of the Parts of the Body (Ithaca, N. Y.: Cornell University Press, 1968).

[22] On the composition and dating of the *De usu partium*, see May, *Galen:* On the Usefulness of the Parts, 3–4.

[23] K 3.25.5–13.

[24] K 3.24.16–17.

[25] Boudon-Millot and Jouanna, *Galien:* Ne pas se chagriner, 161.

says, "to make enquiry of a man with millions – seven or more! – who neither shares what he owns nor enjoys it." When Galen asked after the man's way of life, his interlocutor explained his thinking: "Just as we carefully guard the parts of our body, so also it is necessary for each one to carefully guard his possessions." Noting that he was shocked at the man's statement, Galen implies that he regards the man's interest in preservation as misplaced. The notion of an analogy between the human body and other matters of human interest is something that Galen could appreciate, but from his perspective, the rich man's conclusion is false. For Galen, as he explains in *UP*, the value of the parts of the body lies in their capacity for activity, and he would conclude that the same should hold for wealth and other goods. Putting this compulsion to activity immediately into play (a humorous touch worthy of Socrates), Galen says the encounter prompted him to compose and dictate another book, *On Money-Loving Rich People*, which he sent to his correspondent (apparently) along with the present treatise.

When Galen mentions his encounter with the rich man, he dramatizes the philosophical claim to dynamic intellectual productivity that he has just described in more abstract terms. The rich man of Galen's anecdote assumes that wealth is to be preserved – not shared with others, nor spent to acquire goods, but preserved. This, he suggests, is as obvious as the notion that the parts of one's body are to be guarded. But for Galen, both the healthy body and the healthy soul are dynamic systems defined by motion, ἐνέργεια. For this reason, Galen's ethical bottom line is an injunction against the kind of "hoarding" the rich man represents, even in an extended, intellectual setting. The incident that motivated the writing of *Ind.* was a failure of security, but protection – either of wealth, of the physical body, or of scholarly work – is not the issue. The perfect consolation is to show that value of intellectual property is located in its dynamism. In *Ind.*, he prepares this point by itemizing his losses with a focus on the dynamics of the creation of scientific knowledge, rather than on the products, and in the second half of the treatise he elaborates a philosophical context for this focus. The rich man offers a final foil for Galen, and in this brief encounter at the end of the treatise, he immediately gives an example of the relentless dynamism he has claimed for his intellectual activity: in response to philosophical provocation in a social context, he writes another ethical treatise.

This is a perspective on "intellectual property" that Galen has assimilated in some sense by the time he composes his bio-bibliographical treatise *Lib.Prop*.[26] As he explains at the beginning of that treatise, Galen composed this catalogue of his own works as a descriptive guide for those who may encounter his various writings in the ancient book markets, where they may be difficult to distinguish from spurious texts circulating under his name. Recently, he says, among the bookstalls of Rome he came upon two men in a dispute over the status of a

---

[26] The text is translated in Singer, *Galen: Selected Works*, 1997.

text entitled "Galen the Doctor." One man had bought it under the impression that it was genuinely Galenic. The other – "a man of letters" (*Lib.Prop* Intro. [K 19.9.1]: φιλολόγων), as Galen describes him – was suspicious of the title and, upon inspecting the first two lines, decided immediately that it could not be by Galen for, he asserted, "this is not Galen's language (*Lib.Prop* Intro. [K 19.9.4: λέξις])." Galen appreciates the learning of the second individual and laments the rarity of such philological acumen in his day: diction and style *should* establish a close relationship between himself and his literary production. Indeed, he describes his corpus as mutilated (ἐλωβήσατο) by the scattered process of the exchange of manuscripts that has meant a loss of his authorial control. Yet, in writing this treatise as a guide to his works, he implicitly accepts that a more open process of transmission is a reality. Aside from formal publication and verification by authorial subscription, the world of knowledge has its own dynamic ἐνέργεια, which works by supplement and intervention – by carrying on the conversation.[27] Just as his response to his encounter with the misguided rich man, at the end of *Ind.*, was to compose another treatise, so in *Lib.Prop.* Galen's way of managing his authorial and scientific contributions and setting his literary output in order is by way of another creative intervention.[28]

Conclusion

My purpose in this paper has been to identify the distinctive contribution of *Ind.* to Galen's autobiographical portfolio. Here, in unique fashion, Galen articulates the link between his ethical values and his scientific research, and manages, thus, to offer a philosophically consistent justification of his professional activities. Galen's touchstone in this treatise is his research-based observation that dynamism – ἐνέργεια – is the fundamental characteristic of life – of human life and of the life of all beings: "I observe," he says, "that everything wants to be active both in body and *psyche*" (68). He manages, then, to ground his philo-

---

[27] Galen frequently wrote for friends (often at their request) who then made copies of the texts and disseminated them further. Mattern sketches the complicated publication scenario and comments: "Galen's own attitude toward the written word is skeptical; to him a text is not a fixed phenomenon but something constantly in flux, subject to deliberate or accidental alteration, falsification, and deterioration … it was something to be scrutinized, questioned and, if possible, corrected" (Mattern, *Rhetoric of Healing*, 12). Tomas Hägg notes the contrast between Galen's discussion of his writing and publication process, and Plotinus' working method as described by Porphyry (*The Art of Biography in Antiquity* [Cambridge: Cambridge University Press, 2012]), 372–4.

[28] Cf. Jacques Bompaire, "Quatre styles d'autobiographie au IIe siècle après J.-C.: Aelius Aristide, Lucien, Marc-Aurèle, Galien," in *L'Invention de l'autobiographie: d'Hésiode à Saint Augustin* (ed. M.-F. Baslez, P. Hoffmann, and L. Pernot; Paris: Presses de L'Ecole Normale Supérieure, 1993), 199–209 [209], on the autobiographical qualities of *Lib.Prop*. He describes it as "l'histoire d'une intelligence, d'une quête intellectuelle et épistémologique …"

sophical ideals of detachment in a comprehensive view of the world that allows him precisely to value his own work as a scientific writer and researcher. When he describes his writings as composed "by way of entertainment" he describes them as fully participating in the dynamism that is as innately characteristic of the intellect as it is of the body.

The principle of dynamism is expressed playfully in the paradox at the heart of the text. Galen makes sense of the world and his place in it according to the key term he introduces at the center of this text, the ἐνέργεια of the engaged mind. This intellectual process – and not its products – is the key to his existence as an intellectual and a scientist.[29] Mental dynamism is the core mechanism of Galen's personal ἄσκησις – a philosophical practice inherited from his father and extended through his own research. In working his reasoned way through this treatise on not being grieved, Galen enacts intellectual ἐνέργεια – dynamism – as he makes the fundamental discovery of his scientific life the foundation of his professional commitment and personal integrity.

---

[29] As Maud W. Gleason, "Shock and Awe: The Performance Dimension of Galen's Anatomy Demonstrations," in *Galen and the World of Knowledge* (ed. C. Gill, T. Whitmarsh, and J. Wilkins; Cambridge: Cambridge University Press, 2009), 85–114 [88], notes, writing of his anatomical demonstrations, Galen's intellectual curiosity and drive ran deeper than an urge to public performance: "alone and unobserved on a desert island, (Galen) would have dissected whatever came in on the tide."

Irony

Ralph M. Rosen

Philology and the Rhetoric of Catastrophe in Galen's *De indolentia*

In sections 3–6 of *De indolentia*, Galen catalogues the losses he suffered in the great fire of Rome in 192 CE which had inspired his correspondent to write to him.[1] Galen's description in this passage is a rhetorical *tour de force* in miniature. He opens by distancing himself from the things that most people would immediately find especially difficult to lose because of their financial value, namely, his silver and gold, and the "loan documents" which he would presumably no longer be able to collect on. He alludes to the surprise his friend had felt at his ability to minimize the loss of such things, and in doing so obliquely urges his readers likewise to stand amazed at his virtue.[2] As his friend realized, it was far more remarkable that Galen could bear the loss of a different sort, the "further mass of things stored there" (4) which included drugs, medical instruments, books, and astonishing quantities of theriac and medicinal cinnamon ("more than can be found in all the retail shops put together"). With such a rhetorical climax, Galen hoped to leave no doubt in his readers that he cared more about the practice of medicine than the pursuit of wealth and possessions. All the more extraordinary, therefore, that he claimed to feel no distress even at the loss of these medical accouterments.

Although the actual quantity of Galen's losses was intended to raise an eyebrow, there is nothing especially unusual about the content of his inventory – most of the items he lists are things we would readily expect to find in the storage unit of a doctor of his prominence and stature. He does seem to spend an unusual

---

[1] Unless otherwises indicated, I cite from Véronique Boudon-Millot and Jacques Jouanna (with Antoine Pietrobelli), *Galien:* Ne pas se chagriner (Budé; Paris: Les Belles Lettres, 2010). English translations of *Ind.* are taken (with occasional minor modifications) from Vivian Nutton's translation, "Avoiding Distress," in *Galen: Psychological Works* (ed. P. N. Singer; Cambridge: Cambridge University Press, 2014), 43–106.
[2] See also Galen *Aff.Dig.* 10 (K 5.54 = Wilko De Boer, *De propriorum animi cuiuslibet affectuum dignotione et curatione. De animi cuiuslibet peccatorum dignotione et curatione, De atra bile* [*CMG* 5.4.1.1; Leipzig/Berlin: Teubner, 1937], 36.2–7 = Iosepha Magnaldi, *Claudii Galeni Pergameni Περὶ ψυχῆς παθῶν καὶ ἁμαρτημάτων* [Rome: Tipys Officinae Polygraphicae, 1999], 62), where Galen tells the story of a sybaritic acquaintance who had accused him of being 'not-human' (ἀπάνθρωπος) because he always seemed to cheerful (φαιδρός). This anecdote referred to Galen's overall disposition, not just his ability to overcome specific traumas, but it does allow Galen a good measure of oblique self-praise for what he would regard as an uncommon moral stability.

amount of time, however, cataloguing and describing the various books he lost in the fire, and several aspects of his account merit further exploration. Almost a third of the entire treatise, as it happens, (esp. 12–36, with other references scattered elsewhere throughout), is devoted in one way or another to his books and writings, as well as to the books housed in the adjacent Palatine libraries, and his detailed narrative reveals just how traumatic their destruction was for him.[3] In fact, I will argue in this essay that Galen's account of his books seems ultimately (and deliberately) to work at odds with the consolatory aims of the treatise,[4] and that his fixation on the significance of their loss ironizes his claims to having achieved psychological equilibrium himself. Instead, the profound importance with which he invests the entire enterprise of scholarship and publication throughout this work, serves to amplify the persistence of the trauma Galen experienced when he suddenly lost access to so many tools for scientific research. As we shall see, the very logic of Galen's advice for avoiding the depression brought on by *material* loss, seems to work *against* the very point he is trying to make in his section about his books and scholarly activity. In the end, as I shall argue, the treatise is more rhetorically persuasive as a brief for the critical importance of scholarship for the "philanthropic" project of medicine at the highest level, than as a practical guide to "avoiding distress."

Galen's specific advice for avoiding or purging oneself of mental λύπη is postponed until the second half of the work, sections 38–48, presumably so that he could first detail the magnitude of his losses and prepare the reader to be impressed by his ability to cope. The actual advice he offers is not especially profound and borders on the platitudinous. To illustrate his basic idea that one should train oneself not to become too attached to material possessions, he tells several exemplary stories in this section about Aristippus of Cyrene, the contro-

---

[3] On the topography and archaeology of the Roman libraries and storage areas which Galen would have used to, see Matthew C. Nicholls, "Galen and Libraries in the *Peri Alupias*," *Journal of Roman Studies* 101 (2011): 123–42. Cf. Pier Luigi Tucci, "Flavian Libraries in the City of Rome," in *Ancient Libraries* (ed. J. König, K. Oikonomopoulou, and G. Woolf; Cambridge University Press, 2013), 277–311, and in the same volume, Alexei V. Zadorojnyi, "Libraries and *paideia* in the Second Sophistic: Plutarch and Galen," 389–400.

[4] On the question of the treatise as a work of *consolatio*, see Boudon-Millot and Jouanna, *Galien:* Ne pas se chagriner, ix, and Paraskevi Kotzia, "Galen, περὶ ἀλυπίας: Title, Genre and Two *Cruces*," in *Studi sul* De indolentia *di Galeno* (ed. D. Manetti; Biblioteca di "Galenos": Contributi alla ricerca sui testi medici antichi 4; Pisa/Roma: Fabrizio Serra, 2012), 69–91 [esp. 69–70]. Boudon-Millot and Jouanna as well as Kotzia note that *Ind.* is not quite a proper *consolatio*, in that it was not written to offer consolation to someone else in a state of grief (Kotzia, "Galen, περὶ ἀλυπίας: Title, Genre and Two *Cruces*," 76), though this objection may be too rigid. The work is a description of a method of what we might call "self-consolation," and as such, most of the advice he applies to himself would be be equally applicable to other people if he were consoling them instead of himself. See Nutton, "Avoiding Distress," 51: "it resembles other treatises ... aimed at providing consolation or giving advice to others on the way in which they should face difficulties in their lives."

versial follower of Socrates and founder of the Cyrenaic school.[5] In one of these, Aristippus has just lost one of three fields he owned. One of Aristippus' friends tried to commiserate with him, but, according to Galen (42–46), Aristippus

> said with a laugh: 'Why should you commiserate with me for having three fields when you haven't even one? Or should I commiserate with you?', showing very neatly ... that one should not focus on what has been lost, but consider how those who have inherited three fields from their father will not abide looking at others with thirty ...

In 43 Galen derides the many people he sees who remain unsatisfied with what they have, who continually crave more and consider themselves "poor" relative to others who own more. His conclusion – that people should not grieve over material losses as long as they are left with *something* – is not especially remarkable, but the detail he adds in 45 is revealing and will be relevant when we return below to his specific attitude about the loss of his books:

> **44.** But if someone is not looking all the time at the number of fields that someone else has but at what is enough for his own outgoings, he will bear unconcernedly the loss of what is superfluous. **45.** But if someone with just a single field loses that, he will be completely impoverished, *and so will be justifiably* (εἰκότως) *grieved.*

Galen concludes, then, at 46: "So it was no great thing for me not to be grieved at all at the loss of my property, for what was left was much more than sufficient."[6] As recent commentators have pointed out, this advice is neither new nor exceptional. The story of Aristippus was well known and often adduced to make a similar point,[7] but he acknowledges that there is such a thing as "justifiable grief" if the loss is overwhelming and leaves one utterly destitute.

Galen adds further detail, with historical color, to his qualification of ἀλυπία. His remarks at 54–55 make it clear that living under Commodus was bound to make anyone as highly placed as Galen anxious about his safety:

> **54.** You yourself ... are convinced that the crimes committed by Commodus in a few years are worse than any in the whole of recorded history. So when I saw all of these things happening daily, I schooled my imagination to prepare for the total loss of everything that I had. **55.** As well as being moved to pity myself, I also expected to be sent to a desert island, like other innocent victims. When someone expected to be sent to a desert island with the total loss of everything he had, he prepared himself to bear it, and, if he lost only a part, he was not going to be distressed since he was not deprived of the rest.

---

[5] See Diog. Laert. 2.65–87. Cf. Françoise Caujolle-Zaslawsky, "Aristote de Cyrène," *Dictionnaire des philosophes antiques* 1:370–5 and Boudon-Millot and Jouanna, *Galien:* Ne pas se chagriner, 115–6.

[6] Or reading the sentence, as Boudon-Millot and Jouanna, as a question: "Eh bien donc, pour moi en quoi est-ce une grande affaire si je n'ai absolument pas été affligé par la perte de mes biens?" See further, Boudon-Millot and Jouanna, *Galien:* Ne pas se chagriner, 128.

[7] See Boudon-Millot and Jouanna, *Galien:* Ne pas se chagriner, 118–9, also for the versions of the story in the Arabic tradition.

It is interesting and significant that Galen does not take a fully Stoic view that a truly wise man can rise entirely above pain and suffering, nor does he advocate the pursuit of complete Epicurean ἀταραξία (68), a state in which one would feel *completely* undisturbed by one's troubles or the state of affairs more generally.[8] In this little vignette, we see Galen trying to prepare for the worst, literally conjuring up and "exercising" (ἐγύμνασα) his mind with images (φαντασίας) of ultimate disaster (ἀπώλειαν), i.e., the loss of *all* property and exile. Galen mentioned in 52 that this method of training for hard times derived from a speech of Theseus in a play by Euripides (fr. 814 Mette = fr. 964 Nauck). Theseus' specific claim in this passage, however, seems to be a method more to blunt the shock of unanticipated misfortune than an actual remedy against ἀλυπία. As he says, he tries to imagine every possible calamity for himself so that if any such things should ever happen "it might not gnaw (δάκῃ) at my soul because it was a novel arrival." The emphasis here, in other words, is on the *novelty* of such misfortune, not the distress itself. By always imagining disasters, when they occur one may bear the distress better, but not necessarily feel no pain.

It is not entirely clear how carefully Galen was reading the fragment of Euripides on this point, but his own approach to preparing for disaster likewise does not seem to offer an entirely straightforward path towards ἀλυπία. We might well ask, for example, when would be the moment in this scenario when one could actually claim to be "without distress?" If the emperor had actually confiscated all his goods and banished him to a desert island, Galen as much as admits that he would have been irremediably distressed. Because he has been training himself to be acutely aware that such a fate *might* at any time await him, he could withstand plenty of other hardship – short of complete exile and impoverishment – without true distress. Like Euripides' Thesesus, Galen too would have avoided the *shock* of sudden misfortune thanks to his mental training, but he does not envision himself as ever avoiding the grief that would accompany total destitution and deprivation. One also wonders what his frame of mind would have been all the while he was training himself to prepare for the worst. The fear and anxiety he implies he felt throughout Commodus' reign, even while in full possession of his property and freedoms, certainly seems to be a form of psychological λύπη, and he implies, too, that none of this training would prepare him to be ἄλυπος if the unthinkable actually did happen to him. Exile under Commodus, in short, would elicit the sort of "justifiable" or "appropriate" λύπη that he ascribes in section 45 to the man who loses the sole field he owned.

Indeed, in the subsequent sections, 58–68, Galen seems to be struggling to come to terms in his own mind with what he even means by ἀλυπία. He endorses

---

[8] See Boudon-Millot and Jouanna, *Galien: Ne pas se chagriner*, 55; Nutton, "Avoiding Distress," 95 n. 108.

the example of his father,[9] who espoused a life of μετριοπάθεια rather than of Stoic ἀπάθεια or Epicurean ἀταραξία (62):

> **62.** ... But he never praised those who despise such pleasures [sex, in this example] and who are simply satisfied that their soul is never pained or distressed, proclaiming that the good was of its own nature something bigger and better than this, not confined to being merely free from pain and distress.

As he sums up at 68, "Some people consider that remaining undisturbed is something good, although I know that neither I nor any other human being nor any animal supports this."[10] If being free from ἄλγος, λύπη, and ὄχλησις is not to be thought of as something good, or at least not a state of mind one should necessarily always be striving for in life, it is not entirely clear why Galen would be quite so proud of proclaiming himself utterly unaffected by the loss of his property in the fire. It would be one thing if he simply wanted to make the point that one should always keep one's misfortune in proper perspective and never let one's grief become debilitating. So much of the rhetoric of the treatise, however, especially in the early sections, is concerned to portray Galen as almost preternaturally free from *any* kind of mental suffering, and all the qualifications of ἀλυπία we find in the middle sections only serve to confuse matters. Does his strong endorsement of ἀλυπία, for example, not bring him closer to the Epicurean life he is trying also to argue against?[11]

There are signs throughout *Ind.* that the work was written informally and somewhat hastily,[12] and it is not difficult to form the impression that Galen was asking himself some of these questions as he was writing it. This may well account for the fact that at 69–70, he realizes he needs to distance himself from the position that "none of the wise will ever suffer distress." At 71–72, he lays his cards on the table on this matter, offering what turns out to be a position far

---

[9] Galen speaks at length of his father's influence on him, and with equal admiration, at *Aff. Dig.* 3 (K 5.9 = *CMG* 5.4.1.1 8.3–7). See Ralph M. Rosen, "Galen, Satire and the Compulsion to Instruct," in *Hippocrates and Medical Education* (ed. M. Horstmanshoff; Leiden: Brill, 2010), 338–9; Boudon-Millot and Jouanna, *Galien:* Ne pas se chagriner, 149–52, and Nutton, "Avoiding Distress," 63–64.

[10] An argument against Epicurean ἀοχλησία ("freedom from aggravation"). As he concludes the sentence: "... we have established this in several of our tracts, especially in *Against* (or *On*) *Epicurus*." See Boudon-Millot and Jouanna, *Galien:* Ne pas se chagriner, 162–5.

[11] Nutton, "Avoiding Distress," 95 n. 108, explains Galen's point: "Although the text is again unclear, Galen appears to argue that such an untroubled life advocated by the Epicureans can be achieved only by inaction, yet activity is a natural and essential part of all human and animal life, and hence the Epicurean position is a denial of what makes life life." But Galen seems not quite able to practice fully what he preaches here; see further below.

[12] He repeats in 77, for example, the quotation from Euripides he had just quoted in 52. See Alessandro Lami, "Il nuovo Galeno e il fr. 964 di Euripide," *Galenos: Rivista di filologia dei testi medici antichi* 3 (2009): 11–19. Following Lami, Nutton, "Avoiding Distress," n. 114, sees the repetition "as a sign of the relative informality and hurried composition of this tract."

more qualified than one might have expected from the opening sections, with all their bravado about Galen's legendary display of ἀλυπία after the great fire:

> **71.** ... I do not care about the loss of possessions without quite being deprived of them all and sent to a desert island, or of [about?] bodily pain without quite making light of being placed in the bull of Phalaris. **72.** What will distress me is the ruination of my homeland, or a friend being punished by a tyrant, and other similar things, and I pray to the gods that none of this should ever happen to me. So since nothing of this sort has happened to me until now, you have thus seen never seen me distressed.

This is, of course, a variation on the point he was making a few sections earlier when he mentioned the fear that he would suffer just such a fate under Commodus. Once again, we can see that Galen does have his limits when it comes both to the loss of his possessions and his ability to endure physical pain, and he acknowledges that any normal human being would be highly distressed by either of the misfortunes he mentions in the passage above. Galen adduces these examples as extremes, as if to show that, despite his advocacy of ἀλυπία, he is realistic enough to concede that no sane person could be burned alive in a bronze bull and be happy about it. One must be reasonable, in the end, about what one can expect from training oneself to become ἄλυπος.

The conclusion to be drawn from this section, then, is that, despite Galen's claim throughout the work, and stated succinctly at 65, that he simply did not put much value in "leisure, instruments, drugs, books, reputation and riches" (μικρὰ πάντα) or take them seriously (<πῶς ἂν> ἄξια σπουδῆς ὑπολάβοιμι), he nevertheless felt that they are necessary, at least in some measure, for a worthy and happy life, and that one would be justified in feeling distress without access to *any* of them. The ἀλυπία he claims to have maintained earlier in his life in the face of similarly profound losses is consistent with this position, since he seems not in either case to have been left destitute. He mentions in section 1 the loss of "nearly all his slaves" during an attack of plague at Rome, as well as "three or four other times" when he had suffered similar losses. In each case, one infers that he could always replace what he lost easily enough, by acquiring new slaves or buying new property with resources he still had.

We might expect, therefore, that Galen would display the same attitude specifically towards the loss of his books, since these too are just another form of property and, as such, are easily replaceable. Indeed, he routinely includes his books in his list of material things to which he has avoided becoming too attached (e.g., sections 10, 50, 65). One wonders, however, just how honest Galen is in his account of how he responded to the loss of his books, especially given how often in the work he calls attention to just how amazing it was that he was able to avoid a response of despair. Moreover, the more detail Galen offers about the nature of the books he lost – not only his library of works by others, but many works in his own hand, whether copies of his published works or of unpublished works in progress – the more it becomes clear that in his mind, these books do *not* belong in the same category of replaceable material possessions as slaves or even rare drugs. It would have been true that he had many other books that were not lost in the fire (we learn from 20–23 that he kept some books at his house in Campania and presumably he had some at his residence in Rome), and at least some of the volumes he lost in the fire he could presumably just buy again. There is little doubt that he had the money to do so, and this makes it easy enough for him to keep his losses in perspective, as he recommends to his reader.

Many of the books, however, that Galen showcases among his losses could not, in fact, be replaced for any amount of money, and this issue becomes a veritable *leitmotif* of the entire work. The very point of the treatise, in fact, seems to be to highlight exactly *how great* these losses were, and how any normal person would find them depressing. Galen *claims* that he avoided feeling upset at his material losses and that his losses were so profound that his ἀλυπία constituted a "prime display of nobility and something approaching magnanimity":

> **50.** ... but not to be distressed at the loss of all my drugs, *all my books, and, besides, the recipes of major drugs, as well as the writings on them I had prepared for publication along with many other treatises*, any one of which by itself would have shown the great efforts I have put in gladly throughout my life, that is already a prime display of nobility and something approaching magnanimity (μεγαλοψυχία).[13]

We seem to have here a version of what a modern psychotherapist might call "transference": he tells the story of his incredible losses to a friend as an example of his own self-control, but his point can only be made when his friend is made to experience vicariously the true depth of his own loss. Galen's account suggests with little doubt that his losses *were* in fact quite distressing to him. What else could he mean when at 12 he uses the word δεινότατον to describe the total destruction of the libraries on the Palatine, and the loss of unique manuscripts, and even, perhaps, autograph copies? Sections 12–14, in fact, present a litany of reasons why the loss of his books was truly monumental (with Galen's rhetoric of catastrophe indicated in italics):

> **12.** ... and you haven't even realized that the *most terrible thing* (δεινότατον) about the loss of the books is that there's *no hope* (μηδὲ ἐλπίδα) left for any copies, since all the Palatine libraries were destroyed by fire on that day. **13.** For there is *no possibility of finding* not only the rarities and *works that were available nowhere else* (οὔτε οὖν ὅσα σπάνια καὶ ἀλ(λ)αχόθι μηδαμόθεν κείμενα δυνατόν ἐστιν εὑρεῖν), but also copies of common works that were prized because of the precision of their text, like those of Callinus, Atticus, Peducaeus and even Aristarchus, including the two Homers, and the Plato of Panaetius and many others of that sort; within these writings were preserved things written by or copied for the individuals whose name they bore. There were also many autograph copies of ancient grammarians, orators, doctors and philosophers.

---

[13] A difficult sentence; see Boudon-Millot and Jouanna, *Galien: Ne pas se chagriner*, 135, for detailed syntactic analysis of the Greek. On the Stoic background to Galen's use of the term "magnanimity" (μεγαλοψυχία) here, see Nutton, "Avoiding Distress," 62.

14. *Besides these books, so numerous and so important, I also lost on that day* (ἐπὶ τούτοις οὖν τοιούτοις καὶ τοσούτοις ἀπώλεσα κατὰ τὴν αὐτὴν ἡμέραν ὅσα ...) copies of many books that had been unclear as a result of scribal mistakes, but which after correction I had had transcribed afresh to provide almost a new edition.

Perhaps Galen is just saying here that he was at first distressed after the fire, as anyone would have been, but then quickly applied his philosophical training in ἀλυπία to overcome his distress.[14] But the fact still remains that in order to make his point most forcefully, he needs to convince his addressee (and his readers) that the loss of his books, in particular, was, as we might say, "really, really bad," a true calamity. If one could truly avoid distress over such a loss, it would indeed be a mark of "nobility" and "magnanimity," perhaps, but the rhetoric Galen uses for describing the loss is so strong that one is tempted to conclude that his claims to imperturbability are somewhat disingenuous to say the least.

Such disingenuousness seems especially evident in his decision to describe at length the loss of his grammatical works on Attic Greek (especially those on Old Comedy) and of his collection of pharmacological recipes. Consider, for example, how he introduces and sums up these sections. If Galen himself can claim to be unruffled by the total loss of his work on Old Comedy, his addressee, as Galen notes almost triumphantly, probably could not:

20. *You will perhaps find particularly distressing* (ἴσως δέ ⟨σ⟩ε λυπ(ήσ)ει...) the fate of my work on words in Attic Greek and everyday language, which, as you know, was in two parts, one drawn from Old Comedy, the other from prose-writers. But, by chance, copies of the second part had already been transported to Campania, and had things in Rome been burnt two months later, we would have already sent copies of all of our works to Campania.

Does Galen actually want his friend *not* to be distressed at the thought of such losses, and instead to share in Galen's equanimity as he conjures up in his mind the image of so many scrolls turned to ashes? This seems rhetorically unlikely, since that would minimize the gravity of the losses Galen is trying to impress on his addressee, and that, in turn, would remove the fireworks from his psychological feat of ἀλυπία. The long and detailed description of his lost works on Old Comedy at 20–30 seems directed at getting his friends to feel the maximum amount of vicarious pain, so that we all end up amazed at Galen's final flourish at the very end of 30 – a short four-word sentence: "But none of this distressed me" (αλλ' οὐδὲ ταῦτα ἐλύπησαν).

---

[14] "His own preference ... is for an Platonic-Aristotelian emphasis on moderating one's emotions through a combination of natural talent, habituation and education" [Nutton, "Avoiding Distress," 63]. Galen glosses over in his account whether at *any* point after he first heard the news of his losses he felt any distress. I does not seem pedantic to wonder whether at first he felt profound distress at the news, but then *applied* the full force of his training and self-help method to expunge that distress, or whether he had so calibrated his behavior from years of ἄσκησις that he would claim simply never to have felt any distress.

As if this were not enough to convince his readers *both* of just how depressing his losses really were *and* how astounding it was that he was able to remain unaffected by them, he continues – with rhetoric reminiscent of a circus barker – with an attempt to outdo his narrative about the grammatical works with an even more plaintive description of his recipe-books:

> **31.** *What then, you will say, is there even worse than* all that I have just described that could cause distress (τί ποτε οὖν, φήσεις, ἔτι μεῖζον ἁπάντων τῶν εἰρημένων ἐστὶν ὃ λυπεῖν ⟨ἂν⟩ δύναιτο)? Well, I shall tell you. I was convinced that I had in my possession more remarkable drug recipes than anyone in the whole of the Roman world, some put in my way by chance, others that I had added myself.

There follows in the following sentences (32–37) a remarkably detailed narrative of the various sources of his recipe collection: the rich collector of recipes "back home" who had carefully assembled his recipes in "two folded parchment volumes" which ended up in Galen's hands; his friend and schoolmate Teuthras who left his own vast collection of recipes (a collection he had himself obtained from a doctor named Eumenes) to Galen after his death of plague at Rome. All of these works were destroyed in the fire as well, a loss which Galen has just called "even worse" (μεῖζον ἁπάντων τῶν εἰρημένων ... ὃ λυπεῖν ⟨ἂν⟩ δύναιτο) than the loss of his works on Old Comedy:

> **37.** Not only were all these parchments destroyed in the fire – and I still thought this was no great loss – but so also was my treatise on the composition of drugs, which I had prepared with great precision and where I described how one might make up the most important drugs.

By now Galen has developed his narrative of calamity with such insistence that his claim here that he "still thought this was no great loss" begins to strain credulity. Galen's exact phrasing, καὶ γὰρ καὶ τοῦτο ἔτι μικρὸν ἐνόμιζον ("and even this too I thought was a small thing"), in fact, seems to contradict the very point he has been trying to make, namely that precisely *because* the loss of these books was in fact such a *huge* thing, his claim to be able to transcend the distress such a loss would have on a normal person is all the more wondrous. It may be unfair to accuse Galen here of actually dissembling about his real emotional state after the fire, but the amount of rhetorical energy he puts into the section about his books does suggest that he remained in at least some conflict about the trauma of their loss, despite whatever success he had in minimizing its effect on his state of mind.

Indeed, the striking amount of detail Galen lavishes on his description of his works on Old Comedy and Attic colloquial language further supports the idea that the loss of these scrolls was particularly momentous for him. Why, to put it simply, did Galen feel compelled to go on at such length about a body of work that has, at first glance at least, no obvious connection to his medical or philosophical concerns? He brings up these works at the beginning of 20, as we saw, as an example of losses that ought to impress (or perhaps more accurately, depress) his addressee, so it is worth considering what it was exactly about this particular body of work that Galen found significant enough to dilate on at such length. This is not the first time Galen has told us of his work on Greek comedy – he mentions them as well in his work, *De libris propriis*, at the very end in a brief section that lists his grammatical works (K 19.48 = BM 173.5–15 [section 20]), where he refers to "three volumes on *Everyday Terms* (ὀνόματα) *in Eupolis*; five on *Everyday Terms in Aristophanes*; two on *Everyday Terms in Cratinus*; one of *Examples of Words Specific to the Writers of Comedy*; *Whether Reading Ancient Comedy is Useful for Students* ..." Boudon-Millot notes on this passage that Galen's interest in Attic comedy should come as no surprise, given the fact that he often uses comic vocabulary throughout his writings to explain contemporary usage.[15] *De indolentia*, however, offers considerably more detail about these non-medical works, and suggests that Galen was idiosyncratically invested in them.

When the fire broke out, Galen was away from Rome, staying in Campania (where he may have kept a country estate) and he writes to his friend in sections 20–23 (quoted above) how he had intended to have all his books copied and sent there. Only the copies of his books on Attic prose (48 of them) made it out in time, and the ones on Old Comedy were completely destroyed:

> **23.** ... But Fate ambushed me, by destroying, along with many other of my books, most especially my work on the vocabulary of the entire Old Comedy, **24a** of which, as you know, Didymus had already made a study, both the everyday words and those requiring explanation, in fifty books, of which I made an epitome in 6,000 lines.

The rest of the passage offers an unusually detailed defense of the utility of this kind of philology particularly for medical research:

> **24b.** Such a procedure seemed to be of some value for orators and grammarians, or in general for anyone who might want to use an Attic idiom, **25.** or words that have a significant bearing on practicalities (πράγματα χρήσιμα), like the question that arose recently in Rome when a respected doctor announced that groats (χόνδρος) were not yet in use in the time of Hippocrates, and that that was why in *Regimen in acute diseases* he advocated barley gruel (πτισάνη) over all other cereal foodstuffs; for if groats (χόνδρος) had been known to the Greeks, he would not have chosen anything else in preference. **26.** But groats (χόνδρος) are mentioned particularly in *Regimen for health*, which some ascribe to him but others to Philistion or Ariston, both very early doctors, and particularly in the writers of Old Comedy. Words like "informer's-haircut" (ἀβυδοκόμης) or "leek sauce" (ἀβυρτάκη) <and>[16] **27.** whatever else that was unclear

---

[15] Véronique Boudon-Millot, *Galien: Introduction générale*. Sur l'ordre de ses propres livres. Sur ses propres livres. Que l'excellent médecin est aussi philosophe (Budé; Paris: Les Belles Lettres, 2007), 233. See also Heinrich von Staden, "Gattung und Gedächtnis: Galen über Wahrheit und Lehrdichtung," in *Gattungen wissenschaftlicher Literatur in der Antike* (ed. W. Kullmann, J. Althoff, and M. Asper; Tübingen: Gunter Narr, 1998), 81–82.

[16] Nutton departs here from Boudon-Millot and Jouanna, who had emended the confusing Greek to list two comic poets, Aristomenes and Aristophanes (discussion at Boudon-Millot

to the audience were defined in our treatise – and was anticipated nicely in Didymus' exposition – as follows: emmer, chick peas, vetch, groats and the other cereals, vegetables and late-summer fruits, wines made from the marc of grapes, with or without the addition of water, bushes, fruits, plants, animals, instruments, equipment, tools, and everything else in daily life, and their names.

Galen's interest in comparative philology of this sort is not out of line with intellectual preferences of his day,[17] but the particular philological detail in this passage seems at first a curious rhetorical strategy for someone trying to persuade his readers how momentous the loss of his books was. The last sentence (27), in fact, may even have been written with a touch of comedy itself, alluding, perhaps, to the long lists foods and other items of the daily life that we often find in poets of Old Comedy.[18] Why, we might ask, did Galen feel it was so important in this passage to offer such a fine-grained explanation of his philological work on comic poets? The answer becomes clearer when we understand that this passage, which might seem to us slightly pedantic, reflects several of Galen's beliefs about how good science is to be accomplished. These are methodological concerns that begin with the use of language in general, and ramify to specific questions of history, textual authority and logic. In the case of Galen's word-lists of Attic comic colloquialisms, the example he offers of the utility of philological pursuits is modest, but there were larger issues at stake for him, and they had nothing to do with the Atticizing trends so fashionable with other intellectuals of his age.[19]

As the passage makes clear, Galen wants to show that a good knowledge of contemporary fifth-century Attic speech can settle questions about the authenticity of Hippocratic texts. Since Hippocrates was Galen's most revered medical authority, establishing a genuine Hippocratic provenance of his texts was no slight matter. In the anecdote Galen relates in the passage above, he evidently alludes to a Roman doctor's claim that the Hippocratic *De victus ratione* (*Regimen*) was inauthentic because it used a term that was not known to Greeks in Hippocrates' time (χόνδρος, groats).[20] Galen "disproves" his claim by

---

and Jouanna, *Galien:* Ne pas se chagriner, 87–88). Nutton endorses the suggestion of Ioannis Polemis, "ΔΙΟΡΘΩΤΙΚΑ ΣΤΟ ΠΕΡΙ ΑΛΥΠΙΑΣ ΤΟΥ ΓΑΛΗΝΟΥ," Επιστημονική Επετηρίς της φιλοσοφικής σχολής του Πανεπιστημίου Αθηνών 43 (2011/12): 3–4, that the manuscript preserved two unusual Greek words beginning with alpha, here mentioned by Galen as the kind of lemmata he would have included in his lexicographical works. See Nutton, "Avoiding Distress," 86 n. 57.

[17] von Staden, "Gattung und Gedächtnis," esp. 67–78.

[18] See John Wilkins, *The Boastful Chef: The Discourse of Food in Ancient Greek Comedy* (Oxford: Oxford University Press, 2000), 45–7, 85.

[19] On Galen's disdain for the stylistic fetishes of many intellectuals of the Second Sophistic period, see Ben Morison, "Language," in *The Cambridge Companion to Galen* (ed. R. J. Hankinson; Cambridge: Cambridge University Press, 2008), 144–5.

[20] More or less the same story is told by Galen in his commentary, *In Hippocratis de Acutorum Morborum Victu* (Georg Helmreich, *In Hippocratis De victu acutorum commentaria IV*

noting that the term can be found in Old Comedy, or at least, as we might say, his opponent's *linguistic* argument for spuriousness is repudiated by evidence from other contemporary texts. Arguments such as this are small, but for Galen, essential, contributions to the larger goal of ἀκρίβεια – the scientific precision that he continually champions throughout his writings – and much of the time his interest in ἀκρίβεια begins with language and its ability to communicate and assess logical argument.[21] We have the titles of 21 treatises he wrote on linguistic topics alone, and although nearly all are lost, these, along with the evidence of other treatises, show his deep commitment to linguistics as foundational for all other scientific and philosophical discussion. Galen's linguistics was, however, always practical: he valued clarity of expression over style and so had no embarrassment about using common or colloquial language – language of the polis, πολιτικός) – if it served the purpose of communicating clearly to other doctors, their patients or readers of his treatises.

Something of Galen's unpretentious attitude towards everyday speech can be seen in a comment he makes about Aristophanes in the treatise *De nominibus medicis* (which exists only in an Arabic translation),[22] where he noted that Aristophanes' vocabulary had to be accessible to the wider public in order for his plays to have been successful in the theater. It follows, then, that if Aristophanic words can also be found in Hippocrates, such words may appear to us to be obscure, but were actually common, since comic poets would not have been able to get away with using obscure words. Further, if they were ordinary words in comedy, then their meaning can be straightforwardly ascertained, and this, in turn, can illuminate Hippocratic usage. The anecdote from *Ind.* shows just how important the argument from "ordinariness" was for Galen: it was useful not only for demystifying fifth-century medical terminology, but also for deter-

---

[*CMG* 5.9.1; Leipzig and Berlin: Teubner, 1914], 134–5). See Véronique Boudon-Millot, "Un traité perdu de Galien miraculeusement retrouvé, *Le Sur l'inutilité de se chagriner*: texte grec et traduction française," in *La science médicale antique. Nouveaux regards. Études réunies en l'honneur de J. Jouanna* (ed. V. Boudon-Millot, A. Guardasole, and C. Magdelaine; Paris: Beauchesne, 2008), 110 n. 264, and further discussion at Boudon-Millot and Jouanna, *Galien: Ne pas se chagriner*, 86. For some reason Galen here refers to *Regimen in Health* when he seems to mean just *Regimen*. See Nutton, "Avoiding Distress, 86 n. 56.

[21] From the extensive bibliography on Galen's logical method and scientific enterprise, see, e.g., R. J. Hankinson, "Galen on the foundations of science," in *Galeno: Obra, Pensamento e Influencia* (ed. J. A. López Féres; Madrid: Universidad Nacional de Educacion a Distancia 1991), 15–29; R. J. Hankinson, "Galen's philosophical eclecticism," *ANRW* 36.5: 3571–89, and R. J. Hankinson, "Galen's concept of scientific progress," in *ANRW* 37.2: 1775–89; also, in general, von Staden, "Gattung und Gedächtnis." Galen sums up his commitment to his logical method with customary passion in *Pecc.Dig.* 2 (K 5.62 = De Boer 43.12–44.20 = Magnaldi 70), where he describes the rigorous process for the "one who wants to be free of error" that will ultimately lead him to the questions of happiness.

[22] *Med.Nam.* 31–32 (Max Meyerhof and Joseph Schacht, *Galen:* Über die medizinischen Namen, *Arabisch und Deutsch* [Berlin: Walter de Gruyter, 1931]); see Nutton, "Avoiding Distress," 84 n. 45.

mining the authenticity of Hippocratic treatises in cases where contemporary linguistic usage might settle the matter. For Galen, then, the better we understand the language of Attic comedy, the closer we can get to talking like a Greek of Hippocrates' era, and so the better we can understand the master himself. What is so interesting about this formulation is what it says about Galen's conceptualization of Hippocratic style. In aligning it explicitly with a popular genre such as Old Comedy, one that tries to reach an entire community, not just an educated or literate élite, Galen acknowledges, by implication in any case, that Hippocrates too was a populist of sorts insofar as his writings were supposed to spread medical knowledge for the good of all humankind. This seems to be what Galen has in mind when at *De placitis Hippocratis et Platonis* 9.5.6 (K 5.763), he says that the truly great doctors (and he includes Hippocrates in his list) treat people out of a sense of φιλανθρωπία, not for profit or fame.

> Some practice the medical art for monetary gain, some because of exemptions granted them by the laws, some from *love of their fellow men* (διὰ φιλανθρωπίαν), others again for the fame and honor that attend the profession. Accordingly, as artisans of health they will all share the name physicians, but insofar as they act with different ends in view, one will be called a *lover of mankind* (φιλάνθρωπος) another a lover of honor, another of fame, still another a money-maker. The goal of the physician qua physician is not fame or profit, as Menodotus the Empiric wrote; this is the goal for Menodotus, but not for Diocles, and not for Hippocrates and Empedocles either ... who treated men through *love of mankind* (διὰ φιλανθρωπίαν).[23]

Hippocratic *literary* style would, in turn, reflect the philanthropic style of his practice – unelevated, lucid, and therapeutically efficacious.

Since Galen's philological work on Old Comedy ultimately served to elucidate Hippocrates, the loss of these works meant a genuine setback for Galen's desire to improve, and extend the reach of, medical knowledge with more accurate Hippocratic texts. Brushing off such a setback as trivial and not worthy of mental distress hardly seems in keeping with the philanthropic self-image that Galen usually adopts for himself, and the more energy he devotes to describing these particular losses the more one is left with the feeling that he is in fact trying to make the opposite point, namely that this is a situation in which distress *is* called

---

[23] Phillip De Lacy, *Galen:* On the Doctrines of Hippocrates and Plato (3 vols.; *CMG* 5.4.1.2; Berlin: Akademie, 1980–4), 2.565. Galen is here tapping into a long ethico-philosophical trope of φιλανθρωπία as a mark of high-level virtue, which we can trace as far back as Aeschylus *PV* 11, and it can even be detected in the Hippocratic corpus. See, e.g., *Praec.* 6, "I encourage you *not to stray too far from your humanity*, but to keep an eye on whether your patient is financially well endowed or not ... For if *love of humanity* is present, there will also be love of the art (of medicine)" (παρακελεύομαι δὲ μὴ λίην **ἀπανθρωπίην** εἰσάγειν, ἀλλ' ἀποβλέπειν ἔς γε περιουσίην καὶ οὐσίην· ... ἢν γὰρ παρῇ **φιλανθρωπίη**, πάρεστι καὶ φιλοτεχνίη). See also the related remarks at Hippocratic *Praec.* 5, where the author contrasts a list of virtues associated with the wise doctor, beginning with ἀφιλαργυρίη (avoidance of monetary greed), with a considerable list of vices to be avoided.

for. The loss of the commentaries on Old Comedy may not be quite analogous to finding oneself inside the bull of Phalaris, which, as we noted earlier, Galen concedes would warrant true distress, but at the same time, since these scrolls were irreplaceable there was nothing to which Galen could point to soften the trauma of their loss as he could in the other examples he offers of material loss.[24] Galen would like his reader to believe him when he says that the loss of all these writings was not upsetting to him, but in singling out his works on Old Comedy for such detailed discussion, he more readily leaves the impression that it really *was*. His rhetorical strategy is transparent – the more profound he can make his losses seem, the more amazed will everyone be at his ability to remain emotionally unaffected by them. But clearly he wanted at least *someone* to feel distress at his losses or he would not have taken the trouble to persuade us, and his friend, how terrible they really were. Galen's readers can choose to believe him or not when claims to have transcended the trauma of losing his commentaries, but either way he has made his point that this is important work and that his particular contributions to it are as significant as his ability to endure their loss with equanimity.

It would be an overstatement, not to say idle speculation, to accuse Galen of dissembling about his "real" feelings in this treatise, but we have seen how effectively his rhetorical skills have conveyed several points that seem at times in conflict with one another, at least according to the internal logic of the treatise. A passage towards the end, however, may guide us to a proper understanding of the tone of these inconcinnities. Within the section 58–68 (see above p. 162–63), in which Galen notes his father's influence on his own moral and intellectual formation ("every time I remember him, I feel my soul improved"), with the main point (61) that, like his father, he too "despised human affairs as of little worth," Galen makes the following curious remark:

67. If you peruse what I have written about each of these things [sc. "leisure, instruments, drugs, books, reputation and riches" in 65], you will discover that I have not just baldly declared my opinion about each of these trivial matters but provided a logical proof. And, by God, I did *not do this with zealous enthusiasm* (μετὰ σπουδῆς) *or as something tremendous, but simply as a sort of hobby* (ἐν παιδιᾶς μο(ίρᾳ)).

What exactly does Galen mean when he says that he did not write *Ind.* μετὰ σπουδῆς, but rather ἐν παιδιᾶς μο(ίρᾳ)? Nutton's translation suggests that Galen wanted to avoid being too rigid or doctrinaire in his repudiation of human affairs and material things, and that his advice in the treatise is supposed to be read with a sense of play and without too much systematic reflection. Boudon-Millot and Jouanna's translation implies an even stronger contrast between the

---

[24] Of course, it would have been possible for Galen to attempt to rewrite the unique texts that were lost, but does not entertain the idea and does not offer it as a source of consolation. It could well be that avoided the idea entirely in the work because doing so would have muted the rhetorical advantage he gained from stressing the irreplaceability of the texts.

serious and playful: "Mais, par les dieux, ce *n'est pas avec sérieux* ni comme si j'accomplissais une grande chose que je les ai composés, mais *en manière de divertissement.*"[25] Boudon-Millot and Jouanna explain that the contrast is intended to reflect the tone of the treatise and serves as a good illustration of his "détachement devant les choses humaines qu'il considère comme petites."[26] It is as if Galen had anticipated someone asking him why, if he cared so little about all his losses, he composed the treatise in the first place. Again, Galen seems caught in a bit of a logical bind: he wants to brush off his losses as trivial, but he also felt inspired to write an elaborate treatise about them. If he cannot claim that his losses were worthy of a "serious" work, he is left to explain *Ind.* as an exercise in "playfulness."[27]

Scholars have generally assumed that in conceptualizing the work as a "form of play" he means that it is serio-comic in a Socratic sense,[28] delivering serious content through playful literary forms. Among the many literary devices we associate with Socratic play, of course, is irony, and it seems likely that Galen wants his readers to realize that much about the tone of this work is ironic in exactly this sense. Like Socrates, who was famous for making claims that often strained credulity in the service of a philosophical position, Galen here presents his addressee, first with the claim that he felt no distress at his losses in the fire (presented as practically an ἀδύνατον in the eyes of most people, given the amount of property he lost), then with example after example of why no normal person *ought* to be free from distress in such circumstances. The fact that Galen manages to write calmly and lightly about such trauma, on the one hand, is certainly testimony to his ability to attain some measure of ἀλυπία. But the detailed litany of his specific losses, along with his commentary about exactly how significant they were both for himself and for all humanity, become more than slightly comic and ironic in the face of his persistent counter-claims to mental calmness. This is the playful aspect of the treatise that Galen seems to be referring to in 67, and it is here, I would argue, where the brilliance of his rhetorical strategy really shines. For in the end, the reader may admire well enough Galen's psychological feat of ἀλυπία, but the real force of the work lies in the narrative of his losses, their extent and gravity. Galen thus spotlights not only aspects of his moral character, but at the same time, his equally admirable achievements as polymath, philologist and humanitarian.[29]

---

[25] Boudon-Millot and Jouanna, *Galien:* Ne pas se chagriner, 21.

[26] Boudon-Millot and Jouanna, *Galien:* Ne pas se chagriner, 161.

[27] The phrase ἐν παιδιᾶς μο(ίρᾳ) seems to mean something like "in the service of play"; see Boudon-Millot and Jouanna, *Galien:* Ne pas se chagriner, 161.

[28] As Ivan Garofalo and Alessandro Lami, in their edition of the text, *Galeno: L'anima e il dolore.* De indolentia, De propriis placitis (Milan: Biblioteca Universale Rizzoli, 2012), 43. They translate the phrase ἀλλ' ἐν παιδιᾶς μο(ίρᾳ) here as "ma come per scherzo."

[29] I thank Vivian Nutton and P. N. Singer for their helpful suggestions on an earlier draft of this chapter.

CLARE K. ROTHSCHILD

The Apocolocyntosis of Commodus[1] or The Anti-imperial *Tendenz* of Galen's *De indolentia*

In A. D. 192, the last year of his reign, Commodus threw restraint to the winds and had the senate declare him a god. He assumed such titles as Conqueror of the World, Roman Hercules, and All-Surpasser and named the twelve months of the year after himself. Founding Rome anew, he gave it the name *Colonia Commodiana* and ordered the legions likewise to be called *Commodianae*. Before the year was out, on 31 December, he was murdered, his memory cursed.[2]

Introduction

Although Galen, like Seneca, lived and worked under the inarguably worst emperor of his age, and although he wrote more than almost any member of the literati in his generation and is not known for mincing words, he left very few comments on the political strife of his day. A measure of this silence is undoubtedly related to his role in the royal court as physician to the emperor. Yet fear and decorum do not completely dissolve the tension between Galen's

---

[1] The title Apocolocyntosis (Ἀποκολοκύντωσις, "Pumpkinification" a pun on ἀποθέωσις) comes from Cassius Dio who attributed authorship of a satirical text on the death of Claudius by this name to Seneca the Younger (61.35). Only much later was the work referred to by Cassius Dio identified as the anonymous "Ludus" text (i.e., *Ludus de Morte Claudii*). If Seneca wrote this work, it is his only satirical, political (i.e., anti-imperial) sketch. As W. H. D. Rouse observes in his LCL introduction (rev. ed. 1975), this authorship is impossible to prove or disprove, however, nothing in the text fits Cassius Dio's title very well. John Scott Campbell ("Pisspots and Pumpkins: Three Notes to the Apocolocyntosis," in *Veritatis Amicitiaeque Causa: Essays in Honor of Anna Lydia Motto and John R. Clark* [ed. S. N. Byrne and E. P. Cueva; Wauconda, IL: Bolchazy-Carducci, 1999], 41–52) argues that Latin readers of such a Greek title might have interpreted the title to mean "piss-" or "chamber-pot" and that this title *would* make sense in terms of the text. The text mocks a murdered yet deified emperor – true of both Claudius and Commodus (deified in 197), raising the question of Cassius Dio's interest in the work. On ancient satire, see Ralph M. Rosen, *Making Mockery: The Poetics of Ancient Satire* (Classical Culture and Society; Oxford: Oxford University Press, 2007).

[2] M. P. Speidel, "Commodus the God-Emperor and the Army," *JRS* (1993): 109–14 [here: 109].

documented loquacity and pomposity[3] on one hand, and his silence on the other.[4] It is particularly difficult to imagine how he kept quiet about the events leading up to Commodus' death on December 31st of the year 192 – events he lived through in the city of Rome.[5]

The newly discovered letter-treatise,[6] *De indolentia* catalogues Galen's catastrophic loss and reaction to the great fire in Rome in the winter of 191–2.[7] Commentators agree that the text was written shortly after the fire.[8] Commentators also agree that Galen remained in Rome during this time.[9] Nevertheless, the flurry of publications following its recent discovery accepts that *Ind.* is, with

---

[3] Vivian Nutton refers to Galen as a "bombast" in "The Patient's Choice: A New Treatise by Galen," *CQ* 40, no. 1 (1990): 236–57 [here: 249].

[4] Galen does not always name his contemporary opponents; see, e.g., Teun L. Tieleman, "Galen and the Stoics, or: the Art of Not Naming," in *Galen and the World of Knowledge* (ed. C. Gill, T. Whitmarsh, and J. Wilkins; Cambridge: Cambridge University Press, 2009), 282–99.

[5] General reference work consulted for this essay: Peter Garnsey, Dominic Rathbone, and Alan K. Bowman, eds., *The High Empire, A. D. 70–192* (*The Cambridge Ancient History* 11; 2d. ed.; Cambridge: Cambridge University Press, 2000).

[6] *De indolentia* is, technically speaking, a letter; however, like some of Seneca's letters, Galen gives it a title (however misleading this title might be concerning the first half of the treatise [discussed below]) as if it is a moral treatise intended for a wider readership. We have, therefore, selected to refer to it as both: a letter-treatise.

[7] The Greek text of *Ind.* is based on the following two critical editions: Véronique Boudon-Millot and Jacques Jouanna (with Antoine Pietrobelli), *Galien:* Ne pas se chagriner (Budé; Paris: Les Belles Lettres, 2010; hereafter: BMJ) and Paraskevi Kotzia and Panagiotis Sotiroudis, "Γαληνού περὶ ἀλυπίας," *Hellenica* 60 (2010): 63–148; (hereafter: KS). The ET (Clare K. Rothschild and Trevor W. Thompson) can be found on pp. 21–36 of the present volume; footnotes in the ET explain various textual decisions. For other references to the Galenic corpus, I have followed the abbreviation system in R. J. Hankinson, ed., *The Cambridge Companion to Galen* (Cambridge; Cambridge University Press, 2008). In addition, I include the edition of Karl Gottlieb Kühn as a baseline for all references, facilitating TLG access, which, then, directs to other editions. Unless otherwise designated, the English translations of other Greek and Latin texts were taken from LCL editions, modified (as I have indicated) if necessary.

The date of *Ind.* is based on the following factors. First, the text focuses on Galen's response – or lack thereof – to a fire in the city of Rome, attested by multiple sources (e.g., Cassius Dio 72 (73).24; Herodian 1.14.2–6) during the winter of 191–92 CE. The fire thus functions as a solid *terminus post quem*. Second, near the beginning of the treatise (2), Galen writes, "The very recent (νῦν ἔναγχος) event that happened to me – when all of my possessions deposited in the storehouses on the Sacred Way perished in the great fire." The sense of this passage is that Galen is writing not long after the fire. However, the phrase, ἥττω γεγονέναι κακὰ τοῖς ἀνθρώποις ὧν νῦν ἔπραξεν Κόμοδος ὀλίγοις ἔτεσιν (54) suggests that it was written sometime after the emperor's death on December 31, 192 CE. If it was composed during 193, then it may have been written under any one of five emperors (i.e., Pertinax, Didius Julianus, Pescennius Niger, Clodius Albinus, and Septimius Severus). One must allow for the fire to take place, messengers to get word to Galen's friend that despite the fire Galen is without distress, and the friend to write a letter to Galen inquiring how he has managed to maintain composure in the face of the loss of many of his most prized belongings (*Ind.* 1–3).

[8] See n. 7.

[9] See Vivian Nutton, *Ancient Medicine* (London: Routledge, 2004), 225, and Vivian Nutton, "The Chronology of Galen's Career," *CQ* 23, no. 1 (1973): 158–71.

the possible exception of one discreet comment, essentially silent on the exceptionally turbulent political events of its time.¹⁰

Prior to the discovery of *Ind.*, R. J. Hankinson postulated a few potential examples of political commentary in Galen's oeuvre.¹¹ He cites, for example, Galen's interest in the ineffectiveness of nurture on nature (*Quod animi mores corporis temperamenta sequuntur*; *QAM*),¹² suggesting a possible allusion to Commodus' failings vis-à-vis his father, Marcus Aurelius.¹³ He also notes Galen's reference to the slaves of Perennis who, Galen says, lack a decent upbringing, yet are able to resist, even under torture, the evil prefect of the Roman Praetorian Guard.¹⁴ And, Hankinson mentions Galen's expression of regret over the emperor's disposal of valuable imperial stores of *materia medica*.¹⁵

Maud Gleason, too, explores a political dimension of Galen's life and work. Gleason does not identify explicit political allusions in Galen's writings. Rather, she interprets his public anatomical displays as more than mere medical repar-

---

¹⁰ Véronique Boudon-Millot writes: "La façon dont Galien parle de Commode devenu empereur est une nouveauté assez exceptionnelle par rapport à ce que l'on connaissait: la condamnation de son règne court, prononcée avec un certaine grandiloquence par une comparaison entre le passé et la présent, est sans appel. Pour les historiens, ce nouveau témoignage est important. C'est le réquisitoire le plus ancien que l'on possède contre la tyrannie de Commode. Bien que Galien reste fort discret sur ses déboires à la cour impériale (voir déjà comm. à § 49,16, 4 sq.) une rupture a dû se produire dans les relations entre Commode et Galien" (commentary on § 55,18,7 in BMJ, 145).

¹¹ Commodus is seldom mentioned in the Galenic corpus. In *De libris propriis* 19.7, Galen comments on how he cared for Commodus as a child: διάθεσιν ἀποστήματος ἔχοντα διέσωσε, προσκυνήσας τὸν θεὸν καὶ περιμεῖναί με τὴν ἐπάνοδον αὐτοῦ κελεύσας – ἤλπιζε γὰρ ἐν τάχει κατορθώσειν τὸν πόλεμον – αὐτὸς μὲν ἐξῆλθε, <u>καταλιπὼν δὲ τὸν υἱὸν Κόμμοδον, παιδίον ἔτ' ὄντα κομιδῇ νέον</u>, ἐνετείλατο τοῖς τρέφουσιν αὐτὸ πειρᾶσθαι μὲν ὑγιαῖνον φυλάττειν, εἰ δέ ποτε νοσήσειε, καλεῖν ἐπὶ τὴν θεραπείαν ἐμέ. κατὰ τοῦτον οὖν τὸν χρόνον συνελεξάμην τε καὶ εἰς ἕξιν ἤγαγον μόνιμον ἅ τε παρὰ τῶν διδασκάλων ἐμεμαθήκειν ἅ τ' αὐτὸς εὑρήκειν, ἔτι τε ζητῶν ἔνια. Cf. *Ant.* 14.65.3 and *Hipp.Epid.* 17b.150.7. As for *On Moral Character*, Nutton does not think Galen would have made the comment about Perennis' slaves prior to Commodus' death (Richard Walzer, "New Light on Galen's Moral Philosophy," *CQ* 43, no. 1–2 [1949]: 82–96; Nutton, *Ancient Medicine*, 225–6). Hankinson, however, does not see this conclusion as necessary ("The Man and His Work," in *Cambridge Companion to Galen* [Cambridge: Cambridge University Press, 2008], 32 n. 76). It remains a question as to whether Galen's lost (partly biographical) work entitled *On Slander* (*De calumnia in quo et de vita sua*) contained political commentary; see, Hankinson, "The Man and His Work," 19.

¹² K 4.767–822; cf. Herodian 1.2.1.

¹³ Hankinson, "The Man and His Work," 21. Cf. *QAM* 4.816–8; *Prot.* 1.7.11–13. Galen defines "nurture" vis-à-vis training, diet, etc. in *QAM* 4.813.

¹⁴ Story preserved in the Arabic epitome of *On Moral Character*; see Hankinson, "The Man and His Work," 21.

¹⁵ *Ant.* 14.65.3: διαδεξαμένου δ' αὐτὸν Κομμόδου, μήτε τῆς θηριακῆς ἀντιδότου μήτε τοῦ κινναμώμου πεφροντικότος, ἐκείνου τε τοῦ δένδρου τὸ περιττὸν, ὅσον τ' ἄλλο μετὰ τοὺς Ἁδριανοῦ χρόνους ἐκομίσθη, διαπώλετο τὸ πᾶν, ὥστε τοῦ νῦν ὄντος ἡμῶν αὐτὸ κράτορος Σεβήρου, κελεύσαντος αὐτῷ κατὰ τὸν αὐτὸν τρόπον ὃν ἐσκεύαζον Ἀντωνίνῳ συνθεῖναι τὴν ἀντίδοτον, ἠναγκάσθην ἐκ τῶν ἐπὶ Τραϊανοῦ καὶ Ἀδριανοῦ κατατεθειμένων ἐκλέγειν, καί μοι σαφῶς ἀσθενέστερα γεγονέναι νῦν ἐφαίνετο.

tee among court physicians. According to Gleason, they were "truth-contests," availing themselves of "the complex discourse of power and privilege" in much the same way as Commodus exploited amphitheater entertainment.[16] While Galen certainly did not fear the contests, he did, he says, fear possible political repercussions over his victories in them. He was particularly afraid (he says) of a summons to serve the emperor based on his successes.[17] In *De praenotione ad Epigenem* 9, he explains how friends asked him whether they might inform Marcus Aurelius of his triumphs over the other court physicians. Galen begged them not to, he says, because he hoped to return home to Pergamum. He describes his getaway: "For I was scared that one of the very influential men (in Rome), or even the emperor himself, might discover my escape like a runaway slave and send a soldier to order my return to Rome."[18]

In addition to these observations by Hankinson and Gleason, we might also examine Galen's occasional explicit references to the emperors and the royal court.[19] He refers to Commodus six times in the extant corpus.[20] Three of the references concern Galen's charge to care for Commodus in his youth. None

---

[16] "Shock and Awe: The Performance Dimension of Galen's Anatomy Demonstrations," in *Galen and the World of Knowledge* (ed. C. Gill, T. Whitmarsh, and J. Wilkins; Cambridge: Cambridge University Press, 2009), 85–114, here: 113.

[17] E.g., *Praen.* 14.647–9 (*CMG* 5.8.1 8.20–9.4).

[18] ET: Nutton. Galen does, in the end, make it home, but is immediately summoned back to Rome. On return, however, he persuades Marcus Aurelius to allow him to stay in the city rather than join the military campaign; what is more, to avoid the city, he uses Commodus as an excuse, hiding in one imperial residence after the next. Galen also tells us that Marcus is away longer than originally anticipated, permitting Galen to write quite a number of tractates before returning to Rome (*Praen.* 14.647–51 = *CMG* 5.8.1 8.20–9.10).

[19] Cf. *Aff.Dig.* 3 (K 5.13 and 43–44); *Ant.* 14.65.3; *Comp.Med.Gen.* 13.435. The two passages from *Aff.Dig.* are the most relevant here: *Aff.Dig.* 3 (K 5.13): "If, then, someone of great power or wealth desires to become a good and upright man, he must first put those things from him – especially so today. For where will he now find a Diogenes, to tell the same truth irrespective of wealth and power – even to a king?" And: *Aff.Dig.* 8 (K 5.43–44): "I have not up to this point suffered such a severe financial loss as to have insufficient resources left to provide for my bodily health, nor any dishonor of the kind that I have seen many encounter when stripped of honour by the Senate" (ET: Peter Singer, *Galen: Selected Works* [Oxford World's Classics; Oxford, Oxford University Press, 1997], 105, 120–21).

[20] (1) *Praen.* 14.650 (*CMG* 5.8.1 9.5–8): Galen follows young Commodus from one imperial residence to the next, while Marcus is on a campaign away from Rome; (2) *Praen.* 14.657 (*CMG* 5.8.1 10.20–22): regarding Galen's cure of Commodus as child; (3) *Praen.* 14.661 (*CMG* 5.8.1 11.9–10): concerning treatment of young Commodus known to be extremely remarkable; (4) *Lib.Prop.* 19.18–19: on Marcus' leaving Galen in charge of young Commodus' medical care; (5) *Ant.* 14.65.3: on Commodus' discarding stores of theriac and cinnamon laid up since time of Hadrian; (6) *Hipp.Epid.* 17b.150.7: the identification of Marcus Aurelius as Commodus' father. For discussion favoring authenticity of *Ant.*, see Vivian Nutton, "Galen on Theriac: Problems of Authenticity," in *Galen on Pharmacology: Philosophy, History and Medicine* (ed. A. Debru; Leiden/New York: Brill, 1997), 133–51. *Ind.* is more explicitly critical about Commodus and written much closer to the time of his death. Discussing Severus' need of theriac, *Ant.* 14.1–209 was most likely composed after Commodus' death during the reign of Severus (Nutton, "Galen on Theriac," 148–9).

of the six references is critical of Commodus' regime, perhaps because all treat Commodus', younger days or were written prior to his more turbulent years. The discovery of *Ind.* adds three explicit references to this total of six (*Ind.* 49, 50a, 54–55). Although these references are currently being read as free from engagement in the power struggles of the political milieu of its day, this essay argues that they, together with six other remarks, convey obliquely disapproving political commentary. The essay concludes that, although the purpose of *Ind.* may be closely compared with Plutarch's *De tranquillitate animi* and Seneca's *Ep.* 91 as moral instruction,[21] it also possesses a certain satirical sharpness absent from these other works.[22] This bitter, even brittle, quality reveals Galen's participation in the anti-imperial literary-visual program of his day – a program characterized by disguise and double meaning, playful yet at every moment teetering on the brink of panic and despair.[23] Commodus created a political space at once impishly pugnacious and shockingly base. In this atmosphere, Galen took part in "moral-philosophical combat" selecting a highly defensive posture in both his public contests with doctors and in his preemptive approach to dolor, the latter being the primary focus of the instruction in *Ind.* This program included well-known statuary and numismatic evidence, as well as certain works of Lucian, Cassius Dio, Herodian, and the sources of the *Scriptores Historia Augusta*. The purpose of this program was to express political disdain while avoiding direct confrontation and punishment.[24]

Explicit Anti-Imperial Commentary: *Ind.* 49, 50a, 54–55

Three times in *Ind.*, Galen refers specifically to his life in the imperial court. The language is pointed: Galen is unhappy with the current situation.

---

[21] For at least two reasons, *Ind.* is not a reliable example of the consolation genre. First, the most common consolation *topoi* – calling upon every human being's ultimate mortality, the fragility of life in general, the meaninglessness of possessions, the fickleness of fortune, the futility of planning ahead, and others – are not present in this text. Second, in contrast, *Ind.* repeatedly affirms that, although not impervious to distress, Galen has *never* suffered from it. He has, therefore, never been consoled or in need of consolation. In fact, *Ind.* leaves unanswered how Galen *would* deal with distress *were* it to occur. See esp. Christopher Gill, *Naturalistic Psychology in Galen and Stoicism* (Oxford: Oxford University Press, 2011), 251; cf. also Gill's earlier essay: "Peace of Mind and Being Yourself: Panaetius to Plutarch," *ANRW* 2.36.7: 4599–640.

[22] We might even ask why Galen entitled it *Ind.* when only half treats moral issues. It is somewhat misleading as compared with other works treating consolation and related topics. Of nine examples in this essay (*Ind.* 49, 50a, 54–55, 74, 76, 71, 49, 23b, 6, 62), eight occur in the second half (i.e., *Ind.* 39–84) of the treatise.

[23] Dio (72 [73].19.5) writes: "After that the contests no longer resembled child's play, but were so serious that great numbers of men were killed." Similarly, SHA *Comm.* 10.3: *in iocis quoque perniciosus*. See esp. Maud Gleason, "Identity Theft: Doubles and Masquerades in Cassius Dio's Contemporary History," *Classical Antiquity* 30, no. 1 (2011): 33–86.

[24] Expression of disdain provided the release of pent up anger and disappointment.

(1) In *Ind.* 49, Galen states that he dislikes life at court, having made numerous attempts in the past to leave. The imagery is violent: although he repeatedly attempts to get away, "fate" drags him back.

> Hence, I have accomplished nothing significant by shunning the manifold loss of my possessions, just as I shun life in the imperial court. Not only did I not aspire to such a life back then, but in point of fact I held my ground against it – not once, not twice, but many times. Fate dragged me into it by force.

(2) In *Ind.* 50a, Galen comments that he has so many accusers in the court that he is nearly driven mad.

> No, not even this was a significant achievement: not to be driven utterly mad, despite the many accusers in the imperial court (οὐδὲ γὰρ οὐδὲ τοῦτο μέγα μὴ μανῆναι τὴν μανίαν πολλῶν τῶν ἐν αὐλῇ βασιλικῇ κατηγορησάντων).

Although Galen does not specify what he means by "madness" in this excerpt, elsewhere he describes it as a form of anger (*Aff.Dig.* 5 [K 5.22]), possessing an "overwhelming [negative] effect" (*QAM* 4.788) on the body.[25] According to *Aff.Dig.* 4–5 (K 5.16–24), Galen's avoidance of distress is matched only by his avoidance of anger. Both are to be eschewed, he says, because both provoke life-threatening illnesses (cf. *Ind.* 7).[26] Thus, we learn in this passage that in addition to the more obvious dangers (e.g., poison, exile, murder), court life poses the lethal risks of both distress (λύπη) and madness (μανία).[27]

(3) In *Ind.* 54–55, Galen places blame for the current, nasty, political situation squarely at the feet of the emperor. In all of recorded history, daily life has never been so corrupt as under Commodus. Such corruption, he says, demands extreme measures. One must (he says) imagine at every moment, the worst possible misfortune in order that, should such an event occur, its most deleterious aspect, surprise, will be removed. Galen writes:

> You are persuaded, I think, that in all of recorded history there have never been atrocities as severe as those you encountered recently during the brief reign of Commodus. Day after day, witnessing each of them, I trained my *phantasiai*[28] for the loss of everything I own, including the possibility of being cut off myself – just as others who

---

[25] ET: Singer, *Galen*, 109–10 and 160, respectively. Madness is not a metaphor here, but a medical condition – in this case, a self-diagnosis.

[26] *Ind.* 7: "You also learned that Philides the grammarian's books perished in the fire. Wasting away, he died as a result of discouragement and distress. What is more, for quite some time, people paraded around in black garments – thin and pale like mourners." Again, "discouragement" and "distress" offer Galen's medical identification of the cause of death.

[27] On the emotional confusion Commodus' frightening and erratic behavior caused, see Gleason, "Identity Theft," 50.

[28] The three occurrences of φαντασία in *Ind.* share two important similarities. First, all three speak of the "training" of the φαντασίαι – *Ind.* 54 and 74 using the verb, ἀσκεῖν, *Ind.* 54–55, the verb, γυμνάζειν. And, second, *Ind.* 54–55 and 77 both suggest that the purpose of the training is to endure future loss without distress.

have done nothing wrong – expecting to be sent to a deserted island. When someone anticipates banishment to such-and-such an island including the loss of all of his possessions, he prepares himself to endure it.[29] If somehow (he would have anticipated) losing only part of his possessions – deprived of none of the others – he would have been distressed. (*Ind*. 54–55)

The above three references to Commodus and life at court (i.e., including service under prior and subsequent emperors) are explicit and pejorative. As noted, such political commentary is rare in the Galenic corpus. Only references to the slaves of Perennis tortured by the Praetorian Guard or the emperor discarding valuable stores of theriac compare in their overt sense of political disapproval. These three direct criticisms point both generally to life in the late second-century and specifically to the severity of the year 192. They also raise the possibility of additional allusions to these circumstances in the letter-treatise.

Six Anti-Imperial Historical Allusions

The explicit references to Commodus and his court above warrant an investigation of the rest of the text for anti-imperial historical allusions.[30] I propose the following six possibilities: (1) head smashing; (2) Hercules; (3) Phalaris' Bull; (4) Fate (5) theriac and cinnamon; and (6) bird-breeding.

(1) Head-smashing

In *Ind*. 72a, Galen admits that if a tyrant destroys his homeland, punishes a friend, or does anything similar, he expects his strategy of avoiding distress to crumple and expects to experience λύπη (*Ind*. 72a). He says that he marvels[31] at Musonius (*Ind*. 73) known to pray for crises. Unlike this Stoic philosopher exiled by Nero and Vespasian, Galen will never, he says, pray for exile. On the contrary, *he* prays and *trains* for *good* health (*Ind*. 74–75). But, he adds, no strength can

---

[29] Gordon P. Kelly, *A History of Exile in the Roman Republic* (Cambridge: Cambridge University Press, 2006), 137–41. Galen's reference to "such-and-such an island" may imply strictures on an exile's choice of foreign land. Kelly writes, "The mainland of Greece and Asia was off-limits, as well as an island within fifty miles, with the exception of Cos, Rhodes, Samos, and Lesbos" (137 n. 9).

[30] The argument is cumulative – explicit references providing grounds upon which other possible allusions are based. On allusion and intertextuality, see Tim Whitmarsh, *Greek Literature and the Roman Empire: The Politics of Imitation* (Oxford: Oxford University Press, 2001); Stephen Hinds, *Allusion and Intertext: Dynamics of Appropriation in Roman Poetry* (Roman Literature and its Contexts; Cambridge: Cambridge University Press, 1998); Lowell Edmonds, *Intertextuality and the Reading of Roman Poetry* (Baltimore: John Hopkins University, 2003); Konstantin Doulamis, ed., *Echoing Narratives: Studies of Intertextuality in Greek and Roman Prose Fiction* (Groningen: Barkhuis, 2011).

[31] By which, in this case, Galen probably means "disdains"; cf. *Ind*. 16.3; 19.15; 19.20; 20.21; 21.20; 22.1; 24.3 (BMJ).

protect him from "a head smashed on the ground" (καταγείσης τῆς κεφαλῆς, *Ind.* 74). The reference to head smashing is surprising. In this context, it is an uncharacteristically dramatic exaggeration of the converse of good health. Demanding an explanation, it may possess an historical referent. In the first of two such incidents documented by Cassius Dio,[32] Commodus shoots off an ostrich's head, walks over to where senators are sitting in the arena, and – waving the bird's head in one hand and his own bloody sword in the other – threatens to do the same to them. Present on this occasion, Dio writes that he chewed laurel leaves to disguise his amusement:

> And here is another thing that he did to us senators, which gave us every reason to look for our death. Having killed an ostrich and cut off his head, he came up to where we were sitting, holding the head in his left hand and in his right hand raising aloft his bloody sword; and though he spoke not a word, yet he wagged his head with a grin, indicating that he would treat us in the same way. And many would indeed have perished by the sword on the spot, for laughing at him (for it was laughter rather than indignation [λύπη] that overcame us), if I had not chewed some laurel leaves, which I got from my garland, myself, and persuaded the others who were sitting near me to do the same, so that in the steady movement of our jaws we might conceal the fact that we were laughing. (Cassius Dio 72 [73].21.1–2)[33]

Maud Gleason interprets the senators' laughter as confusion resulting from shock at the Emperor's behavior. She writes:

> As terror fought with a hysterical urge to laugh, Dio concealed his emotions by chewing leaves from his garland and persuaded his neighbors to do the same. The problem was not just that senators under this kind of pressure dared not show what they were feeling; they did not even *know* what they were feeling.[34]

---

[32] General work consulted on Dio: Fergus Millar, *Study of Cassius Dio* (Oxford: Oxford University Press, 1964).

[33] ET: Earnest Cary (LCL)

[34] "Identity Theft," 49, emphasis original. Elsewhere, with respect to his own and others' fear of Julianus, Dio notes how senators attempted to disguise their λύπη (74.13.1–5): "Having thus secured confirmation of the imperial power by decrees of the senate also, he proceeded up to the palace. And finding the dinner that had been prepared for Pertinax, he made great fun of it, and sending out to every place, which by any means whatever something expensive could be procured at that time of night, he proceeded to gorge himself, while the corpse was still lying in the building, and then to play at dice. Among others that he took along with him was Pylades, the pantomime. The next day we went up to pay our respects to him, molding our faces, so to speak, and posturing, so that our grief (λύπη) should not be detected. The populace, however, went about openly with sullen looks, spoke its mind as much as it pleased, and was getting ready to do anything it could." Gleason translates πλαττόμενοι τρόπον τινὰ καὶ σχηματιζόμενοι ὅπως μὴ κατάφωροι ἐπὶ τῇ λύπῃ γενώμεθα as follows: "modeling ourselves as it were, and posturing lest we be caught in the act of grief" ("Identity Theft," 50), commenting: "The Greek words πλαττόμενοι τρόπον τινὰ καὶ σχηματιζόμενοι describe the process of sculpting ones facial expressions and body language to suppress the display of unacceptable emotions. (Thus the usurper makes us impostors of ourselves). The common crowd felt no such inhibitions, and made scowling faces openly: ὁ δὲ δῆμος ἐσκυθρώπαζε φανερῶς. At this point in Dio's narrative the crowd seems to function as the externalization of the senators' concealed feelings …" (50).

Commodus' public threat to behead the senators served as a warning to all that at any given moment, should Commodus choose, one's head could be the bloody object of the emperor's slaughter-crazed whim.

Alternatively, the reference to head smashing (*Ind.* 74) may allude to the deaths of Commodus' chamberlain, Cleander, and his son. Dio records this event as follows:

> And Commodus was so terrified (he was ever the greatest coward) that he at once ordered Cleander to be slain, and likewise his son, who was being reared in the emperor's charge. The boy was dashed to the earth and so perished (καὶ τὸ μὲν παιδίον προσουδίσθη καὶ διεφθάρη); and the Romans, taking the body of Cleander, dragged it away and abused it and carried his head all about the city on a pole. They also slew some other men who had enjoyed great power under him.[35]

Whether these precise allusions are intended or not, the unexpected reference to head smashing is best understood in the terror-filled months of Commodus' late reign.

(2) Hercules

Toward the end of the letter-treatise, Galen admits that, although he strives to have the strength to endure most physical maladies, he does not have "the strength of Hercules" (*Ind.* 76), that is, *his* powers of recovery are only human. The "strength of Hercules" is a very common mythical allusion. Here it certainly connotes superior physical strength. In its current context, however, it probably also possesses political overtones. Olivier Hekster comments on the Empire's saturation with Commodus-Hercules propaganda in the late second century:

> Referring to Hercules in this period *must have* brought 'Commodus-Hercules' to mind.[36]

A possible clue to Galen's polyvalent usage of this phrase in this context is the unusual words employed. The "might" of Hercules is typically expressed by the adjective, βίαιος or the noun, ἡ βία.[37] In *Aff.Dig.*, a treatise covering many of the same topics as *Ind.*, Galen refers to Herculean strength as εὐεξία.[38] In *Ind.*

---

[35] Cassius Dio 72 (73).13.6.

[36] *Commodus: An Emperor at the Crossroads* (Amsterdam: Gieben, 2002), 188. Cf. Cassius Dio 72 (73).7.2; 15.5–6; 16.1; 20.2; Herodian 1.14.8, 9; 1.15.8; SHA *Comm.* 10.9; 11.8, 14; 17.9, 11.

[37] E.g., Hesiod *Theog.* 289, 982; *[Scut.]* 115, 349, 416.

[38] Twice in *Aff.Dig.* 4 (5.15–16): (1) "One would by all means attempt to improve it, even if one were not able to achieve a Heraclean sort of good condition (πάντως <δ'> ἂν ἐπειράθη βέλτιον αὐτὸ κατασκευάσαι, καίτοι τὴν Ἡράκλειον εὐεξίαν οὐ δυνάμενος σχεῖν)"; (2) "If he had refused this, we would have requested of him the second, third, or fourth from the first in good condition. It would be a highly desirable outcome even if we could not get the body of a Heracles, to have at least that of an Achilles, and failing that, that of an Ajax, a Diomedes, an Agamemnon, a Patroclus; and failing those, the body of some other fine hero (εἴ γ' οὖν ἐφ' ἡμῖν ἦν γινομένοις ἐντυχεῖν τῷ προνοουμένῳ τῆς γενέσεως ἡμῶν δεομένοις τε τοῦ λαβεῖν σῶμα γενναιότατον, ὁ δ' [ἢ] ἠρνήσατο, πάντως ἂν ἐφεξῆς ἐδεήθημεν αὐτοῦ δεύτερον γοῦν ἢ τρίτον ἢ

76, however, he refers to Hercules' strength with the word ῥώμη, a homonym in Greek for the city of Rome (Ῥώμη). He writes: "I do not expect my body to have τὴν Ἡρακλέους ῥώμην." The astute reader – aware of Commodus' association with Hercules, Commodus' recent claim to be the founder of the city, and his renaming the city and some of its institutions after himself (among other megalomaniacal acts)[39] – hardly could have missed this allusion to "Hercules' Rome." If correct, then by this phrase, Galen snidely expresses (as Cassius Dio, above) that – continually over the course of Commodus' reign – he did not expect to survive.[40] The statement resembles Cassius Dio's: "And here is another thing that he did to us senators, *which gave us every reason to look for our death*" (72 [73].21, emphasis added).[41]

Coins minted in the year 192 attest a similarly surreptitious – playful yet dangerous – sparring with imperial power. Hekster describes them as follows:

> They are, at first appearance, the same as other coins from that year, with on the reverse Commodus' final names (*Hercules Romanus Augustus*) fully spelled out, divided into two parts by Hercules' club.[42] It has been noted, however, that in a few cases, the way the name was split was somewhat peculiar, making a bawdy interpretation of the legend possible. Reading the right part of the legend from the top down, the words *culi ano usto* appear. This might have been an accident, of course. Coins with a slightly different layout, or with an abbreviated name on the legend, could then be seen as an improvement on this type after the 'wrong' interpretation was spotted.[43]

If such a prank was deliberate against the Emperor *during his reign*, as some scholars suppose, then Commodus was openly mocked in his final days. Galen, of course, does not openly mock the emperor; rather, he waits.[44] Yet once Com-

---

τέταρτον αὐτὸ σχεῖν ἀπὸ τοῦ πρώτου κατ᾽ εὐεξίαν. ἀγαπητὸν γὰρ εἰ καὶ μὴ τὸ τοῦ Ἡρακλέους, ἀλλὰ τό γε τοῦ Ἀχιλλέως σχεῖν, ἢ εἰ μηδὲ τούτου, τό γε τοῦ Αἴαντος ἢ Διομήδους ἢ Ἀγαμέμνονος ἢ Πατρόκλου, εἰ δὲ μὴ τούτων, ἄλλων γέ τινων ἀγαστῶν ἡρώων)" (ET: Singer, *Galen*, 106).

[39] Gleason notes that Commodus' renaming project demonstrates the terror he generated among the senators insofar as new names required their vote. She writes: "But Commodus monkeyed with traditional names and titles. We may imagine how little the conscript fathers enjoyed being addressed by their emperor as 'the fortunate Commodian senate.' Commodus' name-games also distorted the familiar parameters of space and time. Rome herself was now to be called 'Commodiana;' the months of the year were renamed 'Amazonius,' 'Invictus,' etc., echoing Commodus' boastful titles. To make matters worse, it was the senate itself that voted these changes, succumbing, Cassius Dio says, to fear" ("Identity Theft," 48, citing Cassius Dio 72 [73].15. 1–3).

[40] Cf. SHA *Comm*. 11.7: *imitatus est et medicum, ut sanguinem hominibus emitteret scalpris feralibus.*

[41] Concerning Galen's comportment during Commodus' reign, Vivian Nutton writes: "After all, Galen had lived through the reign of Commodus, when it was doubtless his tact and political sense which saved him from the dangers of assassination that others around him came to fear" ("Galen on Theriac," 150, citing *Hipp. Epid. CMG* 5.10.2.2 494).

[42] *RIC* 3, no. 638; *BMCRE* 4, no. 713.

[43] Hekster, *Commodus*, 207.

[44] See n. 7 (above).

modus is dead, Galen, too, takes part in a limited way in the collective intellectual expression of frustration and disgust over Commodus' rule.

In *Ind.* 52, Galen remarks that only Euripides (the most tragic of tragedians, according to Aristotle)[45] suffices in times like the present.

> You are well aware that political spectacles[46] also educate through experience, recalling the art of medicine.[47] No maxim is more effective than the one Euripides placed in the mouth of Theseus.

Galen provides Euripides' text next – verses from an unknown play cited by Galen twice (*Ind.* 77) as well as by Cicero and Plutarch.[48] Galen informs his reader: "Upon hearing the verses, you will recognize them." Presumably, the addressee will not just recognize the verses, but their pertinence to his argument. In case he does not, Galen spells it out in *Ind.* 54–55: exile, untimely death, and the other misfortunes that Theseus thrusts into his mind to prepare himself for a crisis *are the very fears Galen harbors* also. That is why this maxim perfectly suits the present circumstances and that is what, with the verses themselves, Galen's friend is expected to recognize. Additionally, Theseus was to the Athenians as Hercules was to the Dorians – that is, a rival founding hero. As Commodus styled himself the new Hercules, Galen's endorsement of Theseus may also reflect political commentary.

(3) Phalaris' Bull
Ind. 69 begins a new section of Galen's argument with the claim that, having completed the answer to his friend's question on the avoidance of distress (*Ind.* 1–38), Galen intends, as he closes the letter-treatise, to introduce a few exceptions to the rule. In *Ind.* 71–72b, Galen admits that it *is* possible for him to become distressed.

> For my part, I cannot say if such a wise man, unaffected with respect to everything, exists. But, I do have accurate knowledge of the kind of person I am. I can overlook the loss of money as long as I am not sent to a deserted island, deprived of everything. And, I can overlook bodily pain up to the point of pledging that I disregard the bull of Phalaris.

Of interest in this passage is the reference to Phalaris' bull – the hollow bronze sculpture built by Perillos of Athens and used by the fifth-century BCE Sicilian tyrant to burn enemies alive (including its sculptor).[49] According to Cicero – in an outrageous claim to detachment – Epicureans maintained that they would ad-

---

[45] *Poet.* 13.
[46] Double entendre: θέα political spectacles and theatrical drama.
[47] That is, how experience is a very important component to diagnosing disease, prescribing medicine, etc. E.g., *Nat. Fac.* 2.41.8; 42.2; *MM* 10.5.8; 10.334.15; 10.375.16.
[48] Cicero *Tusc.* 3.29 (cf. 3.32); Plutarch [*Cons. Apoll.*] 112D; *Ind.* 52, 77; cf. also, *PHP* 5.418; see BMJ 17 (text), 139–42 (commentary).
[49] Cicero *Verr.* 4.73; Diodorus Siculus 9.19.1.

mit no distress ever, not even inside Phalaris' bull.⁵⁰ Galen's statement possesses clear anti-Epicurean sentiments. However, the reference to Phalaris' bull may also imply a political critique. In the late seventeenth century, Richard Bentley argued against the authenticity of the *Letters of Phalaris* on account of anachronisms. He speculated, rather, that Commodus' personal secretary, Adrianus of Tyre forged them as a spoof, exonerating the Sicilian tyrant.⁵¹ Lucian, too, takes up the theme of this tyrant, referring to Phalaris as Hercules (*Phal.* 1).⁵² In all likelihood, the nexus of connections between Phalaris, bull, Hercules, late second century and Commodus derives from the fact that Commodus went to great lengths to ensure his reputation as bull-slayer *and* demanded honors as Hercules in the month of the bull or *taurus* (i.e., October).⁵³ As noted above, according to Olivier Hekster, during the late second century, references to Hercules could hardly be understood as other than allusions to Commodus.⁵⁴ Moreover, this instrument of torture killed its victims by incineration (i.e., roasting alive). Its first victim was evidently the brazen bull's own craftsman – the inventor killed by his invention. It is difficult to imagine a more apt metaphor of political critique in a treatise on substantial losses in the great fire of 192 by a physician who had saved the emperor's life more than once.⁵⁵ I can avoid distress if you burn my belongings, Galen writes; but not if you burn my body.

---

⁵⁰ Cicero *Tusc.* 2.7.

⁵¹ *Dissertation upon the Epistles of Phalaris* (London: W. Bowyer and J. Nichols, 1777).

⁵² Furthermore, during the first century, Seneca borrowed the allusion to Phalaris for Nero. "Contrast *On Anger* 2.5.1, where Phalaris is an example not of 'cruelty' but of the 'bestiality' just discussed, which inflicts pain for the pleasure of doing so, irrespective of the victim's desert" (eds. Robert A. Kaster and Martha C. Nussbaum, *Lucius Annaeus Seneca: Anger, Mercy, Revenge*, [Chicago/London: University of Chicago], 193 n. 162). Phalaris becomes the example *par excellence* of bestial human behavior. Cf. "Our case is like the story of the Hydra: the more heads we lop, the more occasions for punishing grow up under our eyes" (*Phal.* 8; ET: A. M. Harmon [LCL]). Lucian also composes a spoof on Hercules and Seneca wrote two plays on Hercules representing the Neronian court. Additionally, Dio (72 [73].15.3) notes a statue erected to Commodus featuring the emperor with a bull and a cow: "In his honor a gold statue was erected of a thousand pounds weight, representing him together with a bull and a cow (καὶ ἀνδριάς τε αὐτῷ χρυσοῦς χιλίων λιτρῶν μετά τε ταύρου καὶ βοὸς θηλείας ἐγένετο)." One might also compare the Capitoline statue of Commodus as Hercules. The globe upon which Hercules rests features zodiac signs, including a bull, a goat, and a scorpion.

⁵³ Speidel, "Commodus the God-Emperor and the Army," 109.

⁵⁴ See n. 36 above. "It remains to account for this special devotion to Hercules on the part of Commodus. Ancient writers attribute it to his inclination to the profession of a gladiator, an explanation accepted by most modern historians. According to this view, Hercules was for Commodus the great hero of sport, the great killer of men and animals, the patron of gladiators. To me the contrary seems more probable: Commodus became a gladiator because he wanted to imitate and to equal the god of his choice, not vice-versa. His devotion to Hercules may be traced back earlier; it was founded indeed on a firmly-established tradition" (Michael Rostovtseff and Harold Mattingly, "Commodus-Hercules in Britain," *JRS* 13 [1923]: 91–109 [here: 101]). It is a possible rendition of the myth for political purposes, e.g., Nero *redivivus*.

⁵⁵ Although Galen undoubtedly knew about Phalaris' bull from philosophical literature, legend claims that Domitian roasted Antipas the bishop of Pergamum alive in a brazen bull ca. 92 CE.

If, by the reference to Phalaris' bull, Galen offers – in addition to a critique of Epicureanism – an allusion to Commodus, then in this passage he is saying that his distress-avoidance strategy (i.e., training the φαντασίαι) cannot be guaranteed in the case of unjustified punishment of the type Commodus was known to exact.[56] The sentence following the comment about Phalaris suggests precisely this interpretation:

> And, I can overlook bodily pain up to the point of pledging that I disregard the bull of Phalaris. A homeland destroyed, a friend *punished by a tyrant* (καὶ φίλος ὑπὸ τυράννου κολαζόμενος), and anything else like this will distress me and I pray to the gods that none of these things ever happens to me (emphasis added).

In all likelihood, Phalaris' bull represents more than just anti-Epicurean sentiment. It simultaneously expresses Galen's opinion that, whereas fire destroying a life's work is tolerable, unjust political punishment would break his resolve.

(4) Fate

Galen claims to have harbored fantasies of escaping life at court.[57] In *Ind.* 49 (corroborated in *Praen.* 14.647–9), he says that he repeatedly attempted to flee the royal court, but was unsuccessful against "fate" (τύχη). The word, τύχη occurs nine times in *Ind.* This occurrence rate is relatively high; TLG reports 273 total hits for this word in the Galenic corpus. Of the nine occurrences of τύχη in *Ind.*, seven refer to a positive causal influence over which human beings have lit-

---

[56] The idea of meditating on future woes can be traced back through Posidonius and Chrysippus to Zeno and even perhaps Diogenes of Sinope. Many associate the practice with Cicero (*praemeditatio futuri mali*; *Tusc.* 3.28–29) and Seneca (*Ep.* 98.7: *Quodcumque laesurum est, multo ante quam accidat, speculare et averte*). The latter's emphasis can at times, however, can be different. In *Ep.* 98, although like Galen Seneca advises: "Be sure to foresee whatever can be foreseen by planning. Observe and avoid, long before it happens, anything that is likely to do you harm"; he immediately adds: "... there is nothing more wretched or foolish than premature fear. What madness it is to anticipate one's troubles ... He suffers more than is necessary, who suffers before it is necessary." That is, Seneca deemphasizes mental practice of misfortune because of its potential ruination of the present. Likewise, later in this epistle, Seneca writes: "It is tragic for the soul to be apprehensive of the future and wretched in anticipation of wretchedness ... For such a soul will never be at rest; in waiting for the future it will lose the present blessings which it might enjoy" (*Ep.* 98.5–6). The precise phrase "exercise the φαντασίαι" occurs numerous times in *Arrian's Discourses* (*Disc.* 2.18.25, 28; 3.8."t," 1; 3.12.7, 16; 4.4.26; cf. also Philo *Sacr.* 85.2). Anthony A. Long refers to the phrase as Epictetus' "favorite slogan" and "cardinal rule" (*Epictetus: A Stoic and Socratic Guide to Life* [Oxford: Clarendon Press, 2002]; "favorite slogan," 175; "cardinal rule," 85 and 212). Like Galen, Epictetus argues that daily practice of misfortune involves calling to mind φαντασίαι of death and exile: "Furthermore, at the very moment when you are taking delight in something, call to mind the opposite φαντασίαι (τὰς ἐναντίας φαντασίας σαυτῷ πρόβαλε). What harm is there if you whisper to yourself, at the very moment you are kissing your child ... 'Tomorrow you will die?' So likewise to your friend, 'Tomorrow you will go abroad, or I shall, and we shall never see each other again?'" (*Disc.* 3.24.88–89; cf. Marcus Aurelius *Meditations* 11.34).

[57] As did Dio and others: Gleason, "Identity Theft," 49. Cf. Galen's escape in *Praen.* 14.648–9 (*CMG* 5.8.1 9.2–4).

tle or no control. Twice, however, in *Ind.* 23b and 49, it refers to a negative such influence.[58] In *Ind.* 23b, the verb with τύχη is ἐνεδρεύω: "Fate *laid in wait* for me" or "ambushed me." In *Ind.* 49, the verb with τύχη is ἑλκύω: "Fate *dragged* me."[59] I address both examples, the second one first.

In the second example, "fate" almost certainly refers to the emperor. Galen says that, although he resisted life in the royal court, τύχη forced him to remain.

> Hence, I have accomplished nothing significant by shunning[60] the manifold loss of my possessions, just as I shun life in the imperial court. Not only did I *not* aspire to such a life back then, but in point of fact I held my ground against it – not once, not twice, but many times. Fate dragged me into it by force. (*Ind.* 49)

Véronique Boudon-Millot argues that this passage corresponds to *Lib.Prop.* 19.17, a passage treating Galen's imperial summons to Rome for what will be his second sojourn to the city.[61] On Boudon-Millot's argument, the expression, ἐξ

---

[58] Although "fortune" is the more expected English translation of τύχη and makes sense for the other occurrences in *Ind.*, I translate it as "fate" in *Ind.* 23b and *Ind.* 49 to better capture the sense in English of its negative consequences in these two passages.

[59] Technically speaking τύχη (when referring to an agent or cause as opposed to its result) is the act of a god or another agent or cause beyond human control. Galen spells out the details of a furtive attempt to evade imperial summons *circa* 166 in *Praen.* 14.647–9 (*CMG* 5.8.1 9.4).

[60] The verb καταφρονεῖν occurs with some frequency in *Ind.* We have translated based upon the context as "to shun" (*Ind.* 49.16.3); "to dismiss" (*Ind.* 61.19.14; 62.19.20; 66.20.21; 78.24.3); "to overlook" (*Ind.* 71.21.20; 71.22.1).

[61] According to Nutton, Galen was extraordinarily productive in his tenure (especially the first years) under Marcus Aurelius: "The Chronology of Galen's Early Career," *CQ* 23/1 (1973): 158–71 [here: 170]. Cf. also Singer, *Galen*, li. In the later phase, however, we cannot be sure about his level of productivity. Hankinson traces *Ant.*, *Aff.Dig.*, *Aff.Pecc.*, *Mor.*, and *Hipp.Epid.* VI, VIII to this later period and suspects each of veiled references to Commodus. Although chronologically ordering the texts comprising Galen's oeuvre is difficult and although Galen wrote some commentaries on Hippocrates between 176–80 and others between 180–92 (Singer, *Galen*, li), it is, nevertheless, likely that *Hipp.Epid.* 6, 8 (see above) was composed after the accession of Commodus in 180. Singer traces *De alimentis facultatibus*, the last book of *De sanitate tuenda*, *De ordine librorum propriorum*, and number of Hippocratic commentaries, including those on *The Nature of Man* and *Airs, Waters, Places* to this period also (between 180–92) (*Galen*, li). Most scholars suspect that works including *Aff.Dig.*, *Aff.Pecc.*, and *Mor.* should be clustered toward the end of Galen's life as part of a more philosophical phase. Gill and others note proximity of the central ideas in *Aff.Dig.*, *Aff.Pecc.*, and *Ind.* Gill thinks *Aff.Dig.* and *Aff.Pecc.* develop the distress-avoidance strategy first discussed in *Ind.* (*Naturalistic Psychology in Galen and Stoicism*, 267). Others, such as Hankinson, however, think that Galen's silence regarding the great fire in those works requires explanation, hypothesizing that *Ind.* is a quick summary of Galen's grief strategy first spelled out in *Aff.Dig.* and later applied to his losses in the fire. As noted above, Hankinson speculates that Galen's exploration of the relationship between 'nature and nurture' in, for example, *QAM* 4.768–9, 814–21 may have something to do with Commodus' illustrious paternity and education. These observations, together with Commodus' rise to power in this period, suggest that remarks or allusions to Commodus in Galen's works are clustered together later in Galen's career, that is, around the same time as he wrote *Ind.* As above, *Praen.* 14.647–9 (*CMG* 5.8.1 9.1–3) describes Galen's desire to leave Rome and his hope that he will not be summoned back, whereas these two passages in *Lib.Prop.* and *Ind.*

ἀνάγκης in the phrase, ἐπορεύθην μὲν οὖν ἐξ ἀνάγκης (FT: "Je fus donc contraint de me mettre en route"; ET: "I was forced") corresponds to βιαίως in the phrase ἀλλὰ καὶ τῆς τύχης βιαίως εἰς αὐτὴν ἑλκούσης (FT: "mais auquel, au moment où la fortune m'y entraînait violemment"; ET: "but Fate dragged me") in *Ind.* 49.⁶² While this seems certainly to be the case, both the French and English translations mask the further correspondence in the two Greek phrases between their personifications of "fate," ἀνάγκη and τύχη. In both passages, Galen personifies the emperor as "fate" – analogizing the irrefutability of imperial orders as a goddess. I provide English translations of the two passages (repeating *Ind.* 49 from above) for comparison:

> *Lib.Prop.* 19.17 On return from Rome, then, I established myself in my home city and was minding my own business; but there immediately arrived from Aquileia *a summons under the imperial seal.* The emperors had decided to attack the Germans in winter. *So I was forced* to travel (ἐπορεύθην μὲν οὖν ἐξ ἀνάγκης).⁶³

> *Ind.* 49 Hence, I have accomplished nothing significant by shunning the manifold loss of my possessions, just as I shun *life in the imperial court.* Not only did I not aspire to such a life back then, but in point of fact I held my ground against it … *Fate dragged me into it* by force (ἀλλὰ καὶ τῆς τύχης βιαίως εἰς αὐτὴν ἑλκούσης).

Personifying τύχη as the emperor recalls Herodian's report of Commodus' speech upon the death of his father. In this speech, referring to his status as 'born in the purple,' Commodus personifies the emperor Marcus Aurelius as τύχη:

> Fate has appointed me as emperor after him (ἔδωκε δὲ μετ' ἐκεῖνον ἐμὲ βασιλέα ἡ τύχη), not as an adopted heir like my predecessors who prided themselves on the added power they gained, but as the only one of your emperors to be born in the palace.⁶⁴

The accusative demonstrative in the prepositional phrase μετ' ἐκεῖνον lacks an antecedent in the context and, thus, points to the emperor.

Τύχη in *Ind.* 49, likewise, recalls Dio's statement about Cleander. Although Commodus was responsible for Cleander's promotion, Dio attributes it to Fortune: "So Cleander, raised to greatness by Fortune, bestowed and sold senatorships, military commands, procuratorships, governorships, and, in a word, everything" (ὁ δ' οὖν Κλέανδρος μέγας ὑπὸ τῆς τύχης ἀρθεὶς καὶ ἐχαρίσατο καὶ ἐπώλησε βουλείας, στρατείας, ἐπιτροπείας, ἡγεμονίας, πάντα πράγματα).⁶⁵

---

refer to an imperial summons to return – the one he had hoped to avoid. Also, *Praen.* 14.648–9 (*CMG* 5.8.1 9.1–3) does not refer to "fate."

⁶² Boudon-Millot and Jouanna, *Galien:* Ne pas se chagriner, 132.
⁶³ ET: Singer, 7.
⁶⁴ 1.5.5 (ET: modified); cf. 2.2.8 (Pertinax).
⁶⁵ Cassius Dio 72 (73).12.3; ET: LCL, modified. Contrast SHA *Comm.* 2.9 (*fortuna*) and Herodian 1.8.3; 1.9.5; 1.13.6; 2.2.8; 2.4.5, where usage appears to be typical of historiography of this period. Occasionally it is responsible for reversals (e.g., Herodian 1.8.2; 1.13.6); in Stoic doctrine, as the divine will, τύχη may also select the emperor. See C. R. Whitaker's note on Herodian 1.13.6 (LCL), (44 n. 1 and 86 n. 1).

If *Ind.* 49 personifies the emperor as "fate," it would not be the first time Galen personifies imperial power. Prior to the discovery of *Ind.*, in her essay entitled, "Demiurge and Emperor in Galen's World of Knowledge," Rebecca Fleming persuasively argues that Galen coalesces positive concepts – including, δύναμις, δικαιοσύνη, τέχνη, πρόνοια, φύσις, and δημιουργός – in the figure of the emperor. While her thesis is plausible for admired leaders such as Marcus Aurelius, these concepts can hardly refer to Commodus, least of all during his late reign.[66] The additional such concept, τύχη – which Galen sometimes uses to refer to a negative force – may, however, cleave to the reviled figure of Commodus:[67] wise πρόνοια, referring to the father, is exchanged for unpredictable, untrustworthy, even inane τύχη, for the son. Alternatively (or by synecdoche), it may represent all aspects of the court Galen dislikes. Galen's description of τύχη in *Protr.* 1.2.3–7 supports this claim:

> To put in graphic form how miserable a creature Fortune (τύχη) is, the ancients portrayed her, not just as a woman – *as if this were not a sufficient sign of inanity* – but also with a rudder in her hands, with a spherical support for her feet, and without eyes. All this was intended to indicate the instability of Fortune.[68]

Given these arguments, we return to the first occurrence of "fate" in *Ind.* 23b. Here, also, τύχη appears to represent the emperor. In this passage, Galen discusses *when* the fire "broke out."

> The fire, then, broke out at the end of winter. I planned, at the beginning of summer, to transport books to Campania, both those copies to be kept there and those to be sent to Asia when the Etesian winds blow. Fortune, then, ambushed me depriving me of many of my other books. (*Ind.* 23a)

The verb ἐκγίγνομαι, translated in the above citation as "broke out," often means "to spring from [a source]" or "to be born of [a father]."[69] In this passage, however, the source *from* which the fire sprung is elided; Galen delineates only the season in which the event took place. Elision of the fire's source may suggest that the source is obvious. Alternatively, it may simply imply that the source is unknown,[70] that Galen is ignorant of the source, or that Galen is dissembling

---

[66] "Demiurge and Emperor in Galen's World of Knowledge," in *Galen and the World of Knowledge* (ed. C. Gill, T. Whitmarsh, and J. Wilkins; Cambridge: Cambridge University Press, 2009), 59–84, here: 69. Fleming notes at the end that her essay was written prior to the publication of *Ind.* (84 n. 87). On Commodus' dressing as a woman, see SHA *Comm.* 13.4.

[67] Herodian, too, contrasts τύχη with the concepts of πρόνοια and βουλή (e.g., 3.7.1).

[68] ἧς τὴν μοχθηρίαν ἐμφανίσαι βουληθέντες οἱ παλαιοὶ γράφοντες καὶ πλάττοντες αὐτὴν οὐ μόνον ἐν εἴδει γυναικὸς ἠρκέσθησαν (καίτοι <καὶ> τοῦθ' ἱκανὸν ἦν ἀνοίας σύμβολον) ἀλλὰ καὶ πηδάλιον ἔδοσαν ἐν χεροῖν ἔχειν αὐτῇ καὶ τοῖν ποδοῖν ὑπέθεσαν βάσιν σφαιρικήν, ἐστέρησαν δὲ καὶ τοῖν ὀφθαλμοῖν, ἐνδεικνύμενοι διὰ τούτων ἁπάντων τὸ τῆς τύχης ἄστατον (ET: Singer, 35–36). On translating τύχη as "Fortune" or "Fate," see n. 58 above.

[69] LSJ "A."

[70] Elision of source of origin is common in historiography of the period; cf. references to what incites various wars.

about what prompted the blaze. However, in the next sentence, Galen blames Fate for the crisis. It is possible that the friend to whom Galen addresses *Ind.* would understand by this reference to Fate that Galen, like others, blames Commodus for the fire. The reference to the emperor as τύχη in *Ind.* 49 augments this suspicion. Both usages also support the impression – raised in the next section and formed on other grounds – that Galen faults Commodus for his loss of theriac and cinnamon, valuable instruments, and irreplaceable books.

(5) Theriac, Cinnamon, and Impenetrable Repositories
De indolentia's catalogue of losses begins with Galen's assertion that his friend (the addressee) did *not* express amazement at Galen's avoidance of distress over the loss of replaceable items like silver and gold, but over his loss of irreplaceable items like personal writings and a rich repository of therapeutic drugs.[71] He writes:

> Of items deposited in the storehouses that were destroyed in the fire, you marveled, not that I appeared to endure without distress, the loss of silver, gold, silver-plates, and many contracts, but a considerable number of my writings, a wide assortment of medicines both simple and compound, and various instruments. (*Ind.* 4)

In *Ind.* 6, Galen, then, specifies which of his lost books and remedies were the most valuable:

> … it is no longer possible to recover the books – both the ancient works corrected by my hand and those that I composed – and the so-called remedies, of which you said that you knew I had many. It is especially impossible to recover the so-called theriac of eighty pounds in weight, the cinnamon, of a quantity surpassing all the retail-dealers (in Rome) put together, and, likewise, all the other rare (therapeutic substances) in abundance with me. (*Ind.* 6)

Emphasis on book loss here does not come as a surprise. Galen took pride in his personal library – both his own works and those of others.[72] Emphasis on the loss of theriac and cinnamon – *as if on a par with these valuable writings and instruments* – is, however, surprising. Theriac and cinnamon, while valuable, were replaceable. Galen had admittedly stockpiled more of each than (he says) anyone else in Rome. Nevertheless, these materials were not – unlike many of his books, and even some of his medical instruments – unique. After stating that his loss of books in the fire constituted a valid source of distress, Galen returns to expound

---

[71] On the rhetorical strategy of 'writing on request,' see Jason König, "Conventions of Prefatory Self-Presentation in Galen's On the Order of My Own Books," in *Galen and the World of Knowledge* (ed. C. Gill, T. Whitmarsh, and J. Wilkins; Cambridge: Cambridge University Press, 2009), 35–58.

[72] On Galen's library, see Vivian Nutton, "Galen's Library," in *Galen and the World of Knowledge* (ed. C. Gill, T. Whitmarsh, and J. Wilkins; Cambridge: Cambridge University Press, 2009), 19–34, esp. 23 n. 23.

this claim. The first half of the letter-treatise details at length the precise nature of the numerous writings Galen lost in the fire, including some evidently very rare books ("parchment codices," *Ind.* 33), containing drug recipes collected from all over the world (*Ind.* 32–37). He never, however, returns to the topic of the lost theriac. Why does Galen compare lost theriac (a few of the numerous ingredients of which are rare but not unique) to irreplaceable recipes and instruments, rather than to ultimately recoverable silver, gold, silver-plates, and contracts?

As noted above, Galen laments the destruction of theriac elsewhere in his corpus. In *Ant.*,[73] he records how Commodus rashly destroyed theriac, cinnamon, and other precious *materia medica* stored since the time of Hadrian.[74] From this testimony, we might deduce that the effectiveness of theriac was a matter of dispute between Galen and the emperor, Commodus. While Marcus Aurelius relied heavily on theriac,[75] Commodus, it seems, finds it useless, demolishing all imperial reserves. Since Commodus destroyed theriac once, we might ask whether Galen's unusual emphasis on lost theriac in the beginning of *Ind.* – as on a par with lost irreplaceable items – implicitly expresses a suspicion that Commodus did so again, that is, that Commodus set fire to the storehouses.[76] Such an inference would certainly stretch beyond the evidence, if Galen were alone in implicating Commodus in the cause of this great fire. However, just as some people accused Nero of starting the fire in Rome in July of 64,[77] various reports circulated blaming Commodus for the fire of 192. SHA *Comm.* 16.7–8[78] records that Commodus *ordered* the burning of the city:

> He gave an order, also, for the burning of the city, as though it were his private colony, and this order would have been executed had not Laetus, the prefect of the guard, deterred him.[79]

Cassius Dio characterizes the fire as a portent of Commodus' death. Concerning the fire's cause, Cassius Dio says only that it began (as fires often did) in a private house. He notes that only once the fire was raging out of control did Commodus arrive from the suburbs to encourage the firefighters:

---

[73] 14.65.3

[74] *Ant.* 14.65.3.

[75] *Praen.* 14.660 (*CMG* 5.8.1 11.6–9); cf. *De theriaca ad Pisonem* 14.283–85.

[76] For *Ant.*, Nutton, "Galen On Theriac," 148–9, proposes a date later in the reign of Severus. See n. 15 above. E.g., cf. Cassius Dio's comment that the fire burned "the storehouses of Egyptian and Arabian wares" (72 [73].24).

[77] Cassius Dio 62.16–17; Suetonius *Nero* 38; Tacitus *Ann.* 15.38–44.

[78] *Commodus* is attributed to Aelius Lampridius. On the historical reliability of the SHA, see the brief introduction in the LCL edition. Ronald Syme argues that one author (not six) wrote the "papers," representing "fictional history" (*Historia Augusta Papers* [Oxford: Oxford University Press, 1983]).

[79] *urbem incendi iusserat, utpote coloniam suam, quod factum esset, nisi Laetus praefectus praetorii Commodum deterruisset.*

Before the death of Commodus there were the following portents: many eagles of ill omen soared about the Capitol and moreover uttered screams that boded nothing peaceful, and an owl hooted there; and *a fire that began at night in some dwelling* leaped to the temple of Pax and spread to the storehouses of Egyptian and Arabian wares, whence the flames, borne aloft, entered the palace and consumed very extensive portions of it, so that nearly all the State records were destroyed (πῦρ τε νύκτωρ ἀρθὲν ἐξ οἰκίας τινὸς καὶ ἐς τὸ Εἰρηναῖον ἐμπεσὸν τὰς ἀποθήκας τῶν τε Αἰγυπτίων καὶ τῶν Ἀραβίων φορτίων ἐπενείματο, ἔς τε τὸ παλάτιον μετεωρισθὲν ἐσῆλθε καὶ πολλὰ πάνυ αὐτοῦ κατέκαυσεν, ὥστε καὶ τὰ γράμματα τὰ τῇ ἀρχῇ προσήκοντα ὀλίγου δεῖν πάντα φθαρῆναι). This, in particular, made it clear that the evil would not be confined to the City, but would extend over the entire civilized world under its sway. For the conflagration could not be extinguished by human power, though vast numbers both of civilians and soldiers carried water, and Commodus himself came in from the suburb and encouraged them (οὐδὲ γὰρ κατασβεσθῆναι ἀνθρωπίνῃ χειρὶ ἠδυνήθη, καίτοι παμπόλλων μὲν ἰδιωτῶν παμπόλλων δὲ στρατιωτῶν ὑδροφορούντων, καὶ αὐτοῦ τοῦ Κομμόδου ἐπελθόντος ἐκ τοῦ προαστείου καὶ ἐπισπέρχοντος). Only when it had destroyed everything on which it had laid hold did it spend its force and die out. (72 [73].24)

Herodian too comments on the cause of the fire, attributing it to either a flash of lightning or an earthquake.[80]

De indolentia does not specify the cause of the fire. In *Ind.* 8–9, however, Galen writes that his storehouses on the Sacred Way burned in spite of three deliberate precautions he took. The first precaution contradicts Cassius Dio's report. The storehouses on the Sacred Way in which he deposited his valuables were *not*, Galen says, near private houses. One may wonder whether by listing this precaution first Galen betrays an eagerness to defend himself against those claiming that his prized possessions were foolishly deposited in storehouses too near private dwellings. Fires broke out at least daily in or near such dwellings in Rome.[81]

Galen continues by claiming that many people placed their most valuable possessions in the storehouses because they were *not* made of wood and were guarded by a military garrison. They were, thus, inflammable:

> Placing confidence in the storehouses along the Sacred Way, that is, that they would certainly not succumb to fire, these people used to deposit their most valuable possessions in them. They said that they trusted them because they were not made of wood – apart from the doors – were not in the vicinity of a private house, and were guarded by a military garrison. The district archives of four procurators of Caesar were stored there. For this very reason, those of us who leased the storehouse units paid more rent, boldly storing very valuable possessions there.

---

[80] εἴτε σκηπτοῦ νύκτωρ κατενεχθέντος, εἴτε καὶ πυρός ποθεν ἐκ τοῦ σεισμοῦ διαρρυέντος (1.14.2).

[81] E.g., Juvenal *Sat.* 3.7.

Thus, although Galen does not mention the fire's cause, in testifying to the virtual inflammability of the repositories in which he placed his belongings (and, no doubt, to his own wisdom [backed by others] in selecting such storehouses), Galen raises the question of origin: If the storehouses were not near a private house and not made of wood, they were virtually impenetrable. If a military garrison guards the storehouses, a random arsonist is unlikely. Logical deduction here implicates the garrison – or someone from whom it takes orders.

Emphasis on loss of theriac at the introduction to the letter-treatise coupled with Galen's comments on the impenetrability of his storehouses may suggest that Galen agreed with the SHA's report that Commodus ordered the great fire – only disagreeing that this command was never heeded.[82] While the supposition is tentative, Galen's comments on fate, addressed in the prior section, lend support to this claim.

(6) Bird-breeding

Finally, toward the end of the tractate, as a part of his "eclectic" philosophical discussion,[83] Galen explains that his father regarded those leading lives of pleasure (τοὺς ἥδιστα βεβιωκότας) with disdain. To support this point, he draws an analogy between those seeking pleasure and birds led around by bird-breeders in the city of Rome:

> Correspondingly, my father regarded those who lead lives of pleasure to be nothing more than the birds we see in the city of Rome led around by their owners to mount female birds for a price.[84] (*Ind.* 62)

---

[82] SHA *Comm.* 15.7–8; cf. n. 79 above.

[83] See Pierluigi Donini, "The History of the Concept of Eclecticism," in *The Question of Eclecticism: Studies in Later Greek Philosophy* (ed. J. M. Dillon and A. A. Long; Hellenistic Culture and Society 3; Berkeley/Los Angeles: University of California, 1997), 15–33, here: 30.

[84] Καὶ μὴν καὶ τοὺς ἥδιστα βεβιωκότας οὐδὲν ἔσχε πλείω τῶν οἰωνῶν τούτων οὓς κατὰ <τὴν> τῶν Ῥωμαίων πόλιν ὁρῶμεν ὑπὸ τῶν δεσποτῶν περιαγομένους ἕνεκα τοῦ τὰς θηλείας ὀχεύειν ἐπὶ μισθῷ. In *Ind.* 62, περιαγομένους may refer to the calling of a harem. Perhaps, a *double entendre*: birds of Rome led by owners as Commodus led boys and girls to orgies. Cf. e.g., SHA *Comm.* 5.4, 11. Some debate exists as to Vlatadon's reading of τῶν οἰωνῶν – BMJ *Ind.* 62.19.16–17 (s. v. οἰωνός, "bird"). In our first English translation, we accept "birds" based on our commitment to remaining with the manuscript reading wherever possible. In our second English version in this volume, we reconsidered this choice based on a proposed emendation of Tommaso Raiola, "'Asini per uccelli': una noterella al testo di de Indolentia," *Galenos: Rivista di filologia dei testi medici antichi* 5 (2011): 21–26. Ivan Garofalo and Alessandro Lami indicate that E. W. Handley offers the same reading *apud* Nutton (*Galeno: L'anima e il dolore.* De indolentia, De propriis placitis [BUR Rizzoli. Classici greci e latini. Milan: Biblioteca Universale Rizzoli, 2012]), 41 n. 62, "asini." Raiola reads οἱ ὄνοι ("domestic asses"). Currently, however, we do not feel that the emendation is justified. Our reasoning is as follows. First, evidence of bird mounting may be traced as far back as Aristotle *Hist. an.* 539b25–540a3 (ἐν τούτοις γὰρ ὁ ἄρρην ἐπιπηδῶν ὀχεύει τὴν θήλειαν, καὶ συγγίνεται ὥσπερ καὶ τὰ στρουθία ὀξέως) and 560b16–561a3 (Ἴδια δὲ περὶ τὰς περιστερὰς συμβαίνει καὶ τάδε περὶ τὴν ὀχείαν. Κυνοῦσί τε γὰρ ἀλλήλας, ὅταν μέλλῃ ἀναβαίνειν ὁ ἄρρην, ἢ οὐκ ἂν ὀχεύσειεν), a passage describing how birds "mount" each other in the act of copulation. Aristotle's language is very close to Galen's.

Since Galen polemicizes against various types of philosophers in this part of the tractate, we might assume that the analogy refers to Epicureans. What is more, referring to philosophers as birds is not uncommon. Dio Chrysostom refers to different kinds of philosophers as different species of birds (*De dei cognitione* [*Or.* 12]). Likewise, Plotinus refers to Epicureans as heavy birds incapable of flight.[85] In *Ind.*, Galen generalizes the *topos*, referring not just to a certain sect or sects of philosophers as birds, but to anyone living according to the pleasure principle.[86] The specific reference to bird breeding (i.e., stud birds led around by their owners to mount female birds for a price) is, however, compact and, as a result, difficult to understand.[87] During the second century, bird breeding was common in Rome. It was undertaken primarily for rock pigeons (i.e., carrier pigeons) and doves.[88] On account of this widespread practice, birds were frequently accused of sexually indiscriminate behavior. The partridge (*perdix*/πέρδιξ) may have the most famous libido. Aristotle describes both quails and

---

This reading is, moreover, supported by the following three contextual observations. (1) This part of *Ind.* most likely reflects a critique of contemporary Epicureanism. Galen caricatures "those who lead lives of pleasure" as slave-like in their obsession with pleasure. In antiquity, although the male wild ass (ὄναγρος or ὄνος ἄγρος) was known for unconstrained sexual desire, donkeys are generally characterized as sluggish and apathetic. Not only is laziness missing from Galen's critique in this passage, it contradicts his emphasis on *passionate* insatiability. (2) Also, wild asses (ὄναγροι) often represent sexual abstinence, insofar as fathers were known to castrate the young males (Oppian *Cyn.* 3.191–207; Pliny *Nat.* 8.46; *Physiologus* 9). (3) Finally, where as philosophers are frequently caricatured as birds (e.g., σπερμολόγος), they are seldom if ever (to our knowledge) lampooned as donkeys. See Janet E. Spittler, *Animals in the Apocryphal Acts of the Apostles* (WUNT 247; Tübingen: Mohr Siebeck, 2011), 209–16.

[85] Plotinus *Enn.* 5.9.1: "Forced of necessity to attend first to the material, some of them elect to abide by that order and, their life throughout, make its concerns their first and their last; the sweet and the bitter of sense are their good and evil; they feel they have done all if they live along pursuing the one and barring the doors to the other. And those of them that pretend to reasoning have adopted this as their philosophy; they are like the *heavier birds* which have incorporated much from the earth and are so weighted down that they cannot fly high for all the wings Nature has given them" (emphasis added).

[86] In *Lib. Prop.* (19.48.1–9), Galen lists works concerning the philosophy of Epicurus – lost today. By "pleasure principle," I do not imply Freud's theory specifically but generally. Whereas Freud juxtaposed the pleasure principle with the reality principle to explain how children and adolescents learn to delay gratification, I simply wish to discuss any ancient person driven toward pleasure and away from pain (not necessarily exclusively), without formal attachment to any single philosophical school.

[87] As with any obscure epistolary detail, the writer may rely for its interpretation on a bank of shared knowledge to which only the addressee is privy.

[88] Sg. κολυμβίς. About the practice, Pliny says: "Many go to absurd extremes as pigeon-fanciers. They build pigeon-lofts above their roofs for these birds and tell stories about the high breeding and pedigrees of individual birds, for which there is now a long standing precedent" (*Nat.* 10.110; ET: John F. Healy, *Pliny the Elder, Natural History: A Selection* [London: Penguin, 1991], 146). Varro goes into detail about various species of pigeons as well as how such birds are to be bred, raised, and kept (*Rust.* 3.7–8). He also mentions pricing. Columella has different views from Varro on how pigeons are to be raised and kept; he also mentions pricing (*Rust.* 8.3.8).

partridges as so intent on sexual union that they often inadvertently attempt to mate with decoys (*Hist. An.* 539b25–540a3).[89] Xenophon (*Mem.* 2.1.4) knows a similar tradition:

> "Don't you think that with this education he [the male pigeon] will be less likely to be caught by his enemy than other creatures? Some of them, you know, are so greedy, that in spite of extreme timidity in some cases, they are drawn irresistibly to the bait to get food, and are caught; and others are snared by drink."
> "Yes, certainly."
> "Others again – quails and partridges, for instance – are so amorous, that when they hear the cry of the female, they are carried away by desire and anticipation, throw caution to the winds and blunder into the nets. Is it not so?"

Aelian (*Nat. an.* 3.5) describes the partridge (primarily the male) as "unrestrained in indulgence" (ἀκράτορες … ἀφροδίτης). Likewise, Pliny (*Nat.* 10.101) records the "intemperance of his libido" (*intemperantia libidinis*) and his acting "promiscuously" (*promiscue*). Athenaeus, too, comments on partridges and quails:

> Partridges and quails (ὄρτυγες) are excited to such a degree over the act of copulation that they throw themselves among the decoy birds, alighting upon their heads. They even say that the female partridges, which are led as decoys to the hunt, the moment they catch sight or smell of the males become pregnant, and some even lay immediately.[90]

Finally, Clearchus discusses the mating habits of sparrows, partridges, cocks, and quails:

> Sparrows, partridges, cocks, also, and quails emit semen not merely if they see the females, but even if they hear their call. The cause of this is the imaginative thought of union arising in their consciousness. This becomes most obvious at the season of mating, when you place a mirror directly in their path; for, deceived by the reflection, they run up to it and so are caught; they then emit semen – all, that is, excepting the barn-yard fowls. The latter are simply provoked to fight by the sight of the reflection.[91]

While it is difficult to say exactly what Galen intends by his analogy to stud birds, one possibility is that he identifies inherent hypocrisy in the pleasure principle.[92] This principle makes slaves out of its adherents, in the way that stud birds

---

[89] Οὕτω δὲ σφόδρα καὶ οἱ πέρδικες καὶ οἱ ὄρτυγες ἐπτόηνται περὶ τὴν ὀχείαν, ὥστ' εἰς τοὺς θηρεύοντας ἐμπίπτουσι καὶ πολλάκις καθιζάνουσιν ἐπὶ τὰς κεφαλάς.

[90] *Deipn.* 9.389E.

[91] *Deipn.* 9.389E–F.

[92] Galen *MM* 10.1.9–2.5 κεφάλαιον μὲν οὖν ἁπασῶν αὐτῶν ἐστι τὸ κινδυνεῦσαι μάτην γράψαι, μηδενὸς τῶν νῦν ἀνθρώπων ὡς ἔπος εἰπεῖν ἀλήθειαν σπουδάζοντος, ἀλλὰ χρήματά τε καὶ δυνάμεις πολιτικὰς καὶ ἀπλήστους ἡδονῶν ἀπολαύσεις ἐζηλωκότων ἐς τοσοῦτον ὡς μαίνεσθαι νομίζειν εἴ τις ἄρα καὶ γένοιτο σοφίαν ἀσκῶν ἡντιναοῦν. "The chief reason of all is the risk of writing in vain, as almost nobody nowadays is, one might say, eager for truth. Instead, people strive after money, political power, and an insatiable enjoyment of pleasures to such an extent that they would consider someone mad if he were to gain expertise in any area whatsoever." (ET: Ian Johnston and G. H. R. Horsley, *Galen:* Method of Medicine [3 vols.; LCL: Cambridge,

are the slaves of their bird-breeders. The birds spend their lives in little more than food and intemperate sexual behavior.[93] While such a life may be thought to guarantee continuous pleasure, its addictive and compulsory qualities deny what they are meant to secure.[94] The fact that bird owners receive money for the performance of their stud birds may further suggest an analogy with prostitution, a practice Galen seems to reject at *Ind.* 79b.[95] The point seems to be that pleasure addicts are foolish to imagine that lives devoted solely to pleasure satisfy, let alone can be considered in any respect good (e.g., *Ind.* 62–64, 68).

De indolentia 79b continues this theme by explaining how passions make slaves of those indulging them. This passage contrasts Galen's addressee, a man of restrained character, with slaves to insatiability:

> Although writing, thus far, on the avoidance of distress, at this point, I (think it is appropriate to) offer advice on (a few) other matters. Thanks to nature and education, these things are superfluous to mention to you, someone I know has exercised simplicity in

---

Mass.: Harvard University, 2011], 1:3); cf. also Galen *MM* 10.3.1–7: ἁπάντων δι' ὅλης ἡμέρας ἀσχολουμένων, ἕωθεν μὲν ἐν προσαγορεύσεσι κοινῇ, μετὰ ταῦτα δ' ἤδη σχιζομένων, ἐπὶ μὲν τὴν ἀγορὰν καὶ τὰς δίκας οὐ σμικροῦ τινος ἔθνους, ἐπὶ δ' αὖ τοὺς ὀρχηστάς τε καὶ τοὺς ἡνιόχους ἑτέρου πλείονος, οὐκ ὀλίγου δέ τινος ἄλλου τοῖς κύβοις, ἤ τισιν ἔρωσιν, ἢ λουτροῖς, ἢ μέθαις, ἢ κώμοις σχολάζοντος, ἤ τισιν ἄλλαις ἡδοναῖς τοῦ σώματος. "… for there are no judges of that because they are occupied for the whole day, spending the early mornings in salutations in public, and, after that, when they have already split up, a not inconsiderable crowd goes off to the forum and the law courts, another crowd, larger again, goes off to dances and chariot races, while another crowd, by no means small, spends it time in dicing, amorous adventures, bathing, drinking, carousing, or indulging in certain other pleasures of the body" (ET: Johnston/Horsley, 5).

[93] ὀχεύω refers to the act of copulation primarily of animals; cf. however Plato *Resp.* 586a of humans when behaving as animals. This passage of Plato may be a basis for Galen's reference in *Ind.* 53 to the beast-like behavior of human beings in the context of a discussion of wisdom, virtue, and pleasure.

[94] According to Galen (*UP* 4.144.7–19) all animals (so: birds) experience pleasure during copulation: ἅπασι τοῖς ζῴοις ὄργανά τε κινήσεως ἡ φύσις ἔδωκε καί τινα συνῆψεν αὐτοῖς μὲν τοῖς ὀργάνοις ἐξαίρετον <u>δύναμιν εἰς γένεσιν ἡδονῆς</u>, τῇ χρησομένῃ δ' αὐτοῖς ψυχῇ <u>θαυμαστήν τινα καὶ ἄρρητον ἐπιθυμίαν τῆς χρήσεως</u>, ὑφ' ἧς ἐπεγειρόμενα καὶ κεντριζόμενα, κἂν ἄφρονα κἂν νέα κἂν ἄλογα παντάπασιν ᾖ, προνοεῖται τῆς τοῦ γένους διαμονῆς, ὥσπερ εἰ καὶ τελέως ἦν σοφά. γιγνώσκουσα γάρ, ὡς οἶμαι, τὴν οὐσίαν, ἐξ ἧς ἐδημιούργησεν αὐτά, μὴ προσιεμένη ἀκριβῆ σοφίαν, ἀντὶ ταύτης ἔδωκεν αὐτοῖς ὃ μόνον ἐδύνατο λαβεῖν δέλεαρ εἰς σωτηρίαν τε καὶ φυλακὴν τοῦ γένους, <u>ἡδονὴν σφοδροτάτην</u> τῇ χρήσει τῶν μορίων συνάψασα. Likewise, since Aristotle categorizes human beings as animals, his comment about humans' experiencing pleasure and pain from friction of the genitals at an early age might apply to other animals. Aristotle also describes animals' desire for copulation. See *Hist. an.* 581a and 637b, respectively. Aristotle discusses animals' pursuing natural pleasure in regard to food (*Hist. an.* 589a). Cf. also Philo for whom the pleasure of copulation is described as the highest pleasure available to humans (*Spec.* 1.2.9). The hyena was notoriously libidinous. According to Aelian (*Nat. an.* 5.48), the Kingfisher and Ceryl "desire" each other. I wish to thank Troy Martin and Janet Spittler for these references.

[95] In *Ind.* 79b and elsewhere (e.g., *Ars Med.* 1.371–72), Galen certainly rejects the practice of too much sex. The above passage may be related to 79b insofar as Galen refers to the noise made day and night by those with unquenched desires as moaning or cooing (στένειν), also often used of pigeons. Cf. Theocritus *Id.* 7.141.

food and clothing since you were young. This is not to mention how you have also maintained a controlled approach to sexual pleasures. Slaves to all three are relentlessly driven to want more.

Next, Galen describes a pleasure-slave without money:

> Provided they are not wealthy, at first they lament and moan all day and night. Then, being at a loss for these things, they lie awake every night strategizing how to fulfill their desires. Not obtaining them, they roar. Yet, even upon obtaining them, they are not satisfied. Therefore, falling victim to their insatiable desires, they incline themselves toward a more wretched life. (*Ind.* 80)

Then, he contrasts this poor pleasure-slave with a wealthy one:

> (If, however, they are wealthy), they are not distressed in the same way as the masses. Some grasp at honor, riches, reputation, and political power in a moderate way. However, a wealthy person found grasping at these things without moderation is compelled to live most wretchedly. He does not know the first thing about the virtue of the *psyche*. In fact, he increases the vices in it because he is unable to obtain the objects of his desire. All the while, he remains distressed.

De indolentia 82 sums up the problem of insatiability in the form of a moral maxim:

> For, it is true that the most powerful passions have an insatiable goal. No one, living according to nature, should assent to them, just as I have never trusted them.

In sum, Galen argues that the insatiable wealthy do not know "the first thing about virtue."[96] He contrasts such a lifestyle with that of his reader whom he describes as most self-controlled or *enkratic* (ἐγκρατέστατον) and not in need of advice on excesses (*Ind.* 79b).[97] He concludes by linking insatiability to everyday life: We should trust neither insatiable desires, *nor those possessing them* (*Ind.* 82).

He, then, adds that insatiable pleasure-seekers can never master his distress-avoidance strategy. Training the φαντασίαι[98] is the most effective means

---

[96] Προσγίνονταί τινες οὖν [οὐχ ὡς οἱ πολλοὶ λυποῦνται] οἳ μετρίως ἅπτονται τιμῆς καὶ πλούτου καὶ δόξης καὶ δυνάμεως πολιτικῆς, ὧν [γὰρ] ἂν τούτων εὑρεθῇ τις ἀμέτρως, κακοδαιμονέστατα βιοῦν ἀναγκάζεται, ψυχῆς μὲν ἀρετὴν μηδὲ τὴν ἀρχὴν ὅλως τίς ἐστιν ἐπιστάμενος, αὐξήσας δὲ τὰς ἐν αὐτῇ κακίας ἅμα τῷ λυπεῖσθαι διὰ παντὸς ὡς ἂν οὗ προὔθετο τυχεῖν οὐ δυνάμενος. Κακοδαίμων is mythologized in Epictetus *Diatr.* 4.4.38: "Otherwise, I would have you see that you must be ever the slave of the man who is able to secure your release, to the man who is able to hinder you in everything, and you must serve him as an Evil Genius." The theme of this passage is very close to Galen's (*Ind.* 79b–83). A corresponding mythologized ET of *Ind.* 81 might be: "compelled to live as a most evil genius."

[97] Commodus is reputed to have maintained a harem of 300 girls and 300 boys, hosting huge orgies. According to SHA *Comm.* 10.9, "He also had in his company a man with a male member larger than that of most animals, whom he called Onos."

[98] Background on the treatise's strategy of "training the φαντασίαι" is provided in n. 56 above.

of avoiding distress, but it is not an option for those ill disposed by nature to moral education (cf. *Ind.* 57), least of all those guided by the pleasure principle. In such cases, he says, "experience is a teacher of the unexpected" (*Ind.* 83). This final statement expresses the same content as the well-known adage attributed to Julius Caesar that experience is a teacher.[99] For Caesar, the idea was positive. At some level Galen agrees.[100] For Galen, however, an important outcome of education is the ability to anticipate, even predict, what will happen before it happens – that is, *not* (always) to be at the mercy of experience.[101] To learn from experience is, in a sense for Galen, not to have learned at all (cf. *Ind.* 52). If Hankinson is correct (above) that Galen's remarks about 'natural' potential for moral education allude to Commodus vis-à-vis Marcus Aurelius,[102] then this moral adage from Caesar may also critique Commodus. As a pleasure seeker, despite his excellent pedigree and education, Commodus learns everything from experience.

Apart from Galen, was Commodus ever viewed as, in any sense, guided by the pleasure principle? Both Cassius Dio and Herodian attest precisely this point. According to Cassius Dio:

> Commodus was wholly devoted to pleasure (εὐθυμίαις) and gave himself up to chariot racing, caring nothing for anything of that nature [i.e., those things related to the duties of his office].[103]

Herodian (1.13.7–8), too, comments on Commodus' addiction to pleasure. The passage shares important points in common with *Ind.* 80 (see above).

> He [Commodus] cut himself off from his interest in moral studies and continually gave his whole mind to the slavish pursuit of unrestrained physical pleasure day and night (ἀλλὰ τῆς μὲν περὶ τὰ καλὰ σπουδῆς ἀπῆγεν ἑαυτόν, δεδούλωντο δὲ πᾶσαν αὐτοῦ τὴν ψυχὴν νύκτωρ τε καὶ μεθ' ἡμέραν ἐπάλληλοι καὶ ἀκόλαστοι σώματος ἡδοναί). Any person of moderation (μετρίως) or anyone who even mildly reminded him still of what he had been taught was driven from the court on a charge of conspiracy, while clowns and performers of scurrilous acts gained complete control over him.

It would seem, then, that although Galen's discussion of pleasure-seekers in *Ind.* 62 caricatures Epicureans as birds, further advice on this topic in *Ind.* 79b – *to someone Galen says does not need it* – imbues both passages with a layer of political critique.

---

[99] Cf. *rerum omnium magister usus* (*Bell. civ.* 2.8).

[100] For Galen, experience plays an important role in the art of medicine. See E.g., *Nat.Fac.* 2.41.8; 2.42.2; *MM* 10.5.8; 10.334.15; 10.375.16.

[101] Galen's superior ability at prediction is the topic of *On Prognosis* (*Praen.* 14.599–673).

[102] See p. 177 above.

[103] 72 (73).10.2: Ὅτι ὁ Κόμμοδος εὐθυμίαις τε πάνυ προσέκειτο καὶ ἁρματηλασίᾳ προσεῖχε, καὶ οὔτ' ἀρχὴν τῶν τοιούτων τι αὐτῷ ἔμελεν. E. Cary (LCL) speculates that the referent is most likely Commodus' role as emperor. Elsewhere, Cassius Dio says that Commodus devoted himself to a life of ease (72 [73].10.3).

Conclusion

De indolentia is almost certainly a product of the months immediately following the death of Commodus. Although Galen usually exercises restraint with respect to political commentary, in a letter to an old friend in which he spells out his combative philosophical strategy for maintaining composure in the face of devastating loss – having just survived a reign of terror in which many like him were suddenly, unexpectedly exiled, poisoned, or killed – he broaches the topic. Since the climate of the city remains chaotic, he does not abandon all caution. Five claimants to the title of Roman emperor in one year, following a terrifying and mad despot, are not circumstances promoting reckless παρρησία. The year of 193 quakes with the aftershocks of a year more frightening than anyone could remember.[104] Yet in the wake of Commodus' death and in response to a friend's request, Galen publishes his most extensive critical opinions of the imperial palace (*Ind.* 51).

---

[104] On his death, the Senate declared Commodus a public enemy and restored the original name to the city of Rome and its institutions. Many of his statues were destroyed. In 197, however, Septimius Severus had the Senate deify him (SHA *Sev.* 11.3–4; 12.8; cf. *Did. Iul.* 2.6; *Comm.* 17.6; 20.5). See Eric R. Varner, *Mutilation and Transformation: Damnatio Memoriae and Roman Imperial Portraiture* (Monumenta Graeca et Romana 10; Leiden: Brill, 2004), 136–55.

Christian Trajectories

John T. Fitzgerald

Galen's *De indolentia* in the context of Greco-Roman Medicine, Moral Philosophy, and Physiognomy

Introduction: *De indolentia* and the Galenic Renaissance

Since its discovery in January of 2005, Galen's *De indolentia* (*Ind.* = περὶ ἀλυπίας),[1] sometimes also referred to as περὶ ἀλυπησίας,[2] has generated considerable discussion because of its relevance for multiple areas of contemporary research, including medicine, philosophy, the emotions, the New Testament, textual criticism, the composition and editing of ancient books, public and private libraries, storage facilities, fires, the Second Sophistic, and the history of the Antonine Age of imperial Rome. Credit for bringing this fascinating document to the attention of biblical scholars belongs to Clare K. Rothschild and Trevor W. Thompson, who not only organized a number of sessions at various conferences where it was discussed[3] but also provided scholars with the first translation of the work into

---

[1] The work is preserved in a 15th century codex housed in the Vlatades monastery in Thessaloniki. Known as *Vlatadon* 14, the codex contains 27 complete Galenic and pseudo-Galenic treatises, and for that reason it is important not only for the treatise on freedom from distress (περὶ ἀλυπίας) but also for other works in the Galenic corpus (especially *De ordine librorum propriorum* and *De propriis placitis*). *De indolentia* had gone unrecognized because it had been preserved under two corrupted titles, περὶ ἀλυγισίας and περὶ ἀλογισίας. On the discovery of the work, the codex in which it is preserved, and the corrupted titles, see Véronique Boudon-Millot, "Un traité perdu de Galien miraculeusement retrouvé, *Le Sur l'inutilité de se chagriner*: texte grec et traduction française," in *La science médicale antique. Nouveaux regards. Études réunies en l'honneur de J. Jouanna* (ed. V. Boudon-Millot, A. Guardasole, and C. Magdelaine; Paris: Beauchesne, 2008), 72–123, and Véronique Boudon-Millot, "The Library of a Greek Scholar in the Roman Empire: New Testimony from Galen's Recently Discovered *Peri Alupias*," in *Asklepios: Studies on Ancient Medicine* (ed. L. Cilliers; Acta Classica Supplementum 2; Bloemfontein: Classical Association of South Africa, 2008), 7–18.

[2] Véronique Boudon-Millot and Jacques Jouanna (with Antoine Pietrobelli), *Galien:* Ne pas se chagriner (Budé; Paris: Les Belles Lettres, 2010), 2 and 27–29, amend the title to περὶ ἀλυπησίας (see *Ind.* 69, where the reading of the manuscript, ἀλυπεισίας, is corrected to ἀλυπησίας). Inasmuch as lexical support for ἀλυπησία is lacking, it is preferable to refrain from using otherwise unattested Greek words and to use περὶ ἀλυπίας as the treatise's title (see Galen *Lib. Prop.* 12 [K 19.45.17 = BM 169.13–170.13; Véronique Boudon-Millot, *Galien: Introduction générale. Sur l'ordre de ses propres livres. Sur ses propres livres. Que l'excellent médecin est aussi philosophe* [Budé; Paris: Les Belles Lettres, 2007]).

[3] An earlier version of this article was presented at the Christian Scholars' Conference at Pepperdine University in June of 2011, where my task for that session was to situate the work within the Greco-Roman world. This revised version maintains that same emphasis.

English.⁴ Their industry has had the salutary effect of prompting more biblical scholars to pay closer attention to Galen (whom we have generally neglected),⁵ both in his own right as an author and in his relevance for both Hellenistic Judaism and early Christianity. The sheer quantity of his literary corpus demands such attention. Inasmuch as Galen's "writings in Greek amount to approximately ten percent of all surviving Greek literature before AD 350,"⁶ we neglect his treatises at our own peril. Increased attention to Galen by biblical scholars will coincide with a resurgence of interest in Galen by classicists, historians of ancient medicine, and specialists in ancient philosophy that began in the 1960s and is ongoing.⁷ Indeed, as Vivian Nutton wrote already in 1973, this current resurgence of interest "is without parallel since the early seventeenth century,"⁸ with some experts on ancient philosophy now beginning to use Galen to elucidate early Christians authors and texts.⁹ Such multi-disciplinary contributions are to

---

⁴ Clare K. Rothschild and Trevor W. Thompson, "Galen: 'On the Avoidance of Grief,'" *EC* 2, no. 1 (2011): 110–29. See also their more recent discussion: Clare K. Rothschild and Trevor W. Thompson, "Galen's *On the Avoidance of Grief*: The Question of a Library at Antium," *CP* 107, no. 2 (2012): 131–45.

⁵ Important exceptions to this general neglect are Robert L. Wilken, *The Christians as the Romans Saw Them* (New Haven: Yale University Press, 1984), and Loveday C. A. Alexander, "Paul and the Hellenistic Schools: The Evidence of Galen," in *Paul in his Hellenistic Context* (ed. T. Engberg-Pedersen; Minneapolis: Fortress, 1995), 60–83, and Loveday C. A. Alexander, "The Passions in Galen and the Novels of Chariton and Xenophon," in *Passions and Moral Progress in Greco-Roman Thought* (ed. J. T. Fitzgerald; New York: Routledge, 2008), 175–97.

⁶ Vivian Nutton, *Ancient Medicine* (2d. ed.; London: Routledge, 2004), 391 n. 21. His estimate excludes what survives in Arabic and other languages.

⁷ For an orientation to Galen and recent bibliography, see R. J. Hankinson, ed., *The Cambridge Companion to Galen* (Cambridge: Cambridge University Press, 2008), and for the standard abbreviations of the titles of Galen's works see pages 399–403. In discussing Galen, I sometimes provide my own translations and in such cases indicate where I have done so. In general, however, I have used the standard translations of Galen's works, sometimes with slight modifications. These translations are as follows: *Protrepticus* (*Exhortation to the Arts*), *Ars Medica* (*The Art of Medicine*), *De temperamentis* (*On Mixtures*), *De optima corporis nostri constitutione* (*The Best Constitution of Our Bodies*), *Quod animi mores corporis temperatura sequuntur* (*The Faculties of the Soul Follow the Mixtures of the Body*), and *De pulsibus ad Tirones* (*On the Pulse for Beginners*): Peter N. Singer, *Galen: Selected Works* (Oxford: Oxford University Press, 1997). *De usu partium* (*On the Utility of the Parts*): Margaret T. May, *Galen: On the Usefulness of the Parts of the Body* (2 vols.; Ithaca: Cornell University Press, 1968). *De propriorum animi cuiuslibet affectuum dignotione et curatione* (*Aff.Dig.*; *The Passions of the Soul*): Paul W. Harkins, *Galen: On the Passions and Errors of the Soul* (Columbus: Ohio State University Press, 1963); *De placitis Hippocratis et Platonis* (*On the Doctrines of Hippocrates and Plato*): Phillip De Lacy, *Galen: On the Doctrines of Hippocrates and Plato* (3 vols.; *CMG* 5.4.1–2; Berlin: Akademie, 1980–4); *De methodo medendi* (*On the Therapeutic Method*): Ian Johnston and G. H. R. Horsley, *Galen: Method of Medicine* (3 vols.; LCL; Cambridge: Harvard University Press, 2011); *De praenotione ad Epigenem* (*On Prognosis*): Vivian Nutton, *Galen: On Prognosis* (*CMG* 5.8.1; Berlin: Akademie Verlag, 1979); *Ind.* (*On the Avoidance of Grief*): Rothschild and Thompson, "Galen: 'On the Avoidance of Grief.'"

⁸ Vivian Nutton, "The Chronology of Galen's Early Career," *CQ* 23 (1973): 158–71 [esp. 158].

⁹ See, for example, Jaap Mansfeld, "Galen, Papias, and Others on Teaching and Being Taught," in *Things Revealed: Studies in Early Jewish and Christian Literature in Honor of*

be welcomed, for they are often extremely useful in sharpening our understanding of the ancient Mediterranean world.

Christian interest in Galen is not new. Already during Galen's own lifetime, during the late second and early third centuries, some Roman Christians were so enamored of Galen that one critic accused these Christian "Galenists" of practically worshipping (προσκυνεῖται) him (Eusebius, *Hist. eccl.* 5.28.14).[10] Later in the third century, it is highly probable that Origen, as Robert M. Grant suggested long ago,[11] had read Galen and has his *De usu partium* particularly in mind when he says,

> Each member of our bodies has been made by God, the Craftsman (τεχνίτου), for some work, but it is not for all to know what is the power and use (χρεία) of the members, even the least significant part. For those among physicians (ἰατρῶν) who are involved in dissection are able to say for what use (χρήσιμον) each part, even the smallest part (μόριον), has been deemed by Providence (προνοίας) (*Philoc.* frg. 2.2 = *Hom. Jer.* 39).[12]

As a physician, Galen was famous for his dissections, and his *De usu partium* is thoroughly teleological, "a huge example of the argument from design."[13] Furthermore, he uses the word πρόνοια at least 73 times in this treatise, which he calls both a *hieros logos*[14] and "a genuine hymn" (ὕμνον ἀληθινόν) with which he praises (ὑμνείσθω) the Demiurge, to whom he makes repeated ref-

---

Michael E. Stone (ed. E. G. Chazon, D. Satran, and R. A. Clements; Supplements to the Journal for the Study of Judaism 89; Leiden: Brill, 2004), 317–29.

[10] The critic was the author of *The Little Labyrinth*, which is known only from three quotations given by Eusebius in *Hist. eccl.* 5.28. These Christians were similarly enthusiastic about Aristotle and Theophrastus, and they appear to have applied Aristotelian logic to the interpretation of Scripture. Their veneration of Galen was also quite likely related to his logic, and as Hermann Schöne, "Ein Einbruck der antiken Logik und Textkritik in die altchristliche Theologie," in *Pisciculi: Studien zur Religion und Kultur des Altertums* (ed. T. Klauser and A. Rücker; Münster: Aschendorff, 1939), 252–65 [esp. 260], suggests, it is very likely that they used Galen's *Institutio logica* (see John S. Kieffer, *Galen's* Institutio Logica: *English Translation, Introduction, and Commentary* [Baltimore: Johns Hopkins, 1964]), which was possibly written in the 190's. For additional discussion and bibliography, see John T. Fitzgerald, "Eusebius and *The Little Labyrinth*," in *The Early Church in Its Context: Essays in Honor of Everett Ferguson* (ed. A. J. Malherbe, F. W. Norris, and J. W. Thompson; NovTSup 90; Leiden: Brill, 1998), 120–46 [esp. 121–3].

[11] Robert M. Grant, "Paul, Galen, and Origen," *JTS* 34 (1983): 533–6 [esp. 535]. My comments are intended to strengthen Grant's suggestion. Grant also argues that Origen's (mistaken) idea that Celsus was an Epicurean derives from *Lib.Prop.* 16 (K 19.48.8 = BM 172.14–173.3), where a letter to "Celsus the Epicurean" is mentioned, and that Origen uses Galen as a source for the argument in *Cels.* 1.9–10.

[12] The translation, slightly modified, is by James C. Smith, *Origen:* Homilies on Jeremiah, Homily on 1 Kings 28 (FC 97; Washington, DC: Catholic University of America Press, 1998), 279.

[13] May, *Galen:* On the Usefulness of the Parts of the Body, 1:11.

[14] On the *hieros logos*, see esp. Roland Baumgarten, *Heiliges Wort und Heilige Schrift bei den Griechen: Hieroi Logoi und verwandte Erscheinungen* (ScriptOralia 110; Reihe A: Altertumswissenschaftliche Reihe 26. Tübingen: Gunther Narr, 1998).

erence throughout the work. This praise, he says, is superior to innumerable and costly sacrifices, and composing it is an act of "genuine piety" (τὴν ὄντως εὐσέβειαν) on his part.[15] He also occasionally calls the divine designer "Craftsman" (τεχνίτης) as Origen does in the passage cited above, as well as "Nature."[16] Consequently, if Origen is not thinking of Galen here, he is at least referring to the medical-philosophical tradition exemplified by him.

For his part, Galen certainly knew about both Jews and Christians,[17] and he may even have read some biblical books.[18] Although he admired their stress on virtue, he rejected their insistence on absolute divine omnipotence and emphasis on faith, insisting instead on the necessity of proof. Ironically, one of his formulations in this regard sounds rather Pauline: "I shall show [this] not by persuasive words but by clear demonstrations" (δείξειν οὐ λόγοις πιθανοῖς, ἀλλ' ἐναργέσιν ἀποδείξεσιν: *UP* 14.7 [K 4.169.7–8 = Helmreich 2.302]), which sounds remarkably like some textual versions of 1 Cor 2:4 (οὐκ ἐν πειθοῖ[ς] σοφίας [λόγοις] ἀλλ' ἐν ἀποδείξει). This is unlikely to be an echo of Paul[19] but rather a remarkably similar antithetical rhetorical formulation.

The purpose of this article is not to pursue such possible parallels in thought and expression between Galen and various Christian authors, as interesting as such a study might be. My goal is much more modest. My primary aims are to contribute to contextualizing the treatise within the larger Greco-Roman world and to elucidate some of its more neglected features. Following some introductory comments on the translation of the Greek word λύπη, I shall briefly seek to situate Galen's treatise within its philosophical and medical contexts,[20] and then turn to the treatise itself, where I shall focus on one statement in the third section of the work and indicate how Galen draws at this point on Greco-Roman physiognomic traditions.

---

[15] *UP* 3.10 (K 3.237 = Helmreich 1.174).

[16] See, for example, *UP* 10.9 (K 3.803.11–12 = Helmreich 2.86), where Galen repudiates sophists because they accuse Nature of lacking skill in the design of the human body. Defending the utility of the supposedly useless and insignificant eyelid, he says, "And they are so senseless as not yet to admit that the One forming and framing so many wonderful parts is a Craftsman" (τεχνίτην).

[17] See esp. Richard Walzer, *Galen on Jews and Christians* (London: Oxford University Press, 1949), which is fundamental for all treatments of Galen's views regarding the two groups. See also Wilken, *The Christians as the Romans Saw Them*, 68–93.

[18] Given Galen's comments on the Jewish and Christian view of creation, it is probable that he had read Genesis (so also Wilken, *The Christians as the Romans Saw Them*, 87). For the possibility that Galen had read the Gospels, see Eduard Norden, *Die antike Kunstprosa* (2 vols.; 3rd ed.; Leipzig: Teubner, 1915), 2:518–19 n. 1, and Grant, "Paul," 534; for Galen's reading of any NT books as unlikely, see Wilken, *The Christians as the Romans Saw Them*, 87.

[19] *Contra* Grant, "Paul," 534.

[20] I omit here any consideration of rhetorical and non-discursive contexts for the discussion and treatment of grief. On Greco-Roman funerals as consolatory rituals in regard to grief, see esp. Donovan J. Ochs, *Consolatory Rhetoric: Grief, Symbol, and Ritual in the Greco-Roman Era* (Studies in Rhetoric/Communication; Columbia: University of South Carolina, 1993).

Translating the Term λύπη

The title of this work has been variously translated into English. Renderings include *On the Avoidance of Grief,*[21] *On Freedom from Grief,*[22] *On Not Feeling Grief,*[23] *On the Absence of Grief,*[24] *On Consolation from Grief,*[25] *The Avoidance of Pain,*[26] and *Avoiding Distress.*[27] Such different translations raise the issues of how best to render λύπη into English, and what nuance to give the alpha-privative in ἀλυπία (or ἀλυπησία). As for the term λύπη and how best to render it into English, I think that depends principally on the temporal context in which the word occurs. If the reference is to someone that an individual once knew, admired, or loved, but who is now dead, or to something that an individual once owned but has now been lost, or to things said or done in the past that one now regrets, rendering λύπη by the words "grief" or "distress" or even "despair" seems best. If, however, λύπη is being used in regard to a present situation or to a future contingency, "anxiety" or "worry" or some such synonym is often preferable.[28] In his corpus Galen in fact uses the noun λύπη and the verb λυπεῖν in regard to the past, the present, and the future. As Susan Mattern points out, "When Galen discusses grief or *lupe* in *On diagnosing and treating the disorders of the soul,* he describes it as psychic pain over something either treasured and lost or desired and unattainable: especially material comforts, reputation, or sex."[29] Since, however, the chief reference in his *Ind.* is to possessions that have been lost, it is advisable to render it using "grief" or "distress." My own preference is for the latter, and how one renders the alpha privative of ἀλυπία depends on whether one wishes to emphasize that Galen claims to be free from distress (*The Absence of Distress* or *On Freedom from Distress*) or that he is advising how to avoid distress (*The Avoidance of Distress* or *Avoiding Distress*). Galen

---

[21] See, for example, Christopher Gill, Tim Whitmarsh, and John Wilkins, eds., *Galen and the World of Knowledge* (Greek Culture in the Roman World; Cambridge: Cambridge University Press, 2009), 1, and Rothschild and Thompson, "Galen: 'On the Avoidance of Grief,'" 110.

[22] Singer, *Galen*, 21.

[23] Christopher P. Jones, "Books and Libraries in a Newly-Discovered Treatise of Galen," *Journal of Roman Archaeology* 22 (2009): 390–7 [esp. 390].

[24] Susan P. Mattern, *Galen and the Rhetoric of Healing* (Baltimore: Johns Hopkins University Press, 2008), 134.

[25] Matthew C. Nicholls, "Galen and Libraries in the *Peri Alupias*," *JRS* 101 (2011): 123–42 [esp. 123].

[26] Boudon-Millot, "Library of a Greek Scholar," 7.

[27] Christopher Gill, *Naturalistic Psychology in Galen and Stoicism* (Oxford: Oxford University Press, 2010), 243, and Nutton, *Ancient Medicine*, 232, 234. Nutton's annotated translation of *Ind.* in *Galen: Psychological Writings* (ed. P. N. Singer; Cambridge Galen Translations; Cambridge: Cambridge University Press, 2014), 43–106, will also use this title for the work.

[28] So also Mattern, *Galen*, 132, who notes that λύπη "can be translated as 'grief' (for something lost) or 'anxiety' (about a present situation or future contingency)."

[29] Mattern, *Galen*, 134.

in fact does both in this work, and each of these possible English renderings corresponds to these two aspects of the work.

λύπη in Its Philosophical and Medical Contexts

Regardless, however, of how we render the term λύπη, someone may ask, What does λύπη have to do with ἀρετή? That is, what do distress and grief or, indeed, the emotions in general, the πάθη, have to do with virtue and ethics? For Hellenistic moral philosophy, the answer is "everything." As I have argued elsewhere, "Thoughtful people throughout the ancient Mediterranean world gave great attention to the πάθη because they recognized that the emotions were inextricably linked to proper conduct. From both a theoretical and a practical standpoint, to speak of virtue without giving due attention to the emotions was as impossible as it was inconceivable. Understanding the nature of the emotions was viewed as the basis of all ethical philosophy."[30] As Galen himself argued in his *De placitis Hippocratis et Platonis*, "The doctrine of the virtues follows necessarily from the doctrine of the emotions" (*CMG* 5.4.1.2 5.6.1 [327] = K 5.469, my trans.). Without control over one's emotions, progress in the moral life was not possible.[31]

As a philosopher and ethicist, therefore, Galen was necessarily interested in the emotions, but his activity as a physician also required him to give attention to the emotions, and especially to λύπη. This was because he understood that grief and the other emotions have physiological effects. Basic to Galen's understanding of good health was his theory of the four humours (blood, yellow bile, black bile, and phlegm). These humours or bodily fluids must be in the proper mixture (εὐκρασία) in the human frame for a person to be healthy; if they are not properly mixed (δυσκρασία) and thus not balanced, the consequence of this imbalance is disease and emotional distress.[32]

In *De optima corporis nostri constitutione* he notes two causes of harm to the body – external influences and excretions from foods – and he places exhaustion, grief (λύπας), insomnia, and worry in the category of external influences (*Opt. Corp.Const.* 3 [K 4.742.10–12]). Well-proportioned, properly functioning bodies

---

[30] John T. Fitzgerald, "Anger, Reconciliation, and Friendship in Matthew 5:21–26," in *Israel's God and Rebecca's Children: Christology and Community in Early Judaism and Christianity: Essays in Honor of Larry W. Hurtado and Alan F. Segal* (ed. D. B. Capes, A. D. DeConick, H. K. Bond, and T. A. Miller; Waco: Baylor University Press, 2007), 359–70, 462–73 [esp. 362].

[31] See the essays in John T. Fitzgerald, ed., *Passions and Moral Progress in Greco-Roman Thought* (London: Routledge, 2008).

[32] The theory of the four humours is Hippocratic, but its prestige, according to Jacques Jouanna, *Greek Medicine from Hippocrates to Galen* (trans. N. Allies; Studies in Ancient Medicine 40; Leiden: Brill, 2012), 338, derives from Galen, who showed "in his *Commentary on Hippocrates' The Nature of Man* that this theory was the foundation of Hippocrates' work."

with a good mixture of the four humours are relatively immune to these external influences, for such bodies "will automatically be endowed with the best humours of all, and thus will be better able to withstand grief (λύπη), anger, insomnia, worry, rain, drought, plague, and indeed all causes of disease. It is ill-humoured bodies which most readily succumb to such causes, since they are in themselves already near to a state of disease" (*Opt.Corp.Const.* 3 [K 4.743.3–9]).

It is imperative, therefore, for everyone, but especially for those most susceptible to disease, to be wary of the emotions. In his treatise *Quod animi mores corporis temperatura sequuntur*, he warns that the soul is a slave (δουλεύειν) to the mixtures, which have the power (ἐξουσίαν) to make the soul "sadder (λυπηροτέραν), less bold (ἀτολμοτέραν) and more disheartened (ἀθυμοτέραν)" (*QAM* 3 [K 4.779.15–18], my trans.).

In *Ars Medica* he argues that "one must abstain from excess of all affections of the soul: anger, grief (λύπης), pride, fear, envy, and worry, for these will change the natural composition of the body" (*Ars Med.* 24 [K 1.371.10–14]). They do so by increasing yellow bile – one of the four humours – and this buildup affects the liver. "Worry, anger, grief (λῦπαι), labour, physical exercise, sleeplessness, and lack of food, as well as other sorts of lack, are further causes of the accumulation of yellow bile, because they increase its production in the liver" (*Temp.* 2.6 [K 1.633.11–15]). The mouth of the stomach can also be affected, making one, quite literally, "sick to the stomach." "Yellow bile collects in the stomachs of persons who are distressed" (τοῖς λυπηθεῖσι), and "this is why distressed persons (οἱ λυπηθέντες) vomit bile."[33] The resulting imbalance of mixtures in the body is not only physically uncomfortable but also potentially dangerous, even fatal, and necessitates treatment.[34]

Galen, in keeping with longstanding philosophical tradition, uses a medical term, θεραπεία, "care, healing, treatment," to refer to how to deal with these emotional "diseases."[35] In his *De propriorum animi cuiuslibet affectuum digno-*

---

[33] *PHP* 2.8.15–7 (K 5.239–40 = *CMG* 5.4.1.2 161.15–17). For yellow bile flowing from the liver into the stomach, see *Temp.* 2.6 (K 1.630.7–8). For a concern with foods and ingredients that might "upset" (λυπῆσαι) the stomach and affect the taste, see Galen, *Alim.Fac.* 1 (K 6.478.5), 8 (K 6.572.7), and 14 (K 6.685.4). For the stomach becoming imbalanced (*dyskratic*) after being upset, see *MM* 7.11 (K 10.514.14–16).

[34] For death on account of λύπη, see Galen *Ind.* 7; *Loc.Aff.* 8.302.1; *Comp.Med.Gen.* 13.459.4–5; 861.13–14, and Mattern, *Galen*, 135, 199 [esp. her case numbers 314–16]. On the two passages from *De compositione medicamentorum per Genera*, see Jean-Marie Jacques, "La méthode de Galien pharmacologue dans les deux traités sur les médicaments composés," in *Galen on Pharmacology: Philosophy, History and Medicine* (Studies in Ancient Medicine 16; Leiden: Brill, 1997), 105. See also *MM* 12.6 (K 10.847.1–5) for Galen's reference to some patients having the appearance of a cadaver (νεκρώδης) on their faces – the so-called "Hippocratic face" that portends impending death – with the sleepless and the distressed (λυπηθῶσιν) reckoned among such patients.

[35] Richard J. Duling, *A Dictionary of Medical Terms in Galen* (Leiden: Brill, 1993), 178, defines it as "*medical* or *surgical treatment* or *cure*," and gives some of the principal texts in

tione et curatione,³⁶ he argues that all the emotions are diseases of the soul (*Aff. Dig.* 7 [K 5.35], 10 [K 5.54]), and like the diseases that attack the body, they are potentially dangerous; left unchecked, they will grow and become "incurable" (ἀνίατος) and thus ultimately fatal (7 [K 5.36], 9 [K 5.52]). Treatment of such diseases requires surgery that entails the "excision" (7 [K 5.36, 55]: ἐκκόπτειν; 7 [K 5.56]: ἀποκόπτειν) of the diseased part of the soul. This is the only way to "save" (σωθῆναι) the patient (7 [K 5.55]; see also 2–3 [K 5.7]; 5 [K 5.25]; 7 [K 5.53]), and this afflicted and infectious psychic part must be removed at the root; otherwise it will grow back and once again become a threat (7 [K 5.36]).

All of this is particularly true of λύπη, an ancient (*Aff.Dig* 5 [K 5.24]) and universally acknowledged emotion/disease (2–3 [K 5.7]). "No one fails to see clearly that λύπη is an evil of the soul, just as pain is an evil for the body" (7 [K 5.37]). Furthermore, "all grief is a disease, and envy is the worst grief, whether we call it an emotion or a kind of pain that borders on grief" (7 [K 5.35]).³⁷ λύπη, he says, is a disease to which the young are especially susceptible (7 [K 5.38]), but they are not the only ones, as Galen's own case histories demonstrate. Furthermore, he is fully aware of the wide range of events that can occasion grief. In his commentary on the Hippocratic treatise *Prognostics*, he mentions such precipitating events as the deaths of children, members of the household, relatives, and friends, the anticipated disturbance of one's entire homeland, the loss of possessions, the loss of honor, and a host of things associated with erotic love (*Hipp. Prog.* 18b.19.2–8; see also *Aff.Dig.* 7 [K 5.43]).

As Galen's comments and case histories clearly prove, ancient medicine was acutely aware of the role of the emotions in physical health and of the tendency of the physically ill to become emotionally distraught. This awareness was ancient. For example, Thucydides, in his discussion of the plague that broke out in Athens in 430 during the second year of the Peloponnesian War, comments that "the most terrible thing of all was the despair (ἀθυμία) into which people fell when they realized that they had caught the plague; for they would immediately adopt an attitude of utter hopelessness (ἀνέλπιστον), and, by giving in this way, would lose their powers of resistance" (2.51.4).³⁸ Doctors' awareness of the crucial role played by the emotions caused them to look for symptoms of λύπη and to ask questions of patients to determine their emotional state. For instance,

---

which Galen uses the term. For a treatment of Galen's "therapy of emotions" with attention to its philosophical dimensions, see Gill, *Naturalistic Psychology*, 246–80.

³⁶ This work (*Aff.Dig.* [K 5.1–57]) is closely related to *De animi cuiuslibet peccatorum dignotione et curatione* (*Pecc.Dig.* [K 5.58–103]). Because they are complementary, Singer, *Galen*, 100–49, translates them together as two parts of a single treatise and uses a combined title (*The Affections and Errors of the Soul*) to refer to them.

³⁷ Because envious people are grieved when they observe the success of others, Galen here considers envy a form of λύπη, indeed, the most insidious.

³⁸ The translation is that of Rex Warner, *Thucydides:* History of the Peloponnesian War (Harmondsworth, Middlesex: Penguin, 1972), 154.

Rufus of Ephesus, who was active in the early second century during the reign of Trajan (98–117), wrote a work on interrogating the patient, known as *Medical Questions*. He says,

> One must put questions to the patient, for thereby certain aspects of the disease can be better understood, and the treatment rendered more effective. And I place the interrogation of the patient himself first, since in this way you can learn how far his mind is healthy or otherwise; ... As to the physical strength or weakness of patients, you will recognize these clearly if you have to do, on the one hand, with an individual possessing full vocal power, and who relates events in a straightforward way; while another makes frequent pauses and speaks in a feeble voice. ... Thus excessive boldness (θρασύτης) and untimely grief (ἄκαιρος λύπη) are signs of *melancholia*, and it is chiefly by his speech that an individual shows boldness (θαρρῶν) or distress (ἀνιώμενος).[39]

In contrast to Rufus, Galen in his medical practice did not focus on the patient's speech as indicative of grief, though he did write a work in four books *On the Voice* (*Ord.Lib.Prop.* 2 [K 19.55 = Boudon-Millot 93.6–7]). Instead, Galen paid attention primarily to the pulse,[40] arguing that "mental states, anger, pleasure, grief and fear, are revealed by the pulses first of all."[41] An irregular pulse beat, for example, indicates that the soul of a patient is disturbed (*Praen.* 6.8 [K 14.632.15–633.1 = *CMG* 5.8.1 102.14–18]). He indicates the different kinds of pulses associated with the emotions in his *De pulsibus ad Tirones*. Whereas "in anger the pulse is deep, large, vigorous, quick, and frequent, ... in grief it is small, slow, faint, and sparse" (*Puls.* 12 [K 8.473.13–14, 17]; see also *Caus.Puls.* 9.160.4–5). He also notes somatic changes that may occur in connection with grief, such as chills (*Caus.Puls.* 9.160.7), fevers (*MM* 10.4 [K 10.679.5–6]; 10.5 [K 10.687.6]; 10.6 [K 10.687.15–17]; *Hipp.Epid.* 17a.786.12), and fatigue (*MM* 10.2 [K 10.671.1–2]). In *De praenotione ad Epigenem* Galen tells several stories

---

[39] Rufus *Quaest. med.* 1–2, 4. The translation (slightly modified) is that of Arthur J. Brock, *Greek Medicine: Being Extracts Illustrative of Medical Writers from Hippocrates to Galen* (London: Dent, 1929), 114, who renders ἄκαιρος λύπη as "depression." The same translation ("Niederschlagenheit") is given by Hans Gärtner, ed., *Rufus von Ephesos* (*CMG* Suppl. 4; Berlin: Akademie Verlag, 1962), 27, 53. My translation follows that of Charles Daremberg and Charles-Émile Ruelle, *Oeuvres de Rufus d'Éphèse* (Paris: L'Imprimerie Nationale, 1879), 196, who render it literally as "une tristesse intempestive" ("untimely sadness"). The phrase does not occur elsewhere in Rufus' preserved writings, but Galen, in describing signs of an incipient disease, mentions those that deviate from the norm by occurring at a time that is not customary (μὴ κατὰ τὸν συνήθη καιρόν) and uses ἄκαιρος of a desire for sex at an unusual time (*Ars Med.* 21 [K 1.360.14]; for the correct time for sexual activity, see *Ars Med.* 24 [K 1.371.18–372.7]). That suggests that Rufus has in mind a grief that is not connected with a usual or recognized occasion for sorrow, such as the loss of a loved one.

[40] Galen wrote at least seven works on the pulse that are extant, including *On the Function of the Pulse, On the Pulse for Beginners, Differences of Pulses, Diagnosis by Pulses, Causes of Pulses, Prognosis by Pulses* and *Synopsis on Pulses*. He mentions λύπη at least eleven times in these works.

[41] Nutton, *Galen:* On Prognosis, 197. On Galen's use of the pulse as a diagnostic method, see Mattern, *Galen*, 78, 93–94, 120, 148, 151, 154–7.

in which changes in the beats of the patient's pulse are the basis for correctly diagnosing what is wrong with that individual. One such story or "case history" involves a woman that he was called in to see because she

> was said to lie awake at night, constantly tossing from one position to another. When I found that she was not suffering from fever, I asked about each of the details that had happened to her from which we know the presence of insomnia (ἀγρυπνίας). She replied hesitatingly or not at all, as if to show the folly of such questions, and finally turned over, buried herself completely deep in the blankets, covered her head with a small wrap and lay there as if wanting to sleep. On my departure I decided she was suffering from one of two things: from a depression (δυσθυμεῖν) caused by black bile or from some worry (λυπουμένην) (*Praen.* 6.2–4 [K 14.631.6–16 = *CMG* 5.8.1 100.15–102.2]).

As the story goes on, it was the latter. Conversations with the woman's maid revealed that the patient "was racked with grief" (λύπη τειρομένην) and "that the woman was troubled by some psychological disturbance" (*Praen.* 6.5–6 [K 14.632.8–9 = *CMG* 5.8.1 102.2–10]). It turned out that the woman was in love with a certain Pylades, and that when she heard his name, her pulse began to beat wildly. When other names were mentioned, the pulse remained regular.

A second story involves a slave of a rich man who was anxious (*Praen.* 6.11 [K 14.633.18 = *CMG* 5.8.1 102.29–104.2]): λυπούμενος) because he was about to be audited by his master. He knew that the books would not balance and that a considerable sum of money was missing. As with the lovesick woman, λύπη manifested itself in sleeplessness.[42] "He was kept awake by the thought

---

[42] The close connection between sleeplessness and grief in Galen's thinking is also indicated by the fact that he quite frequently gives them together or in close proximity in various lists; see, for instance, *CAM* 1.302.10; *Temp.* 2.6 (K 1.633.12–13); *Opt.Corp.Const.* 3 (K 4.743.5); *Loc. Aff.* 8.185.1; *Praes.Pul.* 9.388.8–9; *Cris.* 9.696.2–3; 698.7, 11; 700.5; *MM* 8.2 (K 10.535.11–12); 8.2–3 (K 10.555.13–14); 10.2 (K 10.666.4, 9; 671.1); 10.4 (K 10.679.6; 681.14); 10.5 (K 10.685.7; 687.6); 10.6 (K 10.692.16–17); 12.6 (K 10.847.3–4); *MMG* 11.12.4, 9; 13.17–18; 16.7; *Puer.Epil.* 11.360.14; *HNH* 15.114.7–8; 117.10; *HVA* 15.866.1–2; 867.4; *Hipp.Epid.* 17a.998.9; *Hipp.Aph.* 17b.356.9–11; *Hipp.Prog.* 18b.35.10 ("the insomnia of grief"); 53.7. See also *Aff.Dig.* 7 (K 5.37), where he tells the story of a young man who had been awake all night because he was troubled by grief. In *MM* 8.3 (K 10.555.13–15), he advises, "To those who are sleepless, grieving, or overanxious, [give something that] moistens and induces sleep." On insomnia more generally, see also Galen's *De dignotione ex insomniis*. The most famous patient that Galen treated for insomnia was Marcus Aurelius (who suffered from chronic chest pain and abdominal problems), treating him with theriac, the universal antidote of the Greco-Roman world (*Ant.* 14.3–5). Theriac was a compound drug that contained the opium poppy, but the prescribed dosage was too small to create addiction. On theriac, see John Scarborough, "The Opium Poppy in Hellenistic and Roman Medicine," in *Drugs and Narcotics in History* (ed. R. Porter and M. Teich; Cambridge: Cambridge University Press, 1995), 4–23. On Galen's use of this drug to treat Marcus Aurelius, see Scarborough, "Opium Poppy," 17–18, and François P. Retief, "Marcus Aurelius: Was He an Opium Addict?" in *Asklepios: Studies on Ancient Medicine* (ed. L. Cilliers; Acta Classica Supplementum 2; Bloemfontein: Classical Association of South Africa, 2008), 131–7. There are two treatises in the Galenic corpus that deal with theriac, with one regarded by Nutton as genuine (*De theriaca ad Pisonem*) and the other as

of this and was worn out by anxiety" (λυπούμενος) and considerably "worried" (λυποῖτο) (*Praen.* 6.11 [K 14.633.15–634.2 = *CMG* 5.8.1 102.29–104.2]). The slave's emotional turmoil was so great that his "sudden death" was a distinct possibility (*Praen.* 6.12 [K 14.634.5–6 = *CMG* 5.8.1 104.2–6]). But when he was told by his master that a full statement of accounts wasn't necessary, just an indication of the current balance, the slave became ἄλυπος, free from worry and anxiety, "and in three days recovered his natural physical condition" (*Praen.* 6.13 [K 14.634.9–10 = *CMG* 5.8.1 104.6–8]).

Elsewhere, Galen tells the story of a woman who developed hectic fever because of insomnia and λύπη (*MM* 10.5 [K 10.685.7]); and in Book 6 of his commentary on the Hippocratic *Epidemics*, he narrates a series of stories that describe "patients who die of fever caused by the insomnia that results from their grief."[43] As these anecdotes indicate, for Galen the emotions, especially λύπη, were "causative factors that might have various deleterious effects."[44] Grief had to be combated because it "destroys patients by causing insomnia, which in turn causes fever and sometimes wasting."[45] From a medical standpoint, λύπη is perhaps even more dangerous than anger, for "it hounds its victims, gnawing at them internally, destroying their sleep, wasting their bodies, and driving them mad or to their deaths."[46]

Since λύπη was an important topic both philosophically and physiologically,[47] it is not surprising that Galen wrote a work that he called περὶ ἀλυπίας. But we could not possibly have guessed its precise contents and what occasioned it were it not for the discovery of this text and its publication. That is part of the charm of this text and why it merits our attention.

Galen's *De indolentia* 3 and Greco-Roman Physiognomy

De indolentia is Galen's response to a letter (1) written to him by an old school-boy acquaintance (51, 57) who has learned about the loss of Galen's possessions in the fire of 192 CE (2) and has heard from a third party that Galen was not at all troubled (ἀνιᾶσθαι; see also 11, 29, 38, 46) by this grievous loss (3). Galen assures his acquaintance, who was "amazed" (θαυμασιώτερον) by Galen's re-

---

spurious (*De theriaca ad Pamphilianum*). See Vivian Nutton, "Galen on Theriac: Problems of Authenticity," in *Galen on Pharmacology: Philosophy, History and Medicine* (ed. A. Debru; Studies in Ancient Medicine 16; Leiden: Brill, 1997), 133–51.

[43] Mattern, *Galen*, 135.
[44] S. W. Jackson, "Galen, On Mental Disorder," *Journal of the History of the Behavioral Sciences* 5 (1969): 365–84 [esp. 371], cited by Nutton, *Galen: On Prognosis*, 197.
[45] Mattern, *Galen*, 135.
[46] Mattern, *Galen*, 136.
[47] Grief is by no means unique in this regard. As Mattern, *Galen*, 136, rightly notes, character (ἦθος) is not only an ethical concept for Galen but a medical one as well.

sponse to this tragedy (11), that the reports about his loss and his reaction to it are indeed true. In fact, his loss was worse than his acquaintance had imagined (12b). Whereas others had been emotionally devastated by their losses (7, 38) and one person had died from discouragement and distress (7),[48] Galen had "very easily endured what happened" (38).

That last sentiment – that Galen endured without distress the loss of some of his prize possessions – is the leitmotif of the entire document, occurring in at least a dozen different sections of the work (1, 2, 3, 4, 11, 29, 30, 38, 46, 50b, 70, and 72b), and what he says here about himself is consistent with his self-depiction in *Aff.Dig.*[49] My interest in what follows is focused on one aspect of Galen's self-portrait in this work, namely, his confirmation of the testimony of the third party that, in the aftermath of his loss, he had continued on as before, engaging in his customary activities (τὰ συνήθη) and doing so with a radiant (φαιδρόν) countenance (3). Both of these statements provide evidence that he is truly ἄλυπος in so far as the loss of his books and other items is concerned.[50] The evidence provided by performance of customary activities belongs principally to the medical tradition, which viewed grief as incapacitating. One's ability to carry on with routine activities was thus proof that one was not ill or depressed.[51] The evidence provided by the countenance also has a firm place in the medical

---

[48] For death on account of grief, see note 34 above.

[49] See esp. *Aff.Dig.* 8 (K 5.43–44), 9 (K 5.49, 51–52).

[50] There is at least one occasion on which Galen acknowledges that he has suffered psychic distress. In the *De foetuum formatione*, Galen discusses his futile attempt to find out from philosophers the identity of the Demiurge responsible for skillfully crafting the bodies of humans and animals. Failing to hear an acceptable demonstration from these philosophers, Galen says that he was "greatly distressed (λυπηθεὶς ... μεγάλως) at this" (6 [K 4.695.14–15]) (my trans.).

[51] For Galen on the performance of customary tasks, see *Ars Med.* 37 (1.406.13); *San. Tu.* 6.418.14; *Trem.Palp.* 7.635.17; *Diff.Resp.* 7.877.7; *Loc.Aff.* 8.283.18 ("being healthy and performing customary tasks"); *Di.Dec.* 9.795.15; *MM* 8.3 (K 10.562.18); 10.2 (K 10.668.5); 12.8 (K 10.865.16); *MMG* 11.143.5–6; *Cur.Rat.Ven.Sect.* 6 (K 11.267.8); 10 (K 11.281.1); *Praen.* 14.5 (K 14.672.2–3 = *CMG* 5.8.1 140.15–18); *Hipp.Epid.* 17a.53.7; and *Cons.* 108.9 (Dietz). The performance of usual activities is central to Galen's definition of "sickness" and "disease," constituting the chief criterion. He argues in the *Ars Medica* that people's ability to continue performing their usual activities is what determines whether they are sick (νοσεῖν). As long as such things as a severe headache (such as a migraine) have not prevented individuals from engaging in their usual activities, they may not feel well, but they are not clinically ill (*Ars Med.* 21 [K 1.361.16–362.7]). Of course, at the beginning of a disease, people may still be able to engage in their normal activities (*Di.Dec.* 9.795.15), which makes the actual inception point of disease difficult to determine (*Di.Dec.* 9.795.17–18). Patients who have been sick, on the other hand, but who are improving, will begin to "undertake a small amount of their regular tasks" (*Ars Med.* 37 [K 1.406.13–14]), and a patient who is no longer suffering from a fever "will attempt to carry out his customary tasks" (*MM* 10.2 [K 10.668.4–5]). But if the fever returns, he will break off his normal activities and return to bed (*Trem.Palp.* 7.635.16–636.1). In short, physicians such as Galen used the performance of regular tasks as a factor in assessing whether their patients were emotionally distraught or physically ill. The fact that Galen's customary schedule was not impacted by the loss of his possessions in the fire is thus empirical, medical evidence that he is neither ill nor afflicted by λύπη.

tradition, for ancient physicians examined the face as one part of their diagnosis of illness and disease. Yet in examining the face, medical practitioners were also influenced by physiognomy, for which the face was the primary focus of interest. As we shall see, physiognomy provides the best context for understanding the significance of Galen's radiant countenance.

Physiognomy regards physical traits and features as visible signs of the soul's invisible traits of character (Iamblichus *VP* 17.71) and thus endeavors to discern "the character and dispositions of people by an inference drawn from their facial appearance and expression, and from the form and bearing of their whole body" (Aulus Gellius *Noct. att.* 1.9.2).[52] Interest in physiognomy was widespread,[53] especially in the second century CE,[54] with philosophers, physicians, seers, rhetoricians, historians, biographers, and artists among those who gave attention to it.[55] In Greek tradition, Pythagoras was widely viewed as the inventor of phys-

---

[52] The translation, slightly modified, is that of the LCL. On ancient physiognomy, see esp. Elizabeth C. Evans, *Physiognomics in the Ancient World* (TAPA, n.s., 59:5; Philadelphia: The American Philosophical Society, 1969), and Simon Swain, ed., *Seeing the Face, Seeing the Soul: Polemon's Physiognomy from Classical Antiquity to Medieval Islam* (Oxford: Oxford University Press, 2007), which contains the major physiognomic treatises along with translations by various scholars. Unless otherwise indicated, all translations of these treatises (Pseudo-Aristotle, Polemon, Adamantius, and Anonymous Latinus) are drawn from Swain's volume. For reasons of space, I have largely restricted myself to the physiognomic treatises in discussing the phenomenon of physiognomy.

[53] Sustained interest in physiognomy in the Greek world was comparatively late, especially in comparison with Assyria and Babylon. For physiognomy in ancient Mesopotamia, see Barbara Böck, "Physiognomy in Ancient Mesopotamia and Beyond: From Practice to Handbook," in *Divination and Interpretation of Signs in the Ancient World* (ed. A. Annus; University of Chicago Oriental Institute Seminars 6; Chicago: Oriental Institute of the University of Chicago, 2010), 199–224. For physiognomy in early Judaism, see Mladen Popović, *Reading the Human Body: Physiognomics and Astrology in the Dead Sea Scrolls and Hellenistic-Early Roman Period Judaism* (STDJ 67; Leiden: Brill, 2007). For a pioneering attempt to use physiognomy in the study the New Testament and other early Christian literature, see Mikeal C. Parsons, *Body and Character in Luke and Acts: The Subversion of Physiognomy in Early Christianity* (Grand Rapids: Baker Academic, 2006).

[54] See esp. Elizabeth C. Evans, "The Study of Physiognomy in the Second Century A. D.," *TAPA* 72 (1941): 96–108, who argues that interest in physiognomy "was observable in the latter part of the first century, reached its height in the second century, continued to some extent in the third, and became marked again in the fourth" [96]. See also Maud Gleason, "The Semiotics of Gender: Physiognomy and Self-Fashioning in the Second Century C. E.," in *Before Sexuality: The Construction of Erotic Experience in the Ancient Greek World* (ed. D. M. Halperin, J. J. Winkler, and F. I. Zeitlin; Princeton: Princeton University Press, 1990), 389–415, and Maud Gleason, *Making Men: Sophists and Self-Presentation in Ancient Rome* (Princeton: Princeton University Press, 1995), 55–81.

[55] Clement of Alexandria *Strom.* 1.21.135, associates physicians and seers with the practice of physiognomy. Its importance in rhetoric derives from the keen attention paid to the voice and gesture (including facial expressions) in oratory. Artists were interested in physiognomy because of the importance of properly portraying the ethical traits and characteristic emotions of their subjects; see, for example, Xenophon's account of Socrates' conversation with Parrhasius the painter and Cleiton the sculptor (*Mem.* 3.10, esp. 3.10.8): "The sculptor must represent in his figures the activities of the soul" (trans. LCL). For the use of physiognomy by biographers

iognomy,[56] but Galen attributes this honor to his hero Hippocrates, calling him in this connection "the first of all doctors and philosophers" (*QAM* 7 [K 4.798.4–5], my trans.).[57] He discusses physiognomy most fully in his treatise *Quod animi mores corporis temperamenta sequuntur* (*QAM*), quoting especially Plato, Aristotle, and the Hippocratic *Airs, Waters, Places* and *Epidemics*.[58]

Physiognomy's concern with grief and other emotions was long-standing and is reflected already in the first extant physiognomic treatise, which is Pseudo-Aristotle's *Physiognomonica*, probably written towards the end of the fourth century or the beginning of the third century BCE.[59] Already in the opening of this work the author notes that "the body is clearly affected along with the affections (παθήμασι) of the soul in cases of love and fear and grief (λύπας) and pleasure" (1 [805a5–8]). A psychosomatic connection involving the emotions is also elaborated later in the treatise, where the author says,

> Soul and body seem to me to affect each other sympathetically. A change in the state of the soul alters the appearance of the body, and conversely, when the appearance of the body changes, it changes the state of the soul as well. Grief (ἀνιᾶσθαι) and joy (εὐφραίνεσθαι), to take an instance, are states of the soul, and everyone knows that grief involves a gloomy (σκυθρωπότεροι) and joy a cheerful (ἱλαροί) countenance (4 [808b11–17]).[60]

---

and historians, see Elizabeth C. Evans, "Roman Descriptions of Personal Appearance in History and Biography," *HSCP* 46 (1935): 43–84.

[56] Hippolytus *Haer.* 1.2.5; see also Aulus Gellius *Noct. att.* 1.9.1–2; Porphyry *Vit. Pyth.* 13; Iamblichus *VP* 17.71.

[57] Galen acknowledges, however, that Pythagoras also linked body and soul (*QAM* 1 [K 4.768]).

[58] See also *Temp.* 2.6 (K 1.624); *PHP* 5.5.22–25 (K 5.464 = *CMG* 5.4.1.2 320.29–322.10); *Sem.* 2.5 (K 4.629). On Galen and physiognomy, see esp. Elizabeth C. Evans, "Galen the Physician as Physiognomist," *TAPA* 76 (1945): 287–98, and Evans, *Physiognomics in the Ancient World*, 24–26; Tamsyn S. Barton, *Power and Knowledge: Astrology, Physiognomics, and Medicine under the Roman Empire* (Ann Arbor: University of Michigan Press, 1994), 98–99; and George Boys-Stones, "Physiognomy and Ancient Psychological Theory," in *Seeing the Face, Seeing the Soul: Polemon's Physiognomy from Classical Antiquity to Medieval Islam* (ed. S. Swain; Oxford: Oxford University Press, 2007), 19–124 [esp. 99–109].

[59] The first Greek treatise on physiognomy may have been by Antisthenes (Diogenes Laertius 6.16). The pseudo-Aristotelian treatise on physiognomy is in fact a composite document that incorporates works by two different Peripatetic authors, with the first preserved in *Physiog.* 805a1–808b10, and the second in *Physiog.* 808b11–814b9. For a recent discussion, see Boys-Stones, "Physiognomy and Ancient Psychological Theory," 55–75. For the dating of the work, see Sabine Vogt, trans., *Aristoteles:* Physiognomonica (Aristoteles, Werke in deutscher Übersetzung 18.6; Berlin: Akademie Verlag, 1999), 197, who identifies two treatises but argues unpersuasively that they derive from the same author.

[60] These are the opening words of the second treatise preserved in Pseudo-Aristotle's work. For differences between the two treatises, see Boys-Jones, "Physiognomy," 55–75. For the impact of emotions on the body, see also Pseudo-Aristotle *Physiog.* 6 [812a]: "People with sullen (σκυθρωπά) [that is, wrinkled] brows are vexed (δυσάνιοι); this is owing to the emotion (πάθος), for the troubled (ἀνιώμενοι) are sullen (σκυθρωποί) (my trans.). See also the descrip-

Similarly, Polemon (ca. 88–144 CE), a student of Dio Chrysostom (Philostratus *Vit. soph.* 1.25.539), gives attention to physical signs of sadness and grief, though he focuses on characteristic physical features rather than on temporary expressions of emotion.[61] He argues that very thick eyebrows are indicative of grief and sadness (*Physiog.* 2.37),[62] and he even devotes an entire chapter of his work to "the sign of the depressed and sad man," which he gives as follows:

> His sign is that you see he has a peeling face, bringing together what is between the eyes, with a huge forehead, eyebrows locked together, a furtive gaze, eyelids joined together, and frightened by fear (*Physiog.* 2.51).

Polemon was followed in this regard by the physiognomic author known as the Anonymous Latinus (late fourth century CE), who says:

> The sad (*tristis*) man should be understood as follows: his face is thin, his brow wrinkled, his eyebrows turned in and his eyelids taut (*Physiog.* 97).

Pseudo-Aristotle identifies three major physiognomic methods, with the third of these taking "as its basis the characteristic facial expressions which are observed to accompany different conditions of mind, such as anger, fear, erotic excitement, and all the other passions" (1 [805a28–31]).[63] In commenting on the limitations of this third method, he notes that a person's facial expression is not constant. When the emotions change, so does the person's facial expression. For example, "a naturally cheerful (εὔθυμον) man, if he is distressed (λυπηθῆναι), will change his expression accordingly" (1 [805b8–9]).[64]

As the preceding discussion indicates, Pseudo-Aristotle's third method, which is sometimes referred to as the "expressive" or "anatomical" method,[65] focuses on the face, which he regards as the part of the body that gives the clearest signs (6 [814b2–5]). This focus is not only consistent with the Hippocratic insistence

---

tion of the sad man in Anonymous Latinus *Physiog.* 97: "his brow wrinkled" (*frons rugosa*), and also 88: "those whose whole face is wrinkled" (*vultus omnis rugosus*).

[61] On Polemon and his treatise, see Gleason, *Making Men*, 21–54, and Swain, "Polemon's Physiognomy," 125–201.

[62] See also Anonymous Latinus *Physiog.* 12, who regards eyebrows as one of the "sure signs" of a person's mind, and says, "When the eyebrows meet, they signify a very sad man, but one who is also not very wise" (18).

[63] The three methods are also mentioned by Anonymus Latinus *Physiog.* 9, where Pseudo-Aristotle's third method is given as the second one.

[64] See also Adamantius *Physiog.* 1.3 ("Sometimes there are alterations of the appearance from what is normal in those who are rejoicing or grieving [λυπουμένων].") and Anonymous Latinus *Physiog.* 11. For a catalog of passages in Latin authors who characterize individuals by describing their momentary appearance, see Evans, "Roman Descriptions," 76–77.

[65] A. MacC Armstrong, "The Methods of the Greek Physiognomists," *Greece & Rome*, 2nd ser., 5 (1958): 52–56, refers to the third method as the "expression" method [53], whereas Jacques André, ed. and trans., *Anonyme Latin:* Traité de physiognomonie (Budé; Paris: Belles Lettres, 1981), 12, calls it the "anatomical" method.

on the face as a focus in medical diagnosis of health and disease[66] but also is in keeping with a widespread Greco-Roman belief that the countenance was the image of a person's mind and revealed his or her character.[67] Physiognomists such as Pseudo-Aristotle are primarily interested in facial features that are permanent (1 [806a7–12]), but they also give attention to pathognomics, that is, the physical manifestations of the emotions, especially in the face.[68] The eyes are viewed as particularly expressive of emotions, with Polemon devoting approximately a third of his *Physiognomonica* to the eyes.[69] The voice is also deemed important in this regard, with Cicero arguing that Nature "has assigned to every emotion a particular look and tone of voice and bearing of its own; and the whole of a person's frame and every look on his face and utterance of his voice are like the strings of a harp, and sound according as they are struck by each successive emotion" (*De or.* 3.216, trans. LCL).[70]

As far as facial and other physical signs of despondency, grief, and sadness are concerned, the Anonymous Latinus author argues that "those whose whole face is wrinkled are sad (*tristes*), that is, δύσθυμοι " (*Physiog.* 88).[71] A change in voice is also regarded as indicative of despondency. Pseudo-Aristotle remarks, "A voice which, starting low, rises to a high pitch, indicates despondency (δυσθυμικοί) and querulousness" (*Physiog.* 6 [813a32–33]). He is followed in this regard by Anonymous Latinus, who similarly says, "Those who begin with a deep voice and finish with a sharp one are prone to weeping and have a mournful mind" (*Physiog.* 78).

Heaviness in speech is given by Polemon as a sign of sadness (*Physiog.* 2.42), and both he and Adamantius (fourth century CE) note that grief can also be in-

---

[66] See esp. [Hippocrates], *Prog.* 2; translated by James Longrigg, *Greek Medicine: From the Heroic to the Hellenistic Age: A Source Book* (New York: Routledge, 1998), 136–7. For the tongue as an important diagnostic aid, see Diogenes of Apollonia (Diels-Krantz 64A19) in Longrigg, *Greek Medicine*, 36.

[67] See, for example, Cicero *De or.* 3.221 (*imago animi vultus*); *Leg.* 1.27 (*vultus ... indicat mores*).

[68] Pseudo-Aristotle *Physiog.* 2 (806b28–29), refers to τὰ παθήματα τὰ ἐπιφαινόμενα ἐπὶ τῶν προσώπων, "the emotions appearing on the face" (my trans.). For the term pathognomics, see Jennifer Montagu, *The Expression of the Passions: The Origin and Influence of Charles Le Brun's "Conférence sur l'expression générale et particulière"* (New Haven: Yale University Press, 1994), 1, and Rosemary Jann, "Sherlock Holmes Codes the Social Body," *ELH* 57 (1990), 685–708 [esp. 693–4].

[69] Evans, "Physiognomy in the Second Century," 97. For the importance of the eyes, see also Theocritus *Epig.* 11; Cicero *De or.* 3.221–3; *Leg.* 1.27; Quintilian *Inst.* 11.3.66–67; Adamantius *Physiog.* 1.4; 2.1; Anonymous Latinus *Physiog.* 10, 19, 45.

[70] See above for the physician Rufus' emphasis on the voice as a diagnostic tool in medical practice.

[71] He attributes this idea to Aristotle, but no such statement appears in the *Physiognomonica*. Its absence lends support to Richard Förster's contention that a fuller version of the work once existed; see Richard Förster, ed., *Scriptores Physiognomonici Graeci et Latini* (2 vols.; Leipzig: Teubner, 1893), 1: xx.

dicated by one's breathing, with both men utilizing images drawn from bodies of water. For Polemon, "If the calmness of the breath is excessive, so that it is as if it were stagnant, motionless water, know that he is sad" (*Physiog.* 2.41). Adamantius, who is usually heavily dependent on Polemon and often paraphrases him (*Physiog.* 1.1), gives a different indication of grief disclosed by breathing: "If the breath, having been still, comes on all at once as if from the ebb and flow of the sea, he is afflicted by some grief (λύπη)" (*Physiog.* 2.41). Similarly, the Anonymous Latinus writer remarks, "When the breath is sometimes quiet, but after a long interval is drawn or expelled excessively as if tossed in a swell, it indicates a man set in great sadness" (*Physiog.* 77).

Galen's reference to his radiant countenance belongs to this physiognomic tradition. His radiant face is suggestive of joy, not grief and the gloomy (σκυθρωπός) visage commonly associated with it. Indeed, Galen's face shows none of the customary signs of grief. If he had been distressed by the loss of his possessions, his face would have changed and shown the emotional impact that the loss was having on his soul. As in the case of his customary activities, his countenance remains just as it was before the fire, completely unchanged (3). Furthermore, the same connection between φαιδρός and freedom from distress that appears here is also present in the treatise *Aff.Dig.*, where Galen says, "In fact, when this man saw me joyful (φαιδρόν) day in and day out for a considerable period of time, he asked me to teach him how to be free from grief (ἀνιῶτο)" (*Aff.Dig.* 10 [K 5.54]) – which was exactly the kind of psychagogic guidance that his old schoolboy acquaintance wanted to receive from Galen (*Ind.* 1, 38; see also *Aff.Dig.* 7 [K 5.37]). Earlier in that same work on the emotions, he contrasts the faces of children – some are "always radiant" (φαιδρά), whereas others are "sullen" (σκυθρωπά) (*Aff.Dig.* 7 [K 5.37]).[72] As that comparison suggests, being φαιδρός is aligned with being εὔθυμος, "cheerful" and "in good spirits" (*San.Tu.* 6.186), just as λύπη is closely associated with δυσθυμία (*Ind.* 7).[73]

Finally, Galen, in keeping with the physiognomic tradition, also associates a radiant countenance with virtue. In his *Protrepticus*, he observes that painters and sculptors depict Hermes with "radiant (φαιδρός) eyes," and he explains this standard physiognomic rendering of the god by saying that artists wish to show the natural beauty of the virtue of his soul (τὴν τῆς ψυχῆς ἀρετήν) shining through them (3 [K 1.3.5]). Furthermore, the god's worshippers, which include his attendants and deputies Socrates, Hippocrates, and Plato (5 [K 1.5.17–19]),

---

[72] Similarly, Polemon *Physiog.* 1.5, says that "luminous and shining" eyes are a good sign, and associates this facial feature with children. See also Anonymous Latinus *Physiog.* 21, 33–34, 96.

[73] These connections and contrasts are neither new nor unique to Galen and the physiognomic treatises. Xenophon, for example, in discussing the facial expression of emotions, contrasts those who look radiant (φαιδροί) because of their good fortune with those who are gloomy and sullen (σκυθρωποί) because of their ill fortune (*Mem.* 3.10.4).

"are as radiant (φαιδρούς) as the god who leads them" (3 [K 1.3.8]). They are contrasted with the uneducated followers of Tyche, who, in striking contrast to Hermes, is depicted as "without eyes," indicating her blindness (2 [K 1.1.6–7]).[74]

In conclusion, Galen was the quintessential ἰατροφιλόσοφος[75] or "physician-philosopher" of the ancient Mediterranean world and a pivotal figure in the history of medicine. Yet he was also very much a man of his own time, deeply indebted to the philosophical, medical, and physiognomic traditions of his world, even while making his own distinctive contributions to each of these traditions. His treatise on distress, like the other writings in his vast corpus, reflects those traditions and Galen's informative use of them.

---

[74] Galen's description of Tyche and her followers shares much in common with the depiction found in the *Tabula of Cebes* 7–8, but in that work she is contrasted with True Education, who, as in some depictions of Hermes, stands on a square rock (18.3; compare Galen *Protr.* 3 [K 1.5.6–7]). See John T. Fitzgerald and L. Michael White, trans., *The Tabula of Cebes* (SBLTT 24; Chico: Scholars Press, 1983), 141 n. 27 and 150 n. 61.

[75] The term occurs on an inscription given by Jules Baillet, ed., *Inscriptions grecques et latines des tombeaux des rois ou syringes à Thebes* (Mémoires publiés par les membres de l'Institut français d'archéologie orientale du Caire 42; Le Caire: Institut français d'archéologie orientale, 1920–6), 1298.

L. MICHAEL WHITE

The Pathology and Cure of Grief (λύπη): Galen's *De indolentia* in Context

Introduction[1]

Early in the year 193 CE the noted physician-philosopher from Pergamum, Galen, who was then living in Italy, wrote a letter of personal advice and exhortation to an unnamed friend. The friend had heard that Galen had lost a great number of books and other valuable possessions during the fire of the previous year in Rome. Galen says that portions of his library along with valuable instruments and medical concoctions were stored "in a warehouse along the *Via Sacra*."[2] Yet reports had spread among his friends that Galen, unlike some others, had taken the tragic losses without distress or grief. The friend had thus written him to ask how he was able to do so. Galen replied with the paraenetic letter[3] *On Being Ungrieved* (Περὶ ἀλυπίας).[4] Known previously only by its title, recorded in the list of Galen's books,[5] the letter-treatise was rediscovered in 2005 in a mixed codex of manuscripts dating to the 15th century from the Vlatadon Monastery at

---

[1] I want to offer a note of thanks to Clare K. Rothschild and Trevor W. Thompson for organizing this volume of studies and the several sessions at the SBL Annual and Regional Meetings that contributed to it.

[2] *De indolentia* 8; there is also a brief (and vaguely critical) reference to the later part of Commodus' reign in *Ind.* 54, but no mention of his successors or the tumultuous events that ensued. On the date and the place of this work in the Galenic corpus see also Christopher Gill, *Naturalistic Psychology in Galen and Stoicism* (Oxford: Oxford University Press, 2010), 252–3 (with further references).

[3] On its epistolary and hortatory features relative to discussions of paraenesis see L. Michael White, "'*Thus the Sage Constantly Reminds Himself*': Personal Epistolary Paraenesis in Galen and Paul," in *The One Who Sows Bountifully: Essays in Honor of Stanley K. Stowers* (ed. C. J. Hodge, S. M. Olyan, D. Ullucci, and E. Wasserman; BJS; Providence: Brown Judaic Studies, 2013), 255–68.

[4] Internally the manuscript consistently uses the deviant orthography ἀλυπησία, -ς. The critical editions noted the problem but did not correct the ms. to the proper ancient form, ἀλυπία, -ς, as found in Galen's list of books (see next note); the standard Latin title has been rendered as *De indolentia*. See also n. 52 below.

[5] *De libris propriis* 12 (K 19.45.16): περὶ ἀλυπίας ἕν ("on being ungrieved, one [book]"). All translations are my own unless otherwise noted.

Thessaloniki.[6] Its rediscovery offers important social and personal information on Galen and his times.[7]

The letter opens as follows:[8]

Ἔλαβόν σου τὴν ἐπιστολὴν ἐν ᾗ παρεκάλεις μοι δηλωσαί σοι τίς ἄσκησις ἢ λόγοι τίνες ἢ δόγματα <τίνα> παρεσκεύασάν με μηδέποτε λυπεῖσθαι. ("I received your letter in which you urged me to clarify for you what sort of training or arguments or doctrines prepared me never to be grieved.")[9]

In *Ind.* 1–11 then, we have an epistolary preamble specifying the friend's request, with numerous references to the fact that he had heard about Galen's amazing fortitude. This opening section then concludes as follows (*Ind.* 10b–11):

Ταῦτ' οὖν οὕτω γενόμενα καὶ αὐτὰ μὲν ἔφης πεπύσθαι, βούλεσθαι δ' (ἀσ)φαλέστερον ἀκοῦσαι παρ' ἐμοῦ. 11 Τὸ γὰρ μηδὲ τῶν τοιούτων ἁπάντων ἁπτομένων ἀνιαθῆναί με θαυ(μα)σι(ώ)τερον ἐδόκει σοι καὶ [τοῦ] πάνυ μοι τοῦτ' ἐφαίνου γράψαι ἀληθῶς· ἐν (γὰρ) τῇ (Κ)αμπανίᾳ πυθόμ(εν)ος καὶ α(ὐτὰ) διεφθάρθαι, πάνυ ῥᾳδίως ἤνεγκα τὸ πρᾶγμα, μήτε βραχὺ κινηθείς. (...) δ' εἰς Ῥώμη(ν) ε (...).[10] ("So then you said that you had learned [from others] that these things had indeed happened, but that you wanted to hear it confirmed by me. For the fact that not even having all manner of things consumed by fire distressed me seemed amazing to you, and you appeared to write very accurately about this. In Campania, when I learned that these things were destroyed, I bore it all very easily, not even a little 'moved.'[11] And even when I returned?] to Rome ....")

---

[6] The manuscript is now classified as *Vlatadon* 14. For the circumstances of the discovery and the publication of the text, see Antoine Pietrobelli, "Variation autour du *Thessalonicensis Vlatadon* 14: un manuscrit copié au xénon du Kral, peu avant la chute de Constantinople," *Revue des Etudes Byzantines* 68 (2010): 95–126. It was first published by Véronique Boudon-Millot, "Un traité perdu de Galien miraculeusement retrouvé, *Le Sur l'inutilité de se chagriner*: texte grec et traduction française," in *La science médicale antique. Nouveaux regards. Études réunies en l'honneur de J. Jouanna* (ed. V. Boudon-Millot, A. Guardasole, and C. Magdelaine; Paris: Beauchesne, 2008), 72–123. The critical text was published by Véronique Boudon-Millot and Jacques Jouanna (with Antoine Pietrobelli), *Galien:* Ne pas se chagriner (Budé; Paris: Les Belles Lettres, 2010). The first English translation was published by Clare K. Rothschild and Trevor W. Thompson, "Galen: 'On the Avoidance of Grief,'" *EC* 2, no. 1 (2011): 110–29. Another English translation by Vivian Nutton is forthcoming under the title "Avoiding Distress." It is being published in *Galen: Psychological Writings* (ed. P. N. Singer; Cambridge: Cambridge University Press, 2014), 43–106.

[7] Also to be treated by other articles in the present volume. Cf. Pier Luigi Tucci, "Galen's Storeroom, Rome's Libraries, and the Fire of A. D. 192," *Journal of Roman Archaeology* 21 (2008): 133–49; Pier Luigi Tucci, "Antium, the Palatium, and the Domus Tiberiana Again," *Journal of Roman Archaeology* 22 (2009): 398–401; Christopher P. Jones, "Books and Libraries in a Newly-Discovered Treatise of Galen," *Journal of Roman Archaeology* 22 (2009): 390–8.

[8] *Ind.* 1. I follow the Greek text of Boudon-Millot and Jouanna from the Budé edition noted above.

[9] For a further comment on the translation of λύπη and ἀλυπία see n. 53 below.

[10] There is a lacuna in the ms. at this point.

[11] The use of the verb κινεῖν ("to move," here in passive "be moved or stirred up") places the discussion into the classic Stoic definition of how the passions disturb the soul by causing motion (κίνησις) within it. We shall return to this issue below.

From the very beginning, then, the letter uses several key technical terms that will locate the discussion of grief (λύπη) and its avoidance within ancient treatments of the soul, its passions, and their cure. It thus contains widespread physiological and philosophical assumptions about grief central to the Roman moralist tradition that will be the focus of this study. The basic outline of the letter is as follows:

I. §§ 1–11 Galen's reply to the unnamed friend who has inquired, having heard reports both about Galen's misfortune and about his extraordinary fortitude. Includes numerous direct references to the correspondent's impressions and requests of Galen.

II. §§ 12–37 A detailed description of Galen's losses in terms of his books, medicines, recipes, etc.

III. §§ 38–57 How he managed to avoid becoming "grieved" by the experience:

(a) reflection on questions of magnitude and perspective in light of the maxim (from Euripides) that it is the lot of humans to suffer misfortune;

(b) reflection on the need for training and habituation in order to avoid grief in such circumstances.

IV. §§ 58–68 On his upbringing; the compelling examples offered by his father and grandfather that equipped him to be as he is.

V. §§ 69–84 Concluding discussion on self-mastery and the attainment of ἀλυπία (being ungrieved).

Λύπη in the physiology of the soul and its passions

We may begin with the classic definition of the soul and its passions from Aristotle's *Ethica nichomachea*. There he opens the definition of ethical behavior by defining the four cardinal virtues as median or balanced states[12] and asserting that "virtue is the quality of acting in the best way relative to pleasure and pain (περὶ ἡδονὰς καὶ λύπας), while vice is the opposite."[13] He then argues that, since the soul has three primary types of "states" (γινόμενα), either "passion" (πάθη), "capacity" (δυνάμεις), or "disposition" (ἕξεις), virtue must be one of these three.[14]

---

[12] *Eth. nic.* 2.2.7 1104b.
[13] *Eth. nic.* 2.3.6 1104b.
[14] *Eth. nic.* 2.5.1 1105b.

> The capacities (δυνάμεις) are the faculties [of the soul] according to which we may be said to be subject to passion (παθητικός), such as the ability to become angry, experience pain [or grief], or feel mercy (δυνατοί ὀργισθῆναι ἢ λυπηθῆναι ἢ ἐλεῆσαι). The dispositions (ἕξεις) are formed states of character, in view of which we are well or ill-disposed toward the passions (πρὸς τὰ πάθη ἔχομεν εὖ ἢ κακῶς); for example, we have a bad disposition [and hence a vice] in regard to anger if we are disposed to become angry too violently or to mildly ... and similar in respect to the other passions. Now the virtues and vices are not passions, because we are not called noble or base according to our passions [because they are natural states of the soul]. ... And the same considerations also show that the virtues and vices are not capacities, since we are not pronounced noble or base, neither praised nor blamed, merely by reason of our capacity for a passion. If then the virtues are neither passions nor capacities, it remains that they are dispositions [of the soul].[15]

The παθαί (emotions or passions) include ἐπιθυμία (desire), ὀργή (anger or wrath), φόβος (fear), θράσος (confidence, *but connoting* brash self-confidence), φθόνος (envy), χαρά (joy), φιλία (friendship), μίσος (hatred), πόθος (longing), ζῆλος (jealousy), and ἔλεος (pity). More generally, Aristotle classifies them as "those states that are accompanied by pleasure or pain (ἡδονὴ ἤ λύπη)."[16] The first point to note, then, is that both passion and virtue are defined in relation to "pleasure and pain," and as we shall see, the painful side of this balance is the locus of grief. The word λύπη, of course, means both "pain" (generally in the physical sense) and "grief or distress" (in the emotional sense), a key point to which we shall return later. Second, for Aristotle the passions are neither virtues nor vices, but the actions or dispositions prompted by them are.[17]

Here Aristotle is following the basic line earlier espoused by Plato, that the passions or emotions, are (a) intrinsic "capacities" (or faculties) within the corporeal human soul, and (b) in themselves both natural and unavoidable.

> And they [humans] on receiving the immortal principle of soul, framed around it a mortal body, and gave it all the body to be its vehicle (or vessel, ὄχημα), and housed besides another, the mortal species of soul, which has within it certain unavoidable passions (παθήματα), first pleasure (ἡδονήν), a mighty lure to evil; next pains/griefs (λύπας), which cause good to flee; and besides these yet are rashness and fear, thoughtless counselors both; and anger, hard to console; and hope, ready to seduce. And blending these with irrational sense-perception (αἰσθήσει τε ἀλόγῳ) and with an aggressive lust for everything, they thus compounded of necessity the mortal form of the soul.[18]

What transforms these "capacities" (i.e., the natural drives and "emotions") into passions is when they are prone to go beyond proper balance or measure,

---

[15] *Eth. nic.* 2.5.2–6 1105b. For other similar lists of the passions in Aristotle, see *Eth. eud.* 2.2 1220b; *De an.* 1.1 403a; and *Rhet.* 2.1 1378a; cf. 2.2 1418a.

[16] *Eth. nic.* 2.5.2 1105b.

[17] *Eth. nic.* 2.3.1–5 1104b; note especially the end of 2.3.5 1104b, which refers to the alternative view of the Stoics, to be discussed below.

[18] Plato *Tim.* 69cd.

and when such extremes become abiding or habitual (i.e., as a "disposition"), then they become vice. Moreover, in both Plato and Aristotle, the extremes are marked by the dichotomy of "pleasure" (ἡδονή) vs. "pain" (λύπη).[19] Of course, the latter is more often translated "grief, distress, suffering, or vexation." In one sense, then, "pleasure" (ἡδονή) and "pain" (λύπη), are not exactly passions (as reflected in Aristotle), even though both he and Plato at times seem to label them as such in these same texts. The key, in part, is the notion of passion (πάθη, παθός, πάθημα, all derived from πάσχειν – "to suffer") as a "disease" of the soul caused by imbalance in any of its basic drives. For example, hunger is a natural drive, but carried to excess, and overwhelmed by ἡδονή, it becomes gluttony (a vice). Similarly, the impulse to procreate is natural, but as a passion it becomes "lust" (ἐπιθυμία), if associated primarily with pleasure, or that "fierce *eros*" described by Plato, when accompanied by pain.[20]

It was the Stoics who more formally developed these ideas, both by way of establishing a taxonomy of the passions and in view of their generally more negative attitude toward them. They advocated complete extirpation of the passions as diseases of the soul; the σοφός (sage or "wise person") must strive to be "impassible" (or without passion, ἀπαθῆ).[21] With regard to their taxonomy, in contrast to Aristotle, it should be noticed that they understood the natural capacities not as passions *per se*, but only the extremes that cause them to change; when they become "abiding dispositions," they are then called "diseases." In other

---

[19] On Epicurean vs. Stoic interpretation of the role of "pain" from Aristotle, see especially David Armstrong, "'Be Angry and Sin Not': Philodemus versus the Stoics on the Natural Bites and Natural Emotions," in *Passions and Progress in Greco-Roman Thought* (ed. J. T. Fitzgerald; London: Routledge, 2008), 79–121.

[20] Plato *Leg*. 837a–d: "Friendship is how we name the affection of like for like, in accordance with virtue, and of equal for equal, but likewise that of the needy for the rich, which is opposite in kind. And when either of these becomes intense (γίγνηται σφοδρόν), we call it "love" (ἔρωτα). ... The friendship which occurs between opposites is terrible and fierce and seldom reciprocal amongst men, while that based on similarity is gentle and reciprocal throughout life. The kind which arises from a blend of these presents difficulties ... because the man himself is dragged in opposite directions by two tendencies – of which one bids him to enjoy the bloom of his beloved, while the other forbids him. For he that is in love with the body and hungering after its youthful flesh as though it were ripe fruit, urges himself to take his fill, paying no respect to the disposition of the beloved. Whereas, he that counts the bodily desire as but secondary, and content to look rather than to make love, and truly desiring the other's soul with his own soul, thinks that the bodily satisfaction of the body is an outrage. Such a man respects and indeed reveres self-control, manliness, greatness, prudence, and would prefer to remain continually chaste with a beloved who is chaste. This type of friendly love, which is a combination of the other two, is the one that we have just described as the third type."

[21] Diog. Laert. 7.117; cf. R. J. Hankinson, "Galen's Anatomy of the Soul," *Phronesis* 36 (1991): 197–224. On the notion of training, including constant self-reminders, see also B. L. Hijmans, *ΑΣΚΗΣΙΣ: Notes on Epictetus Educational System* (Assen: Van Gorcum, 1959), 12–13.

words, for the Stoics the passions (as bodily diseases) are also the vices. In his *De propriorum animi cuiuslibet affectuum dignotione et curatione*, Galen says:[22]

> Since sins are said to come about from false opinions (ἁμαρτήματα διὰ τὴν ψευδῆ[ν] δόξαν γίγνονται) and passion from some unreasoned impulse (πάθη διὰ τιν᾽ ἄλογον ὁρμὴν), it seems to me that one should first free oneself from the passions (παθῶν), for these also make us judge wrongly. Now the passions of the soul which all acknowledge are temper, anger, fear, grief, envy, and extreme desire (ἔστι δὲ πάθη ψυχῆς, ἅπερ ἅπαντες γινώσκουσι, θυμὸς καὶ ὀργὴ καὶ φόβος καὶ λύπη καὶ φθόνος καὶ ἐπιθυμία σφοδρά).[23]

For Stoics, then, there are three natural states of the passions within the soul, and they are good (εὐπάθεια) because they are rational and thus at rest or "stable." They are joy (χαρά), caution (εὐλάβεια), and well-wishing (βούλησις). When "stirred up" or provoked (κινηθείς) they become imbalanced, thereby turning to vices instead, as pleasure (ἡδονή), fear (φόβος), and sexual desire (ἐπιθυμία), respectively.[24] So, Galen elsewhere quotes Chrysippus as saying:

> Of motions (κινήσεως) there are two sorts, alteration and change of place; when the alteration becomes an abiding disposition (διάθεσιν), it is named disease (νόσημα), being clearly a disposition contrary to nature (παρὰ φύσιν οὖσα δηλονότι διάθεσις). And sometimes, while misapplying the term, we call this [diseased] disposition *passion* (πάθος).[25]

---

[22] *The Passions of the Soul* (*Aff.Dig.*) 2–3 (K 5.7 = SM 1.5 = CMG 5.4.1.1 6). The full title of the work in Greek is Περὶ Διαγνώσεως καὶ Θεραπείας τῶν ἐν [τῇ] ἑκάστου Ψυχῇ ἰδίων Παθῶν (*Concerning the Diagnosis and Treatment of the Particular Passions in Each Person's Soul*). The companion piece, *De animi cuiuslibet peccatorum dignotione et curatione* (*Pecc.Dig.*), is entitled Περὶ Διαγνώσεως καὶ Θεραπείας τῶν ἐν τῇ ἑκάστου Ψυχῇ Ἁμαρτημάτων (*Concerning the Diagnosis and Treatment of the Sins in Each Person's Soul*). On the rendering of these titles, see also Gill, *Naturalistic Psychology in Galen and Stoicism*, 244, which follows the forthcoming work of Singer, *Galen: Psychological Writings* (n. 6 above).

[23] On the use of the term "sin" (either ἁμάρτημα or ἁμαρτία) in connection with the passions compare the contemporary Clement of Alexandria *Protr.* 11 (115.2): ὑμεῖς δὲ οὐ βούλεσθε τὸν οὐράνιον αὐτὸν περιάψασθαι, τον σωτῆρα λόγον, καὶ τῇ ἐπῳδῇ τοῦ θεοῦ πιστεύσαντες ἀπαλλαγῆναι μὲν παθῶν, ἃ δὴ ψυχῆς νόσοι, ἀποσπασθῆναι δὲ ἁμαρτίας; ("But do you not wish to have the heavenly, saving word fastened to you [as an amulet] and, trusting in a charm [incantation] of God, to be set free from the passions, which are diseases of the soul, and to be delivered from sin?"). Cf. L. Michael White, "Moral Pathology: Passions, Progress, and Protreptic in Clement of Alexandria," in *Passions and Moral Progress in Greco-Roman Thought* (ed. J. T. Fitzgerald; London: Routledge, 2008), 284–321.

[24] Diog. Laert. 7.116 (= SVF 3.431): εἶναι δὲ καὶ εὐπαθείας φασὶ τρεῖς, χαράν, εὐλάβειαν, βούλησιν. καὶ τὴν μὲν χαρὰν ἐναντίαν φασὶν εἶναι τῇ ἡδονῇ, οὖσαν εὔλογον ἔπαρσιν, τὴν δὲ εὐλάβειαν τῷ φόβῳ, οὖσαν εὔλογον ἔκκλισιν.

[25] Galen *De locis affectis* 1.3 (K 8.32 = SVF 3.429); cf. Diog. Laert. 7.115b (= SVF 3.422); Stobaeus 2.93.1 (= SVF 3.421); Clement of Alexandria *Strom.* 2.13 (59.6; Otto Stählin, *Clemens Alexandrinus* [5 vols.; *Die griechischen christlichen Schriftsteller der ersten Jahrhunderte*; Leipzig: Hinrichs, 1905–9]).

Diogenes Laertius puts it this way:

> Now they [the Stoics] say that the soul is eightfold. Its parts are the five senses (πέντε αἰσθητήρια), and the vocal faculty (φωνητικόν), the intellectual faculty (διανοητικόν), which is the mind itself,[26] and the procreative faculty (γεννητικόν). Now from falsehood results perversion upon the mind (ἐπιγίνεσθαι τὴν διαστροφὴν ἐπὶ τὴν διάνοιαν), and from it [perversion] arise many passions (πολλὰ πάθη βλαστάνειν), which are also the causes of instability (ἀκαταστασίας αἴτια). Passion, then, according to Zeno, is an irrational *motion* of the soul contrary to nature, or an excessive impulse (πάθος κατὰ Ζήνωνα ἡ ἄλογος καὶ παρὰ φύσιν ψυχῆς κίνησις ἢ ὁρμὴ πλεονάζουσα).[27]

Cicero's rendering of this key definition (in *Tusc.* 4.6.11–12) provides the equivalent Latin terms, *commotio* and *perturbatio*:

> This, therefore, is Zeno's definition of disturbance (*perturbatio*), which he calls πάθος, that is a (com)motion of the soul alien from right reason and contrary to nature (*a recta ratione contra naturam animi commotio*).[28]

A fundamental notion here is that the passions (πάθη/αι, παθήματα), as diseases (νοσήματα, παθοί), are caused by stirring or motion (κίνησις) in the soul that agitates and disturbs the natural drives. Elsewhere, Galen himself says:

> Properly, then, an excessive impulse (ὁρμὴ πλεονάζουσα) is called "passion" (τὸ πάθος), just as one might say an excessive motion (πλεονάζουσαν κίνησιν) is a motion that agitates, when the excess comes from a distortion of the rational and what would be safe, apart from this excess. For when the impulse goes beyond reason and all at once works against it, it may properly be termed excessive and becomes in this way contrary to nature and irrational (παρὰ φύσιν γίγνεσθαι καὶ εἶναι ἄλογος), as we have written elsewhere.[29]

It is this notion that Galen is using in *Ind.* 11 (quoted in full above), when he says,

> In Campania, when I learned that these things were destroyed, I bore it all very easily, not even a little *"moved"* (πάνυ ῥᾳδίως ἤνεγκα τὸ πρᾶγμα, μήτε βραχὺ κινηθείς).[30]

Galen will also refer to the bites and stings (δάκος, δάκνειν, sometimes translated "pangs"), especially associated with the pain of grief and misfortune but

---

[26] In other texts, the mind is also called the "ruling or governing part" (ἡγεμονικόν) or the "logical part" (λογικόν).
[27] Diog. Laert. 7.110.
[28] Compare *Tusc.* 3.11.24: "For all disturbance is a movement of the soul (*omnis perturbatio sit animi motus*) either having no part of reason or rejecting reason or disobedient to reason, and as such the motion is incited in two ways, either by an idea of good or evil, and thus we have four (types of) disturbances equally divided."
[29] *PHP* 4.5.10 (*CMG* 5.4.1.2 264 = K 5.397 = *SVF* 3.479). In this section, Galen also cites Zeno and Chrysippus as his sources; so, respectively *PHP* 4.2.7–10, 13–14 (*CMG* 5.4.1.2 240 = K 5.368 = *SVF* 3.462).
[30] Compare *Ind.* 2: ἔφης αὐτὸς ἑωρακέναι με μηδὲ ἐπὶ βραχὺ κινηθέντα ("You said that you yourself had never seen me even a little '*moved*'").

also the stirrings of desire or anger, and this is another way that they understood how the soul becomes stirred up, as though pricked or shocked (ἐκπλήσσειν) by an external force.[31] Similarly, in *Ind.* 38, another important transitional passage, Galen says,

> Now perhaps you will say that your own desire has been further piqued (ἐπιτάττεσθαί σου τὴν ἐπιθυμίαν) and you wish to know all the more how it was that I – having lost such an array of possessions, each one of which by itself would have become most grievous (λυπηρότατον ἂν ἐγένετο) for other people – was not distressed, as certain others might be, but rather took what befell me very easily (οὐκ ἠνιάθην ὡς ἕτεροί τινες, ἀλλὰ πάνυ <ῥᾳδίως> ἤνεγκα τὸ συμβάν).

This last passage is significant for several reasons in the epistolary structure of the letter, as I have discussed elsewhere.[32] Returning to exhort his friend directly, it marks the transition from his detailed description of his losses (*Ind.* 12–37) to a series of exemplary tales on responding to hardship and loss (*Ind.* 38–57), about which we shall say more later. Finally, we note another key synonym in both of these passages as Galen regularly switches from λύπη (and its cognates, e.g., ἄλυπόν in 72b) to ἀνία (and cognates).[33] The verb ἀνιαθῆναι ("to be distressed or depressed") occurs frequently throughout the treatise in this sense.[34] Again, this usage shows that Galen is operating within a rather strict Stoic definition of the "species" of grief. On the other hand, Christopher Gill argues that Galen's treatment of the passions in *Ind.* is both internally more consistent and less Stoic than his later, and supposedly more systematic, work *De proprium animi cuiuslibet affectuum dignotione et curatione* (*Aff.Dig.*).[35]

---

[31] *Ind.* 52 (to be discussed below at n. 73); compare *Aff.Dig.* 8 (K 5.43–44 = *SM* 1.33–34 = *CMG* 5.4.1.1 29.6–30.15).
See also (Ps-)Plutarch *Cons. Apoll.* 102C (also quoted below at n. 66). The idea comes from poetry and drama (e.g., Aeschylus *Persae* 846), δακνάζειν being the poetic form of the verb, but becomes a commonplace in later philosophical literature. For προσεκπλήσσειν see Clement of Alexandria *Quis div.* 1.3; cf. Aristophanes *Plutus* 673; Aeschylus *Choephori* 233; although it should be note also that ἔκπληξις ("shock or consternation") is one of the species under fear (Diog. Laert. 7.112).

[32] See White, "Personal Epistolary Paraenesis in Galen and Paul," 262–3.

[33] Quoted at n. 52 below. For an index to the key terms in Galen's letter, see the appendix at the end of this article.

[34] *Ind.* 3, 11, 30, 38, 45, 47, 48; as noun, cf. 29, 73. Ralph M. Rosen has also rendered the title *On Not Being Depressed* ("The New Galen on Old Comedy," paper presented at the 2011 APA Annual Meeting). The modern notion of "clinical depression" is probably the best descriptive sense to apply to this term, especially since it is described as having a deepening and burdensome capacity that becomes harder and harder to escape. While "melancholy" might also be fitting, at least as used popularly since the 19th century, we must remember that *melancholia* (Greek μελαγχολία) was a technical medical term meaning afflicted with "black bile." Galen also has a treatise on this topic, Alexander Olivieri, ed., *De melancholia, apud Aëtium* (*CMG* 8.2; Berlin: Akademie, 1950, 143–6).

[35] Gill, *Naturalistic Psychology in Galen and Stoicism*, 265–8, 276–7.

The Species of Grief in Stoic Thought

The Stoic taxonomy postulated four cardinal passions: **grief (λύπη), fear (φόβος), desire (ἐπιθυμία), and pleasure (ἡδονή)**.[36] In the Stoic system, therefore, pleasure and pain have now become cardinal passions, alongside fear and desire. It is possible to see these both as a spectrum ranging from extreme pain to extreme pleasure and as a way to systematize empirical observations on the different human expressions of passion. According to the Stoic scheme, as described by Diogenes Laertius, each of these four cardinal passions constituted a genus which was subdivided into a number of species. The genus of *Fear* (φόβος) is "anticipation of evil happening" (προσδοκία κακοῦ) and has six species:[37] terror (δεῖμα), timidity (ὄκνος, i.e., shrinking back or cowering), shame (αἰσχύνη), consternation or shock (ἔκπληξις), confusion or panic (θόρυβος), and mental anguish (ἀγωνία). *Desire* (ἐπιθυμία) is "irrational appetency" (ἄλογος ὄρεξις), and it has seven:[38] insatiable craving (σπάνις), hatred (μῖσος), contentiousness (φιλονεικία), anger (ὀργή), *eros* (ἔρως), vengeful wrath (μῆνις), and smoldering temper (θυμός). *Pleasure* (ἡδονή) is "irrational elations at possessing what one wishes" (ἄλογος ἔπαρις ἐφ᾽ αἱρετῷ δοκοῦντι ὑπάρχειν) and has only four:[39] enchantment (κήλησις), malevolent joy (ἐπιχαιρεκακία, i.e., joy at the ills of another), rapturous delight (τέρψις), and dissolution (διάχυσις, i.e., overwhelming excitement).[40] Thus, desire and pleasure now stand on the pleasurable side, while fear and grief are now on the painful, but they are all passions.

Significantly, of the four passions only *Grief* (λύπη; *aegritudo* in Latin) is exclusively negative and has no rational counterpart. Cicero says:

> The wise man, however, is not subject to the affect of present evil; fools are subject to distress (*or* grief – *aegritudo*) and feel its affect in the face of expected evil, and their souls are downcast and shrunken together not in conformity with reason. Therefore, here is the first definition: that grief is a contraction of the soul adverse to reason (*ut aegritudo sit animi adversante rationone contractio*). Thus there are four disturbances (*perturbationes*), but only three constant states (*constantiae*),[41] since there is no constant state in opposition to grief (*quoniam aegritudini nulla constantia opponitur*).[42]

Grief also has the most species, nine, each of which can be seen as some sort of combination of the others, but moving the emotional result in the painful direction. Diogenes Laertius offers the following breakdown of its species:

---

[36] Diog. Laert. 7.111 (attributed to Hecato and Zeno).
[37] Diog. Laert. 7.112.
[38] Diog. Laert. 7.113.
[39] Diog. Laert. 7.114.
[40] For the Latin equivalents compare Cicero *Tusc.* 4.6.11–13.
[41] Equivalent to εὐπάθεια in Greek.
[42] *Tusc.* 4.6.14; cf. 3.11.24.

And Grief (λύπην), they [the Stoics] hold to be an irrational contraction [of the soul] (συστολὴν ἄλογον). Its species are *pity, envy, jealousy, rivalry, heavy sorrow, vexation, distress, anguish,* and *distraction.* **Pity** (ἔλεον), then, is grief felt at undeserved suffering; **envy** (φθόνον) is grief felt at others' prosperity; **jealousy** (ζῆλον), grief at the possession by another of what one ardently desires (ἐπιθυμεῖ) for oneself; **rivalry** (ζηλοτυπίαν), grief at the possession by another of what one has oneself; **heavy sorrow** (ἄχθος) is grief that weighs down (λύπην βαρύνουσαν); **vexation** (ἐνόχλησιν) is grief that crushes (στενοχωροῦσαν) and leaves us in a tight place (δυσχωρίαν παρασκευάζουσαν); **distress** (ἀνίαν) is grief brought on by anxious doubt that lingers and intensifies; **anguish or sorrow** (ὀδύνη) is painful grief (λύπην ἐπίπονον); **distraction** (σύγχυσιν), irrational grief that worries to death (ἀποκναίουσαν) and prevents us from viewing the entire situation (κωλύοσαν τὰ παρόντα συνορᾶν).[43]

So, notice here that "jealousy" is defined in terms of "desire," thus: it is "pain/ grief over something one desires (ἐπιθυμεῖ) for oneself." In that sense, the species of grief represent the most painful extreme of all the other passions.[44] Similarly, "distress" (ἀνία) is defined as "pain/grief (λύπη) that comes from worried doubts (or mental debates – διαλογισμοί) that linger and intensify."[45] In other words, it is akin to fear, but classed under λύπη. Another is "heavy sorrow" (ἄχθος), which is explained by using the synonym βαρύνειν ("to be heavy or burdened"); it is a good example of how these terms carry both empirical physiological observations and folk-etymological derivations. Cognate verb forms are also implied, such as ἄχθεσθαι ("to vex or weigh down with sorrow") and συνάχθεσθαι ("to mourn or commiserate with [someone]"). Similarly, "vexation" (ἐνοχλήσις) is from the word for "crowd" (ὄχλος) but by derivation can also mean "trouble, or vex."[46] Galen uses the apophatic form of this word (ἀοχλησία) in *Ind.* 68. The explanatory term used here, στενοχωρεῖν, means "to tighten or crowd" or, in the passive "to be crushed," but it can also signify "tight or constricted breathing." Although not used directly in *Ind.,* it is used elsewhere by Galen of the effects of the passions.[47] Finally, Diogenes Laertius refers to these as "infirmities"

---

[43] Diog. Laert. 7.111. Cicero (*Tusc.* 4.7.16) gives the Latin equivalents as follows: misericordia, invidentia, aemulatio, obtrectatio, angor, luctus, maeror, aerumna, dolor, lamentatio, sollicitudo, molestia, and adflictatio. (NB: Cicero, however, gives thirteen terms, and they are in slightly different order, with misericordia [ἔλεος] coming after obtrectatio [ζηλοτυπία]).

[44] On this point see also the final section below.

[45] The word "intensify" (ἐπιτεινομένην) here is exactly the same as that used by Clement of Alexandria in suggesting that poverty only increases the passions because it increases anxiety, fear, and agitation. See *Quis div.* 12.2; *Strom.* 2.5 (22.4 Stählin), where he quotes from Plato to support his point; cf. n. 102 below and White, "Moral Pathology," 287 nn. 19–20.

[46] While Paul does not use the word, it appears with this sense in Luke 6:18; Acts 5:16; cf. Acts 17:5.

[47] See *Loc.Aff.* 6 (K 8.120). It may surface in this text (*Ind.* 80) in Galen's antithetical example of those who "wail and sigh" (οἰμώζουσι καὶ στένουσι) over their unfulfilled desires for wealth (quoted n. 94 below). The verb στένειν ("to sigh, groan, or moan") comes from the same root.

(ἀρρωστήματα) of the soul saying, "for infirmity is disease with illness" (τὸ γὰρ ἀρρώστημά ἐστι νόσημα μετ' ἀσθενείας).⁴⁸

Note also that the word στενοχωρεῖν is used by Paul in 2 Cor 4:8 in reference to his response to hardships: "θλιβόμενοι ἀλλ' οὐ στενοχωρούμενοι, ἀπορούμενοι ἀλλ' οὐκ ἐξαπορούμενοι .... ('*afflicted but not **crushed**, perplexed but not driven to despair*')." This use is especially telling in light of his despairing tone in 1:8: "ὅτι καθ' ὑπερβολὴν ὑπὲρ δύναμιν ἐβαρήθημεν ὥστε ἐξαπορηθῆναι ἡμᾶς καὶ τοῦ ζῆν ('*because we were excessively **burdened** beyond capacity, that we even **despaired** for (our) life*')." Thus, our new text from Galen helps to understand not only the general framework of his own epistolary advice on withstanding grief, but also Paul's very personal example of his own hardships in 2 Cor. 4:8–9. Paul uses θλίψις/θλίβεσθαι in the same way that Galen uses περίστασις (*Ind.* 73, 75, 78), meaning "to experience a crisis, or to suffer a misfortune."⁴⁹ Thus Paul uses ἀλλ' οὐ στενοχωρούμενοι (2 Cor 4:8) to mean "but not crushed by grief."⁵⁰ Like Galen, then, Paul claims to be impervious, not to the troubling affliction per se (cf. 2 Cor 1:4. 8), but to the passion of grief or despair that might have overwhelmed him were he not the master of his own emotions.⁵¹

Galen puts it this way (*Ind.* 69–73):

69 Τελείως μὲν οὖν <οἶμαι> ἀποκρίνασθαί σοι πρὸς τὴν ἐρώτησιν ἣν ἐποίησω περὶ τῆς ἀλυπ{ησ}ίας [sic],⁵² ἀτὰρ οὖν ἡγοῦμαι διορισμόν τινα προσθεῖναι. 70 Τάχα γὰρ οἴει με, καθάπερ ἔνιοι τῶν φιλοσόφων ὑπέσχοντο μηδ(έποτε) μηδὲ νῦν λυπηθήσεσθαι [τῶν φιλοσόφων], οὕτως καὶ αὐτὸν ἀποφαίνεσθαι καὶ μάλιστα, ἐπειδὴ φῂς ἑωρακέναι με μηδέποτε λυπούμενον. 71 Ἐγὼ δὲ εἰ μέν τίς ἐστιν τοιοῦτος σοφὸς ὡς ἀπαθὴς εἶναι τὸ πᾶν, οὐκ ἔχω λέγειν, τοῦ δ' αὐτὸς εἶναι τοιοῦτος ἀκριβῆ γνῶσιν ἔχω· χρημάτων μὲν γὰρ ἀπωλείας καταφ<ρ>ονῶ μέχρι τοῦ μὴ πάντων ἀποστερηθεὶς εἰς νῆσον ἐρήμην πεμφθῆναι, πόνου δὲ σωματικοῦ μέχρι τοῦ μὴ καταφρονεῖν ἐπαγγέλ<λ>εσθαι τοῦ Φαλάριδος ταύρου. 72a Λυπήσει δέ με καὶ πατρὶς ἀνάστατος γενομένη καὶ φίλος ὑπὸ τυράννου κολαζόμενος ὅσα τ' ἄλλα τοιαῦτα. 72b Καὶ θεοῖς εὔχομαι μηδέν μοι τούτων συμβῆναί ποτε· καὶ διότι μέχρι τοῦ δεῦρό μοι μηδὲν τοιοῦτον συνέβη, διὰ τοῦτο ἄλυπόν με τεθέασαι. 73 Θαυμάζω δὲ Μουσόνιον ἑκάστοτε λέγειν εἰθισμένον, ὥς φασι ὦ Ζεῦ, πέμπε <ἣν θέλεις> περίστασιν. Ἐγὼ δὲ τοὐναντίον εὔχομαι διὰ παντός, ὦ Ζεῦ, μηδεμίαν μοι πέμψῃς περίστασιν ἀνιᾶσαί με δυναμένην.

---

⁴⁸ Diog. Laert. 7.115.

⁴⁹ See n. 54 below; cf. John T. Fitzgerald, *Cracks in an Earthen Vessel: An Examination of the Catalogues of Hardships in the Corinthian Correspondence* (SBLDS 99; Atlanta: Scholars Press, 1988), 39, 166–75.

⁵⁰ Failing to notice the technical terminology related to grief as a passion of the soul, most commentators do not even discuss the term and miss the point of the antithesis within the four pairs of terms. Thus, θλίβεσθαι and στενοχωρεῖν are typically mistaken as synonyms. Cf. Victor P. Furnish, *II Corinthians* (AB 32A; Garden City: Doubleday, 1984), 254; Murray J. Harris, *The Second Epistle to the Corinthians* (NIGCT; Grand Rapids: Eerdmans, 2005), 341–3.

⁵¹ See especially Stanley K. Stowers, "Paul and Self-Mastery," in *Paul in the Greco-Roman World* (ed. J. P. Sampley; Harrisburg: Trinity Press International, 2003), 524–34.

⁵² This deviant orthography, a corruption for ἀλυπίας, is typical of the late Byzantine copyist of Ms. Vlatadon 14. I have therefore supplied the curved braces throughout.

69 I think I have fully answered the question you asked about my ***imperturbability***.[53] Nevertheless, I think I should add some clarification. 70 For perhaps you think – just as some philosophers have professed that they will not at all, now or ever, be grieved – that I myself appear to do the same and especially so, since you say that you have never seen me grieved. 71 For my part, whether in fact there is any such wise man, who is totally without passion [ἀπαθές] with respect to everything, I have nothing to say. But I do have accurate knowledge of myself to be this kind of person: namely, on the one hand, the loss of my possessions I will utterly disregard, so long as I am not exiled to a deserted island and deprived of every last thing; on the other, [I will disregard] bodily pain so long as I am not compelled to face the Phalarian bull. 72a But it will even cause me grief, if my homeland were laid waste, a friend were punished by a tyrant, or some other such thing. 72b And I pray the gods that nothing of this sort ever befalls me. And whereas until the present moment, nothing of this extreme sort has befallen me, for this very reason, you see me ungrieved. 73 I marvel at Musonius, who, so they say, accustomed himself to utter at every moment, "*O Zeus, send me whatever hardship*[54] *you wish.*" But I, on the contrary, pray continually, "*O Zeus, send me no hardship that is able to cause me despair.*"

Galen's self-critical comparison with the austerity of Musonius Rufus shows a significant degree of modulation within the Stoic system, at least as it might be modified pragmatically based on Aristotelian-Platonic ideas, while still maintaining the need for habituation and training to withstand the effects of the immoderate passions.[55]

That Paul likewise deploys these very technical Stoic notions of the passions and their cure in reference to his own personal afflictions, locates their exem-

---

[53] Noting the definite article, to give the sense of the possessive. In this instance I have chosen to render ἀλυπία with the English "*imperturbability*" in order to preserve the force of the alpha-privative in a way analogous to ἀπαθεία ("*impassibility*"). In Cicero, however, *perturbatio* is the more general term for the "disturbance" in the soul that produces the four cardinal passions (cf. *Tusc.* 4.6.14, quoted at n. 42 above). In the strict sense, then, "imperturbability" would then be the Latin equivalent of ἀπαθεία. But I also note that in *Tusc.* 3.25.61, Cicero renders the Greek word λύπη with Latin *aegritudo* (meaning "sickness or distress"), but when he speaks of the more serious forms of grief, he calls it *gravis aegritudinis perturbatio*.

[54] The word περίστασις, as used here, literally means "circumstance," but in context, and typically in the moralist literature, it refers to the "adverse circumstances" or hardships of the sage; cf. Epictetus *Diat.* 2.6.16–17 (discussing the common "misuse" of the term in this sense). It refers especially to physical afflictions and other external conditions of hardship: sickness, poverty, shipwreck, exile, and death. A common synonym is συμφορά as used in the quotation of Euripides in *Ind.* 52 and 77 (see n. 73 below). In a derived sense, the verb συμβαίνειν (and cognate forms) is virtual synonym; it literally means "to fall to one's lot" but comes to mean "troubles that befall one," especially those common to human existence. So note its use here a few lines above in *Ind.* 72b; cf. *Letter of Aristeas* 197 and 232 (where the context is avoidance of grief). See especially Fitzgerald, *Cracks in an Earthen Vessel*, 37–46; David E. Fredrickson, "Paul, Hardships, and Suffering," in *Paul in the Greco-Roman World*, (ed. J. P. Sampley; Harrisburg: Trinity Press International, 2003), 172–97. For συμφορά and other key terms related to the topos on hardships see Fitzgerald, *Cracks in an Earthen Vessel*, 39.

[55] On this particular passage, and its "non-Stoic" elements see Gill, *Naturalistic Psychology in Galen and the Stoics*, 265–7. We shall return to the issue of training and habituation in the last section of the study.

plary and hortatory function in the same orbit as Galen's letter. It also helps to understand the role of Paul's peristasis catalogue and the references to consolation (in 2 Cor 4–5) in relation to the surrounding sections of the letter, in which Paul refers to his earlier "painful or grievous visit" to Corinth (2 Cor 2:1: τὸ μὴ πάλιν ἐν λύπῃ πρὸς ὑμᾶς ἐλθεῖν), and the "painful or aggrieved letter" he wrote to them as a reprimand in order to bring them to "godly grief" and repentance for their actions (2 Cor 2:2–4: εἰ γὰρ ἐγὼ λυπῶ ὑμᾶς ... καὶ ἔγραψα τοῦτο αὐτό,[56] ἵνα μὴ ἐλθὼν λύπην σχῶ ... ἐκ γὰρ πολλῆς θλίψεως καὶ συνοχῆς καρδίας ἔγραψα ὑμῖν διὰ πολλῶν δακρύων, οὐκ ἵνα λυπηθῆτε ἀλλὰ τὴν ἀγάπην ἵνα γνῶτε ... εἰς ὑμᾶς; cf. 7:8–9).[57] These different uses in Paul when compared with Galen show that grief operates in several spheres or realms of human life.

The Realms of Grief

In Galen's letter, as in Paul, grief is a common response or outgrowth of suffering hardship. As noted previously, Galen refers to his loss and hardship simply as "what befell me" (τὸ συμβάν),[58] and he uses this term synonymously with "misfortune" (συμφορά) and "hardships" (περιστάσεις).[59] In *Ind.* 10 he further contrasts his "personally troubling circumstances" (δυσχερὲς ἴδιον) with the ordinary range of "common misfortunes" that are the lot of all humans (συνέβη δέ μοι πρὸς τῷ κοινῷ τούτῳ καὶ ἄλλο τι δυσχερὲς ἴδιον). In *Ind.* 7 Galen mentions another philosopher and friend who had actually "wasted away and died from despondency and grief" (ἀπὸ δυσθυμίας καὶ λύπης διεφθάρη συντακείς) over his own losses in the same fire at Rome.

In general, then, among the Stoics, grief operates in four spheres or realms of human life: (a) in suffering hardship or loss, (b) at the death of a loved one, (c) in finding oneself ill-treated by others, and, finally, (d) as the consequences of one's own cravings, passions, and vice. In this section, we shall focus on the first three. For reasons that will become clear, we shall reserve discussion of the fourth until the final section of this study. Based on English usage, we might

---

[56] I take τοῦτο αὐτό (*literally* "in the same manner" or "with respect to the same") to refer back to ἐγὼ λυπῶ ὑμᾶς ("I pained you"), and thus "I caused you *grief* with my *aggrieved letter* so that I would not have *grief* in coming [to you again]." Note also the parallelism of λύπη and θλίψις in the final two clauses, while συνοχῆς is a metaphorical term for affliction deriving from the sense of tight constraint (thus similar to ἐνόχλησις). Finally, Paul refers to their "godly *grief* that produced repentance" (7:9–10: ἡ γὰρ κατὰ θεὸν λύπη μετάνοιαν εἰς σωτηρίαν ἐργάζεται). Both the sense of being aggrieved at a wrong and the grief that brings a wrongdoer to repentance will arise later in this discussion.

[57] See the discussion by Fredrickson, "Paul, Hardships, and Suffering," 176–8.

[58] *Ind.* 2, 38. The term (and its verbal cognates) usually connotes unfortunate circumstances and is sometimes just translated "misfortune."

[59] See nn. 49 and 54 above.

assume the most common realm of grief to be in mourning that accompanies the death of a loved one, but that may be misleading, as this particular kind of loss can be seen from a different perspective as but one more type of misfortune or suffering common to humans.

In Ps-Demetrius' *Epistolary Types,* for example, the "consoling type" (παραμυθητικός) is framed thus, rather than in reference to bereavement, as "written to those in a state of grief because of some troubling circumstances that have come about (τοῖς ἐπὶ λύπης καθεστηκόσι δυσχεροῦς τινος γεγονότος)."[60] The word "troubling circumstances" (δυσχεροῦς) is yet another term used by Galen in reference to his losses in the fire.[61] In Ps-Libanius' *Epistolary Styles,* this same basic wording is called the "sympathetic style" (συμπαθητική).[62] So, too, the first three spheres are likewise connected to suffering, loss, and unfulfilled desires. For example, among the nine species of grief outlined by Diogenes Laertius (above), the first item, pity (ἔλεον) is defined as "grief felt at underserved suffering" (or c above). The next three, envy (φθόνον), jealousy (ζῆλον), and rivalry (ζηλοτυπίαν), all arise from hard feelings regarding one's own possessions in comparison with those of others (i.e., between a and d). In fact, none of the rest is explicitly or exclusively identified with the death and mourning.[63] A funerary monument from Galen's own day, found at Ostia, port city for Rome, welcomes the visitor to the tomb saying, "hither (is) the end of grief" (ὧδε παυσίλυπος).[64] That is to suggest, that death, rather than being the cause of grief, is actually the end of ordinary human toil and suffering.[65]

To be sure, grief and mourning were principal concerns at death, and seem especially to have been felt in the Roman world with the death of children, and particularly older children or young adults. (Ps-)Plutarch's *Consolatio ad Apollonium* is a good example of the common feelings of grief and the place of friendly consolation to alleviate it. It opens by referring to the death of a young

---

[60] Ps-Demetrius *Epistolary Types* 5 (Abraham J. Malherbe, *Ancient Epistolary Theorists* [SBLSBS; Atlanta: Scholars Press 1991]). The sample letter that follows also refers to the "terrible things befalling from the hands of fate" and the expression of the writer's sharing in their grief.

[61] *Ind.* 10.

[62] *Epistolary Styles* 65 (ed. Malherbe); it opens: "I was severely sorrowful in soul ... when I heard of the terrible things that had befallen you. ..." (Σφόδρα κατὰ ψυχὴν ἠχθέσθην ...).

[63] *Lamentatio* appears in Cicero's list (see n. 43 above); see also n. 66 below.

[64] The inscription is in a mosaic depicting boats approaching the lighthouse of Ostia, at the entrance to Tomb 43 in the Isola Sacra necropolis, date ca. 190–230 CE; for text, *EDR* 112306; Giulia Sacco, *Inscrizione greche d'Italia. Porto* (Rome: Edizioni di storia e letteratura), no. 60; cf. *IG* 14.2136. The inscription flanks the lighthouse directly in front of the door of the tomb.

[65] The boats and especially the lighthouse are typical Ostian iconography; however, some have speculated that the harbor imagery may also be metaphorical in either philosophical or vulgar ways. If it were intended philosophically, then it might depict the tomb as a "haven of rest after the storm-tossed seas of life."

man, just coming of age, and the sense of grief and loss felt by his father; he calls it a "misfortune" (συμφορά):[66]

> For some time now I have shared your pain and commiserated together with you (σοι συνήλγησα καὶ συνηχθέσθην), Apollonius, having heard about the untimely passing from life of your son, who was very dear to all of us. ... At that moment, then, hard upon the time of his death, (for me) to visit you and urge you to bear what has befallen you in human fashion (παρακαλεῖν ἀνθρωπίνως φέρειντὸ συμβεβηκὸς) was unfitting, since you were weakened in both body and soul by the unaccountable misfortune (παρειμένῳ τό τε σῶμα καὶ τὴν ψυχὴν ὑπὸ τῆς παραλόγου συμφορᾶς), and even I was compelled to sympathize (feel compassion) with your plight (καὶ συμπαθεῖν δ' ἦν ἀναγκαῖον). ... Now therefore, since time, which usually soothes all, has passed since your misfortune (συμφορᾷ), and since your disposition (ἡ περὶ σὲ διάθεσις)[67] seems to demand the help of friends, I assumed it good to share with you some words of consolation towards the mitigation of grief (ἄνεσιν τῆς λύπης) and an end of mournful and vain lamentations (παῦλαν τῶν πενθικῶν καὶ ματαίων ὀδυρμῶν). For
> > "words are the physicians of the diseased soul (ψυχῆς νοσούσης εἰσὶν ἰατροί), when in time one may indeed soothe the heart."[68]
> For according to the wise Euripides,
> > "But then against all sorts of ailments are set all manner of drugs; now the pleasant fables of friends for the one who grieves; then admonitions for the one too much playing the fool."[69]
> For of the many passions that afflict the soul, grief by its nature is the harshest of all. For as they say,
> > "On account of grief mania comes to many and incurable disease, and on account of grief have some even killed themselves."[70]
>
> So then, to feel the pain and sting (τὸ μὲν οὖν ἀλγεῖν καὶ δάκνεσθαι) when a son has died is the natural cause of grief, and we are not (in control) of ourselves. But I, for my part, cannot condone those who hymn the praise of that fierce and harsh *apatheia*, which is beyond our ability and unprofitable.[71] ... But to be carried beyond the limits of moderation and to exaggerate mourning is, I say, contrary to nature, and results from vulgar opinions which dwell within us. Wherefore, even this must be dismissed as injurious and vulgar and completely unbecoming of earnest men (σπουδαίοις ἀνδράσιν),[72]

---

[66] *Cons. Apoll.* 101F–102A, 102B–D.

[67] The word διάθεσις can refer either to a condition, or, more technically, the abiding disposition (equivalent to ἕξεις); cf. nn. 14, 25 above. It can also refer to a report about some situation. One cannot help but think here that the author is worried that Apollonius' grief is becoming dangerously entrenched. But given the syntax with περὶ σὲ, it might be best to translate the phrase, "and since the situation reports concerning you (or your state of mind) ..."

[68] Aeschylus *Prom.* 379.

[69] Euripides *Fr.* 962 (August Nauck, *Tragicorum Graecorum Fragmenta* [Leipzig: Teubner, 1856]), also quoted in *Adul. amic.* 69D.

[70] Philemon *Fr.* 106. (Theodor Kock, *Comicorum Atticorum Fragmenta* [Leipzig: Teubner, 1880–8)].

[71] Cf. Cicero *Tusc.* 3.6.12.

[72] I shall not attempt to address the gender issue inherent here, but it is worth noting and deserves a fuller treatment. To be more specific, these thoughts are addressed quite directly to a man, the father of the deceased youth, and the clear assumption is that such an excessive degree

and even a moderate degree of passion (μετριοπάθειαν) is not to be approved [when it comes to mourning].

The treatment of mourning in (Ps-)Plutarch operates very much within this same taxonomy of the passions. While Galen does not address this kind of grief in his letter, his treatment of grief as a result of hardship and loss bears marked similarities in language and tone. We may note also that when it comes to grief, among all the passions, Galen, like (Ps-)Plutarch, seems to falls somewhere between the extreme Stoic position (characterized as "fierce ἀπάθεια") and the Aristotelian "mean" (μετριοπάθεια).

In the third section of the treatise (*Ind.* 58–68), Galen frames his exhortation to his friend in terms of a similar maxim of Euripides about the plight of human suffering. The comment is in the form of a proverb attributed to Theseus (*Ind.* 51–52):

Ἐγὼ δὲ παρὰ σοφοῦ μαθὼν	*Now I, having learned from a certain Sage,*
εἰς φροντίδ᾽ ἀεὶ συμφορὰς ἐβαλλόμην,	*ever to cast misfortunes into my mind,*
φυγάς τ᾽ ἐμαυτῷ προστιθεὶς πάτρας ἐμῆς	*imposing on myself even exile from my homeland,*
θανάτους τ᾽ ἀώρους καὶ κακῶν ἄλλας ὁδούς,	*untimely deaths, and various manner of ills,*
ἵν᾽, εἴ τι πάσχοιμ᾽ ὧν ἐδόξαζόν ποτε,	*so that, if I should ever suffer any of those things I used to imagine,*
μή μοι νεῶρες προσπεσὸν ψυχὴν δάκῃ.[73]	*befalling me afresh, it will not sting my soul.*

The same maxim is quoted by (Ps-)Plutarch, *Consolatio ad Apolloninum* 112D–E, likewise referring to it as a work of Euripides in which Theseus is the speaker. It seems to have served as a *locus classicus* for discussions of grief and consolation, as it also appears in Cicero's *Tusc.* 3.14.29.[74]

---

of grief is "unmanly," while women may be expected to fall more into grief and mourning. So compare Plutarch's letter of consolation to his wife at the death of their two-year-old daughter (*Cons. ad uxorem* 608C): "Only, my dear wife, keep both me and yourself in customary bounds with your passion. For I know and can set a boundary appropriate to the loss, but if I should find that you are distressed in the extreme, that would be far more vexatious to me than what has happened (ἂν δὲ σὲ τῷ δυσφορεῖν ὑπερβάλλουσαν εὕρω, τοῦτό μοι μᾶλλον ἐνοχλήσει τοῦ γεγοννότος)." Note that this comment employs two technical terms for grief (ἐνοχλήσει and δυσφορεῖν, viz. δυσχωρίαν) consistent with the Stoic definition in Diog. Laer. 7.111 (quoted above). Plutarch further addresses the customary mourning rituals and dress of women in *Cons. ad uxorem* 608F–609B, noting how amazed others were that his wife did not exhibit such behavior at the funeral.

[73] Euripides *Fr.* 964 (Nauck = 392 Dindorf/814 Mette) from a lost tragedy of Euripides, similar to the *Hypsipyle*, in which Theseus also appears (see next note). Galen quotes the same refrain in *Ind.* 77; he also quotes it in *PHP* 4.7.10 (*CMG* 5.4.1.2 282 = K 5.418) in the context of the Posidonian view of Chrysippus.

[74] The Latin as quoted by Cicero is his own, slightly variant rendering. Compare *Tusc.* 3.25.59 (Euripides *Fr.* 757 Nauck/Dindorf = 60.90 Bond; a similar sentiment from the lost *Hypsipyle*); and *Tusc.* 3.29.71 (Sophocles *Frag.* 964 Dindorf; from the lost *Locrian Ajax*).

It is noteworthy, too, that this section of Cicero's treatise concerns the philosophical debates between Chrysippus and Carneades on dealing with fate and misfortune. Book 3 of *Tusc.* deals with the alleviation of distress/grief (*aegritudo*), on the premise that even the wise man is subject to distress but is unusually equipped through philosophy to endure it with fortitude. Just as training the body to endure pain and discomfort, so too one must train the soul to ward off distress and grief.[75] But, as Cicero notes, distress is in many ways the worst of the passions because of its degrading effects on body and soul.

> Do you suppose then that it is possible that the wise man might be crushed by distress, that is, wretched misery (*ut aegritudine opprimatur, id est, miseria*)? Now, while all disturbance is misery (*omnis perturbatio miseria est*), distress is torture (*carnificina*). Lust involves ardor; exuberant joy involves fickleness; fear, humiliation. But distress involves far worse things, plague, torture, beaten down, (smothered in) foulness (*tabem, cruciatum, adflictationem, foeditatem*); it tears at the soul and eats away at it, and wears it out completely (*lacerat, exest animum planeque conficit*).[76]

More than death itself, says Cicero, it is the irrational and anxious anticipation of evil and suffering that produces this kind of withering distress or grief.

By extension, to be "aggrieved" at receiving ill treatment undeservedly is a related sphere of grief's operation. We noted it in passing earlier when commenting on Paul's "grievous or aggrieved" letter to the Corinthians where he likewise links it to his ability to endure hardships without becoming excessively grieved. While this aspect of grief is not directly addressed in Galen's letter, to some extent is implied in the role of friendly exhortation that seeks moral progress both for oneself and one's friends. We saw the same idea at work in the role of a friend's consolation as an effort to snatch the grieving father from the clutches of consuming sorrow.[77] In part, this is where the *sophos* as moral adviser functions as a doctor for the soul, a sentiment not at all lost on Galen, who said:

> The character of the soul (τὸ τῆς ψυχῆς ἦθος) is corrupted by poor habits in food, drink, exercise, sights, sounds, and all the arts. Therefore the one pursuing medicine should be practiced in all these things, and should not think that it is proper only for the philosopher to shape the character of the soul.[78]

Dio Chrysostom put it this way, likening the philosophers frank criticism (παρρησία) to a surgeon's treatment:

> Therefore toward oneself first of all, and next toward those dearest and nearest to us, one should behave with both complete frankness and (full) freedom (μετὰ πλείστης

---

[75] *Tusc.* 3.4.7–8. The need to despise rather than fear death is the topic in Book 1 of *Tusc.*, while enduring pain is the topic of Book 2.

[76] *Tusc.* 3.12.27. Cicero's quotation of the maxim from Euripides (nn. 73–74 above) follows on this description of the degrading effects of grief/distress.

[77] (Ps-)Plutarch *Cons. Apoll.* 102 (quoted above at n. 62).

[78] Galen *San.Tu.* 1.8 (K 6.40).

παρρησίας τε καὶ ἐλευθερίας προσφέρεσθαι), neither shrinking back nor slackening in our words. For worse by far than a corrupt and diseased body is a soul which is corrupt, not, by Zeus, because of salves or potions or some consuming poison, but rather because of ignorance and depravity and insolence, and, indeed, jealousy, and grief, and a myriad desires (ἀλλ' ὑπό τε ἀγνοίας καὶ πονηρίας καὶ ὕβρεως καὶ φθόνου δὴ καὶ λύπης καὶ μυρίων ἐπιθυμιῶν). This disease and *pathos* (τοῦτο τὸ νόσημα καὶ τὸ πάθος) is more grievous than that of Heracles, and requires a far stronger, white-hot, cautery.[79]

Significantly, two of the corrupting vices here, "jealousy and grief" (φθόνου δὴ καὶ λύπης) come from the species of grief.

Among the epistolary handbooks, a number of rebuking letters appear, each one reflecting a different grade or degree of harshness owing to the nature of the offense. In Ps-Libanius' *Epistolary Styles* these include one called the "grievious or aggrieved style" (λυπητική), and it reads as follows:

> You have grieved me severly and in the extreme by acting in this manner. Wherefore I am exceedingly vexed at you, and I am grieved with an un incurable grief. For the griefs experienced from friends on friends can hardly be healed and carry an even more wanton afront than that from enemies. (Σφόδρα καθ' ὑπερβολὴν λελύπηκας τόδε τὸ πρᾶγμα διαπραξάμενος. ὅθεν ἰσχυρῶς ἄχθομαι πρὸς σὲ καὶ δυσίατόν τινα λυποῦμαι λύπην. αἱ γὰρ ἐκ φίλων εἰς φίλους γινόμεναι λῦπαι δυσθεράπευτοι λίαν τυγχάνουσι καὶ μείζους τῶν ἐχθρῶν ἔχουσι τὰς ἐπηρείας.)[80]

In addition, Ps-Libanius gives an example of the "remedial or conciliatory style" (θεραπευτική), which some call the "apologetic" (ἀπολογητική), under the description "that through which we offer a remedy to someone who has been aggrieved against us in some matter (δι' ἧς θεραπεύομέν τινα λυπηθέντα πρὸς ἡμᾶς περί τινος)."[81] The sample letter goes as follows:

> On the one hand, over and above what things I myself[82] said in words, I carried out in deed, for I did not think any of it would ever cause you grief. But, on the other hand, since you were vexed by what was said or done, most excellent sir, know that I shall not at all make mention of the things that transpired ever again. For it is my goal always to provide remedies for my friends rather than cause them grief. (Ἐγὼ μὲν ἐφ' οἷς εἶπον λόγοις μετῆλθον ἔργῳ, τὸ γὰρ σύνολον οὐκ ἐνόμιζόν σέ ποτε λυπηθήσεσθαι· εἰ δ' ἐπὶ τοῖς λεχθεῖσιν ἢ πραχθεῖσιν ἠχθέσθης, ἴσθι, κράτιστε ἀνδρῶν, ὡς οὐκέτι τῶν ῥηθέντων λόγον ὅλως ποτὲ ποιήσομαι. σκοπὸς γάρ μοι θεραπεύειν ἀεὶ τοὺς φίλους ἐστὶν ἤπερ λυπεῖν.)[83]

---

[79] *Invid.* 45; cf. Seneca *Ep.* 75.6–7.
[80] Ps-Libanius *Epistolary Styles* 90 (ed. Malherbe).
[81] Ps-Libanius *Epistolary Styles* 19 (ed. Malherbe).
[82] The parallelism of the two verbs (εἶπον and μετῆλθον) taken in concert with the emphatic ἐγώ, strongly supports the first person reading, as given here and as translated by Malherbe, *Ancient Epistolary Theorists*, 77; however, the third person plural is at least grammatically feasible, assuming some sort of contrast (they vs. I) as a note of regret.
[83] Ps-Libanius *Epistolary Styles* 66 (ed. Malherbe).

One reason why there seem to be so many distinct types or grades of rebuke is because the caring friend or moral physician needed to diagnose the correction needed owing to the nature of the offense or the degree of recalcitrance of the perpetrator. The goal was to apply just the right amount of medicine through the "tone" of frank criticism.[84] The more intransigent the disease, the harsher the medicine and the greater the pain required in order to effect the cure. To take such rebuke "ungrievedly" (ἀλύπως), says Plutarch, is a sign of an ignoble, uneducated, and "slavish" person.[85] Plutarch continues:

> ... to hear a rebuke or admonition (ἐπαφῆς καὶ νουθεσίας) to reform character, delivered in words reproachful as a stinging drug (ὥσπερ φαρμάκῳ δάκοντι λόγῳ χρωμένης ἐλέγχοντι), and not to be humbled, not to run in a dizzy sweat, not to burn with shame in the soul, is a notable sign (of a vicious character). ... But with respect to the sting from philosophy (τὸν ἐκ φιλοσοφίας ... δηγμὸν) which takes root in a youth of good disposition (ἐμφυόμενον εὐφυέσι νέοις), the very word that wounds also heals (αὐτὸς ὁ τρώσας λόγος ἰᾶτραι). On account of this, it is also necessary for the one receiving reproach to suffer some pain and be stung (δεῖ πάσχειν μέν τι καὶ δάκνεσθαι), although he should not be thoroughly crushed or made despondent (μὴ συντρίβεσθαι δὲ μηδ' ἀθυμεῖν), ... in hopes that something sweet and splendid will follow from his present anguish and disorder (ἀδημονίας καὶ ταραχῆς).[86]

Thus, the sting and pain of the aggrieved rebuke, delivered with sincerity and frankness (παρρησία), can also have a curative effect.[87] While grief is, on the one hand, the worst of the passions (because of its degrading effects), it can also be part of the cure, on the other.

---

[84] Cf. Plutarch *Adul. amic.* 69E–F.

[85] *Rect. rat. aud.* 46D. Plutarch's treatise "on listening to lectures" deals with "young men" who are in rhetorical education, but the physical and psychological assumptions about rebuke and moral progress are more generally applicable; cf. Lucian, *Nigrinus* 35–36. See also Loveday C. A. Alexander, "The Passions in Galen, Chariton, and Xenophon," in *Passions and Moral Progress in Greco-Roman Thought* (ed. J. T. Fitzgerald; London: Routledge, 2008), 175–98 [179], citing especially Galen *Aff. Dig.* 7. (K 5.38–39 = *SM* 1.29–30 = *CMG* 5.4.1.1 25.26–27.10).

[86] *Rect. rat. aud.* 46D–47A. See L. Michael White, "Rhetoric and Reality in Galatians: Framing the Social Demands of Friendship," in *Early Christianity and Classical Culture: Comparative Studies in Honor of Abraham J. Malherbe* (ed. J. T. Fitzgerald, T. H. Olbricht, and L. M. White; NovTSup 110; Leiden: Brill, 2003), 327–9; White, "Moral Pathology," 301–7. See also Fredrikson, "Paul, Hardship, and Suffering," 176; and J. Paul Sampley, "Paul's Frank Speech with the Galatians and Corinthians," in *Philodemus and the New Testament World* (ed. J. T. Fitzgerald, D. Obbink, and G. S. Holland; NovTSup 111; Leiden: Brill, 2004), 295–321.

[87] On Philodemus' notion of frank criticism and the role of its "stings," see now Armstrong, "Be Angry and Sin Not," 88–95 (responding in part to Richard Sorabji, *Emotions and Peace of Mind: From Stoic Agitation to Christian Temptation* [Oxford: Oxford University Press, 2000], 201–4).

Vice, Habituation, and the Avoidance of Grief

This brings us to the final arena of grief; it comes in the form of a "life of grief," i.e., a miserable and wretched life as the consequence of vice. Yet it is connected to the foregoing sphere, as stinging frank criticism might sometimes be needed to reclaim the person mired in vice and grief. To understand this equation, then, let us return to Galen's personal advice (*Ind.* 56), based on the proverbial lines of Euripides:[88]

> Therefore, since I have proven the saying of Euripides to be otherwise quite true,[89] I encourage you likewise **to train**[90] **the imaginative faculties of your soul** [to prepare for such loss] almost at every moment of time. (Ἐγὼ τοίνυν πεπειραμένος τῶν ἄλλων ἀληθέστατον εἶναι τὸν Εὐριπίδου λόγον, ἀσκεῖν παρακελεύομαι τὰς φαντασίας σου τῆς ψυχῆς μόνον οὐ καθ' ἑκάστην καιροῦ ῥοπήν.)

In this section of the letter (*Ind.* 38–57), Galen deals with his achievement of "disdaining" (καταφρονήσαντι, *Ind.* 49) his losses, by citing exempla about proportionality and magnitude relating to possessions. The point here it seems is to gain some perspective from which to maintain his equilibrium or tranquility (ἀκηδῶς)[91] and thereby avoid grief. Plutarch talks similarly about cultivating tranquility of mind or soul (εὐθυμία) as the steady state that resists the "impulses" (ὁρμαί) that threaten to stir up the passions.[92] Galen had used δυσθυμία as its antithesis back in *Ind.* 2 and 7. Galen reflects on his experience as follows (*Ind.* 50a–51):

> For even this – not being driven to utter mania (μὴ μανῆναι τὴν μανίαν), by having many detractors in the imperial court – was not a great thing. Instead, not being grieved (μὴ λυπηθῆναι) [was a great achievement] – despite having lost all my medicines, all my books, even the recipes containing effective cures, in addition to the published editions about them, at the same time as the many other treatises, each one of which itself demonstrated the considerable industry of my whole life – now this is a further demonstration of one who is well bred (γενναῖον) and a prime example of magnanimity (μεγαλοψυχία).[93] And what first led me to such magnanimity (μεγαλοψυχίαν ἤγαγέ

---

[88] Given in *Ind.* 51–52 (quoted above, at n. 73).

[89] Or "to be the truest of all."

[90] Note the use of ἀσκεῖν in the sense of "training and habituation," as a tool of self-mastery similar to Epictetus and Musonius. Galen's friend had asked him to discuss what "training, arguments, and doctrines" prepared him to be ungrieved (*Ind.* 1, n. 9 above).

[91] *Ind.* 44, taken in a positive sense as a synonym for εὐθυμία ("tranquility").

[92] See *Tranquil. an.* 471D (the role of "impulses" (ὁρμαί) in interfering with tranquility; 473B (on discontentment stirring up the passions). Plutarch also seems to know the same basic tradition as found in *Tabula of Cebes* regarding discontentment arising from *Tyche* (467B–C); cf. also Plutarch *An corp.* 500C.

[93] Or "great-souled;" the antithesis of μεγαλοψυχία here is ὀλιγοψυχία ("pusillanimity"), which we also get in 1 Thess 5:14, the ones who are to be "encouraged." Likewise, μακροθυμία (also in 1 Thess 5:14), is the analogous self-management against a rising passion of anger.

με) you yourself know, since you were from the beginning nourished up and educated together with us.[94]

His point is that μεγαλοψυχία is what comes with upbringing, training, and conditioning. He concludes by saying, "Therefore the wise man reminds himself continually of those things it is possible to suffer" (*Ind.* 53). "I even trained my imaginative faculties (ἐγύμνασά μου τὰς φαντασίας) for the loss of everything" (55). And "I urge you to train (ἀσκεῖν) the imaginative faculties of your soul almost at every moment" (56). "This cannot come about," he continues, "for those who are not favorably disposed by nature to be courageous, nor for those lacking an excellent education (τοῖς μὴ πεφυκόσιν εὖ πρὸς ἀνδρείαν, μήτ' ἀρίστῃ παιδείᾳ χρησαμένοις) ..." (57).

From here (*Ind.* 58–68) he goes on to talk about his own upbringing, using the examples of his grandfather and his father to suggest that he came by his strength of soul from them.[95] After concluding the personal side of his discussion, Galen finally summarizes his advice on the matter (*Ind.* 79b–81):

79b Τὰ δ' ἄλλα γεγραφὼς εἰς ἀλυπ{ησ}ίαν συνεβούλευσα, περιττά σοι λέγειν ὃν ἐξ ἀρχῆς οἶδα καὶ φύσει καὶ παιδείᾳ τοῖς εὐτελέσιν ἐδέσμασι καὶ ἱματίοις ἀεὶ χρώμενον, ἀφροδισίων τε ἐγκρατέστατον οἷς οἱ δουλεύοντες ἀναγκάζονται δεῖσθαι χρημάτων πλειόνων <εἴτε πολυτοῦσιν>. 80 εἴτε δὲ μὴ πλουτοῦσι, πρῶτον οἰμώζουσι καὶ στένουσι μεθ' ἡμέραν καὶ νύκτα, ... ὡς ἐμπιπλάναι τὰς ἐπιθυμίας σκοπούμενοι, ... καὶ μὴ τυχόντες μὲν αὐτῶν ὠρύονται, τυχόντες δὲ οὐκ ἐμπίπλανται, τοῦτο δὲ τῷ μοχθηροτέρῳ βίῳ περιπίπτουσι ταῖς ἀπλήστοις ἐπιθυμίαις. 81 Προσγίνονταί τινες οὖν [οὐχ ὡς οἱ πολλοὶ λυποῦνται] οἳ μετρίως ἄπτονται τιμῆς καὶ πλούτου καὶ δόξης καὶ δυνάμεως πολιτικῆς, ὧν [γὰρ] ἂν τούτων εὑρεθῇ τις ἀμέτρως, κακοδαιμονέστατα βιοῦν ἀναγκάζεται, ψυχῆς μὲν ἀρετὴν μηδὲ τὴν ἀρχὴν ὅλως τίς ἐστιν ἐπιστάμενος, αὐξήσας δὲ τὰς ἐν αὐτῇ κακίας ἅμα τῷ λυπεῖσθαι διὰ παντὸς ὡς ἂν οὗ προὔθετο τυχεῖν οὐ δυνάμενος·

79b Having written other things on being ungrieved, I offer you this advice on the subject,[96] even though it is superfluous to mention [such things] to you, whom I know both by nature and by education always to have made use of simple food and clothing, as well as being extremely self-controlled in regard to sexual pleasures – the slaves of

---

[94] The ms. reads συναναστραφεὶς καὶ συμπαιδευθεὶς, but the former seems to be a corruption for συνανατρεφεὶς, as we translate here. Compare Ps-Demetrius *Epistolary Types* 1B (ed. Malherbe).

[95] He does not give their names, assuming that they are already known by his correspondent and friend, who apparently grew up with Galen; cf. *Ind.* 51. His father, Aelius Nikon, was a noted architect and a leading civic benefactor at Pergamum under Antoninus Pius, although he was a new man in town. See Glen W. Bowersock, *Greek Sophists in the Roman Empire* (Oxford: Clarendon, 1969), 59–62, citing *PIR²*, G24; cf. *IGRR* 4.502–6. His grandfather's name is not given, although it may well be Aelius Nikon too, since *IGRR* 4.504 refers to a Nikon the Younger (Νείκων νέος), who is apparently the architect and Galen's father. Apparently the family was already in Pergamum when Galen was born in 129, and this suggests that the family received citizenship and enfranchisement under Trajan or Hadrian.

[96] I read συνεβούλευσα here as an epistolary aorist, and I understand εἰς ἀλυπίαν to be placed in an intentionally ambiguous position syntactically so that it goes with both the preceding and following clauses, as translated here.

> which are compelled to be in need of more possessions if they are rich. 80 But even if they are not rich, at first they wail and sigh day and night ... fretting how to fulfill their desires. If they do not obtain them, they complain; if they do obtain them, they are not satisfied. **Thus they fall into a most wretched life with insatiable desires.** 81 Some in addition, grasp at honor, wealth, glory and political power in a moderate way, but when one of them is found (to do so) immoderately, **he is compelled to live most wretchedly. One who does not know the first principles about the soul,** *augments the vices within it, while at the same time being perpetually grieved*, **because he was not able to obtain what he purposed.**

There are two key points here. First, to resist the sting of loss that initiates grief, one should train oneself by constantly imagining such loss, until one is habituated to it. This is a basic Stoic tenant on training and habituation, as reflected in the following exhortation of Epictetus, who also frames it in terms of "augmenting the passions:"[97]

> In general, therefore, if you want to do something, make a habit (or *habitual disposition*, ἑκτικόν) of it. If you do wish *not* to do something, do not do it, but rather accustom yourself (ἔθισον) to practice other things in its place. The same principle [of habituation] holds true in matters of the soul (ψυχικῶν): whenever you become angry (ὀργισθῇς), know that not only has this particular vice come upon you, but also that you have **augmented the habit**, and you have, as it were, tossed fuel on the fire (τὴν ἕξιν ηὔχησας καὶ ὡς πυρὶ φρύγανα παρέβαλες).[98] ... In this way also, of course, the diseases (ἀρρωστήματα) [of the soul] <u>erupt</u> (ὑποφύεσθαι) [like a tumor or pustule],[99] as the philosophers say. For whenever you once develop a desire for money (ἐπιθυμήσῃς ἀργυρίου), if reason is applied to bring about a sense perception of the vice (αἴσθησιν ἄξων τοῦ κακοῦ), then the desire will be arrested and our governing principle will be restored to its original state (πέπαυταί τε ἡ ἐπιθυμία καὶ τὸ ἡγεμονικὸν ἡμῶν εἰς τὸ ἐξαρχῆς ἀποκατέστη). But if you do not apply anything as a curative, then the governing principle is not restored ... And if this happens repeatedly, then the remaining part becomes calloused and the disease strengthens the avarice. For a man who develops a fever and then it is arrested, is yet not the same as before developing the fever, unless he has been cured once and for all. This is what happens also with passions of the soul (ἐπὶ τῶν τῆς ψυχῆς παθῶν).

---

[97] Epictetus *Diatr.* 2.18.5, 8–10; cf. Gill, *Naturalistic Psychology in Galen and the Stoics*, 266. The word "habit" (ἕξις) is the same as that used of the "disposition" in Aristotle; see n. 14 above.

[98] On this maxim, see n. 100 below.

[99] See White, "Moral Pathology," 288–9. This unusual word, a cognate of φύω/φύσις, appears mostly in early writings of the fourth century BCE dealing with medicine (Hippocrates), agriculture (Theophrastus *De causis plantarum; Historia plantarum*), and animal husbandry (Aristotle *Historia animalium*). It means to grown up underneath either as an attachment (like a tumor) or as a substitute (like teeth or hooves). The term seems to come into use again during the second cent. CE, proximate to the time of Epictetus, and occurs in Galen's medical writings and Diogenes of Oenoanda *Epicurus* 29 (see LSJ, *sv*). In the context here, it seems to be a reference to something growing under the skin (thus my translation); so note the reference a few lines later to the forming of callouses (τυλοῦται) as a next stage.

Just after this, Epictetus gives two examples of the need for daily conditioning to withstand the impulse toward passion, first anger and then grief. Both are framed in terms of making progress toward self-mastery in controlling the passion. The passage continues as follows:

> If therefore you wish not to be wrathful (ὀργίλος), do not nourish your habit (μὴ τρέφε σου τὴν ἕξιν); toss nothing on it to fan the flames (μηδὲν αὐτῇ παράβαλλε αὐξητικόν). At first remain quiet and number the days on which you did not become angry. ... And should you pass even thirty days (without becoming angry), then offer a sacrifice to god. For the habit is at first loosened, and then totally destroyed (ἡ γὰρ ἕξις ἐκλύεται τὴν πρώτην, εἶτα καὶ παντελῶς ἀναιρεῖται). "Today I was not grieved (ἐλυπήθην)," – nor the next day, nor thereupon for two or three months – "rather, I paid close attention when anything came to pass by way of provocation (ἐρεθιστικῶν)." Know that it is getting better for you (κομψῶς σοί).[100]

The second point is that to fail to cultivate such self-mastery by training and habituation inevitably leads to a life of grief, wretchedness, and misery, because one's passions and desires are never sufficiently satisfied, and one is further mired in vice. Thus, the life of vice is a life of grief. Conversely, the sage is happy despite suffering and adversity, and thus avoids grief and misery. Again, it is Epictetus who delivers the classic paradigm of the ideal Stoic sage:

> Who then is a Stoic? ... Show me someone who though sick is yet happy, though in danger is yet happy, though dying is yet happy, though exiled is yet happy, though defamed is yet happy. Show one! By the gods, I desire to see a Stoic. ... Let someone show us the soul of a person who wishes to be of one mind with God, and no longer blaming either God or man (for misfortune), no longer failing to accomplish something (purposed), nor falling into something (to be avoided), not becoming angry, not becoming envious (μὴ φθονῆσαι), not becoming rivalrous (μὴ ζηλοτυπῆσαι) – why must we speak in riddles? – one who earnestly desires to become a god from a man, and, even in this paltry body of death, wishes for fellowship with Zeus.

The species of grief specifically dealing with possessions[101] appear again, now as the vices to be avoided and the miseries that accrue with vice.

In particular, then, attitudes toward wealth and possessions, and their potential loss constituted a central trope among the Stoics concerning the common hardships of human life. Galen's contemporary, the Christian Clement of Alexandria, argued, therefore, that poverty would only heighten ones distress and grief. He said:

---

[100] *Diatr.* 2.18.12–14. The wording in the second clause (μηδὲν αὐτῇ παράβαλλε αὐξητικόν) harks back to the phrase used earlier in 2.18.5 (n. 98 above): "tossed fuel on the fire." For the metaphor used typically of *"fanning the flames"* of the passions or *"pouring fire on fire,"* compare Plutarch *Adul. amic.* 61A and Clement of Alexandria *Quis div.* 1.2; cf. White, "Moral Pathology," 285 and n. 3.

[101] For φθόνον ("grief felt at others' prosperity") and ζηλοτυπίαν ("grief at the possession by another of what one has oneself") see Diog. Laert. 7.111 (quoted at n. 43 above).

When pain (ἀλγηδόνος) is present, the soul appears to shrink back from it and consider riddance of its presence a gift. At that moment, it also becomes sluggish (ῥαθυμεῖ) with regard to its lessons, whence the other virtues are utterly neglected (ἀπημέληνται). And yet we do not say that virtue itself suffers (for virtue is not affected by disease). But the person who is composed jointly of both – virtue and disease – is distressed (θλίβεται) by the pressing urgency (κατεπείγοντος). And if he happens not to be extremely high minded (καταμεγαλοφρονῶν), not heretofore establishing the habit of self-control (τὴν ἕξιν τῆς ἐγκρατείας), he becomes distraught (ἐξίσταται), and he discovers that not enduring (τὸ μὴ ὑπομῆναι) is equivalent to fleeing. The same reasoning holds true concerning poverty. For it forces the soul to desist (αὕτη τῶν ἀναγκαίων ... ἀπασχολεῖν βιάζεται τὴν ψυχήν) from what is necessary ...[102]

He argued further that giving away one's possessions, following the saying attributed to Jesus, was no better.[103] Ultimately, Clement, like Galen, advocates being unmoved or agitated by passions such as anger or greed: "salvation belongs to passionless and pure souls (ἀπαθῶν καὶ καθαρῶν ψυχῶν)" mastered through self-control (ἐγκράτεια and ἀπάθεια).[104] Thus, the goal should be to habituate oneself to a proper attitude toward wealth and possessions and thus attain self-mastery in response.

This idea is most clearly reflected in the *Tabula of Cebes*, a first century CE Stoic text attributed to a member of the Socratic circle.[105] It brings together the notion of the passions and vice, stimulated by deceit and false opinions about possessions,[106] with the notion of grief and retribution. Modeled on the "choice of Herakles,"[107] the treatise is in the form of an allegorical *mythos* about the two ways of virtue and vice, leading respectively to happiness (εὐδαιμονία) or wretched despair (κακοδαιμονία). Here is the central scene (*Tabula of Cebes* 9.1–11.1) regarding the place of Grief.

9.1. "Then do you see that when you pass beyond this gate there is another enclosure farther up, and standing outside it are women adorned as courtesans usually are?"

"Certainly."

---

[102] Clement of Alexandria *Strom.* 4.5 (20.1–21.1 Stählin), but the idea is based directly on Plato; cf. White, "Moral Pathology," 295–6.

[103] This is the point of his treatise (oration), called "Who is the Rich Man that shall be saved?" (*Quis dives salvetur?*); cf. White, "Moral Pathology," 284–7.

[104] *Quis div.* 20.6; cf. *Strom.* 3.7 (59.4–60.1 Stählin) and 4.23 (147.1–148.2 Stählin), which link true ἀγάπη with ἐγκράτεια and ἀπάθεια. See Theodor Rüther, *Die sittliche Forderung der Apatheia in den beiden ersten christlichen Jahrhunderten und bei Klemens von Alexandrien* (Freiburger Theologische Studien 62; Freiburg: Verlag Herder, 1949), 56.

[105] See John T. Fitzgerald and L. Michael White, *The Tabula of Cebes: Text and Translation with Introduction and Notes* (SBLTTS 24, GRR 7; Chico: Scholars Press, 1983), 1–7.

[106] On the role of ἀπάτη (deceit) see *Tabula of Cebes* 5–6 and 22 (quoted below); the same idea is reflected in Cicero (*Tusc.* 3.1.2) and Dio Chrysostom (*4 Regn.* 115–6).

[107] Also known as the Prodicus myth or Herakles at the crossroads; cf. Fitzgerald and White, *Tabula of Cebes*, 14–16.

"Now, they are as follows: one is called Incontinence (ἀκρασία), another Profligacy (ἀσωτία), another Covetousness (ἀπληστία), and the other Flattery (κολακεία)."

2. "And why are they standing here?"

"They are closely watching," he said, "those who have received something from Fortune (Τύχης)."

"What then?"

"They jump up and embrace them, and flatter and coax them to stay with them, saying that they will have a life that is pleasant (ἡδύν) and painless (ἄπονον), with no misery (κακοπάθειαν) at all. 3. Then, if someone is persuaded by them to enter into Luxury (ἡδυπάθειαν), the diversion seems pleasant (ἡδεῖα) up to a point, so long as it titillates (γαργαλίζῃ) the person, but not beyond. For when he comes to his senses, he realizes that he was not doing the eating but was being devoured and violated (ὑβρίζετο) by her. 4. Therefore, whenever he has squandered all that he has received from Fortune, he is compelled to be a slave to these women, to submit in everything, to act disgracefully, and, for their sake, to commit all that is injurious, such as fraud, desecration, perjury, treason, pillage, and all such things. Then when they have committed all these deeds, they are delivered to Retribution (τιμωρίᾳ)."

10.1. "And what sort is she?"

"Do you see a bit behind them, up above, something like a small door and some sort of dark, narrow place? <...> And does it not appear that some ugly, filthy women dressed in rags are gathering?"

2. "Yes, indeed."

"Well, these women," he said, "are the following: **the one with the whip is called Retribution (τιμωρία), the one with her head on her knees is Grief (λύπη), and the one pulling out her own hair is Sorrow (ὀδύνη).**"

3. "And this other man who is standing by them, someone deformed, emaciated, and naked, and with him there is another woman who resembles him, ugly and emaciated; who is he?"

"**He is called Lamentation (ὀδυρμὸς),**" he said, "**and she, Despondency (ἀθυμία); she is his sister.** 4. So, he is being handed over to them and dwells with them while being punished. Next, from there he is once again being thrown into this other house here, into wretched Unhappiness (κακοδαιμονιαν), unless from her own choice, Repentance (μετάνοια) happens to encounter him."

11.1. "Then what happens if Repentance encounters him?"

"She releases him from his ills and introduces to him another Opinion (δόξαν) [and Desire (ἐπιθυμίαν)], who leads him to true Education (ἀληθινὴν Παιδείαν). ..."

Thus, only when one reforms one's opinions and perceptions of the realities of human life can one then live virtuously. Using the *agon* motif, the allegory then poses the Stoic ideal of self-mastery as the antedote to vice, passions, and a life of grief. Thereby the sage becomes the doctor and guide for others (*Tabula of Cebes* 22.1–23.1).

22.1. "When someone arrives here what does she [Happiness] do?"

"Happiness crowns (στεφανοῖ) him with her power ... as do all the other Virtues, in the same way that one crowns those who have been victorious in the mightiest contests (ὥσπερ τοὺς νενικηκότας τοὺς μεγίστους ἀγῶνας)."

"Well, what kinds of contests has he won?"
2. "The mightiest ... overcoming even the mightiest beasts (τὰ μέγιστα θηρία), which previously used to devour, abuse, and enslave him. ... He has mastered himself (κεκράτηκεν), so that these beasts are his slaves just as he was once theirs."
"What kinds of beasts do you mean? I really want to know."
"In the first place," he said, "Ignorance and Deceit (τὴν Ἄγνοιαν καὶ τὸν Πλάνον). Or don't you think that they are beasts?"
23.1. "Yes, and bad ones at that," I said.
2. "Next come Grief, Lamentation, Avarice, Incontinence, and every other Vice (λύπην καὶ τὸν ὀδυρμὸν καὶ τὴν φιλαργυρίαν καὶ τὴν ἀκρασίαν καὶ τὴν λοιπὴν ἅπασαν κακίαν). All these he masters and is not mastered as before."

Conclusion: Psychagogy and Psychology

By way of conclusion we should note that Galen's works show that medical knowledge and assumptions had changed significantly since the Classical period.[108] In part, these changed assumptions (and the debates that go with them) also reflect the changing social climate and cultural orientations of the shift to Roman power.[109] The soul was the "organ" of sense and perception, but one must be on guard against those things which might distort the healthy judgments, including false perceptions (φαντασίαι), false opinions (ψευδοδόξαι), or undue stimuli that hamper one's rational powers.[110] The passions likewise propel one deeper into vice by distorting or clouding the soul's ability to reason.[111] Cicero, for example, also discusses these Stoic debates (as well as popular opinions)

---

[108] Galen *Loc.Aff.* 1.3 (K 8.32; cf. *SVF* 3.429). On passions in Stoic physiology see Robert J. Rabel, "Diseases of the Soul in Stoic Psychology," *GRBS* 22 (1981): 392; for Galen see R. J. Hankinson, "Actions and Passions: Affection, Emotion, and Moral Self-Management in Galen's Philosophical Psychology," in *Passions and Perceptions: Studies in the Hellenistic Philosophy of Mind* (ed. J. Brunschwig and M. Nussbaum; Proceedings of the Fifth Symposium Hellenisticum; Cambridge: Cambridge University Press, 1993), 184–220.

[109] See Aline Rousselle, *Porneia: On Desire and the Body in Antiquity* (Oxford: Blackwells, 1988), 31–33; Owsei Timken, *Galenism: Rise and Decline of a Medical Philosophy* (Ithaca: Cornell University Press, 1973), 10–48.

[110] On Galen's contributions to the Stoic debates see White, "Moral Pathology," 295. Cf. Richard Sorabji, *Emotions and Peace of Mind,* 29–47, 244–52; Martha C. Nussbaum, *Therapy of Desire: Theory and Practice in Hellenistic Ethics* (Princeton: Princeton University Press, 1994), 366–9. The key terms are δόξα and ψευδοδόξα ("opinion" or belief, and "false opinion/belief"), κρίσις ("judgment"), and ὑπόληψις ("supposition, understanding"); see Diog. Laert. 7.111; *Tabula of Cebes* 11; Plutarch *De esu* 1.6 (*Mor.* 995F–996A). In Latin the terms are *opinio* and *iudicium* (corresponding to the first two in Greek); note the usage in Cicero *Tusc.* 3.25.61 (on Chrysippus' definition of λύπη), quoted below n. 113.

[111] Galen *Aff.Dig.* 2–3 (K 5.7 = *SM* 1.5 = *CMG* 5.4.1.1 6); cf. Dio Chrysostom *Invid.* 45; Plutarch *An. corp.* 2 (500D–F).

based on the views of Chrysippus,[112] in one instance specifically in terms of λύπη:[113]

> ... this reflection [on the lot of humans – *a reference to the debate between Carneades and Chrysippus, based on a passage from Euripides' Hypsipyla*] is a great relief to sorrow ... For we must, as it were, shore up in every way those who are knocked down and unable to cohere on account of the magnitude of their distress (*aegritudinis*). From this Chrysippus gave sickness or distress (*aegritudinem*) its own name, λύπη, since it is a "dissolution" (*solutionem*)[114] of the whole person. It can be entirely rooted out only when we have explicated the principal cause of distress (*aegritudinis*). For it is nothing other than the [false] opinion and judgment (*opinio et iudicium*) of a present and pressing evil. Thereupon, a bodily pain (*dolor corporis*) whose bite (*morsus*) is very sharp, is endured (*perferetur*), when we can see before us the hope of good. And a life spent honorably and brilliantly affords consolation (*consolationem*) so complete that either distress is not able to attack us (*aut non attingat aegritudo*), or else pain pricks the soul very lightly (*aut perleviter pungat anima dolor*). But when, in addition to this opinion of serious evil, we accede to a further [false] opinion that one is obliged – that it is right, that it is a duty (*officium*) – to be distressed at something that has happened, then, and not before, is produced **the disturbance of grave distress (*gravis aegritudinis perturbatio*)**.[115]

In response to earlier criticisms of the Chrysippean position, Posidonius had relegated all the passions and their effects to the irrational parts of the soul alone, thus creating a discontinuous, disjointed, or "conflicted" sense of the human self.[116] By contrast, following Seneca's efforts to harmonize some of these ideas,[117] some of the more practical Roman Stoics, notably Musonius Rufus and Epictetus, reverted to a more "physicalist" approach to the problem by asserting

---

[112] Cicero *Tusc.* 4.10.23 also attributes the idea to Chrysippus: "Just as when the blood is in a bad state, or there is an excess of phlegm or bile, disorder and sickness of the body are born. So also, the disturbing effect of corrupt beliefs warring against one another despoils the soul of health and introduces disorders. Moreover, from disorders are produced, first, disease, which are called νοσήματα, and besides these are affections which are the opposite of such disease and which are accompanied by unhealthy aversion and loathing for certain things. Secondly, are produced sicknesses, which are called ἀρρωστήματα by the Stoics, and these too have corresponding aversions which are their opposites. On this point too much attention is devoted by the Stoics, especially by Chrysippus, to making comparisons between diseases of the body and those of the soul." See David Sedley, "Chrysippus on Psychophysical Causality," in *Passions and Perceptions: Studies in the Hellenistic Philosophy of Mind* (ed. by J. Brunschwig and M. Nussbaum; Proceedings of the Fifth Symposium Hellenisticum; Cambridge: Cambridge University Press, 1993), 313–31, which discusses Galen's appropriation of Chrysippean psychology.

[113] *Tusc.* 3.25.61; the discussion continues to 3.27.66.

[114] There is a folk-etymology here that derives λύπη from λύω (as in διάλυσις), ascribed generally to Plato *Crat.* 419c. So, note also απολλύμενοι in *Ind.* 7; cf. 2 Cor 4:9.

[115] Cicero goes on to associate this type of grief especially with the mourning of women or parents, citing Bion's quip regarding the grief of Agamemnon (Homer *Il.* 10.15); see also n. 72 above.

[116] Sorabji, *Emotions and Peace of Mind*, 93–132.

[117] See Sorabji, *Emotions and Peace of Mind*, 61–63, discussing Seneca's *De Ira*.

that how one trains and cares for the body can affect the rational powers, *and thereby* the condition of one's soul. Galen, the physician, likewise adopted the "physicalist" position, even though he did not always follow a thoroughly Stoic line.[118]

Thus, in keeping with his humoural theory of medicine, care (θεραπεία) of the soul required attention to the health and condition of the body.[119] So, too, in the last section of his letter (*Ind.* 69–84) Galen likewise returns to his views on grief and its avoidance, by talking about training and conditioning, in both body and soul in order to achieve self-mastery (*Ind.* 75–76):

> 75 For, by following closely the quality of my condition, I accurately perceive (αἰσθάνομαι) what condition I have in body and soul. ... 76 In fact, I do not neglect their good condition, but continually, insofar as I am able, endeavor to instill in both [body and soul] a sufficient strength to ward off things that cause grief.

In the final analysis, then, Galen's letter, while very personal and paraenetic, is nonetheless quite sophisticated and complex in its philosophical and medical assumptions regarding the passion of grief and its cure. At the same time, the complex and interwoven place of grief, as outlined here, shows its more central role in Stoic thought regarding the passions than has sometimes been assumed. In one sense, for the Stoics, at least, grief is the supreme passion as a disease of the soul; it marks the extreme to which all the passions might lead, both as emotions and as state of life. As we have seen, Galen also shows a more subtle and realistic approach to the medical condition than the traditional notion of the "stiff-upper-lipped" Stoic. For he, in marked contrast to Musonius (*Ind.* 69–73), acknowledges that misfortune or hardship can hardly go unnoticed, nor is it to be desired. He maintains the goal of self-mastery as the proper response that keeps it from turning into true grief, i.e., emotional and physical despair, misery, and wretchedness. At the same time, he advocates a model of therapeutic progress by cultivating the self through habituation and training. In that sense, his medically informed psychagogy is also genuine psychology.[120] We may close then with Galen's own words of exhortation, displaying a personal tone while echoing perhaps the *Tabula of Cebes*:

> But if there is someone who is still in some measure enslaved to the passions (ἔτι μετρίοις δουλεύῃ πάθεσι), yet who is able to gain knowledge of them from the foregoing words, then, just as I have said earlier, let him appoint for himself (ἐπιστήσας

---

[118] Galen *San.Tu.* 1.8 (K 6.40); see n. 79 above. For Galen's discussion of the internal conflict in the Chrysippan position, see *PHP* 4.2.12 (*CMG* 5.4.1.2 240 = K 5.368–9); cf. Sorabji, *Emotions and Peace of Mind*, 60. See also Gill, *Naturalistic Psychology in Galen and the Stoics*, 278–9, 290–5.

[119] Sorabji, *Emotions and Peace of Mind*, 258–60; *contra* Romano C. Lilla (*Clement of Alexandria: A Study in Christian Platonism and Gnosticism* [London: Oxford University Press, 1971], 68), who aligns Galen *and* Clement directly with the position of Posidonius.

[120] Gill, *Naturalistic Psychology in Galen and the Stoics*, 314–21.

ἑαυτῷ) someone as a overseer [*or* mystagogue] and paedagogue (ἐπόπτην τινὰ καὶ παιδαγωγόν), who will at every turn remind (ἀναμιμνήσκων), chastise (ἐπιπλήττων), exhort (προτρέπων), and urge (παρορμῶν) him to be better, all the while offering himself as a model (παράδειγμα) of what he both says and exhorts, one who will be able thus to prepare him with reason to be both free and good in soul. For it would be shameful to make much of freedom according to human laws, and yet not to strive for that (freedom) which is by nature, and instead to be enslaved to those shameful, wanton, and tyrannical mistresses – avarice, pettiness, love of reputation, love of rule, and love of honor (αἰσχραῖς καὶ ἀσελγέσι καὶ τυραννικαῖς δεσποίναις δουλεύειν φιλοχρηματίᾳ καὶ σμικρολογίᾳ καὶ φιλοδοξίᾳ καὶ φιλαρχίᾳ καὶ φιλοτιμίᾳ). Yet I do not hesitate to say that the foundation of all these is greedy desire (πλεονεξίαν).[121]

The Semantic Complex of Grief & its Cure in *De indolentia*

ἀνιαθῆναι – 3, 11, 30, 38, 45, 47, 48, 73
ἀνία – 29, 73
ἀπορία – 11 ἀπορεῖν – 80
 ἀκηδῶς – 44
 ἀλυπῶς – 4, 45

ἀλυπησία (sic. ἀλυπία) – 69, 70, 79b
ἀοχλησία – 68
δυσθυμία – 2, 7 (*sv.* ἀθυμία)
κινήσθαι – 2, 11
λύπη – 7 λυπός – 38
λυπεῖν – 1, 16, 20, 31, 45, 47, 50b, 55,
 62(2x), 66, 70(2x), 72, 76
πόνος – 71, 79a ἀλγεῖν – 62(2x), 78b
φρονίζειν/καταφρονεῖν – 66 (*once each*), 71

ἄσκησις – 1, 74, 76 ἀσκεῖν – 74
αἰσθανέσθαι – 75
γυμνάζειν – 54

ἐγκράτεια – 79b
ἕξις – 75, 76
καρτερία –74, 79a φέρειν – 11, 38
μεγαλοψυχία – 50b, 51
παθεῖν (to suffer a misfortune) – 53
 ἀπαθής – 71
περίστασις – 73, 75, 78
συλλυπεῖν (to commiserate) – 42(3x)
ψυχή – 56, 58, 60(2x), 68, 75(2x), 76, 81

---

[121] *Aff.Dig.* 9–10 (K 5.52–53 = *SM* 1.40–41 = *CMG* 5.4.1.1 34–35) for the role of unfulfilled desire in leading to grief, see *Ind.* 79b–81 (quoted above). For "enslavement" to the passions (as courtesans), see *Tabula of Cebes* 9.2–4 (quoted above). For the need of a personal pedagogue to help with one's progress, compare Clement of Alexandria *Quis div.* 41.

RICHARD A. WRIGHT

Possessions, Distress, and the Problem of Emotions: *De indolentia* and the Gospel of Luke in Juxtaposition[1]

Galen's somewhat sympathetic critique of early Christianity has been recognized as important for understanding the development of Christianity in the second century of the Common Era and for insight into what the movement looked like to non–Christian observers.[2] Galen, however, has been an infrequent conversation partner for help in illuminating ideas and concepts that appear in the New Testament.[3] The recent discovery of the text of Galen's *De indolentia* provides the opportunity to explore what comes into focus when this text is juxtaposed with texts from the New Testament – in this case, the Gospel of Luke.[4]

---

[1] This essay is a revision of a paper presented at the annual meeting of the Christian Scholars' Conference, Malibu, Calif., 2011. I am grateful to Clare K. Rothschild and Trevor W. Thompson for suggestions that have no doubt improved the essay.

[2] In a text preserved only in Arabic, Galen observes that although Christians sometimes derive their faith from parables and miracles, at other times they act like philosophers. For the text and commentary, see Richard Walzer, *Galen on Jews and Christians* (London: Oxford University Press, 1949). For a reassessment of the Arabic evidence that calls into question the authenticity of part of the quotation provided in Walzer, see Stephen Gero, "Galen on the Christians: A Reappraisal of the Arabic Evidence," *OCP* 56 (1990): 371–411. Even with Gero's corrections, Galen's qualified, favorable, assessment of Christian actions still stands. For discussions of Galen's observations on Christianity, see, for example, Stephen Benko, "Pagan Criticism of Christianity During the First Two Centuries A. D.," *ANRW* 23.2:1055–118; Robert L. Wilken, *The Christians as the Romans Saw Them* (New Haven: Yale University Press, 1984); Dale B. Martin, *Inventing Superstition: From the Hippocratics to the Christians* (Cambridge, Mass.: Harvard University Press, 2004).

[3] Those comparing Galen with early Christianity include Robert M. Grant, "Paul, Galen, and Origen," *JTS* (1983): 533–6; Loveday C.A. Alexander, "Paul and the Hellenistic Schools: The Evidence of Galen," in *Paul in his Hellenistic Context* (ed. T. Engberg-Pedersen; Minneapolis: Fortress, 1995), 60–83; Loveday C.A. Alexander, "*IPSE DIXIT*: Citation of Authority in Paul and in the Jewish and Hellenistic Schools," in *Paul Beyond the Judaism/Hellenism Divide* (ed. T. Engberg-Pedersen; Louisville: Westminster John Knox, 2001), 103–28; L. Michael White, "Moral Pathology: Passion, Progress, and Protreptic in Clement of Alexandria," in *Passions and Moral Progress in Greco-Roman Thought* (ed. J. T. Fitzgerald; New York: Routledge, 2008), 284–321.

[4] Though I believe there are good reasons to compare Galen with early Christianity, I am convinced by Jonathan Z. Smith's argument that there is no such thing as a "natural" comparison. All comparisons are intellectual constructs based on the interests of the researcher: "In the case of the study of religion, as in any disciplined inquiry, comparison, in its strongest form, brings differences together within the space of the scholar's mind for the scholar's own intellectual reasons. It is the scholar who makes their cohabitation – their 'sameness' – possible,

The first cluster of ideas that comes into focus when comparing these two authors has to do with the assessment of possessions – both inappropriate and appropriate evaluations. Related to this topic are issues of wealth and poverty: people who can respond appropriately in poverty are remarkable; wealth will likely inhibit a person's ability to respond appropriately.

The second shared focus concerns the validity of emotions – distress in particular.[5] Galen reflects in some complicated ways the philosophical concern regarding the negative affect that distress in particular – and the emotions in general – have on moral health. Luke infrequently describes people experiencing distress. But the few references he does provide, and the way he edits the use of the term in his source(s), suggest that he shares a similar assessment of distress to what we find in Galen.

Good comparisons involve a consideration of both difference and similarity. As Fitz John Porter Poole has put it, "Difference makes a comparison interesting, similarity makes it possible."[6] I call attention to an evaluation of possessions and a perspective toward emotions that appear to me to be at work in both Galen's letter and Luke's gospel, although the contexts in which we find the language at work are different for each author.

Comparison of New Testament texts with texts from the broader Greco-Roman world has, in the history of New Testament scholarship, been subject to many pitfalls.[7] The challenge is to find a particular social entity with which to compare Christianity and then appropriately nuance comparisons.[8] The philosophical schools have been a source of much scholarly exploration, and Paul,

---

not 'natural' affinities of processes of history" (*Drudgery Divine: On the Comparison of Early Christianities and the Religions of Late Antiquity* [Chicago: The University of Chicago Press, 1990], 51).

[5] It is difficult to choose an appropriate translation for παθή. "Emotion," "passion," or "affection" are all candidates but each presents its own set of limitations. I follow recent trends and use "emotion" throughout (see Juha Sihvola and Troels Engberg-Pedersen, "Introduction," in *The Emotions in Hellenistic Philosophy* [ed. J. Sihvola and T. Engberg-Pedersen; London: Kluwer Academic Publishers, 1998], viii). For λυπή, I use the translation "distress" throughout because this English word covers a broader range of experiences than "grief" which is the term one sometimes sees in translation.

[6] "Metaphors and Maps: Toward Comparison in the Anthropology of Religion," *JAAR* 54 (1986): 417.

[7] For a brief treatment of some of the failures in the task of comparing "Early Christianities" to the religions of Late Antiquity, see Smith, *Drudgery Divine*. For a detailed discussion of the history of scholarship comparing early Christianities with Greco-Roman religions and philosophies, see L. Michael White and John T. Fitzgerald, "Quod est comparandum: the Problem of Parallels," in *Early Christianity and Classical Culture: Comparative Studies in Honor of Abraham J. Malherbe* (ed. J. T. Fitzgerald, T. H. Olbricht, and L. M. White; NovTSup 110; Atlanta: Society of Biblical Literature, 2003), 13–39.

[8] See, for example, Stanley K. Stowers' discussion of the challenges in selecting appropriate groups with which to compare early Christianity ("Does Pauline Christianity Resemble a Hellenistic Philosophy?," in *Paul Beyond the Judaism/Hellenism Divide* [ed. T. Engberg-Pedersen; Louisville: Westminster John Knox, 2001], 81–102; esp. 81–89).

in particular, is a favorite candidate.⁹ Yet no single philosophical school has seemed adequate to explain the thought world of Paul or other forms of early Christianity. Galen represents an interesting person for comparison insofar as his work draws from moral philosophers, but is not aligned with any particular philosophical school. Juxtaposing him with Luke expands our exploration of the early Christian thought world beyond Paul.

Galen: Introduction

In 192 C. E. the physician-philosopher Galen lost many of his literary and medical possessions in a fire that destroyed sections of the city of Rome.¹⁰ Upon learning of this situation, one of Galen's associates sent him a letter inquiring how he had managed not to experience distress (παρεσεύασάν με μηδέποτε λυπεῖσθαι) at this terrible loss (*Ind.* 1).¹¹ Galen responded to the friend's letter

---

⁹ For the broader question of what Christians looked like to non-Christians, see Wilken, *The Christians as the Romans Saw Them*; Wayne A. Meeks, *The First Urban Christians: The Social World of the Apostle Paul* (2d ed.; New Haven: Yale University Press, 2003), chapter 3. For the comparison between Christians and moral philosophers, see Abraham J. Malherbe, "Hellenistic Moralists and the New Testament," *ANRW* 26.1:267–333; Stowers, "Does Pauline Christianity Resemble a Hellenistic Philosophy?"

Stoicism has received the most extensive treatment. See for example, Richard Sorabji, *Emotion and Peace of Mind: From Stoic Agitation to Christian Temptation* (Oxford: Oxford University Press, 2000); Troels Engberg-Pedersen, *Paul and the Stoics* (Louisville: Westminster John Knox, 2000); Troels Engberg-Pedersen, *Cosmology and Self in the Apostle Paul: The Material Spirit* (Oxford: Oxford University Press, 2010); Runar Thorsteinsson, *Roman Christianity and Roman Stoicism: A Comparative Study of Ancient Morality* (Oxford: Oxford University Press, 2010); Tuomas Rasimus, Troels Engberg-Pedersen, and Ismo Dunderberg, eds., *Stoicism in Early Christianity* (Grand Rapids: Baker Academic, 2010). The latter is notable in that it expands the comparison beyond the letters of Paul. It includes essays dealing with Matthew and John (but not Luke).

For comparisons to Epicureanism, see Norman DeWitt, *St. Paul and Epicurus* (Minneapolis: University of Minnesota Press, 1954); Clarence Glad, *Paul and Philodemus: Adaptability in Epicurean and Early Christian Psychagogy* (NovTSup 81; Leiden: Brill, 1995); Richard A. Wright, "Christians, Epicureans, and the Critique of Greco-Roman Religion" (Ph.D. diss., Brown University, 1994); John T. Fitzgerald, Dirk Obbink, and Glenn S. Holland, eds., *Philodemus and the New Testament World* (NovTSup 111; Leiden: Brill, 2004).

¹⁰ For a discussion of Galen's library, see Matthew C. Nicholls, "Galen and Libraries in *Peri Alupias*," *JRS* 101 (2011): 123–42; Vivian Nutton, "Galen's Library," in *Galen and the World of Knowledge* (ed. C. Gill, T. Whitmarsh, and J. Wilkin; Cambridge: Cambridge University Press, 2009), 19–34; George W. Houston, "Galen, His Books, and the Horrea Piperataria at Rome," *Memoirs of the American Academy in Rome* 48 (2003): 41–51.

¹¹ References to *Ind.* refer to the section numbers in Véronique Boudon-Millot and Jacques Jouanna (with Antoine Pietrobelli), *Galien:* Ne pas se chagriner (Budé; Paris: Les Belles Lettres, 2010). Unless otherwise indicated, translations of Galen's *Ind.* are from Clare K. Rothschild and Trevor W. Thompson, "Galen: 'On the Avoidance of Grief,'" *EC* 2, no. 1 (2011): 110–29. Galen's ideas on ethics are concentrated in a few treatises. The exact order of composition for Galen's ethical works is uncertain. His earliest work on questions of ethical

with a discussion of how not to feel distress. The role that Galen adopts in *Ind.* is that of a mature spiritual or moral guide – a psychagogue, leading others along the road toward moral health.[12] While Galen does not explicitly comment on the necessity of such relationships in *Ind.*, the relationship is repeatedly emphasized in *Aff.Dig.* In that text, Galen argues that people are blind to their own weaknesses and so must find someone else to monitor their behavior.[13]

The ideal setting for moral instruction was one in which both the teacher and the student could be present together. If necessary, however, a letter could substitute for the presence of the teacher. Like Seneca's *Epistulae morales*, Galen's advice to an unnamed friend takes the form of a letter bridging the physical gap between Galen as spiritual guide and his friend, seeking advice on this topic.[14]

---

psychology are discussed in *De placitis Hippocratis et Platonis* (*PHP* 4–5 = K 5.360–504; this work, written ca. 162–6 C. E., is not dedicated to ethics but contains ethical observations – primarily against the Stoic concept of a unified soul). According to Christopher Gill, *Ind.* was the first of the cluster of ethical treatises written later in Galen's career – after the fire in Rome. *Ind.* was followed by *De moribus* (*Mor.* which only survives in an Arabic summary). *De propriorum animi cuiuslibet affectuum dignotione et curatione* (*Aff.Dig.* which is paired with *De animi cuiuslibet peccatorum dignotione et curatione* [*Pecc.Dig.*]) refers to *Mor.* and so must have been written later – and is, therefore, later than *Ind.* The other ethical treatise is *Quod animi mores corporis temperamenta sequuntur* (*QAM*), which also refers to *Mor.* and so must be later than *Ind.* (*Naturalistic Psychology in Galen and Stoicism* [Oxford: Oxford University Press, 2010], 252). Gill describes the similarities between *Aff.Dig.* and *Ind.* observing that similar themes are raised in both documents but that *Ind.* is more tightly organized and more autobiographical (262).

[12] See Glad for discussion of the development of the role and its relation to philosophy (*Adaptability,* 15–23, 53–69).

[13] Of the ten chapters into which the book is divided, Galen insists on finding such a person in five of them (3, 5, 6, 7, and 10). He recommends that this person should be mature or older (6, 7, 10) and that the person should be proven (3, 6, 10). Translations from *Aff.Dig.*, unless otherwise noted, are from Peter N. Singer, *Galen: Selected Works* (Oxford: Oxford University Press, 1997) occasionally slightly altered. I provide two sets of references for *Aff.Dig.* It begins, like *Ind.*, with a request from a friend for advice (in this case a question regarding an Epicurean treatise (1 [K 5.1 = *CMG* 5.4.1.1 3.4–7]). Galen also refers in this text to a friend who had noticed that Galen was not distressed over important matters while the friend felt distress over small matters (7 [K 5.37 = *CMG* 5.4.1.1 25.15–19]). Loveday C.A. Alexander compares Galen's *Aff.Dig.* with two Greek narratives ("The Passions in Galen and the Novels of Chariton and Xenophon," in *Passions and Moral Progress in Greco-Roman Thought* [ed. J. T. Fitzgerald; New York: Routledge, 2008], 175–97).

[14] That *Ind.* is a letter is suggested by the opening lines of the document where Galen indicates that he has received a letter from his friend asking advice and addresses his friend in the second person singular. But there is no formal salutation or conclusion; Galen just begins his topic and then, eventually, rather abruptly stops. The standard introduction to psychagogy in Seneca is Ilsetraut Hadot, *Seneca und die griechisch-römische Tradition der Seelenleitung* (Berlin: de Gruyter, 1969). See also Hildegard Cancik-Lindemaier, "Seneca's Collection of Epistles: A Medium of Philosophical Communication," in *Ancient and Modern Perspectives of the Bible and Culture: Essays in Honor of Hans Dieter Betz* (ed. A. Yarbro Collins; Atlanta: Scholars Press, 1998), 88–109 [esp. 102–9].

Galen, Distress, and Emotion

The concern with distress (λυπή) connects Galen's work to the topos of consolation.[15] Consolation literature frequently focused on death, although other topics were also addressed. Galen's work is a variation on the genre because Galen is not writing to eliminate distress from his friend but to explain the absence of distress in his own experience of loss.

Philosophers considered distress an emotion to be moderated or eliminated.[16] Galen claimed that everyone acknowledged distress as problematic. He writes:

> There are emotions of the soul that are universally acknowledged as such: anger [θυμός], wrath [ὀργή], fear [φόβος], distress [λύπη)], envy [φθόνος], and excessive desire [ἐπιθυμία σφοδρά]; and I would add excessive haste in forming love or hatred for any object as another emotion. 'Moderation is best' seems to me a good saying: nothing that happens without moderation is good.[17] (*Aff.Dig.* 2 [K 5.7 = *CMG* 5.4.1.1 7.2–6])

Here Galen aligns himself with the Aristotelian notion of moderation of the emotions. This position is consistent with Galen's part-based understanding of the construction of the soul, deriving from the Platonic-Aristotelian assessment.[18] Even though Galen does not directly address the construction of the soul in *Ind.*,

---

[15] Gill describes *Ind.* as a work of consolation (introduction to *Galen and the World of Knowledge*, 1). Standard works on consolation include: Karl Buresch, *Consolationum a Graecis Romanisque Scriptarum Historia Critica* (Leipzig: J. B. Hirschfeld, 1886); Rudolf Kassel, *Untersuchungen zur Griechischen und Romischen Konsolationsliteratur* (Munich, 1958); Mary E. Fern, *The Latin Consolatio as a Literary Type* (St. Meinrad, Ind.: The Abbey Press, 1941); J. H. D. Scourfield, *Consoling Heliodorus: A Commentary on Jerome, Letter 60* (Oxford: Clarendon Press, 1993). For a discussion of consolation in Greco-Roman antiquity with an eye toward Paul's letter to the Philippians, see Paul A. Hollaway, *Consolation in Philippians: Philosophical Sources and Rhetorical Strategy* (Cambridge: Cambridge University Press, 2001), 55–83. For a discussion of letters of consolation with examples, see Stanley K. Stowers, *Letter Writing in Greco-Roman Antiquity* (Philadelphia: Westminster Press, 1986), 142–52. Amanda Wilcox illustrates the ways in which the genre served as a medium for competition among friends ("Sympathetic Rivals: Consolation in Cicero's Letters," *AJP* 126 [2005]: 237–55).

[16] Galen distinguished "emotions" (παθή; which he believed derived from irrational powers in the soul) from "errors" (ἁμαρτία; which he attributed to faulty reasoning). He wrote separate treatises dealing with each (*Aff.Dig.* and *Pecc.Dig.*) – although he admitted that both were often labeled as "errors" (on the confusion, see *Pecc.Dig.* 1 (K 5.58 = *CMG* 5.4.1.1 41.10–14). For discussions of the role of the emotions among moral philosophers, see Julia Annas, *Hellenistic Philosophy of Mind* (Berkeley: University of California Press, 1992); John M. Cooper, *Reason and Emotion: Essays on Ancient Moral Psychology and Ethical Theory* (Princeton, New Jersey: Princeton University Press, 1999); Richard Sorabji, *Emotion and Peace of Mind;* Sihvola and Engberg-Pedersen, *The Emotions in Hellenistic Philosophy*; Jacques Brunschwig and Martha C. Nussbaum, eds., *Passions and Perceptions: Studies in Hellenistic Philosophy of Mind* (Cambridge: Cambridge University Press, 1993).

[17] Singer inexplicably omits "distress" (λύπη) from his translation. For similar lists of emotions see *Aff.Dig.* 5 (K 5.24 = *CMG* 5.4.1.1 17.8–10) and 7 (K 5.35 = *CMG* 5.4.1.1 24.10–16).

[18] See Gill, *Psychology in Galen*, 256; also, R. J. Hankinson, "Galen's Anatomy of the Soul," *Phronesis* 36 (1991): 198; R. J. Hankinson, "Actions and Passions: Affection, Emotion, and Moral Self-Management in Galen's Philosophical Psychology," in *Passions and Perceptions:*

his discussion of distress assumes such an understanding.[19] The brief contrast between training (ἄσκησις) and teachings (δόγματα) at the beginning of *Ind.* (1) depends on the Platonic-Aristotelian view about ethical development and supports the idea of a division between rational (which responds to teaching) and non-rational (which can be trained) parts of the psyche. Other features of the text that derive from the Platonic-Aristotelian view include the role that Galen allows for non-cognitive components in moral formation.[20] Galen indicates that lack of distress is the sign of a well-bred individual (*Ind.* 50b). He suggests that unless one has been properly disposed by nature, one will not be able to train (*Ind.* 57–62). Galen further indicates that he himself was born with the proper habits (*Ind.* 60). He makes similar points about his friend (*Ind.* 51, 79). Galen uses his father as an example of one who lived a life free from distress but he acquired these abilities without the use of philosophy – he possessed this life by nature (*Ind.* 58).[21]

However, Galen's characterization of his response to the fire as absence of distress looks rather like a Stoic (ἀπάθεια) or Epicurean (ἀταραξία) value. Galen writes that he did not experience distress (μηδέποτε λυπεῖσθαι; *Ind.* 1), which would seem to indicate the absence of the emotion; not the Aristotelian goal of moderation. The metaphor that the emotions are sicknesses or diseases that must be diagnosed and healed or removed is also associated with the Stoics and Epicureans.[22] Leaving aside the subgenre, consolation (see above), the genre of emotional therapy (into which *Ind.* can be placed) is typically associated with those schools.[23]

Although he allows for non-rational means of moral formation, Galen's strategies in *Ind.* focus on rational methods of controlling emotions. In particular, he advocates a method recommended by some philosophers according to which a person prepares for disasters by imagining them in advance (51–56; 76–79).[24] Such an approach presumes that emotions are subject to rational arguments.

Studies in Hellenistic Philosophy of Mind (ed. J. Brunschwig and M. Nussbaum; Cambridge: Cambridge University Press, 1993), 186, 189, 203.

[19] Gill, *Psychology in Galen*, 266. The rational and non-rational division is described in chapter six of *Aff.Dig.*

[20] Gill, *Psychology in Galen*, 257.

[21] Galen uses the example of his father in *Aff.Dig.* as well. In this text, Galen contrasts the admirable example of his father with the poor example of his mother who was "so bad-tempered that she would sometimes bite her maids; she was perpetually shouting and fighting with my father, treating him worse than Xanthippe did Socrates" (7–8 [K 5.40–41 = *CMG* 5.4.1.1 27.20–28]).

[22] Gill, *Psychology in Galen*, 253. For an exploration of Hellenistic moral philosophy on the analogy of medical practices see Martha C. Nussbaum, *The Therapy of Desire: Theory and Practice in Hellenistic Ethics* (Princeton, N. J.: Princeton University Press, 1994).

[23] Hankinson, "Actions and Passions," 191; Gill, *Psychology in Galen*, 253.

[24] Gill, *Psychology in Galen*, 266. Wilcox also notes this strategy ("Sympathetic Rivals," 240 n. 9, 243). For the use of the Euripidean fragment, see also Cicero *Tusc.* 3.30 and Plutarch

Even so, Galen indicates that while he has not yet experienced distress at the loss of possessions, he cannot say that he will never experience this emotion.[25] In fact, under certain circumstances he fully expects to experience distress: on the occasion of having his homeland destroyed; on learning of a friend who had been punished by a tyrant; and there could be other, similar events that would result in the experience of distress (*Ind.* 71–72a). He describes himself as someone who prays that he not have to experience the kinds of situations that could lead to distress.[26] This prayer is in contrast with Musonius who reputedly prayed that misfortune be sent to him so that he might demonstrate his lack of distress (72b–74). Galen also seems to leave open the possibility that if he in fact lost all of his possessions or lost shelter and clothing, that he might legitimately experience distress.[27]

The above observations illustrate how Galen's writings resist reduction to a single philosophical perspective.[28] He presents to his readers a mix of elements drawn from the diversity of his philosophical background.[29] Perhaps this is the result of the strategy recommended by Galen's father, who discouraged Galen from affiliating with one school over another before he had independently evaluated the validity of the analyses offered by these teachers (*Aff.Dig.* 8 [K 5.42 = *CMG* 5.4.1.1 28.3–29]).

Galen and Possessions

Ind. divides into two sections. Galen spends the first part of the text describing in some detail what he lost in the fire (roughly sections 4–38). The effect of this

---

[*Cons. Apoll.*] 112D. Cicero attributes this strategy to the Cyrenaics who argued that distress is (or at least can be) caused by unanticipated misfortune (*Tusc.* 3.31).

[25] Galen writes in *Aff.Dig.*: "There is no loss that has the power to cause me distress (except perhaps the loss of all my possessions – that I have not so far experienced" (8 [K 5.43 = *CMG* 5.4.1.1 29.17–19]).

[26] In *Aff.Dig.* he suggests that the loss of honor from the council (βουλή) would be cause for distress (8 [K 5.44 = *CMG* 5.4.1.1 30.2–3]).

[27] He writes in *Aff.Dig.*: "I have not up to this point suffered such a severe financial loss as to have insufficient resources left to provide for my bodily health, …" (8 [K 5.43 = *CMG* 5.4.1.1 29.21–30]).

[28] Gill describes Galen as an eclectic (*Psychology in Galen*, 279). Hankinson prefers to see Galen as a syncretist rather than an eclectic – defining syncretism as the attempt to show that various strands say the same thing ("Anatomy of the Soul," 198 n. 5). Elizabeth Asmis has suggested that "personal philosophy" is a more satisfactory label for what Galen is doing (paper presented at the annual meeting of the SBL, San Francisco, 19 November 2011). See her essay "Galen's Περὶ ἀλυπίας and the Creation of a Personal Philosophy" in this volume.

[29] Galen describes how he began his philosophical studies around the age of fourteen. He studied with a Stoic, a Platonist, a Peripatetic, and finally an Epicurean (*Aff.Dig.* 8 [K 5.41–42 = *CMG* 5.4.1.1 28.9–20]).

section on the reader is to reinforce Galen's friend's perception of the enormity of Galen's loss – even though he himself considers it trivial. He writes:

> Perhaps then you will say that your desire [ἐπιθυμία] is enjoined to want to know even more how, despite having lost such a great variety of (my) possessions – each of which alone, in and of itself, would have been most distressing [λυπηρότατος] for other human beings – I was not troubled [ἀνιᾶσθαι] like some others. Rather, I very easily endured what happened (*Ind.* 38).[30]

Having provided an inventory, Galen then addresses himself to the question asked by the friend (sections 39–84).

Four aspects of Galen's approach in this passage resonate with how Luke illustrates relationships between people and possessions. Galen observes that: (1) many people evaluate their need based on what others have; (2) people who do not experience distress understand that the purpose of possessions is to provide basic sustenance; (3) the truly remarkable person is the one who loses everything and does not experience distress; and (4) wealth complicates one's ability to avoid distress.

The focus of Galen's response to his friend's request centers on the problem of insatiability (ἀπληστία; *Ind.* 48).[31] Galen discusses the concept in sections 39–48. In *Aff. Dig.*, Galen identifies insatiability as the single cause for all varieties of distress. He writes:

> You should know that every type of distress has the same cause, which is known either as 'insatiability' or 'acquisitiveness'. [Insatiability (ἀπληστία) is so called after the desires which are not fulfilled: insatiable people always desire more of the thing they already have. Thus, even if they have twice as much of something, they still desire to have three times as much, and if they have three times as much they desire to have four times as much. And they look always to those who have more than them, not to those who have less, seeking always to surpass them in the amount that they possess.] (9 [K 5.49 = *CMG* 5.4.1.1 33.5–12])

Galen first argues that one reason people experience distress is because they are not content with what they have.[32] These people determine their "need" by observing what other people have. He writes:

> For even if they have thirty (fields), they will see others who have fifty (fields). And, if they themselves, in the same way, again acquire an equal amount, they will see some others with seventy (fields). And if they have those, they will see many others who have more than one hundred. As a result, advancing little by little, they will desire

---

[30] By way of contrast, Galen notes that Philides the grammarian, who also lost books in the fire, died from distress (*Ind.* 7).

[31] Galen suggests that he will provide two responses in his explanation. The first deals with insatiability. The second is not clear from the flow of the argument.

[32] Cicero attributes the strategy that insists that a perceived evil is not in fact evil – which is essentially what Galen is arguing – to Cleanthes (*Tusc.* 3.31). Galen insists that, except under certain circumstances, the loss of a certain portion of one's possessions is not a bad thing.

everything. In this respect, they will always be poor, their desire [ἐπιθυμία] being unfulfilled. (*Ind.* 43)

Galen describes a person who is constantly comparing his own possessions with those of others. Such a person's appetite can never be satisfied because that person will always encounter someone with more.[33]

Galen contrasts this type of person who has an insatiable desire for more with a person who is able to place his or her possessions in proper perspective. He offers as an example Aristippus[34] who, when his financial situation became difficult, sold one of his four fields. Galen writes:

> Then, a certain one of his fellow citizens, who was intending to console [συλλυπεῖσθαι] (him) for the loss, met (him). Aristippus laughingly said, "Why exactly will you console [συλλυπεῖσθαι] me who owns three such fields when you yourself have only one? Should I not be consoling [συλλυπεῖσθαι] you?" (Aristippus) demonstrates very well what you have often heard from me; namely, one should not look upon what is lost ... . (*Ind.* 42)

Aristippus does not experience distress and therefore does not need consolation because he knows he still has resources. The loss of one field does not put him at any risk; he still has three more. Furthermore, if a good life is determined by the number of possessions one has, then Aristippus (who still has three fields) should be consoling the consoler (who has only one). Assessment is based on comparison but one must know the appropriate locus of comparison. A person who looks to what they have, rather than what they have lost, will not be troubled by distress when they lose only a portion of their possessions.

A person such as Aristippus understands the function of possessions. Galen argues: " ... if someone, instead of continually looking into the number of fields (that) another has, rather (looks into the number of fields) sufficient to meet his own expenses, then he will bear the loss of the excess without concern" (*Ind.* 44).[35] Towards the end of the document, Galen returns to this point stating: "... it is for this reason that I continually try to tell my companions ... that, ... I disregard every loss of money as long as a sufficient amount is left so as to avoid hunger, cold, or thirst" (*Ind.* 78b).[36]

---

[33] Galen makes a similar point in *Aff.Dig.*: "... they look always to those who have more than them, not to those who have less, seeking always to surpass them and in the amount that they possess" (9 [K 5.49 = *CMG* 5.4.1.1 33.10–12]). Later he states: "And therefore you will not be the richest of men, but in perpetual want because of your boundless desires" (9 [K 5.50 = *CMG* 5.4.1.1 33.28–29]).

[34] This anecdote also occurs in Plutarch *Tranq. an.* 469C–D. Aristippus was one of Socrates' students who lived circa 435–356 B. C. E. He had a reputation for enjoying a luxurious life.

[35] A point emphasized in *Aff.Dig.* "If you were to measure the correct amount of possessions, taking their usefulness as your criterion, you would already number yourself among the rich ... I count myself in this category, although I have less than you do" (9 [K 5.50 = *CMG* 5.4.1.1 33.29–34]).

[36] Galen makes similar observations in *Aff.Dig.* He says that his father advised him not to be

Possessions serve to sustain a person; anything beyond what is required for sustenance is expendable. To evaluate whether I have enough I must make the appropriate comparison: I look to my own circumstance, not those of my neighbor. Galen illustrates for his friend that, if one wishes to avoid distress, property must be viewed from the proper perspective: not as objects to be accumulated but as a tools for sustenance; they provide food, drink, and warmth.

In *Aff.Dig.* Galen extends this point. It is not just the case that one can afford to lose property beyond what one needs. An important aspect of not experiencing distress is using surplus property to benefit others. He tells his friend in that text that the friend should use possessions for good works (8 [K 5.44 = *CMG* 5.4.1.1 30.13–15]). Later, Galen contrasts the friend's habits with Galen's own. Galen writes: "Nor can you be seen giving your clothes to others, or assisting people with food or medical care – as I do all the time. You have even see me discharge other people's debts" (9 [K 5.48 = *CMG* 5.4.1.1 32.19–21]). Galen indicates that he spends the inheritance left to him by his father (9 [K 5.48 = *CMG* 5.4.1.1 32.21–23]). He uses his wealth, he does not store it.

A third observation made by Galen concerns the fact that his friend is impressed by how Galen has handled the loss of property. Properly considered, Galen's ability to endure the loss of his possessions without distress is unremarkable. It is only because people tend to seek to accumulate more than they already have, rather than focusing on what they need to live, that Galen's disposition is noteworthy. The remarkable person is the one who endures without distress the loss of everything. Galen writes: "But it is fitting (for us) to be amazed – if indeed (it is fitting to be amazed) – at all of those (people) who, although having lost everything, are not in any way troubled [ἀνιᾶσθαι]" (*Ind.* 48). A few lines earlier, he observes: "It is a great accomplishment, when someone who does not even possess a single field endures poverty without distress [ἀλύπως] – as Crates[37] endured (poverty). And, for this reason, it is even more so, if someone who does not even own a house, as in the case of Diogenes,[38] (endures poverty without distress)" (*Ind.* 45).

Galen has behaved in an appropriate manner but that should not impress his friend; Galen still has ample resources on which to live. If the friend is to be impressed, he should rather be impressed by people who respond appropriately

---

distressed as long as he had possessions enough to care for his bodily needs (8 [K 5.44 = *CMG* 5.4.1.1 30.8–12]). He determined sufficiency by what he needed for health: food, clothing, housing (9 [K 5.46 = *CMG* 5.4.1.1 31.20–23]). Galen tells his friend: "And I know (I said) that you possess twice what I do, and you enjoy honour in the City; so that I cannot see what cause for distress you could have, other than insatiability" (8–9 [K 5.44–45 = *CMG* 5.4.1.1 30.16–18]).

[37] Crates was from Thebes and a student of Diogenes the Cynic circa 365–285 B. C. E. who gave away his possessions (Diog. Laert. 6.5.87).

[38] From Sinope circa 403–321 B. C. E. See Diog. Laert. 6.22–23 for Diogenes sleeping in his cloak and in a tub.

to truly exceptional circumstances; the person who does not experience distress when they do not have enough resources with which to live.

Finally, Galen indicates that the rich will experience difficulty in the avoidance of distress. He concludes *Ind.* by observing that: "I actually dared to inquire of a certain man with millions – seven million or more – who neither shares what he owns with others nor enjoys (them). The man replied: 'Just as we carefully guard the parts of our body, so also it is necessary for each one to carefully guard his possessions'" (*Ind.* 83). This encounter shocked Galen and prompted him to write a book "On Money-Loving Rich People" (περὶ τῶν φιλοχρημάτων πλουσίων; *Ind.* 84). Such an outlook goes against Galen's belief that an excessive amount of possessions should be used for good. Galen emphasizes in *Aff. Dig.* the challenge that wealth will present to those who want to avoid distress. He writes: "If, then, someone of great power or wealth desires to become a good and upright man, he must first put those things from him ..." (3 [K 5.13 = *CMG* 5.4.1.1 10.21–11]).

Luke: Introduction

Similar to *Ind.*, Luke's narrative connects possessions and the experience of distress. In all likelihood, Luke does not envision his gospel as a treatise on how to avoid distress. Nevertheless, certain episodes in this gospel offer insight into the author's perspective of the proper relationship between human beings and possessions, and on the appropriateness of distress and other emotions.

Luke and Possessions

Commentators have frequently observed that how a person uses possessions is an important concern in Luke's narratives.[39] An example from early in the gospel helps illustrate the point. When Luke introduces the ministry of John the Baptist, he inserts into his description a scene that focuses on possessions. He writes:

> And the crowds asked him, "What then should we do?" In reply he said to them, "Whoever has two coats must share with anyone who has none; and whoever has food must do likewise." Even tax collectors came to be baptized, and they asked him, "Teacher,

---

[39] Recent volumes on this topic include: Hans-Georg Gradl, *Zwischen Arm und Reich: Das lukanische Doppelwerk in leserorientierter und textpragmatischer Perspectiv* (Würzburg: Echter, 2005); James A. Metzger, *Consumption and Wealth in Luke's Travel Narrative* (Biblical Interpretation Series, 88; Leiden: Brill, 2007); Christopher M. Hays, *Luke's Wealth Ethics: A Study in Their Coherence and Character* (WUNT 2.275; Tübingen: Mohr Siebeck, 2010); Nils Neumann, *Armut und Reichtum im Lukasevangelium und in der kynischen Philosophie* (SBS 220; Stuttgart: Verlag Katholisches Bibelwerk, 2010).

what should we do?" He said to them, "Collect no more than the amount prescribed for you." Soldiers also asked him, "And we, what should we do?" He said to them, "Do not extort money from anyone by threats or false accusation, and be satisfied with your wages." (Luke 3:10–14)[40]

In this scene, when the crowds ask what they must do to avoid the wrath that is coming, the answer involves directions for the use of possessions: sharing a coat; sharing food; not collecting more taxes that are prescribed; and not extorting money.[41]

The role of possessions and their assessment comes into focus in Luke 12. The author presents a pair of scenes in which Jesus teaches about possessions to the crowd (vv. 13–21) and then to his disciples (vv. 22–34). The first scene consists of a challenge and response between a person in the crowd and Jesus, followed by a parable. Jesus is accosted by a man who wants him to settle an inheritance dispute (v. 13).[42] He resists being drawn into the dispute (v. 14)[43] instead, turning to the audience and challenging them not to be greedy (v. 15).[44]

---

[40] Unless otherwise noted, translations from the biblical texts are from NRSV.

[41] One sees a spectrum in Luke of what appear to be appropriate relationships between people and their property. On the one hand, there are the women in chapter eight who provide for the ministry of Jesus out of their resources but are not described as selling everything that they own (8:1–3). At the other end is the command by Jesus to crowds who are following him that they cannot be his disciples if they do not give up all their possessions (οὕτως οὖν πᾶς ἐξ ὑμῶν ὃς οὐκ ἀποτάσσεται πᾶσιν τοῖς ἑαυτοῦ ὑπάρχουσιν οὐ δύναται εἶναί μου μαθητής; 14:33). Zacchaeus recieves "salvation" for giving half of his possessions and repaying with interest people he had defrauded (19:8–9). It is in relation to this spectrum that one places Judas who in Acts uses the money he received for betraying Jesus to purchase property; he does not return the money as in Matthew (contrast Acts 1:16–20 with Matt 27:3–10).

[42] The inheritance question and Jesus' response to the crowd occur only in Luke. A form of vv. 13–14 (but not v. 15) is found in the *Gos. Thom.* 72. Ronald F. Hock emphasizes the importance of inheritance in this world ("The Parable of the Foolish Rich Man [Luke 12:16–20] and Graeco-Roman Conventions of Thought and Behavior," in *Early Christianity and Classical Culture: Comparative Studies in Honor of Abraham J. Malherbe* [ed. J. T. Fitzgerald, T. H. Olbricht, and L. M. White; NovTSup 110; Atlanta: Society of Biblical Literature, 2003], 183).

[43] The criticism from Jesus is not directed at the dispute per se but rather at the attempt to involve him ("who set me to be a judge or arbiter over you"). Hock suggests that it would not have been unusual for someone to approach Jesus to assume the role of informal judge ("Foolish Rich Man," 183 n. 11). The connection between the question asked and Jesus' response is not unambiguous. Are we to judge the interlocutor as greedy? That would be the implication from Jesus' response to the crowd. But Jesus' remarks to the man only chastise him for trying to make Jesus arbitrate. Joseph A. Fitzmyer (*The Gospel According to Luke X–XXIV: Introduction, Translation, and Notes* [AB 28A; Garden City: Doubleday, 1985], 968) and John Nolland (*Luke 9:21–18:34* [WBC 35B; Nashville: Thomas Nelson Publishers, 1993], 684) suggest v. 15 was not originally connected to the material in vv. 13–14; I. Howard Marshall argues in favor of them being connected (*The Gospel of Luke: A Commentary on the Greek Text* [NIGTC; Grand Rapids: Eerdmans, 1978], 521).

[44] Hays calls attention to the similarity with 8:14 where riches, worries, and pleasure are placed together (*Wealth Ethics,* 126 n. 185). Several commentators have observed that one finds concern about greed in the writings of the Hellenistic moral philosophers. Luke Timothy Johnson cites Plutarch *Cupid. divit.* (*The Gospel According to Luke* [SP 3; Collegeville, MN:

Jesus says: "Take care! Be on your guard against all kinds of greed [πάσης πλεονεξίας]; for one's life does not consist in the abundance of possessions [οὐκ ἐν τῷ περισσεύειν τινὶ ἡ ζωὴ αὐτοῦ ἐστιν ἐκ τῶν ὑπαρχόντων αὐτῷ]."[45]

A parable follows this exhortation.[46] A rich man's land produces abundantly, creating a storage problem (vv. 16–17).[47] The man decides to build newer, larger barns (v. 18). At this point, he determines he has sufficient resources for many years (v. 19).[48] Before he can enjoy his enhanced property however, God announces that the man will lose his life.[49] In verse 21, Jesus then warns the crowd not to store up riches for themselves but to be "rich toward God" (ὁ θησαυρίζων ἑαυτῷ καὶ μὴ εἰς θεὸν πλουτῶν).

For the purposes of this essay, two points are noteworthy. First, as with Galen, the Gospel of Luke seems to argue (albeit parabolically) that life ought not be evaluated on the basis of an abundance of possessions. The episode begins with a request that is in some ways similar to that of the insatiable man described by Galen in *Ind.* 39–48. The question about inheritance derives from a man comparing his inheritance with that of his brother and wanting more. The words of Jesus that follow connect the man's desire with greed, and ultimately, with defining life by the relative number of one's possessions. Jesus tells him a parable about

---

The Liturgical Press, 1991], 198); Fitzmyer compares this story to Seneca, *Ep.* 17.5 (*Luke,* 972). Abraham J. Malherbe has argued that Luke adapts the Hellenistic topos of greed ("The Christianization of a Topos [Luke 12:13–34]," *NovT* 38 [1996]: 123–35); Malherbe's approach has been further developed by Hock ("Foolish Rich Man"); Matthew Rindge has recently argued that viewing the parable within the greed topos does not do justice to the aspect of death that is so prominent in the parable (*Jesus' Parable of the Rich Fool: Luke 12:13–34 Among Ancient Conversations on Death and Possessions* [Early Christianity and Its Literature 6; Atlanta: Society of Biblical Literature, 2011]).

[45] The translation of the final phrase in v. 15 is difficult because of the word order and the syntactical relationship between the clauses. C. F. D. Moule has argued that the verse consists of the combination of two originally separate sayings ("H. W. Moule on Acts iv.25," *ExpTim* 65 [1953–54]: 220–1). As Nolland notes, the phrase περισσεύειν τινὶ can mean either "to have in abundance" or "to have more than enough" (*Luke 9:21–18:34,* 685). The latter meaning would resonate particularly strongly with the argument in Galen. Hays prefers "superfluity" to abundance (*Wealth Ethics,* 126).

[46] Hock argues that formally, the anecdote is an ἠθοποιΐα – a speech that reveals character ("Foolish Rich Man," 186–9). A much shorter version of this parable is also found in *Gos. Thom.* 63 (though, it does not contain Jesus' warning against storing up possessions for oneself [v. 21]). Verse 21 is missing in manuscripts D, a, and b.

[47] Hock identifies the man as an aristocrat because he is called πλοῦτος and the decision to lead a hedonistic lifestyle represents an urban view ("Foolish Rich Man," 185).

[48] The notion of eating, drinking, and being merry is found in numerous places in ancient literature. See the discussion and references in Fitzmyer (*Luke X–XXIV,* 973). Nolland provides a more focused comparison suggesting that the saying in Luke's context is most similar to Sir 11:19: "I have found rest and now I will eat of my good things" (but not with the criticism of the means of gaining wealth found in v. 18) (*Luke 9:21–18:34,* 686). The verse is omitted in D.

[49] ταύτῃ τῇ νυκτὶ τὴν ψυχήν σου ἀπαιτοῦσιν ἀπὸ σοῦ. It is not exactly clear to whom the first person plural refers. For the interpretation that it refers to God, see Fitzmyer (*Luke X–XXIV,* 974). For the interpretation that it refers to angels, see Marshall (*Luke,* 524).

a man who comes into possession of, and stores, an abundance of possessions. As a result of this stored wealth, he tells himself that he may now relax. This man is not insatiable, nor did he acquire his possessions in order to compete with someone else who had more.[50] He does not want more than he now has; he only believes that he may now relax because he has sufficient wealth on which to survive. This relationship to his acquired wealth, however, raises a second point.

The man stores his wealth. The man in *Ind.* (83) who suggested that possessions ought to be protected like a person protects their body is similar to this man in Jesus' parable. Galen was shocked by the man's attempt to protect his possessions. He considered such a view inappropriate. In *Aff.Dig.*, Galen emphasized that excess wealth should be used to do good works (8 [K 5.44 = *CMG* 5.4.1.1 30.13–15]). Galen himself used his wealth to help others (9 [K 5.48 = *CMG* 5.4.1.1 32.19–21]). He even spent his inheritance (9 [K 5.48 = *CMG* 5.4.1.1 32.21–23]). Even though the parable does not explicitly criticize the man for not distributing the wealth, the larger context of the gospel invites such a reading.[51] We have already seen in Luke 3 that when the crowds asked John the Baptist what they needed to do, he directed some of them to distribute their property (v. 11). In the next scene of this section of chapter 12, Jesus tells the disciples to sell their possessions and give alms (v. 33). In chapter 14 the crowd is told that they cannot become disciples without giving up all of their possessions (v. 33). The rich ruler (whom I will discuss below) is told to sell his possessions and give to the poor (18:22). In short, numerous examples within the gospel suggest that a person ought to distribute excess wealth to the poor.[52]

After the parable, Jesus turns to his disciples, challenging them not to worry about what they will eat, drink, or wear:[53] "Therefore I tell you, do not worry about your life [μὴ μεριμνᾶτε τῇ ψυχῇ], what you will eat, or about your body, what you will wear. For life is more than food, and the body more than clothing

---

[50] It is worth noting that it is clear from the parable that the wealth was not obtained illegitimately, and therefore the parable is not attacking the means of accumulation. Also, as Rindge has pointed out, the variable in this story that is not in Galen is mortality (*Rich Fool*, 123, 239). The man dies and so does not have the opportunity to enjoy the wealth.

[51] See, for example, the discussion in Fitzmyer (*Luke X–XXIV*, 972); Marshall, (*Luke*, 524); Nolland (*Luke 9:21–18:34*, 687).

[52] One can also compare the women who use their possessions to provide for Jesus (8:3) and Zacchaeus who promises to gives half of his possessions to the poor and to pay back those whom he has cheated (19:8–9). So I disagree with Hock's assessment that criticizing the man for not sharing his wealth is too narrow an interpretation of the parable ("Foolish Rich Man," 195). I find his argument that the man has made a category error persuasive (the man believes that what is good for the body [the abundant harvest] is good for the soul; 192). But I think both the evidence from Galen and the larger context of the gospel ask us to include a criticism that the man did not distribute his windfall.

[53] A form of v. 22 appears in *Gos. Thom.* 36. The material in 12:22–34 loosely parallels Matt 6:25–34. Determining the editorial history for this section is quite difficult. Do Matthew and Luke work from the same source or are they working with different versions of the story? For a discussion of Luke's compositional activity in this section, see Fitzmyer (*Luke X–XXIV*, 976).

[ἡ γὰρ ψυχὴ πλεῖόν ἐστιν τῆς τροφῆς καὶ τὸ σῶμα τοῦ ἐνδύματος]" (vv. 22–23).[54] In these verses the focus is on the basic necessities of life: nourishment and protection for the body.[55] Jesus exhorts the disciples not to concern themselves with basic necessities, as life is more than these things. If, in the preceding scene, life ought not be defined by an abundance of possessions, neither can it be reduced to basic needs. In v. 24, Jesus tells the disciples to observe the ravens; in v. 27 they are told to consider the lilies. God provides what ravens and lilies need; the disciples are more valuable than these entities; therefore, God will provide the basic necessities (24, 28).[56] Furthermore, being anxious will not accomplish anything positive (v. 25). The disciples are challenged not to strive after food and drink [καὶ ὑμεῖς μὴ ζητεῖτε τί φάγητε καὶ τί πίητε καὶ μὴ μετεωρίζεσθε] (v. 29). Rather, they should strive for the kingdom of the Father, which will result in receiving the basic necessities (v. 31). God knows that they need these things (v. 30b) and he will provide them. Jesus then tells them to sell their possessions and give alms (πωλήσατε τὰ ὑπάρχοντα ὑμῶν καὶ δότε ἐλεημοσύνην; v. 33).[57]

Both Galen and Luke exhibit a concern for the basic necessities of life. Neither author treats food and clothing as trivial. As we have seen, Galen claimed to be able to disregard any loss of wealth as long as he had a sufficient food and clothing (*Ind.* 78b). Luke also testifies to the importance of these basic necessities. The disciples are told not to worry about them not because they are unimportant but because God will provide them. God provides for ravens and lilies and will therefore provide for human beings. Different from *Ind.*, Luke introduces the concept of God as a source for alleviating anxiety. Galen prays to the gods that he not experience events that could result in feeling distress (*Ind.* 72b). However, the gods do not play a role in the avoidance of distress. In contrast, God factors prominently in Luke's discussion: God knows what people need, provides those needs and thus eliminates the need to worry.

Galen and Luke write from similar, though not identical perspectives. Galen writes for people in a position of sufficiency – even abundance. His discussion focuses on people with resources who lose them.[58] He confesses that should he

---

[54] In contrast with Galen, Luke does not set this advice in the context of avoiding distress – or at least does not label the experience as distress – but rather he is concerned with the related issue of anxiousness and striving. For the association of "anxiety" with "distress" see Paul A. Hollaway, "Bona Cogitare: An Epicurean Consolation in Phil 4:8–9," *HTR* 91 (1998): 90 n. 4.

[55] Hays calls attention to the similarity with the Lord's Prayer and the request: τὸν ἄρτον ἡμῶν τὸν ἐπιούσιον δίδου ἡμῖν τὸ καθ' ἡμέραν (11:3; *Wealth Ethics*, 128).

[56] Compare also 12:6–7 where Jesus tells the disciples that they are more valuable to God than sparrows – he will not forget them.

[57] Another form of this saying appears in *Gos. Thom.* 76. The command to sell possessions occurs only in Luke. Again, the compositional history is difficult to sort out (see Fitzmyer, *Luke X–XXIV*, 981).

[58] Except of course for the remarkable people. But this is what makes them remarkable. A person with resources should be able to lose some of them and not feel distress.

lose sufficient resources to provide the basic necessities, he might experience distress (Aff.Dig. 8 [K 5.43–44 = CMG 5.4.1.1 29.17–30]). Likewise, the Lukan Jesus sometimes addresses individuals in states of sufficiency.[59] The disciples, however, are exhorted to trust God for the basic necessities – perhaps suggesting states of need.[60] Moreover, it is from this position of want that they are told to give alms. God can be trusted to provide for all, for some directly and for others through them. This point is illustrated again in a short episode about a widow. Jesus observes rich people (πλουσίους) placing gifts into the temple treasury. He then spots a poor widow making her gift. She gives all that she has (21:1–4).[61] He says: "Truly I tell you, this poor widow has put in more than all of them; for all of them have contributed out of their abundance [ἐκ τοῦ περισσεύοντος], but she out of her poverty has put in all she had to live on [ἐκ τοῦ ὑστερήματος αὐτῆς πάντα τὸν βίον ὃν εἶχεν ἔβαλεν]."[62] The scene reinforces Jesus' words to the disciples in chapter 12 – that they sell their possessions and give alms to the poor.

Jesus' approval of the widow is similar to Galen's observation that the noteworthy individual is the one who can lose all that s/he has and not experience distress (Ind. 45, 48). Again, the details are not precisely the same. In Luke, the widow does not lose possessions but rather gives them as alms. She gives not out of abundance but out of poverty. Galen does not describe a similar situation. He provides examples of those who endure poverty without distress; he does not provide examples of those in poverty who use their possessions to benefit others.

Luke also illustrates a belief that the wealthy will experience difficulty in making appropriate decisions with respect to possessions. In Luke's version of the beatitudes, Jesus says, in contrast with the poor who possess the kingdom of God (ὑμετέρα ἐστὶν ἡ βασιλεία τοῦ θεοῦ; 6:20): "... woe to you who are rich, for you have received your consolation (Πλὴν οὐαὶ ὑμῖν τοῖς πλουσίοις, ὅτι ἀπέχετε τὴν παράκλησιν ὑμῶν; 6:24). The wealthy do not possess the kingdom of God because they have received another kind of compensation. In the parable of the rich man (Ἄνθρωπος δέ τις ἦν πλούσιος) and Lazarus (πτωχὸς δέ τις ὀνόματι Λάζαρος; 16:19–31), Lazarus dies and is rewarded by God. The rich man on the

---

[59] One thinks, for example of the rich ruler (Luke 18:18–25 discussed below) and Zacchaeus (Luke 19:1–10).

[60] Reflected, for example, in Peter's statement to Jesus in Luke 18:28: "Look, we have left our homes and followed you (ἰδοὺ ἡμεῖς ἀφέντες τὰ ἴδια ἠκολουθήσαμέν σοι.). As Robert C. Tannehill observes, the disciples are in a difficult position having left everything to follow Jesus; being sent out without provisions (9:3; 10:4); and now following Jesus dependent upon the hospitality of strangers (The Narrative Unity of Luke-Acts: A Literary Interpretation. Volume 1: the Gospel According to Luke [Philadelphia: Fortress Press, 1986], 246).

[61] This pericope also occurs in Mark 12:41–44. Luke simplifies the description of the scene. He highlights the basic contrast between the gifts of the rich and the gift of the poor widow.

[62] Addison G. Wright argues that Jesus does not praise the widow but laments that she has been deceived by the Scribes and their piety ("The Widow's Mites: Praise or Lament? – A Matter of Context," CBQ 44 [1982]: 256–65). Given the larger context within Luke of the importance of one using one's possessions in the service of God, Wright's conclusion seems unlikely.

other hand is tormented after his death. He seeks comfort but is reminded by Abraham that he received good things during his lifetime.

The most telling illustration of challenges presented by wealth is the rich ruler who wants to know what he must do to inherit eternal life.[63] After insisting that he has done everything that Jesus identifies (18:20–21), Jesus says to him: "There is still one thing lacking. Sell all that you own and distribute the money to the poor [πάντα ὅσα ἔχεις πώλησον καὶ διάδος πτωχοῖς], and you will have treasure in heaven; then come, follow me" (v. 22). Two aspects of this episode assist the reader in assessing the man. First, Luke edits the encounter to create a negative assessment by the reader. In Mark, after the man asks the question, Jesus is sympathetic to the man – he loves him (ἠγάπησεν αὐτὸν, 10:21). Luke identifies the man as a "ruler" (not part of Mark's description) and removes Jesus' initial positive evaluation. Jesus just looks at the man and states that entrance into the kingdom will be difficult for the wealthy.[64]

Secondly, Luke intensifies the form. In all three of the Synoptics, the man's response is described using a form of λύπη.[65] Luke, however, writes that the man became very distressed because he was rich (ὁ δὲ ἀκούσας ταῦτα περίλυπος ἐγενήθη ἦν γὰρ πλούσιος σφόδρα, v. 23).[66]

As in Galen, wealth in Luke complicates a person's ability to use his or her possessions appropriately. This scene is especially noteworthy because the ruler responds inappropriately not to an actual loss of possessions but to the idea of losing possessions. At this point in the narrative, the reader knows that the man has made an inadequate assessment. The rich ruler cannot imagine that selling and distributing his possessions can be good. From chapter 12, the reader knows that God provides the basic necessities for those who use their possessions to help others.

Finally, the episode explicitly connects the loss of possessions with the emotion of distress – the theme of Galen's text. I turn now to a discussion of Luke's assessment of distress.

---

[63] Hays identifies this pericope as pivotal in Luke because it echoes Luke's command to abandon all things and specifies that the ruler should sell and divide the proceeds among the poor combining elements from 14:33 and 12:33 (*Wealth Ethics,* 166).

[64] As Johnson has pointed out, "This man is exceedingly wealthy, he has kept all the laws, and he is a ruler; the portrait of those closed to the prophet's visitation is complete" (*Luke,* 280). Hays makes a similar observation (*Wealth Ethics,* 167). L. Michael White deals with the issue of wealth in early Christianity in his article dealing with Clement of Alexandria ("Moral Pathology"). He looks at Clement's "Who is the Rich Man that can be Saved?"

[65] ἀπῆλθεν λυπούμενος (Mark 10:22; Matt 19:22).

[66] In v. 24 of some manuscripts the narrator repeats the identification of the ruler as the one who became very distressed, thereby emphasizing this point even more: "But when he heard this, he became very distressed; for he was very rich. Jesus looked at him (the one who had become very distressed) and said ... " (my translation). The repeated words are included in A, D (as well as a few others) but are not part of ℵ, B (and some others).

Luke, Distress, and Emotion

Luke infrequently describes people experiencing distress. Forms of λύπη occur in the gospel in only two pericope and not at all in Acts.[67] Besides the rich ruler, where an inappropriate response to possessions is characterized by the term λύπη, the only other appearance of the term occurs after Jesus' last supper with his disciples (22:39–46). In Luke, Jesus leads the disciples to a garden to pray.[68] Two features of the Lucan narrative stand out: (1) in Luke (but not in the other Synoptics), the author attributes the disciples' sleep to distress; (2) in contrast, in the other Synoptics (but *not* in Luke), *Jesus* experiences distress in the garden. First, when the disciples arrive in the garden, Jesus instructs them to pray (v. 40); he himself withdraws from them to pray (vv. 41–44).[69] When he returns, he finds the disciples asleep (v. 45). The narrator explains that the disciples are asleep because of their distress (ἀπὸ τῆς λύπης). How is the reader to evaluate the disciples in this scene? Many commentators suggest that Luke is excusing the disciples by explaining away their sleep.[70] Given the clearly negative association with the term in 18:23, the reader must at least entertain the possibility that the disciples' behavior is inappropriate.[71]

Luke's editing of Mark's garden narrative with respect to the depiction of Jesus supports a negative reading of the term in association with the disciples. In both Matthew and Mark, Jesus experiences distress before he is arrested (Matt 26:36–38; Mark 14:33–35). In Luke, however, that experience is removed. Combining Luke's explanation that the disciples sleep because of distress with the fact that Luke chooses to remove the attribution of distress to Jesus while

---

[67] By way of comparison, forms of λύπη appear in four pericopes in Mark and in six pericopes in Matthew.

[68] Once again, sorting out the editorial history for this pericope is complex. Scholars do not agree on whether Luke is heavily editing Mark or is dependent on some other source. See Fitzmyer (*Luke X–XXIV,* 1436–40) for discussion.

[69] Some mss omit vv. 43–44. See Fitzmyer (*Luke X–XXIV,* 1443–4) for discussion. Fitzmyer decides against their inclusion. See Jerome Neyrey for a persuasive account of how the verses are appropriate for what Luke is doing in this narrative ("The Absence of Jesus' Emotions – The Lucan Redaction of Lk 22:39–46," *Bib* 61, no .2 [1980]: 153–71).

[70] E.g., Fitzmyer, *Luke X–XXIV,* 1439; Alfred Plummer, *A Critical and Exegetical Commentary on the Gospel According to Luke* (ICC; New York: T & T Clark, 1989), 511; Marshall, *Luke,* 833; Nolland, *Luke 9:21–18:34,* 1084.

[71] Johnson, attending to the philosophical background of λύπη, connects their sleep to envy or cowardice/fear. He argues that Luke does not depict Jesus as afraid which indicates that he faces his death as a philosopher should (*Luke,* 352). Gregory E. Sterling also connects Luke's treatment of the death of Jesus with an attempt to depict Jesus as a philosopher. He connects the depiction more generally to the philosophical adaptation of the noble death tradition without specifying a particular philosophical tradition ("Mors philosophi: The Death of Jesus in Luke," *HTR* 94 [2002]: 383–402). Neyrey demonstrates how Luke's treatment of "distress" in connection with Jesus and the disciples is similar to the negative assessment of distress one sees in Stoic philosophers ("Absence," 154–5). Tannehill, drawing on the work of Neyrey, describes the response by the disciples to be a "sign of spiritual weakness" (*Narrative Unity,* 271).

he prays in the garden, it seems reasonable to conclude that Luke judges the experience of λύπη to be negative.[72]

Luke's treatment of another text, that in Mark contains a form of λύπη, further suggests that he is making editorial decisions based on a nuanced understanding of the experience of distress. At the Last Supper in Matthew and Mark, when Jesus tells the disciples that the betrayer is at the table, the disciples experience distress (λυπούμενοι σφόδρα ἤρξαντο [Matt 26:22]; ἤρξαντο λυπεῖσθαι [Mark 14:19]). In Luke, however, the disciples ask questions among themselves (ἤρξαντο συζητεῖν πρὸς ἑαυτοὺς); they do not experience distress (Luke 22:23).[73] One wonders why Luke removes the experience of distress from the disciples; in this episode, the editorial motivation is even more ambiguous. Marshall tentatively suggests that the author might take exception to depicting the disciples as grieving.[74] This likely is not the case because, as we have seen, Luke attributes distress to the disciples in the Garden. Nor is it likely that Luke excuses the dispute between the disciples.[75]

Perhaps Luke considered distress the wrong emotion with which to characterize the disciples for the point he wished to illustrate. Philosophers did in fact use λύπη to describe the emotion experienced by those striving for honor and glory.[76] However, the focus in vv. 24ff is not on ambition. Instead, Luke appears to be interested in the proper behavior of those who are leaders. As Tannehill observes, "[Luke] does not speak of those who wish to become great, as in Matthew and Mark, but simply of those who are greater and are leaders (22:26), for the issue is not the general tendency toward ambitious striving but the standard behavior for recognized leaders in the church."[77] So, while "distress" might appropriately

---

[72] See also Neyrey, "Absence," 168–9.

[73] Once again the editorial history is difficult to untangle. Verses 21–23 are either a reworking of Mark or dependent on a parallel tradition, derived from elsewhere. But even if Luke is not using Mark as his source for this episode, he must be aware that Mark characterizes the disciples as experiencing distress.

[74] *Luke*, 810.

[75] Tannehill, for example, suggests that much of the discourse at the table is exposing the failure of the disciples (*Narrative Unity*, 263).

[76] Galen writes, for example, "the desire for universal praise is analogous to the desire to own all the world's possessions" (*Aff.Dig.* 8 [K 5.44 = *CMG* 5.4.1.1 30.4–6]). Earlier in the text he writes: "And what must I say of envy (φθόνου). It is the worst of evils. I call it envy whenever someone is distressed over the success of others (τις ἐπ᾽ ἀλλοτρίοις ἀγαθοῖς λυπῆται). All distress is a disease, and envy is the worst distress, whether we call it an emotion or a kind of pain which borders on distress (*Aff.Dig.* 7 [K 5.35 = *CMG* 5.4.1.1 24.12–15]; translation by Paul W. Harkins, *Galen on the Passions and Errors of the Soul* [with Introduction and Interpretation by Walter Riese; Ohio State University Press, 1963], slightly altered; Singer omits these lines from his translation). See also Galen's discussion in *Aff.Dig.* 8 (K 5.43 = *CMG* 5.4.1.1 29.18–30).

[77] *Narrative Unity*, 257. François Bovon makes a similar point: "... the exchange of words deals more with the future of the Christian community of the disciples, thus with ecclesiology, than with the Master's imminent fate, with Christology" (*Luke 3* [Hermeneia; Minneapolis: Fortress, 2012], 188). The episode in Mark (10:35–45) occurs earlier in Jesus' ministry and

be used to characterize the disciples' experience in Mark's episode, it would not be accurate in the Lukan context because the issue does not concern ambition.

Both Luke's own use of λύπη and his editorial decisions involving the use of the term in his sources support our suspicion that distress in Luke, as in Galen, is a negative experience – an inappropriate response.[78] Can we observe a similar pattern in Luke with respect to other emotions? Of the emotions identified by Galen (anger [θυμός], wrath [ὀργή], fear [φόβος], distress [λύπη], envy [φθόνος], and excessive desire [ἐπιθυμία σφοδρά]), all of them with the exception of envy appear in one form or another in Luke-Acts. A thorough analysis of Luke's illustrations of these emotions is beyond the scope of this paper but some general observations can be made.

Luke narrates three scenes that involve θυμός. Each scene demonstrates that this is an inappropriate emotion. Those in the synagogue in Nazareth become filled with rage (καὶ ἐπλήσθησαν πάντες θυμοῦ ἐν τῇ συναγωγῇ ἀκούοντες ταῦτα, 4:28). The people in Ephesus become enraged at the story told by the silversmiths regarding Paul (Ἀκούσαντες δὲ καὶ γενόμενοι πλήρεις θυμοῦ ἔκραζον λέγοντες· μεγάλη ἡ Ἄρτεμις Ἐφεσίων, Acts 19:28). And finally, Herod is described as becoming enraged with the people of Tyre and Sidon (Ἦν δὲ θυμομαχῶν Τυρίοις καὶ Σιδωνίοις, Acts 12:20). In the scene that follows, Herod is hailed as a god and subsequently struck down dead for not refusing (or deflecting in any way) living deification (vv. 21–23). Luke shares with Galen a negative assessment of θυμός.

Luke's use of the term wrath (ὀργή) is more complicated but shows a predictable pattern. On the one hand, wrath appears to be something appropriate for God; it is a component of God's judgment. John the Baptist questions the crowds concerning who warned them about the wrath to come (presumably coming from God; Luke 3:7). A similar description occurs in 21:23 where Jesus describes days when there will be "wrath against this people (ἔσται γὰρ ἀνάγκη μεγάλη ἐπὶ τῆς γῆς καὶ ὀργὴ τῷ λαῷ τούτῳ). In the parable of the banquet (14:16–24), the host (presumably God) becomes enraged (ὀργισθείς) when no one accepts his invitation.[79] The description of God as one who acts in wrath comes to Luke (and his sources) from the LXX. The prophets described the day of the Lord as being

---

involves James and John. Luke appears to move that scene to the Last Supper; remove the focus on James and John; and alter the point Jesus makes from the argument.

[78] Luke omits one additional scene that features the experience of distress. In both Matthew and Mark, Herod experiences distress when he is asked to behead John the Baptist (Matt 14:9 [καὶ λυπηθεὶς ὁ βασιλεύς]; Mark 6:26 [περίλυπος γενόμενος ὁ βασιλεὺς]). Luke omits the narrative of the death of John the Baptist. He narrates why Herod is upset with John in 3:19–20 and that Herod beheaded John in 9:9; but he does not narrate the execution. In this instance, the omission of the scene involving distress can be accounted for on the basis of plot concerns rather than out of concern for the use of the term distress. See the discussion in Joseph A. Fitzmyer (*The Gospel According to Luke I–X: Introduction, Translation, and Notes* [AB 28; Garden City: Doubleday, 1985], 476).

[79] In each of these scenes, Luke inherits the wrath vocabulary from his sources.

a day of wrath. So it is not surprising that Luke might consider the description appropriate for God and therefore not edit it out of his gospel.[80]

However, when human beings express wrath, Luke consistently characterizes them in negative ways. In the parable of the Prodigal Son, the elder son becomes enraged (ὠργίσθη) upon learning of the celebration for the younger son (15:28). In the scene where Jesus heals a man with a withered hand (an episode in all three Synoptics), Luke removes wrath from Jesus' look (6:10).[81] It appears, then, that ὀργή is something appropriate for (or belonging to) God but inappropriate for Jesus and other human beings. With regard to ὀργή, Luke, thus, seems to share Galen's perspective.

"Fear" (φόβος) occurs more frequently in Luke than any of the other emotions and its usage is too complex to evaluate with precision in this essay. However, three tentative observations can be offered. First, the fear of God is an appropriate emotion for humans to experience. Zechariah experiences fear when he sees the angel (1:12); the angel tells him not to fear (1:13). The shepherds experience great fear when the angel of the Lord appears (καὶ ἐφοβήθησαν φόβον μέγαν; 2:9); the angel tells them not to be afraid (2:10). By way of contrast, in the parable of the unjust judge, the man does not fear God (18:2, 4); this helps indicate his injustice. In 12:4–5, Jesus tells the disciples not to fear the person who can destroy the body. He says: "But I will warn you whom to fear: fear him who, after he has killed, has authority to cast into hell. Yes, I tell you, fear him!" (Luke 12:5).[82] At the crucifixion, one of the thieves questions the other: do you not fear God? (23:40). The question is asked in order to rebuke – fearing God is something one ought to do.

Second, God's people ought not fear for their lives. Jesus tells his disciples not to be afraid because they are more valuable to God than sparrows (12:7).[83] In 12:32, Jesus tells the disciples not to be afraid because it is the Father's pleasure to give them the kingdom (12:32). Jesus tells Jairus not to fear but trust, despite the fact that he has just received word that his daughter died (8:50).[84] Each of these occasions pertains to a concern for one's life. Jesus exhorts these people not to fear in such circumstances – the lives of God's people belong to God who never neglects them.

Third, three scenes in the gospel are suggestive of what Luke might be doing with the emotion of fear in his gospel. First, Mary is perplexed when Gabriel

---

[80] See, for example, Isa 13:9; Zeph 1:14–16. See the brief discussion in Fitzmyer (*Luke I–X*, 148).

[81] περιβλεψάμενος αὐτοὺς μετ' ὀργῆς (Mark 3:5). Matthew removes the whole element of having Jesus look at the crowd after questioning whether it is lawful to do good on the Sabbath (Matt 12:10–13).

[82] These sayings also appear in Matt 10:28–29. Matthew has φοβεῖσθε; Luke has φοβηθῆτε.

[83] This is also in Matt 10:31. So it does not necessarily derive from Luke but he does not feel obligated to edit it out.

[84] Luke finds this language in Mark (5:36) but does not edit it out.

appears to her but is not characterized as experiencing fear (ἡ δὲ ἐπὶ τῷ λόγῳ διεταράχθη καὶ διελογίζετο ποταπὸς εἴη ὁ ἀσπασμὸς οὗτος, 1:29).[85] Second, in the Gospel of Mark, the woman suffering from hemorrhages who touches Jesus is characterized as fearful, even trembling (ἡ δὲ γυνὴ φοβηθεῖσα καὶ τρέμουσα, 5:33).[86] Luke, in contrast, characterizes her as merely trembling. That is, Luke removes fear in the characterization of her response.[87] Finally, in Matthew and Mark, the women who leave the tomb are characterized as fearful: in Matthew, the women leave the tomb with fear and joy, running to tell the apostles; in Mark, the women flee from the tomb because they are seized with terror (16:8). In Luke, the women remember the words of Jesus and make a report to the eleven and the rest. No emotions are reported. In all three scenes, the absence of fear appears to be characteristic of remarkable people.[88] So here one may also observe how Luke's approach to fear is consistent with Galen's approach.

It is difficult to assess the use of ἐπιθυμία in Luke. This emotion is characterized as clearly negative in only one episode. In Paul's speech to the Ephesian elders, he tells them: "'I coveted [ἐπεθύμησα] no one's silver or gold or clothing'" (Acts 20:33). In this scene, ἐπιθυμία is clearly a negative emotion; one that Paul does not possess. In the other occurrences, the emotion is best interpreted as neutral.[89] Galen's own discussion of the emotion is ambiguous. His introduction of the term in *Aff.Dig.* indicates that the problem is with excess; Galen identifies his concern with "excessive desire" (ἐπιθυμία σφοδρά, *Aff.Dig.* 2–3 [K 5.7 = *CMG* 5.4.1.1 7.2–6]), although in later lists he uses the term without modification. Without full analysis it is difficult to say but preliminarily we see further congruence on emotion in general between Galen and Luke.

Conclusion

This essay calls attention to features in the Gospel of Luke that resonate with Galen's *Ind*. In both the Third Gospel and *Ind.*, greed – the concern for abundant possessions – is inappropriate. Possessions should be used and not stored.

---

[85] Nevertheless, Gabriel tells her not to fear (1:30).

[86] The episode is intercalated between Jairus arriving to ask Jesus' help and the completion of that episode.

[87] This aspect of the episode is missing in Matthew. In that gospel, after she touches Jesus, Jesus immediately turns to her and affirms her (9:21–22).

[88] One might also consider that Jesus tells Simon not to be afraid after the startling number of fish caught (5:10). However, Luke does not characterize Simon as afraid – although Simon tells Jesus to go away identifying himself as sinful: ἰδὼν δὲ Σίμων Πέτρος προσέπεσεν τοῖς γόνασιν Ἰησοῦ λέγων· ἔξελθε ἀπ' ἐμοῦ, ὅτι ἀνὴρ ἁμαρτωλός εἰμι, κύριε (5:8).

[89] Nolland states that Luke uses ἐπιθυμία as a positive term throughout the gospel (*Luke 9:21–18:34*, 386). This seems unwarranted to me.

For both Luke and Galen, it is important for human beings to have sufficient possessions for living: food and clothing. On this issue one sees the greatest differences between Luke and Galen. Galen writes to persons with wealth. If they have excess they should use it for others but he does not provide any examples of people giving out of poverty. Furthermore, if he does not have enough resources to provide the basic necessities, Galen can imagine experiencing distress. Although Luke's Jesus does address persons with wealth, he also includes persons without resources. Luke writes that worrying about the acquisition of these necessities is inappropriate. God will provide what disciples require. Because of the role of God in the lives of disciples, they can use whatever resources they have (whether they are wealthy or poor) for the benefit of others.[90]

Both Luke and Galen seem to reflect that an appropriate assessment of possessions is difficult for the wealthy. The comparison suggests that Luke's approach toward distress specifically, and the emotions generally, resonates with Galen's position in *Ind*.

---

[90] As noted above (n. 41), there appears to be a spectrum along which a person might appropriately use their possessions. In the scenes highlighted by comparison with *Ind.*, however, Luke emphasizes selling or distributing.

III. Ancillary Material

Trevor W. Thompson

Collation of the Critical Editions of Galen's *De indolentia*[1]

The collation records the differences between the three critical editions of Galen's *De indolentia*:

Paraskevi Kotzia and Panagiotis Sotiroudis. "Γαληνοῦ Περὶ ἀλυπίας." *Hellenica* 60 (2010): 63–148. Abbreviated here as KS.

Véronique Boudon-Millot and Jacques Jouanna (with Antoine Pietrobelli). *Galien: Ne pas se chagriner*. Collection des universités de France, publiée sous le patronage de l'Association Guillaume Budé. Paris: Les Belles Lettres, 2010. Abbreviated here as BMJ.

Ivan Garofalo and Alessandro Lami. *Galeno: L'anima e il dolore*. De indolentia, De propriis placitis. Milan: Biblioteca Universale Rizzoli, 2012. Abbreviated here as GL.

The differences among the editions are listed in the following format:

KS Section.Page.Line   Kotzia and Sotiroudis text
BMJ Section.Page.Line   Boudon-Millot and Jouanna text
GL Section.Page   Garofalo and Lami text

The edition of Kotzia and Sotiroudis differs in the divison of sections from the edition of Boudon-Millot and Jouanna; the edition of Garofalo and Lami follows the divisions of Boudon-Millot and Jouanna with minor variation. The text of Kotzia and Sotiroudis includes thirty-one sections in total; both the text of Boudon-Millot and Jouanna and that of Garofalo and Lami divide the text into eighty-four sections. Kotzia and Sotiroudis offer continuous line numbers (#1–384). The edition of Garofalo and Lami does not include line numbers but does provide the page divisions of the codex.

An earlier draft of this collation charted the differences between the edition of Kotzia and Sotiroudis and the edition of Boudon-Millot and Jouanna. It was electronically shared with Garofalo via email (August 8, 2011). Garofalo and Lami included their own text and the texts of Boudon-Millot and Jouanna and Kotzia and Sotiroudis respectively in a collation of differences (Garofalo and Lami, *Galeno: L'anima e il dolore*, 149–55). The collation printed here includes not only differences in words and proposed emendations but also differences

---

[1] Special thanks to Jacob Lollar and Theodore Austin Holt IV for their work in checking the collation for accuracy.

in punctuation and accent. It also records the proposed emendations of Ioannis Polemis and Vito Lorusso, neither included in the existing editions:

Ioannis Polemis. "ΔΙΟΡΘΩΤΙΚΑ ΣΤΟ ΠΕΡΙ ΑΛΥΠΙΑΣ ΤΟΥ ΓΑΛΗΝΟΥ." *Επιστημονική Επετηρίς της φιλοσοφικής σχολής του Πανεπιστημίου Αθηνών* 43 (2011/12): 371–8. Klaus-Dietrich Fischer, Ivan Garofalo, Alessandro Lami, and Vito Lorusso. "Congetture e emendamenti inediti." *Galenos: Rivista di filologia dei testi medici antichi* 6 (2012): 181–90 [esp. 183; proposed emendation of *De indolentia* by Lorusso].

For the difficult section BMJ § 16–18 (KS § 7–8), additional readings and proposed reconstructions are provided.

Collation

KS § 1.66.1	Ἔλαβόν σου τὴν ἐπιστολὴν ἐν ᾗ παρεκάλεις με δηλῶσαί σοι τίς
BMJ § 1.2.3–4	Ἔλαβόν σου τὴν ἐπιστολὴν ἐν ᾗ παρεκάλεις μοι δηλῶσαί σοι τίς
GL § 1.6	[10vVlat] Ἔλαβόν σου τὴν ἐπιστολήν, ἐν ᾗ παρεκάλεις με δηλῶσαί σοι, τίς
KS § 1.66.2	δόγματα παρεσκεύασάν
BMJ § 1.2.4–5	δόγματα <τίνα> παρεσκεύασάν
GL § 1.6	δόγματα παρεσκεύασάν
KS § 1.66.3–4	μεγάλην εἰσβολὴν ἀπολέσαντά
BMJ § 1.2.7	μεγάλην ἐμβολὴν ἀπολέσαντά
GL § 1.6	μεγάλην εἰσβολὴν ἀπολέσαντά
KS § 1.66.4	οἰκέτας, οὓς σχεδὸν εἶχον
BMJ § 1.2.8	οἰκέτας οὓς σχεδὸν εἶχον
GL § 1.6	οἰκέτας, <ὅσ>ους σχεδὸν εἶχον
KS § 1.66.5–6	πρόσθεν ἤδη μοι γεγονέναι τι τοιοῦτον· εἰς
BMJ § 1.2.9	πρόσθεν ἤδη μοι γεγονέναι τι τοιοῦτον εἰς
GL § 1.6	πρόσθεν ἤδη μοι γεγονέναι τι τοιοῦτον εἰς
KS § 1.66.6	χρήματά τε τρίς που
BMJ § 1.2.10	χρήματά τε τρίς που
GL § 1.6	χρήματα, [τε] τρίς που
KS § 1.66.6	ἀδραῖς ζημίαις
BMJ § 1.2.10	ἀδραῖς ζημίαις
GL § 1.8	ἀδραῖς ζημίαις
KS § 1.66.6–7	περιπεσόντα, ἔφης αὐτὸς
BMJ § 1–§ 2.2.10–11	περιπεσόντα· 2 ἔφης αὐτὸς
GL § 1–§ 2.8 and 10	περιπεσόντι. 2 ἔφης <δ'> αὐτὸς

KS §1.66.7	ἐπὶ βραχὺ ἀνιαθέντα, τὸ δὲ
BMJ §2.2.11–12	ἐπὶ βραχὺ κινηθέντα. Τὸ δὲ
GL §2.8	ἐπὶ βραχὺ κινηθέντα, τὸ δὲ
KS §1.66.8	τὰ πρόσθεν, ἀπολομένων
BMJ §2.2.13	τὰ πρόσθεν, ἀπο<λ>λυμένων
GL §2.8	τὰ πρόσθεν, ἀπολομένων
KS §1.66.9	πάντων <τῶν> ἀποκειμένων μοι πραγμάτων
BMJ §2.2.14	πάντων <τῶν> ἀποκειμένων μοι πραγμάτων
GL §2.8	πάντων <τῶν> ἀποκειμένων μοι πραγμάτων
KS §1–§2.66.10–11	ἀποθήκαις. 2 Ὁπόσα μὲν οὖν καίρια καὶ αὐτὸς
BMJ §2–§3.2.15–16	ἀποθήκαις· 3 ὁπόσα μὲν οὖν καίρια καὶ αὐτὸς
GL §2–§3.8	ἀποθήκαις. 3 ὁπόσα μὲν οὖν <ἦν> καὶ ποῖα, καὶ αὐτὸς
KS §2.66.12	τινος ἀγγείλαντός σοι μηδὲ νῦν
BMJ §3.2.16–3.1	τινος <τῶν> ἀγγε<λ>λόντων σοι μηδὲν νῦν
GL §3.8	τινος ἀγγέλων τῶν σῶν μηδὲ νῦν
KS §2.66.12	με, φαιδρόν τε <ὄντα> καὶ τὰ
BMJ §3.3.1–2	με φαιδρόν τε καὶ τὰ
GL §3.8	με φαιδρόν τε καὶ τὰ
KS §2.66.13	ἔμπροσθεν· θαυμάζειν <δ'> οὐχ ὅτι καὶ
BMJ §3–§4.3.2–3	ἔμπροσθεν. 4 Θαυμάζειν οὐχ ὅτι καὶ
GL §3–§4.8	ἔμπροσθεν· 4 θαυμάζειν <δ'> οὐχ ὅτι, καὶ
KS §2.66.14–15	πολλῶν ἀποκειμένων, ἃ διεφθάρη
BMJ §4.3.4–5	πο<λ>λῶν ἀποκειμένων ἃ διεφθάρη
GL §4.8	πολλῶν ἀποκειμένων, ἃ διεφθάρη
KS §2.66.15	κατὰ τὴν πυρκαϊάν, ἀλύπως ὤφθην φέρων,
BMJ §4.3.5–6	κατὰ τὴν πυρκαϊὰν ἀλύπως ὤφθη<ν> φέρων,
GL §4.8	κατὰ τὴν πυρκαϊάν, ἀλύπως ὤφθη<ν> φέρων,
KS §2.66.16	συγγεγραμμένων
BMJ §4.3.6–7	συ<γγε>γρα<μ>μένων
GL §4.8	σεσωρευμένων
KS §2.66.16–17	δὲ παντοῖα πάμπολλα,
BMJ §4.3.7–8	δὲ παντοῖα πάμπο<λ>λα,
GL §4.8	δὴ παντοῖα πάμπολλα,

KS §2.66.17–18	τὰ μὲν ἁπλᾶ τὰ δὲ συγκείμενα, καὶ ἄρμενα παντοδαπὰ {τὰ μὲν} εἰς τὰς ἰατρικὰς
BMJ §4–§5.3.8–9	τὰ μὲν ἁπλᾶ, τὰ δὲ συγκείμενα, καὶ ἄρμενα παντοδαπά, 5 τὰ μὲν εἰς τὰς ἰατρικὰς
GL §4–§5.8	τὰ μὲν ἁπλᾶ, τὰ δὲ συγκείμενα, καὶ ἄρμενα παντοδαπά, 5 τὰ μὲν εἰς τὰς ἰατρικὰς
KS §2.66.18–67.19	χρείας. <Τὰ> μὲν οὖν ἔφην ἀπολέσαι, ἀλλὰ
BMJ §5.3.9–10	χρείας <ἃ> μὲν οὖν ἔφην ἀπολέσας ἄλλα
GL §5.8	χρείας <ἃ> μὲν οὖν ἔφην ἀπολέσας ἄλλα
KS §2.67.19	κτήσεσθαί τι ἐλπίζειν,
BMJ §5.3.10–11	κτήσασθαι ἔτι ἐλπίζει<ν>,
GL §5.8	κτήσασθαι ἔτι ἐλπίζει<ν>,
KS §2.67.19–20	χρήματα προσευρημένα τῶν ἀρμένων, ὧν τὰ
BMJ §5.3.11–12	[χρήματα] προσευρημένα [τῶν ἀρμένων] ὧν τὰ
GL §5.8	[χρήματα] προσευρημένα τῶν ἀρμένων, ὧν τὰ
KS §2.67.20	πλάττων
BMJ §5.3.12	πλάτ<τ>ων
GL §5.8	πλάττων
KS §2.67.21	ὡς οὐκέθ' οἷόν τε
BMJ §5.3.13	ὡς οὐκ ἔτ' οἷόν τε
GL §5.8	ὡς οὐκέτι οἷόν τε
KS §2.67.21	πολλοῦ
BMJ §5.3.14	πο<λ>λοῦ
GL §5.8	πολλοῦ
KS §2.67.22	τὰ βιβλία τά τε ἐπηνωρθωμένα {καὶ} διὰ
BMJ §6.3.15	τὰ βιβλία τά τε ἐπηνωρθωμένα καὶ διὰ
GL §6.8	τὰ βιβλία, τά τε ἐπηνωρθωμένα [καὶ] διὰ
KS §2.67.22–23	χειρός, ἀνδρῶν
BMJ §6.3.16	χειρὸς ἀνδρῶν
GL §6.8	χειρὸς ἀνδρῶν
KS §2.67.23	τὰ συγγράμματα, τά θ'
BMJ §6.3.16	τὰ συγγράμματα τά θ'
GL §6.8	[τὰ] συγγράμματα, τά θ'
KS §2.67.23	συντεθέντα· καὶ
BMJ §6.3.17	συντεθέντα, καὶ
GL §6.8	συντεθέντα· καὶ

KS §2.67.24	ἀντιδότους, ἃς
BMJ §6.3.17–4.1	ἀντιδότους ἃς
GL §6.8	ἀντιδότους, ἃς

KS §2.67.24	ἔφης
BMJ §6.4.1	<ἔ>φης
GL §6.8	<ἔ>φης

KS §2.67.24–25	παμπόλλας
BMJ §6.4.1	παμπό<λ>λας
GL §6.8	παμπόλλας

KS §2.67.26	λιτρῶν κιννάμωμόν τε τοσοῦτον, ὅσον
BMJ §6.4.3	λιτρῶν κιννάμωμόν τε τοσοῦτον ὅσον
GL §6.8	λιτρῶν, κιννάμωμόν τε τοσοῦτον, ὅσον

KS §2.67.27	ταῦτα καπηλεύουσιν ἔστιν
BMJ §6.4.4	ταῦτα καπηλεύουσιν ἔστιν
GL §6.10	ταῦτα καπηλεύουσιν ἔστιν

KS §2.67.27	καὶ τἄλλα πάντα
BMJ §6.4.5	καὶ τἄλλα πάντα
GL §6.10	καὶ τὰ ἄλλα πάντα

KS §3.67.29	Κάλλιστος
BMJ §7.4.6	Φιλίδης
GL §7.10	Φιλι<στ>ίδης

KS §3.67.29–30	ἀπολομένων αὐτῷ
BMJ §7.4.7	ἀπολλυμένων αὐτῷ
GL §7.10	ἀπολομένων αὐτῷ

KS §3.67.30	κατὰ <τὴν> πυρκαϊὰν
BMJ §7.4.7	κατὰ πυρκαϊὰν
GL §7.10	κατὰ <τὴν> πυρκαϊὰν

KS §3.67.30	ὑπὸ δυσθυμίας
BMJ §7.4.7–8	ἀπὸ δυσθυμίας
GL §7.10	ἀπὸ δυσθυμίας

KS §3.67.31	συντακείς, ἄλλος δὲ καὶ ἄλλος
BMJ §7.4.8–9	συντακείς, ἄλλος δὲ καὶ ἄλλος
GL §7.10	συντακείς, πολλοὶ δὲ καὶ ἄλλοι

KS §3.67.31–32	προῖεσαν ἄχρι πολλοῦ, λεπτοὶ
BMJ §7.4.9–10	προήεσαν ἄχρι πολλοῦ λεπτοὶ
GL §7.10	προήεσαν ἄχρι πολλοῦ λεπτοὶ

KS § 3.67.33	ἀποθήκαις, ὡς δὴ οὐδὲν
BMJ § 8.4.11–12	ἀποθήκαις ὡς δὴ οὐδὲ
GL § 8.10	ἀποθήκαις, ὡς οὐδὲν
KS § 3.67.34–35	ἀπετίθεντο, θαρρεῖν
BMJ § 8.4.13–14	ἀπετίθεντο· θαρρεῖν
GL § 8.10	ἀπετίθεντο, θαρρεῖν
KS § 3.67.35	δὲ αὐταῖς διὰ
BMJ § 8.4.14	δὲ αὐταῖς διὰ
GL § 8.10	δὲ αὐτοὺς διὰ
KS § 3.67.35	αὐτάς, ὅτι
BMJ § 8.4.14	αὐτὰς ὅτι
GL § 8.10	αὐτάς, ὅτι
KS § 3.67.36	τῷ φρουρεῖσθαι
BMJ § 8.4.16	τὸ φρουρεῖσθαι
GL § 8.10	τῷ φρουρεῖσθαι
KS § 3.67.39–40	ἐτελοῦμεν οἳ ἐμισθούμεθα κατὰ τὰς ἀποθήκας ἐκείνας οἰκήματα τά τε σπουδῆς
BMJ § 9.4.19–20	ἐτελοῦμεν οἱ μεμισθωμένοι τὰ κατὰ τὰς ἀποθήκας ἐκεῖνα οἰκήματα, τά τε σπουδῆς
GL § 9.10	ἐτελοῦμεν, οἳ ἐμεμισθώμεθα κατὰ τὰς ἀποθήκας ἐκεῖνα <τὰ> οἰκήματα, τά δὲ σπουδῆς
Polemis	ἐτελοῦμεν οἳ μεμισθώμεθα κατὰ τὰς ἀποθήκας ἐκείνας οἰκήματα τά τε σπουδῆς
KS § 3.67.40	ἐκεῖ
BMJ § 9.4.21	ἐκεῖ[να]
GL § 9.10	ἐκεῖ[να]
KS § 4.67.42	ἐξιών, ἅπαντα
BMJ § 9.4.23	ἐξιών, ἅπαντα
GL § 9.10	ἐξιὼν ἅπαντα
KS § 4.67.43	κατεθέμην
BMJ § 10.4.24–25	κατετεθείμην
GL § 10.12	κατετεθείμην
KS § 4.67.43–44	ἀποθήκην, ὡς
BMJ § 10.4.25	ἀποθήκην ὡς
GL § 10.12	ἀποθήκην, ὡς
KS § 4.67.44	τὴν ἀποδημίαν· τοιγαροῦν
BMJ § 10.5.1	τὴν ἀποδημίαν· τοιγαροῦν
GL § 10.12	τὴν ἀποδημίαν. τοιγαροῦν

KS § 4.68.46	αὐτὸς μὲν
BMJ § 10.5.3	αὐτὰ μὲν
GL § 10.12	αὐτὸς μὲν
KS § 4.68.46–47	βούλεσθαι δὲ ἀσφαλέστερον
BMJ § 10.5.4	βούλεσθαι δ' (ἀσ)φαλέστερον
GL § 10.12	βούλεσθαι δὲ ἀσφαλέστερον
KS § 4.68.47	ἐμοῦ· τὸ
BMJ § 10–§ 11.5.4–5	ἐμοῦ. 11 Τὸ
GL § 10–§ 11.12	ἐμοῦ. 11 τὸ
KS § 4.68.47	ἁπτομένων
BMJ § 11.5.5	ἁπτομένων
GL § 11.12	ἀπολομένων
KS § 4.68.48	θαυμασιώτερον
BMJ § 11.5.6	θαυ(μα)σι(ώ)τερον
GL § 11.12	θαυμασιώτερον
KS § 4.68.48	σοι καὶ πάνυ
BMJ § 11.5.6–7	σοι καὶ [τοῦ] πάνυ
GL § 11.12	σοι, καὶ, Ζεῦ, πάνυ
KS § 4.68.49	ἀληθῶς· ἐν [γὰρ] τῇ Καμπανίᾳ πυθόμενος
BMJ § 11.5.7–8	ἀληθῶς· ἐν (γὰρ) τῇ (Κ)αμπανίᾳ πυθόμ(εν)ος
GL § 11.12	ἀληθῶς. ἐν γὰρ Καμπανίᾳ πυθόμενος
KS § 4.68.49	ἅ[παν]τα
BMJ § 11.5.8	α(ὐτὰ)
GL § 11.12	αὐτὰ
KS § 4.68.50	πρᾶγμα μήτε
BMJ § 11.5.9	πρᾶγμα, μήτε
GL § 11.12	πρᾶγμα μηδὲ
Polemis	πρᾶγμα μήδε
KS § 4.68.50	ἀνιαθείς.
BMJ § 11.5.9	κινηθείς.
GL § 11.12	κινηθείς.
KS § 4.68.50–51	['Επεὶ] δ' εἰς Ῥώμην ἐπ[ανῆλθον,]
BMJ § 11.5.9–10	(…) δ' εἰς Ῥώμη(ν) ε(…)
GL § 11.12	**** δ' εἰς Ῥώμην ἔβην ******
KS § 4.68.51–52	κατα[σκ]ευάσαι· <ἐν> βραχεῖ <δὲ> χρόνῳ τῆς δ[υσχερείας]
BMJ § 12a.5.11–12	κατα(σκ)ευάσαι β(ραχεῖ) χρόνῳ τ(ῆς δ …….)
GL § 12a.12	κατασκευάσαι· ε*** χρόνῳ τῆς *******[11r]

KS § 4.68.53	ἠσθόμην, ὥσπερ
BMJ § 12a.5.12	ἠσθόμην ὥσπερ
GL § 12a.12	ἠσθόμην, ὥσπερ
KS § 4.68.54	φαρμάκου καθιστάμενος ἐν
BMJ § 12a.5.14	φαρμάκου καθιστάμενος ἐν
GL § 12a.12	φαρμάκου καθιστάμενος ἐν
KS § 4.68.55	σε, μηδὲ
BMJ § 12b.5.16	σε μηδὲ
GL § 12b.12	σε, μηδὲ
KS § 4.68.56	ὑπολειπομένην, ὡς ἂν
BMJ § 12b.5.17	ὑπολειπομένην ὡς ἂν
GL § 12b.12	ὑπολειπομένης, ὡς ἂν
KS § 5.68.58	ἀλλαχόθι
BMJ § 13.5.19	ἀλ<λ>αχόθι
GL § 13.12	ἀλλαχόθι
KS § 5.68.58–59	δυνατὸν ἐστιν εὑρεῖν {ἐστιν} οὔτε <τινὰ> τῶν μέσων διὰ
BMJ § 13.5.20	δυνατὸν ἐστιν εὑρεῖν [ἐστιν], οὔτε τῶν μέσων, διὰ
GL § 13.14	δυνατὸν ἔτι εὑρεῖν ἔστιν, οὔτε τῶν μὲν μέσων, διὰ
KS § 5.68.60	ἐσπουδασμένων, Καλλίνεια καὶ
BMJ § 13.5.21	ἐσπουδασμένων, Καλλίνια καὶ
GL § 13.14	ἐσπουδασμένων· Καλλίνεια καὶ
KS § 5.68.60	καὶ Πεδουκίνεια, καὶ μὴν
BMJ § 13.5.22	καὶ Πεδουκίνια καὶ μὴν
GL § 13.14	μὲν καὶ Πεδουκίνεια καὶ μὴν
KS § 5.68.61	Ἀριστάρχεια, οἵτινές
BMJ § 13.5.22	Ἀριστάρχεια οἵτινές
GL § 13.14	Ἀριστάρχεια, οἵτινές
KS § 5.68.61	δύο, καὶ
BMJ § 13.6.1	δύο καὶ
GL § 13.14	δύο, καὶ
KS § 5.68.62–63	διασῳζομένων ἔν τισι τῶν γραμμάτων ἐκείνων αὐτῶν
BMJ § 13.6.2–3	διασῳζομένων ἐντὸς τῶν γραμμάτων ἐκείνων αὐτῶν
GL § 13.14	διασῳζομένων ἐντὸς τῶν γραμμάτων ἐκείνων αὐτῶν,
KS § 5.68.63	ἀνεγράψαντο
BMJ § 13.6.4	ἀν<τ>εγράψαντο
GL § 13.14	ἀνεγράψαντο
Lorusso	ἀνεγράψαντο

KS §5.68.63	οἱ ἄνδρες ὧν ἦν
BMJ §13.6.4	οἱ ἄνδρες ὧν ἦν
GL §13.14	οἱ ἄνδρες, ὧν ἦν

KS §5.68.64	αὐτόγραφα
BMJ §13.6.5	ἀντίγραφα
GL §13.14	αὐτόγραφα

KS §6.68.67–68	μετὰ τὴν ἐπανόρθωσιν εἰς καθαρὸν ἔδαφος ἐγέγραπτο βιβλία τῶν ἀσαφῶν ἡμαρτημένων δὲ κατὰ τὰς γραφάς,
BMJ §14.6.8–10	μετὰ τὴν ἐπανόρθωσιν εἰς καθαρὸν ἔδαφος ἐγέγραπτό <μοι> βιβλία τῶν ἀσαφῶν <μέν>, ἡμαρτημένων δὲ κατὰ τὰς γραφάς
GL §14.14	μετὰ τὴν ἐπανώρθωσιν τῶν ἀσαφῶν, ἡμαρτημένων δὲ κατὰ τὰς γραφάς, εἰς καθαρὸν ἔδαφος ἐγέγραπτο βιβλία,

KS §6.68.68–69.69	οἷον τῶν προειρημένων, <ὡς> ἔκδοσιν ἐμὴν
BMJ §14.6.10–11	οἷον ἐμοῦ προηρημένου ἔ<κ>δοσιν ἐμὴν
GL §14.14	κοινὴν προηρημένου ἔκδοσιν ἐμοῦ

KS §6.69.69–70	ἐκπεπονημένων, ὡς
BMJ §14.6.12	ἐκπεπονημένων ὡς
GL §14.14	ἐκπεπονημένων, ὡς

KS §6.69.70	{χρήματα} μήτε ἐλλείπειν,
BMJ §14.6.13	ῥήματα μήτε ἐλλείπει<ν>,
GL §14.14	[χ]ρήμα[τα] μήτε ἐλλείπειν,

KS §6.69.71	διπλῆν ἢ
BMJ §14.6.14	διπλῆν, ἢ
GL §14.14	διπλῆν ἢ

KS §6.69.71	κορωνίδα <μὴ> προσηκόντως
BMJ §14.6.14	κορωνίδα προσηκό<ν>τως
GL §14.14	κορωνίδα προσηκόντως

KS §6.69.72	βιβλίων· τί δὲ λέγειν
BMJ §14.6.15	βιβλίων· τί δὲ λέγειν
GL §14.14	βιβλίων. τί δὲ δεῖ λέγειν
Polemis	βιβλίων· τί δεῖ λέγειν

KS §6.69.72	στιγμῆς ἢ ὑποστιγμῆς, ἃς οἶσθα
BMJ §14.6.15–16	στιγμῆς ἢ ὑποστιγμῆς ὡς οἶσθα
GL §14.14	στιγμῆς ἢ ὑποστιγμῆς ὡς οἶσθα

KS §6.69.73	βιβλίοις, ὥστε
BMJ §14.6.17	βιβλίοις ὥστε
GL §14.14	βιβλίοις, ὥστε

KS § 6–§ 7.69.74–75	δεῖσθαι. 7 Τοιαῦτα
BMJ § 14–§ 15.6.18	δεῖσθαι; 15 Τοιαῦτα
GL § 14–§ 15.14	δεῖσθαι; 15 τοιαῦτα
KS § 7.69.75	Θεοφράστου καὶ Ἀριστοτέλους
BMJ § 15.6.18–19	Θεοφράστου καὶ Ἀριστοτέλους
GL § 15.14	Θεοφράστου, καὶ μάλιστα τὰ κατὰ τὰς ἐπιστημονικὰς πραγματείας, καὶ Ἀριστοτέλους
KS § 7.69.76	Κλειτομάχου
BMJ § 15.6.19	Κλειτ<ομάχ>ου
GL § 15.16	Κλειτ<ομάχ>ου
Polemis	Κλύτου
KS § 7.69.76	Χρυσίππου
BMJ § 15.6.20	Χρυσίπ<π>ου
GL § 15.16	Χρυσίππου
BMJ § 16.6.21–7.5	
B-M	Λυπήσει δέ σε καὶ ταῦτα μάλιστα ὡς τῶν ἐν τοῖς καλουμένοις πίναξι τούτων γεγραμμένων βιβλίων ἔξωθεν ηὗρόν τινα, κατά τινά τε τῆς ἐν τῷ Παλατίῳ βιβλιοθήκης, καὶ τὰ[ς] ἐναντία ἃ φανερῶς ἦν οὗπερ ἐγέγραπτο κατὰ τὴν λέξιν, οὔτε κατὰ διάνοιαν ὅμοια μὲν αὐτῷ,
Jones (2009)	λυπήσει δέ σε καὶ ταῦτα μάλιστα, ὡς τῶν ἐν τοῖς καλουμένοις πίναξι τῶν <προ>γεγραμμένων βιβλίων ἔξωθεν ηὗρόν τινα, καί τινά {τε} τῆς ἐν τῷ Παλατίῳ βιβλιοθήκης καὶ τὰ [τινα?] ἐν Ἀντίῳ, ἃ φανερῶς <οὐκ> ἦν οὗπερ ἐγέγραπτο κατὰ τὴν λέξιν, οὔτε κατὰ διάνοιαν ὅμοια μὲν [delendum?] αὐτῷ,
KS § 7.69.77–81	Λυπήσει δέ σε καὶ ταῦτα μάλιστα, ὡς τῶν ἐν τοῖς καλουμένοις πίναξι {τῶν} γεγραμμένων βιβλίων ἔξωθεν εὗρόν τινα κατὰ {τε} τὰς ἐν τῷ Παλατίῳ βιβλιοθήκας καὶ τὰ ἐναντία, ἃ φανερῶς <οὐκ> ἦν οὗπερ ἐγέγραπτο κατὰ τὴν λέξιν, οὔτε κατὰ <τὴν> διάνοιαν ὅμοια {μὲν} αὐτῷ,
BMJ § 16.6.21–7.5	Λυπήσει δέ σε καὶ ταῦτα μάλιστα ὡς τῶν ἐν τοῖς καλουμένοις πίναξι [τῶν] γεγραμμένων βιβλίων ἔξωθεν εὗρόν τινα κατά τε τὰς ἐν τῷ Παλατίῳ βιβλιοθήκας καί τ<ιν>α[ς] ἐναντίω<ς> ἃ φανερῶς <οὐκ> ἦν οὗπερ ἐγέγραπτο, <οὔτε> κατὰ τὴν λέξιν οὔτε κατὰ <τὴν> διάνοιαν ὁμοιούμενα αὐτῷ.
Stramaglia (2011)	Λυπήσει δέ σε καὶ ταῦτα μάλιστα, ὡς τῶν ἐν τοῖς καλουμένοις πίναξι {τῶν} γεγραμμένων βιβλίων ἐκσωθέν<τα> εὗρόν τινα κατά τε τὰς ἐν τῷ Παλατίῳ βιβλιοθήκας καὶ τὰς ἐν Ἀντίῳ, ἃ φανερῶς ἦν <οὐχ> οὗ ἐπεγέγραπτο κατὰ τὴν λέξιν, οὔτε κατὰ διάνοιαν ὁμοιούμεν<α> αὐτῷ.
Rashed (2011)	Λυπήσει δέ σε καὶ ταῦτα μάλιστα ὡς τῶν ἐν τοῖς καλουμένοις πίναξιν ἀναγεγραμμένων βιβλίων ἔξωθεν εὗρόν τινα κατά τε τὰς ἐν τῷ Παλατίῳ βιβλιοθήκας καὶ τὰς ἐν Ἀντίῳ ἃ φανερῶς ἦν οὗπερ ἐπεγέγραπτο, κατὰ τὴν λέξιν τε καὶ διάνοιαν ὁμοιούμενα αὐτῷ·

GL § 16.16   λυπήσει δέ σε καὶ τοῦτο μάλιστα, ὡς τῶν ἐν τοῖς καλουμένοις πίναξι [τῶν] γεγραμμένων βιβλίων ἔξωθεν εὑρόν τινα κατά τε τὰς ἐν τῷ Παλατίῳ βιβλιοθήκας καὶ τὰς ἐν Ἀντίῳ, ἃ φανερῶς οὔτ᾽ ἦν οὗπερ <ἐπ>εγέγραπτο κατὰ τὴν λέξιν, οὔτε κατὰ διάνοιαν ὅμοια ἦν αὐτῷ,

BMJ § 16–§ 17.7.5–9
B-M   καὶ τὰ Θεοφράστου καὶ μάλιστα τὰ κατὰ τὰς ἐπιστημονικὰς πραγματείας· 17 ἔστιν ἄλλα τὰ περὶ φυτῶν βιβλία κατὰ δύο πραγματείας ἐκτεταμένας ἡρμενευμένα <ἃ> πάντες ἔχουσι·

Jones (2009)   καὶ τὰ Θεοφράστου καὶ μάλιστα τὰ κατὰ τὰς ἐπιστημονικὰς πραγματείας. (17) ἔστιν ἄλλα τὰ περὶ φυτῶν βιβλία κατὰ δύο πραγματείας ἐκτεταμένας ἡρμηνευμένα [ἡρμενευμένα, unless this is a misprint] <ἃ> πάντες ἔχουσι·

KS § 7.69.81–83   καὶ τὰ Θεοφράστου καὶ μάλιστα τὰ κατὰ τὰς ἐπιστημονικὰς πραγματείας. Ἔστιν ἄλλα τὰ περὶ φυτῶν βιβλία κατὰ δύο πραγματείας ἐκτεταμένας ἡρμηνευμένα, <ἃς> πάντες ἔχουσι·

BMJ § 16–§ 17.7.5–9   Καὶ τὰ Θεοφράστου καὶ μάλιστα τὰ κατὰ τὰς ἐπιστημονικὰς πραγματείας 17 – ἔστιν ἄλλα τὰ περὶ φυτῶν βιβλία κατὰ δύο πραγματείας ἐκτεταμένας ἡρμηνευμένα – πάντες ἔχουσι·

Stramaglia (2011)   –
Rashed (2011)   <καὶ γὰρ εἰ παραπλήσια ἀλλήλοις τὰ Ἀριστοτέλους> καὶ τὰ Θεοφράστου καὶ μάλιστα τὰ κατὰ τὰς ἐπιστημονικὰς πραγματείας 17 ἔστιν, ἄλλα τά <γε> περὶ φυτῶν βιβλία κατὰ δύο πραγματείας ἐκτεταμένας ἡρμηνευμένα πάντες ἔχουσιν,

GL § 16–§ 17.16   καὶ τὰ Θεοφράστου, καὶ μάλιστα τὰ κατὰ τὰς ἐπιστημονικὰς πραγματείας, 17 – ἔστιν ἄλλα τὰ Περὶ φυτῶν βιβλία κατὰ δύο πραγματείας ἐκτεταμένας ἡρμηνευμένα ἃ πάντες ἔχουσι –

KS § 7.69.83   ἡ δὲ <τῇ> Ἀριστοτέλους
BMJ § 17.7.9   ἡ δ᾽ Ἀριστοτέλ(ει)
GL § 17.16   ἡ δ᾽ Ἀριστοτέλ<ους>

KS § 7.69.84   μεταγραφεῖσα, ἡ
BMJ § 17.7.10   μεταγραφεῖσα ἡ
GL § 17.16   μεταγραφεῖσα, ἡ

KS § 7.69.85   ἀπολομένη. Κατὰ δὲ τὸν
BMJ § 17.7.10–11   ἀπολομένη· Κατὰ δὲ τὸν
GL § 17.16   ἀπολομένη, κατὰ δὲ τὸν

KS § 7.69.85   καὶ Θεοφράστου καὶ ἄλλων τινῶν
BMJ § 17.7.11–12   καὶ Θεοφράστου καὶ ἄλλων τινῶν
GL § 17.16   καὶ τὰ Θεοφράστου καὶ Ἀριστοτέλους καὶ ἄλλων τινῶν

KS § 7.69.87   μὲν μὴ
BMJ § 17.7.13   μέν, μὴ
GL § 17.16   μέν, μὴ

KS § 7.69.89	τὰ δ' ἐναντία
BMJ § 17.7.15	τ<ιν>ὰ δ' ἐναντίως
GL § 17.16	τὰ δ' ἐν Ἀντίῳ
KS § 8.69.91	λυμηναμένης, ἀλλὰ
BMJ § 18.7.19	λυμηναμένης ἀλλὰ
GL § 18.18	λυμηναμένης, ἀλλὰ
KS § 8.69.93	οἰκίαν, ἐν
BMJ § 18.8.1	οἰκίαν ἐν
GL § 18.18	οἰκίαν, ἐν
KS § 8.70.94	ἦν, πολλῶν
BMJ § 18.8.2	ἦν πολλῶν
GL § 18.18	ἦν πολλῶν

BMJ § 18.8.3–6
B-M   τὰ δὲ ἐναντία διὰ τὴν ἀμέλειαν τῶν ἑκάστοτε λῃστευομένων ἐκ διαδοχῆς αὐτὰ (…) καθ' ὃν χρόνον ἐγὼ ἀνέβην εἰς Ῥώμην πρῶτον ἐγγὺς ἦν τοῦ διεφθάρθαι.

Jones (2009)   –

KS § 8.70.94–96   τὰ δὲ ἐναντία διὰ τὴν ἀμέλειαν τῶν ἑκάστοτε λυμαινομένων ἐκ διαδοχῆς αὐτὰ μ[.]σι [……..] καθ' ὃν χρόνον ἐγὼ ἀνέβην εἰς Ῥώμην <τὸ> πρῶτον ἐγγὺς ἦν τοῦ διεφθάρθαι.

BMJ § 18.8.3–6   τ<ιν>ὰ δὲ ἐναντίως διὰ τὴν ἀμέλειαν τῶν ἑκάστοτε λῃστευομένων ἐκ διαδοχῆς αὐτὰ (…) καθ' ὃν χρόνον ἐγὼ ἀνέβην εἰς Ῥώμην πρῶτον, ἐγγὺς ἦν τοῦ διεφθάρθαι.

Stramaglia (2011)   τὰ δὲ ἐν Ἀντίῳ, διὰ τὴν ἀμέλειαν τῶν ἑκάστοτε λῃστευομενων ἐκ διαδοχῆς αὐτὰ μεσι[τείαι]ς, καθ' ὃν χρόνον ἐγὼ ἀνέβην εἰς Ῥώμην πρῶτον ἐγγὺς ἦν τοῦ διεφθάρθαι.

Rashed (2011)   τὰ δὲ ἐν Ἀντίῳ, διὰ τὴν ἀμέλειαν τῶν ἑκάστοτ' ἐμπιστευομένων ἐκ διαδοχῆς αὐτά, μ<υ>σὶ <βεβρωμένα> καθ' ὃν χρόνον ἐγὼ ἀνέβην εἰς Ῥώμην πρῶτον ἐγγὺς ἦν τοῦ διεφθάρθαι.

Puglia (2011)   Τὰ δὲ ἐν Ἀντίῳ, διὰ τὴν ἀμέλειαν τῶν ἑκάστοτ' ἐμπιστευομένων ἐκ διαδοχῆς αὐτὰ μ[ὴ] σή[πηται, ἤδ]η καθ' ὃν χρόνον ἐγὼ ἀνέβην εἰς Ῥώμην πρῶτον ἐγγὺς ἦν τοῦ διεφθάρθαι.

GL § 18.18   τὰ δὲ ἐν Ἀντίῳ διὰ τὴν ἀμέλειαν τῶν ἑκάστοτ' ἐμπιστευομένων ἐκ διαδοχῆς αὐτὰ (lac. 13 fere litt.) καθ' ὃν χρόνον ἐγὼ ἀνέβην εἰς Ῥώμην πρῶτον ἐγγὺς ἦν [11v] τοῦ διεφθάρθαι.

KS § 8.70.97	19 Ταῦτ' ἄρα
BMJ § 19.8.6	19 Ταῦτ' ἄρα
GL § 19.18	19 τοῦτ' ἄρα
KS § 8.70.97	μικρὸν ἐγγραφομένοις αὐτά.
BMJ § 19.8.7	μικρὸν ἐγγραφομένοις αὐτά·
GL § 19.18	μικρὸν ἐκγραφομένοις αὐτά·

KS §8.70.97–98	αὐτά. Νυνὶ
BMJ §19.8.7	αὐτά· νυνὶ
GL §19.18	αὐτά· νυνὶ
KS §8.70.98–99	κεκολλῆσθαι τὰς χάρτας
BMJ §19.8.8–9	κεκολλῆσθαι τὰς χάρτας
GL §19.18	κεκολλῆσθαι τοὺς χάρτας
KS §8.70.99	σηπεδόνος· ἔστι
BMJ §19.8.9	σηπεδόνος· ἔστι
GL §19.18	σηπεδόνος. ἔστι
KS §8.70.100	μάλιστα καὶ
BMJ §19.8.10	μάλιστα, καὶ
GL §19.18	μάλιστα καὶ
KS §9.70.101	9 Ἴσως δὲ ἐλύπει <σε ἂν> καὶ ἡ τῶν Ἀττικῶν ὀνομάτων
BMJ §20.8.11–12	20 Ἴσως δέ <σ>ε λυπ<ήσ>ει καὶ ἡ τῶν Ἀττικῶν ὀνομάτων
GL §20.18	20 ἴσως δέ <σ>ε λύπ<ήσ>ει καὶ ἡ των Ἀττικῶν ὀνομάτων
Polemis	Ἴσως δὲ λείπει καὶ ἡ τῶν Ἀττικῶν ὀνομάτων
KS §9.70.102	πραγματεία, διττὴ
BMJ §20.8.12–13	πράγματα <καὶ ὀνόματα πραγματεία> διττὴ
GL §20.18	πραγματεία, διττὴ
KS §9.70.103	μέτρου γραψάντων. Ἀλλὰ
BMJ §20.8.15	μέτρου γραψάντων· ἀλλὰ
GL §20.18	μέτρων γραψάντων· ἀλλὰ
KS §9.70.104	τἀντίγραφα· καὶ
BMJ §20.8.16	τἀντίγραφα. Καὶ
GL §20.18	τἀντίγραφα, καὶ
KS §9.70.105	μετὰ δύο μῆνας
BMJ §20.8.17	μετὰ δύο μῆνας
GL §20.18	μετὰ δύο μῆνας
KS §9.70.105	ἔφθανον ἂν εἰς
BMJ §20.8.18	ἔφθανον <ἂ>ν οὖν εἰς
GL §20.18	ἔφθανε ἂν οὖν εἰς
KS §9.70.109–10	πραγματείας, ὅπως ἐν βιβλιοθήκῃ δημοσίᾳ στῶσι, καθάπερ
BMJ §21.9.2–3	πραγματείας ὅπως ἐν βιβλιοθήκῃ δημοσίᾳ στῶσι, καθάπερ
GL §21.18	πραγματείας, ὅπως ἐν βιβλιοθήκῃ δημοσίᾳ τεθῶσι, καθάπερ
Polemis	πραγματείας, ὅπως ἐν βιβλιοθήκαις δημοσίαις θῶσι, καθάπερ
KS §9.70.110	ἄλλοι
BMJ §21.9.3	ἄλλοι[ς]
GL §21.20	ἄλλοι[ς]

KS § 9.70.113	μένειν, ὡς ἔφην.
BMJ § 22.9.7	μένειν ὡς ἔφην.
GL § 22.20	μένειν, ὡς ἔφην.
KS § 10.70.115	ἐνενόουν
BMJ § 23a.9.9	ἐνόουν
GL § 23a.20	ἐν<εν>όουν
KS § 10.70.115	κομίσαι
BMJ § 23a.9.9	κομίσαι
GL § 23a.20	κομίσαι
KS § 10.70.116	τὰ πεμφθησόμενα
BMJ § 23a.9.10	τὰ πεμφ<θ>ησόμενα
GL § 23a.20	τὰ πεμφ<θ>ησόμενα,
KS § 10.70.116–7	τῶν ἐτησίων πνεόντων εἰς Ἀσίαν.
BMJ § 23a.9.11	τῶν ἐ[ν]τησίων πνεόντων εἰς Ἀσίαν.
GL § 23a.20	τῶν ἐ[ν]τησίων πνεόντων, εἰς Ἀσίαν.
KS § 10.70.118–9	πραγματείαν, ἣν ἐξελεξάμην <ἐκ> τῆς
BMJ § 23b.9.14	πραγματείαν ἣν ἐξέλεξα[το] τῆς
GL § 23b.20	πραγματείαν, ἣν ἐξέλεξα ἐκ τῆς
KS § 10.70.119	ὅλης. Ἦν δ' ὡς οἶσθα
BMJ § 23b–24a.9.15	ὅλης, 24a ἧς [δ'] ὡς οἶσθα
GL § 23b–§ 24a.20	ὅλης. 24a τῶνδ' ὡς οἶσθα
KS § 10.70.119–71.120	τὰ πολιτικὰ <ἃ> ἔφθασεν Δίδυμος
BMJ § 24a.9.15–16	τὰ πολιτικὰ ἔφθανεν Δίδυμος
GL § 24a.20	τὰ πολιτικὰ ἔφθαν' ὁ Δίδυμος
Polemis	καὶ τὰ πολιτικὰ, <ἃ> φθάνων Δίδυμος
KS § 11.71.124	ἢ οἵτινες ὅλως ἀττικίζειν
BMJ § 24b.9.20	ἢ οἵτινες ὅλως ἀττικίζειν
GL § 24b.20	ἢ εἴ τινες ἄλλως ἀττικίζειν
KS § 11.71.124–5	βούλοιντό τινα {καὶ} τῶν εἰς {τὰ} πράγματα
BMJ § 24b–§ 25.9.20–21	βούλοιντο <ἢ> τινα 25 καὶ τῶν εἰς τὰ πράγματα
GL § 24b–§ [25].20	βούλοιντό [25] τινα καὶ τῶν εἰς τὰ πράγματα
KS § 11.71.125–6	καὶ τὸ παρατεθὲν ἔναγχος εἰπόντος <τινὸς> ἐν Ῥώμῃ
BMJ § 25.9.22–23	καὶ τὸ παρατεθὲν ἔναγχος, εἰπόντος <τινὸς> ἐν Ῥώμῃ
GL § [25].20	καὶ τὸ παρατεθὲν ἔναγχος ὑπό τινος ἐν Ῥώμῃ
KS § 11.71.126	ἰατρῶν οὔπω
BMJ § 25.9.23–10.1	ἰατρῶν οὔπω
GL § [25].20	ἰατρῶν· οὔπω

KS §11.71.127	χόνδρου κατὰ τοὺς Ἱπποκράτους χρόνους·
BMJ §25.10.1–2	χόνδρου κατ<ὰ τ>οὺς Ἱπποκράτους χρόνους,
GL §[25].20	χόνδρου κατ<ὰ τ>οὺς Ἱπποκράτους χρόνους.
KS §11.71.130	προελέσθαι τοῦδε· μάλιστα
BMJ §25–§26.10.5–6	προελέσθαι τοῦδε. 26 Μάλιστα
GL §[25]–§26.22	προελέσθαι τοῦδε. 26 μάλιστα
KS §11.71.130	καὶ κατὰ τὸ περὶ
BMJ §26.10.6	καὶ κατὰ τὸ περὶ
GL §26.22	καὶ κἂν τῷ περὶ
KS §11.71.131	ὑγιεινόν, ὅ
BMJ §26.10.6–7	ὑγιεινὸν ὅ
GL §26.22	ὑγιεινῷ ὅ
KS §11.71.131	εἶναι ἔνιοι
BMJ §26.10.7	εἶναι, ἔνιοι
GL §26.22	εἶναι, ἔνιοι
KS §11.71.131	Φιλιστίωνος ἕτεροι
BMJ §26.10.7–8	Φιλιστίωνος, ἕτεροι
GL §26.22	Φιλιστίωνος, ἕτεροι
KS §11.71.132	Ἀρίστωνος, ἀνδρῶν
BMJ §26.10.8	Ἀρίστωνος ἀνδρῶν
GL §26.22	Ἀρίστωνος, ἀνδρῶν
KS §11.71.132–3	ὁ χόνδρος, ἀλλὰ καὶ
BMJ §26.10.9	ὁ χόνδρος, ἀλλὰ καὶ
GL §26.22	ὁ χόνδρος, ἀλλὰ καὶ
Polemis	ὁ χόνδρος. Ἀλλὰ καὶ
KS §11–§12.71.133–4	κωμικοῖς †Ἀβυδομᾶν ἢ Ἀβυστακινεῖν†. 12 Ἀλλ'
BMJ §26–§27.10.10	κωμικοῖς, Ἀριστομένει ἢ Ἀριστοφάνει. 27 Ἀλλ'
GL §26–§27.22	κωμικοῖς, †ἀβυδομῆν ἢ ἀβυστακινεῖν.† 27 ἀλλ'
Polemis	κωμικοῖς, Ἀβυδοκόμαν ἢ ἀβυρτάκην <ἢ> ἄλλ'
KS §12.71.135	πραγματείαν, ἃ
BMJ §27.10.12	πραγματείαν – ἃ
GL §27.22	πραγματείαν, ἃ
KS §12.71.135	καλῶς οὑτωσί·
BMJ §27.10.13	καλῶς – οὑτωσί·
GL §27.22	καλῶς, οὑτωσί·
KS §12.71.136	δημήτρια
BMJ §27.10.14	Δημήτρια
GL §27.22	Δημήτρια

KS §12.71.137	{καὶ θάμναι} καὶ δένδρα
BMJ §27.10.15	καὶ θάμναι καὶ δευτερίαι
GL §27.22	[καὶ θάμναι] καὶ δένδρα
KS §12.71.138	καὶ τἄλλα
BMJ §27.10.17	καὶ τἄλλα
GL §27.22	καὶ τἄλλα
KS §12.71.139	οὖν λοιπὰ ἐκ
BMJ §28.10.18	οὖν [λοιπὰ] ἐκ
GL §28.22	οὖν [λοιπὰ] ἐκ
KS §12.71.140	οὐκ ἔφθασεν
BMJ §28.10.19	οὐκ ἔφθασαν
GL §28.22	οὐκ ἔφθασεν
KS §12.71.141	εἰς Καμπανίαν μετενεχθῆναι, τὰ δὲ <τῶν> ἄνευ
BMJ §28.10.20	εἰς Καμπανίαν μετενεχθῆναι, τὰ δὲ < ἐκ τῶν> ἄνευ
GL §28.22	εἰς Καμπανίαν [12r] μετενεχθῆναι, τὰ δ' ε<κ τῶν> ἄνευ
KS §12.71.141–2	ἤδη μετενήνεκτο κατὰ τὴν τύχην,
BMJ §28.10.21	ἤδη μετενήνεκτο κατὰ τὴν τύχην,
GL §28.24	ἤδη μετενήνεκτο κατά τινά τύχην
KS §12.71.142	μεγάλοις, ὧν
BMJ §28.10.22	μεγάλοις ὧν
GL §28.24	μεγάλοις, ὧν
KS §12.71.143	δίχα, πλειόνων
BMJ §28.10.23	δίχα πλειόνων
GL §28.24	δίχα πλειόνων
KS §12.71.143	ἑξαμέτρων ὄντα.
BMJ §28.10.24	ἐξάριθμον ἐχόντων.
GL §28.24	ἐξάριθμον ἔχοντα.
KS §13.71.144	13 Τούτων οὖν οὐδὲν
BMJ §29.10.24	29 Τούτων οὖν οὐδὲν
GL §29.24	29 τούτων οὖν οὐδὲν
KS §13.71.144	με, καίτοι
BMJ §29.10.25	με καίτοι
GL §29.24	με καί τοι
KS §13.72.145	τῶν ἐμῶν ὑπομνημάτων
BMJ §29.11.1	τῶν ἡμ<ετέρ>ων ὑπομνημάτων
GL §29.24	τῶν ἡμετέρων ὑπομνημάτων

KS §13.72.146	σύμμετρα, ὡς
BMJ §29.11.3	σύμμετρα ὡς
GL §29.24	σύμμετρα ὡς
KS §13.72.147	χρήσιμα, τινὰ δὲ ἐμοὶ μόνῳ καὶ τῷ
BMJ §29.11.4	χρήσιμα, τινὰ δὲ ἐμοὶ μόνῳ καίτοι
GL §29.24	χρήσιμα, τινὰ δ' ἐμοὶ μόνῳ καί τοι
KS §13.72.147–8	παρασκευήν. Εἰς ἀνάμνησιν ἔπειτα αἱ κεφαλαιώδεις πλεῖσται
BMJ §29–§30.11.4–5	παρασκευὴν εἰς ἀνάμνησιν, 30 ἔπειτα αἱ κεφαλαιώδεις πλεῖσται
GL §29–§30.24	παρασκευὴν εἰς ἀνάμνησιν. 30 ἔπειτα αἱ κεφαλαιώδεις πλεῖσται
KS §13.72.149	φιλοσόφων· ἀλλ' οὐδὲ ταῦτα ἐλύπησεν.
BMJ §30.11.6–7	φιλοσοφ<ικ>ῶν· ἀλλ' οὐδὲ ταῦτα ἐλύπησαν.
GL §30.24	φιλοσόφων. ἀλλ' οὐδὲ ταῦτα ἐλύπησεν.
KS §13.72.150–1	ὃ λυπεῖν δύναιτο; καὶ
BMJ §31.11.8–9	ὃ λυπεῖν <ἂν> δύναιτο; Καὶ
GL §31.24	ὃ λυπεῖν <ἂν> δύναιτο; καὶ
KS §13–§14.72.151–2	φράσω τοῦτο. 14 Γραφὰς φαρμάκων θαυμασιωτέρας
BMJ §31.11.9–10	φράσω τοῦτο· γραφὰς φαρμάκων θαυμασιωτέρας
GL §31.24	φράσω τοῦτο. γραφὰς φαρμάκων θαυμασιωτάτας
KS §14.72.153	Ῥωμαίων
BMJ §31.11.11	Ῥωμαίους
GL §31.24	Ῥωμαίων
KS §14.72.154	συλλαβούσης
BMJ §31.11.12	συ<λ>λαμβανούσης,
GL §31.24	συλλαμβανούσης
KS §14.72.154	συμπροθυμηθέντος.
BMJ §31.11.13	συμπροτιμηθέντος.
GL §31.24	συμπροθυμηθέντος.
KS §14.72.154–5	Διττὴ δὴ τύχη προυξένησέ
BMJ §32.11.13–14	Διττὴ δὲ τύχη προὐξένησέ
GL §32.24	διττὴ δὲ τύχη προὐξένησέ
KS §14.72.156	ἐσπούδασεν εὑρεῖν
BMJ §32.11.16	ἐσπούδασεν εὑρεῖν
GL §32.24	ἐσπούδασεν ἔχειν
KS §14.72.157	γνῶσιν, ὡς
BMJ §32.11.16–17	γνῶσιν ὡς
GL §32.24	γνῶσιν, ὡς

KS § 14.72.157	ἑκατὸν χρυσῶν ἐνίας
BMJ § 32.11.17	ἑκατὸν χρυσῶν ἐνίας
GL § 32.24	ἑκατὸν χρυσίων ἐνίας
KS § 14.72.157–8	πλέον· ὃς
BMJ § 32.11.17–18	πλέον, ὃ<ς>
GL § 32.24	πλέον, ὃ<ς>
KS § 14.72.158	ἔργον ἐπετηδεύσατο, <ὡς> μὴ μόνον
BMJ § 32.11.18–19	ἔργον ἐπετηδεύσατο <οἷον> μὴ μόνον
GL § 32.26	ἔργον ἐπετηδεύσατο ὡς μὴ μόνον
KS § 14.72.158–59	κατὰ τὴν οὐσίαν
BMJ § 32.11.19	κατὰ τὴν Ἀσίαν
GL § 32.26	κατὰ τὴν Ἀσίαν
KS § 14.72.159	τῶν <νῦν> ἰατρῶν, ἀλλὰ
BMJ § 32.11.20	τῶν <νῦν> ἰατρῶν, ἀλλὰ
GL § 32.26	τῶν <νῦν> ἰατρῶν, ἀλλὰ
KS § 14.72.159–60	τῶν παλαιῶν ἐξωνήσασθαι.
BMJ § 32.11.20–21	τῶν παλαιῶν ἐξωνήσασθαι.
GL § 32.26	τῶν παλαιῶν ἐξωνήσασθαι,
KS § 14.72.160	Τούτων τῶν φαρμάκων πάντων αἱ γραφαὶ
BMJ § 33.11.21	Τούτων τῶν φαρμάκων πάντων αἱ γραφαὶ
GL § 33.26	τούτων τῶν φαρμάκων πάντων αἱ γραφαὶ
KS § 14.72.161	πυκτὰς
BMJ § 33.12.1	π<τ>υκτὰς
GL § 33.26	π<τ>υκτὰς
KS § 14.72.161	ἀσφαλείας, ἅστινας
BMJ § 33.12.2	ἀσφαλείας ἅστινας
GL § 33.26	ἀσφαλείας, ἅστινας
KS § 14.72.163–4	εὐπορίας, τὴν δὲ {δὲ}
BMJ § 34.12.5	εὐπορίας· τήνδε δὲ <τὴν>
GL § 34.26	εὐπορίας, τὴν δὲ [δὲ]
KS § 14–§ 15.72.164–5	δευτέραν ἐφεξῆς ἄκουσον. 15 Ὡς
BMJ § 34.12.5–6	δευτέραν ἐφ<εξ>ῆς ἄκουσον· ὡς
GL § 34.26	δευτέραν ἐφ<εξ>ῆς ἄκουσον. ὡς
KS § 15.72.165–6	ἔτος ἄγων τρίτον πρὸς τοῖς τριάκοντα,
BMJ § 34.12.6–7	ἔτος ἄγων τρίτον πρὸς τοῖς τριάκοντα,
GL § 34.26	ἔτος ἄγων τρίτον πρὸς τοῖς τριάκοντα,

KS §15.72.167	εὗρον, ὃς
BMJ §34.12.8–9	εὗρον ὃς
GL §34.26	εὗρον ὃς
KS §15.72.167	Εὐμένους
BMJ §34.12.9	Εὐμενοῦς
GL §34.26	Εὐμενοῦς
KS §15.72.168	καὶ αὐτοῦ Περγαμηνοῦ, φιλοφαρμάκου δὲ καὶ
BMJ §34.12.10	καὶ αὐτοῦ περγαμηνοῦ φιλοφαρμάκου δὲ καὶ
GL §34.26	καὶ αὐτοῦ Περγαμηνοῦ, φιλοφαρμάκου δὲ καὶ
KS §15.73.169	αἱ διφθέραι
BMJ §35.12.12	αἱ γραφαὶ
GL §35.26	αἱ διφθέραι
KS §15.73.171	ἀποδημίας αὐτοῦ, μεθ'
BMJ §35.12.13–14	ἀποδημίας αὐτῷ μεθ'
GL §35.26	ἀποδημίας αὐτῷ μεθ'
KS §15.73.171	Ῥώμῃ διετέλεσεν ἄχρι θανάτου.
BMJ §35.12.14	Ῥώμῃ διετέλεσεν ἄχρι θανάτου.
GL §35.26	Ῥώμῃ διετέλεσεν μέχρι θανάτου.
KS §15.73.173	ἀνόδου, τὸ
BMJ §35.12.17	ἀνόδου τὸ
GL §35.26	ἀνόδου τὸ
KS §15.73.173–4	Ῥώμην μοι γεγονότι.
BMJ §35.12.17	Ῥώμην μοι γεγονέναι.
GL §35.26	Ῥώμην ἐμοὶ γεγονέναι.
KS §15.73.174	παρασκευῶν εἴ
BMJ §36.12.18	παρασκευῶν εἴ
GL §36.26	παρασκευῶν, εἴ
KS §15.73.175	εἶχε φαρμάκων ἐλάμβανον
BMJ §36.12.19	εἶχε φαρμάκων ἐλάμβανον
GL §36.26 and 28	εἶχε φαρμάκων, ἐλάμβανον
KS §15.73.175	χαλεπῶς ἀντιδιδοὺς
BMJ §36.12.19–20	χαλεπῶς ἀντιδιδοὺς
GL §36.28	χαλεπῶς, ἀντιδιδοὺς
KS §15.73.177	ἐνόμιζον – ἀλλὰ <καὶ> πραγματεία
BMJ §37.12.22	ἐνόμιζον –, ἀλλὰ πραγματεία
GL §37.28	ἐνόμιζον – ἀλλὰ πραγματεία

KS § 15.73.178–9	ἀκριβείας, ἡ περὶ συνθέσεως φαρμάκων, ἐν ᾗ πως αὐτὸς αὖθις συνθείην φαρμάκων
BMJ § 37.12.23–24	ἀκριβείας ἡ περὶ συνθέσεως φαρμάκων ἐν ᾗ πῶς αὐτὸς αὖθις συνθείην φαρμάκων
GL § 37.28	ἀκριβείας, ἡ περὶ συνθέσεως φαρμάκων, ἐν ᾗ πῶς ἄν τις αὖθις συνθείη[ν] φαρμάκων
KS § 15.73.179	ἄμεινον τὰ δοκιμώτατα, καὶ
BMJ § 37.13.1	ἐμήνυον τὰ δοκιμώτατα· καὶ
GL § 37.28	ἐμήνυον τὰ δοκιμώτατα, καὶ
KS § 15.73.180	σῴζονται ὀλίγων γραφαὶ <οὐ> φθάνουσαι διδόσθαι τοῖς ἑταίροις.
BMJ § 37.13.1–2	σῴζονται ὀλίγων γραφαὶ φθάνουσαι διδόσθαι τοῖς ἑταίροις.
GL § 37.28	σῴζονται ὀλίγων γραφαὶ φθάνουσαι δίδοσθαι τοῖς ἑταίροις.
KS § 16.73.181	16 Ἴσως οὖν φήσεις ἐπιτάττεσθαί
BMJ § 38.13.3	38 Ἴσως ἂν οὖν φήσεις ἐπιτάττεσθαί
GL § 38.28	38 ἴσως οὖν φήσεις ὑποτάττεσθαί
Polemis	Ἴσως οὖν φήσεις ἐπιτετάσθαι
KS § 16.73.182–3	ποικιλίαν κτημάτων, ὧν ἕκαστον αὐτὸ καθ'
BMJ § 38.13.5	ποικιλίαν κτημάτων ὧν ἕκαστον αὐτὸ καθ'
GL § 38.28	ποικιλίαν κτημάτων, ὧν ἕκαστον αὐτὸ καθ'
KS § 16.73.183–4	ἐγένετο τοῖς ἄλλοις ἀνθρώποις, οὐκ ἠνιάθην, ὡς ἕτεροί τινες,
BMJ § 38.13.6–7	ἐγένετο τοῖς ἄλλοις ἀνθρώποις, οὐκ ἠνιάθην ὡς ἕτεροί τινες,
GL § 38.28	ἐγένετο [12v] τοῖς ἄλλοις ἀνθρώποις, οὐκ ἠνιάθην ὡς ἕτεροί τινες,
KS § 16.73.184	πάνυ ἤνεγκα
BMJ § 38.13.7	πάνυ <ῥᾳδίως> ἤνεγκα
GL § 38.28	πᾶν ἤνεγκα
KS § 16.73.185	πρὸς τοῦτο ποιήσομαι· τὴν μὲν ἑτέραν, ὑπὲρ ἧς
BMJ § 39.13.8–9	πρὸς τοῦτο ποιήσομαι, τὴν μὲν ἑτέραν ὑπὲρ ἧς
GL § 39.28	πρὸς τοῦτο ποιήσομαι, τὴν μὲν ἑτέραν ὑπὲρ ἧς
KS § 16.73.186–7	χρὴ πολλάκις <ἐμοῦ> ἀκηκοότα διερχομένου τοιούτους λόγους, ὧνπερ νῦν
BMJ § 39.13.10–11	χρὴ πολλάκις ἀκηκοότα διερχομένου <ἐμοῦ> τοιούτος λόγους ὧν καὶ νῦν
GL § 39.28	χρὴ πολλάκις ἀκηκοέναι διερχομένου μου τοὺς λόγους ὧν καὶ νῦν

KS §16–§17.73.187–8	ἀναμνήσεως. 17 Φιλήδονος <ὢν> Ἀρίστιππος οὐκ ἀρκούμενος διαίτῃ εὐτελεῖ
BMJ §39.13.11–12	ἀναμνήσεως· φιλότιμος Ἀρίστιππος, οὐκ ἀρκούμενος διαίτῃ εὐτελεῖ
GL §39.28	ἀναμνήσεως· <ὁ> φιλότιμος Ἀρίστιππος, οὐκ ἀρκούμενος διαίτῃ εὐτελεῖ,
KS §17.73.188–9	ἀλλὰ καὶ πολυτελῶς ὀψωνῶν ἑκάστης ἡμέρας ἐδίδου
BMJ §39.13.13–14	ἀλλὰ καὶ πολυτελείαις ὄψων [ἂν] ἑκάστης ἡμέρας διδοὺς
GL §39.28	ἀλλὰ καὶ πολυτελῶς ὀψωνῶν ἑκάστης ἡμέρας, διδοὺς
KS §17.73.190	ταῖς εὐμορφοτέραις
BMJ §39.13.14	τοῖς θερμοτέροις
GL §39.28	ταῖς θερμοτέραις
KS §17.73.190	ἑταιρῶν· ὅμως καίτοι
BMJ §39.13.15	ἑταίρων – ὅμως καί τι
GL §39.28 and 30	ἑταίρων, ὅμως καί τοι
Polemis	ἑταιρῶν· ὅμως καὶ ἔτι
KS §17.74.191–2	δεόμενος ὁ ἀνὴρ ἐκεῖνος, ἀνιών ποτε ἐκ Πειραιῶς – εἰώθει <γάρ> ἀεὶ βαδίζειν οὐ μόνον τὰς οὕτω βραχείας ὁδοὺς ἀλλὰ καὶ τὰς μακρὰς –,
BMJ §39–§40.13.15–18	δεόμενος ὁ ἀνὴρ ἐκεῖνος –, 40 ἀνιών ποτε ἐκ Πειραιῶς – εἰώθει ἀεὶ βαδίζειν οὐ μόνον τὰς οὕτω βραχείας ὁδούς, ἀλλὰ καὶ τὰς μακρὰς –,
GL §39–§40.30	δεομένος – 40 ὁ οὖν ἀνὴρ ἐκεῖνος ἀνιών ποτε ἐκ τοῦ Πειραιῶς (εἰώθει ἀεὶ βαδίζειν οὐ μόνον τὰς οὕτω βραχείας ὁδούς, ἀλλὰ καὶ τὰς μακράς),
KS §17.74.193–4	τῷ φορτίῳ, φασκώλιον δὲ ἦν τοῦτο χρυσίων μεστόν, ἐκέλευσεν ἀποχέαι τοσοῦτον, ὡς τὸ λοιπὸν
BMJ §40.13.19–21	τῷ φορτίῳ – φασκώλιον δὲ ἦν τοῦτο χρυσίων μεστόν –, ἐκέλευσεν ἀποχέαι τοσοῦτον ὡς τὸ λοιπὸν
GL §40.30	τῷ φορτίῳ (φασκώλιον δὲ ἦν τοῦτο χρυσίων μεστόν) ἐκέλευσεν ἀποχέαι τοσοῦτον ὡς τὸ λοιπὸν
KS §18.74.196–7	τέσσαρας ἔχων ἀγροὺς ἐπὶ τῆς πατρίδος,
BMJ §41.13.22–14.1	τέσσαρας ἔχων ἀγροὺς ἐπὶ τῆς πατρίδος,
GL §41.30	τέτταρας ἔχων ἀγροὺς ἐν τῇ πατρίδι,
KS §18.74.197–8	τῶν πραγμάτων ἐξ αὐτῶν ἀπώλεσεν, ὡς λοιπὸν ἔχειν τρεῖς.
BMJ §41.14.1–2	τῶν πραγμάτων ἐξ αὐτῶν ἀπήλασεν ὡς λοιπὸν ἔχειν τρεῖς.
GL §41.30	τῶν πραγμάτων αὐτῶν ἀπώλεσεν ὡς λοιποὺς ἔχειν τρεῖς.

KS § 18.74.199	ἦν ἐπὶ τῇ ζημίᾳ συλλυπεῖσθαι <...>, γελάσας οὖν ὁ Ἀρίστιππος ἔφη·
BMJ § 42.14.3–4	ἦν ἐπὶ τῇ ζημίᾳ συλλυπεῖσθαι· γελάσας οὖν ὁ Ἀρίστιππος ἔφη·
GL § 42.30	ἦν τῇ ζημίᾳ συλλυπεῖσθαι. γελάσας οὖν ὁ Ἀρίστιππος ἔφη·
KS § 18.74.200	ἐμοὶ συλλυπεῖ σὺ
BMJ § 42.14.5	ἐμοὶ <σὺ> συλλυπήσῃ
GL § 42.30	ἐμοὶ συλλυπήσῃ
KS § 18.74.200	τοιούτους, οἷον μόνον αὐτὸς ἔχεις,
BMJ § 42.14.6	τοιούτους οἷον <ἕνα> μόνον αὐτὸς ἔχεις
GL § 42.30	τοιούτους οἷον μόνον αὐτὸς <οὐκ> ἔχεις·
KS § 18.74.202	πολλάκις ἤκουσας παρ' ἐμοῦ λεγόμενον, ὡς
BMJ § 42.14.7–8	πολλάκις ἤκουσας παρ' ἐμοῦ λεγόμενον ὡς
GL § 42.30	πολλάκις παρ' ἐμοῦ ἤκουσας λεγόμενον ὡς
KS § 18.74.203	ἐμβλέπειν ἀλλὰ λογίζεσθαι
BMJ § 42.14.9	ἐμβλέπειν καὶ λογίζεσθαι
GL § 42.30	ἐπιβλέπειν καὶ λογίζεσθαι
KS § 18.74.203–4	τοῦ πατρὸς {οὐκ ἀνέξοντο} βλέπειν οὐκ ἀνέξονται ἑτέρους
BMJ § 42.14.10–11	τοῦ πατρὸς οὐκ ἀνέξονται βλέπειν ἑτέρους
GL § 42.30	τοῦ πατρὸς [οὐκ ἀνέξοντο] βλέπειν οὐκ ἀνέξονται ἑτέρους
KS § 18.74.205	τριάκοντα ἔχωσιν, ἑτέρους ὄψονται
BMJ § 43.14.11–12	τριάκοντα ἔχωσιν, ἑτέρους ὄψονται
GL § 43.30	τριάκοντα ἔχωσιν, ἑτέρους ὄψονται
KS § 18.74.205–6	ἔχοντας· ἐὰν {ταῦτα} πάλιν
BMJ § 43.14.12–13	ἔχοντας· ἐὰν <κατὰ> ταὐτὰ πάλιν
GL § 43.30	ἔχοντας, ἐὰν <κατὰ> ταὐτὰ πάλιν
KS § 18.74.206	κτήσωνται τοσούτους, ἔχοντας
BMJ § 43.14.13	κτήσωνται τοσούτους, ἔχοντας
GL § 43.30	κτήσωνται τοσούτους, ἔχοντας
KS § 18.74.207	ἑβδομήκοντα· κἂν
BMJ § 43.14.14	ἑβδομήκοντα, κἂν
GL § 43.32	ἑβδομήκοντα, κἂν
KS § 18.74.208–9	ἔχοντας. Ὥστε κατὰ βραχὺ προϊόντες ἁπάντων ἐπιθυμήσουσιν· καὶ
BMJ § 43.14.15–17	ἔχοντας, ὥστε κατὰ βραχὺ προϊόντες ἁπάντων ἐπιθυμήσουσιν, καὶ
GL § 43.32	ἔχοντας, ὥστε κατὰ βραχὺ προϊόντες ἁπάντων ἐπιθυμήσουσιν, καὶ

KS §18.74.210	Ἐὰν δέ τις μὴ ὁπόσους ἀγροὺς
BMJ §44.14.18	44 Ἐὰν δέ τις μὴ πόσους ἀγροὺς
GL §44.32	44 ἐὰν δέ τις μὴ ὁπόσους ἀγροὺς
KS §18.74.210–1	σκοπῇ ἀλλ' ἢ τοὺς
BMJ §44.14.19	σκοπῇ, ἀλλ' ἤ<δη> τοὺς
GL §44.32	σκοπῇ, ἀλλ' εἰ τοὺς
KS §18.74. 211–2	ἐξαρκοῦντας αὐτῷ, τὴν τῶν περιττωμάτων ἀπώλειαν εὐκόλως οἴσει.
BMJ §44.15.1–2	ἐξαρκοῦντας αὐτῷ, τὴν τῶν περιττωμάτων ἀπώλειαν ἀκηδῶς οἴσει.
GL §44.32	ἐξαρκοῦντας αὐτός, τὴν τῶν περιττῶν ἀπώλειαν ἀλύπως οἴσει.
KS §18.74.213	ἄπορος
BMJ §45.15.3	ἄπορο<ς>
GL §45.32	ἄπορος
KS §18.74.213–4	ἀνιαθήσεται, ἕνα δὲ ἀπολέσας ἐκ
BMJ §45.15.4–5	ἀνιαθήσεται, ἕνα δὲ ἀπολέσας <τις> ἐκ
GL §45.32	ἀνιαθήσεται. ἕνα δ' ἀπολέσας ἐκ
KS §18.74.214	τεσσάρων ἐν ἴσῳ
BMJ §45.15.5	τεσσάρων, ἐν ἴσῳ
GL §45.32	τεττάρων ἐν ἴσῳ
KS §18.74.214–5	τοῖς τρεῖς ἔχουσιν ἐξ ἀρχῆς·
BMJ §45.15.5–6	τοῖς τρεῖς ἔχουσιν ἐξ ἀρχῆς,
GL §45.32	τοῖς τρεῖς ἀγροὺς ὑπολοίπους ἔχουσιν ἐξ ἀρχῆς,
KS §18.74.215–6	τοῦτο μὲν μέγα οὐδέν, μὴ λυπεῖσθαι τρεῖς ἀγροὺς ὑπολοίπους ἔχοντα,
BMJ §45.15.6–7	τούτῳ μὲν μέγα οὐδὲν μὴ λυπεῖσθαι τρεῖς ἀγροὺς ὑπολοίπους ἔχοντι,
GL §45.32	τοῦτο μὲν μέγα οὐδὲν μὴ λυπεῖσθαι τρεῖς ἀγροὺς ἔχοντι,
KS §18.74.216	μέγα δὲ τὸ μηδὲ τὸν
BMJ §45.15.7–8	μέγα δὲ τὸ τὸν μηδὲ
GL §45.32	μέγα δὲ τὸν μηδὲ
KS §18.75.217	Κράτης ἔφερε· καὶ
BMJ §45.15.9	Κράτης ἔφερε, καὶ
GL §45.32	Κράτης ἔφερε, καὶ
KS §18.75.217	καὶ διὰ τοῦτο μᾶλλον εἰ μηδὲ οἰκίαν ἔχει
BMJ §45.15.9–10	καὶ διὰ τοῦτο μᾶλλον εἴ <τις> μηδὲ οἰκίαν ἔχει[ν]
GL §45.32	καὶ δὴ τοῦτο μᾶλλον εἰ μηδὲ οἰκίαν ἔχει[ν]

KS §19.75.219	19 Οὐκ οὖν ἐμοί τι πρᾶγμα μέγα μηδόλως ἀνιαθέντι
BMJ §46.15.10–11	46 Οὐκοῦν ἐμοὶ τί πρᾶγμα μέγα μηδ' ὅλως ἀνιαθέντι
GL §46.32	46 οὔκουν ἐμοί τι πρᾶγμα μέγα μηδ' ὅλως ἀνιαθέντι
KS §19.75.220	ἀπώλειαν· ἦν
BMJ §46.15.11–12	ἀπώλειαν; Ἦν
GL §46.32	ἀπώλειαν· ἦν
KS §19.75.220	ἱκανῶν. Ἀλλὰ
BMJ §46–47.15.12–13	ἱκανῶν. 47 Ἀλλὰ
GL §46–47.32	ἱκανῶν, 47 ἀλλὰ
KS §19.75.221–2	μὲν ἐνίοτε μυρίας δραχμὰς ἐκ προσόδων μυριάδων δέκα,
BMJ §47.15.14–15	μὲν ἐνίοτε μυρίας δραχμὰς ἐκ προσόδων μυριάδων δέκα,
GL §47.32	μὲν <ἐν> ἐνιαυτῷ μυρίας δραχμὰς ἐκ προσόδου μυριάδων δέκα,
KS §19.75.222–3	ἀπώλειαν. Κατὰ
BMJ §47.15.15–16	ἀπωλείᾳ· κατὰ
GL §47.32	ἀπωλείᾳ. κατὰ
KS §19.75.223	εἴ τις τὰς ὑπολοίπους
BMJ §47.15.16	εἰ τὰς ἀπολοίπους
GL §47.32	εἴ τὰς ὑπολοίπους
KS §19.75.223	ἀπολλύοι
BMJ §47.15.17	ἀπόλλυσιν
GL §47.32	ἀπόλλυσιν
KS §19.75.224	ἀνιᾶσθαι τῶν
BMJ §47.15.17–18	ἀνιᾶσθαι, τῶν
GL §47.32	ἀνιᾶσθαι, τῶν
KS §19.75.226–7	ἐργαζομένους· ἐκείνους δ' εἴπερ ἄρα θαυμάζεσθαι προσήκει, ὅσοι
BMJ §48.15.20–21	ἐργαζομένους· ἐκείνους δ' εἴπερ ἄρα θαυμάζεσθαι προσήκει ὅσοι
GL §48.34	ἐργαζομένους, ἐκείνους δ' εἴ περ ἄρα θαυμάζεσθαι προσήκει ὅσοι
KS §19.75.227	οὐδόλως
BMJ §48.15.22	οὐδ' ὅλως
GL §48.34	οὐδ' ὅλως
KS §19.75.227–8	ὁ Κιτιεὺς Ζήνων, ὥς φ[ασιν], ἀπαγγελθείσης
BMJ §48.15.22–23	ὁ Κιτιεὺς Ζήνων, ὥς φ(ασιν), ἀπαγγελθείσης
GL §48.34	ὁ Κιτιεὺς Ζήνων, ὅς, φασιν, [13r] ἀπαγγελθείσης

KS § 19.75.228	ναυαγίας, ἐν
BMJ §48.15.23–16.1	ναυαγίας ἐν
GL §48.34	ναυαγίας ἐν
KS §19.75.229	ἀπώλεσεν, εὖ γε ποιεῖς εἶπεν,
BMJ §48.16.1	ἀπώλεσεν· "εὖ γε ποιεῖς, εἶπεν,
GL §48.34	ἀπώλεσεν· εὖ γε ποιεῖς, εἶπεν,
KS §19.75.229–30	συνελαύνουσα ἡμᾶς εἰς τὸν τρίβωνα καὶ τὴν στοάν.
BMJ §48.16.2	συνελαύ<νου>σα ἡμᾶς εἰς τὸν τρίβωνα καὶ τὴν στοάν".
GL §48.34	συνελαυ<νου>σα ἡμᾶς πρὸς τὸν τρίβωνα καὶ τὴν στοάν.
KS §20.75.232–3	κτημάτων, ὥσπερ τῆς ἐν αὐλῇ μοναρχικῇ διατριβῆς, ἣν οὐ μόνον οὐκ ἐπεθύμησά ποτ' ἔχειν,
BMJ §49.16.4–6	κτημάτων, ὥσπερ τῆς ἐν αὐλῇ μοναρχικῇ διατριβῆς ἣν οὐ μόνον οὐκ ἐπεθύμησα τότ' ἔχειν,
GL §49.34	κτημάτων, ὥσπερ τῆς ἐν αὐλῇ μοναρχικῇ διατριβῆς, ἣν οὐ μόνον οὐκ ἐπεθύμησά ποτ' ἔχειν,
KS §20.75.233–4	ἑλκούσης ἀντέσχον
BMJ §49.16.7	ἑλκούσης ἀντέσχον
GL §49.34	ἑλκούσης, ἀντέσχον
KS §20.75.234	οὐχ ἅπαξ οὐδὲ δὶς ἀλλὰ καὶ πολλάκις. Οὐ γὰρ
BMJ §49–§50a.16.7–8	οὐχ ἅπαξ οὐδὲ δὶς ἀλλὰ καὶ πολλάκις· 50a οὐδὲ γὰρ
GL §49–§50a.34	οὐχ ἅπαξ οὐδὲ δὶς ἀλλὰ καὶ πάνυ πολλάκις. 50a οὐδὲ γὰρ
KS §20.75.235–6	μέγα, <τὸ> μὴ μανῆναί <με> τὴν μανίαν πολλῶν τῶν ἐν αὐλῇ βασιλικῇ καταγηρασάντων,
BMJ §50a.16.8–10	μέγα μὴ μανῆναι τὴν μανίαν πολλῶν τῶν ἐν αὐλῇ βασιλικῇ κατηγορησάντων,
GL §50a.34	μέγα, μὴ μανῆναι τὴν αὐτὴν μανίαν πολλοῖς τῶν ἐν αὐλῇ βασιλικῇ καταγηράσαντων,
Polemis	μέγα μὴ μανῆναί τὴν <αὐτὴν> μανίαν πολλοῖς τῶν ἐν αὐλῇ βασιλικῶν καταγηρασάντων.
KS §20.75.236	ἀπολέσαντα φάρμακα,
BMJ §50b.16.10–11	ἀπολέσαντα <τὰ> φάρμακα,
GL §50b.34	ἀπολέσαντα <τὰ> φάρμακα,
KS §20.75.237	πάντα δὲ βιβλία καὶ προσέτι
BMJ §50b.16.11	πάντα δὲ <τὰ> βιβλία, καὶ προσέτι
GL §50b.34	πάντα δὲ <τὰ> βιβλία, καὶ προσέτι
KS §20.75.238–9	ἄλλαις, καὶ
BMJ §50b.16.14	ἄλλαις καὶ
GL §50b.34	ἄλλαις καὶ

KS §20.75.239–40	φιλοπονίαν ἐδείκνυτο, μὴ λυπηθῆναι
BMJ §50b.16.15	φιλοπονίαν ἐδείκνυτο μὴ λυπηθῆναι
GL §50b.34	φιλοπονίαν <ἄν> ἐπεδείκνυτο, μὴ λυπηθῆναι,
KS §20.75.240–1	μεγαλοψυχίας ἐχόμενον ἐπίδειγμα πρῶτον.
BMJ §50b.16.16–17	μεγαλοψυχίας ἐχόμενον ἐπίδειγμα πρῶτον.
GL §50b.36	μεγαλοψυχίας ἐσόμενον ἐπίδειγμα πρῶτον,
KS §21.76.242–3	ἃ σὺ γινώσκεις αὐτός,
BMJ §51.16.18	ἃ σὺ γινώσκεις αὐτός,
GL §51.36	ἃ σὺ καὶ γινώσκεις αὐτός,
Polemis	ἃ σὺ γινώσκειν αὐτός,
KS §21.76.243	συναναστραφεὶς
BMJ §51.16.19	συναναστραφεὶς
GL §51.36	συνανα[σ]τραφεὶς
KS 76.243–4	συμπαιδευθεὶς ἡμῖν φῇς, δεύτερον <δὲ> τὰ προσγενόμενα
BMJ §51.16.19–20	συμπαιδευθεὶς ἡμῖν [ἔφης], δεύτερον <δὲ> τὰ προσγινόμενα
GL §51.36	συμπαιδευθεὶς ἡμῖν [ἔφης], δεύτερον <δὲ> τὰ προσγινόμενα
Polemis	συμπαιδευθεὶς ἡμῖν ἔφης, δεύτερον <δὲ> τὰ προσγινόμενα
KS §21.76.245	Εὖ γάρ, ἴσθι,
BMJ §52.16.21	52 Εὖ γάρ ἴσθι,
GL §52.36	52 εὖ γάρ ἴσθι,
KS §21.76.246	τῶν τῆς τέχνης ἔργων. Ὁ
BMJ §52.16.22–17.1	τῶν τῆς τέχνης ἔργων· ὃ
GL §52.36	τῶν τῆς τύχης ἔργων. ὃ
KS §21.76.247	Θησέα παντὸς μᾶλλον ἀληθές ἐστιν, ἀκούσας δὲ τῶν ἐπῶν εἴσει·
BMJ §52.17.2–3	Θησέα, παντὸς μᾶλλον ἀληθές ἐστιν· ἀκούσας δὲ τῶν ἐπῶν εἴσει.
GL §52.36	Θησέα, παντὸς μᾶλλον ἀληθές ἐστιν· ἀκούσας δὲ τῶν ἐπῶν εἴσῃ·
KS §21.76.249	εἰς φροντίδας νοῦν
BMJ §52.17.5	εἰς φροντίδ' ἀεὶ
GL §52.36	εἰς φροντίδας καὶ
KS §21.76.249	συμφοράς τ' ἐβαλλόμην,
BMJ §52.17.5	συμφορὰς ἐβαλλόμην,
GL §52.36	συμφορὰς ἐβαλλόμην
KS §21.76.252	ἵν', εἴ
BMJ §52.17.8	ἵν', εἴ
GL §52.36	ἵν' εἴ

KS § 21.76.253	μή μοι νεῶρες προσπεσὸν
BMJ § 52.17.9	μή μοι νεῶρες προσπεσὸν
GL § 52.36	μή μοι νεωρῶς προσπεσὸν
KS § 21.76.253	δάκοι.
BMJ § 52.17.9	δάκῃ.
GL § 52.36	δάκῃ.
KS § 22.76.257–8	παρ' ὅλον τὸν χρόνον, ὡς τὰς ἱστορίας ἔγραψαν
BMJ § 54.18.1–2	παρ' ὅλον τὸν χρόνον, ὡς τὰς ἱστορίας ἔγραψαν
GL § 54.38	παρ' ὅλον τὸν χρόνον οὗ τὰς ἱστορίας ἔγραψαν
Polemis	παρ' ὅλον τὸν χρόνον, ὡς <ἐν> ταῖς ἱστορίαις ἔγραψαν
KS § 22.76.258	οἱ τοῦτ' ἔργον ἔχοντες,
BMJ § 54.18.2–3	οἱ τοῦτ' ἔργο<ν> ἔχοντες,
GL § 54.38	οἱ τοῦτ' ἔργον ἔχοντες
KS § 22.76.259	ἔπραξας <ἐν> Κομμόδου ὀλίγοις ἔτεσιν,
BMJ § 54.18.4	ἔπραξεν Κόμοδος ὀλίγοις ἔτεσιν,
GL § 54.38	ἔπραξε Κόμμοδος ἐν ὀλίγοις ἔτεσιν,
Polemis	ἔπραξαν <ἐν> Κομμόδου ὀλίγοις ἔτεσιν,
KS § 22–§ 23.76.261–2	ἔχω. 23 Μετὰ τοῦτο καὶ αὐτός τι κλασθῆναι προσδοκᾷς,
BMJ § 54–§ 55.18.6–7	ἔχω, 55 μετὰ τοῦ καὶ αὐτός τι κλασθῆναι προσδοκήσας,
GL § 54–§ 55.38	ἔχω, 55 μετὰ τοῦ καὶ αὐτὸς ἐπικλασθῆναι, προσδοκῶν
Polemis	ἔχω. Μετὰ τοῦτο καὶ αὐτὸς δικασθῆναι προσδόκα,
KS § 23.76.262–3	ἄλλοι μηδὲν ἀδικήσαντες,
BMJ § 55.18.8	ἄλλοι μηδὲ ἀδικήσαντες,
GL § 55.38	ἄλλοι μηδὲ<ν> ἀδικήσαντες
KS § 23.76.264–77.265	τις πεμφθῆναι προσδοκήσας ἅμα τῇ πάντων ἀπωλείᾳ τούτων ὧν εἶχε παρεσκεύασεν
BMJ § 55.18.9–11	τις πεμφθῆναι προσδοκήσας ἅμ(α) τῇ πάντων ἀπωλείᾳ τῶν <κτημάτων> ὧν εἶχε παρεσκεύασεν
GL § 55.38	τις προσδοκήσας πεμφθῆναι ἅμα τῇ πάντων ἀπωλείᾳ [τῶν] ὧν εἶχε, παρεσκεύασεν
Polemis	τις πεμφθῆναι προσδοκήσας ἅμα τῇ πάντων ἀπωλείᾳ τῶν ὧν εἶχε παρεσκεύασεν
KS § 23.77.265	εἴ που ἕν τι ἀπολέσας μόνον μηδενὸς
BMJ § 55.18.11–12	ἢ που κατά τι ἀπολέσας (γοῦν μη)δενὸς
GL § 55.38	ἢ που καί τι ἀπολέσας μηδενὸς
KS § 23.77.266	ἀφαιρεθείς, <οὐκ> ἔμελλε λυπήσεσθαι.
BMJ § 55.18.12–13	ἀφαιρεθείς, <οὐκ ἂν> ἔμελλε λυπηθήσεσθαι.
GL § 55.38	ἀφαιρεθεὶς ἔμελλε λυπηθήσεσθαι;

KS §23.77.267–8	εἶναι τὸν Εὐριπίδου λόγον ἀσκεῖν παρακελεύομαι τὰς φαντασίας σου τῆς ψυχῆς
BMJ §56.18.14–16	εἶναι τὸν Εὐριπίδου λόγον, ἀσκεῖν παρακελεύομαι τὰς φαντασίας σου τῆς ψυχῆς
GL §56.38	εἶναι τὸν Εὐριπίδου λόγον, ἀσκεῖν παρακελεύομαι τὰς φαντασίας σου τῆς ψυχῆς
KS §24.77.270	εὖ πρὸς ἀνδρείαν μήτ' ἀρίστῃ παιδείᾳ χρησαμένοις, ἣν
BMJ §57.18.18–19	εὖ πρὸς ἀνδρείαν, μήτ' ἀρίστῃ παιδείᾳ χρησαμένοις, ἣν
GL §57.38	εὖ πρὸς ἀνδρείαν, μήτ' ἀρίστῃ παιδείᾳ διαχρησαμένοις ἣν
KS §24.77.271	ἐμοὶ προυξένησε τύχη τις ἀγαθή, ὥς που
BMJ §57.18.19	ἐμοὶ προὐξένησε τύχη τις ἀγαθὴ ὥς που
GL §57.38	ἐμοὶ προὐξένησε τύχη τις ἀγαθή· ὥς που
KS §24.77.271–2	οἶσθα ὁποίαν. Ἣν μοι πατὴρ οὗ ἐγὼ
BMJ §57–§58.18.20–21	οἶσθα ὁποῖον. 58 Ἣν μοι πατὴρ οἵου ἐγὼ
GL §57–§[58].38	οἶσθα ὁποῖος [58] ἣν μοι πατήρ, οὗ ἐγὼ
KS §24.77.272–3	ἑκάστοτε βελτίων ἐμαυτοῦ τὴν ψυχὴν
BMJ §58.18.21–22	(ἑκάστο)τε βελτίων ἐμ(αυτοῦ) τὴν ψυχὴν
GL §[58].38	(ἑκάστ)οτε βελτίων ἐμαυτοῦ τὴν ψυχὴν
KS §24.77.274	τις ἀκριβῶς καὶ ὡς οὗτος ἐτίμησε δικαιοσύνην
BMJ §58.18.23–19.1	τις <οὕτως> ἀκριβῶς ὡς καὶ οὗτος ἐτίμησε δικαιοσύνην τε καὶ σωφροσύνην
GL §[58].38	[13v] τις ἀκριβῶς ὡσαύτως ἐτίμησε δικαιοσύνην
KS §24.77.274–5	καὶ δι' αὐτὰς <καὶ τὰς ἄλλας ἀρετάς.> {κἀκείνας} Ἔσχε <δὲ>
BMJ §58.19.1–2	σωφροσύνην καὶ δι' αὐτὰς κἀκείνας ἔσχε
GL §[58].40	σωφροσύνην· καὶ δὴ αὐτὸς κἀκείνας ἔσχε
KS §24.77.275	φύσει τοῦτο χωρὶς
BMJ §58.19.2	φύσει τοῦτο χωρὶς
GL §[58].40	φύσει [τοῦτο] χωρὶς
KS §24.77.276	λόγων· οὐ
BMJ §58–§59.19.3	λόγων. 59 Οὐ
GL §[58]–§59.40	λόγων. 59 οὐ
KS §24.77.276	νεότητι παρὰ
BMJ §59.19.3–4	νεότητι, παρὰ
GL §59.40	νεότητι παρὰ
KS §24.77.277	πάππῳ δὲ ἐμῷ,
BMJ §59.19.4	πάππῳ δὲ ἐμῷ,
GL §59.40	πάππῳ δ' ἐμῷ,

KS §24.77.277	ἀρετὴν τὸ
BMJ §59.19.5	ἀρετήν, τὸ
GL §59.40	ἀρετήν, τὸ
KS §24.77.278	κατὰ τὴν ἀρχιτεκτονίαν
BMJ §59.19.5	κατὰ τὴν ἀρχιτεκτονίαν
GL §59.40	κατ' ἀρχιτεκτονίαν
KS §24.77.278–9	ἀσκηθείς, ἐν αἷς καὶ αὐτὸ ἐκείνῳ ἦν πρῶτον. Ἔλεγε
BMJ §59.19.6	ἀσκηθεὶς ἐν οἷς καὶ αὐτὸ ἐκείνῳ πρῶτον· ἔλεγε
GL §59.40	ἀσκηθείς, ἐν αἷς καὶ αὐτὸς ἐκεῖνος ἦν πρῶτος. ἔλεγε
Polemis	ἀσκηθεὶς, ἐν αἷς καὶ αὐτὸ ἐκείνῳ ἦν πατρῷον. Ἔλεγε
KS §24.77.280	αὐτός, ἀλλὰ
BMJ §59.19.8	αὐτὸς ἀλλὰ
GL §59.40	αὐτὸς ἀλλὰ
KS §24.77.281	βεβιωκέναι, τὸν μὲν ἀρχιτέκτονα τὸν
BMJ §59.19.9	<βε>βιωκέναι, τὸν μὲν ἀρχιτέκτονα, τὸν
GL §59.40	βεβιωκέναι, τὸ μὲν ἀρχιτέκτονα, τὸν
KS §25.77.283–4	παιδείαν ὁμοίαν
BMJ §60.19.12–13	παιδείαν ὁμοίαν
GL §60.40	παιδείαν, ὁμοίαν
KS §25.77.286	Καὶ μὴν καὶ
BMJ §62.19.16	Καὶ μὴν καὶ
GL §62.40	καὶ μὴν οὖν
KS §25.77.286–7	βεβιωκότας οὐδὲν ἔσχε πλείω τῶν οἰωνῶν τούτων, οὓς
BMJ §62.19.16–17	βεβιωκότας οὐδὲν ἔσχε πλείω τῶν οἰωνῶν τούτων οὓς
GL §62.40	<βε>βιωκότας οὐδὲν ἔχειν πλέον τῶν ὄνων τούτων οὓς
KS §25.77.287	κατὰ <τὴν> τῶν Ῥωμαίων πόλιν
BMJ §62.19.17–18	κατὰ <τὴν> τῶν Ῥωμαίων πόλιν
GL §62.40	κατὰ τὴν τῶν Ῥωμαίων πόλιν
KS §25.77.288	περιαγομένους ἕνεκα τοῦ
BMJ §62.19.18–19	περιαγομένους ἕνεκα τοῦ
GL §62.40	περιαγομένους ἕνεκα τοῦ
KS §25.77.288–9	μισθῷ, τοὺς
BMJ §62.19.19	μισθῷ· τοὺς
GL §62.40	μισθῷ, τοὺς
KS §25.77.289	τοὺς δὲ τῶν τοιούτων ἡδονῶν καταφρονοῦντας,
BMJ §62.19.19–20	τοὺς δὲ τῶν τοιούτων ἡδονῶν καταφρονοῦντας,
GL §62.40	τοὺς δὲ τῶν τοιούτων καταφρονοῦντας,

KS § 25.77–78.290–1	ἔπεισεν ἀπομαντευόμενος
BMJ § 62.19.22	ἐπήνεσεν ἀπομαντευόμενος
GL § 62.40	ἐπήνεσεν, ἀπομαντευόμενος
KS § 25.78.291	κρεῖττον <εἶναι> τὸ ἀγαθὸν
BMJ § 62.19.22–20.1	κρεῖττον <ὂν> τὸ ἀγαθὸν
GL § 62.40	κρεῖττον τὸ ἀγαθὸν
KS § 25.78.291	ἰδίαν ἔχον φύσιν,
BMJ § 62.20.1	ἰδίαν ἔχειν φύσιν,
GL § 62.40	ἰδίαν ἔχειν φύσιν,
KS § 25.78.293	ἐπιστήμην θείων καὶ ἀνθρωπίνων πραγμάτων
BMJ § 63.20.3–4	ἐπισ<τ>ήμην θείων καὶ ἀνθρωπίνων πραγμάτων
GL § 63.42	ἐπιστήμην θείων τε καὶ ἀνθρωπίνων πραγμάτων
KS § 25.78.295	ἐλάχιστον, δῆλον
BMJ § 63.20.6	ἐλάχιστον, δῆλον
GL § 63.42	ἐλάχιστον δῆλον
KS § 25.78.295–6	καὶ τῶν ἄλλων ἁπάντων ἀκριβῆ γνῶσιν οὐκ ἔχομεν. Ὁ
BMJ § 63–§ 64.20.6–7	καὶ τῶν ἄλλων ἁπάντων ἀκριβῆ γνῶσιν οὐκ ἔχομεν· 64 ὁ
GL § 63–§ 64.42	καὶ ἄλλων ἁπάντων ἀκριβῆ γνῶσιν οὐκ ἔχομεν. 64 ὁ
KS § 25.78.297	πράγματά ἐστιν,
BMJ § 64.20.9	πράγματά εἰσιν,
GL § 64.42	πράγματά ἐστιν,
KS § 25.78.297–8	κατὰ μέρος, οὐδ'
BMJ § 64.20.9	κατὰ μέρος, οὐδ'
GL § 64.42	κατὰ μέρος οὐδ'
KS § 25.78.298	τι ἐλέσθαι καὶ φυγεῖν
BMJ § 64.20.10	τι ἐλέσθαι καὶ φυγεῖν
GL § 64.42	τι ἐλέσθαι ἢ φυγεῖν
KS § 25.78.300	πολλοὺς ὁρᾶν ὑπὸ
BMJ § 64.20.13	πολλοὺς ὁρᾶν ὑπὸ
GL § 64.42	πολλοὺς ὁρῶν ὑπὸ
KS § 26.78.302	26 Ἐν τούτῳ τρεφόμενος
BMJ § 65.20.14	65 Ἐν τούτῳ τρεφόμενος
GL § 65.42	65 ἐν τούτῳ δὲ τρεφόμενος
Polemis	Ἐν τούτῳ στρεφόμενος
KS § 26.78.302–3	μικρὰ πάντα εἶναι νομίζω καὶ σχολὰς καὶ ἄρμενα
BMJ § 65.20.15	μικρὰ πάντα εἶναι νομίζω. Καὶ σχολὴν καὶ ἄρμενα
GL § 65.42	μικρὰ πάντα εἶναι νομίζω, καὶ σχολῇ γ' ἂν ἄρμενα
Polemis	μικρὰ πάντα εἶναι νομίζω καὶ σχολῇ καὶ ἄρμενα

KS §26.78.303–4	πλοῦτον <καὶ οὐκ> ἄξια σπουδῆς ὑπολάβοιμι <ἄν>· τῷ
BMJ §65.20.16–17	πλοῦτον <πῶς ἄν> ἄξια σπουδῆς ὑπολάβοιμι; Τῷ
GL §65.42	πλοῦτον ἄξια σπουδῆς ὑπολάβοιμι. τῷ
Polemis	πλοῦτον ἄξια σπουδῆς ὑπολάβοιμι· τῷ
KS §26.78.305	εἶναι, τίς ἂν
BMJ §65.20.18	εἶναι, τί ἂν
GL §65.42	εἶναι τί ἂν
KS §26.78.305	ἀκόλουθον γάρ ἐστι
BMJ §66.20.19	66 Ἀκόλουθον γάρ ἐστι
GL §66.42	66 ἀκόλουθόν ἐστι,
KS §26.78.306	μεγαλεῖα ἐστερῆσθαι λυπεῖσθαί
BMJ §66.20.20	μεγαλεῖα ἐστερῆσθαι, λυπεῖσθαί
GL §66.42	μεγάλων ἐστερῆσθαι, λυπεῖσθαί
KS §26.78.307	σμικρῶν ἀεὶ διὰ τέλους καταφρονοῦντι <μή>.
BMJ §66.20.21–22	σμικρῶν ἀεὶ διὰ τέλους καταφρονοῦντι, <μηδέποτε λυπεῖσθαι>.
GL §66.42	σμικρῶν, ἀεὶ διατελεῖν καταφρονοῦντι.
KS §26.78.308	σμικρὸν εἶναι
BMJ §67.21.1	σμικρῶν εἶναι
GL §67.42	σμικρῶν εἶναι
KS §26.78.308–9	ἀλλὰ μετὰ πολλῆς <ἀκριβείας>, {εἰσὶ}
BMJ §67.21.1–2	ἀλλὰ μετὰ πολλῆς <ἀκριβείας> εἴσει
GL §67.42	ἀλλὰ μετ' ἀποδείξεως, τὰ γεγραμμένα
KS §26.78.309–10	{ἃ} διελθὼν εὑρήσεις· ἀλλὰ
BMJ §67.21.3	διελθὼν ἃ εὑρήσει(ς· ἀλλὰ)
GL §67.42	[ἃ] διελθὼν εὑρήσεις· ἀλλὰ
KS §26.78.310	σπουδῆς οὐδὲ
BMJ §67.21.4	σπουδῆς, οὐδὲ
GL §67.42	σπουδῆς, οὐδὲ
KS §26.78.311	μέρει συνέθηκα.
BMJ §67.21.5	μο(ίρᾳ) συνέθηκα.
GL §67.42	μοίρᾳ συνέθηκα.
KS §26.78.311	ἀοχλησίαν
BMJ §68.21.5	ἀοχλ<ησ>ίαν
GL §68.42	ἀοχλησίαν
KS §26.78.312	νομίζουσιν εἶναι, ὃ οὔτε
BMJ §68.21.6	νομίζουσιν εἶναι ὃ οὔτε
GL §68.42 and 44	νομίζουσιν ὃ οὔτε

KS §26.78.312	οὔτε ἄλλον ἄνθρωπον
BMJ §68.21.6–7	οὔτε ἄλλον ἄνθρωπον
GL §68.44	οὔτε ἄλλον ἀνθρώπων
KS §26.78.312–3	τι φέρειν οἶδα·
BMJ §68.21.7	τι φέρον οἶδα·
GL §68.44	τι φέρον οἶδα.
KS §26.79.314	κατὰ ψυχήν. Ἀλλὰ
BMJ §68.21.8	κατὰ ψυχήν· ἀλλὰ
GL §68.44	κατὰ ψυχήν· ἀλλὰ
KS §26.79.314	ὑπομνήσεων ἐπέστησα
BMJ §68.21.9	ὑπομνήσεων ἐπεστησάμην
GL §68.44	ὑπομνημάτων ἐπεστήσαμεν,
KS §26.79.315	τοῖς κατ' Ἐπικούρου.
BMJ §68.21.10	τῷ κατ' Ἐπίκουρον.
GL §68.44	τῷ κατ' Ἐπικούρου.
KS §27.79.316	27 Τελέως μὲν οὖν <οἶμαι> ἀποκρίνασθαί
BMJ §69.21.10–11	69 Τελείως μὲν οὖν <οἶμαι> ἀποκρίνασθαί
GL §69.44	69 τελείως μὲν οὖν ἀποκρίνασθαί
KS §27.79.316–7	ἐρώτησιν ἣν ἐποιήσω περὶ τῆς ἀλυπίας· αὐτὰρ
BMJ §69.21.11–12	ἐρώτησιν ἣν ἐποιήσω περὶ τῆς ἀλυπησίας, ἀτὰρ
GL §69.44	ἐρώτησιν ἥν ἐποιήσω περὶ τῆς ἀλυπίας· αὐτὰρ
KS §27.79.318–20	ὑπέσχοντο, οὕτως καὶ αὐτὸν ἀποφαίνεσθαι μηδέποτ[ε δ]ὴ μηδὲ νῦν λυπήσεσθαι, {τῶν φιλοσόφων} καὶ μάλιστα ἐπειδὴ φῂς
BMJ §70.21.14–16	ὑπέσχοντο μηδ(έποτε) μηδὲ νῦν λυπηθήσεσθαι [τῶν φιλοσόφων], οὕτως καὶ αὐτὸν ἀποφαίνεσθαι καὶ μάλιστα, ἐπειδὴ φῂς
GL §70.44	ὑπέσχοντο μηδέποτε μηδένα [14r] λυπηθήσεσθαι τῶν [φιλο] σοφῶν, οὕτως καὶ αὐτὸν ἀποφαίνεσθαι, καὶ μάλιστα ἐπειδὴ φῂς
Polemis	ὑπέσχοντο, οὕτως καὶ αὐτὸν ἀποφαίνεσθαι μηδέποτ[ε δ]ὴ μηδὲ νῦν λυπήσεσθαι τὸν φιλόσοφον καὶ μάλιστα ἐπειδὴ φῂς
KS §27.79.321	Ἐγὼ δέ, εἰ μέν τίς ἐστιν τοιοῦτος
BMJ §71.21.17	Ἐγὼ δὲ εἰ μέν τίς ἐστιν τοιοῦτος
GL §71.44	ἐγὼ δὲ εἰ μέν τίς ἐστι τοιοῦτος
KS §27.79.321–2	τὸ πᾶν, οὐκ ἔχω λέγειν· τοῦ δ' αὐτὸς <μὴ> εἶναι τοιοῦτος ἀκριβῆ γνῶσιν
BMJ §71.21.18–19	τὸ πᾶν, οὐκ ἔχω λέγειν, τοῦ δ' αὐτὸς εἶναι τοιοῦτος ἀκριβῆ γνῶσιν
GL §71.44	τὸ πᾶν, οὐκ ἔχω λέγειν, τοῦ δ' αὐτὸς <μὴ> εἶναι τοιοῦτος ἀκριβῆ γνῶσιν

KS § 27.79.322	ἔχω. Χρημάτων
BMJ §71.21.19	ἔχω· χρημάτων
GL §71.44	ἔχω. χρημάτων
KS §27.79.323	καταφρονῶ
BMJ §71.21.20	καταφ<ρ>ονῶ
GL §71.44	καταφρονῶ
KS §27.79.325	ἐπαγγέλλεσθαι
BMJ §71.22.1	ἐπαγγέλ<λ>εσθαι
GL §71.44	ἐπαγγέλλεσθαι
KS §27.79.326–7	τοιαῦτα, καὶ θεοῖς εὔχομαι
BMJ §72a–72b.22.4	τοιαῦτα. 72b Καὶ θεοῖς εὔχομαι
GL §72.44	τοιαῦτα, καὶ <τοῖς> θεοῖς εὔχομαι
KS §27.79.327	ποτε· καὶ
BMJ §72b.22.5	ποτε· καὶ
GL §72.44	ποτε, καὶ
KS §27.79.328	συνέβη, διὰ
BMJ §72b.22.6	συνέβη, διὰ
GL §72.44	συνέβη διὰ
KS §28.79.329	Μουσώνιον
BMJ §73.22.7	Μουσόνιον
GL §72.44	Μουσώνιον
KS §28.79.329–30	ὥς φασιν, ὦ Ζεῦ,
BMJ §73.22.8	ὥς φασι, ὦ Ζεῦ,
GL §73.46	ὥς φασιν, ὦ Ζεῦ,
KS §28.79.330	πέμπε περίστασιν.
BMJ §73.22.8–9	πέμπε <ἢν θέλεις> περίστασιν.
GL §73.46	πέμπε περίστασιν.
KS §28.79.330	διὰ παντός· ὦ Ζεῦ,
BMJ §73.22.9	διὰ παντός, ὦ Ζεῦ,
GL §73.46	διὰ παντός, ὦ Ζεῦ,
KS §28.79.331	μοι
BMJ §73.22.10	μοι
GL §73.46	μοι
KS §28.79.332–3	αὐτό, βουλόμενος οὐ
BMJ §74.22.12–13	αὐτὸ βουλόμενος <ἀλλ'> οὐ
GL §74.46	αὐτὸ βουλόμενος οὐ

KS § 28.79.333–4	τῆς κεφαλῆς ἐπιδείξασθαι καρτερίαν· ἀσκεῖν <δ'> ἀξιώσας
BMJ § 74.22.13–14	τῆς κεφαλῆς ἐπιδείξασθαι καρτερίαν· ἀσκεῖν <δ'> ἀξιώσας
GL § 74.46	τῆς κεφαλῆς ἐπιδείξασθαι καρτερίαν, ἀσκεῖν δ' ἀξιώσας
KS § 28.79.334	δεινόν, ὡς
BMJ § 74.22.14	δεινόν, ὡς
GL § 74.46	δεινὸν ὡς
KS § 28.79.334–5	περιπεσεῖν {δὲ} οὐκ ἂν εὐξαίμην
BMJ § 74.22.15	περιπεσεῖν [δὲ] οὐκ ἂν εὐξαίμην
GL § 74.46	περιπεσεῖν [δὲ] οὐκ ἂν εὐξαίμην
KS § 28.79.335	τῶν λυπῆσαί με δυναμένων.
BMJ § 74.22.16	τῶν λυπῆσαί με δυναμένων.
GL § 74.46	τῶν λυπῆσαί με δυναμένων.
KS § 28.79.337	τῶν ἔξωθεν αἰτίων
BMJ § 75.22.19	τῶν ἔξωθεν αἰτίων
GL § 75.46	τῶν ἔξωθεν αἰτιῶν
KS § 28.79.338–80.339	βουλοίμην <ἂν> ὡς διαφθεῖραί μου τὴν ὑγείαν, οὔτε
BMJ § 75.22.19–20	βουλοίμην <ἂν> ὡς διαφθεῖραί μου τὴν ὑγείαν, οὔτε
GL § 75.46	βουλοίμην ἂν ὡς διαφθεῖραί μου τὴν ὑγείαν οὔτε
KS § 28.80.340	αὐτῶν, ἀλλὰ διὰ παντός, ὅση <ἂν> δύναμις ἐμοὶ ᾖ,
BMJ § 76.22.22–23	αὐτῶν, ἀλλὰ διὰ παντὸς ὅση δύναμις ἐμοὶ ᾖ,
GL § 76.46	αὐτῶν, ἀλλὰ διὰ παντὸς ὅση δύναμις ἐμοὶ ἐστι,
KS § 28.80.341	ἐντεθῆναι πειρῶμαι τοσαύτην, ὡς ἀντέχειν
BMJ § 76.22.23–23.1	ἐντεθῆναι πειρῶμαι τοσαύτην ὡς ἀντέχειν
GL § 76.46	ἐντιθέναι πειρῶμαι τοσαύτην ὡς ἀντέχειν
KS § 28.80.343	μήτε τὴν ψυχήν, ἣν ἐμοί φασι ὑπάρχειν οἱ σοφοί,
BMJ § 76.23.3–4	μήτε τὴν ψυχὴν ἣν ἐμοί φασι ὑπάρχειν οἱ σοφοί,
GL § 76.46	μήτε τὴν ψυχὴν ἣν ἔνιοί φασιν ὑπάρχειν τοῖς σοφοῖς,
KS § 28.80.344	παραλιπεῖν – ἐπαινῶ
BMJ § 76–§ 77.23.5	παραλιπεῖν. 77 Ἐπαινῶ
GL § 76–§ 77.46	παραλιπεῖν. 77 ἐπαινῶ
KS § 28.80.345–51	delete {ὅπερ ὑπὲρ Εὐριπίδους … ψυχὴν δάκῃ}
BMJ § 77.23.5–6	ὅ<σ>περ ὑπὲρ Εὐριπίδου
GL § 77.46	ὅπερ παρ' Εὐριπίδει
BMJ § 77.23.7	παρά τινος σοφοῦ
GL § 77.46	παρὰ σοφοῦ τινος
BMJ § 77.23.8	φροντίδ' ἀεὶ
GL § 77.46	φροντίδας καὶ

BMJ §77.23.10	θανάτους τ' ἀώρους
GL §77.48	θανάτους τε ἀώρους
BMJ §77.23.11	ἵν', εἴ
GL §77.48	ἵν' εἴ
BMJ §77.23.12	μάτην <νεῶρες>
GL §77.48	μή μοι <νεωρῶς>
KS §28.80.352–3	περιστάσεις <ὁδόν>. Οὐ μὴν ὑπεράνω
BMJ §78a–§78b.23.14	περιστάσεις. 78b Οὐ μὴν ὑπεράνω
GL §78a–§78b.48	περιστάσεις, 78b οὐ μὴν ὑπεράνω
KS §28.80.353–4	ἑκάστοτε λέγειν πειρῶμαι ὡς οὐδὲν οὐδέποτε ἐπαγγειλάμενος
BMJ §78b.23.15–24.1	ἑκάστοτε λέγειν πειρώμενος, ὡς οὐδὲν οὐδέποτε ἐπαγγειλάμενος
GL §78b.48	ἑκάστοτε λέγειν εἰώθαμεν, ὡς οὐδέποτε ἐπηγγειλάμην
Polemis	ἑκάστοτε λέγειν πειρῶμαι ὡς οὐδὲν οὐδέποτε ἐπηγγειλάμην
KS §28.80.355	ἐπεδειξάμην, ὅτι χρημάτων
BMJ §78b.24.2	ἐπεδειξάμην, ὅτι χρημάτων
GL §78b.48	ἐπεδειξάμην, ὅτι χρημάτων
Polemis	ἐπεδειξάμην, ἔτι χρημάτων
KS §28.80.355–6	καταφρονῶ, μέχρις
BMJ §78b.24.3	καταφρονῶ μέχρις
GL §78b.48	καταφρονῶ μέχρις
KS §28.80.356	αὐτῶν, ὡς
BMJ §78b.24.4	αὐτῶν ὡς
GL §78b.48	αὐτῶν ὡς
KS §28.80.357	ῥιγοῦν – τὸ γὰρ διψῆν ὑπάρχει καὶ αὐτὸ τούτοις –, {ἕπεσθαι}
BMJ §78b.24.4–6	ῥιγοῦν <μήτε διψῆν> [τὸ γὰρ διψῆν ὑπάρχει καὶ αὐτὸ τούτοις ἕπεσθαι],
GL §78b.48	ῥιγοῦν – [14v] τῷ γὰρ διψῆν ὑπάρχει καὶ αὐτῷ τούτοις ἕπεσθαι] –
KS §28.80.358	ἂν ἐπιτρέπῃ μοι καὶ †τοῦτο δύνασθαι
BMJ §78b.24.6–7	ἂν ἐπιτρέπηταί μοι καὶ [τοῦ]τὸ δύνασθαι
GL §78b.48	ἂν ἐπιτρέπῃ μὲν καὶ τοῦτο,
KS §28.80.359	φίλῳ, καί
BMJ §78b.24.7	φίλῳ καί
GL §78b.48	φίλῳ καί
KS §28.80.359	βιβλίον ἕπεσθαι τοῖς λεγομένοις. Οἱ
BMJ §78b–§79a.24.8–9	βιβλίον ἕπεσθαι τοῖς λεγομένοις· 79a οἱ
GL §78b–§79.48	βιβλίον ἕπεσθαι τοῖς λεγομένοις. 79 οἱ

KS § 28.80.360-1	στερίσκουσι, ἀγαπῴην δ' <ἂν> ἐν αὐτοῖς εἰ καρτερίαν ἐπιδείξασθαι δυνηθείην.
BMJ § 79a.24.9-11	στερίσκουσι· ἀγαπᾶν δὲ <δεῖ> ἐν αὐτοῖς εἴ τις καρτερίαν ἐπιδείξασθαι ἐδυνήθη.
GL § 79.48	στερίσκουσι, ἀγαπῶ δὲ ἐν αὐτοῖς εἰ καρτερίαν ἐπιδείξασθαι δυνηθείην.
KS § 29.80.362	29 Τὰ δ' ἄλλα <ἃ> γράφων
BMJ § 79b.24.11	79b Τὰ δ' ἄλλα γεγραφὼς
GL § 79.48	ἃ δ' ἄλλοις γράφων
Polemis	Ἃ δ' ἄλλα γράφων
KS § 29.80.362	εἰς ἀλυπίαν
BMJ § 79b.24.11	εἰς ἀλυπησίαν
GL § 79.48	εἰς ἀλυπίαν
KS § 29.80.362-3	συνεβούλευσα, περιττὰ σοὶ λέγειν, ὃν
BMJ § 79b.24.12	συνεβούλευσα περιττά σοι λέγειν ὃν
GL § 79.48	συνεβούλευσα περιττά σοι λέγειν, ὃν
KS § 29.81.364	χρώμενον ἀφροδισίων
BMJ § 79b.24.14	χρώμενον, ἀφροδισίων
GL § 79.48	χρώμενον, ἀφροδισίων
KS § 29.81.364	ἐγκρατέστατον, οἷς
BMJ § 79b.24.14	ἐγκρατέστατον οἷς
GL § 79.48	ἐγκρατέστατον, οἷς
KS § 29.81.365	πλειόνων. Εἰ {τε} δὲ μὴ πλουτοῦσι,
BMJ § 79b–§ 80.24.15–16	πλειόνων <εἴτε πλουτοῦσιν>, 80 εἴτε δὲ μὴ πλουτοῦσι,
GL § 79–§ 80.48	πλειόνων. 80 εἰ [τε] δὲ μὴ πλουτοῦσι,
KS § 29.81.366	μεθ' ἡμέραν καὶ νύκτα· εἶτ'
BMJ § 80.24.17–25.1	μεθ' ἡμέραν καὶ νύκτα, εἶτ'
GL § 80.48	μεθ' ἡμέραν καὶ νύκτα, εἶτ'
KS § 29.81.366-7	ὧν ἀπορήσουσιν
BMJ § 80.25.1	ὧν <οὐκ> ἀπορήσουσιν
GL § 80.48 and 50	ὧν εὐπορήσουσιν
Polemis	ὧν εὐπορήσουσιν
KS § 29.81.367	σκοπούμενοι δι'
BMJ § 80.25.2	σκοπούμενοι, δι'
GL § 80.50	σκοπούμενοι δι'
KS § 29.81.368	ἀναγκάζονται. Καὶ
BMJ § 80.25.3	ἀναγκάζονται, καὶ
GL § 80.50	ἀναγκάζονται, καὶ

KS §29.81.368–9	ὀλοφύρονται, τυχόντες
BMJ §80.25.3–4	ὠρύονται, τυχόντες
GL §80.50	ὠρύ[ρ]ονται, τυχόντες
Polemis	ὀδύρονται. τυχόντες

KS §29–§30.81.369–71	τούτω δὲ τῷ μοχθηροτάτῳ βίῳ περιπίπτουσι <καὶ> ταῖς ἀπλήστοις ἐπιθυμίαις προσγίνονται. 30 Τινὲς οὖν οὐχ ὡς οἱ πολλοὶ λυποῦνται, οἳ μετρίως ἅπτονται
BMJ §80–§81.25.4–7	τοῦτο δὲ τῷ μοχθηροτέρῳ βίῳ περιπίπτουσι ταῖς ἀπλήστοις ἐπιθυμίαις. 81 Προσγίνονταί τινες οὖν [οὐχ ὡς οἱ πολλοὶ λυποῦνται] οἳ μετρίως ἅπτονται
GL §80–§81.50	τούτου δ᾽ ἔτι μοχθηροτέρῳ βίῳ περιπίπτουσιν οἷς ἄπληστοι ἐπιθυμίαι προσγίνονται. 81 τίνες οὖν οὐχ ὡς οἱ πολλοὶ λυποῦνται; οἳ μετρίως ἅπτονται

KS §30.81.372–3	πολιτικῆς· ᾧ γὰρ ἂν τούτων εὑρεθῇ τις ἀμέτρως,
BMJ §81.25.8–9	πολιτικῆς, ὧν [γὰρ] ἂν τούτων εὑρεθῇ τις ἀμέτρως,
GL §81.50	πολιτικῆς. ὃς γὰρ ἂν τούτων ἐρασθῇ τινος ἀμέτρως,

KS §30.81.374–5	αὐξήσει δὲ τὰς ἐν αὐτῇ κακίας
BMJ §81.25.11	αὐξήσας δὲ τὰς ἐν αὐτῇ κακίας
GL §81.50	αὐξήσει δὲ τὰς ἐν αὐτῇ κακίας

KS §30.81.375	παντός, ὡς
BMJ §81.25.12	παντὸς ὡς
GL §81.50	παντὸς ὡς

KS §30.81.375	προύθετο
BMJ §81.25.12	προύθετο
GL §81.50	προύθετο

KS §30.81.375–6	δυνάμενος. Αἱ γάρ τοι μέγισται τῶν ἐπιθυμιῶν
BMJ §81–§82.25.12–13	δυνάμενος· 82 αἱ γάρ τοι μέγισται τῶν ἐπιθυμιῶν
GL §81–§82.50	δυνάμενος· 82 αἱ γάρ τοι μέγισται τῶν ἐπιθυμιῶν

KS §30.81.377	ὥστε οὐδεὶς <ἂν> πιστεύσειε
BMJ §82.25.14	ὥστε οὐδεὶς <ἂν> πιστεύσειε
GL §82.50	ὥστε οὐδεὶς ἂν πιστεύσειε

KS §30.81.377–8	διακείμενος, ὥσπερ οὐδὲ τῷ ποτε πιστεύοντι, ἀλλ᾽
BMJ §82–§83.25.14–15	διακείμενος ὥσπερ οὐδὲ τῷ ποτε πιστεύοντι. 83 Ἀλλ᾽
GL §82–§83.50	διακείμενος, ὥσπερ οὐδ᾽ ἐγώ ποτ᾽ ἐπίστευόν τι. 83 ἀλλ᾽

KS §30–§31.81.378–9	γίνεται. 31 Καί
BMJ §83.25.16	γίνεται· καί
GL §83.50	γίνεται, καί

KS §31.81.379–80	τὰς μυριάδας μὲν ἔχοντος ἑπτακισχιλίας
BMJ §83.25.17–18	τὰς μυριάδας μὲν ἔχοντος, ἑπτακισχιλίους
GL §83.50	τοῦ μυριάδας μὲν ἔχοντος, ἑπτακισχιλίους
KS §31.81.380–1	οὔτε δὲ κοινωνοῦντος ὧν εἶχεν ἑτέροις οὔτ' ἀπολαύοντος. Ὁ
BMJ §83.25.18–19	οὔτε δὲ κοινωνοῦν<τος> ὧν εἶχεν ἑτέροις, οὐτ' ἀπολαβόντος· ὁ
GL §83.50	οὐδὲν δὲ κοινωνοῦντος ὧν εἶχεν ἑτέροις, οὔτε ἀπολαύοντος· ὁ
KS §31.81.383	τοῦ ἀνδρὸς ὑπηγόρευσα χωρισθεὶς
BMJ §84.26.1–2	τοῦ ἀνδρός, ὑπηγόρευσα χωρισθεὶς
GL §84.52	τοῦ ἀνδρός, ὑπηγόρευσα χωρισθεὶς
KS §31.81.384	πλουσίων, ὃ καὶ αὐτό σοι πέπομφα.
BMJ §84.26.3	πλουσίων ὃ καὶ αὐτὶ σοὶ πέπομφα.
GL §84.52	πλουσίων, ὃ καὶ αὐτό σοι πέπομφα.

Index of Ancient Authors and Texts

I. Galen

Protrepticus (Kühn)
1.1 K	220
1.2 K	190
1.3 K	219–20
1.5 K	219–20
1.7 K	177

De optima doctrina
1.41 K	118

Quod optimus medicus sit quoque philosophus
1.60 K	138
1.61 K	138

De sectis ad eos qui introducuntur
1.64–105 K	53

De constitutione artis medicae
1.224–304 K	54
1.244–5 K	139
1.302 K	212

Ars Medica
1.305–412 K	53
1.360 K	211
1.361 K	214
1.371 K	211
1.371–2 K	197, 209
1.406 K	214

De temperamentis
1.609 K	150–1
1.624 K	216
1.630 K	209
1.633 K	209, 212

De naturalibus facultatibus
2.41 K	185, 199
2.42 K	185, 199
2.52–53 K	139
2.141 K	140
2.179 K	139

De usu partium
3.7–9 K	137
3.24 K	152
3.25 K	152
3.237 K	206
3.365–6 K	139
3.803 K	206
4.144 K	197
4.169 K	206
4.360–1 K	137

De semine
4.629 K	216

De foetuum formatione
4.695 K	214

De optima corporis nostri constitutione
4.742 K	208
4.743 K	209

Quod animi mores corporis temperamenta sequuntur
4.767–822 K	177
4.768 K	216
4.768–9 K	188
4.779 K	209
4.788 K	180
4.798 K	216

4.813 K	177	5.53 K	95, 138, 210
4.814–21 K	188	5.54 K	93, 95, 135, 159, 210, 219
4.816–8 K	177	5.55 K	210
		5.56 K	210

De propriorum animi cuiuslibet affectuum dignotione et curatione

De animi cuiuslibet peccatorum dignotione et curatione

5.1 K	254		
5.5 K	13	5.58 K	255
5.7 K	210, 226, 246, 255, 272	5.61 K	133
5.9 K	163	5.62 K	170
5.11 K	115	5.67 K	137
5.13 K	178, 261	5.72 K	96
5.14 K	115	5.78–79 K	139
5.15 K	115, 118	5.92–93 K	139
5.15–16 K	183		
5.16–24 K	180	*De atra bile*	
5.22 K	180	5.104–48 K	54
5.24 K	210, 255		
5.25 K	210	*De usu pulsuum*	
5.27 K	135	5.149 K	139
5.35 K	210, 255, 269		
5.36 K	210	*De placitis Hippocratis et Platonis*	
5.37 K	11, 94–5, 97, 135, 145, 210, 212, 219, 254	5.239 K	209
		5.239–40 K	209
5.37–41 K	107	5.360–504 K	254
5.37–57 K	135	5.368 K	227
5.38 K	210	5.368–9 K	248
5.38–59 K	239	5.397 K	227
5.40–41 K	256	5.415–42 K	12
5.40–43 K	135	5.417 K	113–5
5.41–42 K	128, 257	5.417–8 K	110–1
5.42 K	257	5.418 K	185, 236
5.42–43 K	139	5.420–1 K	92
5.43 K	11, 94, 135, 143, 210, 257, 270	5.421 K	121
		5.464 K	216
5.43–44 K	105, 135, 178, 214, 228, 266	5.469 K	208
		5.471 K	101
5.44 K	104, 257, 260, 264, 269	5.472 K	101
5.44–45 K	260	5.472–3 K	101
5.45 K	103, 135	5.763 K	171
5.45–52 K	135	5.783 K	138
5.46 K	260	5.815 K	138
5.48 K	106, 125, 260, 264		
5.49 K	101, 214, 258–9	*De parvae pilae exercitio*	
5.50 K	105, 259	5.899–910 K	54
5.51–2 K	214		
5.52 K	94, 103, 210	*De sanitate tuenda*	
5.52–3 K	249	6.40 K	237, 248

6.186 K	93, 219	*De pulsibus ad Tirones*	
6.418 K	214	8.473 K	211

De alimentorum facultatibus
6.478 K 209
6.572 K 209
6.685 K 209

De causis pulsuum
9.160 K 211

De dignotione ex insomniis
6.832–5 K 54

De crisibus
9.550–766 K 54
9.620 K 139

De morborum differentiis
6.836–80 K 53

De diebus decretoriis
9.795 K 214

De causis morborum
7.1–41 K 53

De methodo medendi
10.1–2 K 196
10.2 K 133
10.3 K 197
10.5 K 185, 199
10.14–17 K 137
10.77 K 140
10.117–8 K 140
10.334 K 185, 199
10.375 K 139, 185, 199
10.514 K 209
10.535 K 212
10.555 K 212
10.562 K 214
10.666 K 212
10.668 K 214
10.671 K 211–2
10.679 K 211–2
10.685 K 212–3
10.687 K 211–2
10.692 K 212
10.847 K 209, 212
10.865 K 214

De symptomatum differentiis
7.42–84 K 54

De symptomatum causis
7.85–146 K 54
7.147–204 K 54
7.205–272 K 54

De morborum temporibus
7.406–39 K 53
7.440–62 K 53

Adversus eos qui de typis scripserunt
7.475–512 K 54

De plenitudine
7.513–83 K 54

De tremore, palpitatione, convulsione et rigore
7.635–6 K 214

Ad Glauconem de methodo medendi
11.12 K 212
11.13 K 212
11.16 K 212
11.143 K 214

De difficultate respirationis
7.877 K 214

De locis affectis
8.32 K 226, 246
8.90 K 139
8.120 K 230
8.283 K 214
8.302 K 209

De curandi ratione per venae sectionem
11.267 K 214
11.281 K 214

De purgantium medicamentorum facultate
11.323–42 K   54

Quos, Quibus catharticis medicamentis et quando purgare oporteat
11.343–56 K   54

Puero epileptico consilium
11.357–78 K   53
11.360 K   212

De compositione medicamentorum per genera
13.435 K   178
13.459 K   209
13.861 K   209

De antidotis
14.1–209 K   178
14.3–5 K   212
14.65 K   177–8, 192

De theriaca ad Pisonem
14.215   81
14.283–85   192

De praenotione ad Epigenem
14.599–673 K   54, 199
14.602 K   137–9
14.627 K   54
14.631 K   212
14.631–3 K   136
14.632 K   212
14.632–3 K   211
14.633 K   212
14.634 K   212
14.647–9 K   178, 187–8
14.647–51 K   178
14.648–9 K   187–9
14.650 K   178
14.657 K   178
14.660 K   127, 192
14.661 K   178
14.672 K   214

Introductio seu medicus
14.674–797 K   53

In Hippocratis de natura hominis
15.114 K   212
15.117 K   212

In Hippocratis de acutorum morborum victu
15.418–919 K   54
15.866 K   212
15.867 K   212

In Hippocratis de praedictionibus
16.489–840 K   54

In Hippocratis epidemiarum libri, I–VI
17a.53 K   214
17a.786 K   211
17a.998 K   212
17b.150 K   177–8

In Hippocratis aphorismos
17b.352 K   140
17b.356 K   212

In Hippocratis epidemiarum librum VI (Wenckebach and Pfaff)
486 WP   136
486–7 WP   136

In Hippocratis prognosticum
18b.19 K   116, 210
18b.35 K   212
18b.53 K   212

Quomodo simulantes morbum
19.1–7 K   54
19.7 K   177

De libris propriis
19.8–9 K   83
19.8–48 K   54
19.9 K   154
19.13 K   139
19.14 K   128
19.17 K   188–9
19.18–19 K   178
19.39–45 K   136
19.44 K   118
19.45 K   11, 91, 144, 204, 221

Index of Ancient Authors and Texts

19.45–46 K	11, 134	8–9 BMJ	77, 193
19.45–48 K	136	10 BMJ	84, 164, 233–4, 254
19.48 K	120, 168, 195, 205	10b–11 BMJ	222
		11 BMJ	213–4, 227–8
De ordine librorum propriorum/suorum		12 BMJ	65, 67, 79, 165
19.49–61 K	54	12–13 BMJ	78
19.55 K	211	12–14 BMJ	165–6
19.58 K	139	12–36 BMJ	160
19.59 K	138	12–37 BMJ	131, 223, 228
		12a BMJ	84
Quod qualitates incorporeae sint		12b BMJ	214
19.463–84 K	54	12b–22 BMJ	84
		13 BMJ	65, 73, 82–83, 121
De consuetudinibus		13–14 BMJ	61
108	214	13–26 BMJ	91
115	151	14 BMJ	14, 65, 83–84, 145
		15–17 BMJ	65
De nominibus medicis		15–18 BMJ	83
31–32	170	16 BMJ	14, 66, 68, 72, 82, 146–7, 181
De optimo medico cognoscendo		17 BMJ	66, 68, 72–3, 82–84, 185
9	139	18 BMJ	65–66, 68, 74
		19 BMJ	73, 76, 83, 181
De propriis placitis (Nutton)		20 BMJ	60, 146–7, 166, 181
2–4 N	137	20–23 BMJ	165, 168
7 N	137	20–30 BMJ	166
11 N	137	21 BMJ	14, 66, 82, 84, 70, 181
14–15 N	137	22 BMJ	181
		23–24a BMJ	168
De indolentia (Boudon-Millot and Jouanna)		23a BMJ	190
1 BMJ	13, 91, 94–95, 108, 131, 134, 213–4, 219, 222, 240, 253, 256	23b BMJ	179, 188, 190
		23b–26 BMJ	14
		23b–28 BMJ	82, 85
1–11 BMJ	222, 223	24 BMJ	181
1–38 BMJ	185	24b–27 BMJ	168–9
2 BMJ	12, 176, 214, 227, 233, 240	27 BMJ	169
3 BMJ	213–20, 228, 254	28 BMJ	65
3–6 BMJ	159	29 BMJ	14, 83, 85, 213–4, 228
4 BMJ	58, 79, 159, 191, 214	30 BMJ	166, 214, 228
4–5 BMJ	14, 145	31 BMJ	14, 79, 85–86, 167
4–38 BMJ	257	31–37 BMJ	131
5 BMJ	226, 254	32 BMJ	85
6 BMJ	69, 74, 83–84, 86, 179, 191, 254	32–37 BMJ	167, 192
		33 BMJ	85, 192
7 BMJ	79, 131, 146, 180, 209, 214, 219, 233, 240, 247, 254, 258	34 BMJ	11, 15
		34–35 BMJ	85
		34–36 BMJ	87
8 BMJ	221	35 BMJ	79, 85

36 BMJ	85–86	58–68 BMJ	162, 172, 223, 236, 241
37 BMJ	85–86, 167	59 BMJ	11
38 BMJ	14, 97, 131, 146–8, 213–4, 219, 228, 233, 257	60 BMJ	12, 256
		61 BMJ	58, 124, 134, 172, 188
38–48 BMJ	13, 160	62 BMJ	12, 120, 124, 133, 163, 179, 188, 194
38–57 BMJ	223, 228, 240		
39 BMJ	94, 97, 100, 131, 147	62–64 BMJ	197
39–42 BMJ	131	64 BMJ	133
39–48 BMJ	263	65 BMJ	79, 164
39–84 BMJ	179, 258	66 BMJ	124, 134, 188
40 BMJ	98, 100, 147	67 BMJ	15, 114, 133, 172–3
41 BMJ	58	67–68 BMJ	149
41–42 BMJ	147	68 BMJ	12, 120, 133, 154, 162–3, 197
42 BMJ	94, 100–1, 259		
42–46 BMJ	58, 161	69 BMJ	115, 133, 203, 185
43 BMJ	101, 105, 148, 161, 259	69–70 BMJ	163
44 BMJ	240, 259	69–73 BMJ	231
44–45 BMJ	161	69–84 BMJ	223, 248
45 BMJ	92, 105, 132, 161–2, 228, 260, 265	70 BMJ	134, 214
		71 BMJ	124, 134, 179, 188
46 BMJ	105, 131, 148, 161, 213–4	71–72 BMJ	164
47 BMJ	105, 228	71–72a BMJ	257
48 BMJ	101, 106, 132, 228, 240, 258, 260, 265	71–72b BMJ	185
		72a BMJ	14, 117, 181
49 BMJ	107, 124, 134, 177, 179–80, 187–91, 258–9	72b BMJ	116, 214, 228, 232, 265
		72b–74 BMJ	257
49–50 BMJ	132	73 BMJ	117–8, 134, 181, 228, 231
50 BMJ	132, 164–5, 259	74 BMJ	118, 179–81
50–51 BMJ	149	74–75 BMJ	181, 183
50a BMJ	179–80	75 BMJ	12, 126, 231
50a–51 BMJ	240	75–76 BMJ	248
50b BMJ	79, 85–86, 124–5, 214, 256	76 BMJ	12, 118–9, 179, 182–4
51 BMJ	13, 132, 200, 213, 241, 256	76–79 BMJ	256
		77 BMJ	12, 180, 185, 232, 236
51–52 BMJ	236	78 BMJ	13, 134, 188, 231
51–56 BMJ	256	78a BMJ	116
52 BMJ	12, 92, 107–9, 114, 185, 199, 228, 232	78a–b BMJ	14
		78b BMJ	124–5, 259, 265
52–56 BMJ	91, 133	79 BMJ	14, 256
53 BMJ	113–4, 197, 241	79b BMJ	95, 197–9
54 BMJ	108, 114, 176, 180, 222	79b–81 BMJ	241
54–55 BMJ	11–12, 161, 179–81, 185	79b–82 BMJ	59
55 BMJ	12, 108, 114, 177, 241	79b–83 BMJ	198
55b BMJ	83	80 BMJ	101, 198, 230
56 BMJ	13, 95, 108, 114, 150, 240–1	81 BMJ	12, 120, 198
		82 BMJ	198
57 BMJ	13, 97, 107, 199, 213, 241	83 BMJ	125, 199, 261, 264
57–62 BMJ	97, 108, 132, 256	84 BMJ	14, 93, 261
58 BMJ	256		

II. Other Ancient Authors and Texts

Adamantius

Physiognomonica
1.1	219
1.3	217
1.4	218
2.1	218

Aelian

De natura animalium
3.5	196
5.48	197

Varia historia
14.6	109

Aeschylus

Choephori
233	228

Persae
846	228

Prometheus vinctus
379	235

Alexander of Aphrodisias

De fato
212.1–8	96

Anonymous Latinus

Physiognomonica
10	218
11	217
12	217
18	217
19	218
21	219
33–34	219
45	218
77	219
78	218
88	217–8
96	219
97	217

Letter of Aristeas
197	232
232	232

Aristophanes

Plutus
673	228

Thesmophoriazusae
542	34

Aristotle

De anima
403a	224
581a	197
637b	197

Ethica eudemia
1220b	224

Ethica nichomachea
1095b	114
1095b–1096a	114
1100b	124
1104b	223–4
1105b	223–4
1106b	120
1119a	120
1124a	120, 124

Historia animalium
539b–540a	194, 196
560b–561a	194
581a	197
589a	197
637b	197

Rhetorica
1378a	224
1418a	224

Pseudo-Aristotle

Physiognomonica
805	217
805a	216–7
805a–808b	216
806a	218
806b	218
808b	216
808b–814b	216
812a	216
813a	218
814b	217

Athenaeus

Deipnosophistae
9.389	196
12.544	109

Aulus Gellius

Noctes atticae
1.9	215–216
2.3–5	23
12.5	123
19.5	70

Bion

Fragmenta
34	102
40	98

Caesar

Bellum civile
2.8	199

Cassius Dio

Historia romana
17.57	69
38.18	108, 119
58.25	69
61.35	175
62.16–17	192
72 (73).7	183
72 (73).10	199
72 (73).12	189
72 (73).13	183
72 (73).15	183–5
72 (73).16	183
72 (73).19	179
72 (73).20	183
72 (73).21	182, 184
72 (73).24	11, 176, 192–3
74.13	182

Cicero

Academicae quaestiones
1.35	141
1.43	141
2.66	141
2.70	141
2.135	117, 120–1

Epistulae ad Atticum
4.4	70
4.5	69–70
4.8	69–70
4.10	72
4.41	69
5.3	69–70
9.11	72
12.14	70
13.44	70

Epistulae ad familiares
16.22	70

De fato
5	122

De finibus
4.23	123
4.79	121

De legibus
1.27	218

De officiis
1.46	122
1.61–92	124, 132
1.66	124
1.80–81	113
1.110	126
2.7–8	141

2.60	121	4.26	103
3.7	121	4.82	94, 101

De oratore

3.216	218
3.221	218
3.221–3	218

In Verrem

4.73	185

Clement of Alexandria

Protrepticus

11	226

De natura deorum

1.6	122

Stromateis

1.21	215
2.5	230
2.13	226
3.7	244
4.5	244
4.23	244

Tusculanae disputationes

1.79	121
2.7	185
2.17	116
3.1	244
3.4	237
3.6	235
3.11	227–9
3.12	120, 237
3.13	93
3.14	115, 236
3.15	115
3.18	115
3.19	124
3.22	93
3.23	101
3.24	97
3.25	97, 232, 236, 246–7
3.27	247
3.28	109, 120
3.28–29	187
3.29	108–9, 185, 236
3.30	111, 256
3.31	109, 257–8
3.32	120, 185
3.52	109
3.54	117
3.56	98
3.56–58	98
3.57	98
3.61	101
3.71	120
3.81	116
4.6	227, 229, 232
4.7	230
4.10	247

Quis dives salvetur

1.2	243
1.3	228
12.2	230
20.6	244
41	249

Corpus Inscriptionum Latinarum (CIL)

5.5262	70
10.4670	70
10.6638	70

Dio Chrysostom

De aegritudine (*Or.* 16)

3	116

De invidia (*Or.* 77/78)

45	238, 246

De regno iv (*Or.* 4)

115–6	244

Diodorus Siculus

9.19	185

Diogenes Laertius

1.21	127

2.13	110	4	87
2.55	110	5	87–88
2.65–87	161		
2.77	98	*Epictetus*	
4.47	98		
4.51–52	99	*Diatribai*	
6.2	100	1.6	117–9
6.5	260	2.6	232
6.15	107	2.18	187, 242–3
6.16	216	3.8	187
6.22–23	260	3.12	187
6.70	118	3.24	108, 112, 187
6.87	106	4.1	96
6.104	92	4.4	187, 198
7.92	107	4.5	104
7.103	123		
7.106	118	*Enchiridion*	
7.110	227	5.1	97
7.111	103, 229–30, 236, 243–4	16.1	97
7.112	228, 229		
7.113	229	Epicurus	
7.114	229	*Epistula ad Menoeceum*	
7.115	226, 231	127	120
7.116	226	313	120
7.117	115, 225		
7.127–8	123	Epistle of Aristeas	
7.128	123	197	232
9.20	110, 113	232	232

Pseudo-Demetrius

Epistolary Types
1B	241
5	234

Euripides

Fragmenta
757	236
962	235
964	162, 236

Diogenes of Oenoanda

Epicurus
29	242

Poet
13	185

Dionysius of Halicarnassus

Eusebius

Antiquitates romanae
10.21.5.2	69

Praeparatio evangelica
15.13.8	106

Dioscurides

Historia ecclesiastica
5.28.14	205

De materia medica
3	87

Favorinus

De exilio
96   95, 108

Fronto

Epistulae
2.5   75

Gospel of Thomas

36   264
63   263
72   262
76   265

Gregory of Nazianzus

Epistulae
32   116

Hebrew Bible

Isaiah
13:9   271

Zephaniah
1:14–16   271

Herodian

1.2   177
1.5   189
1.8   189
1.9   189
1.13   189, 199
1.14   11, 176, 183, 193
1.15   183
2.2   189
2.4   189
3.7   190

Hesiod

Theogonia
289   183
982   183

[Scutum]
115   183
349   183
416   183

Hippocrates / Hippocratic Corpus

De morbis mulierum (Γυναικεῖα)
1.75   49

Epidemiae (Ἐπιδημίαι)
486   136
486–7   136
494   184

Praeceptiones (Παραγγελίαι)
5   171
6   171

Prognostica (Προγνωστικόν)
2   218

Hippolytus

Refutatio omnium haeresium
1.2.5   216

Homer

Illiad
10.15   247

Horace

Carmina
2.2.13–16   101
3.16.28   105

Epistulae
2.2.60   99
2.2.146–9   103

Satirae
2.3.99–102 98

Iamblichus

De vita pythagorica
17.71   215–6

Inscriptiones Graecae (IG)

14.2136	234

Inscriptiones Graecae ad Res Romanas Pertinentes (IGRR)

4.502–6	241
4.504	241

Juvenal

Satirae

3.7	193

Pseudo-Libanius

Epistolary Styles

19	238
65	234
66	238
90	238

Lucian

Phalaris

1	186
8	186

Musonius Rufus

9	106
17	93

Nepos

Atticus

13.3	70
13.3–4	70

New Testament

Matthew

6:25–34	264
9:21–22	272
10:28–29	271
10:31	271
12:10–13	271
14:9	270
19:22	262
26:22	269
26:36–38	268
27:3–10	262

Mark

3:5	271
5:36	271
6:26	270
10:21	267
10:22	267
10:35–45	270
12:41–44	266
14:19	269
14:33–35	268

Luke

1:12	271
1:13	271
1:29	272
1:30	272
2:9	271
2:10	271
3:7	270
3:10–14	261–2
3:11	264
3:19–20	270
4:28	270
5:8	272
5:10	272
5:33	272
6:10	271
6:18	230
6:20	267
6:24	267
8:1–3	260
8:3	264
8:14	262
8:50	271
9:3	266
9:9	270
10:4	266
11:3	265
12:4–5	271
12:5	271
12:6–7	265
12:7	271
12:13	262

12:13–14	262	22:41–44	268
12:13–21	262	22:45	268
12:13–34	263	23:40	271
12:14	262		
12:15	262–3	Acts	
12:16–17	263	1:16–20	262
12:16–20	262	4:25	263
12:18	263	5:16	230
12:19	263	12:20	270
12:20	270	12:21–23	270
12:21	263	17:5	230
12:21–23	270	20:33	272
12:22	265		
12:22–23	265	1 Corinthians	
12:22–34	262, 264		
12:24	265	2:4	206
12:25	265	5:9–13	15
12:27	265		
12:28	265	2 Corinthians	
12:29	265	1:4	231
12:30b	265	1:8	231
12:31	265	2:1	233
12:32	271	2:2–4	233
12:33	264–5, 267	4–5	233
14:16–24	270	4:8	231
14:33	262, 264, 267	4:8–9	231
15:28	271	4:9	247
16:8	272	7:8–9	233
16:19–31	267	7:9–10	233
16:23	267		
18:2	271	Philippians	
18:4	271	4:8–9	265
18:18–25	266		
18:20–21	267	1 Thessalonians	
18:22	264, 267	5:14	240
18:22–23	265		
18:23	268	Panaetius	
18:28	266		
19:1–10	266	*Fragmenta*	
19:8–9	262, 264	45	113
19:28	270	115	113
21:1–4	266		
21:23	270	Oppian	
22:21–23	269		
22:23	269	*Cynegetica*	
22:26	269	3.191–207	195
22:39–46	268		
22:40	268		

Origen

Contra Celsum
1.9–10   205

Homiliae in Jeremiam
39   205

Philo

De sacrificiis Abelis et Caini
85.2   187

De specialibus legibus
1.2   197

De virtutibus
5.68   93

Philodemus

Index Stoicorum
61.2–4   121

Philostratus

Vita Apollonii
20.8   70

Physiologus
9   195

Plato

Cratylus
419c   247

Leges
837a–d   225

Phaedrus
276d   133
276d–e   114
277e   115

Protagoras
310a–d   135

Respublica
586a   197

Timaeus
69cd   224

Pliny the Elder

Naturalis historia
8.46   195
10.101   196
10.110   195

Pliny the Younger

Epistulae
1.8   70
2.17   71

Plotinus

Enneads
5.9.1   259

Plutarch

Animine an corporis affectiones sint peiores
500C   240
500D–F   244

Brutus
21.1   21

Cicero
27   72

[*Consolatio ad Apollonium*]
101F–102A   235
102   237
102B–D   235
102C   228
102C–D   120
112C–D   112–3
112D   185, 256–7
112D–E   236
112E   112
118D   111

Consolatio ad uxorem
608C   236
608F–609B   236

De capienda ex inimicis utilitate
87A   107

De cohibenda ira
463D   113

De esu
995F–996A 246

De cupiditate divitiarum
524A–B   102
524B   101–2
524C–D   103
524D   105
524D–E   105

De Pythiae oraculis
402E   96

De recta ratione audiendi
46D   239
46D–47A   239

De tranquillitate animi
465A–B   93
465B–C   108
466E   106
467B–C   240
467C–D   106
467E   98
468F–469A 98
469C–D   259
469D   100
471D   240
473B   240
474D   111–2
474E   112
474E–F   112
476C   96

Lucullus
42   74

Marcius Coriolanus
26   69

Quomodo adulator ab amico internoscatur
61A   243
69D   235
69E–F   239

Sulla
26   72

Polemon

Physiognomonica
1.5   219
1.25   217
2.37   217
2.41   219
2.42   218
2.51   217

Polybius

13.2.2   101

Porphyry

Vita Pythagorae
13   216

Proclus

In Platonis Alcibiadem
3.158   115

Quintilian

Institutio oratoria
11.3.66–67 218

Rufus

Quaestiones medicinales
1–2   211
4   211

Scriptores Historiae Augustae

Commodus
2.9   189
5.4   194
5.11   194

10.3	179		108.35–36	119
10.9	183, 198		116	122
11.7	184			
11.8	183		*Ira*	
11.14	183		2.31.4	112
13.4	190			
15.7–8	194		Simplicius	
16.7–8	192		*In Enchiridion Epicteti*	
17.6	200		1.23	107
17.9	183		45.25–34	107
17.11	183		54.22	112
20.5	200			

Didius Iulianus
2.6   200

Severus
11.3–4   200
12.8   200

Seneca

Ad Helviam
5.2   114
5.2–3   109, 112
11.3   101
11.4   105

De tranquillitate animi
7.4   116
11.6   111
11.9   112
14.3   106
16.2   98

Dialogi
10.4   116

Epistulae morales
2.6   105
66.18   116
75.6–7   238
76.34   108
76.34–5   113
76.35   111
91.3–4   108
98.5–6   187
98.7   187

Sirach
11:19   263

Sophocles

Fragmenta
964   236

Stobaeus

Eclogae
2.93   226
2.99   114
2.102   114
3.10   101

Strabo

Geographica
13.1.54   72

Suetonius

Nero
9   69
38   192

Stoicorum Veterum Fragmenta (SVF)

1.187   123
1.190–2   117
1.216   114
1.277   106
1.422   115
1.434   115
2.35–36   133
3.49   123

3.117–23	117	Teles	
3.127	118	Περὶ αὐταρκείας	
3.127–39	117	2	106
3.144	115		
3.201	115	Περὶ συγκρίσεως πενίας καὶ πλούτου	
3.264	132	38.4–39.1	99
3.264–5	118		
3.265	107	Περὶ φυγῆς	
3.269	107, 118	3	116
3.269–70	118		
3.270	107	Theocritus	
3.274–5	107	*Epigrams*	
3.417	110	11	218
3.421	226		
3.422	226	*Idylls*	
3.429	226, 246	7.141	197
3.431	226		
3.443–55	115	Thucydides	
3.448	115	*Historia*	
3.456	103	2.51.4	210
3.462	227		
3.479	227	Varro	
3.481	115	*De re rustica*	
3.543	115	3.7–8	195
3.567	114	8.3	195
3.586	116		

The Tabula of Cebes

Vitruvius

5–6	244	6.4.1	76
7–8	220		
9	248–9	Xenophon	
9–11	244–5	*Memorabilia*	
11	246	2.1.4	196
18	220	2.1.17	105
22	244	3.10	215, 219
22–23	245–6		

Tacitus

Symposium

Annales		4.34	105
14.27	69	4.35	105
15.38–44	192	4.37	104

Modern Author Index

Alesse, Francesca 113, 121–4, 126
Alexander, Loveday C. A. 204, 239, 251, 261
Alexander, Sidney 98
Alexanderson, Bengt 54
Anastassiou, Anargyros 16, 48, 104
André, Jacques 217
Annas, Julia 255
Armisen-Marchetti, Mireille 109
Armstrong, A. MacC 217
Armstrong, David 225, 239
Arrighetti, Graziano 104
Asmis, Elizabeth 12, 124–5, 127–42, 257
Athanasopoulou, Ioanna-Maria 16
Atkins, E. Margaret 113, 122

Babbitt, F. C. 113
Baillet, Jules 220
Bardong, Kurt 54
Barigazzi, Adelmo 95, 108
Barnes, Jonathan 96, 115, 130, 137, 140–1
Barton, Tamsyn S. 216
Basore, John W. 109
Bassi, Domenico 43
Baumgarten, Roland 205
Becchi, Francesco 16
Beck, Lily S. 87
Béguin, Daniel 53
Benko, Stephen 251
Bergsträsser, Gotthelf 57
Billerbeck, Margarethe 99, 105
Bio, Anna Maria Ieraci 16, 67
Böck, Barbara 215
Bompaire, Jacques 154
Bosman, Philippus R. 15
Boudon-Millot, Véronique 3–5, 8–9, 14–16, 21, 41–55, 58, 66, 68, 73, 75, 77, 79, 81, 83, 91, 104, 118, 128, 131–2, 143–7, 149–50, 152, 159, 160–3, 165, 168, 170, 172–3, 176–7, 188, 203, 207, 211, 222, 253, 277
Bovon, François 270
Bowersock, Glen W. 241
Bowman, Alan K. 176
Boys-Stones, George 216
Brancacci, Aldo 107, 125
Brink, Charles O. 103
Brittain, Charles 117
Brock, Arthur J. 151, 211
Bruce, Lorne 71
Brunschwig, Jacques 246–7, 255–6
Buchheim, Rudolf 80
Buresch, Karl 255

Campbell, John Scott 175
Cancik-Lindemaier, Hildegard 254
Cary, Earnest 182, 199
Caujolle-Zaslawsky, Françoise 161
Chazan, Robert 59
Chiaradonna, Riccardo 127
Cilliers, Louise 16, 203, 212
Claassen, Jo-Marie 119
Cohn, Leopold 93
Collard, Christopher 109
Cooper, John M. 123, 255
Cousin, Victor 115

Daremberg, Charles 211
De Boer, Wilko 54, 93, 159, 170
Debru, Armelle 80, 88, 115, 178
De Lacy, Phillip 92, 102, 110–1, 122, 127, 171, 204
Del Mastro, Gianluca 17
DeWitt, Norman 253
Diehl, Ernst 106
Diels, Hermann 5, 54, 111
Dietz, Fridericus R. 151, 214

Dillon, John 128, 194
Dindorf, Wilhelm 236
Donini, Pierluigi 115, 127–8, 130, 194
Dorandi, Tiziano 17, 121
Doulamis, Konstantin 181
Duling, Richard J. 209
Dunderberg, Ismo 253
Dyck, Andrew R. 121–2, 124

Edelstein, Ludwig 101, 115, 121–3
Edmonds, Lowell 181
Ehlert, Jürgen 54
Eijk, Philip J. van der 9, 115
Engberg-Pedersen, Troels 123, 204, 251–3, 255
Eustratiades, Sophronius 4–5, 41–42
Evans, Elizabeth C. 215–8

Fabricius, Cajus 80–82
Fairclough, Henry R. 103
Fern, Mary E. 255
Festugière, André-Jean 130, 142
Fischer, Klaus-Dietrich 16, 67, 104, 278
Fitzgerald, John T. 115, 122, 203–20, 225–6, 231–2, 239, 244, 251–3, 261–2
Fitzmyer, Joseph A. 262–5, 268, 270–1
Fleming, Rebecca 9, 190
Formentin, Mariarosa 53
Förster, Richard 218
Fortuna, Stefania 54
Frede, Michael 128–9, 140
Fredrickson, David E. 232–3
Furnish, Victor P. 231

Garnsey, Peter 176
Garofalo, Ivan 9, 16–17, 21–22, 28–30, 35, 42, 54, 67, 75, 118, 173, 194, 277–8
Gärtner, Hans 211
Gero, Stephen 251
Gerson, Lloyd P. 142
Gill, Christopher 11, 17, 124–7, 143, 151, 155, 176, 178–9, 188, 190–1, 207, 210, 221, 226, 228, 232, 242, 248, 253–7
Glad, Clarence 253–4
Gleason, Maud W. 155, 177–80, 182, 184, 187, 215, 217
Gomoll, Heinz 123

Goulet-Caze, Marie-Odile 99, 118
Gourevitch, Danielle 80
Gourinat, Jean-Baptiste 17, 121
Gradl, Hans-Georg 261
Grant, Robert M. 205–6, 251
Graver, Margaret R. 92–93, 110, 116
Griffin, Miriam T. 113, 122, 130, 141
Grmek, Mirko D. 80
Guardasole, Alessia 16
Guidorizzi, Giulio 54
Guillaumont, François 16
Gummere, R. M. 109
Gundert, Beate 43–44, 54
Gutas, Dimitri 57

Hadot, Ilsetraut 254
Hadot, Pierre 142
Hägg, Tomas 154
Halkin, Abraham 17, 57
Handley, E. W. 194
Hankinson, R. J. 10, 46, 54, 128, 169–70, 176–8, 188, 199, 204, 225, 246, 255–7
Harkins, Paul W. 204, 269
Harlfinger, Dieter 43
Harmon, A. M. 186
Harris, Murray J. 231
Harris, William V. 15, 17
Harvey, Steven 59
Hatzimichali, Myrto 127–8
Hays, Christopher M. 261, 263, 265, 267
Healy, John F. 195
Helmreich, Georg 53, 54, 137, 139, 169, 206
Henderson, Jeffrey 9
Hense, Otto 99, 106, 114, 117–8
Hijmans, B. L. 225
Hinds, Stephen 181
Hock, Ronald F. 99, 262–4
Holland, Glenn S. 239, 253
Hollaway, Paul A. 255, 265
Horsley, G. H. R. 9, 196–7, 204
Houston, George W. 17, 70, 73, 253

Inwood, Brad 115, 122
Irmer, Dieter 48, 104

Jackson, S. W. 213
Jacques, Jean-Marie 209

Jaia, Alessandro 71, 76
Jann, Rosemary 218
Jayyusi-Lehn, Ghada 60
Johnson, Luke Timothy 262, 267–8
Johnson, William A. 17
Johnston, Ian 9, 21, 196–7, 204
Jones, Christopher P. 9, 17, 66–69, 73, 207, 222, 286–88
Jouanna, Jacques 5, 8, 16–17, 21, 34, 42–43, 48, 53, 58, 66, 68, 73, 75, 77, 79, 91, 118, 131–2, 143–7, 149–50, 151–2, 159–63, 165, 168–70, 173, 176, 203, 208, 222, 253, 277

Kannicht, Richard 30, 34, 109
Kassel, Rudolf 255
Kaster, Robert A. 15, 186
Kelly, Gordon P. 181
Kidd, Ian G. 96, 101, 110, 115, 121–3
Kieffer, John S. 205
Kindstrand, Jan F. 98, 102
Klugman-Barkan, Roberta 60
Kock, Theodor 235
König, Jason 17–18, 160, 191
Konstan, David 15, 115
Kotzia, Paraskevi 9, 16–17, 21, 23, 27, 34, 58, 75, 91–126, 145, 160, 176, 277
Kousoulis, Antonis A. 16
Kranz, Walther 111

Lami, Alessandro 9, 16–17, 21–23, 27, 29, 30, 35, 42, 54, 67, 163, 173, 194, 277–8
Laurence, Patrick 16
Leszl, Walter 125–6
Levy, Carlos 17
Lilla, Romano C. 248
Littré, Émile 49, 53
Lloyd-Jones, Hugh 106
Long, Anthony A. 97, 125, 128, 187, 194
Longrigg, James 218
Lord, Carnes 72
Lorenz, Hendrik 110
Lorusso, Vito 16, 278, 284
Lucarini, Carlo M. 17
Lutz, Cora 93, 107, 117–8

Magdelaine, Caroline 16
Magnaldi, Iosepha 159, 170
Malherbe, Abraham J. 205, 234, 238–9, 241, 252–3, 262–3
Manetti, Daniela 16–18, 43, 67, 91, 114, 118, 160
Manning, Charles E. 109
Mansfeld, Jaap 115, 204
Marganne, Marie-Hélène 81
Marquardt, Johannes 118
Marshall, Anthony J. 72
Marshall, I. Howard 262–4, 268–9
Martin, Dale B. 251
Martini, Emidio 43
Marzano, Annalisa 69
Matini, Maria Luisa Morricone 71
Mattern, Susan P. 18, 144, 154, 207, 209, 211, 213
Mattingly, Harold 186
Mattock, John N. 134
May, Margaret T. 152, 204–5
Meeks, Wayne A. 253
Metzger, James A. 261
Meyerhof, Max 170
Millar, Fergus 182
Mioni, Elpidio 48, 53
Mitsis, Phillip 96
Moles, John L. 99
Mondrain, Brigitte 43, 49, 50
Montagu, Jennifer 218
Moraux, Paul 128, 137
Morison, Ben 169
Moule, C. F. D. 263

Nauck, August 162, 235–6
Nesselrath, Heinz-Günther 117
Neumann, Nils 261
Newman, Robert J. 109
Neyrey, Jerome 268–9
Nicholls, Matthew C. 14, 18, 23–24, 65–78, 160, 207, 253
Nolland, John 262–4, 268, 272
Norden, Eduard 206
Nussbaum, Martha C. 124, 186, 246–7, 255–6
Nutton, Vivian 3, 9, 16–18, 27, 42–43, 54, 68, 82, 127–8, 137, 159–60, 162–3, 165–6, 168–9, 170, 172–3, 176–8, 184,

188, 191–2, 194, 204, 207, 211–2, 222, 253

Obbink, Dirk 239, 253
Ochs, Donovan J. 206
Oikonomopoulou, Katerina 17–18, 160
Oldfather, W. A. 108, 112, 119
Olivieri, Alexander 228
O'Neil, Edward N. 99, 102, 104, 106

Parsons, Mikeal C. 215
Parsons, Peter J. 106
Petit, Caroline 47, 51, 53
Perilli, Lorenzo 16, 104
Piacente, Luigi 18
Pietrobelli, Antoine 5, 16–18, 21, 41–43, 46–47, 49–50, 53–54, 58, 66, 79, 91, 131, 143, 159, 176, 203, 222, 253, 277
Plummer, Alfred 268
Pohlenz, Max 122
Polemis, Ioannis 18, 24–26, 28–29, 31–33, 35, 169, 278, 282–3, 285–6, 289–91, 296–7, 301–5, 307, 309, 311–3
Polito, Robert 141
Poole, Fitz John Porter 252
Popović, Mladen 215
Poulakou-Rebelakou, Effie 16
Puglia, Enzo 18, 67, 75, 76, 288

Rabel, Robert J. 246
Raiola, Tommaso 18, 32, 194
Ramelli, Ilaria 115
Rashed, Marwan 18, 53, 67, 73, 75, 83, 286–88
Rasimus, Tuomas 253
Rathbone, Dominic 176
Retief, François P. 212
Rich, Audrey N. M. 104
Richard, Marcel 4
Riddle, John M. 80, 86
Rindge, Matthew 263–4
Rist, J. M. 142
Ritter, Hellmut 60
Robinson, James T. 59
Rodopoulos, Panteleimon 3
Rolfe, J. C. 123

Roselli, Amneris 16–18, 67, 75, 104, 114, 124
Rosen, Ralph M. 14, 159–73, 175, 228
Rosenthal, Franz 57
Roskam, Geert 96, 115, 121–2, 126
Rostovtseff, Michael 186
Rothschild, Clare K. 3–17, 21–36, 66–68, 73, 76, 145, 175–200, 203–4, 207, 221–2, 251, 253
Rouse, W. H. D. 175
Rousselle, Aline 246
Ruelle, Charles-Émile 211
Rüther, Theodor 244

Sacco, Giulia 234
Sampley, J. Paul 231–2, 239
Scarborough, John 80, 82, 212
Schacht, Joseph 170
Schmekel, August 120
Schmiedeberg, Oswald 80
Schöne, Hermann 205
Scourfield, J. H. D. 255
Sedley, David N. 97, 122, 130, 141, 247
Sellars, John 104
Shackleton Bailey, David R. 72
Sihvola, Juha 123, 252, 255
Singer, Peter N. 9, 13, 16, 103–4, 151, 153, 159, 178, 180, 184, 188–90, 204, 207, 210, 222, 226, 254–5, 269
Smith, James C. 205
Smith, Jonathan Z. 251–2
Sorabji, Richard 123, 239, 246–8, 253, 255
Sotiroudis, Panagiotis 9, 15, 21, 24, 34, 58, 75, 91, 124, 145, 176, 277
Speidel, M. P. 175, 186
Spittler, Janet E. 195, 197
Staden, Heinrich von 115, 127, 168–70
Stählin, Otto 226, 230, 244
Stannard, Jerry 80
Starr, Raymond J. 72
Sterling, Gregory E. 268
Stewart, Zeph 125
Stogioglou, Georgiou 4
Stowers, Stanley K. 221, 231, 252–3, 255
Straaten, Modestus van 113, 121–4, 126
Stramaglia, Antonio 18, 25, 66, 68–69, 75, 286–8

Swain, Simon 215–7
Syme, Ronald 192

Tannehill, Robert C. 266, 268–9
Thompson, Trevor W. 3–17, 21–36, 66–68, 73, 76, 145, 176, 203–4, 207, 221–2, 251, 253, 277–314
Thorsteinsson, Runar 253
Tieleman, Teun L. 110, 121, 124, 176
Timken, Owsei 246
Touwaide, Alain 13, 79–88
Tucci, Pier Luigi 9, 18, 24, 66, 76–78, 160, 222

Usener, Hermann 104, 116, 120

Varner, Eric R. 200
Vegetti, Mario 10, 16
Vimercati, Emmanuele 113, 122
Vogt, Sabine 216
Voloudakis, Konstantinos 3–4

Wachsmuth, Curt 114
Walzer, Richard 60, 128, 135, 177, 206, 251
Warner, Rex 210
Warren, James 125
Wellmann, Max 87
West, Martin L. 94
Whitaker, C. R. 189
White, L. Michael 220–49, 251–2
Whitmarsh, Tim 11, 17, 127, 143, 151, 155, 176, 178, 181, 190–1, 207, 253
Wilcox, Amanda 255–6
Wilken, Robert L. 204, 206, 251, 253
Wilkins, John 11, 17, 127, 143, 151, 155, 169, 176, 178, 190–1, 207
Woolf, Greg 17–18, 160
Wright, Addison G. 266
Wright, Richard A. 251–73

Zadorojnyi, Alexei V. 18, 160
Zeller, Eduard 128
Zonta, Mauro 59, 60

Studien und Texte zu Antike und Christentum
Studies and Texts in Antiquity and Christianity

Editors:
CHRISTOPH MARKSCHIES (Berlin)
MARTIN WALLRAFF (Basel)
CHRISTIAN WILDBERG (Princeton)

Ahmed, Luise: see *Fürst, Alfons*
Aland, Barbara / Hahn, Johannes / Ronning, Christian (Ed.): Literarische Konstituierung von Identifikationsfiguren in der Antike. 2003. *Volume 16.*
Albrecht, Michael: see *Hirsch-Luipold, Rainer*
Behrmann, Ingrid: see *Breytenbach, Cilliers*
Betz, Hans Dieter: The „Mithras Liturgy". 2003. *Volume 18.*
Bracht, Katharina: Hippolyts Schrift In Danielem. 2014. *Volume 85.*
Bracht Katharina: Vollkommenheit und Vollendung. 1999. *Volume 2.*
Bremer, Jan Maarten: see *Furley, William D.*
Brent, Allen: Ignatius of Antioch and the Second Sophistic. 2006. *Volume 36.*
Breytenbach, Cilliers / Behrmann, Ingrid (Ed.): Frühchristliches Thessaloniki. 2007. *Volume 44.*
Bumazhnov, Dmitrij: Der Mensch als Gottes Bild im christlichen Ägypten. 2005. *Volume 34.*
– : Visio mystica im Spannungsfeld frühchristlicher Überlieferungen. 2009. *Volume 52.*
– (Ed.): Christliches Ägypten in der spätantiken Zeit. Akten der 2. Tübinger Tagung zum Christlichen Orient, 7.–8. Dezember 2007. 2013. *Volume 79.*
– / *Seeliger, Hans Reinhard* (Ed.): Syrien im 1.–7. Jahrhundert nach Christus. 2011. *Volume 62.*
Burgsmüller, Anne: Die Askeseschrift des Pseudo-Basilius. 2005. *Volume 28.*
Cancik, Hubert / Schäfer, Alfred / Spickermann, Wolfgang (Ed.): Zentralität und Religion. 2006. *Volume 39.*
Conring, Barbara: Hieronymus als Briefschreiber. 2001. *Volume 8.*
Cook, John Granger: The Interpretation of the New Testament in Greco-Roman Paganism. 2000. *Volume 3.*
– : The Interpretation of the Old Testament in Greco-Roman Paganism. 2004. *Volume 23.*
Cosgrove, Charles H.: An Ancient Christian Hymn with Musical Notation. 2011. *Volume 65.*
Cristea, Hans-Joachim: Schenute von Atripe: Contra Origenistas. 2010. *Volume 60.*
Denzey Lewis, Nicola: see *Iricinschi, Eduard*
Dörnemann, Michael: Krankheit und Heilung in der Theologie der frühen Kirchenväter. 2003. *Volume 20.*
Dümler, Bärbel: Zeno von Verona zu heidnischer Kultur und christlicher Bildung. 2013. *Volume 75.*
Egelhaaf-Gaiser, Ulrike / Schäfer, Alfred (Ed.): Religiöse Vereine in der römischen Antike. 2002. *Volume 13.*
Elliott, Mark W.: The Song of Songs and Christology in the Early Church. 2000. *Volume 7.*
Fauth, Wolfgang: Jao-Jahwe und seine Engel. 2014. *Band 74.*
Förster, Hans: Die Anfänge von Weihnachten und Epiphanias. 2007. *Volume 46.*
– : Die Feier der Geburt Christi in der Alten Kirche. 2000. *Volume 4.*
Frateantonio, Christa: Religiöse Autonomie der Stadt im Imperium Romanum. 2003. *Volume 19.*
Fürst, Alfons / Ahmed, Luise / Gers-Uphaus, Christian / Klug, Stefan (Ed.): Monotheistische Denkfiguren in der Spätantike. 2013. *Volume 81.*

Furley, William D. / Bremer, Jan Maarten: Greek Hymns I. 2001. *Volume 9.*
– : Greek Hymns II. 2001. *Volume 10.*
Gemeinhardt, Peter: Das lateinische Christentum und die antike pagane Bildung. 2007. *Volume 41.*
Gers-Uphaus, Christian: see *Fürst, Alfons*
Gleede, Benjamin: Platon und Aristoteles in der Kosmologie des Proklos. 2009. *Volume 54.*
Goehring, James E.: Politics, Monasticism, and Miracles in Sixth Century Upper Egypt. 2012. *Volume 69.*
Görgemanns, Herwig: Philologos Kosmos. 2013. *Volume 73.*
– : see *Hirsch-Luipold, Rainer*
Gonzalez, Eliezer: The Fate of the Dead in Early Third Century North African Christianity. 2014. *Volume 83.*
Greschat, Katharina: Die *Moralia in Job* Gregors des Großen. 2005. *Volume 31.*
Gutsfeld, Andreas / Koch, Dietrich-Alex (Ed.): Vereine, Synagogen und Gemeinden im kaiserzeitlichen Kleinasien. 2006. *Volume 25.*
Hahn, Johannes: see *Aland, Barbara*
Hartmann, Götz: Selbststigmatisierung und Charisma christlicher Heiliger der Spätantike. 2006. *Volume 38.*
Heiser, Andreas: Die Paulusinszenierung des Johannes Chrysostomus. 2012. *Volume 70.*
Henner, Jutta: Fragmenta Liturgica Coptica. 2000. *Volume 5.*
Henze, Matthias: The Syriac Apocalypse of Daniel. 2001. *Volume 11.*
Heyden, Katharina: Die „Erzählung des Aphroditian". 2009. *Volume 53.*
Hirsch-Luipold, Rainer: Plutarchs Denken in Bildern. 2002. *Volume 14.*
– / *Görgemanns, Herwig / Albrecht, Michael von* (Hg.): Religiöse Philosophie und philosophische Religion der frühen Kaiserzeit. *Ratio Religionis Studien I.* 2009. *Volume 51.*
Horn, Cornelia / Phenix, Robert R. (Ed.): Children in Late Ancient Christianity. 2009. *Volume 58.*
Die ikonoklastische Synode von Hiereia 754. Einleitung, Text, Übersetzung und Kommentar ihres Horos, besorgt von *Torsten Krannich, Christoph Schubert* und *Claudia Sode,* nebst einem Beitrag zur *Epistula ad Constantiam* des Eusebius von Cäsarea von *Annette von Stockhausen.* 2002. *Volume 15.*
Iricinschi, Eduard / Jenott, Lance / Denzey Lewis, Nicola / Townsend, Philippa (Ed.): Beyond the Gnostic Gospel. 2013. *Volume 82.*
Jenott, Lance: The Gospel of Judas: Coptic Text, Translation, and Historical Interpretation of 'the Betrayer's Gospel'. 2011. *Volume 64.*
– : see *Iricinschi, Eduard*
Kany, Roland: Augustins Trinitätsdenken. 2007. *Volume 22.*
Kisić, Rade: Patria Caelestis. 2011. *Volume 61.*
Klug, Stefan: see *Fürst, Alfons*
Koch, Dietrich-Alex: see *Gutsfeld, Andreas*
Köckert, Charlotte: Christliche Kosmologie und kaiserzeitliche Philosophie. 2009. *Volume 56.*
Krannich, Torsten: Von Leporius bis zu Leo dem Großen. 2005. *Volume 32.*
– : see Die ikonoklastische Synode von Hiereia 754.
Lange, Christian: Mia Energeia. 2012. *Volume 66.*
Leuenberger-Wenger, Sandra: Ethik und christliche Identität bei Gregor von Nyssa. 2008. *Volume 49.*
Lubomierski, Nina: Die Vita Sinuthii. 2007. *Volume 45.*
Luijendijk, AnneMarie: Forbidden Oracles? 2014. *Volume 89.*
Maas, Michael: Exegesis and Empire in the Early Byzantine Mediterranean. 2003. *Volume 17.*
Mastrocinque, Attilio: From Jewish Magic to Gnosticism. 2005. *Volume 24.*
Moschos, Dimitrios: Eschatologie im ägyptischen Mönchtum. 2010. *Volume 59.*
Müller, Andreas: Das Konzept des geistlichen Gehorsams bei Johannes Sinaites. 2006. *Volume 37.*
Müller, Barbara: Führung im Denken und Handeln Gregors des Grossen. 2009. *Volume 57.*

Studies and Texts in Antiquity and Christianity

Mutschler, Bernhard: Irenäus als johanneischer Theologe. 2004. *Volume 21.*
Nesselrath, Heinz-Günther / Rühl, Meike (Ed.): Der Mensch zwischen Weltflucht und Weltverantwortung. 2014. *Volume 87.*
Patterson, Paul A.: Visions of Christ. 2012. *Volume 68.*
Pevarello, Daniele: The Sentences of Sextus and the Origins of Christian Ascetiscism. 2013. *Volume 78.*
Phenix, Robert: Rhetoric and Interpretation in Fifth Century Syriac Literature. 2008. *Volume 50.*
– : see *Horn, Cornelia*
Pietzner, Katrin: Ungebildete Konkurrenten? 2013. *Volume 77.*
Quiroga Puertas, Alberto J. (Ed.): The Purpose of Rhetoric in Late Antiquity. 2013. *Volume 72.*
Reutter, Ursula: Damasus, Bischof von Rom (366–384). 2009. *Volume 55.*
Ritter, Adolf Martin: STUDIA CHRYSOSTOMICA. 2013. *Volume 71.*
Ronning, Christian: Herrscherpanegyrik unter Trajan und Konstantin. 2007. *Volume 42.*
–: see *Aland, Barbara*
Rothschild, Clare K. / Thompson, Trevor W. (Ed.): Galen's *De indolentia.* 2014. *Volume 88.*
Rühl, Meike: see *Nesselrath, Heinz-Günther*
Rüpke, Jörg (Ed.): Festrituale in der römischen Kaiserzeit. 2008. *Volume 48.*
–: Gruppenreligionen im römischen Reich. 2007. *Volume 43.*
– / *Woolf, Gregory D.* (Ed.): Religious Dimensions of the Self in the Second Century CE. 2013. *Volume 76.*
Samellas, Antigone: Death in the Eastern Mediterranean (50–600 A.D.). 2002. *Volume 12.*
Sanzo, Joseph E.: Scriptural Incipits on Amulets from Late Antique Egypt. 2014. *Volume 84.*
Schäfer, Alfred: see *Cancik, Hubert*
–: see *Egelhaaf-Gaiser, Ulrike*
Schulze, Christian: Medizin und Christentum in Spätantike und frühem Mittelalter. 2005. *Volume 27.*
Schurig, Sebastian: Die Theologie des Kreuzes beim frühen Cyrill von Alexandria. 2005. *Volume 29.*
Schubert, Christoph: see *Die ikonoklastische Synode von Hiereia 754.*
Seeliger, Hans Reinhard: see *Bumazhnov, Dmitrij*
Sode, Claudia: see *Die ikonoklastische Synode von Hiereia 754.oklastische*
Spickermann, Wolfgang: see *Cancik, Hubert*
Steimle, Christopher: Religion im römischen Thessaloniki. 2008. *Volume 47.*
Stockhausen, Annette von: see *Die ikonoklastische Synode von Hiereia 754.*
Stöcklin-Kaldewey, Sara: Kaiser Julians Gottesverehrung im Kontext der Spätantike. 2014. *Volume 86.*
Thom, Johan C.: Cleanthes' Hymn to Zeus. 2005. *Volume 33.*
Thompson, Trevor W.: see *Rothschild, Clare K.*
Thümmel, Hans Georg (Ed.): Origenes' Johanneskommentar Buch I–V. 2011. *Volume 63.*
Thum, Tobias: Plutarchs Dialog *De E apud Delphos. Ratio religionis Studien II.* 2013. *Volume 80.*
Tiersch, Claudia: Johannes Chrysostomus in Konstantinopel (398–404). 2002. *Volume 6.*
Tloka, Jutta: Griechische Christen – Christliche Griechen. 2005. *Band 30.*
Townsend, Philippa: see *Iricinschi, Eduard*
Der Tractatus Tripartus aus Nag Hammadi Codex I (Codex Jung). Neu übersetzt von Peter Nagel. 1998. *Volume 1.*
Tuschling, R.M.M.: Angels and Orthodoxy. 2007. *Volume 40.*
Uhle, Tobias: Augustin und die Dialektik. 2012. *Volume 67.*
Woolf, Gregory D.: see *Rüpke, Jörg*
Zuntz, Günther: Griechische philosophische Hymnen. 2005. *Volume 35.*

For a complete catalogue of this series please write to the publisher
Mohr Siebeck • P.O. Box 2040 • D–72010 Tübingen/Germany
Up-to-date information on the internet at www.mohr.de